# IMMIGRATION AND NATIONALITY LAWS OF THE UNITED STATES

## SELECTED STATUTES, REGULATIONS AND FORMS

As Amended to February 1, 1991
(including amendments effective October 1, 1991)

Selected By

**T. Alexander Aleinikoff**
*Professor of Law*
*University of Michigan Law School*

**David A. Martin**
*Professor of Law*
*University of Virginia School of Law*

**WEST PUBLISHING CO.**
ST. PAUL, MINN., 1991

COPYRIGHT © 1990 WEST PUBLISHING CO.
COPYRIGHT © 1991 By WEST PUBLISHING CO.
                     50 West Kellogg Boulevard
                     P.O. Box 64526
                     St. Paul, MN 55164-0526

United States.
    Immigration and nationality laws of the United States : selected
statutes, regulations, and forms / [edited by] T. Alexander
Aleinikoff, David A. Martin.
        p.       cm.
    Includes index.
    ISBN 0-314-88742-3
    1. Emigration and immigration law—United States. I. Aleinikoff,
Thomas Alexander, 1951–     . II. Martin, David A., 1948–       .
III. Title.
KF4806   1991
342.73'082—dc20
[347.30282]                                              91-11446
                                                         CIP

**ISBN** 0-314-88742-3

# EDITOR'S NOTE

The Immigration and Nationality Act as set forth herein incorporates amendments made by the Immigration and Nationality Act of 1990 (Pub.L. 101–649) due to take effect October 1, 1991.

*

# WESTLAW® ELECTRONIC RESEARCH GUIDE

---

## 1. Coordinating Legal Research with WESTLAW

This statutory compilation provides essential aid in solving legal problems involving federal immigration law. WESTLAW provides additional resources. This guide will assist your use of WESTLAW to supplement research begun in this pamphlet.

## 2. Databases

A database is an aggregation of documents with one or more features in common. A database may contain statutes, court decisions, administrative materials, or commentaries. Every database has its own identifier. Database identifiers, such as DCT (decisions of the United States District Courts), are used to identify the database to be searched. The WESTLAW Directory is a comprehensive listing of databases, with information about each database, including the types of documents each contains.

## 3. Updating Statutes

A WESTLAW search may be used to ascertain whether a particular statutory section has been amended after this pamphlet was printed. After checking the WESTLAW Directory for coverage, sign on to the USC database and using the desired title number and section number, a query is entered in the following form:

ci (8 +3 1258)

This will retrieve section 1258 of Title 8 of the United States Code.

## 4. Retrieving a Regulation in the Code of Federal Regulations

To find the text of a federal regulation, sign on to the CFR database and enter a query in the following form:

ci (8 + 213.1)

This will retrieve section 213.1 of the Code of Federal Regulations.

## 5. Retrieving Cases Citing a Statute

To retrieve cases citing a statutory provision, sign on to any caselaw database and enter a query in this form:

(Immigration +7 211) ("8 U.S.C.***" "Title 8" +7 1181)

This will retrieve cases citing section 211 of the Immigration and Nationality Act, 8 U.S.C.A. 1181.

## 6. Retrieving Cases Citing a Constitutional Provision

To find cases citing a particular constitutional provision, sign on to any of the caselaw databases. Using the desired citations, a query is entered in the following form:

A constitutional amendment such as the Eighth Amendment

(eighth +5 amendment) (const.amend +2 VIII 8)
(U.S.C.A.Const.Amend +2 8)

A constitutional article such as Article 4

(U.S.C.A.Const. "U.S. Const." +2 4 IV) (constitution /5 4 IV)

A particular section of a constitutional article such as Article 4 section 1

(U.S.C.A.Const. "U.S.C.A. Const." +2 IV 4 +2 1)
(constitution /5 4 IV /2 1)

## 7. Retrieving Cases Citing a Court Rule

To find cases citing a particular rule, sign on to a caselaw database. Using the desired citation a query is entered in the following form:

Federal Rules of Civil Procedure such as Rule 11

Fed.R.Civ! F.R.Civ! Civ.Proc! F.R.C.P. Civ** /8 11

Federal Rules of Criminal Procedure such as Rule 16

Fed.R.Cr! F.R.Cr! Crim.Proc! Crim**** F.R.Cr.P. 18 16

Federal Rules of Appellate Procedure such as Rule 22

F.R.A.P. F.R.Ap! Fed.R.Ap! App.Proc. Appellate /3 22

## 8. Key Number Search

WESTLAW may be used to search any topic and key number in West's Key Number System. To retrieve cases with at least one headnote classified to the topic Aliens ☞53.9, sign on to a caselaw database and enter:

24k53.9

The topic name Aliens is replaced by its numerical equivalent 24 and the ☞ by the letter k. A list of topics and their numerical equivalents is in the WESTLAW Reference Manual and is also available in the WESTLAW Directory.

## 9.  Retrieving a Cited Case

WESTLAW's FIND command can be used to quickly retrieve a cited case.  Simply enter a command in this form:

fi 866 F.2d 258

## 10.  Using Insta-Cite ® for Case History and Parallel Citations

Insta-Cite ® may be used to find any parallel citations and the history of a reported case.  Enter a command in this form:

ic 673 F.2d 225

All parallel cites will be displayed together with the history of the case reported at 673 F.2d 225.

## 11.  Shepardizing™ a Case with WESTLAW

Shepard's ® Citations may be displayed for a reported case.  Enter a command in this form:

sh 88 S.Ct. 1970

The Shepard's information for the case reported at 88 S.Ct. 1970 will be displayed.

## 12.  Additional Information

The information provided above illustrates some of the ways WESTLAW can complement research using U.S.C.A.  However, this brief overview illustrates only some of the power of WESTLAW.  The full range of WESTLAW search techniques is available to support your research from this series.  Please consult the WESTLAW manual for additional information.

*

# TABLE OF CONTENTS

*

# TABLE

## IMMIGRATION AND NATIONALITY ACT SECTION CLASSIFICATION TO U.S.C.A.

| Date | Pub.L. | Ch. | Sec. | 66 Stat. Page | U.S.C.A. Title | U.S.C.A. Section |
|------|--------|-----|------|---------------|-------|---------|
| 1952—June 27 | 414 | 477 | 101 | 166 | 8 | 1101 |
| | | | 102 | 173 | 8 | 1102 |
| | | | 103 | 173 | 8 | 1103 |
| | | | 104 | 174 | 8 | 1104 |
| | | | 105 | 175 | 8 | 1105 |
| | | | 106 | — | 8 | 1105a |
| | | | 201 | 175 | 8 | 1151 |
| | | | 202 | 176 | 8 | 1152 |
| | | | 203 | 178 | 8 | 1153 |
| | | | 204 | 179 | 8 | 1154 |
| | | | 205 | 180 | 8 | 1155 |
| | | | 206 | 181 | 8 | 1156 |
| | | | 207 | — | 8 | 1157 |
| | | | 208 | — | 8 | 1158 |
| | | | 209 | — | 8 | 1159 |
| | | | 210 | — | 8 | 1160 |
| | | | 210A | — | 8 | 1161 |
| | | | 211 | 181 | 8 | 1181 |
| | | | 212 | 181 | 8 | 1182 |
| | | | 213 | 188 | 8 | 1183 |
| | | | 214 | 189 | 8 | 1184 |
| | | | 215 | 190 | 8 | 1185 |
| | | | 216 | — | 8 | 1186a |
| | | | 216A | — | 8 | 1186b |
| | | | 217 | — | 8 | 1187 |
| | | | 218 | — | 8 | 1188 |
| | | | 221 | 191 | 8 | 1201 |
| | | | 222 | 193 | 8 | 1202 |
| | | | 223 | 194 | 8 | 1203 |
| | | | 224 | 195 | 8 | 1204 |
| | | | 231 | 195 | 8 | 1221 |
| | | | 232 | 196 | 8 | 1222 |
| | | | 234 | 198 | 8 | 1224 |
| | | | 235 | 198 | 8 | 1225 |
| | | | 236 | 200 | 8 | 1226 |
| | | | 237 | 201 | 8 | 1227 |
| | | | 238 | 202 | 8 | 1228 |
| | | | 239 | 203 | 8 | 1229 |
| | | | 240 | 204 | 8 | 1230 |
| | | | 241 | 204 | 8 | 1251 |
| | | | 242 | 208 | 8 | 1252 |
| | | | 242A | — | 8 | 1252a |
| | | | 242B | — | 8 | 1252b |
| | | | 243 | 212 | 8 | 1253 |
| | | | 244 | 214 | 8 | 1254 |
| | | | 244A | — | 8 | 1254a |
| | | | 245 | 217 | 8 | 1255 |
| | | | 245A | — | 8 | 1255a |
| | | | 246 | 217 | 8 | 1256 |
| | | | 247 | 218 | 8 | 1257 |
| | | | 248 | 218 | 8 | 1258 |

# TABLE

# TABLE

\*

# IMMIGRATION AND NATIONALITY LAWS OF THE UNITED STATES

## SELECTED STATUTES, REGULATIONS AND FORMS

*

# IMMIGRATION AND NATIONALITY ACT [INA § ___]

## TITLE I—GENERAL PROVISIONS

## TITLE II—IMMIGRATION

### CHAPTER I—SELECTION SYSTEM

# GENERAL PROVISIONS

3

CHAPTER III—ISSUANCE OF ENTRY DOCUMENTS

# IMMIGRATION AND NATIONALITY

## CHAPTER V—DEPORTATION; ADJUSTMENT OF STATUS

9

## TITLE III—NATIONALITY AND NATURALIZATION

### Chapter I—Nationality at Birth and Collective Naturalization

### Chapter II—Nationality Through Naturalization

hostilities, the Vietnam hostilities, or in other periods of military hostilities [8 U.S.C.A. § 1440–1].

    (a) Permitting granting of posthumous citizenship.

    (b) Noncitizens eligible for posthumous citizenship.

    (c) Requests for posthumous citizenship.

    (d) Documentation of posthumous citizenship.

    (e) No benefits to survivors.

330.    Constructive residence through service on certain United States vessels [8 U.S.C.A. § 1441].

331.    Alien enemies [8 U.S.C.A. § 1442].

    (a) Naturalization under specified conditions.

    (b) Procedure.

    (c) Exceptions from classification.

    (d) Effect of cessation of hostilities.

    (e) Apprehension and removal.

332.    Administration [8 U.S.C.A. § 1443].

    (a) Rules and regulations governing examination of petitioners.

    (b) Instruction in citizenship.

    (c) Prescription of forms.

    (d) Administration of oaths and depositions.

    (e) Issuance of certificate of naturalization or citizenship.

    (f) Copies of records.

    (g) Furnished quarters for photographic studios.

    (h) Public education regarding naturalization benefits.

333.    Photographs; number [8 U.S.C.A. § 1444].

334.    Application for naturalization; declaration of intention [8 U.S.C.A. § 1445].

    (a) Evidence and form.

    (b) Who may file.

    (c) Hearings.

    (d) Filing of application.

    (e) Substitute filing place and administering oath other than before Attorney General.

    (f) Redesignated (g).

    (g) Declaration of intention.

335.    Investigation of applicants; examination of applications [8 U.S.C.A. § 1446].

    (a) Waiver.

    (b) Conduct of examinations; authority of designees; record.

    (c) Transmittal of examination.

    (d) Determination to grant or deny application.

    (e) Withdrawal of application.

    (f) Transfer of application.

336.    Hearings on denials of application for naturalization [8 U.S.C.A. § 1447].

    (a) Request for hearing before immigration officer.

    (b) Request for hearing before district court.

    (c) Appearance of Attorney General.

    (d) Subpena of witnesses.

    (e) Change of name of petitioner.

337.    Oath of renunciation and allegiance [8 U.S.C.A. § 1448].

    (a) Public ceremony.

    (b) Hereditary titles or orders of nobility.

    (c) Other than public ceremony.

    (d) Rules and regulations.

# GENERAL PROVISIONS

(c) Application for admission to United States under certificate of identity; revision of determination.

# TITLE I

# GENERAL PROVISIONS

## § 101.  Definitions [8 U.S.C.A. § 1101]

(a) As used in this chapter—

(1) The term "administrator" means the Assistant Secretary of State for Consular Affairs.

(2) The term "advocates" includes, but is not limited to, advises, recommends, furthers by overt act, and admits belief in.

(3) The term "alien" means any person not a citizen or national of the United States.

(4) The term "application for admission" has reference to the application for admission into the United States and not to the application for the issuance of an immigrant or nonimmigrant visa.

(5) The term "Attorney General" means the Attorney General of the United States.

(6) The term "border crossing identification card" means a document of identity bearing that designation issued to an alien who is lawfully admitted for permanent residence, or to an alien who is a resident in foreign contiguous territory, by a consular officer or an immigration officer for the purpose of crossing over the borders between the United States and foreign contiguous territory in accordance with such conditions for its issuance and use as may be prescribed by regulations.

(7) The term "clerk of court" means a clerk of a naturalization court.

(8) The terms "Commissioner" and "Deputy Commissioner" mean the Commissioner of Immigration and Naturalization and a

Deputy Commissioner of Immigration and Naturalization, respectively.

**(9)** The term "consular officer" means any consular, diplomatic, or other officer of the United States designated under regulations prescribed under authority contained in this chapter, for the purpose of issuing immigrant or nonimmigrant visas.

**(10)** The term "crewman" means a person serving in any capacity on board a vessel or aircraft.

**(11)** The term "diplomatic visa" means a nonimmigrant visa bearing that title and issued to a nonimmigrant in accordance with such regulations as the Secretary of State may prescribe.

**(12)** The term "doctrine" includes, but is not limited to, policies, practices, purposes, aims, or procedures.

**(13)** The term "entry" means any coming of an alien into the United States, from a foreign port or place or from an outlying possession, whether voluntarily or otherwise, except that an alien having a lawful permanent residence in the United States shall not be regarded as making an entry into the United States for the purposes of the immigration laws if the alien proves to the satisfaction of the Attorney General that his departure to a foreign port or place or to an outlying possession was not intended or reasonably to be expected by him or his presence in a foreign port or place or in an outlying possession was not voluntary: *Provided,* That no person whose departure from the United States was occasioned by deportation proceedings, extradition, or other legal process shall be held to be entitled to such exception.

**(14)** The term "foreign state" includes outlying possessions of a foreign state, but self-governing dominions or territories under mandate or trusteeship shall be regarded as separate foreign states.

**(15)** The term "immigrant" means every alien except an alien who is within one of the following classes of nonimmigrant aliens—

**(A)(i)** an ambassador, public minister, or career diplomatic or consular officer who has been accredited by a foreign government, recognized de jure by the United States and who is accepted by the President or by the Secretary of State, and the members of the alien's immediate family;

**(ii)** upon a basis of reciprocity, other officials and employees who have been accredited by a foreign government recognized de jure by the United States, who are accepted by the Secretary of State, and the members of their immediate families; and

**(iii)** upon a basis of reciprocity, attendants, servants, personal employees, and members of their immediate families, of the officials and employees who have a nonimmigrant status under (i) and (ii) above;

15

**(B)** an alien (other than one coming for the purpose of study or of performing skilled or unskilled labor or as a representative of foreign press, radio, film, or other foreign information media coming to engage in such vocation) having a residence in a foreign country which he has no intention of abandoning and who is visiting the United States temporarily for business or temporarily for pleasure;

**(C)** an alien in immediate and continuous transit through the United States, or an alien who qualifies as a person entitled to pass in transit to and from the United Nations Headquarters District and foreign countries, under the provisions of paragraphs (3), (4), and (5) of section 11 of the Headquarters Agreement with the United Nations (61 Stat. 758);

**(D)(i)** an alien crewman serving in good faith as such in a capacity required for normal operation and service on board a vessel, as defined in section 258(a) [8 U.S.C.A. § 1288a] (other than a fishing vessel having its home port or an operating base in the United States) or aircraft, who intends to land temporarily and solely in pursuit of his calling as a crewman and to depart from the United States with the vessel or aircraft on which he arrived or some other vessel or aircraft;

**(ii)** an alien crewman serving in good faith as such in any capacity required for normal operations and service aboard a fishing vessel having its home port or an operating base in the United States who intends to land temporarily in Guam and solely in pursuit of his calling as a crewman and to depart from Guam with the vessel on which he arrived;

**(E)** an alien entitled to enter the United States under and in pursuance of the provisions of a treaty of commerce and navigation between the United States and the foreign state of which he is a national, and the spouse and children of any such alien if accompanying or following to join him; (i) solely to carry on substantial trade, including trade in services or trade in technology, principally between the United States and the foreign state of which he is a national; or (ii) solely to develop and direct the operations of an enterprise in which he has invested, or of an enterprise in which he is actively in the process of investing, a substantial amount of capital;

**(F)(i)** an alien having a residence in a foreign country which he has no intention of abandoning, who is a bona fide student qualified to pursue a full course of study and who seeks to enter the United States temporarily and solely for the purpose of pursuing such a course of study at an established college, university, seminary, conservatory, academic high school, elementary school, or other academic institution or in a language training program in the United States, particularly designated by him and approved by the Attorney General after consultation with the Secretary of Education, which institution or place of study shall have agreed to report to the Attorney General the termination of attendance of each nonimmigrant student, and if any such institution of learning or place of study fails to make reports promptly the approval shall be withdrawn, and (ii) the alien spouse and minor children of any such alien if accompanying him or following to join him;

**(G)(i)** a designated principal resident representative of a foreign government recognized de jure by the United States, which foreign government is a member of an international organization entitled to enjoy privileges, exemptions, and immunities as an international organization under the International Organizations Immunities Act (59 Stat. 669) [22 U.S.C. 288 et seq.], accredited resident members of the staff of such representatives, and members of his or their immediate family;

**(ii)** other accredited representatives of such a foreign government to such international organizations, and the members of their immediate families;

**(iii)** an alien able to qualify under (i) or (ii) above except for the fact that the government of which such alien is an accredited representative is not recognized de jure by the United States, or that the government of which he is an accredited representative is not a member of such international organization; and the members of his immediate family;

**(iv)** officers, or employees of such international organizations, and the members of their immediate families;

**(v)** attendants, servants, and personal employees of any such representative, officer, or employee, and the members of the immediate families of such attendants, servants, and personal employees;

**(H)** an alien (i)(a) who is coming temporarily to the United States to perform services as a registered nurse, who meets the qualifications described in section 212(m)(1) [8 U.S.C.A. § 1182(m)(1)], and with respect to whom the Secretary of Labor determines and certifies to the Attorney General that an unexpired attestation is on file and in effect under section 212(m)(2) [8 U.S.C.A. § 1182(m)(2)] for each facility (which facility shall include the petitioner and each worksite, other than a private household worksite, if the worksite is not the alien's employer or controlled by the employer) for which the alien will perform the services, or (b) who is coming temporarily to the United States to perform services (other than services described in subclause (a) during the period in which such subclause applies and other than services described in subclause (ii)(a) or in subparagraph (O) or (P)) in a specialty occupation described in section 214(i)(1) [8 U.S.C.A. § 1184(i)(1)] who meets the requirements for the occupation specified in section 214(i)(2) [8 U.S.C.A. § 1184(i)(2)], and with respect to whom the Secretary of Labor determines and certifies to the Attorney General that the intending employer has filed with, and had approved by, the Secretary an application under section 212(n)(1) [8 U.S.C.A. § 1182(n)(1)] or (ii) (a) having a residence in a foreign country which he has no intention of abandoning who is coming temporarily to the United States to perform agricultural labor or services, as defined by the Secretary of Labor in regulations and including agricultural labor defined in section 3121(g) of Title 26 and agriculture as defined in section 203(f) of Title 29, of a temporary or seasonal nature, or (b) having a residence in a foreign country which he has no intention of abandoning who is coming temporarily to the United States to perform other temporary service or labor, if unemployed persons capable of performing such service or labor cannot be found in this country, but this clause shall not apply to graduates of medical schools coming to the United States to perform services as members of the medical profession; or (iii) having a residence in a foreign country which he has no intention of abandoning who is coming temporarily to the United States as a trainee, other than to receive graduate medical education or training and by inserting before the semi, in a training program that is not designed primarily to provide productive employment; and the alien spouse and minor children of any such alien specified in this paragraph if accompanying him or following to join him;

(I) upon a basis of reciprocity, an alien who is a bona fide representative of foreign press, radio, film, or other foreign information media, who seeks to enter the United States solely to engage in such vocation, and the spouse and children of such a representative, if accompanying or following to join him;

(J) an alien having a residence in a foreign country which he has no intention of abandoning who is a bona fide student, scholar, trainee, teacher, professor, research assistant, specialist, or leader in a field of specialized knowledge or skill, or other person of similar description, who is coming temporarily to the United States as a participant in a program designated by the Director of the United States Information Agency, for the purpose of teaching, instructing or lecturing, studying, observing, conducting research, consulting, demonstrating special skills, or receiving training and who, if he is coming to the United States to participate in a program under which he will receive graduate medical education or training, also meets the requirements of section 212(j) [8 U.S.C.A. § 1182(j)], and the alien spouse and minor children of any such alien if accompanying him or following to join him;

**(K)** an alien who is the fiancee or fiance of a citizen of the United States and who seeks to enter the United States solely to conclude a valid marriage with the petitioner within ninety days after entry, and the minor children of such fiancee of fiance accompanying him or following to join him;

**(L)** an alien who, within 3 years preceding the time of his application for admission into the United States, has been employed continuously for one year by a firm or corporation or other legal entity or an affiliate or subsidiary thereof and who seeks to enter the United States temporarily in order to continue to render his services to the same employer or a subsidiary or affiliate thereof in a capacity that is managerial, executive, or involves specialized knowledge, and the alien spouse and minor children of any such alien if accompanying him or following to join him;

**(M)(i)** an alien having a residence in a foreign country which he has no intention of abandoning who seeks to enter the United States temporarily and solely for the purpose of pursuing a full course of study at an established vocational or other recognized nonacademic institution (other than in a language training program) in the United States particularly designated by him and approved by the Attorney General, after consultation with the Secretary of Education, which institution shall have agreed to report to the Attorney General the termination of attendance of each nonimmigrant nonacademic student and if any such institution fails to make reports promptly the approval shall be withdrawn, and (ii) the alien spouse and minor children of any such alien if accompanying him or following to join him;

**(N)(i)** the parent of an alien accorded the status of special immigrant under paragraph (27)(I)(i), but only if and while the alien is a child, or

**(ii)** a child of such parent or of an alien accorded the status of a special immigrant under clause (ii), (iii), or (iv) of paragraph (27)(I);

**(O)** an alien who—

**(i)** has extraordinary ability in the sciences, arts, education, business, or athletics which has been demonstrated by sustained national or international acclaim or, with regard to motion picture and television productions a demonstrated record of extraordinary achievement, and whose achievements have been recognized in the field through extensive documentation, and seeks to enter the United States to continue work in the area of extraordinary ability, but only if the Attorney General determines that the alien's entry into the United

States will substantially benefit prospectively the United States; or

**(ii)(I)** seeks to enter the United States temporarily and solely for the purpose of accompanying and assisting in the artistic or athletic performance by an alien who is admitted under clause (i) for a specific event or events,

**(II)** is an integral part of such actual performance,

**(III)(a)** has critical skills and experience with such alien which are not of a general nature and which cannot be performed by other individuals, or (b) in the case of a motion picture or television production, has skills and experience with such alien which are not of a general nature and which are critical either based on a pre-existing longstanding working relationship or, with respect to the specific production, because significant principal photography will take place both inside and outside the United States and the continuing participation of the alien is essential to the successful completion of the production, and

**(IV)** has a foreign residence which the alien has no intention of abandoning; or

**(iii)** is the alien spouse or child of an alien described in clause (i) or (ii) and is accompanying, or following to join, the alien;

**(P)** an alien having a foreign residence which the alien has no intention of abandoning who—

**(i)(I)** performs as an athlete, individually or as part of a group or team, at an internationally recognized level of performance, or performs as part of an entertainment group that has been recognized internationally as being outstanding in the discipline for a sustained and substantial period of time and has had a sustained and substantial relationship with that group over a period of at least 1 year and provides functions integral to the performance of the group, and

**(II)** seeks to enter the United States temporarily and solely for the purpose of performing as such an athlete or entertainer with respect to a specific athletic competition or performance;

**(ii)(I)** performs as an artist or entertainer, individually or as part of a group, or is an integral part of the performance of such a group, and

**(II)** seeks to enter the United States temporarily and solely for the purpose of performing as such an artist or entertainer or with such a group under a reciprocal exchange program which is between an organization or organizations in the United States and an organization in one or more foreign states and which provides for the temporary exchange of artists and entertainers, or groups of artists and entertainers, between the United States and the foreign states involved;

**(iii)(I)** performs as an artist or entertainer, individually or as part of a group, or is an integral part of the performance of such a group, and

**(II)** seeks to enter the United States temporarily and solely for the purpose of performing as such an artist or entertainer or with such a group under a program that is culturally unique; or

**(iv)** is the spouse or child of an alien described in clause (i), (ii), or (iii) and is accompanying, or following to join, the alien;

**(Q)** an alien having a residence in a foreign country which he has no intention of abandoning who is coming temporarily (for a period not to exceed 15 months) to the United States as a participant in an international cultural exchange program designated by the Attorney General for the purpose of providing practical training, employment, and the sharing of the history, culture, and traditions of the country of the alien's nationality and who will be employed under the same wages and working conditions as domestic workers; or

**(R)** an alien, and the spouse and children of the alien if accompanying or following to join the alien, who—

**(i)** for the 2 years immediately preceding the time of application for admission, has been a member of a religious denomination having a bona fide nonprofit, religious organization in the United States; and

**(ii)** seeks to enter the United States for a period not to exceed 5 years to perform the work described in subclause (I), (II), or (III) of paragraph (27)(C)(ii).

**(16)** The term "immigrant visa" means an immigrant visa required by this chapter and properly issued by a consular officer at his office outside of the United States to an eligible immigrant under the provisions of this chapter.

**(17)** The term "immigration laws" includes this chapter and all laws, conventions, and treaties of the United States relating to the immigration, exclusion, deportation, or expulsion of aliens.

**(18)** The term "immigration officer" means any employee or class of employees of the Service or of the United States designated by the Attorney General, individually or by regulation, to perform the functions of an immigration officer specified by this chapter or any section of this title.

**(19)** The term "ineligible to citizenship," when used in reference to any individual, means, notwithstanding the provisions of any treaty relating to military service, an individual who is, or was at any time, permanently debarred from becoming a citizen of the United States under section 3(a) of the Selective Training and Service Act of 1940, as amended (54 Stat. 885; 55 Stat. 844), or under section 4(a) of the Selective Service Act of 1948, as amended (62 Stat. 605; 65 Stat. 76) [50 App. U.S.C. 454(a)], or under any section of this chapter, or any other Act, or under any law amendatory of, supplementary to, or in substitution for, any of such sections or Acts.

(20) The term "lawfully admitted for permanent residence" means the status of having been lawfully accorded the privilege of residing permanently in the United States as an immigrant in accordance with the immigration laws, such status not having changed.

(21) The term "national" means a person owing permanent allegiance to a state.

(22) The term "national of the United States" means (A) a citizen of the United States, or (B) a person who, though not a citizen of the United States, owes permanent allegiance to the United States.

(23) The term "naturalization" means the conferring of nationality of a state upon a person after birth, by any means whatsoever.

(24) The term "naturalization court", unless otherwise particularly described, means a court authorized by section 210(a) [8 U.S.C.A. § 1421(a)] to exercise naturalization jurisdiction.

(25) The term "noncombatant service" shall not include service in which the individual is not subject to military discipline, court martial, or does not wear the uniform of any branch of the armed forces.

(26) The term "nonimmigrant visa" means a visa properly issued to an alien as an eligible nonimmigrant by a competent officer as provided in this chapter.

(27) The term "special immigrant" means—

(A) an immigrant, lawfully admitted for permanent residence, who is returning from a temporary visit abroad;

(B) an immigrant who was a citizen of the United States and may, under section 324(a) [8 U.S.C.A. § 1435(a)] or 327 [8 U.S.C.A. § 1438], apply for reacquisition of citizenship;

(C) an immigrant, and the immigrant's spouse and children if accompanying or following to join the immigrant, who—

(i) for at least 2 years immediately preceding the time of application for admission, has been a member of a religious denomination having a bona fide nonprofit, religious organization in the United States;

(ii) seeks to enter the United States—

(I) solely for the purpose of carrying on the vocation of a minister of that religious denomination,

(II) before October 1, 1994, in order to work for the organization at the request of the organization in a professional capacity in a religious vocation or occupation, or

(III) before October 1, 1994, in order to work for the organization (or for a bona fide organization which is affiliated with the religious denomination and is exempt from taxation as an organization described in section 501(c)(3) of Title 26) at the request of the organization in a religious vocation or occupation; and

(iii) has been carrying on such vocation, professional work, or other work continuously for at least the 2-year period described in clause (i);

(D) an immigrant who is an employee, or an honorably retired former employee, of the United States Government abroad, and who has performed faithful service for a total of fifteen years, or more, and his accompanying spouse and children: *Provided,* That the principal officer of a Foreign Service establishment, in his discretion, shall have recommended the granting of special immigrant status to such alien in exceptional circumstances and the Secretary of State approves such recommendation and finds that it is in the national interest to grant such status;

(E) an immigrant, and his accompanying spouse and children, who is or has been an employee of the Panama Canal Company or Canal Zone Government before the date on which the Panama Canal Treaty of 1977 (as described in section 3602(a)(1) of Title 22) enters into force [October 1, 1979], who was resident in the Canal Zone on the effective date of the exchange of instruments of ratification of such Treaty [April 1, 1979], and who has performed faithful service as such an employee for one year or more;

(F) an immigrant, and his accompanying spouse and children, who is a Panamanian national and (i) who, before the date on which such Panama Canal Treaty of 1977 enters into force [October 1, 1979], has been honorably retired from United States Government employment in the Canal Zone with a total of 15 years or more of faithful service, or (ii) who, on the date on which such Treaty enters into force, has been employed by the United States Government in the Canal Zone with a total of 15 years or more of faithful service and who subsequently is honorably retired from such employment;

(G) an immigrant, and his accompanying spouse and children, who was an employee of the Panama Canal Company or Canal Zone Government on the effective date of the exchange of instruments of ratification of such Panama Canal Treaty of 1977 [April 1, 1979], who has performed faithful service for five years or more as such an employee, and whose personal safety, or the personal safety of whose spouse or children, as a direct result of such Treaty, is reasonably placed in danger because of the special nature of any of that employment;

(H) an immigrant, and his accompanying spouse and children, who—

(i) has graduated from a medical school or has qualified to practice medicine in a foreign state,

(ii) was fully and permanently licensed to practice medicine in a State on January 9, 1978, and was practicing medicine in a State on that date,

(iii) entered the United States as a nonimmigrant under subsection (a)(15)(H) or (a)(15)(J) of this section before January 10, 1978, and

(iv) has been continuously present in the United States in the practice or study of medicine since the date of such entry;

(I)(i) an immigrant who is the unmarried son or daughter of an officer or employee, or of a former officer or employee, of an international organization described in paragraph (15)(G)(i), and who (I) while maintaining the status of a nonimmigrant under paragraph (15)(G)(iv) or paragraph (15)(N), has resided and been physically present in the United States for periods totaling at least one-half of the seven years before the date of application for a visa or for adjustment of status to a status under this subparagraph and for a period or periods aggregating at least seven years between the ages of five and 21 years, and (II) applies for a visa or adjustment of status under this subparagraph no later than his twenty-fifth birthday or six months after October 24, 1988, whichever is later;

(ii) an immigrant who is the surviving spouse of a deceased officer or employee of such an international organization, and who (I) while maintaining the status of a nonimmigrant under paragraph (15)(G)(iv) or paragraph (15)(N), has resided and been physically present in the United States for periods totaling at least one-half of the seven years before the date of application for a visa or for adjustment of status to a status under this subparagraph and for a period or periods aggregating at least 15 years before the date of the death of such officer or employee, and (II) applies for a visa or adjustment of status under this subparagraph no later than six

24

months after the date of such death or six months after October 24, 1988, whichever is later;

(iii) an immigrant who is a retired officer or employee of such an international organization, and who (I) while maintaining the status of a nonimmigrant under paragraph (15)(G)(iv), has resided and been physically present in the United States for periods totaling at least one-half of the seven years before the date of application for a visa or for adjustment of status to a status under this subparagraph and for a period or periods aggregating at least 15 years before the date of the officer or employee's retirement from any such international organization, and (II) applies for a visa or adjustment of status under this subparagraph before January 1, 1993, and no later than six months after the date of such retirement or six months after October 24, 1988, whichever is later; or

(iv) an immigrant who is the spouse of a retired officer or employee accorded the status of special immigrant under clause (iii), accompanying or following to join such retired officer or employee as a member of his immediate family; or

(J) an immigrant (i) who has been declared dependent on a juvenile court located in the United States and has been deemed eligible by that court for long-term foster care, and (ii) for whom it has been determined in administrative or judicial proceedings that it would not be in the alien's best interest to be returned to the alien's or parent's previous country of nationality or country of last habitual residence; except that no natural parent or prior adoptive parent of any alien provided special immigrant status under this subparagraph shall thereafter, by virtue of such parentage, be accorded any right, privilege, or status under this Act.

(28) The term "organization" means, but is not limited to, an organization, corporation, company, partnership, association, trust, foundation or fund; and includes a group of persons, whether or not incorporated, permanently or temporarily associated together with joint action on any subject or subjects.

(29) The term "outlying possessions of the United States" means American Samoa and Swains Island.

(30) The term "passport" means any travel document issued by competent authority showing the bearer's origin, identity, and nationality if any, which is valid for the entry of the bearer into a foreign country.

(31) The term "permanent" means a relationship of continuing or lasting nature, as distinguished from temporary, but a relationship may be permanent even though it is one that may be dissolved eventually at the instance either of the United States or of the individual, in accordance with law.

(32) The term "profession" shall include but not be limited to architects, engineers, lawyers, physicians, surgeons, and teachers in elementary or secondary schools, colleges, academies, or seminaries.

(33) The term "residence" means the place of general abode; the place of general abode of a person means his principal, actual dwelling place in fact, without regard to intent.

(34) The term "Service" means the Immigration and Naturalization Service of the Department of Justice.

(35) The term "spouse", "wife", or "husband" do not include a spouse, wife, or husband by reason of any marriage ceremony where the contracting parties thereto are not physically present in the presence of each other, unless the marriage shall have been consummated.

(36) The term "State" includes the District of Columbia, Puerto Rico, Guam, and the Virgin Islands of the United States.

(37) The term "totalitarian party" means an organization which advocates the establishment in the United States of a totalitarian dictatorship or totalitarianism. The terms "totalitarian dictatorship" and "totalitarianism" mean and refer to systems of government not representative in fact, characterized by (A) the existence of a single political party, organized on a dictatorial basis, with so close an identity between such party and its policies and the governmental policies of the country in which it exists, that the party and the government constitute an indistinguishable unit, and (B) the forcible suppression of opposition to such party.

(38) The term "United States", except as otherwise specifically herein provided, when used in a geographical sense, means the continental United States, Alaska, Hawaii, Puerto Rico, Guam, and the Virgin Islands of the United States.

(39) The term "unmarried", when used in reference to any individual as of any time, means an individual who at such time is not married, whether or not previously married.

(40) The term "world communism" means a revolutionary movement, the purpose of which is to establish eventually a Communist totalitarian dictatorship in any or all the countries of the world through the medium of an internationally coordinated Communist political movement.

(41) The term "graduates of a medical school" means aliens who have graduated from a medical school or who have qualified to practice medicine in a foreign state, other than such aliens who are of national or international renown in the field of medicine.

(42) The term "refugee" means (A) any person who is outside any country of such person's nationality or, in the case of a person having no nationality, is outside any country in which such person

last habitually resided, and who is unable or unwilling to return to, and is unable or unwilling to avail himself or herself of the protection of, that country because of persecution or a well-founded fear of persecution on account of race, religion, nationality, membership in a particular social group, or political opinion, or (B) in such special circumstances as the President after appropriate consultation (as defined in section 207(e) [8 U.S.C.A. § 1157(e)]) may specify, any person who is within the country of such person's nationality or, in the case of a person having no nationality, within the country in which such person is habitually residing, and who is persecuted or who has a well-founded fear of persecution on account of race, religion, nationality, membership in a particular social group, or political opinion. The term "refugee" does not include any person who ordered, incited, assisted, or otherwise participated in the persecution of any person on account of race, religion, nationality, membership in a particular social group, or political opinion.

**(43)** The term "aggravated felony" means murder, any illicit trafficking in any controlled substance (as defined in section 802 of Title 21), including any drug trafficking crime as defined in section 924(c)(2) of Title 18, or any illicit trafficking in any firearms or destructive devices as defined in section 921 of such title, any offense described in section 1956 of Title 18 (relating to laundering of monetary instruments), or any crime of violence (as defined in section 16 of Title 18, not including a purely political offense) for which the term of imprisonment imposed (regardless of any suspension of such imprisonment) is at least 5 years, or any attempt or conspiracy to commit any such act. Such term applies to offenses described in the previous sentence whether in violation of Federal or State law and also applies to offenses described in the previous sentence in violation of foreign law for which the term of imprisonment was completed within the previous 15 years.

**(44)(A)** The term "managerial capacity" means an assignment within an organization in which the employee primarily—

    **(i)** manages the organization, or a department, subdivision, function, or component of the organization;

    **(ii)** supervises and controls the work of other supervisory, professional, or managerial employees, or manages an essential function within the organization, or a department or subdivision of the organization;

    **(iii)** if another employee or other employees are directly supervised, has the authority to hire and fire or recommend those as well as other personnel actions (such as promotion and leave authorization) or, if no other employee is directly supervised, functions at a senior level within the organizational hierarchy or with respect to the function managed; and

(iv) exercises discretion over the day-to-day operations of the activity or function for which the employee has authority.

A first-line supervisor is not considered to be acting in a managerial capacity merely by virtue of the supervisor's supervisory duties unless the employees supervised are professional.

(B) The term "executive capacity" means an assignment within an organization in which the employee primarily—

(i) directs the management of the organization or a major component or function of the organization;

(ii) establishes the goals and policies of the organization, component, or function;

(iii) exercises wide latitude in discretionary decision-making; and

(iv) receives only general supervision or direction from higher level executives, the board of directors, or stockholders of the organization.

(C) If staffing levels are used as a factor in determining whether an individual is acting in a managerial or executive capacity, the Attorney General shall take into account the reasonable needs of the organization, component, or function in light of the overall purpose and stage of development of the organization, component, or function. An individual shall not be considered to be acting in a managerial or executive capacity (as previously defined) merely on the basis of the number of employees that the individual supervises or has supervised or directs or has directed.

(45) The term "substantial" means, for purposes of paragraph (15)(E) with reference to trade or capital, such an amount of trade or capital as is established by the Secretary of State, after consultation with appropriate agencies of Government.

(b) As used in subchapters I and II of this chapter—

(1) The term "child" means an unmarried person under twenty-one years of age who is—

(A) a legitimate child;

(B) a stepchild, whether or not born out of wedlock, provided the child had not reached the age of eighteen years at the time the marriage creating the status of stepchild occurred;

(C) a child legitimated under the law of the child's residence or domicile, or under the law of the father's residence or domicile, whether in or outside the United States, if such legitimation takes place before the child reaches the age of eighteen years and the child is in the legal custody of the legitimating parent or parents at the time of such legitimation;

(D) an illegitimate child, by, through whom, or on whose behalf a status, privilege, or benefit is sought by virtue of the relationship of the child to its natural mother or to its natural father if the father has or had a bona fide parent-child relationship with the person;

**(E)** a child adopted while under the age of sixteen years if the child has been in the legal custody of, and has resided with, the adopting parent or parents for at least two years: *Provided,* That no natural parent of any such adopted child shall thereafter, by virtue of such parentage, be accorded any right, privilege, or status under this chapter; or

**(F)** a child, under the age of sixteen at the time a petition is filed in his behalf to accord a classification as an immediate relative under section 201(b) [8 U.S.C.A. § 1151(b)], who is an orphan because of the death or disappearance of, abandonment or desertion by, or separation or loss from, both parents, or for whom the sole or surviving parent is incapable of providing the proper care and has in writing irrevocably released the child for emigration and adoption; who has been adopted abroad by a United States citizen and spouse jointly, or by an unmarried United States citizen at least twenty-five years of age, who personally saw and observed the child prior to or during the adoption proceedings; or who is coming to the United States for adoption by a United States citizen and spouse jointly, or by an unmarried United States citizen at least twenty-five years of age, who have or has complied with the preadoption requirements, if any, of the child's proposed residence; *Provided,* That the Attorney General is satisfied that proper care will be furnished the child if admitted to the United States: *Provided further,* That no natural parent or prior adoptive parent of any such child shall thereafter, by virtue of such parentage, be accorded any right, privilege, or status under this chapter.

**(2)** The terms "parent", "father", or "mother" mean a parent, father, or mother only where the relationship exists by reason of any of the circumstances set forth in subdivision (1) of this subsection, except that, for purposes of paragraph (1)(F) (other than the second proviso therein) in the case of an illegitimate child described in paragraph (1)(D) (and not described in paragraph (1)(C)), the term "parent" does not include the natural father of the child if the father has disappeared or abandoned or deserted the child or if the father has in writing irrevocably released the child for emigration and adoption.

**(3)** The term "person" means an individual or an organization.

**(4)** The term "special inquiry officer" means any immigration officer who the Attorney General deems specially qualified to conduct specified classes of proceedings, in whole or in part, required by this chapter to be conducted by or before a special inquiry officer and who is designated and selected by the Attorney General, individually or by regulation, to conduct such proceedings.

Such special inquiry officer shall be subject to such supervision and shall perform such duties, not inconsistent with this chapter, as the Attorney General shall prescribe.

(5) The term "adjacent islands" includes Saint Pierre, Miquelon, Cuba, the Dominican Republic, Haiti, Bermuda, the Bahamas, Barbados, Jamaica, the Windward and Leeward Islands, Trinidad, Martinique, and other British, French, and Netherlands territory or possessions in or bordering on the Caribbean Sea.

(c) As used in subchapter III of this chapter—

(1) The term "child" means an unmarried person under twenty-one years of age and includes a child legitimated under the law of the child's residence or domicile, or under the law of the father's residence or domicile, whether in the United States or elsewhere, and, except as otherwise provided in sections 320–323 [8 U.S.C.A. §§ 1431–1434], a child adopted in the United States, if such legitimation or adoption takes place before the child reaches the age of sixteen years, and the child is in the legal custody of the legitimating or adopting parent or parents at the time of such legitimation or adoption.

(2) The terms "parent", "father", and "mother" include in the case of a posthumous child a deceased parent, father, and mother.

(d) Repealed. Pub.L. 100–525, § 9(a)(3), Oct. 24, 1988, 102 Stat. 2619.

(e) For the purposes of this chapter—

(1) The giving, loaning, or promising of support or of money or any other thing of value to be used for advocating any doctrine shall constitute the advocating of such doctrine; but nothing in this paragraph shall be construed as an exclusive definition of advocating.

(2) The giving, loaning, or promising of support or of money or any other thing of value for any purpose to any organization shall be presumed to constitute affiliation therewith; but nothing in this paragraph shall be construed as an exclusive definition of affiliation.

(3) Advocating the economic, international, and governmental doctrines of world communism means advocating the establishment of a totalitarian Communist dictatorship in any or all of the countries of the world through the medium of an internationally coordinated Communist movement.

(f) For the purposes of this chapter—

No person shall be regarded as, or found to be, a person of good moral character who, during the period for which good moral character is required to be established, is, or was—

(1) a habitual drunkard;

(2) Repealed. Pub. L. 97–116, § 2(c)(1), Dec. 29, 1981, 95 Stat. 1611.

(3) a member of one or more of the classes of persons, whether excludable or not, described in paragraphs (2)(D), (6)(E), and (9)(A) of section 212(a) [8 U.S.C.A. § 1182(a)(2)(D), (6)(E), and (9)(A)]; or subparagraphs (A) and (B) of section 212(a)(2) [8 U.S.C.A. § 1182(a)(2)(A) and (B)] and subparagraph (C) thereof of such section (except as such paragraph relates to a single offense of simple possession of 30 grams or less of marihuana), if the offense described therein, for which such person was convicted or of which he admits the commission, was committed during such period;

(4) one whose income is derived principally from illegal gambling activities;

(5) one who has been convicted of two or more gambling offenses committed during such period;

(6) one who has given false testimony for the purpose of obtaining any benefits under this chapter;

(7) one who during such period has been confined, as a result of conviction, to a penal institution for an aggregate period of one hundred and eighty days or more, regardless of whether the offense, or offenses, for which he has been confined were committed within or without such period;

(8) one who at any time has been convicted of an aggravated felony (as defined in subsection (a)(43) of this section).

The fact that any person is not within any of the foregoing classes shall not preclude a finding that for other reasons such person is or was not of good moral character.

(g) For the purposes of this chapter any alien ordered deported (whether before or after the enactment of this chapter) who has left the United States, shall be considered to have been deported in pursuance of law, irrespective of the source from which the expenses of his transportation were defrayed or of the place to which he departed.

(h) For purposes of section 212(a)(2)(E) [8 U.S.C.A. § 1182(a)(2)(E)], the term "serious criminal offense" means—

(1) any felony;

(2) any crime of violence, as defined in section 16 of Title 18; or

(3) any crime of reckless driving or of driving while intoxicated or under the influence of alcohol or of prohibited substances if such crime involves personal injury to another.

(June 27, 1952, c. 477, Title I, § 101, 66 Stat. 166; Pub. L. 85–316, §§ 1, 2, Sept. 11, 1957, 71 Stat. 639; Pub. L. 85–508, § 22, July 7, 1958, 72 Stat. 351; Pub. L. 86–3, § 20(a), Mar. 18, 1959, 73 Stat. 13; Pub. L. 87–256, § 109(a), (b),

Sept. 21, 1961, 75 Stat. 534; Pub. L. 87–301, §§ 1, 2, 7, Sept. 26, 1961, 75 Stat. 650, 653; Pub. L. 89–236, §§ 8, 24, Oct. 3, 1965, 79 Stat. 916, 922; Pub. L. 89–710, Nov. 2, 1966, 80 Stat. 1104; Pub. L. 91–225, § 1, Apr. 7, 1970, 84 Stat. 116; Pub. L. 94–155, Dec. 16, 1975, 89 Stat. 824; Pub. L. 94–484, Title VI, § 601(b), (e), Oct. 12, 1976, 90 Stat. 2301; Pub. L. 94–571, § 7(a), Oct. 20, 1976, 90 Stat. 2706; Pub. L. 94–484, Title VI, § 602(c), Oct. 12, 1976, as added Pub. L. 95–83, Title III, § 307(q)(3), Aug. 1, 1977, 91 Stat. 395; Pub. L. 95–105, Title I, § 109(b)(3), Aug. 17, 1977, 91 Stat. 847; 1977 Reorg. Plan No. 2, § 7(a)(8), 42 F.R. 62461, 91 Stat. 1637; Pub. L. 96–70, Title III, § 3201(a), Sept. 27, 1979, 93 Stat. 496; Pub. L. 96–212, Title II, § 201(a), Mar. 17, 1980, 94 Stat. 102; Pub. L. 97–116, §§ 2, 5(d)(1), 18(a), Dec. 29, 1981, 95 Stat. 1611, 1614, 1619; Pub. L. 97–241, Title III, § 303(a), Aug. 24, 1982, 96 Stat. 291; Pub. L. 98–47, § 3, Oct. 30, 1984, 98 Stat. 3435; Pub.L. 99–505, § 1, Oct. 21, 1986, 100 Stat. 1806; Pub.L. 99–603, Title III, §§ 301(a), 312, 315(a), Nov. 6, 1986, 100 Stat. 3411, 3434, 3439; Pub.L. 99–653, § 2, Nov. 14, 1986, 100 Stat. 3655; Pub.L. 100–459, Title II, § 210(a), Oct. 1, 1988, 102 Stat. 2203; Pub.L. 100–525, §§ 2(o)(1), 8(b), 9(a), Oct. 24, 1988, 102 Stat. 2613, 2617, 2619; Pub.L. 100–690, Title VII, § 7342, Nov. 18, 1988, 102 Stat. 4469; Pub.L. 101–162, Title VI, § 611(a), Nov. 21, 1989, 103 Stat. 1038; Pub.L. 101–238, § 3(a), Dec. 18, 1989, 103 Stat. 2100; Feb. 16, 1990, Pub.L. 101–246, Title I, § 131(b), 104 Stat. 31; Nov. 29, 1990, Pub.L. 101–649, Title I, §§ 123, 151(a), 153(a), 161, 162(f)(2)(A), Title II, §§ 203(c), 204(a), (c), 205(c)(1), (d), (e), 206(c), 207(a), 208, 209(a), 231, Title IV, § 407(a)(2), Title V, §§ 501(a), 509(a), Title VI, § 603(a)(1), 104 Stat. 4995, 5004, 5005, 5008, 5012, 5018, 5019, 5020, 5022, 5023, 5026, 5027, 5028, 5040, 5048, 5051, 5082.)

## § 102. Diplomatic and semidiplomatic immunities [8 U.S.C.A. § 1102]

Except as otherwise provided in this chapter, for so long as they continue in the nonimmigrant classes enumerated in this section, the provisions of this chapter relating to ineligibility to receive visas and the exclusion or deportation of aliens shall not be construed to apply to nonimmigrants—

(1) within the class described in paragraph (15)(A)(i) of section 101(a) [8 U.S.C.A. § 1101(a)(15)(A)(i)], except those provisions relating to reasonable requirements of passports and visas as a means of identification and documentation necessary to establish their qualifications under such paragraph (15)(A)(i), and, under such rules and regulations as the President may deem to be necessary, the provisions of paragraph (3) (other than subparagraph (E)) of section 212(a) [8 U.S.C.A. § 1182(a)(3)(E)];

(2) within the class described in paragraph (15)(G)(i) of section 101(a) [8 U.S.C.A. § 1101(a)(15)(G)(i)], except those provisions relating to reasonable requirements of passports and visas as a means of identification and documentation necessary to establish their qualifications under such paragraph (15)(G)(i), and the provisions of paragraph (3) (other than subparagraph (E)) of section 101(a) [8 U.S.C.A. § 1182(a)(3)(E)]; and

(3) within the classes described in paragraphs (15)(A)(ii), (15)(G)(ii), (15)(G)(iii), or (15)(G)(iv) of section 101(a) [8 U.S.C.A.

§ 1101(a)(15)(A)(ii), (15)(G)(ii), (15)(G)(iii), or (15)(G)(iv) ], except those provisions relating to reasonable requirements of passports and visas as a means of identification and documentation necessary to establish their qualifications under such paragraphs, and the provisions of paragraph (3) (other than subparagraph (E)) of section 212(a) [8 U.S.C.A. § 1182(a)(3)(E)].

(June 27, 1952, c. 477, Title I, § 102, 66 Stat. 173; Oct. 24, 1988, Pub.L. 100–525, § 9(b), 102 Stat. 2619; Nov. 29, 1990, Pub.L. 101–649, Title VI, § 603(a)(2), 104 Stat. 5082.)

## § 103. Powers and duties [8 U.S.C.A. § 1103]

### (a) Attorney General

The Attorney General shall be charged with the administration and enforcement of this chapter and all other laws relating to the immigration and naturalization of aliens, except insofar as this chapter or such laws relate to the powers, functions, and duties conferred upon the President, the Secretary of State, the officers of the Department of State, or diplomatic or consular officers: *Provided, however,* That determination and ruling by the Attorney General with respect to all questions of law shall be controlling. He shall have control, direction, and supervision of all employees and of all the files and records of the Service. He shall establish such regulations; prescribe such forms of bond, reports, entries, and other papers; issue such instructions; and perform such other acts as he deems necessary for carrying out his authority under the provisions of this chapter. He may require or authorize any employee of the Service or the Department of Justice to perform or exercise any of the powers, privileges, or duties conferred or imposed by this chapter or regulations issued thereunder upon any other employee of the Service. He shall have the power and duty to control and guard the boundaries and borders of the United States against the illegal entry of aliens and shall, in his discretion, appoint for that purpose such number of employees of the Service as to him shall appear necessary and proper. He is authorized to confer or impose upon any employee of the United States, with the consent of the head of the Department or other independent establishment under whose jurisdiction the employee is serving, any of the powers, privileges, or duties conferred or imposed by this chapter or regulations issued thereunder upon officers or employees of the Service. He may, with the concurrence of the Secretary of State, establish officers of the Service in foreign countries; and, after consultation with the Secretary of State, he may, whenever in his judgment such action may be necessary to accomplish the purposes of this chapter, detail employees of the Service for duty in foreign countries.

### (b) Commissioner; appointment

The Commissioner shall be a citizen of the United States and shall be appointed by the President, by and with the advice and consent of the Senate. He shall be charged with any and all responsibilities and authority in the administration of the Service and of this chapter which are conferred upon the Attorney General as may be delegated to him by the Attorney General or which may be prescribed by the Attorney General.

### (c) Statistical information system

(1) The Commissioner, in consultation with interested academicians, government agencies, and other parties, shall provide for a system for collection and dissemination, to Congress and the public, of information (not in individually identifiable form) useful in evaluating the social, economic, environmental, and demographic impact of immigration laws.

(2) Such information shall include information on the alien population in the United States, on the rates of naturalization and emigration of resident aliens, on aliens who have been admitted, paroled, or granted asylum, on nonimmigrants in the United States (by occupation, basis for admission, and duration of stay), on aliens who have been excluded or deported from the United States, on the number of applications filed and granted for suspension of deportation, and on the number of aliens estimated to be present unlawfully in the United States in each fiscal year.

(3) Such system shall provide for the collection and dissemination of such information not less often than annually.

### (d) Annual report

(1) The Commissioner shall submit to Congress annually a report which contains a summary of the information collected under subsection (c) of this section and an analysis of trends in immigration and naturalization.

(2) Each annual report shall include information on the number, and rate of denial administratively, of applications for naturalization, for each district office of the Service and by national origin group.

(June 27, 1952, c. 477, Title I, § 103, 66 Stat. 173; Oct. 24, 1988, Pub.L. 100–525, § 9(c), 102 Stat. 2619, 2620; Nov. 29, 1990, Pub.L. 101–649, Title I, §§ 142, 161, 104 Stat. 5004, 5008.)

## § 104. Powers and duties of Secretary of State; Bureau of Consular Affairs [8 U.S.C.A. § 1104]

### (a) Powers and duties

The Secretary of State shall be charged with the administration and the enforcement of the provisions of this chapter and all other immigration and nationality laws relating to (1) the powers, duties, and functions of diplomatic and consular officers of the United States, except those powers, duties, and functions conferred upon the consular officers relating to the granting or refusal of visas; (2) the powers, duties, and functions of the Bureau of Consular Affairs; and (3) the determination of nationality of a person not in the United States. He shall establish such regulations; prescribe such forms of reports, entries and other papers; issue such instructions; and perform such other acts as he deems necessary for carrying out such provisions. He is authorized to confer or impose upon any employee of the United States, with the consent of the head of the department or independent establishment under whose jurisdiction the employee is serving, any of the powers, functions, or duties conferred or imposed by this chapter or regulations issued thereunder upon officers or employees of the Department of State or of the American Foreign Service.

### (b) Creation of Bureau of Consular Affairs; duties of Assistant Secretary of State for Consular Affairs

There is established in the Department of State a Bureau of Consular Affairs, to be headed by an Assistant Secretary of State for Consular Affairs. The Assistant Secretary of State for Consular Affairs shall be a citizen of the United States, qualified by experience, and shall maintain close liaison with the appropriate committees of Congress in order that they may be advised regarding the administration of this chapter by consular officers. He shall be charged with any and all responsibility and authority in the administration of the Bureau and of this chapter which are conferred on the Secretary of State as may be delegated to him by the Secretary of State or which may be prescribed by the Secretary of State. He shall also perform such other duties as the Secretary of State may prescribe.

### (c) Passport Office, Visa Office, and other offices; directors

Within the Bureau there shall be a Passport Office, a Visa Office, and such other offices as the Secretary of State may deem to be appropriate, each office to be headed by a director. The Directors of the Passport Office and the Visa Office shall be experienced in the administration of the nationality and immigration laws.

### (d) Transfer of duties

The functions heretofore performed by the Passport Division and the Visa Division of the Department of State shall hereafter be performed by the Passport Office and the Visa Office, respectively, of the Bureau of Consular Affairs.

### (e) General Counsel of Visa Office; appointment and duties

There shall be a General Counsel of the Visa Office, who shall be appointed by the Secretary of State and who shall serve under the general direction of the Legal Adviser of the Department of State. The General Counsel shall have authority to maintain liaison with the appropriate officers of the Service with a view to securing uniform interpretations of the provisions of this chapter.

(June 27, 1952, c. 477, Title I, § 104, 66 Stat. 174; Pub. L. 87–510, § 4(a)(2), June 28, 1962, 76 Stat. 123; Pub. L. 88–426, Title III, § 305(43), Aug. 14, 1964, 78 Stat. 428; Pub. L. 95–105, Title I, § 109(b)(1), Aug. 17, 1977, 91 Stat. 847; Oct. 24, 1988, Pub.L. 100–525, § 9(d), 102 Stat. 2620.)

## § 105. Liaison with internal security officers [8 U.S.C.A. § 1105]

The Commissioner and the Assistant Secretary of State for Consular Affairs shall have authority to maintain direct and continuous liaison with the Directors of the Federal Bureau of Investigation and the Central Intelligence Agency and with other internal security officers of the Government for the purpose of obtaining and exchanging information for use in enforcing the provisions of this chapter in the interest of the internal security of the United States. The Commissioner and the Assistant Secretary of State for Consular Affairs shall maintain direct and continuous liaison with each other with a view to a coordinated, uniform, and efficient administration of this chapter, and all other immigration and nationality laws.

(June 27, 1952, c. 477, Title I, § 105, 66 Stat. 175; Pub. L. 95–105, Title I, § 109(b)(2), Aug. 17, 1977, 91 Stat. 847.)

## § 106. Judicial review of orders of deportation and exclusion [8 U.S.C.A. § 1105a]

### (a) Exclusiveness of procedure

The procedure prescribed by, and all the provisions of chapter 158 of Title 28, shall apply to, and shall be the sole and exclusive procedure for, the judicial review of all final orders of deportation heretofore or hereafter made against aliens within the United States pursuant to administrative proceedings under section 242(b) [8 U.S.C.A. § 1252(b)] or comparable provisions of any prior Act, except that—

#### (1) Time for filing petition

a petition for review may be filed not later than 90 days after the date of the issuance of the final deportation order, or, in the case of an alien convicted of an aggravated felony, not later than 30 days after the issuance of such order;

#### (2) Venue

the venue of any petition for review under this section shall be in the judicial circuit in which the administrative proceedings before a special inquiry officer were conducted in whole or in part, or in the judicial circuit wherein is the residence, as defined in this chapter, of the petitioner, but not in more than one circuit;

#### (3) Respondent; service of petition; stay of deportation

the action shall be brought against the Immigration and Naturalization Service, as respondent. Service of the petition to review shall be made upon the Attorney General of the United States and upon the official of the Immigration and Naturalization Service in charge of the Service district in which the office of the clerk of the court is located. The service of the petition for review upon such official of the Service shall stay the deportation of the alien pending determination of the petition by the court, unless the court otherwise directs or unless the alien is convicted of an aggravated felony, in which case the Service shall not stay the deportation of the alien pending determination of the petition of the court unless the court otherwise directs;

### (4) Determination upon administrative record

except as provided in clause (B) of paragraph (5) of this subsection, the petition shall be determined solely upon the administrative record upon which the deportation order is based and the Attorney General's findings of fact, if supported by reasonable, substantial, and probative evidence on the record considered as a whole, shall be conclusive;

### (5) Claim of nationality; determination or transfer to district court for hearing de novo

whenever any petitioner, who seeks review of an order under this section, claims to be a national of the United States and makes a showing that his claim is not frivolous, the court shall (A) pass upon the issues presented when it appears from the pleadings and affidavits filed by the parties that no genuine issue of material fact is presented; or (B) where a genuine issue of material fact as to the petitioner's nationality is presented, transfer the proceedings to a United States district court for the district where the petitioner has his residence for hearing de novo of the nationality claim and determination as if such proceedings were originally initiated in the district court under the provisions of section 2201 of Title 28. Any such petitioner shall not be entitled to have such issue determined under section 360(a) [8 U.S.C.A. § 1503(a)] or otherwise;

### (6) Consolidation

whenever a petitioner seeks review of an order under this section, any review sought with respect to a motion to reopen or reconsider such an order shall be consolidated with the review of the order;

### (7) Challenge of validity of deportation order in criminal proceeding; motion for judicial review before trial; hearing de novo on nationality claim; determination of motion; dismissal of indictment upon invalidity of order; appeal

if the validity of a deportation order has not been judicially determined, its validity may be challenged in a criminal proceeding against the alien for violation of subsection (d) or (e) of section 242 [8 U.S.C.A. § 1252(d) or (e)] only by separate motion for judicial review before trial. Such motion shall be determined by the court without a jury and before the trial of the general issue. Whenever a claim to United States nationality is made in such motion, and in the opinion of the court, a genuine issue of material fact as to the alien's nationality is presented, the court shall accord him a hearing de novo on the nationality claim and determine that issue as if proceedings had been initiated under the provisions of section 2201 of Title 28. Any such alien shall not be entitled to have such issue determined under section 360(a) [8 U.S.C.A. § 1503(a)] or otherwise. If no such hearing de novo as to nationality is conducted, the determination shall be made solely upon the administrative record upon which the deportation order is based and the Attorney General's findings of fact, if supported by reasonable, substantial and probative evidence on the record considered as a whole, shall be conclusive. If the deportation order is held invalid, the court shall dismiss the indictment and the United States shall have the right to appeal to the court of appeals within thirty days. The procedure on such appeals shall be as provided in the Federal rules of criminal procedure. No petition for review under this section may be filed by any alien during the pendency of a criminal proceeding against such alien for violation of subsection (d) or (e) of section 242 [8 U.S.C.A. § 1252(d) or (e)];

**(8) Deferment of deportation; compliance of alien with other provisions of law; detention or taking into custody of alien**

nothing in this section shall be construed to require the Attorney General to defer deportation of an alien after the issuance of a deportation order because of the right of judicial review of the order granted by this section, or to relieve any alien from compliance with subsections (d) and (e) of section 242 [8 U.S.C.A. § 1252(d) or (e)]. Nothing contained in this section shall be construed to preclude the Attorney General from detaining or continuing to detain an alien or from taking him into custody pursuant to subsection (c) of section 242 [8 U.S.C.A. § 1252(c)] at any time after the issuance of a deportation order;

**(9) Typewritten record and briefs**

it shall not be necessary to print the record or any part thereof, or the briefs, and the court shall review the proceedings on a typewritten record and on typewritten briefs; and

**(10) Habeas corpus**

any alien held in custody pursuant to an order of deportation may obtain judicial review thereof by habeas corpus proceedings.

**(b) Limitation of certain aliens to habeas corpus proceedings**

Notwithstanding the provisions of any other law, any alien against whom a final order of exclusion has been made heretofore or hereafter under the provisions of section 236 [8 U.S.C.A. § 1226] or comparable provisions of any prior Act may obtain judicial review of such order by habeas corpus proceedings and not otherwise.

## (c) Exhaustion of administrative remedies or departure from United States; disclosure of prior judicial proceedings

An order of deportation or of exclusion shall not be reviewed by any court if the alien has not exhausted the administrative remedies available to him as of right under the immigration laws and regulations or if he has departed from the United States after the issuance of the order. Every petition for review or for habeas corpus shall state whether the validity of the order has been upheld in any prior judicial proceeding, and, if so, the nature and date thereof, and the court in which such proceeding took place. No petition for review or for habeas corpus shall be entertained if the validity of the order has been previously determined in any civil or criminal proceeding, unless the petition presents grounds which the court finds could not have been presented in such prior proceeding, or the court finds that the remedy provided by such prior proceeding was inadequate or ineffective to test the validity of the order.

(June 27, 1952, c. 477, Title I, § 106, as added Pub. L. 87–301, § 5(a), Sept. 26, 1961, 75 Stat. 651, and amended Pub. L. 97–116, § 18(b), Dec. 29, 1981, 95 Stat. 1620; Pub.L. 100–525, § 9(e), Oct. 24, 1988, 102 Stat. 2620; Pub.L. 100–690, Title VII, § 7347(b), Nov. 18, 1988, 102 Stat. 4472; Nov. 29, 1990, Pub.L. 101–649, Title V, §§ 502(a), 513(a), 545(b), 104 Stat. 5048, 5052, 5065.)

# § 401. Repealed. Pub.L. 91–510, Title IV, § 422(a), Oct. 26, 1970, 84 Stat. 1189 [8 U.S.C.A. § 1106]

# TITLE II

# IMMIGRATION

### CHAPTER I—SELECTION SYSTEM

## § 201. Worldwide level of immigration [8 U.S.C.A. § 1151]

### (a) In general

Exclusive of aliens described in subsection (b) of this section, aliens born in a foreign state or dependent area who may be issued immigrant visas or who may otherwise acquire the status of an alien lawfully admitted to the United States for permanent residence are limited to—

(1) family-sponsored immigrants described in section 203(a) [8 U.S.C.A. § 1153(a)] (or who are admitted under section 211(a) [8 U.S.C.A. § 1181(a)] on the basis of a prior issuance of a visa to their accompanying parent under section 203(a) [8 U.S.C.A. § 1153(a)]) in a number not to exceed in any fiscal year the number specified in subsection (c) of this section for that year, and not to exceed in any of the first 3 quarters of any fiscal year 27 percent of the worldwide level under such subsection for all of such fiscal year;

(2) employment-based immigrants described in section 203(b) [8 U.S.C.A. § 1153(b)] (or who are admitted under section 211(a) [8 U.S.C.A. § 1181(a)] on the basis of a prior issuance of a visa to their accompanying parent under section 203(b) [8 U.S.C.A. § 1153(b)]), in a number not to exceed in any fiscal year the number specified in subsection (d) of this section for that year, and not to exceed in any of the first 3 quarters of any fiscal year 27 percent of the worldwide level under such subsection for all of such fiscal year; and

(3) for fiscal years beginning with fiscal year 1995, diversity immigrants described in section 203(c) [8 U.S.C.A. § 1153(c)] (or who are admitted under section 211(a) [8 U.S.C.A. § 1181(a)] on the basis of a prior issuance of a visa to their accompanying parent under section 203(c) [8 U.S.C.A. § 1153(c)]) in a number not to exceed in any fiscal year the number specified in subsection (e) of this section for that year, and not to exceed in any of the first 3 quarters of any fiscal year 27 percent of the worldwide level under such subsection for all of such fiscal year.

### (b) Aliens not subject to direct numerical limitations

Aliens described in this subsection, who are not subject to the worldwide levels or numerical limitations of subsection (a) of this section, are as follows:

**(1)(A)** Special immigrants described in subparagraph (A) or (B) of section 101(a)(27) [8 U.S.C.A. § 1101(a)(27)].

**(B)** Aliens who are admitted under section 1157 of this title or whose status is adjusted under section 1159 of this title.

**(C)** Aliens whose status is adjusted to permanent residence under section 210, 211, or 245A [8 U.S.C.A. § 1160, 1161, or 1255a].

**(D)** Aliens whose deportation is suspended under section 244A [8 U.S.C.A. § 1254(a)].

**(E)** Aliens provided permanent resident status under section 249 [8 U.S.C.A. § 1259].

**(2)(A)(i) Immediate relatives.**—For purposes of this subsection, the term "immediate relatives" means the children, spouses, and parents of a citizen of the United States, except that, in the case of parents, such citizens shall be at least 21 years of age. In the case of an alien who was the spouse of a citizen of the United States for at least 2 years at the time of the citizen's death and was not legally separated from the citizen at the time of the citizen's death, the alien shall be considered, for purposes of this subsection, to remain an immediate relative after the date of the citizen's death but only if the spouse files a petition under section 204(a)(1)(A) [8 U.S.C.A. § 1154(a)(1)(A)] within 2 years after such date and only until the date the spouse remarries.

**(ii)** Aliens admitted under section 211(a) [8 U.S.C.A. § 1181(a)] on the basis of a prior issuance of a visa to their accompanying parent who is such an immediate relative.

**(B)** Aliens born to an alien lawfully admitted for permanent residence during a temporary visit abroad.

**(c) Worldwide level of family-sponsored immigrants**

**(1)(A)** The worldwide level of family-sponsored immigrants under this subsection for a fiscal year is, subject to subparagraph (B), equal to—

**(i)** 480,000, minus

**(ii)** the number computed under paragraph (2), plus

**(iii)** the number (if any) computed under paragraph (3).

**(B)(i)** For each of fiscal years 1992, 1993, and 1994, 465,-000 shall be substituted for 480,000 in subparagraph (A)(i).

**(ii)** In no case shall the number computed under subparagraph (A) be less than 226,000.

**(2)** The number computed under this paragraph for a fiscal year is the sum of the number of aliens described in subparagraphs (A) and (B) of subsection (b)(2) of this section who were issued immigrant visas or who otherwise acquired the status of aliens lawfully admitted to the United States for permanent residence in the previous fiscal year.

(3) The number computed under this paragraph for a fiscal year is the difference (if any) between the maximum number of visas which may be issued under section 203(b) [8 U.S.C.A. § 1153(b)] (relating to employment-based immigrants) during the previous fiscal year and the number of visas issued under that section during that year.

### (d) Worldwide level of employment-based immigrants

(1) The worldwide level of employment-based immigrants under this subsection for a fiscal year is equal to—

**(A)** 140,000, plus

**(B)** the number computed under paragraph (2).

(2) The number computed under this paragraph for a fiscal year is the difference (if any) between the maximum number of visas which may be issued under section 203(a) [8 U.S.C.A. § 1153(a)] (relating to family-sponsored immigrants) during the previous fiscal year and the number of visas issued under that section during that year.

### (e) Worldwide level of diversity immigrants

The worldwide level of diversity immigrants is equal to 55,000 for each fiscal year.

(June 27, 1952, c. 477, Title II, ch. 1, § 201, 66 Stat. 175; Pub. L. 89–236, § 1, Oct. 3, 1965, 79 Stat. 911; Pub. L. 94–571, § 2, Oct. 20, 1976, 90 Stat. 2703; Pub. L. 95–412, § 1, Oct. 5, 1978, 92 Stat. 907; Pub. L. 96–212, Title II, § 203(a), Mar. 17, 1980, 94 Stat. 106; Pub. L. 97–116, § 20[(a)], Dec. 29, 1981, 95 Stat. 1621; Nov. 29, 1990, Pub.L. 101–649, Title I, §§ 101(a), 161, 104 Stat. 4980, 5008.)

## § 202. Numerical limitations on individual foreign states [8 U.S.C.A. § 1152]

### (a) Per country level

(1) **Nondiscrimination.** Except as specifically provided in paragraph (2) and in sections 101(a)(27), 201(b)(2)(A)(i), and 203 [8 U.S.C.A. §§ 1101(a)(27), 1151(b)(2)(A)(i), and 1153], no person shall receive any preference or priority or be discriminated against in the issuance of an immigrant visa because of the person's race, sex, nationality, place of birth, or place of residence.

(2) **Per country levels for family-sponsored and employment-based immigrants.** Subject to paragraphs (3) and (4), the total number of immigrant visas made available to natives of any single foreign state or dependent area under subsections (a) and (b) of section 203 [8 U.S.C.A. § 1153] in any fiscal year may not exceed 7 percent (in the case of a single foreign state) or 2 percent (in the

case of a dependent area) of the total number of such visas made available under such subsections in that fiscal year.

**(3) Exception if additional visas available.** If because of the application of paragraph (2) with respect to one or more foreign states or dependent areas, the total number of visas available under both subsections (a) and (b) of section 203 [8 U.S.C.A. § 1153] for a calendar quarter exceeds the number of qualified immigrants who otherwise may be issued such a visa, paragraph (2) shall not apply to visas made available to such states or areas during the remainder of such calendar quarter.

**(4) Special rules for spouses and children of lawful permanent resident aliens.**

**(A)** 75 percent of minimum 2nd preference set-aside for spouses and children not subject to per country limitation.

**(i)** In general. Of the visa numbers made available under section 203(a) [8 U.S.C.A. § 1153(a)] to immigrants described in section 203(a)(2)(A) [8 U.S.C.A. § 1153(a)(2)(A)] in any fiscal year, 75 percent of the 2–A floor (as defined in clause (ii)) shall be issued without regard to the numerical limitation under paragraph (2).

**(ii)** 2–A floor defined. In this paragraph, the term "2–A floor" means, for a fiscal year, 77 percent of the total number of visas made available under section 203(a) [8 U.S.C.A. § 1153(a)] to immigrants described in section 203(a)(2)(A) [8 U.S.C.A. § 1153(a)(2)(A)] in the fiscal year.

**(B) Treatment of remaining 25 percent for countries subject to subsection (e).**

**(i)** In general. Of the visa numbers made available under section 203(a) [8 U.S.C.A. § 1153(a)] to immigrants described in section 203(a)(2)(A) [8 U.S.C.A. § 1153(a)(2)(A)]in any fiscal year, the remaining 25 percent of the 2–A floor shall be available in the case of a state or area that is subject to subsection (e) of this section only to the extent that the total number of visas issued in accordance with subparagraph (A) to natives of the foreign state or area is less than the subsection (e) ceiling (as defined in clause (ii)).

**(ii)** Subsection (e) ceiling defined. In clause (i), the term "subsection (e) ceiling" means, for a foreign state or dependent areas, 77 percent of the maximum number of visas that may be made available under section 203(a) [8 U.S.C.A. § 1153(a)] to immigrants who are natives of the state or area under section 203(a)(2) [8 U.S.C.A. § 1153(a)(2)] consistent with subsection (e) of this section.

**(C) Treatment of unmarried sons and daughters in countries subject to subsection (e).** In the case of a foreign state or dependent area to which subsection (e) of this section applies, the number of immigrant visas that may be made available to natives of the state or area under section 203(a)(2)(B) [8 U.S.C.A. § 1153(a)(2)(B)] may not exceed

(i) 23 percent of the maximum number of visas that may be made available under section 203(a) [8 U.S.C.A. § 1153(a)] to immigrants of the state or area described in section 203(a)(2) [8 U.S.C.A. § 1153(a)(2)] consistent with subsection (e) of this section, or

(ii) the number (if any) by which the maximum number of visas that may be made available under section 203(a) [8 U.S.C.A. § 1153(a)] to immigrants of the state or area described in section 203(a)(2) [8 U.S.C.A. § 1153(a)(2)] consistent with subsection (e) of this section exceeds the number of visas issued under section 203(a)(2)(A) [8 U.S.C.A. § 1153(a)(2)(A)]

whichever is greater.

**(D) Limiting pass down for certain countries subject to subsection (e).** In the case of a foreign state or dependent area to which subsection (e) of this section applies, if the total number of visas issued under section 203(a)(2) [8 U.S.C.A. § 1153(a)(2)] exceeds the maximum number of visas that may be made available to immigrants of the state or area under section 203(a)(2) [8 U.S.C.A. § 1153(a)(2)] consistent with subsection (e) of this section (determined without regard to this paragraph), in applying paragraphs (3) and (4) of section 203(a) [8 U.S.C.A. § 1153(a)] under subsection (e)(2) of this section all visas shall be deemed to have been required for the classes specified in paragraphs (1) and (2) of such section.

## (b) Rules for chargeability

Each independent country, self-governing dominion, mandated territory, and territory under the international trusteeship system of the United Nations, other than the United States and its outlying possessions, shall be treated as a separate foreign state for the purposes of a numerical level established under subsection (a)(2) of this section when approved by the Secretary of State. All other inhabited lands shall be attributed to a foreign state specified by the Secretary of State. For the purposes of this chapter the foreign state to which an immigrant is chargeable shall be determined by birth within such foreign state except that (1) an alien child, when accompanied by or following to join his alien parent or parents, may be charged to the foreign state of either parent if such parent has received or would be qualified for an immigrant visa, if necessary to prevent the separation of the child from the parent or parents, and if immigration charged to the foreign state to which such parent has been or would be chargeable has not reached a numerical level established under subsection (a)(2) of this section for that fiscal year; (2) if an alien is chargeable to a different foreign state from that of his spouse, the foreign state to which such alien is chargeable may, if necessary to prevent the separation of husband and wife, be determined by the foreign state of the spouse he is accompanying or following to join, if such spouse has received or would be qualified for an immigrant visa and if immigration charged to the foreign state to which such spouse has been or would be chargeable has not reached a numerical level established under subsection (a)(2) of this section for that fiscal year; (3) an alien born in the United States shall be considered as having been born in the country of which he is a citizen or subject, or, if he is not a citizen or subject of any country, in the last foreign country in which he had his residence as determined by the consular officer; and (4) an alien born within any foreign state in which neither of his parents was born and in which neither of his parents had a residence at the time of such alien's birth may be charged to the foreign state of either parent.

### (c) Chargeability for dependent areas

Any immigrant born in a colony or other component or dependent area of a foreign state overseas from the foreign state, other than an alien described in section 201(b) [8 U.S.C.A. § 1151(b)], shall be chargeable for the purpose of the limitation set forth in subsection (a) of this section, to the foreign state.

### (d) Changes in territory

In the case of any change in the territorial limits of foreign states, the Secretary of State shall, upon recognition of such change, issue appropriate instructions to all diplomatic and consular offices.

### (e) Special rules for countries at ceiling

If it is determined that the total number of immigrant visas made available under subsections (a) and (b) of section 203 [8 U.S.C.A. § 1153] to natives of any single foreign state or dependent area will exceed the numerical limitation specified in subsection (a)(2) of this section in any fiscal year, in determining the allotment of immigrant visa numbers to natives under subsections (a) and (b) of section 203 [8 U.S.C.A. § 1153], visa numbers with respect to natives of that state or area shall be allocated (to the extent practicable and otherwise consistent with this section and section 203 [8 U.S.C.A. § 1153]) in a manner so that—

(1) the ratio of the visa numbers made available under section 203(a) [8 U.S.C.A. § 1153(a)] to the visa numbers made available under section 203(b) [8 U.S.C.A. § 1153(b)] is equal to the ratio of the worldwide level of immigration under section 203(c) [8 U.S.C.A. § 1153(c)] to such level under section 203(d) [8 U.S.C.A. § 1153(d)];

(2) except as provided in subsection (a)(4) of this section, the proportion of the visa numbers made available under each of paragraphs (1) through (4) of section 203(a) [8 U.S.C.A. § 1153(a)] is equal to the ratio of the total number of visas made available under the respective paragraph to the total number of visas made available under section 203(a) [8 U.S.C.A. § 1153(a)], and

(3) the proportion of the visa numbers made available under each of paragraphs (1) through (5) of section 203(b) [8 U.S.C.A. § 1153(b)] is equal to the ratio of the total number of visas made available under the respective paragraph to the total number of visas made available under section 203(b) [8 U.S.C.A. § 1153(b)].

Nothing in this subsection shall be construed as limiting the number of visas that may be issued to natives of a foreign state or dependent area under section 203(a) or 203(b) [8 U.S.C.A. § 1153(a) or 1153(b)] if there is insufficient demand for visas for such natives under section 203(a) or 203(b) [8 U.S.C.A. § 1153(a) or 1153(b)], respectively, or as limiting the number of visas that may be issued under section 203(a)(2)(A) [8 U.S.C.A. § 1153(a)(2)(A)] pursuant to subsection (a)(4)(A) of this section.

(June 27, 1952, c. 477, Title II, ch. 1, § 202, 66 Stat. 176; Pub. L. 87–301, § 9, Sept. 26, 1961, 75 Stat. 654; Pub. L. 89–236, § 2, Oct. 3, 1965, 79 Stat. 911; Pub. L. 94–571, § 3, Oct. 20, 1976, 90 Stat. 2703; Pub. L. 95–412, § 2, Oct. 5, 1978, 92 Stat. 907; Pub. L. 96–212, Title II, § 203(b), Mar. 17, 1980, 94 Stat. 107; Pub. L. 97–116, §§ 18(c), 20(b), Dec. 29, 1981, 95 Stat. 1620, 1622; Pub.L. 99–603, Title III, § 311(a), Nov. 6, 1986, 100 Stat. 3434; Pub.L. 99–653, § 4, Nov. 14, 1986, 100 Stat. 3655, as amended Pub.L. 100–525, § 8(c), Oct. 24, 1988, 102 Stat. 2617; Pub.L. 100–525, § 9(f), Oct. 24, 1988, 102 Stat. 2620; Nov. 29, 1990, Pub.L. 101–649, Title I, §§ 102, 161, 104 Stat. 4982, 5008.)

# § 203. Allocation of immigrant visas [8 U.S.C.A. § 1153]

## (a) Preference allocation for family-sponsored immigrants

Aliens subject to the worldwide level specified in section 201(c) [8 U.S.C.A. § 1151(c)] for family-sponsored immigrants shall be allotted visas as follows:

(1) **Unmarried sons and daughters of citizens.** Qualified immigrants who are the unmarried sons or daughters of citizens of the United States shall be allocated visas in a number not to exceed 23,400, plus any visas not required for the class specified in paragraph (4).

(2) **Spouses and unmarried sons and unmarried daughters of permanent resident aliens.** Qualified immigrants—

(A) who are the spouses or children of an alien lawfully admitted for permanent residence, or

(B) who are the unmarried sons or unmarried daughters (but are not the children) of an alien lawfully admitted for permanent residence,

shall be allocated visas in a number not to exceed 114,200, plus the number (if any) by which such world-wide level exceeds 226,000, plus any visas not required for the class specified in paragraph (1); except that not less than 77 percent of such visa numbers shall be allocated to aliens described in subparagraph (A).

(3) **Married sons and married daughters of citizens.** Qualified immigrants who are the married sons or married daughters of citizens of the United States shall be allocated visas in a number not to exceed 23,400, plus any visas not required for the classes specified in paragraphs (1) and (2).

(4) **Brothers and sisters of citizens.** Qualified immigrants who are the brothers or sisters of citizens of the United States, if such citizens are at least 21 years of age, shall be allocated visas in a number not to exceed 65,000, plus any visas not required for the classes specified in paragraphs (1) through (3).

## (b) Preference allocation for employment-based immigrants

Aliens subject to the worldwide level specified in section 201(d) [8 U.S.C.A. § 1151(d)] for employment-based immigrants in a fiscal year shall be allotted visas as follows:

(1) **Priority workers.** Visas shall first be made available in a number not to exceed 40,000, plus any visas not required for the classes specified in paragraphs (4) and (5), to qualified immigrants

who are aliens described in any of the following subparagraphs (A) through (C):

**(A)** Aliens with extraordinary ability. An alien is described in this subparagraph if—

**(i)** the alien has extraordinary ability in the sciences, arts, education, business, or athletics which has been demonstrated by sustained national or international acclaim and whose achievements have been recognized in the field through extensive documentation,

**(ii)** the alien seeks to enter the United States to continue work in the area of extraordinary ability, and

**(iii)** the alien's entry into the United States will substantially benefit prospectively the United States.

**(B)** Outstanding professors and researchers. An alien is described in this subparagraph if—

**(i)** the alien is recognized internationally as outstanding in a specific academic area,

**(ii)** the alien has at least 3 years of experience in teaching or research in the academic area, and

**(iii)** the alien seeks to enter the United States—

**(I)** for a tenured position (or tenure-track position) within a university or institution of higher education to teach in the academic area,

**(II)** for a comparable position with a university or institution of higher education to conduct research in the area, or

**(III)** for a comparable position to conduct research in the area with a department, division, or institute of a private employer, if the department, division, or institute employs at least 3 persons full-time in research activities and has achieved documented accomplishments in an academic field.

**(C)** Certain multinational executives and managers. An alien is described in this subparagraph if the alien, in the 3 years preceding the time of the alien's application for classification and admission into the United States under this subparagraph, has been employed for at least 1 year by a firm or corporation or other legal entity or an affiliate or subsidiary thereof and who seeks to enter the United States in order to continue to render services to the same employer or to a subsidiary or affiliate thereof in a capacity that is managerial or executive.

**(2) Aliens who are members of the professions holding advanced degrees or aliens of exceptional ability.**

**(A)** In general. Visas shall be made available, in a number not to exceed 40,000, plus any visas not required for the classes specified in paragraph (1), to qualified immigrants who are members of the professions holding advanced degrees or their equivalent or who because of their exceptional ability in the sciences, arts, or business, will substantially benefit prospectively the national economy, cultural or educational interests, or welfare of the United States, and whose services in the sciences, arts, professions, or business are sought by an employer in the United States.

**(B)** Waiver of job offer. The Attorney General may, when he deems it to be in the national interest, waive the requirement of subparagraph (A) that an alien's services in the sciences, arts, or business be sought by an employer in the United States.

**(C)** Determination of exceptional ability. In determining under subparagraph (A) whether an immigrant has exceptional ability, the possession of a degree, diploma, certificate, or similar award from a college, university, school, or other institution of learning or a license to practice or certification for a particular profession or occupation shall not by itself be considered sufficient evidence of such exceptional ability.

**(3) Skilled workers, professionals, and other workers.**

**(A)** In general. Visas shall be made available, in a number not to exceed 40,000, plus any visas not required for the classes specified in paragraphs (1) and (2), to the following classes of aliens who are not described in paragraph (2):

**(i)** Skilled workers. Qualified immigrants who are capable, at the time of petitioning for classification under this paragraph, of performing skilled labor (requiring at least 2 years training or experience), not of a temporary or seasonal nature, for which qualified workers are not available in the United States.

**(ii)** Professionals. Qualified immigrants who hold baccalaureate degrees and who are members of the professions.

**(iii)** Other workers. Other qualified immigrants who are capable, at the time of petitioning for classification under this paragraph, of performing unskilled labor, not of a temporary or seasonal nature, for which qualified workers are not available in the United States.

**(B)** Limitation on other workers. Not more than 10,000 of the visas made available under this paragraph in any fiscal year may be available for qualified immigrants described in subparagraph (A)(iii).

**(C)** Labor certification required. An immigrant visa may not be issued to an immigrant under subparagraph (A) until the consular officer is in receipt of a determination made by the Secretary of Labor pursuant to the provisions of section 212(a)(5)(A) [8 U.S.C.A. § 1182(a)(5)(A)].

**(4) Certain special immigrants.** Visas shall be made available, in a number not to exceed 10,000, to qualified special immigrants described in section 101(a)(27) [8 U.S.C.A. § 1101(a)(27)] (other than those described in subparagraph (A) or (B) thereof), of which not more than 5,000 may be made available in any fiscal year to special immigrants described in subclause (II) or (III) of section 101(a)(27)(C)(ii) [8 U.S.C.A. § 1101(a)(27)(C)(ii)].

**(5) Employment creation.**

**(A) In general.** Visas shall be made available, in a number not to exceed 10,000, to qualified immigrants seeking to enter the United States for the purpose of engaging in a new commercial enterprise—

**(i)** which the alien has established,

**(ii)** in which such alien has invested (after November 29, 1990) or, is actively in the process of investing, capital in an amount not less than the amount specified in subparagraph (C), and

**(iii)** which will benefit the United States economy and create full-time employment for not fewer than 10 United States citizens or aliens lawfully admitted for permanent residence or other immigrants lawfully authorized to be employed in the United States (other than the immigrant and the immigrant's spouse, sons, or daughters).

**(B) Set-aside for targetted employment areas.—**

**(i) In general.** Not less than 3,000 of the visas made available under this paragraph in each fiscal year shall be reserved for qualified immigrants who establish a new commercial enterprise described in subparagraph (A) which will create employment in a targetted employment area.

**(ii) Targetted employment area defined.** In this paragraph, the term "targetted employment area" means, at the time of the investment, a rural area or an area which has experienced high unemployment (of at least 150 percent of the national average rate).

**(iii) Rural area defined.** In this paragraph, the term "rural area" means any area other than an area within a metropolitan statistical area or within the outer boundary of any city or town having a population of 20,000 or more (based on the most recent decennial census of the United States).

**(C) Amount of capital required.—**

**(i) In general.** Except as otherwise provided in this subparagraph, the amount of capital required under subparagraph

50

(A) shall be $1,000,000. The Attorney General, in consultation with the Secretary of Labor and the Secretary of State, may from time to time prescribe regulations increasing the dollar amount specified under the previous sentence.

(ii) Adjustment for targetted employment areas. The Attorney General may, in the case of investment made in a targetted employment area, specify an amount of capital required under subparagraph (A) that is less than (but not less than ½ of) the amount specified in clause (i).

(iii) Adjustment for high employment areas. In the case of an investment made in a part of a metropolitan statistical area that at the time of the investment—

(I) is not a targetted employment area, and

(II) is an area with an unemployment rate significantly below the national average unemployment rate,

the Attorney General may specify an amount of capital required under subparagraph (A) that is greater than (but not greater than 3 times) the amount specified in clause (i).

(c) **Diversity immigrants.**

(1) **In general.** Except as provided in paragraph (2), aliens subject to the worldwide level specified in section 201(e) [8 U.S.C.A. § 1151(e)] for diversity immigrants shall be allotted visas each fiscal year as follows:

(A) Determination of preference immigration. The Attorney General shall determine for the most recent previous 5-fiscal-year period for which data are available, the total number of aliens who are natives of each foreign state and who (i) were admitted or otherwise provided lawful permanent resident status (other than under this subsection) and (ii) were subject to the numerical limitations of section 201(a) [8 U.S.C.A. § 1151(a)] (other than paragraph (3) thereof) or who were admitted or otherwise provided lawful permanent resident status as an immediate relative or other alien described in section 201(b)(2) [8 U.S.C.A. § 1151(b)(2)].

(B) Identification of high-admission and low-admission regions and high-admission and low-admission states. The Attorney General—

(i) shall identify—

(I) each region (each in this paragraph referred to as a "high-admission region") for which the total of the numbers determined under subparagraph (A) for states in the region is greater than ⅙ of the total of all such numbers, and

(II) each other region (each in this paragraph referred to as a "low-admission region"); and

(ii) shall identify—

(I) each foreign state for which the number determined under subparagraph (A) is greater than 50,000 (each such state in this paragraph referred to as a "high-admission state"), and

(II) each other foreign state (each such state in this paragraph referred to as a "low-admission state").

(C) Determination of percentage of worldwide immigration attributable to high-admission regions.   The Attorney General shall determine the percentage of the total of the numbers determined under subparagraph (A) that are numbers for foreign states in high-admission regions.

(D) Determination of regional populations excluding high-admission states and ratios of populations of regions within low-admission regions and high-admission regions.   The Attorney General shall determine—

(i) based on available estimates for each region, the total population of each region not including the population of any high-admission state;

(ii) for each low-admission region, the ratio of the population of the region determined under clause (i) to the total of the population determined under such clause for all the low-admission regions;  and

(iii) for each high-admission region, the ratio of the population of the region determined under clause (i) to the total of the populations determined under such clause for all the high-admission regions.

(E) Distribution of visas.—

(i) No visas for natives of high-admission states.   The percentage of visas made available under this paragraph to natives of a high-admission state is 0.

(ii) For low-admission states in low-admission regions. Subject to clauses (iv) and (v), the percentage of visas made available under this paragraph to natives (other than natives of a high-admission state) in a low-admission region is the product of—

(I) the percentage determined under subparagraph (C), and

(II) the population ratio for that region determined under subparagraph (D)(ii).

(iii) For low-admission states in high-admission regions. Subject to clauses (iv) and (v), the percentage of visas made available under this paragraph to natives (other than natives of a high-admission state) in a high-admission region is the product of—

**(I)** 100 percent minus the percentage determined under subparagraph (C), and

**(II)** the population ratio for that region determined under subparagraph (D)(iii).

**(iv)** Redistribution of unused visa numbers. If the Secretary of State estimates that the number of immigrant visas to be issued to natives in any region for a fiscal year under this paragraph is less than the number of immigrant visas made available to such natives under this paragraph for the fiscal year, subject to clause (v), the excess visa numbers shall be made available to natives (other than natives of a high-admission state) of the other regions in proportion to the percentages otherwise specified in clauses (ii) and (iii).

**(v)** Limitation on visas for natives of a single foreign state. The percentage of visas made available under this paragraph to natives of any single foreign state for any fiscal year shall not exceed 7 percent.

**(F)** Region defined. Only for purposes of administering the diversity program under this subsection, Northern Ireland shall be treated as a separate foreign state, each colony or other component or dependent area of a foreign state overseas from the foreign state shall be treated as part of the foreign state, and the areas described in each of the following clauses shall be considered to be a separate region:

**(i)** Africa.

**(ii)** Asia.

**(iii)** Europe.

**(iv)** North America (other than Mexico).

**(v)** Oceania.

**(vi)** South America, Mexico, Central America, and the Caribbean.

**(2) Requirement of education or work experience.** An alien is not eligible for a visa under this subsection unless the alien—

**(A)** has at least a high school education or its equivalent, or

**(B)** has, within 5 years of the date of application for a visa under this subsection, at least 2 years of work experience in an occupation which requires at least 2 years of training or experience.

**(3) Maintenance of information.** The Secretary of State shall maintain information on the age, occupation, education level, and other relevant characteristics of immigrants issued visas under this subsection.

### (d) Treatment of family members.

A spouse or child as defined in subparagraph (A), (B), (C), (D), or (E) of section 101(b)(1) [8 U.S.C.A. § 1101(b)(1)] shall, if not otherwise entitled to an immigrant status and the immediate issuance of a visa under subsection (a), (b), or (c) of this section, be entitled to the same status, and the same order of consideration provided in the respective subsection, if accompanying or following to join, the spouse or parent.

### (e) Order of consideration.

(1) Immigrant visas made available under subsection (a) or (b) of this section shall be issued to eligible immigrants in the order in which a petition in behalf of each such immigrant is filed with the Attorney General (or in the case of special immigrants under section 101(a)(27)(D) [8 U.S.C.A. § 1101(a)(27)(D)], with the Secretary of State) as provided in section 204(a) [8 U.S.C.A. § 1154(a)].

(2) Immigrant visa numbers made available under subsection (c) of this section (relating to diversity immigrants) shall be issued to eligible qualified immigrants strictly in a random order established by the Secretary of State for the fiscal year involved.

(3) Waiting lists of applicants for visas under this section shall be maintained in accordance with regulations prescribed by the Secretary of State.

### (f) Presumption.

Every immigrant shall be presumed not to be described in subsection (a) or (b) of this section, section 101(a)(27) [8 U.S.C.A. § 1101(a)(27)], or section 201(b)(2) [8 U.S.C.A. § 1151(b)(2)], until the immigrant establishes to the satisfaction of the consular officer and the immigration officer that the immigrant is so described. In the case of any alien claiming in his application for an immigrant visa to be described in section 101(b)(1) [8 U.S.C.A. § 1101(b)(1)] or in subsection (a) or (b) of this section, the consular officer shall not grant such status until he has been authorized to do so as provided by section 1154 of this title.

### (g) Lists.

For purposes of carrying out the Secretary's responsibilities in the orderly administration of this section, the Secretary of State may make reasonable estimates of the anticipated numbers of visas to be issued during any quarter of any fiscal year within each of the categories under subsections (a), (b), and (c) of this section and to rely upon such estimates in authorizing the issuance of visas. The Secretary of State shall terminate the registration of any alien who fails to apply for an immigrant visa within one year following notification to the alien of the availability of such visa, but the Secretary shall reinstate the registration of any such alien who establishes within 2 years following the date of notification of the availability of such visa that such failure to apply was due to circumstances beyond the alien's control.

(June 27, 1952, c. 477, Title II, ch. 1, § 203, 66 Stat. 178; Pub. L. 85–316, § 3, Sept. 11, 1957, 71 Stat. 639; Pub. L. 86–363, §§ 1–3, Sept. 22, 1959, 73 Stat. 644; Pub. L. 89–236, § 3, Oct. 3, 1965, 79 Stat. 912; Pub. L. 94–571, § 4, Oct. 20, 1976, 90 Stat. 2705; Pub. L. 95–412, § 3, Oct. 5, 1978, 92 Stat. 907; Pub. L. 95–417, § 1, Oct. 5, 1978, 92 Stat. 917; Pub. L. 96–212, Title II, § 203(c), (i), Mar. 17, 1980, 94 Stat. 107, 108; Nov. 29, 1990, Pub.L. 101–649, Title I, §§ 111, 121(a), 131, 162(a)(1), Title VI, § 603(a)(3), 104 Stat. 4986, 4987, 4997, 5008, 5009.)

## § 204. Procedure for granting immigrant status [8 U.S.C.A. § 1154]

### (a) Petition for preference status or immediate relative status; spousal second preference petition

**(1)(A)** Any citizen of the United States claiming that an alien is entitled to classification by reason of a relationship described in paragraph (1), (3), or (4) of section 203(a) [8 U.S.C.A. § 1153(a)(1), (3), or (4)] or to an immediate relative status under section 201(b)(2)(A)(i) [8 U.S.C.A. § 1151(b)(2)(A)(i)] may file a petition with the Attorney General for such classification.

**(B)** Any alien lawfully admitted for permanent residence claiming that an alien is entitled to a classification by reason of the relationship described in section 203(a)(2) [8 U.S.C.A. § 1153(a)(2)] may file a petition with the Attorney General for such classification.

**(C)** Any alien desiring to be classified under section 203(b)(1)(A) [8 U.S.C.A. § 1153(b)(1)(A)], or any person on behalf of such an alien, may file a petition with the Attorney General for such classification.

**(D)** Any employer desiring and intending to employ within the United States an alien entitled to classification under section 203(b)(1)(B), 203(b)(1)(C), 203(b)(2), or 203(b)(3) [8 U.S.C.A. §§ 1153(b)(1)(B), 1153(b)(1)(C), 1153(b)(2), or 1153(b)(3)] may file a petition with the Attorney General for such classification.

**(E)(i)** Any alien (other than a special immigrant under section 101(a)(27)(D) [8 U.S.C.A. § 1101(a)(27)(D)], desiring to be classified under section 203(b)(4) [8 U.S.C.A. § 1153(b)(4)], or any person on behalf of such an alien, may file a petition with the Attorney General for such classification.

**(ii)** Aliens claiming status as a special immigrant under section 101(a)(27)(D) [8 U.S.C.A. § 1101(a)(27)(D)] may file a petition only with the Secretary of State and only after notification by the Secretary that such status has been recommended and approved pursuant to such section.

**(F)** Any alien desiring to be classified under section 203(b)(5) [8 U.S.C.A. § 1153(b)(5)] may file a petition with the Secretary of State for such classification.

**(G)(i)** Any alien desiring to be provided an immigrant visa under section 203(c) [8 U.S.C.A. § 1153(c)] may file a petition at the place and time determined by the Secretary of State by regulation. Only one such petition may be filed by an alien with respect to any petitioning period established. If more than one petition is submitted all such petitions submitted for such period by the alien shall be voided.

(ii)(I) The Secretary of State shall designate a period for the filing of petitions with respect to visas which may be issued under section 203(c) [8 U.S.C.A. § 1153(c)] for the fiscal year beginning after the end of the period.

(II) Aliens who qualify, through random selection, for a visa under section 203(c) [8 U.S.C.A. § 1153(c)] shall remain eligible to receive such visa only through the end of the specific fiscal year for which they were selected.

(III) The Secretary of State shall prescribe such regulations as may be necessary to carry out this clause.

(iii) A petition or registration under this subparagraph shall be in such form as the Secretary of State may by regulation prescribe and shall contain such information and be supported by such documentary evidence as the Secretary of State may require.

(2)(A) The Attorney General may not approve a spousal second preference petition filed by an alien who, by virtue of a prior marriage, has been accorded the status of an alien lawfully admitted for permanent residence as the spouse of a citizen of the United States or as the spouse of an alien lawfully admitted for permanent residence, unless—

(i) a period of 5 years has elapsed after the date the alien acquired the status of an alien lawfully admitted for permanent residence, or

(ii) the alien establishes to the satisfaction of the Attorney General by clear and convincing evidence that the prior marriage (on the basis of which the alien obtained the status of an alien lawfully admitted for permanent residence) was not entered into for the purpose of evading any provision of the immigration laws.

In this subparagraph, the term "spousal second preference petition" refers to a petition, seeking preference status under section 203(a)(2) [8 U.S.C.A. § 1153(a)(2)], for an alien as a spouse of an alien lawfully admitted for permanent residence.

(B) Subparagraph (A) shall not apply to a petition filed by an alien whose prior marriage was terminated by the death of his or her spouse.

**(b) Investigation; consultation; approval; authorization to grant preference status**

After an investigation of the facts in each case, and after consultation with the Secretary of Labor with respect to petitions to accord a status under section 203(b)(2) or 203(b)(3) [8 U.S.C.A. §§ 1153(b)(2) or 1153(b)(3)], the Attorney General shall, if he determines that the facts stated in the petition are true and that the alien in behalf of whom the petition is made is an immediate relative specified in section 201(b) [8

U.S.C.A. § 1151(b)], or is eligible for preference under subsection (a) or (b) of section 203 [8 U.S.C.A. § 1153(a) or (b) ], approve the petition and forward one copy thereof to the Department of State. The Secretary of State shall then authorize the consular officer concerned to grant the preference status.

## (c) Restrictions on future entry of aliens involved with marriage fraud

Notwithstanding the provisions of subsection (b) of this section no petition shall be approved if (1) the alien has previously been accorded, or has sought to be accorded, an immediate relative or preference status as the spouse of a citizen of the United States or the spouse of an alien lawfully admitted for permanent residence, by reason of a marriage determined by the Attorney General to have been entered into for the purpose of evading the immigration laws, or (2) the Attorney General has determined that the alien has attempted or conspired to enter into a marriage for the purpose of evading the immigration laws.

## (d) Recommendation of valid home-study

Notwithstanding the provisions of subsections (a) and (b) of this section no petition may be approved on behalf of a child defined in section 101(b)(1)(F) [8 U.S.C.A. § 1011(b)(1)(F)] unless a valid home-study has been favorably recommended by an agency of the State of the child's proposed residence, or by an agency authorized by that State to conduct such a study, or, in the case of a child adopted abroad, by an appropriate public or private adoption agency which is licensed in the United States.

## (e) Subsequent finding of non-entitlement to preference classification

Nothing in this section shall be construed to entitle an immigrant, in behalf of whom a petition under this section is approved, to enter the United States as a [1] immigrant under subsection (a), (b), or (c) of section 203 [8 U.S.C.A. § 1153(a), (b), or (c) ] or as an immediate relative under section 201(b) [8 U.S.C.A. § 1151(b)] if upon his arrival at a port of entry in the United States he is found not to be entitled to such classification.

## (f) Preferential treatment for children fathered by United States citizens and born in Korea, Vietnam, Laos, Kampuchea, or Thailand after 1950 and before October 22, 1982

(1) Any alien claiming to be an alien described in paragraph (2)(A) of this subsection (or any person on behalf of such an alien) may file a petition with the Attorney General for classification under section 201(b), 203(a)(1), or 203(a)(3) [8 U.S.C.A. §§ 1151(b), 1153(a)(1), or 1153(a)(3)], as appropriate. After an investigation of the facts of each case the Attorney General shall, if the conditions described in paragraph (2) are met, approve the petition and forward one copy to the Secretary of State.

**(2)** The Attorney General may approve a petition for an alien under paragraph (1) if—

**(A)** he has reason to believe that the alien (i) was born in Korea, Vietnam, Laos, Kampuchea, or Thailand after 1950 and before October 22, 1982, and (ii) was fathered by a United States citizen;

**(B)** he has received an acceptable guarantee of legal custody and financial responsibility described in paragraph (4); and

**(C)** in the case of an alien under eighteen years of age, (i) the alien's placement with a sponsor in the United States has been arranged by an appropriate public, private, or State child welfare agency licensed in the United States and actively involved in the intercountry placement of children and (ii) the alien's mother or guardian has in writing irrevocably released the alien for emigration.

**(3)** In considering petitions filed under paragraph (1), the Attorney General shall—

**(A)** consult with appropriate governmental officials and officials of private voluntary organizations in the country of the alien's birth in order to make the determinations described in subparagraphs (A) and (C)(ii) of paragraph (2); and

**(B)** consider the physical appearance of the alien and any evidence provided by the petitioner, including birth and baptismal certificates, local civil records, photographs of, and letters or proof of financial support from, a putative father who is a citizen of the United States, and the testimony of witnesses, to the extent it is relevant or probative.

**(4)(A)** A guarantee of legal custody and financial responsibility for an alien described in paragraph (2) must—

**(i)** be signed in the presence of an immigration officer or consular officer by an individual (hereinafter in this paragraph referred to as the "sponsor") who is twenty-one years of age or older, is of good moral character, and is a citizen of the United States or alien lawfully admitted for permanent residence, and

**(ii)** provide that the sponsor agrees (I) in the case of an alien under eighteen years of age, to assume legal custody for the alien after the alien's departure to the United States and until the alien becomes eighteen years of age, in accordance with the laws of the State where the alien and the sponsor will reside, and (II) to furnish, during the five-year period beginning on the date of the alien's acquiring the status of an alien lawfully admitted for permanent residence, or during the period beginning on the date of the alien's acquiring the status of an alien lawfully admitted for permanent residence and ending on the date on which the alien becomes twenty-one years of age, whichever period is longer, such financial support as is necessary to maintain the family in the United States of which the alien is a member at a level equal to at least 125 per centum of the current official poverty line (as established by the Director of the Office of Management and Budget, under section 9902(2) of Title 42 and as revised by the Secretary of Health and Human Services under section 9847 of Title 42) for a family of the same size as the size of the alien's family.

**(B)** A guarantee of legal custody and financial responsibility described in subparagraph (A) may be enforced with respect to an alien against his sponsor in a civil suit brought by the Attorney General in the United States district court for the district in which the sponsor resides, except that a sponsor or his estate shall not be liable under such a guarantee if the sponsor dies or is adjudicated a bankrupt under Title 11.

**(g) Restrictions on petitions based on marriages entered while in exclusion or deportation proceedings**

Notwithstanding subsection (a) of this section, except as provided section 245(e)(3) [8 U.S.C.A. § 1255(e)(3)], a petition may not be approved to grant an alien immediate relative status or preference status by reason of a marriage which was entered into during the period described in section 245(e)(2) [8 U.S.C.A. § 1255(e)(2)], until the alien has resided outside the United States for a 2-year period beginning after the date of the marriage.

(June 27, 1952, c. 477, Title II, ch. 1, § 204, 66 Stat. 179; Pub. L. 87–885, § 3, Oct. 24, 1962, 76 Stat. 1247; Pub. L. 89–236, § 4, Oct. 3, 1965, 79 Stat. 915; Pub. L. 94–571, § 7(b), Oct. 20, 1976, 90 Stat. 2706; Pub. L. 95–417, §§ 2, 3, Oct. 5, 1978, 92 Stat. 917; Pub. L. 96–470, Title II, § 207, Oct. 19, 1980, 94 Stat. 2245; Pub. L. 97–116, §§ 3, 18(d), Dec. 29, 1981, 95 Stat. 1611, 1620; Pub. L. 97–359, Oct. 22, 1982, 96 Stat. 1716; Pub.L. 99–639, §§ 2(c), 4(a), 5(b), Nov. 10, 1986, 100 Stat. 3541, 3543; Pub.L. 100–525, § 9(g), Oct. 24, 1988, 102 Stat. 2620; Nov. 29, 1990, Pub.L. 101–649, Title I, § 162(b), Title VII, § 702(b), 104 Stat. 5010, 5086.)

1. So in original.

## § 205. Revocation of approval of petitions; notice of revocation; effective date [8 U.S.C.A. § 1155]

The Attorney General may, at any time, for what he deems to be good and sufficient cause, revoke the approval of any petition approved by him under section 204 [8 U.S.C.A. § 1154]. Such revocation shall be effective as of the date of approval of any such petition. In no case, however, shall such revocation have effect unless there is mailed to the petitioner's last known address a notice of the revocation and unless notice the revocation is communicated through the Secretary of State to the beneficiary of the petition before such beneficiary commences his journey to the United States. If notice of revocation is not so given, and the beneficiary applies for admission to the United States, his admissibility shall be determined in the manner provided for by sections 235 and 236 [8 U.S.C.A. §§ 1225 and 1226].

(June 27, 1952, c. 477, Title II, ch. 1, § 205, 66 Stat. 180; Pub. L. 86–363, § 5(a), (b), Sept. 22, 1959, 73 Stat. 644; Pub. L. 87–301, §§ 3, 10, Sept. 26, 1961, 75 Stat. 650, 654; Pub. L. 89–236, § 5, Oct. 3, 1965, 79 Stat. 916.)

# § 206. Unused immigrant visas [8 U.S.C.A. § 1156]

If an immigrant having an immigrant visa is excluded from admission to the United States and deported, or does not apply for admission before the expiration of the validity of his visa, or if an alien having an immigrant visa issued to him as a preference immigrant is found not to be a preference immigrant, an immigrant visa or a preference immigrant visa, as the case may be, may be issued in lieu thereof to another qualified alien.

(June 27, 1952, c. 477, Title II, ch. 1, § 206, 66 Stat. 181; Pub. L. 89–236, § 6, Oct. 3, 1965, 79 Stat. 916.)

# § 207. Annual admission of refugees and admission of emergency situation refugees [8 U.S.C.A. § 1157]

**(a) Maximum number of admissions; increases for humanitarian concerns; allocations**

(1) Except as provided in subsection (b) of this section, the number of refugees who may be admitted under this section in fiscal year 1980, 1981, or 1982, may not exceed fifty thousand unless the President determines, before the beginning of the fiscal year and after appropriate consultation (as defined in subsection (e) of this section), that admission of a specific number of refugees in excess of such number is justified by humanitarian concerns or is otherwise in the national interest.

(2) Except as provided in subsection (b) of this section, the number of refugees who may be admitted under this section in any fiscal year after fiscal year 1982 shall be such number as the President determines, before the beginning of the fiscal year and after appropriate consultation, is justified by humanitarian concerns or is otherwise in the national interest.

(3) Admissions under this subsection shall be allocated among refugees of special humanitarian concern to the United States in accordance with a determination made by the President after appropriate consultation.

(4) In the determination made under this subsection for each fiscal year (beginning with fiscal year 1992), the President shall enumerate, with the respective number of refugees so determined, the number of aliens who were granted asylum in the previous year.

**(b) Determinations by President respecting number of admissions for humanitarian concerns**

If the President determines, after appropriate consultation, that (1) an unforeseen emergency refugee situation exists, (2) the admission of certain refugees in response to the emergency refugee situation is justified by grave humanitarian concerns or is otherwise in the national interest, and (3) the admission to the United States of these refugees cannot be accomplished under subsection (a) of this section, the President may fix a number of refugees to be admitted to the United States during the succeeding period (not to exceed twelve months) in response to the emergency refugee situation and such admissions shall be allocated among refugees of special humanitarian concern to the United States in accordance with a determination made by the President after the appropriate consultation provided under this subsection.

**(c) Admission by Attorney General of refugees; criteria; admission status of spouse or child; applicability of other statutory requirements; termination of refugee status of alien, spouse or child**

**(1)** Subject to the numerical limitations established pursuant to subsections (a) and (b) of this section, the Attorney General may, in the Attorney General's discretion and pursuant to such regulations as the Attorney General may prescribe, admit any refugee who is not firmly resettled in any foreign country, is determined to be of special humanitarian concern to the United States, and is admissible (except as otherwise provided under paragraph (3)) as an immigrant under this chapter.

**(2)** A spouse or child (as defined in section 101(b)(1)(A), (B), (C), (D), or (E) [8 U.S.C.A. § 1101(b)(1)(A), (B), (C), (D), or (E)]) of any refugee who qualifies for admission under paragraph (1) shall, if not otherwise entitled to admission under paragraph (1) and if not a person described in the second sentence of section 101(a)(42) [8 U.S.C.A. § 1101(a)(42)], be entitled to the same admission status as such refugee if accompanying, or following to join, such refugee and if the spouse or child is admissible (except as otherwise provided under paragraph (3)) as an immigrant under this chapter. Upon the spouse's or child's admission to the United States, such admission shall be charged against the numerical limitation established in accordance with the appropriate subsection under which the refugee's admission is charged.

**(3)** The provisions of paragraphs (4), (5), (7)(A) of section 212(a) [8 U.S.C.A. § 1182(a)(4), (5), (7)(A)] shall not be applicable to any alien seeking admission to the United States under this subsection, and the Attorney General may waive any other provision of such section (other than paragraph (2)(C) or subparagraphs (A), (B), (C), or (E) of paragraph (3)) with respect to such an alien for humanitarian purposes, to assure family unity, or when it is otherwise in the public interest. Any such waiver by the Attorney General shall be in writing and shall be granted only on an individual basis following an investigation. The Attorney General shall provide for the annual reporting to Congress of the

61

number of waivers granted under this paragraph in the previous fiscal year and a summary of the reasons for granting such waivers.

**(4)** The refugee status of any alien (and of the spouse or child of the alien) may be terminated by the Attorney General pursuant to such regulations as the Attorney General may prescribe if the Attorney General determines that the alien was not in fact a refugee within the meaning of section 101(a)(42) [8 U.S.C.A. § 1101(a)(42)] at the time of the alien's admission.

### (d) Oversight reporting and consultative requirements

**(1)** Before the start of each fiscal year the President shall report to the Committees on the Judiciary of the House of Representatives and of the Senate regarding the foreseeable number of refugees who will be in need of resettlement during the fiscal year and the anticipated allocation of refugee admissions during the fiscal year. The President shall provide for periodic discussions between designated representatives of the President and members of such committees regarding changes in the worldwide refugee situation, the progress of refugee admissions, and the possible need for adjustments in the allocation of admissions among refugees.

**(2)** As soon as possible after representatives of the President initiate appropriate consultation with respect to the number of refugee admissions under subsection (a) of this section or with respect to the admission of refuges in response to an emergency refugee situation under subsection (b) of this section, the Committees on the Judiciary of the House of Representatives and of the Senate shall cause to have printed in the Congressional Record the substance of such consultation.

**(3)(A)** After the President initiates appropriate consultation prior to making a determination under subsection (a) of this section, a hearing to review the proposed determination shall be held unless public disclosure of the details of the proposal would jeopardize the lives or safety of individuals.

**(B)** After the President initiates appropriate consultation prior to making a determination, under subsection (b) of this section, that the number of refugee admissions should be increased because of an unforeseen emergency refugee situation, to the extent that time and the nature of the emergency refugee situation permit, a hearing to review the proposal to increase refugee admissions shall be held unless public disclosure of the details of the proposal would jeopardize the lives or safety of individuals.

### (e) Definition

For purposes of this section, the term "appropriate consultation" means, with respect to the admission of refugees and allocation of refugee admissions, discussions in person by designated Cabinet-level representatives of the President with members of the Committees on the Judiciary of the Senate and of the House of Representatives to review the refugee situation or emergency refugee situation, to project the extent of possible participation of the United States therein, to discuss the reasons for believing that the proposed admission of refugees is justified by humanitarian concerns or grave humanitarian concerns or is otherwise in the national interest, and to provide such members with the following information:

(1) A description of the nature of the refugee situation.

(2) A description of the number and allocation of the refugees to be admitted and an analysis of conditions within the countries from which they came.

(3) A description of the proposed plans for their movement and resettlement and the estimated cost of their movement and resettlement.

(4) An analysis of the anticipated social, economic, and demographic impact of their admission to the United States.

(5) A description of the extent to which other countries will admit and assist in the resettlement of such refugees.

(6) An analysis of the impact of the participation of the United States in the resettlement of such refugees on the foreign policy interests of the United States.

(7) Such additional information as may be appropriate or requested by such members.

To the extent possible, information described in this subsection shall be provided at least two weeks in advance of discussions in person by designated representatives of the President with such members.

(June 27, 1952, c. 477, Title II, ch. 1, § 207, as added Pub. L. 96–212, Title II, § 201(b), Mar. 17, 1980, 94 Stat. 103, and amended Pub.L. 100–525, § 9(h), Oct. 24, 1988, 102 Stat. 2620; Nov. 29, 1990, Pub.L. 101–649, Title I, § 104(b), Title VI, § 603(a)(4), 104 Stat. 4985, 5082.)

## § 208. Asylum procedure [8 U.S.C.A. § 1158]

### (a) Establishment by Attorney General; coverage

The Attorney General shall establish a procedure for an alien physically present in the United States or at a land border or port of entry, irrespective of such alien's status, to apply for asylum, and the alien may be granted asylum in the discretion of the Attorney General if the Attorney General determines that such alien is a refugee within the meaning of section 101(a)(42)(A) [8 U.S.C.A. § 1101(a)(42)(A)].

### (b) Termination of asylum by Attorney General; criteria

Asylum granted under subsection (a) of this section may be terminated if the Attorney General, pursuant to such regulations as the Attorney General may prescribe, determines that the alien is no longer a refugee within the meaning of section 101(a)(42)(A) [8 U.S.C.A. § 1101(a)(42)(A)] owing to a change in circumstances in the alien's country of nationality or, in the case of an alien having no nationality, in the country in which the alien last habitually resided.

### (c) Status of spouse or child of alien granted asylum

A spouse or child (as defined in section 101(b)(1)(A), (B), (C), (D), or (E) [8 U.S.C.A. § 1101(b)(1)(A), (B), (C), (D), or (E)]) of an alien who is granted asylum under subsection (a) of this section may, if not otherwise eligible for asylum under such subsection, be granted the same status as the alien if accompanying, or following to join, such alien.

### (d) Aliens convicted of aggravated felony

An alien who has been convicted of an aggravated felony, notwithstanding subsection (a) of this section, may not apply for or be granted asylum.

(June 27, 1952, c. 477, Title II, ch. 1, § 208, as added Pub. L. 96–212, Title II, § 201(b), Mar. 17, 1980, 94 Stat. 105; Pub.L. 101–649, Title V, 515(a)(1), Nov. 29, 1990, 104 Stat. 5053.)

## § 209. Adjustment of status of refugees [8 U.S.C.A. § 1159]

### (a) Criteria and procedures applicable for admission as immigrant; effect of adjustment

(1) Any alien who has been admitted to the United States under section 207 [8 U.S.C.A. § 1157]—

(A) whose admission has not been terminated by the Attorney General pursuant to such regulations as the Attorney General may prescribe,

(B) who has been physically present in the United States for at least one year, and

(C) who has not acquired permanent resident status,

shall, at the end of such year period, return or be returned to the custody of the Service for inspection and examination for admission to the United States as an immigrant in accordance with the provisions of sections 235, 236, and 237 [8 U.S.C.A. §§ 1225, 1226, and 1227].

(2) Any alien who is found upon inspection and examination by an immigration officer pursuant to paragraph (1) or after a hearing before a special inquiry officer to be admissible (except as otherwise provided under subsection (c) of this section) as an immigrant under this chapter at the time of the alien's inspection and examination shall, notwithstanding any numerical limitation specified in this chapter, be regarded as lawfully admitted to the United States for permanent residence as of the date of such alien's arrival into the United States.

### (b) Maximum number of adjustments; recordkeeping

Not more than 10,000 of the refugee admissions authorized under section 207(a) [8 U.S.C.A. § 1157(a)] in any fiscal year may be made available by the Attorney General, in the Attorney General's discretion and under such regulations as the Attorney General may prescribe, to adjust to the status of an alien lawfully admitted for permanent residence the status of any alien granted asylum who—

(1) applies for such adjustment,

(2) has been physically present in the United States for at least one year after being granted asylum,

(3) continues to be a refugee within the meaning of section 101(a)(42)(A) [8 U.S.C.A. § 1101(a)(42)(A)] or a spouse or child of such a refugee,

(4) is not firmly resettled in any foreign country, and

(5) is admissible (except as otherwise provided under subsection (c) of this section) as an immigrant under this chapter at the time of examination for adjustment of such alien.

Upon approval of an application under this subsection, the Attorney General shall establish a record of the alien's admission for lawful permanent residence as of the date one year before the date of the approval of the application.

### (c) Applicability of other federal statutory requirements

The provisions of paragraphs (4), (5), and (7)(A) of section 212(a) [8 U.S.C.A. § 1182(a)(4), (5), and (7)(A)] shall not be applicable to any alien seeking adjustment of status under this section, and the Attorney General may waive any other provision of such section (other than paragraph (2)(C) or subparagraphs (A), (B), (C), or (E) of paragraph (3)) with respect to such an alien for humanitarian purposes, to assure family unity, or when it is otherwise in the public interest.

(June 27, 1952, c. 477, Title II, ch. 1, § 209, as added Pub. L. 96–212, Title II, § 201(b), Mar. 17, 1980, 94 Stat. 105, and amended Nov. 29, 1990, Pub.L. 101–649, Title I, § 104(a)(1), Title VI, § 603(a)(4), 104 Stat. 4985, 5082.)

## § 210. Special agricultural workers [8 U.S.C.A. § 1160]

### (a) Lawful Residence

#### (1) In general

The Attorney General shall adjust the status of an alien to that of an alien lawfully admitted for temporary residence if the Attorney General determines that the alien meets the following requirements:

(A) Application period

The alien must apply for such adjustment during the 18-month period beginning on the first day of the seventh month that begins after November 6, 1986.

(B) Performance of seasonal agricultural services and residence in the United States

The alien must establish that he has—

(i) resided in the United States, and

(ii) performed seasonal agricultural services in the United States for at least 90 man-days.

during the 12-month period ending on May 1, 1986. For purposes of the previous sentence, performance of seasonal agricultural services in the United States for more than one employer on any one day shall be counted as performance of services for only 1 man-day.

(C) Admissible as immigrant

The alien must establish that he is admissible to the United States as an immigrant, except as otherwise provided under subsection (c)(2) of this section.

**(2) Adjustment to permanent residence**

The Attorney General shall adjust the status of any alien provided lawful temporary resident status under paragraph (1) to that of an alien lawfully admitted for permanent residence on the following date:

(A) Group 1

Subject to the numerical limitation established under subparagraph (C), in the case of an alien who has established, at the time of application for temporary residence under paragraph (1), that the alien performed seasonal agricultural services in the United States for at least 90 man-days during each of the 12-month periods ending on May 1, 1984, 1985, and 1986, the adjustment shall occur on the first day after the end of the one-year period that begins on the later of (I) the date the alien was granted such temporary resident status, or (II) the day after the last day of the application period described in paragraph (1)(A).

(B) Group 2

In the case of aliens to which subparagraph (A) does not apply, the adjustment shall occur on the day after the last day of the two-year period that begins on the later of (I) the date the alien was granted such temporary resident status, or (II) the day after the last day of the application period described in paragraph (1)(A).

(C) Numerical limitation

Subparagraph (A) shall not apply to more than 350,000 aliens. If more than 350,000 aliens meet the requirements of such subparagraph, such subparagraph shall apply to the 350,-000 aliens whose applications for adjustment were first filed under paragraph (1) and subparagraph (B) shall apply to the remaining aliens.

**(3) Termination of temporary residence**

(A) During the period of temporary resident status granted an alien under paragraph (1), the Attorney General may terminate such status only upon a determination under this chapter that the alien is deportable.

(B) Before any alien becomes eligible for adjustment of status under paragraph (2), the Attorney General may deny adjustment to permanent status and provide for termination of the temporary resident status granted such alien under paragraph (1) if—

(i) the Attorney General finds by a preponderance of the evidence that the adjustment to temporary resident status was the result of fraud or willful misrepresentation as set out in section 212(a)(6)(C)(i) [8 U.S.C.A. § 1182(a)(6)(C)(i)], or

(ii) the alien commits an act that (I) makes the alien inadmissible to the United States as an immigrant, except as provided under subsection (c)(2) of this section, or (II) is convicted of a felony or 3 or more misdemeanors committed in the United States.

**(4) Authorized travel and employment during temporary residence**

During the period an alien is in lawful temporary resident status granted under this subsection, the alien has the right to travel abroad (including commutation from a residence abroad) and shall be granted authorization to engage in employment in the United States and shall be provided an "employment authorized" endorsement or other appropriate work permit, in the same manner as for aliens lawfully admitted for permanent residence.

**(5) In general**

Except as otherwise provided in this subsection, an alien who acquires the status of an alien lawfully admitted for temporary residence under paragraph (1), such status not having changed, is considered to be an alien lawfully admitted for permanent residence (as described in section 101(a)(20) [8 U.S.C.A. § 1101(a)(20)]), other than under any provision of the immigration laws.

**(b) Applications for adjustment of status**

**(1) To whom may be made**

(A) Within the United States

The Attorney General shall provide that applications for adjustment of status under subsection (a) of this section may be filed—

(i) with the Attorney General, or

(ii) with a designated entity (designated under paragraph (2)), but only if the applicant consents to the forwarding of the application to the Attorney General.

(B) Outside the United States

The Attorney General, in cooperation with the Secretary of State, shall provide a procedure whereby an alien may apply for adjustment of status under subsection (a)(1) of this section at an appropriate consular office outside the United States. If the alien otherwise qualifies for such adjustment, the Attorney General shall provide such documentation of authorization to enter the United States and to have the alien's status adjusted upon entry as may be necessary to carry out the provisions of this section.

### (2) Designation of entities to receive applications

For purposes of receiving applications under this section, the Attorney General—

**(A)** shall designate qualified voluntary organizations and other qualified State, local, community, farm labor organizations, and associations of agricultural employers, and

**(B)** may designate such other persons as the Attorney General determines are qualified and have substantial experience, demonstrated competence, and traditional long-term involvement in the preparation and submittal of applications for adjustment of status under section 209 or 245 [8 U.S.C.A. § 1159 or 1255], Public Law 89–732 [8 U.S.C.A. § 1255 note], or Public Law 95–145.

### (3) Proof of eligibility

(A) In general

An alien may establish that he meets the requirement of subsection (a)(1)(B)(ii) of this section through government employment records, records supplied by employers or collective bargaining organizations, and such other reliable documentation as the alien may provide. The Attorney General shall establish special procedures to credit properly work in cases in which an alien was employed under an assumed name.

(B) Documentation of work history

(i) An alien applying for adjustment of status under subsection (a)(1) of this section has the burden of proving by a preponderance of the evidence that the alien has worked the requisite number of man-days (as required under subsection (a)(1)(B)(ii) of this section).

(ii) If an employer or farm labor contractor employing such an alien has kept proper and adequate records respecting such employment, the alien's burden of proof under clause (i) may be met by securing timely production of those records under regulations to be promulgated by the Attorney General.

(iii) An alien can meet such burden of proof if the alien establishes that the alien has in fact performed the work described in subsection (a)(1)(B)(ii) of this section by producing sufficient evidence to show the extent of that employment as a matter of just and reasonable inference. In such a case, the burden then shifts to the Attorney General to disprove the alien's evidence with a showing which negates the reasonableness of the inference to be drawn from the evidence.

### (4) Treatment of applications by designated entities

Each designated entity must agree to forward to the Attorney General applications filed with it in accordance with paragraph (1)(A)(ii) but not to forward to the Attorney General applications filed with it unless the applicant has consented to such forwarding. No such entity may make a determination required by this section to be made by the Attorney General.

### (5) Limitation on access to information

Files and records prepared for purposes of this section by designated entities operating under this section are confidential and the Attorney General and the Service shall not have access to such files or records relating to an alien without the consent of the alien.

### (6) Confidentiality of information

Neither the Attorney General, nor any other official or employee of the Department of Justice, or bureau or agency thereof, may—

(A) use the information furnished pursuant to an application filed under this section for any purpose other than to make a determination on the application including a determination under subparagraph (a)(3)(B), or for enforcement of paragraph (7).

(B) make any publication whereby the information furnished by any particular individual can be identified, or

(C) permit anyone other than the sworn officers and employees of the Department or bureau or agency or, with respect to applications filed with a designated entity, that designated entity, to examine individual applications.

Anyone who uses, publishes, or permits information to be examined in violation of this paragraph shall be fined in accordance with Title 18, or imprisoned not more than five years, or both.

### (7) Penalties for false statements in applications

(A) Criminal penalty

Whoever—

(i) files an application for adjustment of status under this section and knowingly and willfully falsifies, conceals, or covers up a material fact or makes any false, fictitious, or fraudulent statements or representations, or makes or

69

uses any false writing or document knowing the same to contain any false, fictitious, or fraudulent statement or entry, or

(ii) creates or supplies a false writing or document for use in making such an application,

shall be fined in accordance with Title 18, or imprisoned not more than five years, or both.

(B) Exclusion

An alien who is convicted of a crime under subparagraph (A) shall be considered to be inadmissible to the United States on the ground described in section 212(a)(19) [8 U.S.C.A. § 1182(a)(19)].

## (c) Waiver of numerical limitations and certain grounds for exclusion

### (1) Numerical limitations do not apply

The numerical limitations of sections 201 and 202 [8 U.S.C.A. §§ 1151 and 1152] shall not apply to the adjustment of aliens to lawful permanent resident status under this section.

### (2) Waiver of grounds for exclusion

In the determination of an alien's admissibility under subsection (a)(1)(C) of this section—

(A) Grounds of exclusion not applicable

The provisions of paragraphs (5) and (7)(A) of section 212(a) [8 U.S.C.A. § 1182(a)(5) and (7)(A)] shall not apply.

(B) Waiver of other grounds

(i) In general

Except as provided in clause (ii), the Attorney General may waive any other provision of section 212(a) [8 U.S.C.A. § 1182(a)] in the case of individual aliens for humanitarian purposes, to assure family unity, or when it is otherwise in the public interest.

(ii) Grounds that may not be waived

The following provisions of section 212(a) [8 U.S.C.A. § 1182(a)] may not be waived by the Attorney General under clause (i):

(I) Paragraphs (2)(A) and (2)(B) (relating to criminals).

(II) Paragraph (4) (relating to aliens likely to become public charges).

(III) Paragraph (2)(C) (relating to drug offenses), except for so much of such paragraph as relates to a single offense of simple possession of 30 grams or less of marihuana.

**(IV)** Paragraph (3) (relating to security and related grounds), other than subparagraph (E) thereof.

**(V)** Omitted.

(C) Special rule for determination of public charge

An alien is not ineligible for adjustment of status under this section due to being inadmissible under section 212(a)(4) [8 U.S.C.A. § 1182(a)(4)] if the alien demonstrates a history of employment in the United States evidencing self-support without reliance on public cash assistance.

**(d) Temporary stay of exclusion or deportation and work authorization for certain applicants**

**(1) Before application period**

The Attorney General shall provide that in the case of an alien who is apprehended before the beginning of the application period described in subsection (a)(1) of this section and who can establish a nonfrivolous case of eligibility to have his status adjusted under subsection (a) of this section (but for the fact that he may not apply for such adjustment until the beginning of such period), until the alien has had the opportunity during the first 30 days of the application period to complete the filing of an application for adjustment, the alien—

**(A)** may not be excluded or deported, and

**(B)** shall be granted authorization to engage in employment in the United States and be provided an "employment authorized" endorsement or other appropriate work permit.

**(2) During application period**

The Attorney General shall provide that in the case of an alien who presents a nonfrivolous application for adjustment of status under subsection (a) of this section during the application period, and until a final determination on the application has been made in accordance with this section, the alien—

**(A)** may not be excluded or deported, and

**(B)** shall be granted authorization to engage in employment in the United States and be provided an "employment authorized" endorsement or other appropriate work permit.

**(3) Use of application fees to offset program costs**

No application fees collected by the Immigration and Naturalization Service (INS) pursuant to this subsection may be used by the INS to offset the costs of the special agricultural worker legalization program until the INS implements the program consistent with the statutory mandate as follows:

**(A)** During the application period as defined in subsection (a)(1)(A) of this section the INS may grant temporary admission

71

to the United States, work authorization, and provide an "employment authorized" endorsement or other appropriate work permit to any alien who presents a preliminary application for adjustment of status under subsection (a) of this section at a designated port of entry on the southern land border. An alien who does not enter through a port of entry is subject to deportation and removal as otherwise provided in this chapter.

**(B)** During the application period as defined in subsection (a)(B)(1)(B) [1] of this section any alien who has filed an application for adjustment of status within the United States as provided in subsection (b)(1)(A) of this section pursuant to the provision of 8 CFR section 210.1(j) is subject to paragraph (2) of this subsection.

**(C)** A preliminary application is defined as a fully completed and signed application with fee and photographs which contains specific information concerning the performance of qualifying employment in the United States and the documentary evidence which the applicant intends to submit as proof of such employment. The applicant must be otherwise admissible to the United States and must establish to the satisfaction of the examining officer during an interview that his or her claim to eligibility for special agriculture worker status is credible.

### (e) Administrative and judicial review

### (1) Administrative and judicial review

There shall be no administrative or judicial review of a determination respecting an application for adjustment of status under this section except in accordance with this subsection.

### (2) Administrative review

(A) Single level of administrative appellate review

The Attorney General shall establish an appellate authority to provide for a single level of administrative appellate review of such a determination.

(B) Standard for review

Such administrative appellate review shall be based solely upon the administrative record established at the time of the determination on the application and upon such additional or newly discovered evidence as may not have been available at the time of the determination.

### (3) Judicial review

(A) Limitation to review of exclusion or deportation

72

There shall be judicial review of such a denial only in the judicial review of an order of exclusion or deportation under section 106 [8 U.S.C.A. § 1105a].

(B) Standard for judicial review

Such judicial review shall be based solely upon the administrative record established at the time of the review by the appellate authority and the findings of fact and determinations contained in such record shall be conclusive unless the applicant can establish abuse of discretion or that the findings are directly contrary to clear and convincing facts contained in the record considered as a whole.

## (f) Temporary disqualification of newly legalized aliens from receiving aid to families with dependent children

During the five-year period beginning on the date an alien was granted lawful temporary resident status under subsection (a) of this section, and notwithstanding any other provision of law, the alien is not eligible for aid under a State plan approved under part A of title IV of the Social Security Act [42 U.S.C.A. § 601 et seq.]. Notwithstanding the previous sentence, in the case of an alien who would be eligible for aid under a State plan approved under part A of title IV of the Social Security Act but for the previous sentence, the provisions of paragraph (3) of section 245A(h) [8 U.S.C.A. § 1255a(h)(3)] shall apply in the same manner as they apply with respect to paragraph (1) of such section and, for this purpose, any reference in section 245A(h) [8 U.S.C.A. § 1255a(h)] to paragraph (1) is deemed a reference to the previous sentence.

## (g) Treatment of special agricultural workers

For all purposes (subject to subsections (a)(5) and (f) of this section) an alien whose status is adjusted under this section to that of an alien lawfully admitted for permanent residence, such status not having changed, shall be considered to be an alien lawfully admitted for permanent residence (within the meaning of section 101(a)(20) [8 U.S.C.A. § 1101(a)(20)]).

## (h) Seasonal agricultural services defined

In this section, the term "seasonal agricultural services" means the performance of field work related to planting, cultural practices, cultivating, growing and harvesting of fruits and vegetables of every kind and other perishable commodities, as defined in regulations by the Secretary of Agriculture.

(June 27, 1952, c. 477, Title II, ch. 1, § 210, as added Pub.L. 99–603, Title III, § 302(a)(1), Nov. 6, 1986, 100 Stat. 3417, and amended Pub.L. 100–202, § 101(a) [Title II, § 211], Dec. 22, 1987, 101 Stat. 1329–18; Pub.L. 100–525, § 2(m), Oct. 24, 1988, 102 Stat. 2613; Dec. 18, 1989, Pub.L. 101–238, § 4, 103 Stat. 2103; Nov. 29, 1990, Pub.L. 101–649, Title VI, § 603(a)(5), 104 Stat. 5082.)

1. So in original.  Probably should be
(a)(1)(B).

## § 210A. Determination of agricultural labor shortages and admission of additional special agricultural workers [8 U.S.C.A. § 1161]

**(a) Determination of need to admit additional special agricultural workers**

### (1) In general

Before the beginning of each fiscal year (beginning with fiscal year 1990 and ending with fiscal year 1993), the Secretaries of Labor and Agriculture (in this section referred to as the "Secretaries") shall jointly determine the number (if any) of additional aliens who should be admitted to the United States or who should otherwise acquire the status of aliens lawfully admitted for temporary residence under this section during the fiscal year to meet a shortage of workers to perform seasonal agricultural services in the United States during the year.  Such number is, in this section, referred to as the "shortage number".

### (2) Overall determination

The shortage number is—

(A) the anticipated need for special agricultural workers (as determined under paragraph (4)) for the fiscal year, minus

(B) the supply of such workers (as determined under paragraph (5)) for that year,

divided by the factor (determined under paragraph (6)) for man-days per worker.

### (3) No replenishment if no shortage

In determining the shortage number, the Secretaries may not determine that there is a shortage unless, after considering all of the criteria set forth in paragraphs (4) and (5), the Secretaries determine that there will not be sufficient able, willing, and qualified workers available to perform seasonal agricultural services required in the fiscal year involved.

### (4) Determination of need

For purposes of paragraph (2)(A), the anticipated need for special agricultural workers for a fiscal year is determined as follows:

(A) Base

The Secretaries shall jointly estimate, using statistically valid methods, the number of man-days of labor performed in seasonal agricultural services in the United States in the previous fiscal year.

74

**(B)** Adjustment for crop losses and changes in industry

The Secretaries shall jointly—

(i) increase such number by the number of man-days of labor in seasonal agricultural services in the United States that would have been needed in the previous fiscal year to avoid any crop damage or other loss that resulted from the unavailability of labor, and

(ii) adjust such number to take into account the projected growth or contraction in the requirements for seasonal agricultural services as a result of—

(I) growth or contraction in the seasonal agriculture industry, and

(II) the use of technologies and personnel practices that affect the need for, and retention of, workers to perform such services.

**(5) Determination of supply**

For purposes of paragraph (2)(B), the anticipated supply of special agricultural workers for a fiscal year is determined as follows:

**(A)** Base

The Secretaries shall use the number estimated under paragraph (4)(A).

**(B)** Adjustment for retirements and increased recruitment

The Secretaries shall jointly—

(i) decrease such number by the number of man-days of labor in seasonal agricultural services in the United States that will be lost due to retirement and movement of workers out of performance of seasonal agricultural services, and

(ii) increase such number by the number of additional man-days of labor in seasonal agricultural services in the United States that can reasonably be expected to result from the availability of able, willing, qualified, and unemployed special agricultural workers, rural low skill, or manual, laborers, and domestic agricultural workers.

**(C)** Bases for increased number

In making the adjustment under subparagraph (B)(ii), the Secretaries shall consider—

(i) the effect, if any, that improvements in wages and working conditions offered by employers will have on the availability of workers to perform seasonal agricultural services, taking into account the adverse effect, if any, of such improvements in wages and working conditions on the economic competitiveness of the perishable agricultural industry,

(ii) the effect, if any, of enhanced recruitment efforts by the employers of such workers and government employment services in the traditional and expected areas of supply of such workers, and

(iii) the number of able, willing and qualified individuals who apply for employment opportunities in seasonal agricultural services listed with offices of government employment services.

**(D)** Construction

Nothing in this subsection shall be deemed to require any individual employer to pay any specified level of wages, to provide any specified working conditions, or to provide for any specified recruitment of workers.

**(6) Determination of man-day per worker factor**

**(A)** Fiscal year 1990

For fiscal year 1990—

**(i)** In general

Subject to clause (ii), for purposes of paragraph (2) the factor under this paragraph is the average number, as estimated by the Director of the Bureau of the Census under subsection (b)(3)(A)(ii) of this section, of man-days of seasonal agricultural services performed in the United States in fiscal year 1989 by special agricultural workers whose status is adjusted under section 1160 of this title and who performed seasonal agricultural services in the United States at any time during the fiscal year.

**(ii)** Lack of adequate information

If the Director determines that—

**(I)** the information reported under subsection (b)(2)(A) of this section is not adequate to make a reasonable estimate of the average number described in clause (i), but

**(II)** the inadequacy of the information is not due to the refusal or failure of employers to report the information required under subsection (b)(2)(A) of this section,

the factor under this paragraph is 90.

**(B)** Fiscal year 1991

For purposes of paragraph (2) for fiscal year 1991, the factor under this paragraph is the average number, as estimated by the Director of the Bureau of the Census under subsection (b)(3)(A)(ii) of this section, of man-days of seasonal agricultural services performed in the United States in fiscal year

1990 by special agricultural workers who obtained lawful temporary resident status under this section.

(C) Fiscal years 1992 and 1993

For purposes of paragraph (2) for fiscal years 1992 and 1993, the factor under this paragraph is the average number, as estimated by the Director of the Bureau of the Census under subsection (b)(3)(A)(ii) of this section, of man-days of seasonal agricultural services performed in the United States in each of the two previous fiscal years by special agricultural workers who obtained lawful temporary resident status under this section during either of such fiscal years.

(7) **Emergency procedure for increase in shortage number**

(A) Requests

After the beginning of a fiscal year, a group or association representing employers (and potential employers) of individuals who perform seasonal agricultural services may request the Secretaries to increase the shortage number for the fiscal year based upon a showing that extraordinary, unusual, and unforeseen circumstances have resulted in a significant increase in the shortage number due to (i) a significant increase in the need for special agricultural workers in the year, (ii) a significant decrease in the availability of able, willing, and qualified workers to perform seasonal agricultural services, or (iii) a significant decrease (below the factor used for purposes of paragraph (6)) in the number of man-days of seasonal agricultural services performed by aliens who were recently admitted (or whose status was recently adjusted) under this section.

(B) Notice of Emergency Procedure

Not later than 3 days after the date the Secretaries receive a request under subparagraph (A), the Secretaries shall provide for notice in the Federal Register of the substance of the request and shall provide an opportunity for interested parties to submit information to the Secretaries on a timely basis respecting the request.

(C) Prompt determination on request

The Secretaries, not later than 21 days after the date of the receipt of such a request and after consideration of any information submitted on a timely basis with respect to the request, shall make and publish in the Federal Register their determination on the request. The request shall be granted, and the shortage number for the fiscal year shall be increased, to the extent that the Secretaries determine that such an increase is justified based upon the showing and circumstances described in subparagraph (A) and that such an increase takes

77

into account reasonable recruitment efforts having been under-taken.

**(8) Procedure for decreasing man-days of seasonal agricultural services required in the case of oversupply of workers**

(A) Requests

After the beginning of a fiscal year, a group of special agricultural workers may request the Secretaries to decrease the number of man-days required under subparagraphs (A) and (B) of subsection (d)(2) of this section with respect to the fiscal year based upon a showing that extraordinary, unusual, and unforeseen circumstances have resulted in a significant decrease in the shortage number due to (i) a significant decrease in the need for special agricultural workers in the year, (ii) a significant increase in the availability of able, willing, and qualified workers to perform seasonal agricultural services, or (iii) a significant increase (above the factor used for purposes of paragraph (6)) in the number of man-days of seasonal agricultural services performed by aliens who were recently admitted (or whose status was recently adjusted) under this section.

(B) Notice of request

Not later than 3 days after the date the Secretaries receive a request under subparagraph (A), the Secretaries shall provide for notice in the Federal Register of the substance of the request and shall provide an opportunity for interested parties to submit information to the Secretaries on a timely basis respecting the request.

(C) Determination on request

The Secretaries, before the end of the fiscal year involved and after consideration of any information submitted on a timely basis with respect to the request, shall make and publish in the Federal Register their determination on the request. The request shall be granted, and the number of man-days specified in subparagraphs (A) and (B) of subsection (d)(2) of this section for the fiscal year shall be reduced by the same proportion as the Secretaries determine that a decrease in the shortage number is justified based upon the showing and circumstances described in subparagraph (A).

**(b) Annual numerical limitation on admission of additional special agricultural workers**

**(1) Annual numerical limitation**

(A) Fiscal year 1990

The numerical limitation on the number of aliens who may be admitted under subsection (c)(1) of this section or who otherwise may acquire lawful temporary residence under such subsection for fiscal year 1990 is—

> **(i)** 95 percent of the number of individuals whose status was adjusted under section 210(a) [8 U.S.C.A. § 1160(a)], minus
>
> **(ii)** the number estimated under paragraph (3)(A)(i) for fiscal year 1989 (as adjusted in accordance with subparagraph (C)).

**(B)** Fiscal years 1991, 1992, and 1993

The numerical limitation on the number of aliens who may be admitted under subsection (c)(1) of this section or who otherwise may acquire lawful temporary residence under such subsection for fiscal year 1991, 1992, or 1993 is—

> **(i)** 90 percent of the number described in this clause for the previous fiscal year (or, for fiscal year 1991, the number described in subparagraph (A)(i)), minus
>
> **(ii)** the number estimated under paragraph (3)(A)(i) for the previous fiscal year (as adjusted in accordance with subparagraph (C)).

**(C)** Adjustment to take into account change in number of H-2 agricultural workers

The number used under subparagraph (A)(ii) or (B)(ii) (as the case may be) shall be increased or decreased to reflect any numerical increase or decrease, respectively, in the number of aliens admitted to perform temporary seasonal agricultural services (as defined in subsection (g)(2) of this section) under section 101(a)(15)(H)(ii)(a) [8 U.S.C.A. § 1101(a)(15)(H)(ii)(a)] in the fiscal year compared to such number in the previous fiscal year.

**(2) Reporting of information on employment**

In the case of a person or entity who employs, during a fiscal year (beginning with fiscal year 1989 and ending with fiscal year 1992) in seasonal agricultural services, a special agricultural worker—

> **(A)** whose status was adjusted under section 210 [8 U.S. C.A. § 1160], the person or entity shall furnish an official designated by the Secretaries with a certificate (at such time, in such form, and containing such information as the Secretaries establish, after consultation with the Attorney General and the Director of the Bureau of the Census) of the number of man-days of employment performed by the alien in seasonal agricultural services during the fiscal year, or
>
> **(B)** who was admitted or whose status was adjusted under this section, the person or entity shall furnish the alien and an

official designated by the Secretaries with a certificate (at such time, in such form, and containing such information as the Secretaries establish, after consultation with the Attorney General and the Director of the Bureau of the Census) of the number of man-days of employment performed by the alien in seasonal agricultural services during the fiscal year.

**(3) Annual estimate of employment of special agricultural workers**

**(A)** In general

The Director of the Bureau of the Census shall, before the end of each fiscal year (beginning with fiscal year 1989 and ending with fiscal year 1992), estimate—

**(i)** the number of special agricultural workers who have performed seasonal agricultural services in the United States at any time during the fiscal year, and

**(ii)** for purposes of subsection (a)(5) of this section, the average number of man-days of such services certain of such workers have performed in the United States during the fiscal year.

**(B)** Furnishing of information to director

The official designated by the Secretaries under paragraph (2) shall furnish to the Director, in such form and manner as the Director specifies, information contained in the certifications furnished to the official under paragraph (2).

**(C)** Basis for estimates

The Director shall base the estimates under subparagraph (A) on the information furnished under subparagraph (B), but shall take into account (to the extent feasible) the underreporting or duplicate reporting of special agricultural workers who have performed seasonal agricultural services at any time during the fiscal year. The Director shall periodically conduct appropriate surveys, of agricultural employers and others, to ascertain the extent of such underreporting or duplicate reporting.

**(D)** Report

The Director shall annually prepare and report to the Congress information on the estimates made under this paragraph.

**(c) Admission of additional special agricultural workers**

**(1) In general**

For each fiscal year (beginning with fiscal year 1990 and ending with fiscal year 1993), the Attorney General shall provide for the admission for lawful temporary resident status, or for the adjustment of status to lawful temporary resident status, of a number of aliens equal to the shortage number (if any, determined under subsection (a) of this section) for the fiscal year, or, if less, the numerical limitation established under subsection (b)(1) of this section for the fiscal year. No such alien shall be admitted who is not admissible to the United States as an immigrant, except as otherwise provided under subsection (e) of this section.

### (2) Allocation of visas

The Attorney General shall, in consultation with the Secretary of State, provide such process as may be appropriate for aliens to petition for immigrant visas or to adjust status to become aliens lawfully admitted for temporary residence under this subsection. No alien may be issued a visa as an alien to be admitted under this subsection or may have the alien's status adjusted under this subsection unless the alien has had a petition approved under this paragraph.

## (d) Rights of aliens admitted or adjusted under this section

### (1) Adjustment to permanent residence

The Attorney General shall adjust the status of any alien provided lawful temporary resident status under subsection (c) of this section to that of an alien lawfully admitted for permanent residence at the end of the 3-year period that begins on the date the alien was granted such temporary resident status.

### (2) Termination of temporary residence

During the period of temporary resident status granted an alien under subsection (c) of this section, the Attorney General may terminate such status only upon a determination under this chapter that the alien is deportable.

### (3) Authorized travel and employment during temporary residence

During the period an alien is in lawful temporary resident status granted under this section, the alien has the right to travel abroad (including commutation from a residence abroad) and shall be granted authorization to engage in employment in the United States and shall be provided an "employment authorized" endorsement or other appropriate work permit, in the same manner as for aliens lawfully admitted for permanent residence.

### (4) In general

Except as otherwise provided in this subsection, an alien who acquires the status of an alien lawfully admitted for temporary residence under subsection (c) of this section, such status not having changed, is considered to be an alien lawfully admitted for permanent residence (as described in section 101(a)(20) [8 U.S.C.A. § 1101(a)(20)]), other than under any provision of the immigration laws.

### (5) Employment in seasonal agricultural services required

**(A)** For 3 years to avoid deportation

In order to meet the requirement of this paragraph (for purposes of this subsection and section 241(a)(1)(F) [8 U.S.C.A. § 1251(a)(1)(F)]), an alien, who has obtained the status of an alien lawfully admitted for temporary residence under this section, must establish to the Attorney General that the alien has performed 90 man-days of seasonal agricultural services—

(i) during the one-year period beginning on the date the alien obtained such status,

(ii) during the one-year period beginning one year after the date the alien obtained such status, and

(iii) during the one-year period beginning two years after the date the alien obtained such status.

**(B)** For 5 years for naturalization

Notwithstanding any provision in subchapter III of this chapter, an alien admitted under this section may not be naturalized as a citizen of the United States under that title unless the alien has performed 90 man-days of seasonal agricultural services in each of 5 fiscal years (not including any fiscal year before the fiscal year in which the alien was admitted under this section).

**(C)** Proof

In meeting the requirements of subparagraphs (A) and (B), an alien may submit such documentation as may be submitted under section 210(b)(3) [8 U.S.C.A. § 1160(b)(3)].

**(D)** Adjustment of number of man-days required

The number of man-days specified in subparagraphs (A) and (B) are subject to adjustment under subsection (a)(8) of this section.

### (6) Disqualification from certain public assistance

The provisions of section 245A(h) [8 U.S.C.A. § 1255a(h)] (other than paragraph (1)(A)(iii)) shall apply to an alien who has obtained the status of an alien lawfully admitted for temporary residence under this section, during the five-year period beginning on the date the alien obtained such status, in the same manner as they apply to an alien granted lawful temporary residence under section 1255a of this title; except that, for purposes of this paragraph, assistance furnished under the Legal Services Corporation Act (42 U.S.C. 2996 et seq.) [42 U.S.C.A. § 2996 et seq.] or under title V of the Housing Act of 1949 [42 U.S.C.A. § 1471 et seq.] shall not be construed to be financial assistance described in section 245A(h)(1)(A)(i) [8 U.S.C.A. § 1255a(h)(1)(A)(i)].

### (e) Determination of admissibility of additional workers

In the determination of an alien's admissibility under subsection (c)(1) of this section—

### (1) Grounds of exclusion not applicable

The provisions of paragraphs (5) and (7)(A) of section 212(a) [8 U.S.C.A. § 1182(a)(5) and (7)(A)] shall not apply.

### (2) Waiver of certain grounds for exclusion

**(A)** In general

Except as provided in subparagraph (B), the Attorney General may waive any other provision of section 212(a) [8 U.S.C.A. § 1182(a)] in the case of individual aliens for humanitarian purposes, to assure family unity, or when it is otherwise in the public interest.

**(B)** Grounds that may not be waived

The following provisions of section 212(a) [8 U.S.C.A. § 1182(a)] may not be waived by the Attorney General under subparagraph (A):

    **(i)** Paragraphs (2)(A) and (2)(B) (relating to criminals).

    **(ii)** Paragraph (2)(C) (relating to drug offenses), except for so much of such paragraph as relates to a single offense of simple possession of 30 grams or less of marihuana.

    **(iii)** Paragraphs and [1] (3) (relating to security grounds), other than subparagraph (E) thereof.

    **(iv)** Paragraph (3)(D) (relating to those who assisted in the Nazi persecutions).

**(C)** Special rule for determination of public charge

An alien is not ineligible for adjustment of status under this section due to being inadmissible under section 212(a)(4) [8 U.S.C.A. § 1182(a)(4)] if the alien demonstrates a history of employment in the United States evidencing self-support without reliance on public cash assistance.

### (3) Medical examination

The alien shall be required, at the alien's expense, to undergo such a medical examination (including a determination of immunization status) as is appropriate and conforms to generally accepted professional standards of medical practice.

### (f) Terms of employment respecting aliens admitted under this section

### (1) Equal transportation for domestic workers

If a person employs an alien, who was admitted or whose status is adjusted under subsection (c) of this section, in the performance of seasonal agricultural services and provides transportation arrangements or assistance for such workers, the employer must provide the same transportation arrangements or assistance (generally comparable in expense and scope) for other individuals employed in the performance of seasonal agricultural services.

### (2) Prohibition of false information by certain employers

A farm labor contractor, agricultural employer, or agricultural association who is an exempt person (as defined in paragraph (5)) shall not knowingly provide false or misleading information to an alien who was admitted or whose status was adjusted under subsection (c) concerning the terms, conditions, or existence of agricultural employment (described in subsection (a), (b), or (c) of section 301 of MASAWPA) [29 U.S.C.A. § 1831].

### (3) Prohibition of discrimination by certain employers

In the case of an exempt person and with respect to aliens who have been admitted or whose status has been adjusted under subsection (c) of this section, the provisions of section 505 of MASAWPA [29 U.S.C.A. § 1855] shall apply to any proceeding under or related to (and rights and protections afforded by) this section in the same manner as they apply to proceedings under or related to (and rights and protections afforded by) MASAWPA [29 U.S.C.A. § 1801 et seq.].

### (4) Enforcement

If a person or entity—

**(A)** fails to furnish a certificate required under subsection (b)(2) of this section or furnishes false statement of a material fact in such a certificate,

**(B)** violates paragraph (1) or (2), or

**(C)** violates the provisions of section 505(a) of MASAWPA [29 U.S.C.A. § 1805(a)] (as they apply under paragraph (3)),

the person or entity is subject to a civil money penalty under section 503 of MASAWPA [29 U.S.C.A. § 1803] in the same manner as if the person or entity had committed a violation of MASAWPA.

### (5) Special definitions

In this subsection:

### (A) MASAWPA

The term "MASAWPA" means the Migrant and Seasonal Agricultural Worker Protection Act (Public Law 97–470) [29 U.S.C.A. § 1801 et seq.].

**(B)** The term "exempt person" means a person or entity who would be subject to the provisions of MASAWPA but for paragraph (1) or (2), or both, of section 4(a) of MASAWPA [29 U.S.C.A. § 1803(a)].

### (g) General definitions

In this section:

(1) The term "special agricultural worker" means an individual, regardless of present status, whose status was at any time adjusted under section 210 [8 U.S.C.A. § 1160] or who at any time was admitted or had the individual's status adjusted under subsection (c) of this section.

(2) The term "seasonal agricultural services" has the meaning given such term in section 210(h) [8 U.S.C.A. § 1160(h)].

(3) The term "Director" refers to the Director of the Bureau of the Census.

(4) The term "man-day" means, with respect to seasonal agricultural services, the performance during a calendar day of at least 4 hours of seasonal agricultural services.

(June 27, 1952, c. 477, Title II, ch. 1, § 210A,¹ as added Pub.L. 99–603, Title III, § 303(a), Nov. 6, 1986, 100 Stat. 3422, and amended Pub.L. 100–525, § 2(n)(1), Oct. 24, 1988, 102 Stat. 2613; Nov. 29, 1990, Pub.L. 101–649, Title VI, § 603(a)(6), (b)(1), 104 Stat. 5083, 5085.)

1. So in original.

## CHAPTER II—ADMISSION QUALIFICATIONS FOR ALIENS; TRAVEL CONTROL OF CITIZENS AND ALIENS

## § 211. Admission of immigrants into the United States [8 U.S.C.A. § 1181]

### (a) Documents required; admission under quotas before June 30, 1968

Except as provided in subsection (b) and subsection (c) of this section no immigrant shall be admitted into the United States unless at the time of application for admission he (1) has a valid unexpired immigrant visa or was born subsequent to the issuance of such visa of the accompanying parent, and (2) presents a valid unexpired passport or other suitable travel document, or document of identity and nationality, if such document is required under the regulations issued by the Attorney General. With respect to immigrants to be admitted under quotas of quota areas prior to June 30, 1968, no immigrant visa shall be deemed valid unless the immigrant is properly chargeable to the quota area under the quota of which the visa is issued.

### (b) Readmission without required documents; Attorney General's discretion

Notwithstanding the provisions of section 212(a)(7)(A) [8 U.S.C.A. § 1182(a)(7)(A)] in such cases or in such classes of cases and under such conditions as may be by regulations prescribed, returning resident immigrants, defined in section 101(a)(27)(A) [8 U.S.C.A. § 1101(a)(27)(A)], who are otherwise admissible may be readmitted to the United States by the Attorney General in his discretion without being required to obtain a passport, immigrant visa, reentry permit or other documentation.

### (c) Nonapplicability to aliens admitted as refugees

The provisions of subsection (a) of this section shall not apply to an alien whom the Attorney General admits to the United States under section 207 [8 U.S.C.A. § 1157].

(June 27, 1952, c. 477, Title II, ch. 2, § 211, 66 Stat. 181; Pub. L. 89–236, § 9, Oct. 3, 1965, 79 Stat. 917; Pub. L. 94–571, § 7(c), Oct. 20, 1976, 90 Stat. 2706; Pub. L. 96–212, Title II, § 202, Mar. 17, 1980, 94 Stat. 106; Pub.L. 101–649, Title VI, § 603(a)(7), Nov. 29, 1990, 104 Stat. 5083.)

## § 212.  Excludable aliens [8 U.S.C.A. § 1182]

### (a) Classes of excludable aliens

Except as otherwise provided in this chapter, the following describes classes of excludable aliens who are ineligible to receive visas and who shall be excluded from admission into the United States:

#### (1) Health-related grounds

##### (A) In general

Any alien—

(i) who is determined (in accordance with regulations prescribed by the Secretary of Health and Human Services) to have a communicable disease of public health significance,

(ii) who is determined (in accordance with regulations prescribed by the Secretary of Health and Human Services in consultation with the Attorney General)—

(I) to have a physical or mental disorder and behavior associated with the disorder that may pose, or has posed, a threat to the property, safety, or welfare of the alien or others, or

(II) to have had a physical or mental disorder and a history of behavior associated with the disorder, which behavior has posed a threat to the property, safety, or welfare of the alien or others and which behavior is likely to recur or to lead to other harmful behavior,

(iii) who is determined (in accordance with regulations prescribed by the Secretary of Health and Human Services) to be a drug abuser or addict,

is excludable.

##### (B) Waiver authorized

For provision authorizing waiver of certain clauses of subparagraph (A), see subsection (g) of this section.

#### (2) Criminal and related grounds

86

**(A)** Conviction of certain crimes

**(i)** In general

Except as provided in clause (ii), any alien convicted of, or who admits having committed, or who admits committing acts which constitute the essential elements of—

**(I)** a crime involving moral turpitude (other than a purely political offense), or

**(II)** a violation of (or a conspiracy to violate) any law or regulation of a State, the United States, or a foreign country relating to a controlled substance (as defined in section 802 of Title 21),

is excludable.

**(ii)** Exception

Clause (i)(I) shall not apply to an alien who committed only one crime if—

**(I)** the crime was committed when the alien was under 18 years of age, and the crime was committed (and the alien released from any confinement to a prison or correctional institution imposed for the crime) more than 5 years before the date of application for a visa or other documentation and the date of application for admission to the United States, or

**(II)** the maximum penalty possible for the crime of which the alien was convicted (or which the alien admits having committed or of which the acts that the alien admits having committed constituted the essential elements) did not exceed imprisonment for one year and, if the alien was convicted of such crime, the alien was not sentenced to a term of imprisonment in excess of 6 months (regardless of the extent to which the sentence was ultimately executed).

**(B)** Multiple criminal convictions

Any alien convicted of 2 or more offenses (other than purely political offenses), regardless of whether the conviction was in a single trial or whether the offenses arose from a single scheme of misconduct and regardless of whether the offenses involved moral turpitude, for which the aggregate sentences to confinement actually imposed were 5 years or more is excludable.

**(C)** Controlled substance traffickers

Any alien who the consular or immigration officer knows or has reason to believe is or has been an illicit trafficker in any such controlled substance or is or has been a knowing assister, abettor, conspirator, or colluder with others in the illicit trafficking in any such controlled substance, is excludable.

**(D)** Prostitution and commercialized vice

Any alien who—

(i) is coming to the United States solely, principally, or incidentally to engage in prostitution, or has engaged in prostitution within 10 years of the date of application for a visa, entry, or adjustment of status,

(ii) directly or indirectly procures or attempts to procure, or (within 10 years of the date of application for a visa, entry, or adjustment of status) procured or attempted to procure or to import, prostitutes or persons for the purpose of prostitution, or receives or (within such 10-year period) received, in whole or in part, the proceeds of prostitution, or

(iii) is coming to the United States to engage in any other unlawful commercialized vice, whether or not related to prostitution,

is excludable.

**(E)** Certain aliens involved in serious criminal activity who have asserted immunity from prosecution

Any alien—

(i) who has committed in the United States at any time a serious criminal offense (as defined in section 101(h) [8 U.S.C.A. § 1101(h)]),

(ii) for whom immunity from criminal jurisdiction was exercised with respect to that offense,

(iii) who as a consequence of the offense and exercise of immunity has departed from the United States, and

(iv) who has not subsequently submitted fully to the jurisdiction of the court in the United States having jurisdiction with respect to that offense,

is excludable.

**(F)** Waiver authorized

For provision authorizing waiver of certain subparagraphs of this paragraph, see subsection (h) of this section.

**(3) Security and related grounds**

(A) In general

Any alien who a consular officer or the Attorney General knows, or has reasonable ground to believe, seeks to enter the United States to engage solely, principally, or incidentally in—

(i) any activity to violate any law of the United States relating to espionage or sabotage or to violate or evade any law prohibiting the export from the United States of goods, technology, or sensitive information,

(ii) any other unlawful activity, or

(iii) any activity a purpose of which is the opposition to, or the control or overthrow of, the Government of the United States by force, violence, or other unlawful means,

is excludable.

(B) Terrorist activities

(i) In general

Any alien who—

(I) has engaged in a terrorist activity, or

(II) a consular officer or the Attorney General knows, or has reasonable ground to believe, is likely to engage after entry in any terrorist activity (as defined in clause (iii)),

is excludable. An alien who is an officer, official, representative, or spokesman of the Palestine Liberation Organization is considered, for purposes of this chapter, to be engaged in a terrorist activity.

(ii) Terrorist activity defined

As used in this chapter, the term "terrorist activity" means any activity which is unlawful under the laws of the place where it is committed (or which, if committed in the United States, would be unlawful under the laws of the United States or any State) and which involves any of the following:

(I) The highjacking or sabotage of any conveyance (including an aircraft, vessel, or vehicle).

(II) The seizing or detaining, and threatening to kill, injure, or continue to detain, another individual in order to compel a third person (including a governmental organization) to do or abstain from doing any act as an explicit or implicit condition for the release of the individual seized or detained.

(III) A violent attack upon an internationally protected person (as defined in section 1116(b)(4) of Title 18) or upon the liberty of such a person.

(IV) An assassination.

(V) The use of any—

(a) biological agent, chemical agent, or nuclear weapon or device, or

**(b)** explosive or firearm (other than for mere personal monetary gain),

with intent to endanger, directly or indirectly, the safety of one or more individuals or to cause substantial damage to property.

**(VI)** A threat, attempt, or conspiracy to do any of the foregoing.

**(iii)** Engage in terrorist activity defined

As used in this chapter, the term "engage in terrorist activity" means to commit, in an individual capacity or as a member of an organization, an act of terrorist activity or an act which the actor knows, or reasonably should know, affords material support to any individual, organization, or government in conducting a terrorist activity at any time, including any of the following acts:

**(I)** The preparation or planning of a terrorist activity.

**(II)** The gathering of information on potential targets for terrorist activity.

**(III)** The providing of any type of material support, including a safe house, transportation, communications, funds, false identification, weapons, explosives, or training, to any individual the actor knows or has reason to believe has committed or plans to commit an act of terrorist activity.

**(IV)** The soliciting of funds or other things of value for terrorist activity or for any terrorist organization.

**(V)** The solicitation of any individual for membership in a terrorist organization, terrorist government, or to engage in a terrorist activity.

**(C)** Foreign policy

**(i)** In general

An alien whose entry or proposed activities in the United States the Secretary of State has reasonable ground to believe would have potentially serious adverse foreign policy consequences for the United States is excludable.

**(ii)** Exception for officials

An alien who is an official of a foreign government or a purported government, or who is a candidate for election to a foreign government office during the period immediately preceding the election for that office, shall not be excludable or subject to restrictions or conditions on entry into the United States under clause (i) solely because of the alien's past, current, or expected beliefs, statements, or associations, if such beliefs, statements, or associations would be lawful within the United States.

### (iii) Exception for other aliens

An alien, not described in clause (ii), shall not be excludable or subject to restrictions or conditions on entry into the United States under clause (i) because of the alien's past, current, or expected beliefs, statements, or associations, if such beliefs, statements, or associations would be lawful within the United States, unless the Secretary of State personally determines that the alien's admission would compromise a compelling United States foreign policy interest.

### (iv) Notification of determinations

If a determination is made under clause (iii) with respect to an alien, the Secretary of State must notify on a timely basis the chairmen of the Committees on the Judiciary and Foreign Affairs of the House of Representatives and of the Committees on the Judiciary and Foreign Relations of the Senate of the identities of the alien and the reasons for the determination.

### (D) Immigrant membership in totalitarian party

#### (i) In general

Any immigrant who is or has been a member of or affiliated with the Communist or any other totalitarian party (or subdivision or affiliate thereof), domestic or foreign, is excludable.

#### (ii) Exception for involuntary membership

Clause (i) shall not apply to an alien because of membership or affiliation if the alien establishes to the satisfaction of the consular officer when applying for a visa (or to the satisfaction of the Attorney General when applying for admission) that the membership or affiliation is or was involuntary, or is or was solely when under 16 years of age, by operation of law, or for purposes of obtaining employment, food rations, or other essentials of living and whether necessary for such purposes.

#### (iii) Exception for past membership

Clause (i) shall not apply to an alien because of membership or affiliation if the alien establishes to the satisfaction of the consular officer when applying for a visa (or to the satisfaction of the Attorney General when applying for admission) that—

(I) the membership or affiliation terminated at least—

(a) 2 years before the date of such application, or

**(b)** 5 years before the date of such application, in the case of an alien whose membership or affiliation was with the party controlling the government of a foreign state that is a totalitarian dictatorship as of such date, and

**(II)** the alien is not a threat to the security of the United States.

**(iv)** Exception for close family members

The Attorney General may, in the Attorney General's discretion, waive the application of clause (i) in the case of an immigrant who is the parent, spouse, son, daughter, brother, or sister of a citizen of the United States or a spouse, son, or daughter of an alien lawfully admitted for permanent residence for humanitarian purposes, to assure family unity, or when it is otherwise in the public interest if the alien is not a threat to the security of the United States.

**(E)** Participants in Nazi persecutions or genocide

**(i)** Participation in Nazi persecutions

Any alien who, during the period beginning on March 23, 1933, and ending on May 8, 1945, under the direction of, or in association with—

**(I)** the Nazi government of Germany,

**(II)** any government in any area occupied by the military forces of the Nazi government of Germany,

**(III)** any government established with the assistance or cooperation of the Nazi government of Germany, or

**(IV)** any government which was an ally of the Nazi government of Germany,

ordered, incited, assisted, or otherwise participated in the persecution of any person because of race, religion, national origin, or political opinion is excludable.

**(ii)** Participation in genocide

Any alien who has engaged in conduct that is defined as genocide for purposes of the International Convention on the Prevention and Punishment of Genocide is excludable.

**(4) Public charge**

Any alien who, in the opinion of the consular officer at the time of application for a visa, or in the opinion of the Attorney General at the time of application for admission or adjustment of status, is likely at any time to become a public charge is excludable.

**(5) Labor certification and qualifications for certain immigrants**

**(A)** Labor certification

**(i)** In general

Any alien who seeks admission or status as an immigrant under paragraph (2) or (3) of section 203(b) [8 U.S.C.A. § 1153(b)] is excludable, unless the Secretary of Labor has determined and certified to the Secretary of State and the Attorney General that—

**(I)** there are not sufficient workers who are able, willing, qualified (or equally qualified in the case of an alien described in clause (ii)) and available at the time of application for a visa and admission to the United States and at the place where the alien is to perform such skilled or unskilled labor, and

**(II)** the employment of such alien will not adversely affect the wages and working conditions of workers in the United States similarly employed.

**(ii)** Certain aliens subject to special rule

For purposes of clause (i)(I), an alien described in this clause is an alien who—

**(I)** is a member of the teaching profession, or

**(II)** has exceptional ability in the sciences or the arts.

**(B)** Unqualified physicians

An alien who seeks admission or status as an immigrant under paragraph (2) or (3) of section 203(b) [8 U.S.C.A. § 1153(b)] who is a graduate of a medical school not accredited by a body or bodies approved for the purpose by the Secretary of Education (regardless of whether such school of medicine is in the United States) and who is coming to the United States principally to perform services as a member of the medical profession is excludable, unless the alien (i) has passed parts I and II of the National Board of Medical Examiners Examination (or an equivalent examination as determined by the Secretary of Health and Human Services) and (ii) is competent in oral and written English. For purposes of the previous sentence, an alien who is a graduate of a medical school shall be considered to have passed parts I and II of the National Board of Medical Examiners if the alien was fully and permanently licensed to practice medicine in a State on January 9, 1978, and was practicing medicine in a State on that date.

**(6) Illegal entrants and immigration violators**

**(A)** Aliens previously deported

Any alien who has been excluded from admission and deported and who again seeks admission within one year of the date of such deportation is excludable, unless prior to the alien's reembarkation at a place outside the United States or attempt to be admitted from foreign contiguous territory the Attorney General has consented to the alien's reapplying for admission.

**(B)** Certain aliens previously removed

Any alien who—

    **(i)** has been arrested and deported,

    **(ii)** has fallen into distress and has been removed pursuant to this or any prior Act,

    **(iii)** has been removed as an alien enemy, or

    **(iv)** has been removed at Government expense in lieu of deportation pursuant to section 242(b) [8 U.S.C.A. § 1252(b)],

and who seeks admission within 5 years of the date of such deportation or removal (or within 20 years in the case of an alien convicted of an aggravated felony) is excludable, unless before the date of the alien's embarkation or reembarkation at a place outside the United States or attempt to be admitted from foreign contiguous territory the Attorney General has consented to the alien's applying or reapplying for admission.

**(C)** Misrepresentation

    **(i)** In general

    Any alien who, by fraud or willfully misrepresenting a material fact, seeks to procure (or has sought to procure or has procured) a visa, other documentation, or entry into the United States or other benefit provided under this chapter is excludable.

    **(ii)** Waiver authorized

    For provision authorizing waiver of clause (i), see subsection (i) of this section.

**(D)** Stowaways

Any alien who is a stowaway is excludable.

**(E)** Smugglers

    **(i)** In general

    Any alien who at any time knowingly has encouraged, induced, assisted, abetted, or aided any other alien to enter or to try to enter the United States in violation of law is excludable.

    **(ii)** Waiver authorized

    For provision authorizing waiver of clause (i), see subsection (d)(11) of this section.

**(F)** Subject of civil penalty

An alien who is the subject of a final order for violation of section 274C [8 U.S.C.A. § 1324c] is excludable.

### (7) Documentation requirements

#### (A) Immigrants

##### (i) In general

Except as otherwise specifically provided in this chapter, any immigrant at the time of application for admission—

**(I)** who is not in possession of a valid unexpired immigrant visa, reentry permit, border crossing identification card, or other valid entry document required by this chapter, and a valid unexpired passport, or other suitable travel document, or document of identity and nationality if such document is required under the regulations issued by the Attorney General under section 211(a) [8 U.S.C.A. § 1181(a)], or

**(II)** whose visa has been issued without compliance with the provisions of section 203 [8 U.S.C.A. § 1153] is excludable.

##### (ii) Waiver authorized

For provision authorizing waiver of clause (i), see subsection (k) of this section.

#### (B) Nonimmigrants

##### (i) In general

Any nonimmigrant who—

**(I)** is not in possession of a passport valid for a minimum of six months from the date of the expiration of the initial period of the alien's admission or contemplated initial period of stay authorizing the alien to return to the country from which the alien came or to proceed to and enter some other country during such period, or

**(II)** is not in possession of a valid nonimmigrant visa or border crossing identification card at the time of application for admission,

is excludable.

##### (ii) General waiver authorized

For provision authorizing waiver of clause (i), see subsection (d)(4) of this section.

##### (iii) Guam visa waiver

For provision authorizing waiver of clause (i) in the case of visitors to Guam, see subsection (*l*) of this section.

##### (iv) Visa waiver pilot program

For authority to waive the requirement of clause (i) under a pilot program, see section 217 [8 U.S.C.A. § 1187].

### (8) Ineligible for citizenship

**(A) In general**

Any immigrant who is permanently ineligible to citizenship is excludable.

**(B) Draft evaders**

Any alien who has departed from or who has remained outside the United States to avoid or evade training or service in the armed forces in time of war or a period declared by the President to be a national emergency is excludable, except that this subparagraph shall not apply to an alien who at the time of such departure was a nonimmigrant and who is seeking to reenter the United States as a nonimmigrant.

### (9) Miscellaneous

**(A)** Practicing polygamists

Any immigrant who is coming to the United States to practice polygamy is excludable.

**(B)** Guardian required to accompany excluded alien

Any alien accompanying another alien ordered to be excluded and deported and certified to be helpless from sickness or mental or physical disability or infancy pursuant to section 237(e) [8 U.S.C.A. § 1227(e)], whose protection or guardianship is required by the alien ordered excluded and deported, is excludable.

**(C)** International child abduction

**(i)** In general

Except as provided in clause (ii), any alien who, after entry of a court order granting custody to a citizen of the United States of a child having a lawful claim to United States citizenship, detains, retains, or withholds custody of the child outside the United States from the United States citizen granted custody, is excludable until the child is surrendered to such United States citizen.

**(ii)** Exception

Clause (i) shall not apply to an alien who is a national of a foreign state that is a signatory to the Hague Convention on the Civil Aspects of International Child Abduction.

### (b) Notices of denials

If an alien's application for a visa, for admission to the United States, or for adjustment of status is denied by an immigration or consular officer because the officer determines the alien to be excludable under subsection (a) of this section, the officer shall provide the alien with a timely written notice that—

(1) states the determination, and

(2) lists the specific provision or provisions of law under which the alien is excludable or ineligible for entry or adjustment of status.

### (c) Nonapplicability of subsection (a)

Aliens lawfully admitted for permanent residence who temporarily proceeded abroad voluntarily and not under an order of deportation, and who are returning to a lawful unrelinquished domicile of seven consecutive years, may be admitted in the discretion of the Attorney General without regard to the provisions of subsection (a) of this section (other than subparagraphs (A), (B), (C), or (E) of paragraph (3)). Nothing contained in this subsection shall limit the authority of the Attorney General to exercise the discretion vested in him under section 211(b) [8 U.S.C.A. § 1181(b)]. The first sentence of this subsection shall not apply to an alien who has been convicted of an aggravated felony and has served a term of imprisonment of at least 5 years.

### (d) Temporary admission of nonimmigrants

(1), (2) Repealed.

(3) Except as provided in this subsection, an alien (A) who is applying for a nonimmigrant visa and is known or believed by the consular officer to be ineligible for such visa under subsection (a) of this section (other than paragraphs (3)(A), (3)(C), and (3)(D) of such subsection), may after approval by the Attorney General of a recommendation by the Secretary of State or by the consular officer that the alien be admitted temporarily despite his inadmissibility, be granted such a visa and may be admitted into the United States temporarily as a nonimmigrant in the discretion of the Attorney General, or (B) who is inadmissible under subsection (a) of this section (other than paragraphs (3)(A), (3)(C), and (3)(D) of such subsection), but who is in is in possession of appropriate documents or is granted a waiver thereof and is seeking admission, may be admitted into the United States temporarily as a nonimmigrant in the discretion of the Attorney General. The Attorney General shall prescribe conditions, including exaction of such bonds as may be necessary, to control and regulate the admission and return of excludable aliens applying for temporary admission under this paragraph.

(4) Either or both of the requirements of paragraph (7)(B)(i) of subsection (a) of this section may be waived by the Attorney General and the Secretary of State acting jointly (A) on the basis of unforeseen emergency in individual cases, or (B) on the basis of reciprocity with respect to nationals of foreign contiguous territory or of adjacent islands and residents thereof having a common nationality with such nationals, or (C) in the case of aliens proceeding in immediate and

continuous transit through the United States under contracts authorized in section 238(c) [8 U.S.C.A. § 1228(c)].

**(5)(A)** The Attorney General may, except as provided in subparagraph (B) or in section 214(f) [8 U.S.C.A. § 1184(f)], in his discretion parole into the United States temporarily under such conditions as he may prescribe for emergent reasons or for reasons deemed strictly in the public interest any alien applying for admission to the United States, but such parole of such alien shall not be regarded as an admission of the alien and when the purposes of such parole shall, in the opinion of the Attorney General, have been served the alien shall forthwith return or be returned to the custody from which he was paroled and thereafter his case shall continue to be dealt with in the same manner as that of any other applicant for admission to the United States.

**(B)** The Attorney General may not parole into the United States an alien who is a refugee unless the Attorney General determines that compelling reasons in the public interest with respect to that particular alien require that the alien be paroled into the United States rather than be admitted as a refugee under section 207 [8 U.S.C.A. § 1157].

**(6)** Repealed.

**(7)** The provisions of subsection (a) (other than paragraph (7)) of said subsection, shall be applicable to any alien who shall leave Guam, Puerto Rico, or the Virgin Islands of the United States, and who seeks to enter the continental United States or any other place under the jurisdiction of the United States. The Attorney General shall by regulations provide a method and procedure for the temporary admission to the United States of the aliens described in this proviso. Any alien described in this paragraph, who is excluded from admission to the United States, shall be immediately deported in the manner provided by section 237(a) [8 U.S.C.A. § 1227(a)].

**(8)** Upon a basis of reciprocity accredited officials of foreign governments, their immediate families, attendants, servants, and personal employees may be admitted in immediate and continuous transit through the United States without regard to the provisions of this section except paragraphs (3)(A), (3)(B), (3)(C), and (7)(B) of subsection (a) of this section.

**(9), (10)** Repealed.

**(11)** The Attorney General may, in his discretion for humanitarian purposes, to assure family unity, or when it is otherwise in the public interest, waive application of clause (i) of subsection (a)(6)(E) of this section in the case of any alien lawfully admitted for permanent residence who temporarily proceeded abroad voluntary[1] and not under an order of deportation, and who is otherwise admissible to the United States as a returning resident under section 211(b) [8 U.S.C.A. § 1181(b)] if the alien has encouraged, induced, assisted, abetted, or aided only the alien's spouse, parent, son, or daughter (and no other individual) to enter the United States in violation of law.

### (e) Educational visitor status; foreign residence requirement; waiver

No person admitted under section 101(a)(15)(J) [8 U.S.C.A. § 1101(a)(15)(J)] or acquiring such status after admission (i) whose participation in the program for which he came to the United States was financed in whole or in part, directly or indirectly, by an agency of the Government of the United States or by the government of the country of his nationality or his last residence, (ii) who at the time of admission or acquisition of status under section 101(a)(15)(J) [8 U.S.C.A. § 1101(a)(15)(J)] was a national or resident of a country which the Director of the United States Information Agency, pursuant to regulations prescribed by him, had designated as clearly requiring the services of persons engaged in the field of specialized knowledge or skill in which the alien was engaged, or (iii) who came to the United States or acquired such status in order to receive graduate medical education or training, shall be eligible to apply for an immigrant visa, or for permanent residence, or for a nonimmigrant visa under section 101(a)(15)(H) or 101(a)(15)(L) [8 U.S.C.A. § 1101(a)(15)(H) or section 1101(a)(15)(L)] until it is established that such person has resided and been physically present in the country of his nationality or his last residence for an aggregate of at least two years following departure from the United States: *Provided*, That upon the favorable recommendation of the Director, pursuant to the request of an interested United States Government agency, or of the Commissioner of Immigration and Naturalization after he has determined that departure from the United States would impose exceptional hardship upon the alien's spouse or child (if such spouse or child is a citizen of the United States or a lawfully resident alien), or that the alien cannot return to the country of his nationality or last residence because he would be subject to persecution on account of race, religion, or political opinion, the Attorney General may waive the requirement of such two-year foreign residence abroad in the case of any alien whose admission to the United States is found by the Attorney General to be in the public interest: *And provided further*, That, except in the case of an alien described in clause (iii), the Attorney General may, upon the favorable recommendation of the Director, waive such two-year foreign residence requirement in any case in which the foreign country of the alien's nationality or last residence has furnished the Director a statement in writing that it has no objection to such waiver in the case of such alien.

### (f) Suspension of entry or imposition of restrictions by President

Whenever the President finds that the entry of any aliens or of any class of aliens into the United States would be detrimental to the interests of the United States, he may by proclamation, and for such period as he shall deem necessary, suspend the entry of all aliens or any class of aliens as immigrants or nonimmigrants, or impose on the entry of aliens any restrictions he may deem to be appropriate.

**(g) Bond and conditions for admission of alien excludable on health-related grounds**

The Attorney General may waive the application of—

(1) section[2] (a)(1)(A)(i) of this section in the case of any alien who—

(A) is the spouse or the unmarried son or daughter, or the minor unmarried lawfully adopted child, of a United States citizen, or of an alien lawfully admitted for permanent residence, or of an alien who has been issued an immigrant visa, or

(B) has a son or daughter who is a United States citizen, or an alien lawfully admitted for permanent residence, or an alien who has been issued an immigrant visa, or

(2) subsection (a)(1)(A)(ii) of this section in the case of any alien,

in accordance with such terms, conditions, and controls, if any, including the giving of bond, as the Attorney General, in his discretion after consultation with the Secretary of Health and Human Services, may by regulation prescribe.

**(h) Waiver of subsection (a)(2)(A)(i)((I), (II), (B), (D), and (E)**

The Attorney General may, in his discretion, waive the application of subparagraphs (A)(i)(I), (B), (D), and (E) of subsection (a)(2) of this section and subparagraph (A)(i)(II) of such subsection insofar as it relates to a single offense of simple possession of 30 grams or less of marijuana in the case of an immigrant who is the spouse, parent, son, or daughter of a citizen of the United States or alien lawfully admitted for permanent residence if—

(1) it is established to the satisfaction of the Attorney General that—

(A) the alien is excludable only under subparagraph (D)(i) or (D)(ii) of such subsection or the activities for which the alien is excludable occurred more than 15 years before the date of the alien's application for a visa, entry, or adjustment of status, and

(B) the admission to the United States of such alien would not be contrary to the national welfare, safety, or security of the United States, and

(C) the alien has been rehabilitated; and

(2) the Attorney General, in his discretion, and pursuant to such terms, conditions and procedures as he may by regulations prescribe, has consented to the alien's applying or reapplying for a visa, for admission to the United States, or adjustment of status.

No waiver shall be provided under this subsection in the case of an alien who has been convicted of (or who has admitted committing acts that constitute) murder or criminal acts involving torture.

**(*i*) Admission of alien excludable for fraud or willful misrepresentation of material fact**

The Attorney General may, in his discretion, waive application of clause (i) of subsection (a)(6)(C) of this section—

**(1)** in the case of an alien who is the spouse, parent, or son or daughter of a United States citizen or of an alien lawfully admitted for permanent residence, or

**(2)** if the fraud or misrepresentation occurred at least 10 years before the date of the alien's application for a visa, entry, or adjustment of status and it is established to the satisfaction of the Attorney General that the admission to the United States of such alien would not be contrary to the national welfare, safety, or security of the United States.

**(j) Limitation on immigration of foreign medical graduates**

**(1)** The additional requirements referred to in section 101(a)(15)(J) [8 U.S.C.A. § 1101(a)(15)(J)] for an alien who is coming to the United States under a program under which he will receive graduate medical education or training are as follows:

**(A)** A school of medicine or of one of the other health professions, which is accredited by a body or bodies approved for the purpose by the Secretary of Education, has agreed in writing to provide the graduate medical education or training under the program for which the alien is coming to the United States or to assume responsibility for arranging for the provision thereof by an appropriate public or nonprofit private institution or agency, except that, in the case of such an agreement by a school of medicine, any one or more of its affiliated hospitals which are to participate in the provision of the graduate medical education or training must join in the agreement.

**(B)** Before making such agreement, the accredited school has been satisfied that the alien (i) is a graduate of a school of medicine which is accredited by a body or bodies approved for the purpose by the Secretary of Education (regardless of whether such school of medicine is in the United States); or (ii)(I) has passed parts I and II of the National Board of Medical Examiners Examination (or an equivalent examination as determined by the Secretary of Health and Human Services), (II) has competency in oral and written English, (III) will be able to adapt to the educational and cultural environment in which he will be receiving his education or training, and (IV) has adequate prior education and training to participate satisfactorily in the program for which he is coming to the United States. For the purposes of this subparagraph, an alien who is a graduate of a medical school shall be considered to have

101

passed parts I and II of the National Board of Medical Examiners Examination if the alien was fully and permanently licensed to practice medicine in a State on January 9, 1978, and was practicing medicine in a State on that date.

(C) The alien has made a commitment to return to the country of his nationality or last residence upon completion of the education or training for which he is coming to the United States, and the government of the country of his nationality or last residence has provided a written assurance, satisfactory to the Secretary of Health and Human Services, that there is a need in that country for persons with the skills the alien will acquire in such education or training.

(D) The duration of the alien's participation in the program of graduate medical education or training for which the alien is coming to the United States is limited to the time typically required to complete such program, as determined by the Director of the United States Information Agency at the time of the alien's entry into the United States, based on criteria which are established in coordination with the Secretary of Health and Human Services and which take into consideration the published requirements of the medical specialty board which administers such education or training program; except that—

(i) such duration is further limited to seven years unless the alien has demonstrated to the satisfaction of the Director that the country to which the alien will return at the end of such specialty education or training has an exceptional need for an individual trained in such specialty, and

(ii) the alien may, once and not later than two years after the date the alien enters the United States as an exchange visitor or acquires exchange visitor status, change the alien's designated program of graduate medical education or training if the Director approves the change and if a commitment and written assurance with respect to the alien's new program have been provided in accordance with subparagraph (C).

(E) The alien furnishes the Attorney General each year with an affidavit (in such form as the Attorney General shall prescribe) that attests that the alien (i) is in good standing in the program of graduate medical education or training in which the alien is participating, and (ii) will return to the country of his nationality or last residence upon completion of the education or training for which he came to the United States.

(2)(A) Except as provided in subparagraph (B), the requirements of subparagraphs (A) and (B)(ii)(I) of paragraph (1) shall not apply between the effective date of this subsection and December 31, 1983, to any alien who seeks to come to the United States to participate in an accredited program of graduate medical education or training if (i) the Secretary of Health and Human Services determines, on a case-by-case basis, that there would be a substantial disruption in the health services provided in such program because such alien was not permitted, because of his failure to meet such requirements, to enter the United States to participate in such program, and (ii) the program has a comprehensive plan to reduce reliance on alien physicians, which plan the Secretary of Health and Human Services finds, in accordance with criteria published by the Secretary, to be satisfactory and to include the following:

(I) A detailed discussion of specific problems that the program anticipates without such waiver and of the alternative resources and methods (including use of physician extenders and other paraprofessionals) that have been considered and have been and will be applied to reduce such disruption in the delivery of health services.

(II) A detailed description of those changes of the program (including improvement of educational and medical services training) which have been considered and which have been or will be applied which would make the program more attractive to graduates of medical schools who are citizens of the United States.

(III) A detailed description of the recruiting efforts which have been and will be undertaken to attract graduates of medical schools who are citizens of the United States.

(IV) A detailed description and analysis of how the program, on a year-by-year basis, has phased down and will phase down its dependence upon aliens who are graduates of foreign medical schools so that the program will not be dependent upon the admission to the program of any additional such aliens after December 31, 1983.

(B) In the administration of this subsection, the Attorney General shall take such action as may be necessary to ensure that the total number of aliens participating (at any time) in programs described in subparagraph (A) does not, because of the exemption provided by such subparagraph, exceed the total number of aliens participating in such programs on the effective date of this subsection. The Secretary of Health and Human Services, in coordination with the Attorney General and the Director of the United States Information Agency, shall (i) monitor the issuance of waivers under subparagraph (A) and the needs of the communities (with respect to which such waivers are issued) to assure that quality medical care is provided, and (ii) review each program with such a waiver to assure that the plan described in subparagraph (A)(ii) is being carried out and that participants in such program are being provided appropriate supervision in their medical education and training.

(C) The Secretary of Health and Human Services, in coordination with the Attorney General and the Director of the United States Information Agency, shall report to the Congress at the beginning of fiscal years 1982 and 1983 on the distribution (by geography, nationality, and medical specialty or field of practice) of foreign medical graduates in the United States who have received a waiver under subparagraph (A), including an analysis of the dependence of the various communities on aliens who are in medical education or training programs in the various medical specialties.

**(3)** The Director of the United States Information Agency annually shall transmit to the Congress a report on aliens who have submitted affidavits described in paragraph (1)(E), and shall include in such report the name and address of each such alien, the medical education or training program in which such alien is participating, and the status of such alien in that program.

**(k) Attorney General's discretion to admit otherwise excludable aliens who possess immigrant visas**

Any alien, excludable from the United States under paragraph (5)(A) or (7)(A)(i) of subsection (a) of this section, who is in possession of an immigrant visa may, if otherwise admissible, be admitted in the discretion of the Attorney General if the Attorney General is satisfied that exclusion was not known to, and could not have been ascertained by the exercise of reasonable diligence by, the immigrant before the time of departure of the vessel or aircraft from the last port outside the United States and outside foreign contiguous territory or, in the case of an immigrant coming from foreign contiguous territory, before the time of the immigrant's application for admission.

**(*l*) Guam; waiver of requirements; nonimmigrant visitors**

**(1)** The requirement of paragraph (7)(B)(i) of subsection (a) of this section may be waived by the Attorney General, the Secretary of State, and the Secretary of the Interior, acting jointly, in the case of an alien applying for admission as a nonimmigrant visitor for business or pleasure and solely for entry into and stay on Guam for a period not to exceed fifteen days, if the Attorney General, the Secretary of State, and the Secretary of the Interior, after consultation with the Governor of Guam, jointly determine that—

**(A)** an adequate arrival and departure control system has been developed on Guam, and

**(B)** such a waiver does not represent a threat to the welfare, safety, or security of the United States or its territories and commonwealths.

**(2)** An alien may not be provided a waiver under this subsection unless the alien has waived any right—

**(A)** to review or appeal under this chapter of an immigration officer's determination as to the admissibility of the alien at the port of entry into Guam, or

**(B)** to contest, other than on the basis of an application for asylum, any action for deportation against the alien.

**(3)** If adequate appropriated funds to carry out this subsection are not otherwise available, the Attorney General is authorized to accept from the Government of Guam such funds as may be tendered to cover all or any part of the cost of administration and enforcement of this subsection.

**(m) Requirements for admission of nonimmigrant nurses during five-year period**

**(1)** The qualifications referred to in section 101(a)(15)(H)(i)(a) [8 U.S.C.A. § 1101(a)(15)(H)(i)(a)], with respect to an alien who is coming to the United States to perform nursing services for a facility, are that the alien—

**(A)** has obtained a full and unrestricted license to practice professional nursing in the country where the alien obtained nursing education or has received nursing education in the United States or Canada;

**(B)** has passed an appropriate examination (recognized in regulations promulgated in consultation with the Secretary of Health and Human Services) or has a full and unrestricted license under State law to practice professional nursing in the State of intended employment; and

**(C)** is fully qualified and eligible under the laws (including such temporary or interim licensing requirements which authorize the nurse to be employed) governing the place of intended employment to engage in the practice of professional nursing as a registered nurse immediately upon admission to the United States and is authorized under such laws to be employed by the facility.

**(2)(A)** The attestation referred to in section 101(a)(15)(H)(i)(a) [8 U.S.C.A. § 1101(a)(15)(H)(i)(a)] is an attestation as to the following:

**(i)** There would be a substantial disruption through no fault of the facility in the delivery of health care services of the facility without the services of such an alien or aliens.

**(ii)** The employment of the alien will not adversely affect the wages and working conditions of registered nurses similarly employed.

**(iii)** The alien employed by the facility will be paid the wage rate for registered nurses similarly employed by the facility.

**(iv)** Either (I) the facility has taken and is taking timely and significant steps designed to recruit and retain sufficient registered nurses who are United States citizens or immigrants who are authorized to perform nursing services, in order to remove as quickly as reasonably possible the dependence of the facility on nonimmigrant registered nurses, or (II) the facility is subject to an approved State plan for the recruitment and retention of nurses (described in paragraph (3)).

(v) There is not a strike or lockout in the course of a labor dispute, and the employment of such an alien is not intended or designed to influence an election for a bargaining representative for registered nurses of the facility.

(vi) At the time of the filing of the petition for registered nurses under section 101(a)(15)(H)(i)(a) [8 U.S.C.A. § 1101(a)(15)(H)(i)(a)], notice of the filing has been provided by the facility to the bargaining representative of the registered nurses at the facility or, where there is no such bargaining representative, notice of the filing has been provided to registered nurses employed at the facility through posting in conspicuous locations.

A facility is considered not to meet clause (i) (relating to an attestation of a substantial disruption in delivery of health care services) if the facility, within the previous year, laid off registered nurses. Nothing in clause (iv) shall be construed as requiring a facility to have taken significant steps described in such clause before December 18, 1989. In the case of an alien for whom an employer has filed an attestation under this subparagraph and who is performing services at a worksite other than the employer's or other than a worksite controlled by the employer, the Secretary may waive such requirements for the attestation for the worksite as may be appropriate in order to avoid duplicative attestations, in cases of temporary, emergency circumstances, with respect to information not within the knowledge of the attestor, or for other good cause.

(B) For purposes of subparagraph (A)(iv)(I), each of the following shall be considered a significant step reasonably designed to recruit and retain registered nurses:

(i) Operating a training program for registered nurses at the facility or financing (or providing participation in) a training program for registered nurses elsewhere.

(ii) Providing career development programs and other methods of facilitating health care workers to become registered nurses.

(iii) Paying registered nurses wages at a rate higher than currently being paid to registered nurses similarly employed in the geographic area.

(iv) Providing adequate support services to free registered nurses from administrative and other nonnursing duties.

(v) Providing reasonable opportunities for meaningful salary advancement by registered nurses.

The steps described in this subparagraph shall not be considered to be an exclusive list of the significant steps that may be taken to meet the conditions of subparagraph (A)(iv)(I). Nothing herein shall require a facility to take more than one step, if the facility can demonstrate that taking a second step is not reasonable.

**(C)** Subject to subparagraph (E), an attestation under subparagraph (A) shall—

(i) expire at the end of the 1–year period beginning on the date of its filing with the Secretary of Labor, and

(ii) apply to petitions filed during such 1–year period if the facility states in each such petition that it continues to comply with the conditions in the attestation.

**(D)** A facility may meet the requirements under this paragraph with respect to more than one registered nurse in a single petition.

**(E)(i)** The Secretary of Labor shall compile and make available for public examination in a timely manner in Washington, D.C., a list identifying facilities which have filed petitions for nonimmigrants under section 101(a)(15)(H)(i)(a) [8 U.S.C.A. § 1101(a)(15)(H)(i)(a)] and, for each such facility, a copy of the facility's attestation under subparagraph (A) (and accompanying documentation) and each such petition filed by the facility.

(ii) The Secretary of Labor shall establish a process for the receipt, investigation, and disposition of complaints respecting a facility's failure to meet conditions attested to or a facility's misrepresentation of a material fact in an attestation. Complaints may be filed by any aggrieved person or organization (including bargaining representatives, associations deemed appropriate by the Secretary, and other aggrieved parties as determined under regulations of the Secretary). The Secretary shall conduct an investigation under this clause if there is reasonable cause to believe that a facility fails to meet conditions attested to.

(iii) Under such process, the Secretary shall provide, within 180 days after the date such a complaint is filed, for a determination as to whether or not a basis exists to make a finding described in clause (iv). If the Secretary determines that such a basis exists, the Secretary shall provide for notice of such determination to the interested parties and an opportunity for a hearing on the complaint within 60 days of the date of the determination.

(iv) If the Secretary of Labor finds, after notice and opportunity for a hearing, that a facility (for which an attestation is made) has failed to meet a condition attested to or that there was a misrepresentation of material fact in the attestation, the Secretary shall notify the Attorney General of such finding and may, in addition, impose such other administrative remedies (including civil monetary penalties in an amount not to exceed $1,000 per violation) as the Secretary determines to be appropriate. Upon receipt of such notice, the Attorney General shall not approve petitions filed with respect to a facility during a period of at least 1 year for nurses to be employed by the facility.

(v) In addition to the sanctions provided under clause (iv), if the Secretary of Labor finds, after notice and an opportunity for a hearing, that a facility has violated the condition attested to under subparagraph (A)(iii) (relating to payment of registered nurses at the prevailing

107

wage rate), the Secretary shall order the facility to provide for payment of such amounts of back pay as may be required to comply with such condition.

(3) The Secretary of Labor shall provide for a process under which a State may submit the Secretary a plan for the recruitment and retention of United States citizens and immigrants who are authorized to perform nursing services as registered nurses in facilities in the State. Such a plan may include counseling and educating health workers and other individuals concerning the employment opportunities available to registered nurses. The Secretary shall provide, on an annual basis in consultation with the Secretary of Health and Human Services, for the approval or disapproval of such a plan, for purposes of paragraph (2)(A)(iv)(II). Such a plan may not be considered to be approved with respect to the facility unless the plan provides for the taking of significant steps described in paragraph (2)(A)(iv)(I) with respect to registered nurses in the facility.

(4) The period of admission of an alien under section 101(a)(15)(H)(i)(a) [8 U.S.C.A. § 1101(a)(15)(H)(i)(a)] shall be for an initial period of not to exceed 3 years, subject to an extension for a period or periods, not to exceed a total period of admission of 5 years (or a total period of admission of 6 years in the case of extraordinary circumstances, as determined by the Attorney General).

(5) For purposes of this subsection and section 101(a)(15)(H)(i)(a) [8 U.S.C.A. § 1101(a)(15)(H)(i)(a)], the term "facility" includes an employer who employs registered nurses in a home setting.

**(n) Labor condition application**

(1) No alien may be admitted or provided status as a nonimmigrant described in section 101(a)(15)(H)(i)(b) [8 U.S.C.A. § 1101(a)(15)(H)(i)(b)] in an occupational classification unless the employer has filed with the Secretary of Labor an application stating the following:

(A) The employer—

(i) is offering and will offer during the period of authorized employment to aliens and to other individuals employed in the occupational classification and in the area of employment wages that are at least—

(I) the actual wage level for the occupational classification at the place of employment, or

(II) the prevailing wage level for the occupational classification in the area of employment,

whichever is greater, determined as of the time of filing the application, and

(ii) will provide working conditions for such aliens that will not adversely affect the working conditions of workers similarly employed.

(B) There is not a strike or lockout in the course of a labor dispute in the occupational classification at the place of employment.

(C) The employer, at the time of filing the application—

(i) has provided notice of the filing under this paragraph to the bargaining representative (if any) of the employer's employees in the occupational classification and area for which aliens are sought, or

(ii) if there is no such bargaining representative, has posted notice of filing in conspicuous locations at the place of employment.

(D) The application shall contain a specification of the number of workers sought, the occupational classification in which the workers will be employed, and wage rate and conditions under which they will be employed. The employer shall make available for public examination, within one working day after the date on which an application under this paragraph is filed, at the employer's principal place of business or worksite, a copy of each such application (and accompanying documentation). The Secretary shall compile, on a current basis, a list (by employer and by occupational classification) of the applications filed under this subsection. Such list shall include the wage rate, number of aliens sought, period of intended employment, and date of need. The Secretary shall make such list available for public examination in Washington, D.C.

(2)(A) The Secretary shall establish a process for the receipt, investigation, and disposition of complaints respecting a petitioner's failure to meet a condition specified in an application submitted under paragraph (1) or a petitioner's misrepresentation of material facts in such an application. Complaints may be filed by any aggrieved person or organization (including bargaining representatives). No investigation or hearing shall be conducted on a complaint concerning such a failure or misrepresentation unless the complaint was filed not later than 12 months after the date of the failure or misrepresentation, respectively. The Secretary shall conduct an investigation under this paragraph if there is reasonable cause to believe that such a failure or misrepresentation has occurred.

(B) Under such process, the Secretary shall provide, within 30 days after the date such a complaint is filed, for a determination as to whether or not a reasonable basis exists to make a finding described in subparagraph (C). If the Secretary determines that such a reasonable basis exists, the Secretary shall provide for notice of such determination to the interested parties and an opportunity for a hearing on the complaint, in accordance with section 556 of Title 5, within 60 days after the date of the determination. If such a hearing is requested, the Secretary shall make a finding concerning the matter by not later than 60 days after the date of the hearing. In the case of similar complaints respecting the same applicant, the Secretary may consolidate the hearings under this subparagraph on such complaints.

**(C)** If the Secretary finds, after notice and opportunity for a hearing, a failure to meet a condition (or a substantial failure in the case of a condition described in subparagraph (C) or (D) of paragraph (1)) or misrepresentation of material fact in an application—

(i) the Secretary shall notify the Attorney General of such finding and may, in addition, impose such other administrative remedies (including civil monetary penalties in an amount not to exceed $1,000 per violation) as the Secretary determines to be appropriate, and

(ii) the Attorney General shall not approve petitions filed with respect to that employer under section 1154 or 1184(c) of this title during a period of at least 1 year for aliens to be employed by the employer.

**(D)** In addition to the sanctions provided under subparagraph (C), if the Secretary finds, after notice and opportunity for a hearing, that an employer has not paid wages at the wage level specified under the application and required under paragraph (1), the Secretary shall order the employer to provide for payment of such amounts of back pay as may be required to comply with the requirements of paragraph (1).

(June 27, 1952, c. 477, Title II, ch. 2, § 212, 66 Stat. 182; July 18, 1956, c. 629, Title III, § 301(a), 70 Stat. 575; Pub. L. 85–508, § 23, July 7, 1958, 72 Stat. 351; Pub. L. 86–3, § 20(b), Mar. 18, 1959, 73 Stat. 13; Pub. L. 86–648, § 8, July 14, 1960, 74 Stat. 505; Pub. L. 87–256, § 109(c), Sept. 21, 1961, 75 Stat. 535; Pub. L. 87–301, §§ 11–15, Sept. 26, 1961, 75 Stat. 654, 655; Pub. L. 89–236, §§ 10, 15, Oct. 3, 1965, 79 Stat. 917, 919; Pub. L. 91–225, § 2, Apr. 7, 1970, 84 Stat. 116; Pub. L. 94–484, Title VI, § 601(a), (c), (d), Oct. 12, 1976, 90 Stat. 2300, 2301; Pub. L. 94–571, §§ 5, 7(d), Oct. 20, 1976, 90 Stat. 2705, 2706; 1966 Reorg.Plan No. 3, §§ 1, 3, 31 F.R. 8855, 80 Stat. 1610; Pub. L. 95–83, Title III, § 307(q)(1), (2), Aug. 1, 1977, 91 Stat. 394; 1977 Reorg.Plan No. 2, § 7(a)(8), 42 F.R. 62461, 91 Stat. 1637; Pub. L. 95–549, Title I, §§ 101, 102, Oct. 30, 1978, 92 Stat. 2065; Pub. L. 96–70, Title III, § 3201(b), Sept. 27, 1979, 93 Stat. 497; Pub. L. 96–88, Title III, § 301(a)(1), Title V, §§ 503, 509(b), Oct. 17, 1979, 93 Stat. 670, 690, 695; Pub. L. 96–212, Title II, § 203(d), (f), Mar. 17, 1980, 94 Stat. 107; Pub. L. 96–538, Title IV, § 404, Dec. 17, 1980, 94 Stat. 3192; Pub. L. 97–116, §§ 4, 5(a)(1), (2), (b), 18(e), Dec. 29, 1981, 95 Stat. 1611, 1612, 1620; Pub. L. 97–241, Title III, § 303(a), Aug. 24, 1982, 96 Stat. 291; Pub. L. 98–454, Title VI, § 602(a), Oct. 5, 1984, 98 Stat. 1737; Pub.L. 98–473, Title II, §§ 220(a), Oct. 12, 1984, 98 Stat. 2028; Pub.L. 99–396, § 14(a), Oct. 27, 1986, 100 Stat. 842; Pub.L. 99–570, Title I, § 1751(a), Oct. 27, 1986, 100 Stat. 3207–47; Pub.L. 99–639, § 6(a), Nov. 10, 1986, 100 Stat. 3544, as amended Pub.L. 100–525, § 7(c)(1), Oct. 24, 1988, 102 Stat. 2617; Pub.L. 99–639, § 6(b), as added Pub.L. 100–525, § 7(c)(3), Oct. 24, 1988, 102 Stat. 2616; Pub.L. 99–653, § 7(a), Nov. 14, 1986, 100 Stat. 3657; Pub.L. 99–653 § 7(d)(2), as added Pub.L. 100–525, § 8(f), Oct. 24, 1988, 102 Stat. 2617; Pub.L. 100–204, Title VIII, § 806(c), Dec. 22, 1987, 101 Stat. 1399; Pub.L.

100–525, §§ 3(1)(A), 9(i), Oct. 24, 1988, 102 Stat. 2614, 2620; Pub.L. 100–690, Title VII, § 7349(a), Nov. 18, 1988, 102 Stat. 4473; Dec. 18, 1989, Pub.L. 101–238, § 3(b), 103 Stat. 2100; Feb. 16, 1990, Pub.L. 101–246, Title I, § 131(a), (c), 104 Stat. 31; Nov. 29, 1990, Pub.L. 101–649, Title I, §§ 161, 162(e)(1), (f)(2)(B), Title II, §§ 202(b), 205(c)(3), 231, Title V, §§ 511(a), 514(a), Title VI, § 601(a), (b), (d), 104 Stat. 5008, 5011, 5012, 5014, 5020, 5028, 5052, 5053, 5067, 5075–5077.)

**1.** So in original. Probably should be "voluntarily".

**2.** So in original. "Subsection" was probably intended.

## § 213. Admission of aliens on giving bond or undertaking; return upon permanent departure [8 U.S.C.A. § 1183]

An alien excludable under paragraph (4) of section 212(a) [8 U.S. C.A. § 1182(a)(4)] may, if otherwise admissible, be admitted in the discretion of the Attorney General upon the giving of a suitable and proper bond or undertaking approved by the Attorney General, in such amount and containing such conditions as he may prescribe, to the United States, and to all States, territories, counties, towns, municipalities, and districts thereof holding the United States and all States, territories, counties, towns, municipalities, and districts thereof harmless against such alien becoming a public charge. Such bond or undertaking shall terminate upon the permanent departure from the United States, the naturalization, or the death of such alien, and any sums or other security held to secure performance thereof, except to the extent forfeited for violation of the terms thereof, shall be returned to the person by whom furnished, or to his legal representatives. Suit may be brought thereon in the name and by the proper law officers of the United States for the use of the United States, or of any State, territory, district, county, town, or municipality in which such alien becomes a public charge, irrespective of whether a demand for payment of public expenses has been made.

(June 27, 1952, c. 477, Title II, ch. 2, § 213, 66 Stat. 188; July 10, 1970, Pub.L. 91–313, § 1, 84 Stat. 413; Nov. 29, 1990, Pub.L. 101–649, Title VI, § 603(a)(8), 104 Stat. 5083.)

## § 214. Admission of nonimmigrants [8 U.S.C.A. § 1184]

### (a) Regulations

(1) The admission to the United States of any alien as a nonimmigrant shall be for such time and under such conditions as the Attorney General may by regulations prescribe, including when he deems necessary the giving of a bond with sufficient surety in such sum and containing such conditions as the Attorney General shall prescribe, to insure that at the expiration of such time or upon failure to maintain the status under which he was admitted, or to maintain any status subsequently acquired under section 248 [8 U.S.C.A. § 1258], such alien will depart from the United States. No alien admitted to Guam

111

without a visa pursuant to section 212(*l*) [8 U.S.C.A. § 1182(*l*)] may be authorized to enter or stay in the United States other than in Guam or to remain in Guam for a period exceeding fifteen days from date of admission to Guam. No alien admitted to the United States without a visa pursuant to section 217 [8 U.S.C.A. § 1187] may be authorized to remain in the United States as a nonimmigrant visitor for a period exceeding 90 days from the date of admission.

**(2)(A)** The period of authorized status as a nonimmigrant under section 101(a)(15)(O) [8 U.S.C.A. § 1101(a)(15)(O)] shall be for such period as the Attorney General may specify in order to provide for the event for which the nonimmigrant is admitted.

**(B)(i)** The period of authorized status as a nonimmigrant described in section 101(a)(15)(P) [8 U.S.C.A. § 1101(a)(15)(P)] shall be for such period as the Attorney General may specify in order to provide for the competition, event, or performance for which the nonimmigrant is admitted. In the case of nonimmigrants admitted as individual athletes under section 101(a)(15)(P) [8 U.S.C.A. § 1101(a)(15)(P)], the period of authorized status may be for an initial period (not to exceed 5 years) during which the nonimmigrant will perform as an athlete and such period may be extended by the Attorney General for an additional period of up to 5 years.

**(ii)** An alien who is admitted as a nonimmigrant under clause (ii) or (iii) of section 101(a)(15)(P) [8 U.S.C.A. § 1101(a)(15)(P) may not be readmitted as such a nonimmigrant unless the alien has remained outside the United States for at least 3 months after the date of the most recent admission. The Attorney General may waive the application of the previous sentence in the case of individual tours in which the application would work an undue hardship.

**(b) Presumption of status; written waiver**

Every alien (other than a nonimmigrant described in subparagraph (H)(i) or (L) of section 101(a)(15) [8 U.S.C.A. § 1101(a)(15)]) shall be presumed to be an immigrant until he establishes to the satisfaction of the consular officer, at the time of application for a visa, and the immigration officers, at the time of application for admission, that he is entitled to a nonimmigrant status under section 101(a)(15) [8 U.S.C.A. § 1101(a)(15)]. An alien who is an officer or employee of any foreign government or of any international organization entitled to enjoy privileges, exemptions, and immunities under the International Organizations Immunities Act or an alien who is the attendant, servant, employee, or member of the immediate family of any such alien shall not be entitled to apply for or receive an immigrant visa, or to enter the United States as an immigrant unless he executes a written waiver in the same form and substance as is prescribed by section 247(b) [8 U.S.C.A. § 1257(b)].

**(c) Petition of importing employer; involvement of Departments of Labor and Agriculture**

(1) The question of importing any alien as a nonimmigrant under section 101(a)(15)(H), (L), (O), or (P)(i) [8 U.S.C.A. § 1101(a)(15)(H), (L), (O), or (P)(i)] in any specific case or specific cases shall be determined by the Attorney General, after consultation with appropriate agencies of the Government, upon petition of the importing employer. Such petition shall be made and approved before the visa is granted. The petition shall be in such form and contain such information as the Attorney General shall prescribe. The approval of such a petition shall not, of itself, be construed as establishing that the alien is a nonimmigrant. For purposes of this subsection with respect to nonimmigrants described in section 101(a)(15)(H)(ii)(a) [8 U.S.C.A. § 1101(a)(15)(H)(ii)(a)], the term "appropriate agencies of Government" means the Department of Labor and includes the Department of Agriculture. The provisions of section 1188 of this title shall apply to the question of importing any alien as a nonimmigrant under section 101(a)(15)(H)(ii)(a) [8 U.S.C.A. § 1101(a)(15)(H)(ii)(a)].

(2)(A) The Attorney General shall provide for a procedure under which an importing employer which meets requirements established by the Attorney General may file a blanket petition to import aliens as nonimmigrants described in section 101(a)(15)(L) [8 U.S.C.A. § 1101(a)(15)(L)] instead of filing individuals petitions under paragraph (1) to import such aliens. Such procedure shall permit the expedited processing of visas for entry of aliens covered under such a petition.

(B) For purposes of section 101(a)(15)(L) [8 U.S.C.A. § 1101(a)(15)(L)] an alien is considered to be serving in a capacity involving specialized knowledge with respect to a company if the alien has a special knowledge of the company product and its application in international markets or has an advanced level of knowledge of processes and procedures of the company.

(C) The Attorney General shall provide a process for reviewing and acting upon petitions under this subsection with respect to nonimmigrants described in section 101(a)(15)(L) [8 U.S.C.A. § 1101(a)(15)(L)] within 30 days after the date a completed petition has been filed.

(D) The period of authorized admission for—

(i) a nonimmigrant admitted to render services in a managerial or executive capacity under section 101(a)(15)(L) [8 U.S.C.A. § 1101(a)(15)(L)] shall not exceed 7 years, or

(ii) a nonimmigrant admitted to render services in a capacity that involved specialized knowledge under section 101(a)(15)(L) [8 U.S.C.A. § 1101(a)(15)(L)] shall not exceed 5 years.

(3) The Attorney General shall approve a petition—

**(A)** with respect to a nonimmigrant described in section 101(a)(15)(O)(i) [8 U.S.C.A. § 1101(a)(15)(O)(i)] only after consultation with peer groups in the area of the alien's ability or, with respect to aliens seeking entry for a motion picture or television production, after consultation with the appropriate union representing the alien's occupational peers and a management organization in the area of the alien's ability, or

**(B)** with respect to a nonimmigrant described in section 101(a)(15)(O)(ii) [8 U.S.C.A. § 1101(a)(15)(O)(ii)] after consultation with labor organizations with expertise in the skill area involved.

In the case of an alien seeking entry for a motion picture or television production, (i) any opinion under the previous sentence shall only be advisory, (ii) any such opinion that recommends denial must be in writing, (iii) in making the decision the Attorney General shall consider the exigencies and scheduling of the production, and (iv) the Attorney General shall append to the decision any such opinion.

**(4)(A)** A person may petition the Attorney General for classification of an alien as a nonimmigrant under clause (ii) of section 101(a)(15)(P) [8 U.S.C.A. § 1101(a)(15)(P)].

**(B)** The Attorney General shall approve petitions under this subsection with respect to nonimmigrants described in clause (i) or (iii) of section 101(a)(15)(P) [8 U.S.C.A. § 1101(a)(15)(P)] only after consultation with labor organizations with expertise in the specific field of athletics or entertainment involved.

**(C)** The Attorney General shall approve petitions under this subsection for nonimmigrants described in section 101(a)(15)(P)(ii) [8 U.S.C.A. § 1101(a)(15)(P)(ii)] only after consultation with labor organizations representing artists and entertainers in the United States, in order to assure reciprocity in fact with foreign states.

**(5)** In the case of an alien who is provided nonimmigrant status under section 101(a)(15)(H)(i)(b) [8 U.S.C.A. § 1101(a)(15)(H)(i)(b)] or 101(a)(15)(H)(ii)(b) [8 U.S.C.A. § 1101(a)(15)(H)(ii)(b)] and who is dismissed from employment by the employer before the end of the period of authorized admission, the employer shall be liable for the reasonable costs of return transportation of the alien abroad.

**(6)** If a petition is filed and denied under this subsection, the Attorney General shall notify the petitioner of the determination and the reasons for the denial and of the process by which the petitioner may appeal the determination.

**(d) Issuance of visa to fiancée or fiancé of citizen**

A visa shall not be issued under the provisions of section 101(a)(15)(K) [8 U.S.C.A. § 1101(a)(15)(K)] until the consular officer has received a petition filed in the United States by the fiancée or fiancé of the applying alien and approved by the Attorney General. The petition shall be in such form and contain such information as the Attorney General shall, by regulation, prescribe. It shall be approved only after satisfactory evidence is submitted by the petitioner to establish that the parties have previously met in person within 2 years before the date of filing the petition, have a bona fide intention to marry and are legally able and actually willing to conclude a valid marriage in the United States within a period of ninety days after the alien's arrival. In the event the marriage with the petitioner does not occur within three months after the entry of the said alien and minor children, they shall be required to depart from the United States and upon failure to do so shall be deported in accordance with sections 242 and 243 [8 U.S.C.A. §§ 1252 and 1253], except that the Attorney General in his discretion may waive the requirement that the parties have previously met in person.

### (e) Professionals from Canada

Notwithstanding any other provision of this chapter, an alien who is a citizen of Canada and seeks to enter the United States under and pursuant to the provisions of Annex 1502.1 (United States of America), Part C—Professionals, of the United States-Canada Free-Trade Agreement to engage in business activities at a professional level as provided for therein may be admitted for such purpose under regulations of the Attorney General promulgated after consultation with the Secretaries of State and Labor.

### (f) Denial of crewmember status in case of certain labor disputes

(1) Except as provided in paragraph (3), no alien shall be entitled to nonimmigrant status described in section 101(a)(15)(D) [8 U.S.C.A. § 1101(a)(15)(D)] if the alien intends to land for the purpose of performing service on board a vessel of the United States (as defined in section 2101(46) of Title 46) or on an aircraft of an air carrier (as defined in section 1301(3) of the Appendix to Title 49) during a labor dispute where there is a strike or lockout in the bargaining unit of the employer in which the alien intends to perform such service.

(2) An alien described in paragraph (1)—

(A) may not be paroled into the United States pursuant to section 212(d)(5) [8 U.S.C.A. § 1182(d)(5)] unless the Attorney General determines that the parole of such alien is necessary to protect the national security of the United States; and

(B) shall be considered not to be a bona fide crewman for purposes of section 252(b) [8 U.S.C.A. § 1282(b)].

(3) Paragraph (1) shall not apply to an alien if the air carrier or owner or operator of such vessel that employs the alien provides documentation that satisfies the Attorney General that the alien—

(A) has been an employee of such employer for a period of not less than 1 year preceding the date that a strike or lawful lockout commenced;

(B) has served as a qualified crewman for such employer at least once in each of 3 months during the 12-month period preceding such date; and

(C) shall continue to provide the same services that such alien provided as such a crewman.

### (g) Temporary workers and trainees; limitation on numbers

(1) The total number of aliens who may be issued visas or otherwise provided nonimmigrant status during any fiscal year (beginning with fiscal year 1992)—

(A) under section 101(a)(15)(H)(i)(b) [8 U.S.C.A. § 1101(a)(15)(H)(i)(b)] may not exceed 65,000,

(B) under section 101(a)(15)(H)(ii)(b) [8 U.S.C.A. § 1101(a)(15)(H)(ii)(b)] may not exceed 66,000, or

(C) under section 101(a)(15)(P)(i) [8 U.S.C.A. § 1101(a)(15)(P)(i)] or section 101(a)(15)(P)(iii) [8 U.S.C.A. § 1101(a)(15)(P)(iii)] may not exceed 25,000.

(2) The numerical limitations of paragraph (1) shall only apply to principal aliens and not to the spouses or children of such aliens.

(3) Aliens who are subject to the numerical limitations of paragraph (1) shall be issued visas (or otherwise provided nonimmigrant status) in the order in which petitions are filed for such visas or status.

(4) In the case of a nonimmigrant described in section 101(a)(15)(H)(i)(b) [8 U.S.C.A. § 1101(a)(15)(H)(i)(b)] the period of authorized admission as such a nonimmigrant may not exceed 6 years.

### (h) Intention to abandon foreign residence

The fact that an alien is the beneficiary of an application for a preference status filed under section 204 [8 U.S.C.A. § 1154] or has otherwise sought permanent residence in the United States shall not constitute evidence of an intention to abandon a foreign residence for purposes of obtaining a visa as a nonimmigrant described in subparagraph (H)(i) or (L) of section 101(a)(15) [8 U.S.C.A. § 1101(a)(15)] or otherwise obtaining or maintaining the status of a nonimmigrant described in such subparagraph, if the alien had obtained a change of status under section 248 [8 U.S.C.A. § 1258] to a classification as such a nonimmigrant before the alien's most recent departure from the United States.

### (i) "Specialty occupation" defined

(1) For purposes of section 101(a)(15)(H)(i)(b) [8 U.S.C.A. § 1101(a)(15)(H)(i)(b)] and paragraph (2), the term "specialty occupation" means an occupation that requires—

(A) theoretical and practical application of a body of highly specialized knowledge, and

(B) attainment of a bachelor's or higher degree in the specific specialty (or its equivalent) as a minimum for entry into the occupation in the United States.

(2) For purposes of section 101(a)(15)(H)(i)(b) [8 U.S.C.A. § 1101(a)(15)(H)(i)(b)], the requirements of this paragraph, with respect to a specialty occupation, are—

(A) full state licensure to practice in the occupation, if such licensure is required to practice in the occupation,

(B) completion of the degree described in paragraph (1)(B) for the occupation, or

(C)(i) experience in the specialty equivalent to the completion of such degree, and (ii) recognition of expertise in the specialty through progressively responsible positions relating to the specialty.

(June 27, 1952, c. 477, Title II, ch. 2, § 214, 66 Stat. 189; Pub. L. 91–225, § 3, Apr. 7, 1970, 84 Stat. 117; Pub. L. 98–454, Title VI, § 602(b), Oct. 5, 1984, 98 Stat. 1737; Pub.L. 99–603, Title III, §§ 301(b), 313(b), Nov. 6, 1986, 100 Stat. 3411, 3438; Pub.L. 99–639, § 3(a), (c), Nov. 10, 1986, 100 Stat. 3542; Pub.L. 99–603, § 301(b), as amended Pub.L. 100–525, § 2(*l* )(1), Oct. 24, 1988, 102 Stat. 2612; Pub. L. 100–449, Title III, § 307(b), Sept. 28, 1988, 102 Stat. 1877; Sept. 28, 1988, Pub.L. 100–449, Title III, § 307(b), 102 Stat. 1877; Nov. 29, 1990, Pub.L. 101–649, Title II, §§ 202(a), 205(a), (b), (b)(1), (2), (c)(2), 206(b), 207(b)(1), (2), 531, 104 Stat. 5014, 5019, 5020, 5023, 5025, 5026, 5028.)

## § 215. Travel control of citizens and aliens [8 U.S.C.A. § 1185]

### (a) Restrictions and prohibitions

Unless otherwise ordered by the President, it shall be unlawful—

(1) for any alien to depart from or enter or attempt to depart from or enter the United States except under such reasonable rules, regulations, and orders, and subject to such limitations and exceptions as the President may prescribe;

(2) for any person to transport or attempt to transport from or into the United States another person with knowledge or reasonable cause to believe that the departure or entry of such other person is forbidden by this section;

(3) for any person knowingly to make any false statement in an application for permission to depart from or enter the United States with intent to induce or secure the granting of such permission either for himself or for another;

(4) for any person knowingly to furnish or attempt to furnish or assist in furnishing to another a permit or evidence of permission to depart or enter not issued and designed for such other person's use;

(5) for any person knowingly to use or attempt to use any permit or evidence of permission to depart or enter not issued and designed for his use;

(6) for any person to forge, counterfeit, mutilate, or alter, or cause or procure to be forged, counterfeited, mutilated, or altered, any permit or evidence of permission to depart from or enter the United States;

(7) for any person knowingly to use or attempt to use or furnish to another for use any false, forged, counterfeited, mutilated, or altered permit, or evidence of permission, or any permit or evidence of permission which, though originally valid, has become or been made void or invalid.

### (b) Citizens

Except as otherwise provided by the President and subject to such limitations and exceptions as the President may authorize and prescribe, it shall be unlawful for any citizen of the United States to depart from or enter, or attempt to depart from or enter, the United States unless he bears a valid passport.

### (c) Definitions

The term "United States" as used in this section includes the Canal Zone, and all territory and waters, continental or insular, subject to the jurisdiction of the United States. The term "person" as used in this section shall be deemed to mean any individual, partnership, association, company, or other incorporated body of individuals, or corporation, or body politic.

### (d) Nonadmission of certain aliens

Nothing in this section shall be construed to entitle an alien to whom a permit to enter the United States has been issued to enter the United States, if, upon arrival in the United States, he is found to be inadmissible under any of the provisions of this chapter, or any other law, relative to the entry of aliens into the United States.

### (e) Revocation of proclamation as affecting penalties

The revocation of any rule, regulation, or order issued in pursuance of this section shall not prevent prosecution for any offense committed, or the imposition of any penalties or forfeitures, liability for which was incurred under this section prior to the revocation of such rule, regulation, or order.

### (f) Permits to enter

Passports, visas, reentry permits, and other documents required for entry under this chapter may be considered as permits to enter for the purposes of this section.

(June 27, 1952, c. 477, Title II, ch. 2, § 215, 66 Stat. 190; Pub.L. 95–426, Title VII, § 707(a)–(d), Oct. 7, 1978, 92 Stat. 992, 993.)

## § 216. Conditional permanent resident status for certain alien spouses and sons and daughters [8 U.S.C.A. § 1186a]

### (a) In general

#### (1) Conditional basis for status

Notwithstanding any other provision of this chapter, an alien spouse (as defined in subsection (g)(1) of this section) and an alien son or daughter (as defined in subsection (g)(2) of this section) shall be considered, at the time of obtaining the status of an alien lawfully admitted for permanent residence, to have obtained such status on a conditional basis subject to the provisions of this section.

#### (2) Notice of requirements

##### (A) At time of obtaining permanent residence

At the time an alien spouse or alien son or daughter obtains permanent resident status on a conditional basis under paragraph (1), the Attorney General shall provide for notice to such a spouse, son, or daughter respecting the provisions of this section and the requirements of subsection (c)(1) of this section to have the conditional basis of such status removed.

##### (B) At time of required petition

In addition, the Attorney General shall attempt to provide notice to such a spouse, son, or daughter, at or about the beginning of the 90-day period described in subsection (d)(2)(A) of this section, of the requirements of subsections (c)(1) of this section.

##### (C) Effect of failure to provide notice

The failure of the Attorney General to provide a notice under this paragraph shall not affect the enforcement of the provisions of this section with respect to such a spouse, son, or daughter.

### (b) Termination of status if finding that qualifying marriage improper

#### (1) In general

In the case of an alien with permanent resident status on a conditional basis under subsection (a), if the Attorney General determines, before the second anniversary of the alien's obtaining the status of lawful admission for permanent residence, that—

119

(A) the qualifying marriage—

(i) was entered into for the purpose of procuring an alien's entry as an immigrant, or

(ii) has been judicially annulled or terminated, other than through the death of a spouse; or

(B) a fee or other consideration was given (other than a fee or other consideration to an attorney for assistance in preparation of a lawful petition) for the filing of a petition under section 204(a) [8 U.S.C.A. § 1154(a)] or 214(d) [8 U.S.C.A. § 1184(d)] with respect to the alien; the Attorney General shall so notify the parties involved and, subject to paragraph (2), shall terminate the permanent resident status of the alien (or aliens) involved as of the date of the determination.

### (2) Hearing in deportation proceeding

Any alien whose permanent resident status is terminated under paragraph (1) may request a review of such determination in a proceeding to deport the alien. In such proceeding, the burden of proof shall be on the Attorney General to establish, by a preponderance of the evidence, that a condition described in paragraph (1) is met.

### (c) Requirements of timely petition and interview for removal of condition

#### (1) In general

In order for the conditional basis established under subsection (a) of this section for an alien spouse or an alien son or daughter to be removed—

(A) the alien spouse and the petitioning spouse (if not deceased) jointly must submit to the Attorney General, during the period described in subsection (d)(2) of this section, a petition which requests the removal of such conditional basis and which states, under penalty of perjury, the facts and information described in subsection (d)(1) of this section, and

(B) in accordance with subsection (d)(3) of this section, the alien spouse and the petitioning spouse (if not deceased) must appear for a personal interview before an officer or employee of the Service respecting the facts and information described in subsection (d)(1) of this section.

### (2) Termination of permanent resident status for failure to file petition or have personal interview

#### (A) In general

In the case of an alien with permanent resident status on a conditional basis under subsection (a) of this section, if—

(i) no petition is filed with respect to the alien in accordance with the provisions of paragraph (1)(A), or

(ii) unless there is good cause shown, the alien spouse and petitioning spouse fail to appear at the interview described in paragraph (1)(B),

the Attorney General shall terminate the permanent resident status of the alien as of the second anniversary of the alien's lawful admission for permanent residence.

**(B)** Hearing in deportation proceeding

In any deportation proceeding with respect to an alien whose permanent resident status is terminated under subparagraph (A), the burden of proof shall be on the alien to establish compliance with the conditions of paragraphs (1)(A) and (1)(B).

**(3) Determination after petition and interview**

**(A)** In general

If—

(i) a petition is filed in accordance with the provisions of paragraph (1)(A), and

(ii) the alien spouse and petitioning spouse appear at the interview described in paragraph (1)(B),

the Attorney General shall make a determination, within 90 days of the date of the interview, as to whether the facts and information described in subsection (d)(1) of this section and alleged in the petition are true with respect to the qualifying marriage.

**(B)** Removal of conditional basis if favorable determination

If the Attorney General determines that such facts and information are true, the Attorney General shall so notify the parties involved and shall remove the conditional basis of the parties effective as of the second anniversary of the alien's obtaining the status of lawful admission for permanent residence.

**(C)** Termination if adverse determination

If the Attorney General determines that such facts and information are not true, the Attorney General shall so notify the parties involved and, subject to subparagraph (D), shall terminate the permanent resident status of an alien spouse or an alien son or daughter as of the date of the determination.

**(D)** Hearing in deportation proceeding

Any alien whose permanent resident status is terminated under subparagraph (C) may request a review of such determination in a proceeding to deport the alien. In such proceeding, the burden of proof shall be on the Attorney General to establish, by a preponderance of the evidence, that the facts and information described in subsection (d)(1) of this section and alleged in the petition are not true with respect to the qualifying marriage.

### (4) Hardship waiver

The Attorney General, in the Attorney General's discretion, may remove the conditional basis of the permanent resident status for an alien who fails to meet the requirements of paragraph (1) if the alien demonstrates that—

(A) extreme hardship would result if such alien is deported,

(B) the qualifying marriage was entered into in good faith by the alien spouse, but the qualifying marriage has been terminated (other than through the death of the spouse) and the alien was not at fault in failing to meet the requirements of paragraph (1), or

(C) the qualifying marriage was entered into in good faith by the alien spouse and during the marriage the alien spouse or child was battered by or was the subject of extreme cruelty perpetrated by his or her spouse or citizen or permanent resident parent and the alien was not at fault in failing to meet the requirements of paragraph (1).

In determining extreme hardship, the Attorney General shall consider circumstances occurring only during the period that the alien was admitted for permanent residence on a conditional basis. The Attorney General shall, by regulation, establish measures to protect the confidentiality of information concerning any abused alien spouse or child, including information regarding the whereabouts of such spouse or child.

## (d) Details of petition and interview

### (1) Contents of petition

Each petition under subsection (c)(1)(A) of this section shall contain the following facts and information:

(A) Statement of proper marriage and petitioning process
The facts are that—

(i) the qualifying marriage—

(I) was entered into in accordance with the laws of the place where the marriage took place,

(II) has not been judicially annulled or terminated, other than through the death of a spouse, and

(III) was not entered into for the purpose of procuring an alien's entry as an immigrant; and

(ii) no fee or other consideration was given (other than a fee or other consideration to an attorney for assistance in preparation of a lawful petition) for the filing of a petition under section 204(a) [8 U.S.C.A. § 1154(a)] or 214(d) [8 U.S.C.A. § 1184(d)] with respect to the alien spouse or alien son or daughter.

**(B)** Statement of additional information

The information is a statement of—

(i) the actual residence of each party to the qualifying marriage since the date the alien spouse obtained permanent resident status on a conditional basis under subsection (a) of this section, and

(ii) the place of employment (if any) of each such party since such date, and the name of the employer of such party.

**(2) Period for filing petition**

**(A)** 90-day period before second anniversary

Except as provided in subparagraph (B), the petition under subsection (c)(1)(A) of this section must be filed during the 90-day period before the second anniversary of the alien's obtaining the status of lawful admission for permanent residence.

**(B)** Date of petitions for good cause

Such a petition may be considered if filed after such date, but only if the alien establishes to the satisfaction of the Attorney General good cause and extenuating circumstances for failure to file the petition during the period described in subparagraph (A).

**(C)** Filing of petitions during deportation

In the case of an alien who is the subject of deportation hearings as a result of failure to file a petition on a timely basis in accordance with subparagraph (A), the Attorney General may stay such deportation proceedings against an alien pending the filing of the petition under subparagraph (B).

**(3) Personal interview**

The interview under subsection (c)(1)(B) of this section shall be conducted within 90 days after the date of submitting a petition under subsection (c)(1)(A) of this section and at a local office of the Service, designated by the Attorney General, which is convenient to the parties involved. The Attorney General, in the Attorney General's discretion, may waive the deadline for such an interview or the requirement for such an interview in such cases as may be appropriate.

### (e) Treatment of period for purposes of naturalization

For purposes of subchapter III of this chapter, in the case of an alien who is in the United States as a lawful permanent resident on a conditional basis under this section, the alien shall be considered to have been admitted as an alien lawfully admitted for permanent residence and to be in the United States as an alien lawfully admitted to the United States for permanent residence.

### (f) Treatment of certain waivers

In the case of an alien who has permanent residence status on a conditional basis under this section, if, in order to obtain such status, the alien obtained a waiver under subsection (h) or (i) of section 212 [8 U.S.C.A. § 1182] of certain grounds of exclusion, such waiver terminates upon the termination of such permanent residence status under this section.

### (g) Definitions

In this section:

(1) The term "alien spouse" means an alien who obtains the status of an alien lawfully admitted for permanent residence (whether on a conditional basis or otherwise)—

(A) as an immediate relative (described in section 201(b) [8 U.S.C.A. § 1151(b)]) as the spouse of a citizen of the United States,

(B) under section 214(d) [8 U.S.C.A. § 1184(d)] as the fiancee or fiance of a citizen of the United States, or

(C) under section 203(a)(2) [8 U.S.C.A. § 1153(a)(2)] as the spouse of an alien lawfully admitted for permanent residence,

by virtue of a marriage which was entered into less than 24 months before the date the alien obtains such status by virtue of such marriage, but does not include such an alien who only obtains such status as a result of section 203(a)(8) [8 U.S.C.A. § 1153(a)(8)].

(2) The term "alien son or daughter" means an alien who obtains the status of an alien lawfully admitted for permanent residence (whether on a conditional basis or otherwise) by virtue of being the son or daughter of an individual through a qualifying marriage.

(3) The term "qualifying marriage" means the marriage described to in paragraph (1).

(4) The term "petitioning spouse" means the spouse of a qualifying marriage, other than the alien.

(June 27, 1952, c. 477, Title II, ch. 2, § 216, as added Pub.L. 99–639, § 2(a), Nov. 6, 1986, 100 Stat. 3537, and amended Pub.L. 100–525, § 7(a)(1), Oct. 24, 1988, 102 Stat. 2616; Pub.L. 100–525, § 7(a)(2), Oct. 24, 1988, 102 Stat. 2616; Pub.L. 101–649, Title VII, § 701(a), Nov. 29, 1990, 104 Stat. 5085.)

## § 216A. Conditional permanent resident status for certain alien entrepreneurs, spouses, and children [8 U.S.C.A. § 1186b]

### (a) In general

#### (1) Conditional basis for status

Notwithstanding any other provision of this chapter, an alien entrepreneur (as defined in subsection (f)(1) of this section), alien spouse, and alien child (as defined in subsection (f)(2) of this section) shall be considered, at the time of obtaining the status of an alien lawfully admitted for permanent residence, to have obtained such status on a conditional basis subject to the provisions of this section.

#### (2) Notice of requirements

**(A)** At time of obtaining permanent residence

At the time an alien entrepreneur, alien spouse, or alien child obtains permanent resident status on a conditional basis under paragraph (1), the Attorney General shall provide for notice to such an entrepreneur, spouse, or child respecting the provisions of this section and the requirements of subsection (c)(1) of this section to have the conditional basis of such status removed.

**(B)** At time of required petition

In addition, the Attorney General shall attempt to provide notice to such an entrepreneur, spouse, or child, at or about the beginning of the 90-day period described in subsection (d)(2)(A) of this section, of the requirements of subsection (c)(1) of this section.

**(C)** Effect of failure to provide notice

The failure of the Attorney General to provide a notice under this paragraph shall not affect the enforcement of the provisions of this section with respect to such an entrepreneur, spouse, or child.

### (b) Termination of status if finding that qualifying entrepreneurship improper

#### (1) In general

In the case of an alien entrepreneur with permanent resident status on a conditional basis under subsection (a) of this section, if the Attorney General determines, before the second anniversary of the alien's obtaining the status of lawful admission for permanent residence, that—

**(A)** the establishment of the commercial enterprise was intended solely as a means of evading the immigration laws of the United States,

**(B)(i)** a commercial enterprise was not established by the alien,

**(ii)** the alien did not invest or was not actively in the process of investing the requisite capital; or

**(iii)** the alien was not sustaining the actions described in clause (i) or (ii) throughout the period of the alien's residence in the United States, or

**(C)** the alien was otherwise not conforming to the requirements of section 203(b)(5) [8 U.S.C.A. § 1153(b)(5)],

then the Attorney General shall so notify the alien involved and, subject to paragraph (2), shall terminate the permanent resident status of the alien (and the alien spouse and alien child) involved as of the date of the determination.

### (2) Hearing in deportation proceeding

Any alien whose permanent resident status is terminated under paragraph (1) may request a review of such determination in a proceeding to deport the alien. In such proceeding, the burden of proof shall be on the Attorney General to establish, by a preponderance of the evidence, that a condition described in paragraph (1) is met.

### (c) Requirements of timely petition and interview for removal of condition

#### (1) In general

In order for the conditional basis established under subsection (a) of this section for an alien entrepreneur, alien spouse, or alien child to be removed—

**(A)** the alien entrepreneur must submit to the Attorney General, during the period described in subsection (d)(2) of this section, a petition which requests the removal of such conditional basis and which states, under penalty of perjury, the facts and information described in subsection (d)(1) of this section, and

**(B)** in accordance with subsection (d)(3) of this section, the alien entrepreneur must appear for a personal interview before an officer or employee of the Service respecting the facts and information described in subsection (d)(1) of this section.

### (2) Termination of permanent resident status for failure to file petition or have personal interview

**(A) In general**

In the case of an alien with permanent resident status on a conditional basis under subsection (a) of this section, if—

**(i)** no petition is filed with respect to the alien in accordance with the provisions of paragraph (1)(A), or

(ii) unless there is good cause shown, the alien entrepreneur fails to appear at the interview described in paragraph (1)(B) (if required under subsection (d)(3) of this section),

the Attorney General shall terminate the permanent resident status of the alien as of the second anniversary of the alien's lawful admission for permanent residence.

**(B)** Hearing in deportation proceeding

In any deportation proceeding with respect to an alien whose permanent resident status is terminated under subparagraph (A), the burden of proof shall be on the alien to establish compliance with the conditions of paragraphs (1)(A) and (1)(B).

**(3) Determination after petition and interview**

**(A)** In general

If—

(i) a petition is filed in accordance with the provisions of paragraph (1)(A), and

(ii) the alien entrepreneur appears at any interview described in paragraph (1)(B),

the Attorney General shall make a determination, within 90 days of the date of the such filing or interview (whichever is later), as to whether the facts and information described in subsection (d)(1) of this section and alleged in the petition are true with respect to the qualifying commercial enterprise.

**(B)** Removal of conditional basis if favorable determination

If the Attorney General determines that such facts and information are true, the Attorney General shall so notify the alien involved and shall remove the conditional basis of the alien's status effective as of the second anniversary of the alien's obtaining the status of lawful admission for permanent residence.

**(C)** Termination if adverse determination

If the Attorney General determines that such facts and information are not true, the Attorney General shall so notify the alien involved and, subject to subparagraph (D), shall terminate the permanent resident status of an alien entrepreneur, alien spouse, or alien child as of the date of the determination.

**(D)** Hearing in deportation proceeding

Any alien whose permanent resident status is terminated under subparagraph (C) may request a review of such determination in a proceeding to deport the alien. In such proceeding,

127

the burden of proof shall be on the Attorney General to establish, by a preponderance of the evidence, that the facts and information described in subsection (d)(1) of this section and alleged in the petition are not true with respect to the qualifying commercial enterprise.

## (d) Details of petition and interview

### (1) Contents of petition

Each petition under subsection (c)(1)(A) of this section shall contain facts and information demonstrating that—

**(A)** a commercial enterprise was established by the alien;

**(B)** the alien invested or was actively in the process of investing the requisite capital; and

**(C)** the alien sustained the actions described in subparagraphs (A) and (B) throughout the period of the alien's residence in the United States.

### (2) Period for filing petition

**(A)** 90-day period before second anniversary

Except as provided in subparagraph (B), the petition under subsection (c)(1)(A) of this section must be filed during the 90-day period before the second anniversary of the alien's obtaining the status of lawful admission for permanent residence.

**(B)** Date petitions for good cause

Such a petition may be considered if filed after such date, but only if the alien establishes to the satisfaction of the Attorney General good cause and extenuating circumstances for failure to file the petition during the period described in subparagraph (A).

**(C)** Filing of petitions during deportation

In the case of an alien who is the subject of deportation hearings as a result of failure to file a petition on a timely basis in accordance with subparagraph (A), the Attorney General may stay such deportation proceedings against an alien pending the filing of the petition under subparagraph (B).

### (3) Personal interview

The interview under subsection (c)(1)(B) of this section shall be conducted within 90 days after the date of submitting a petition under subsection (c)(1)(A) of this section and at a local office of the Service, designated by the Attorney General, which is convenient to the parties involved. The Attorney General, in the Attorney General's discretion, may waive the deadline for such an interview or the requirement for such an interview in such cases as may be appropriate.

### (e) Treatment of period for purposes of naturalization

For purposes of subchapter III of this chapter, in the case of an alien who is in the United States as a lawful permanent resident on a conditional basis under this section, the alien shall be considered to have been admitted as an alien lawfully admitted for permanent residence and to be in the United States as an alien lawfully admitted to the United States for permanent residence.

### (f) Definitions

In this section:

(1) The term "alien entrepreneur" means an alien who obtains the status of an alien lawfully admitted for permanent residence (whether on a conditional basis or otherwise) under section 203(b)(5) [8 U.S.C.A. § 1153(b)(5)].

(2) The term "alien spouse" and the term "alien child" mean an alien who obtains the status of an alien lawfully admitted for permanent residence (whether on a conditional basis or otherwise) by virtue of being the spouse or child, respectively, of an alien entrepreneur.

(June 27, 1952, c. 477, Title II, ch. 2, § 216A, as added Nov. 29, 1990, Pub.L. 101–649, Title I, § 121(b)(1), 104 Stat. 4990.)

## § 217. Visa waiver pilot program for certain visitors [8 U.S.C.A. § 1187]

### (a) Establishment of pilot program

The Attorney General and the Secretary of State are authorized to establish a pilot program (hereinafter in this section referred to as the "pilot program") under which the requirement of paragraph (26)(B) of section 212(a) [8 U.S.C.A. § 1182(a)(26)(B)] may be waived by the Attorney General and the Secretary of State, acting jointly and in accordance with this section, in the case of an alien who meets the following requirements:

### (1) Seeking entry as tourist for 90 days or less

The alien is applying for admission during the pilot program period (as defined in subsection (e)) as a nonimmigrant visitor (described in section 101(a)(15)(B) [8 U.S.C.A. § 1101(a)(15)(B)]) for a period not exceeding 90 days.

### (2) National of pilot program country

The alien is a national of, and presents a passport issued by, a country which—

(A) extends (or agrees to extend) reciprocal privileges to citizens and nationals of the United States, and

(B) is designated as a pilot program country under subsection (c) of this section.

### (3) Executes immigration forms

The alien before the time of such admission completes such immigration forms as the Attorney General shall establish.

### (4) Entry by sea or air

If arriving by sea or air, the alien arrives at the port of entry into the United States on a carrier which has entered into an agreement with the Service to guarantee transport of the alien out of the United States if the alien is found inadmissible or deportable by an immigration officer.

### (5) Not a safety threat

The alien has been determined not to represent a threat to the welfare, health, safety, or security of the United States.

### (6) No previous violation

If the alien previously was admitted without a visa under this section, the alien must not have failed to comply with the conditions of any previous admission as such a nonimmigrant.

### (7) Round-trip ticket

The alien is in possession of a round-trip transportation ticket (unless this requirement is waived by the Attorney General under regulations).

## (b) Waiver of rights

An alien may not be provided a waiver under the pilot program unless the alien has waived any right—

(1) to review or appeal under this chapter of an immigration officer's determination as to the admissibility of the alien at the port of entry into the United States, or

(2) to contest, other than on the basis of an application for asylum, any action for deportation against the alien.

## (c) Designation of pilot program countries

### (1) In general

The Attorney General and the Secretary of State acting jointly may designate any country as a pilot program country if it meets the requirements of paragraph (2).

### (2) Qualifications

A country may not be designated as a pilot program country unless the following requirements are met:

#### (A) Low nonimmigrant visa refusal rate for previous 2-year period

The average number of refusals of nonimmigrant visitor visas for nationals of that country during the two previous full fiscal years was less than 2.0 percent of the total number of nonimmigrant visitor visas for nationals of that country which were granted or refused during those years.

**(B)** Low nonimmigrant visa refusal rate for each of 2 previous years

The average number of refusals of nonimmigrant visitor visas for nationals of that country during either of such two previous full fiscal years was less than 2.5 percent of the total number of nonimmigrant visitor visas for nationals of that country which were granted or refused during that year.

**(C)** Machine readable passport program

The government of the country certifies that it has or is in the process of developing a program to issue machine-readable passports to its citizens.

**(D)** Law enforcement interests

The Attorney General determines that the United States law enforcement interests would not be compromised by the designation of the country.

**(3) Continuing and subsequent qualifications**

For each fiscal year (within the pilot program period) after the initial period—

**(A)** Continuing qualification

In the case of a country which was a pilot program country in the previous fiscal year, a country may not be designated as a pilot program country unless the sum of—

(i) the total of the number of nationals of that country who were excluded from admission or withdrew their application for admission during such previous fiscal year as a nonimmigrant visitor, and

(ii) the total number of nationals of that country who were admitted as nonimmigrant visitors during such previous fiscal year and who violated the terms of such admission,

was less than 2 percent of the total number of nationals of that country who applied for admission as nonimmigrant visitors during such previous fiscal year.

**(B)** New countries

In the case of another country, the country may not be designated as a pilot program country unless the following requirements are met:

(i) Low nonimmigrant visa refusal rate in previous 2-year period

The average number of refusals of nonimmigrant visitor visas for nationals of that country during the two previous full fiscal years was less than 2 percent of the total number of nonimmigrant visitor visas for nationals of that country which were granted or refused during those years.

(ii) Low nonimmigrant visa refusal rate in each of the 2 previous years

The average number of refusals of nonimmigrant visitor visas for nationals of that country during either of such two previous full fiscal years was less than 2.5 percent of the total number of nonimmigrant visitor visas for nationals of that country which were granted or refused during that year.

### (4) Initial period

For purposes of paragraphs (2) and (3), the term "initial period" means the period beginning at the end of the 30-day period described in subsection (b)(1) of this section and ending on the last day of the first fiscal year which begins after such 30-day period.

### (d) Authority

Notwithstanding any other provision of this section, the Attorney General and the Secretary of State, acting jointly, may for any reason (including national security) refrain from waiving the visa requirement in respect to nationals of any country which may otherwise qualify for designation or may, at any time, rescind any waiver or designation previously granted under this section.

### (e) Carrier agreements

### (1) In general

The agreement referred to in subsection (a)(4)(C) of this section is an agreement between a carrier and the Attorney General under which the carrier agrees, in consideration of the waiver of the visa requirement with respect to a nonimmigrant visitor under the pilot program—

(A) to indemnify the United States against any costs for the transportation of the alien from the United States if the visitor is refused admission to the United States or remains in the United States unlawfully after the 90-day period described in subsection (a)(1)(A) of this section,

(B) to submit daily to immigration officers any immigration forms received with respect to nonimmigrant visitors provided a waiver under the pilot program, and

(C) to be subject to the imposition of fines resulting from the transporting into the United States of a national of a designated country without a passport pursuant to regulations promulgated by the Attorney General.

### (2) Termination of agreements

The Attorney General may terminate an agreement under paragraph (1) with five days' notice to the carrier for the carrier's failure to meet the terms of such agreement.

### (f) Definition of pilot program period

For purposes of this section, the term "pilot program period" means the period beginning on October 1, 1988, and ending on September 30, 1994.

(June 27, 1952, c. 477, Title II, ch. 2, § 217, as added Pub.L. 99–603, Title III, § 313(a), Nov. 6, 1986, 100 Stat. 3435, and amended Pub.L. 100–525, § 2(p)(1), Oct. 24, 1988, 102 Stat. 2613; Pub.L. 100–525, § 2(p)(2), Oct 24, 1988, 102 Stat. 2613; Pub.L. 101–649, Title II, § 201(a), Nov. 29, 1990, 104 Stat. 5012.)

## § 218. Admission of temporary H–2A workers [8 U.S. C.A. § 1188]

### (a) Conditions for approval of H–2A petitions

(1) A petition to import an alien as an H–2A worker (as defined in subsection (i)(2) of this section) may not be approved by the Attorney General unless the petitioner has applied to the Secretary of Labor for a certification that—

    (A) there are not sufficient workers who are able, willing, and qualified, and who will be available at the time and place needed, to perform the labor or services involved in the petition, and

    (B) the employment of the alien in such labor or services will not adversely affect the wages and working conditions of workers in the United States similarly employed.

(2) The Secretary of Labor may require by regulation, as a condition of issuing the certification, the payment of a fee to recover the reasonable costs of processing applications for certification.

### (b) Conditions for denial of labor certification

The Secretary of Labor may not issue a certification under subsection (a) of this section with respect to an employer if the conditions described in that subsection are not met or if any of the following conditions are met:

    (1) There is a strike or lockout in the course of a labor dispute which, under the regulations, precludes such certification.

    (2)(A) The employer during the previous two-year period employed H–2A workers and the Secretary of Labor has determined, after notice and opportunity for a hearing, that the employer at any time during that period substantially violated a material term or condition of the labor certification with respect to the employment of domestic or nonimmigrant workers.

    (B) No employer may be denied certification under subparagraph (A) for more than three years for any violation described in such subparagraph.

(3) The employer has not provided the Secretary with satisfactory assurances that if the employment for which the certification is sought is not covered by State workers' compensation law, the employer will provide, at no cost to the worker, insurance covering injury and disease arising out of and in the course of the worker's employment which will provide benefits at least equal to those provided under the State workers' compensation law for comparable employment.

(4) The Secretary determines that the employer has not made positive recruitment efforts within a multi-state region of traditional or expected labor supply where the Secretary finds that there are a significant number of qualified United States workers who, if recruited, would be willing to make themselves available for work at the time and place needed. Positive recruitment under this paragraph is in addition to, and shall be conducted within the same time period as, the circulation through the interstate employment service system of the employer's job offer. The obligation to engage in positive recruitment under this paragraph shall terminate on the date the H–2A workers depart for the employer's place of employment.

### (c) Special rules for consideration of applications

The following rules shall apply in the case of the filing and consideration of an application for a labor certification under this section:

#### (1) Deadline for filing applications

The Secretary of Labor may not require that the application be filed more than 60 days before the first date the employer requires the labor or services of the H–2A worker.

#### (2) Notice within seven days of deficiencies

(A) The employer shall be notified in writing within seven days of the date of filing if the application does not meet the standards (other than that described in subsection (a)(1)(A) of this section) for approval.

(B) If the application does not meet such standards, the notice shall include the reasons therefor and the Secretary shall provide an opportunity for the prompt resubmission of a modified application.

#### (3) Issuance of certification

(A) The Secretary of Labor shall make, not later than 20 days before the date such labor or services are first required to be performed, the certification described in subsection (a)(1) of this section if—

(i) the employer has complied with the criteria for certification (including criteria for the recruitment of eligible individuals as prescribed by the Secretary), and

(ii) the employer does not actually have, or has not been provided with referrals of, qualified eligible individuals who have indicated their availability to perform such labor or services on the terms and conditions of a job offer which meets the requirements of the Secretary.

In considering the question of whether a specific qualification is appropriate in a job offer, the Secretary shall apply the normal and accepted qualifications required by non-H–2A-employers in the same or comparable occupations and crops.

**(B)(i)** For a period of 3 years subsequent to the effective date of this section, labor certifications shall remain effective only if, from the time the foreign worker departs for the employer's place of employment, the employer will provide employment to any qualified United States worker who applies to the employer until 50 percent of the period of the work contract, under which the foreign worker who is in the job was hired, has elapsed. In addition, the employer will offer to provide benefits, wages and working conditions required pursuant to this section and regulations.

**(ii)** The requirement of clause (i) shall not apply to any employer who—

**(I)** did not, during any calendar quarter during the preceding calendar year, use more than 500 man-days of agricultural labor, as defined in section 203(u) of Title 29,

**(II)** is not a member of an association which has petitioned for certification under this section for its members, and

**(III)** has not otherwise associated with other employers who are petitioning for temporary foreign workers under this section.

**(iii)** Six months before the end of the 3-year period described in clause (i), the Secretary of Labor shall consider the findings of the report mandated by section 403(a)(4)(D) of the Immigration Reform and Control Act of 1986 [8 U.S.C.A. § 1186 note] as well as other relevant materials, including evidence of benefits to United States workers and costs to employers, addressing the advisability of continuing a policy which requires an employer, as a condition for certification under this section, to continue to accept qualified, eligible United States workers for employment after the date the H–2A workers depart for work with the employer. The Secretary's review of such findings and materials shall lead to the issuance of findings in furtherance of the Congressional policy that aliens not be admitted under this section unless there are not sufficient workers in the United States who are able, willing, and qualified to perform the labor or service needed and that the employment of the aliens in such labor or services will not adversely affect the wages and working conditions of workers in the United States similarly employed. In the absence of the enactment of Federal legislation prior to three months before the end of the 3-year period described in clause (i) which addresses the subject matter of this subparagraph, the Secretary shall immediately publish the findings required by this clause, and shall promulgate, on an interim or final basis, regulations based on his findings which shall be effective no later than three years from the effective date of this section.

(**iv**) In complying with clause (i) of this subparagraph, an association shall be allowed to refer or transfer workers among its members: *Provided,* That for purposes of this section an association acting as an agent for its members shall not be considered a joint employer merely because of such referral or transfer.

(**v**) United States workers referred or transferred pursuant to clause (iv) of this subparagraph shall not be treated disparately.

(**vi**) An employer shall not be liable for payments under section 655.202(b)(6) of title 20, Code of Federal Regulations (or any successor regulation) with respect to an H–2A worker who is displaced due to compliance with the requirement of this subparagraph, if the Secretary of Labor certifies that the H–2A worker was displaced because of the employer's compliance with clause (i) of this subparagraph.

(**vii**)(**I**) No person or entity shall willfully and knowingly withhold domestic workers prior to the arrival of H–2A workers in order to force the hiring of domestic workers under clause (i).

(**II**) Upon the receipt of a complaint by an employer that a violation of subclause (I) has occurred the Secretary shall immediately investigate. He shall within 36 hours of the receipt of the complaint issue findings concerning the alleged violation. Where the Secretary finds that a violation has occurred, he shall immediately suspend the application of clause (i) of this subparagraph with respect to that certification for that date of need.

**(4) Housing**

Employers shall furnish housing in accordance with regulations. The employer shall be permitted at the employer's option to provide housing meeting applicable Federal standards for temporary labor camps or to secure housing which meets the local standards for rental and/or public accommodations or other substantially similar class of habitation: *Provided,* That in the absence of applicable local standards, State standards for rental and/or public accommodations or other substantially similar class of habitation shall be met: *Provided further,* That in the absence of applicable local or State standards, Federal temporary labor camp standards shall apply: *Provided further,* That the Secretary of Labor shall issue regulations which address the specific requirements of housing for employees principally engaged in the range production of livestock: *Provided further,* That when it is the prevailing practice in the area and occupation of intended employment to provide family housing, family housing shall be provided to workers with families who request it: *And provided further,* That nothing in this paragraph shall require an employer to provide or secure housing for workers who are not entitled to it under the temporary labor certification regulations in effect on June 1, 1986.

### (d) Roles of agricultural associations

#### (1) Permitting filing by agricultural associations

A petition to import an alien as a temporary agricultural worker, and an application for a labor certification with respect to such a worker, may be filed by an association of agricultural producers which use agricultural services.

#### (2) Treatment of associations acting as employers

If an association is a joint or sole employer of temporary agricultural workers, the certifications granted under this section to the association may be used for the certified job opportunities of any of its producer members and such workers may be transferred among its producer members to perform agricultural services of a temporary or seasonal nature for which the certifications were granted.

#### (3) Treatment of violations

**(A)** Member's violation does not necessarily disqualify association or other members

If an individual producer member of a joint employer association is determined to have committed an act that under subsection (b)(2) of this section results in the denial of certification with respect to the member, the denial shall apply only to that member of the association unless the Secretary determines that the association or other member participated in, had knowledge of, or reason to know of, the violation.

**(B)** Association's violation does not necessarily disqualify members

**(i)** If an association representing agricultural producers as a joint employer is determined to have committed an act that under subsection (b)(2) of this section results in the denial of certification with respect to the association, the denial shall apply only to the association and does not apply to any individual producer member of the association unless the Secretary determines that the member participated in, had knowledge of, or reason to know of, the violation.

**(ii)** If an association of agricultural producers certified as a sole employer is determined to have committed an act that under subsection (b)(2) of this section results in the denial of certification with respect to the association, no individual producer member of such association may be the beneficiary of the services of temporary alien agricultural workers admitted under this section in the commodity and occupation in which such aliens were employed by the association which was denied certification during the period such denial is in force, unless such producer member employs such aliens in the commodity and occupation in question directly or through an association which is a joint employer of such workers with the producer member.

### (e) Expedited administrative appeals of certain determinations

(1) Regulations shall provide for an expedited procedure for the review of a denial of certification under subsection (a)(1) of this section or a revocation of such a certification or, at the applicant's request, for a de novo administrative hearing respecting the denial or revocation.

(2) The Secretary of Labor shall expeditiously, but in no case later than 72 hours after the time a new determination is requested, make a new determination on the request for certification in the case of an H–2A worker if able, willing, and qualified eligible individuals are not actually available at the time such labor or services are required and a certification was denied in whole or in part because of the availability of qualified workers. If the employer asserts that any eligible individual who has been referred is not able, willing, or qualified, the burden of proof is on the employer to establish that the individual referred is not able, willing, or qualified because of employment-related reasons.

### (f) Violators disqualified for 5 years

An alien may not be admitted to the United States as a temporary agricultural worker if the alien was admitted to the United States as such a worker within the previous five-year period and the alien during that period violated a term or condition of such previous admission.

### (g) Authorizations of Appropriations

(1) There are authorized to be appropriated for each fiscal year, beginning with fiscal year 1987, $10,000,000 for the purposes—

(A) of recruiting domestic workers for temporary labor and services which might otherwise be performed by nonimmigrants described in section 101(a)(15)(H)(ii)(a) [8 U.S.C.A. § 1101(a)(15)(H)(ii)(a)], and

(B) of monitoring terms and conditions under which such nonimmigrants (and domestic workers employed by the same employers) are employed in the United States.

(2) The Secretary of Labor is authorized to take such actions, including imposing appropriate penalties and seeking appropriate injunctive relief and specific performance of contractual obligations, as may be necessary to assure employer compliance with terms and conditions of employment under this section.

(3) There are authorized to be appropriated for each fiscal year, beginning with fiscal year 1987, such sums as may be necessary for the purpose of enabling the Secretary of Labor to make determinations and certifications under this section and under section 212(a)(14) [8 U.S.C.A. § 1182(a)(14)].

(4) There are authorized to be appropriated for each fiscal year, beginning with fiscal year 1987, such sums as may be necessary for the purposes of enabling the Secretary of Agriculture to carry out the Secretary's duties and responsibilities under this section.

### (h) Miscellaneous Provisions

(1) The Attorney General shall provide for such endorsement of entry and exit documents of nonimmigrants described in section 101(a)(15)(H)(ii) [8 U.S.C.A. § 1101(a)(15)(H)(ii)] as may be necessary to carry out this section and to provide notice for purposes of section 274A [8 U.S.C.A. § 1324a].

(2) The provisions of subsections (a) and (c) of section 214 [8 U.S.C.A. § 1184(a) and (c)] and the provisions of this section preempt any State or local law regulating admissibility of nonimmigrant workers.

### (i) Definitions

For purposes of this section:

(1) The term "eligible individual" means, with respect to employment, an individual who is not an unauthorized alien (as defined in section 274A(h) [8 U.S.C.A. § 1324a(h)]) with respect to that employment.

(2) The term "H–2A worker" means a nonimmigrant described in section 101(a)(15)(H)(ii)(a) [8 U.S.C.A. § 1101(a)(15)(H)(ii)(a)].

(June 27, 1952, c. 477, Title II, ch. 2, § 218, formerly § 216, as added Pub.L. 99–603, Title III, § 301(c), Nov. 6, 1986, 100 Stat. 3411, renumbered and amended Pub.L. 100–525, § 2(*l*)(2), (3), Oct. 24, 1988, 102 Stat. 2612.)

## CHAPTER III—ISSUANCE OF ENTRY DOCUMENTS

## § 221. Issuance of visas [8 U.S.C.A. § 1201]

### (a) Immigrants; nonimmigrants

Under the conditions hereinafter prescribed and subject to the limitations prescribed in this chapter or regulations issued thereunder, a consular officer may issue (1) to an immigrant who has made proper application therefor, an immigrant visa which shall consist of the application provided for in section 222 [8 U.S.C.A. § 1202], visaed by such consular officer, and shall specify the foreign state, if any, to which the immigrant is charged, the immigrant's particular status under such foreign state, the preference, nonpreference, immediate relative, or special immigrant classification to which the alien is charged, the date on which the validity of the visa shall expire, and such additional information as may be required; and (2) to a nonimmigrant who has made proper application therefor, a nonimmigrant visa, which shall specify the classification under section 101(a)(15) [8 U.S.C.A. § 1101(a)(15)] of the nonimmigrant, the period during which the nonimmigrant visa shall be valid, and such additional information as may be required.

### (b) Registration; photographs; waiver of requirement

Each alien who applies for a visa shall be registered in connection with his application, and shall furnish copies of his photograph signed by him for such use as may be by regulations required. The requirements of this subsection may be waived in the discretion of the Secretary of State in the case of any alien who is within that class of nonimmigrants enumerated in sections 101(a)(15)(A) [8 U.S.C.A. § 1101(a)(15)(A)], and 101(a)(15)(G) [8 U.S.C.A. § 1101(a)(15)(G)], or in the case of any alien who is granted a diplomatic visa on a diplomatic passport or on the equivalent thereof.

### (c) Period of validity; requirement of immigrant visa

An immigrant visa shall be valid for such period, not exceeding four months, as shall be by regulations prescribed, except that any visa issued to a child lawfully adopted by a United States citizen and spouse while such citizen is serving abroad in the United States Armed Forces, or is employed abroad by the United States Government, or is temporarily abroad on business, shall be valid until such time, for a period not to exceed three years, as the adoptive citizen parent returns to the United States in due course of his service, employment, or business. A nonimmigrant visa shall be valid for such periods as shall be by regulations prescribed. In prescribing the period of validity of a nonimmigrant visa in the case of nationals of any foreign country who are eligible for such visas, the Secretary of State shall, insofar as practicable, accord to such nationals the same treatment upon a reciprocal basis as such foreign country accords to nationals of the United States who are within a similar class. An immigrant visa may be replaced under the original number during the fiscal year in which the original visa was issued for an immigrant who establishes to the satisfaction of the consular officer that he was unable to use the original immigrant visa during the period of its validity because of reasons beyond his control and for which he was not responsible: *Provided,* That the immigrant is found by the consular officer to be eligible for an immigrant visa and the immigrant pays again the statutory fees for an application and an immigrant visa.

### (d) Physical examination

Prior to the issuance of an immigrant visa to any alien, the consular officer shall require such alien to submit to a physical and mental examination in accordance with such regulations as may be prescribed. Prior to the issuance of a nonimmigrant visa to any alien, the consular officer may require such alien to submit to a physical or mental examination, or both, if in his opinion such examination is necessary to ascertain whether such alien is eligible to receive a visa.

### (e) Surrender of visa

Each immigrant shall surrender his immigrant visa to the immigration officer at the port of entry, who shall endorse on the visa the date and the port of arrival, the identity of the vessel or other means of transportation by which the immigrant arrived, and such other endorsements as may be by regulations required.

### (f) Surrender of documents

Each nonimmigrant shall present or surrender to the immigration officer at the port of entry such documents as may be by regulation required. In the case of an alien crewman not in possession of any individual documents other than a passport and until such time as it becomes practicable to issue individual documents, such alien crewman may be admitted, subject to the provisions of this part, if his name appears in the crew list of the vessel or aircraft on which he arrives and the crew list is visaed by a consular officer, but the consular officer shall have the right to exclude any alien crewman from the crew list visa.

### (g) Non-issuance of visas or other documents

No visa or other documentation shall be issued to an alien if (1) it appears to the consular officer, from statements in the application, or in the papers submitted therewith, that such alien is ineligible to receive a visa or such other documentation under section 212 [8 U.S.C.A. § 1182], or any other provision of law, (2) the application fails to comply with the provisions of this chapter, or the regulations issued thereunder, or (3) the consular officer knows or has reason to believe that such alien is ineligible to receive a visa or such other documentation under section 212 [8 U.S.C.A. § 1182], or any other provision of law: *Provided,* That a visa or other documentation may be issued to an alien who is within the purview of section 212(a)(4) [8 U.S.C.A. § 1182(a)(4)], if such alien is otherwise entitled to receive a visa or other documentation, upon receipt of notice by the consular officer from the Attorney General of the giving of a bond or undertaking providing indemnity as in the case of aliens admitted under section 213 [8 U.S.C.A. § 1183]: *Provided further,* That a visa may be issued to an alien defined in section 101(a)(15)(B) or (F) [8 U.S.C.A. § 1101(a)(15)(B) or (F)], if such alien is otherwise entitled to receive a visa, upon receipt of a notice by the consular officer from the Attorney General of the giving of a bond with sufficient surety in such sum and containing such conditions as the consular officer shall prescribe, to insure that at the expiration of the time for which such alien has been admitted by the Attorney General, as provided in section 214(a) [8 U.S.C.A. § 1184(a)], or upon failure to maintain the status under which he was admitted, or to maintain any status subsequently acquired under section 248 [8 U.S.C.A. § 1258], such alien will depart from the United States.

### (h) Nonadmission upon arrival

Nothing in this chapter shall be construed to entitle any alien, to whom a visa or other documentation has been issued, to enter the United States, if, upon arrival at a port of entry in the United States, he is found to be inadmissible under this chapter, or any other provision of law. The substance of this subsection shall appear upon every visa application.

### (i) Revocation of visas or documents

After the issuance of a visa or other documentation to any alien, the consular officer or the Secretary of State may at any time, in his discretion, revoke such visa or other documentation. Notice of such revocation shall be communicated to the Attorney General, and such revocation shall invalidate the visa or other documentation from the date of issuance: *Provided,* That carriers or transportation companies, and masters, commanding officers, agents, owners, charterers, or consignees, shall not be penalized under section 273(b) [8 U.S.C.A. § 1323(b)] for action taken in reliance on such visas or other documentation, unless they received due notice of such revocation prior to the alien's embarkation.

(June 27, 1952, c. 477, Title II, ch. 3, § 221, 66 Stat. 191; Pub.L. 87–301, § 4, Sept. 26, 1961, 75 Stat. 651; Pub.L. 89–236, §§ 11(a), (b), 17, Oct. 3, 1965, 79 Stat. 918, 919; Pub.L. 97–116, § 18(f), Dec. 29, 1981, 95 Stat. 1620; Pub.L. 99–653, § 5(1)–(3), formerly § 5(a)–(c), Nov. 14, 1986, 100 Stat. 3656, renumbered Pub.L. 100–525, § 8(d)(1), Oct. 24, 1988, 102 Stat. 2617; Pub.L. 101–649, Title VI, § 603(a)(9), Nov. 29, 1990, 104 Stat. 5083.)

## § 222. Application for visas [8 U.S.C.A. § 1202]

### (a) Immigrant visas

Every alien applying for an immigrant visa and for alien registration shall make application therefor in such form and manner and at such place as shall be by regulations prescribed. In the application the immigrant shall state his full and true name, and any other name which he has used or by which he has been known; age and sex; the date and place of his birth; present address and places of previous residence; whether married or single, and the names and places of residence of spouse and children, if any; calling or occupation; personal description (including height, complexion, color of hair and eyes, and marks of identification); languages he can speak, read, or write; names and addresses of parents, and if neither parent living then the name and address of his next of kin in the country from which he comes; port of entry into the United States; final destination, if any, beyond the port of entry; whether he has a ticket through to such final destination; whether going to join a relative or friend, and, if so, the name and complete address of such relative or friend; the purpose for which he is going to the United States; the length of time he intends to remain in the United States; whether or not he intends to remain in the United States permanently; whether he was ever arrested, convicted or was ever in prison or almshouse; whether he has ever been the beneficiary of a pardon or an amnesty; whether he has ever been treated in an institution or hospital or other place for insanity or other mental disease; if he claims to be an immediate relative within the meaning of section 201(b) [8 U.S.C.A. § 1151(b)] or a preference or special immigrant, the facts on which he bases such claim; whether or not he is a member of any class of individuals excluded from admission into the United States, or whether he claims to be exempt from exclusion under the immigration laws; and such additional information necessary to the identification of the applicant and the enforcement of the immigration and nationality laws as may be by regulations prescribed.

### (b) Other documentary evidence for immigrant visa

Every alien applying for an immigrant visa shall present a valid unexpired passport or other suitable travel document, or document of identity and nationality, if such document is required under the regulations issued by the Secretary of State. The immigrant shall furnish to the consular officer with his application a copy of a certification by the appropriate police authorities stating what their records show concerning the immigrant; a certified copy of any existing prison record, military record, and record of his birth; and a certified copy of all other records or documents concerning him or his case which may be required by the consular officer. The copy of each document so furnished shall be permanently attached to the application and become a part thereof. In the event that the immigrant establishes to the satisfaction of the consular officer that any document or record required by this subsection is unobtainable, the consular officer may permit the immigrant to submit in lieu of such document or record other satisfactory evidence of the fact to which such document or record would, if obtainable, pertain.

### (c) Nonimmigrant visas; immigrant registration; form, manner and contents of application

Every alien applying for a nonimmigrant visa and for alien registration shall make application therefor in such form and manner as shall be by regulations prescribed. In the application the alien shall state his full and true name, the date and place of birth, his nationality, the purpose and length of his intended stay in the United States; personal description (including height, complexion, color of hair and eyes, and marks of identification); his marital status; and such additional information necessary to the identification of the applicant and the enforcement of the immigration and nationality laws as may be by regulations prescribed.

### (d) Other documentary evidence for nonimmigrant visa

Every alien applying for a nonimmigrant visa and alien registration shall furnish to the consular officer, with his application, a certi-

143

fied copy of such documents pertaining to him as may be by regulations required.

### (e) Signing and verification of application

Except as may be otherwise prescribed by regulations, each application required by this section shall be signed by the applicant in the presence of the consular officer, and verified by the oath of the applicant administered by the consular officer. The application for an immigrant visa, when visaed by the consular officer, shall become the immigrant visa. The application for a nonimmigrant visa or other documentation as a nonimmigrant shall be disposed of as may be by regulations prescribed. The issuance of a nonimmigrant visa shall, except as may be otherwise by regulations prescribed, be evidenced by a stamp placed by the consular officer in the alien's passport.

### (f) Confidential nature of records

The records of the Department of State and of diplomatic and consular offices of the United States pertaining to the issuance or refusal of visas or permits to enter the United States shall be considered confidential and shall be used only for the formulation, amendment, administration, or enforcement of the immigration, nationality, and other laws of the United States, except that in the discretion of the Secretary of State certified copies of such records may be made available to a court which certifies that the information contained in such records is needed by the court in the interest of the ends of justice in a case pending before the court.

(June 27, 1952, c. 477, Title II, ch. 3, § 222, 66 Stat. 193; Pub. L. 87–301, § 6, Sept. 26, 1961, 75 Stat. 653; Pub. L. 89–236, § 11(c), Oct. 3, 1965, 79 Stat. 918; Pub.L. 99–653, § 6, Nov. 14, 1986, 100 Stat. 3656; Pub.L. 99–653, § 6, as amended Pub.L. 100–525, § 8(e), Oct. 24, 1988, 102 Stat. 2617; Pub.L. 100–525, § 9(j), Oct. 24, 1988, 102 Stat. 2620.)

## § 223.  Re-entry permit [8 U.S.C.A. § 1203]

### (a) Application; contents

(1) Any alien lawfully admitted for permanent residence, or (2) any alien lawfully admitted to the United States pursuant to clause 6 of section 3 of the Immigration Act of 1924, between July 1, 1924, and July 5, 1932, both dates inclusive, who intends to depart temporarily from the United States may make application to the Attorney General for a permit to reenter the United States, stating the length of his intended absence or absences, and the reasons therefor. Such applications shall be made under oath, and shall be in such form, contain such information, and be accompanied by such photographs of the applicant as may be by regulations prescribed.

### (b) Issuance of permit; nonrenewability

If the Attorney General finds (1) that the applicant under subsection (a)(1) of this section has been lawfully admitted to the United

States for permanent residence, or that the applicant under subsection (a)(2) of this section has since admission maintained the status required of him at the time of his admission and such applicant desires to visit abroad and to return to the United States to resume the status existing at the time of his departure for such visit, (2) that the application is made in good faith, and (3) that the alien's proposed departure from the United States would not be contrary to the interests of the United States, the Attorney General may, in his discretion, issue the permit, which shall be valid for not more than two years from the date of issuance and shall not be renewable. The permit shall be in such form as shall be by regulations prescribed for the complete identification of the alien.

### (c) Multiple reentries

During the period of validity, such permit may be used by the alien in making one or more applications for reentry into the United States.

### (d) Presented and surrendered

Upon the return of the alien to the United States the permit shall be presented to the immigration officer at the port of entry, and upon the expiration of its validity, the permit shall be surrendered to the Service.

### (e) Permit in lieu of visa

A permit issued under this section in the possession of the person to whom issued, shall be accepted in lieu of any visa which otherwise would be required from such person under this chapter. Otherwise a permit issued under this section shall have no effect under the immigration laws except to show that the alien to whom it was issued is returning from a temporary visit abroad; but nothing in this section shall be construed as making such permit the exclusive means of establishing that the alien is so returning.

(June 27, 1952, c. 477, Title II, ch. 3, § 223, 66 Stat. 194; Pub. L. 97–116, § 6, Dec. 29, 1981, 95 Stat. 1615.)

## § 224. Immediate relative and special immigrant visas [8 U.S.C.A. § 1204]

A consular officer may, subject to the limitations provided in section 1201 of this title, issue an immigrant visa to a special immigrant or immediate relative as such upon satisfactory proof, under regulations prescribed under this chapter, that the applicant is entitled to special immigrant or immediate relative status.

(June 27, 1952, c. 477, Title II, ch. 3, § 224, 66 Stat. 195; Pub. L. 89–236, § 11(d), Oct. 3, 1965, 79 Stat. 918.)

## Chapter IV—Provisions Relating to Entry and Exclusion

## § 231. Lists of alien and citizen passengers arriving and departing [8 U.S.C.A. § 1221]

**(a) Shipment or aircraft manifest; arrival; form and contents; exclusions**

Upon the arrival of any person by water or by air at any port within the United States from any place outside the United States, it shall be the duty of the master or commanding officer, or authorized agent, owner, or consignee of the vessel or aircraft, having any such person on board to deliver to the immigration officers at the port of arrival typewritten or printed lists or manifests of the persons on board such vessel or aircraft. Such lists or manifests shall be prepared at such time, be in such form and shall contain such information as the Attorney General shall prescribe by regulation as being necessary for the identification of the persons transported and for the enforcement of the immigration laws. This subsection shall not require the master or commanding officer, or authorized agent, owner, or consignee of a vessel or aircraft to furnish a list or manifest relating (1) to an alien crewman or (2) to any other person arriving by air on a trip originating in foreign contiguous territory, except (with respect to such arrivals by air) as may be required by regulations issued pursuant to section 239 [8 U.S.C.A. § 1229].

**(b) Departure; shipment or aircraft manifest; form and contents; exclusions**

It shall be the duty of the master or commanding officer or authorized agent of every vessel or aircraft taking passengers on board at any port of the United States, who are destined to any place outside the United States, to file with the immigration officers before departure from such port a list of all such persons taken on board. Such list shall be in such form, contain such information, and be accompanied by such documents, as the Attorney General shall prescribe by regulation as necessary for the identification of the persons so transported and for the enforcement of the immigration laws. No master or commanding officer of any such vessel or aircraft shall be granted clearance papers for his vessel or aircraft until he or the authorized agent has deposited such list or lists and accompanying documents with the immigration officer at such port and made oath that they are full and complete as to the information required to be contained therein, except that in the case of vessels or aircraft which the Attorney General determines are making regular trips to ports of the United States, the Attorney General may, when expedient, arrange for the delivery of lists of outgoing persons at a later date. This subsection shall not require the master or commanding officer, or authorized agent, owner, or consignee of a vessel or aircraft to furnish a list or manifest relating (1) to an alien crewman or (2) to any other person departing by air on a trip originating in the United States who is destined to foreign contiguous territory, except (with respect to such departure by air) as may be required by regulations issued pursuant to section 239 [8 U.S.C.A. § 1229].

### (c) Record of citizens and resident aliens leaving permanently for foreign countries

The Attorney General may authorize immigration officers to record the following information regarding every resident person leaving the United States by way of the Canadian or Mexican borders for permanent residence in a foreign country: Names, age, and sex; whether married or single; calling or occupation; whether able to read or write; nationality; country of birth; country of which citizen or subject; race; last permanent residence in the United States; intended future permanent residence; and time and port of last arrival in the United States; and if a United States citizen or national, the facts on which claim to that status is based.

### (d) Penalties against noncomplying shipments or aircraft

If it shall appear to the satisfaction of the Attorney General that the master or commanding officer, owner, or consignee of any vessel or aircraft, or the agent of any transportation line, as the case may be, has refused or failed to deliver any list or manifest required by subsection (a) or (b) of this section, or that the list or manifest delivered is not accurate and full, such master or commanding officer, owner, or consignee, or agent, as the case may be, shall pay to the Commissioner the sum of $300 for each person concerning whom such accurate and full list or manifest is not furnished, or concerning whom the manifest or list is not prepared and sworn to as prescribed by this section or by regulations issued pursuant thereto. No vessel or aircraft shall be granted clearance pending determination of the question of the liability to the payment of such penalty, or while it remains unpaid, and no such penalty shall be remitted or refunded, except that clearance may be granted prior to the determination of such question upon the deposit with the collector of customs of a bond or undertaking approved by the Attorney General or a sum sufficient to cover such penalty.

### (e) Waiver of requirements

The Attorney General is authorized to prescribe the circumstances and conditions under which the list or manifest requirements of subsections (a) and (b) of this section may be waived.

(June 27, 1952, c. 477, Title II, ch. 4, § 231, 66 Stat. 195; Pub. L. 97–116, § 18(g), Dec. 29, 1981, 95 Stat. 1620; Pub.L. 101–649, Title V, § 543(a)(1), Nov. 29, 1990, 104 Stat. 5057.)

## § 232. Detention of aliens for observation and examination upon arrival [8 U.S.C.A. § 1222]

For the purpose of determining whether aliens (including alien crewmen) arriving at ports of the United States belong to any of the classes excluded by this chapter, by reason of being afflicted with any of the diseases or mental or physical defects or disabilities set forth in section 212(a) [8 U.S.C.A. § 1182(a)], or whenever the Attorney General has received information showing that any aliens are coming from a country or have embarked at a place where any of such diseases are prevalent or epidemic, such aliens shall be detained by the Attorney General, for a sufficient time to enable the immigration officers and medical officers to subject such aliens to observation and an examination sufficient to determine whether or not they belong to the excluded classes.

(June 27, 1952, c. 477, Title II, ch. 4, § 232, 66 Stat. 196; Pub.L. 99–500, Title I, § 101(b) [Title II, § 206(a), formerly § 206], Oct. 18, 1986, 100 Stat. 1783–56, as renumbered and amended Pub.L. 100–525, § 4(b)(1), (2), Oct. 24, 1988, 102 Stat. 2615.)

## § 233. Repealed. Pub.L. 99–500, Title I, § 101(b) [Title II, § 206(a), formerly § 206], Oct. 18, 1986, 100 Stat. 1783–56, renumbered and amended Pub.L. 100–525, § 4(b)(1), (3), Oct. 24, 1988, 102 Stat. 2615 [8 U.S.C.A. § 1223]

## § 234. Physical and mental examinations; appeal of findings [8 U.S.C.A. § 1224]

The physical and mental examination of arriving aliens (including alien crewmen) shall be made by medical officers of the United States Public Health Service, who shall conduct all medical examinations and shall certify, for the information of the immigration officers and the special inquiry officers, any physical and mental defect or disease observed by such medical officers in any such alien. If medical officers of the United States Public Health Service are not available, civil surgeons of not less than four years' professional experience may be employed for such service upon such terms as may be prescribed by the Attorney General. Aliens (including alien crewmen) arriving at ports of the United States shall be examined by at least one such medical officer or civil surgeon under such administrative regulations as the Attorney General may prescribe, and under medical regulations prepared by the Secretary of Health and Human Services. Medical officers of the United States Public Health Service who have had special training in the diagnosis of insanity and mental defects shall be detailed for duty or employed at such ports of entry as the Attorney General may designate, and such medical officers shall be provided with suitable facilities for the detention and examination of all arriving aliens who it is suspected may be excludable under paragraph (1) of section 212(a) [8 U.S.C.A. § 1182(a)], and the services of interpreters shall be provided for such examination. Any alien certified under paragraph (1) of section 212(a) [8 U.S.C.A. § 1182(a)(1)], may appeal to a board of medical officers of the United States Public Health Service, which shall be convened by the Secretary of Health and Human

Services, and any such alien may introduce before such board one expert medical witness at his own cost and expense.

(June 27, 1952, c. 477, Title II, ch. 4, § 234, 66 Stat. 198; Oct. 24, 1988, Pub.L. 100–525, § 9(k), 102 Stat. 2620; Nov. 29, 1990, Pub.L. 101–649, Title VI, § 603(a)(10), 104 Stat. 5083.)

## § 235. Inspection by Immigration Officers [8 U.S.C.A. § 1225]

### (a) Powers of officers

The inspection, other than the physical and mental examination, of aliens (including alien crewmen) seeking admission or readmission to or the privilege of passing through the United States shall be conducted by immigration officers, except as otherwise provided in regard to special inquiry officers. All aliens arriving at ports of the United States shall be examined by one or more immigration officers at the discretion of the Attorney General and under such regulations as he may prescribe. Immigration officers are authorized and empowered to board and search any vessel, aircraft, railway car, or other conveyance, or vehicle in which they believe aliens are being brought into the United States. The Attorney General and any immigration officer, including special inquiry officers, shall have power to administer oaths and to take and consider evidence of or from any person touching the privilege of any alien or person he believes or suspects to be an alien to enter, reenter, pass through, or reside in the United States or concerning any matter which is material and relevant to the enforcement of this chapter and the administration of the Service, and, where such action may be necessary, to make a written record of such evidence. Any person coming into the United States may be required to state under oath the purpose or purposes for which he comes, the length of time he intends to remain in the United States, whether or not he intends to remain in the United States permanently and, if an alien, whether he intends to become a citizen thereof, and such other items of information as will aid the immigration officer in determining whether he is a national of the United States or an alien and, if the latter, whether he belongs to any of the excluded classes enumerated in section 212 [8 U.S.C.A. § 1182]. The Attorney General and any immigration officer, including special inquiry officers, shall have power to require by subpena the attendance and testimony of witnesses before immigration officers and special inquiry officers and the production of books, papers, and documents relating to the privilege of any person to enter, reenter, reside in, or pass through the United States or concerning any matter which is material and relevant to the enforcement of this chapter and the administration of the Service, and to that end may invoke the aid of any court of the United States. Any United States district court within the jurisdiction of which investigations or inquiries are being conducted by an immigration officer or special inquiry officer may, in the event of neglect or refusal to respond to a subpena issued under this subsection or refusal to testify before an immigration officer or special inquiry officer, issue an order requiring such persons to appear before an immigration officer or special inquiry officer, produce books, papers, and documents if demanded, and testify, and any failure to obey such order of the court may be punished by the court as a contempt thereof.

### (b) Detention for further inquiry; challenge of favorable decision

Every alien (other than an alien crewman), and except as otherwise provided in subsection (c) of this section and in section 273(d) [8 U.S.C.A. § 1323(d)], who may not appear to the examining immigration officer at the port of arrival to be clearly and beyond a doubt entitled to land shall be detained for further inquiry to be conducted by a special inquiry officer. The decision of the examining immigration officer, if favorable to the admission of any alien, shall be subject to challenge by any other immigration officer and such challenge shall operate to take the alien, whose privilege to land is so challenged, before a special inquiry officer for further inquiry.

### (c) Temporary exclusion; permanent exclusion by Attorney General

Any alien (including an alien crewman) who may appear to the examining immigration officer or to the special inquiry officer during the examination before either of such officers to be excludable under subparagraph (A) (other than clause (ii)), (B), or (C) of section 212(a)(3) [8 U.S.C.A. § 1182(a)(3)(B), or (C)] shall be temporarily excluded, and no further inquiry by a special inquiry officer shall be conducted until after the case is reported to the Attorney General together with any such written statement and accompanying information, if any, as the alien or his representative may desire to submit in connection therewith and such an inquiry or further inquiry is directed by the Attorney General. If the Attorney General is satisfied that the alien is excludable under any of such paragraphs on the basis of information of a confidential nature, the disclosure of which the Attorney General, in the exercise of his discretion, and after consultation with the appropriate security agencies of the Government, concludes would be prejudicial to the public interest, safety, or security, he may in his discretion order such alien to be excluded and deported without any inquiry or further inquiry by a special inquiry officer. Nothing in this subsection shall be regarded as requiring an inquiry before a special inquiry officer in the case of an alien crewman.

(June 27, 1952, c. 477, Title II, ch. 4, § 235, 66 Stat. 198; Nov. 29, 1990, Pub.L. 101–649, Title VI, § 603(a)(11), 104 Stat. 5083.)

## § 236.  Exclusion of aliens [8 U.S.C.A. § 1226]

### (a) Proceedings

A special inquiry officer shall conduct proceedings under this section, administer oaths, present and receive evidence, and interrogate, examine, and cross-examine the alien or witnesses. He shall have authority in any case to determine whether an arriving alien who has been detained for further inquiry under section 235 [8 U.S.C.A. § 1225] shall be allowed to enter or shall be excluded and deported. The determination of such special inquiry officer shall be based only on the evidence produced at the inquiry. No special inquiry officer shall conduct a proceeding in any case under this section in which he shall have participated in investigative functions or in which he shall have participated (except as provided in this subsection) in prosecuting functions. Proceedings before a special inquiry officer under this section shall be conducted in accordance with this section, the applicable provisions of sections 235 and 287(b) [8 U.S.C.A. §§ 1225 and 1357(b)], and such regulations as the Attorney General shall prescribe, and shall be the sole and exclusive procedure for determining admissibility of a person to the United States under the provisions of this section. At such inquiry, which shall be kept separate and apart from the public, the alien may have one friend or relative present, under such conditions as may be prescribed by the Attorney General. A complete record of the proceedings and of all testimony and evidence produced at such inquiry, shall be kept.

### (b) Appeal

From a decision of a special inquiry officer excluding an alien, such alien may take a timely appeal to the Attorney General, and any such alien shall be advised of his right to take such appeal. No appeal may be taken from a temporary exclusion under section 235(c) [8 U.S.C.A. § 1225(c)]. From a decision of the special inquiry officer to admit an alien, the immigration officer in charge at the port where the inquiry is held may take a timely appeal to the Attorney General. An appeal by the alien, or such officer in charge, shall operate to stay any final action with respect to any alien whose case is so appealed until the final decision of the Attorney General is made. Except as provided in section 235(c) [8 U.S.C.A. § 1225(c)] such decision shall be rendered solely upon the evidence adduced before the special inquiry officer.

### (c) Finality of decision of special inquiry officers

Except as provided in subsections (b) or (d) of this section, in every case where an alien is excluded from admission into the United States, under this chapter or any other law or treaty now existing or hereafter made, the decision of a special inquiry officer shall be final unless reversed on appeal to the Attorney General.

### (d) Physical and mental defects

If a medical officer or civil surgeon or board of medical officers has certified under section 234 [8 U.S.C.A. § 1224] that an alien has a disease, illness, or addiction which would make the alien excludable under paragraph (1) of section 212(a) [8 U.S.C.A. § 1182(a)], the decision of the special inquiry officer shall be based solely upon such certification. No alien shall have a right to appeal from such an excluding decision of a special inquiry officer.

### (e) Custody of alien

(1) Pending a determination of excludability, the Attorney General shall take into custody any alien convicted of an aggravated felony upon completion of the alien's sentence for such conviction.

(2) Notwithstanding any other provision of this section, the Attorney General shall not release such felon from custody unless the Attorney General determines that the alien may not be deported because the condition described in section 243(g) [8 U.S.C.A. § 1253(g)] exists.

(3) If the determination described in paragraph (2) has been made, the Attorney General may release such alien only after—

(A) a procedure for review of each request for relief under this subsection has been established,

(B) such procedure includes consideration of the severity of the felony committed by the alien, and

(C) the review concludes that the alien will not pose a danger to the safety of other persons or to property.

(June 27, 1952, c. 477, Title II, ch. 4, § 236, 66 Stat. 200; Nov. 29, 1990, Pub.L. 101–649, Title V, § 504(b), Title VI, § 603(a)(12), 104 Stat. 5050, 5083.)

## § 237. Immediate deportation of aliens excluded from admission or entering in violation of law [8 U.S.C.A. § 1227]

### (a) Maintenance expenses

(1) Any alien (other than an alien crewman) arriving in the United States who is excluded under this chapter, shall be immediately deported, in accommodations of the same class in which he arrived, unless the Attorney General, in an individual case, in his discretion, concludes that immediate deportation is not practicable or proper. Deportation shall be to the country in which the alien boarded the vessel or aircraft on which he arrived in the United States, unless the alien boarded such vessel or aircraft in foreign territory contiguous to the United States or in any island adjacent thereto or adjacent to the United States and the alien is not a native, citizen, subject, or national of, or does not have a residence in, such foreign contiguous territory or adjacent island, in which case the deportation shall instead be to the country in which is located the port at which the alien embarked for such foreign contiguous territory or adjacent island. The cost of the maintenance including detention expenses and expenses incident to detention of any such alien while he is being detained, shall be borne by the owner or owners of the vessel or aircraft on which he arrived, except that the cost of maintenance (including detention expenses and expenses incident to detention while the alien is being detained prior to the time he is offered for deportation to the transportation line which brought him to the United States) shall not be assessed against the owner or owners of such vessel or aircraft if (A) the alien was in possession of a valid,

unexpired immigrant visa, or (B) the alien (other than an alien crewman) was in possession of a valid, unexpired nonimmigrant visa or other document authorizing such alien to apply for temporary admission to the United States or an unexpired reentry permit issued to him, and (i) such application was made within one hundred and twenty days of the date of issuance of the visa or other document, or in the case of an alien in possession of a reentry permit, within one hundred and twenty days of the date on which the alien was last examined and admitted by the Service, or (ii) in the event the application was made later than one hundred and twenty days of the date of issuance of the visa or other document or such examination and admission, if the owner or owners of such vessel or aircraft established to the satisfaction of the Attorney General that the ground of exclusion could not have been ascertained by the exercise of due diligence prior to the alien's embarkation, or (C) the person claimed United States nationality or citizenship and was in possession of an unexpired United States passport issued to him by competent authority.

(2) If the government of the country designated in paragraph (1) will not accept the alien into its territory, the alien's deportation shall be directed by the Attorney General, in his discretion and without necessarily giving any priority or preference because of their order as herein set forth, either to—

(A) the country of which the alien is a subject, citizen, or national;

(B) the country in which he was born;

(C) the country in which he has a residence; or

(D) any country which is willing to accept the alien into its territory, if deportation to any of the foregoing countries is impracticable, inadvisable, or impossible.

### (b) Unlawful practice of transportation lines

It shall be unlawful for any master, commanding officer, purser, person in charge, agent, owner, or consignee of any vessel or aircraft (1) to refuse to receive any alien (other than an alien crewman), ordered deported under this section back on board such vessel or aircraft or another vessel or aircraft owned or operated by the same interests; (2) to fail to detain any alien (other than an alien crewman) on board any such vessel or at the airport of arrival of the aircraft when required by this chapter or if so ordered by an immigration officer, or to fail or refuse to deliver him for medical or other inspection, or for further medical or other inspection, as and when so ordered by such officer; (3) to refuse or fail to remove him from the United States to the country to which his deportation had been directed; (4) to fail to pay the cost of his maintenance while being detained as required by this section; (5) to take any fee, deposit, or consideration on a contingent basis to be kept or returned in case the alien is landed or excluded; or (6) knowingly to bring to the United States any alien (other than an alien crewman) excluded or arrested and deported under any provision of law until such alien may be lawfully entitled to reapply for admission to the United States. If it shall appear to the satisfaction of the Attorney General that any such master, commanding officer, purser, person in charge, agent, owner, or consignee of any vessel or aircraft has violated any of the provisions of this section, such master, commanding officer, purser, person in charge, agent, owner, or consignee shall pay to the Commissioner the sum of $2,000 for each violation. No such vessel or aircraft shall have clearance from any port of the United States while any such fine is unpaid or while the question of liability to pay any such fine is being determined, nor shall any such fine be remitted or refunded, except that clearance may be granted prior to the determination of such question upon the deposit with the district director of customs of a bond or undertaking approved by the Attorney General or a sum sufficient to cover such fine.

### (c) Transportation expense of deportation

An alien shall be deported on a vessel or aircraft owned by the same person who owns the vessel or aircraft on which the alien arrived in the United States, unless it is impracticable to so deport the alien within a reasonable time. The transportation expense of the alien's deportation shall be borne by the owner or owners of the vessel or aircraft on which the alien arrived. If the deportation is effected on a vessel or aircraft not owned by such owner or owners, the transportation expense of the alien's deportation may be paid from the appropriation for the enforcement of this chapter and recovered by civil suit from any owner, agent, or consignee of the vessel or aircraft on which the alien arrived.

### (d) Stay of deportation; payment of maintenance expenses

The Attorney General, under such conditions as are by regulations prescribed, may stay the deportation of any alien deportable under this section, if in his judgment the testimony of such alien is necessary on behalf of the United States in the prosecution of offenders against any provision of this chapter or other laws of the United States. The cost of maintenance of any person so detained resulting from a stay of deportation under this subsection and a witness fee in the sum of $1 per day for each day such person is so detained may be paid from the appropriation for the enforcement of this subchapter. Such alien may be released under bond in the penalty of not less than $500 with security approved by the Attorney General on condition that such alien shall be produced when required as a witness and for deportation, and on such other conditions as the Attorney General may prescribe.

### (e) Deportation of alien accompanying physically disabled alien

Upon the certificate of an examining medical officer to the effect that an alien ordered to be excluded and deported under this section is helpless from sickness or mental and physical disability, or infancy, if such alien is accompanied by another alien whose protection or guardianship is required by the alien ordered excluded and deported, such accompanying alien may also be excluded and deported, and the master, commanding officer, agent, owner, or consignee of the vessel or aircraft in which such alien and accompanying alien arrived in the United States shall be required to return the accompanying alien in the same manner as other aliens denied admission and ordered deported under this section.

(June 27, 1952, c. 477, Title II, ch. 4, § 237, 66 Stat. 201; Pub. L. 97–116, § 7, Dec. 29, 1981, 95 Stat. 1615; Pub.L. 99–500, Title I, § 101(b) [Title II, § 206(b)(2)], added Pub.L. 100–525, § 4(b)(4), Oct. 24, 1988, 102 Stat. 2615; Pub.L. 100–525, § 9(*l*), Oct. 24, 1988, 102 Stat. 2620; Pub.L. 101–649, Title V, § 543(a)(2), Nov. 29, 1990, 104 Stat. 5057.)

## § 238. Entry through or from foreign contiguous territory and adjacent islands [8 U.S.C.A. § 1228]

### (a) Contracts with transportation lines; necessity of transportation contract

The Attorney General shall have power to enter into contracts with transportation lines for the entry and inspection of aliens coming to the United States from foreign contiguous territory or from adjacent islands. No such transportation line shall be allowed to land any such alien in the United States until and unless it has entered into any such contracts which may be required by the Attorney General.

### (b) Landing stations

Every transportation line engaged in carrying alien passengers for hire to the United States from foreign contiguous territory or from adjacent islands shall provide and maintain at its expense suitable landing stations, approved by the Attorney General, conveniently located at the point or points of entry. No such transportation line shall be allowed to land any alien passengers in the United States until such landing stations are provided, and unless such stations are thereafter maintained to the satisfaction of the Attorney General.

### (c) Landing agreements

The Attorney General shall have power to enter into contracts including bonding agreements with transportation lines to guarantee the passage through the United States in immediate and continuous transit of aliens destined to foreign countries. Notwithstanding any other provision of this chapter, such aliens may not have their classification changed under section 248 [8 U.S.C.A. § 1258].

### (d) Definitions

As used in this section the terms "transportation line" and "transportation company" include, but are not limited to, the owner, charterer, consignee, or authorized agent operating any vessel or aircraft bringing aliens to the United States, to foreign contiguous territory, or to adjacent islands.

### (e) Redesignated (d)

(June 27, 1952, c. 477, Title II, ch. 4, § 238, 66 Stat. 202; Pub.L. 99–653, § 7(b), Nov. 14, 1986, 100 Stat. 3657.)

## § 239. Designation of ports of entry for aliens arriving by aircraft [8 U.S.C.A. § 1229]

The Attorney General is authorized (1) by regulation to designate as ports of entry for aliens arriving by aircraft any of the ports of entry for civil aircraft designated as such in accordance with law; (2) by regulation to provide such reasonable requirements for aircraft in civil air navigation with respect to giving notice of intention to land in advance of landing, or notice of landing, as shall be deemed necessary for purposes of administration and enforcement of this chapter; and (3) by regulation to provide for the application to civil air navigation of the provisions of this chapter where not expressly so provided in this chapter to such extent and upon such conditions as he deems necessary. Any person who violates any regulation made under this section shall be subject to a civil penalty of $2000 which may be remitted or mitigated by the Attorney General in accordance with such proceedings as the Attorney General shall by regulation prescribe. In case the violation is by the owner or person in command of the aircraft, the penalty shall be a lien upon the aircraft, and such aircraft may be libeled therefor in the appropriate United States court. The determination by the Attorney General and remission or mitigation of the civil penalty shall be final. In case the violation is by the owner or person in command of the aircraft, the penalty shall be a lien upon the aircraft and may be collected by proceedings in rem which shall conform as nearly as may be to civil suits in admiralty. The Supreme Court of the United States, and under its direction other courts of the United States, are authorized to prescribe rules regulating such proceedings against aircraft in any particular not otherwise provided by law. Any aircraft made subject to a lien by this section may be summarily seized by, and placed in the custody of such persons as the Attorney General may by regulation prescribe. The aircraft may be released from such custody upon deposit of such amount not exceeding $500 as the Attorney General may prescribe, or of a bond in such sum and with such sureties as the Attorney General may prescribe, conditioned upon the payment of the penalty which may be finally determined by the Attorney General.

(June 27, 1952, c. 477, Title II, ch. 4, § 239, 66 Stat. 203; Nov. 29, 1990, Pub.L. 101–649, Title V, § 543(a)(3), 104 Stat. 5058.)

## § 240. Records of admission [8 U.S.C.A. § 1230]

(a) The Attorney General shall cause to be filed, as a record of admission of each immigrant, the immigrant visa required by section

221(e) [8 U.S.C.A. § 1201(e)] to be surrendered at the port of entry by the arriving alien to an immigration officer.

**(b)** The Attorney General shall cause to be filed such record of the entry into the United States of each immigrant admitted under section 211(b) [8 U.S.C.A. § 1181(b)] and of each nonimmigrant as the Attorney General deems necessary for the enforcement of the immigration laws.

(June 27, 1952, c. 477, Title II, ch. 4, § 240, 66 Stat. 204.)

## CHAPTER V—DEPORTATION; ADJUSTMENT OF STATUS

## § 241. Deportable aliens [8 U.S.C.A. § 1251]

### (a) Classes of deportable aliens

Any alien (including an alien crewman) in the United States shall, upon the order of the Attorney General, be deported if the alien is deportable as being within one or more of the following classes of aliens:

#### (1) Excludable at time of entry or of adjustment of status or violates status

**(A)** Excludable aliens

Any alien who at the time of entry or adjustment of status was within one or more of the classes of aliens excludable by the law existing at such time is deportable.

**(B)** Entered without inspection

Any alien who entered the United States without inspection or at any time or place other than as designated by the Attorney General or is in the United States in violation of this chapter or any other law of the United States is deportable.

**(C)** Violated nonimmigrant status or condition of entry

(i) Nonimmigrant status violators

Any alien who was admitted as a nonimmigrant and who has failed to maintain the nonimmigrant status in which the alien was admitted or to which it was changed under section 248 [8 U.S.C.A. § 1258], or to comply with the conditions of any such status, is deportable.

(ii) Violators of conditions of entry

Any alien whom the Secretary of Health and Human Services certifies has failed to comply with terms, conditions, and controls that were imposed under section 212(g) [8 U.S.C.A. § 1182(g)] is deportable.

**(D)** Termination of conditional permanent residence

(i) In general

Any alien with permanent resident status on a conditional basis under section 216 [8 U.S.C.A. § 1186a] (relating to conditional permanent resident status for certain alien spouses and sons and daughters) or under section 216A [8 U.S.C.A. § 1186b] (relating to conditional permanent resident status for certain alien entrepreneurs, spouses, and children) who has had such status terminated under such section is deportable.

**(ii)** Exception

Clause (i) shall not apply in the cases described in section 216(c)(4) [8 U.S.C.A. § 1186a(c)(4)] (relating to certain hardship waivers).

**(E)** Smuggling

**(i)** In general

Any alien who (prior to the date of entry, at the time of entry, or within 5 years of the date of entry) knowingly has encouraged, induced, assisted, abetted, or aided any other alien to enter or to try to enter the United States in violation of law is deportable.

**(ii)** Waiver authorized

The Attorney General may, in his discretion for humanitarian purposes, to assure family unity, or when it is otherwise in the public interest, waive application of clause (i) in the case of any alien lawfully admitted for permanent residence if the alien has encouraged, induced, assisted, abetted, or aided only the alien's spouse, parent, son, or daughter (and no other individual) to enter the United States in violation of law.

**(F)** Failure to maintain employment

Any alien who obtains the status of an alien lawfully admitted for temporary residence under section 210A [8 U.S. C.A. § 1161] who fails to meet the requirement of section 210A(d)(5)(A) [8 U.S.C.A. § 1161(d)(5)(A)] by the end of the applicable period is deportable.

**(G)** Marriage fraud

An alien shall be considered to be deportable as having procured a visa or other documentation by fraud (within the meaning of section 212(a)(5)(C)(i) [8 U.S.C.A. § 1182(a)(5)(C)(i)]) and to be in the United States in violation of this chapter (within the meaning of subparagraph (B)) if—

(i) the alien obtains any entry into the United States with an immigrant visa or other documentation procured on the basis of a marriage entered into less than 2 years prior to such entry of the alien and which, within 2 years subsequent to any entry of the alien in the United States, shall be judicially annulled or terminated, unless the alien establishes to the satisfaction of the Attorney General that such marriage was not contracted for the purpose of evading any provisions of the immigration laws, or

(ii) it appears to the satisfaction of the Attorney General that the alien has failed or refused to fulfill the alien's marital agreement which in the opinion of the Attorney General was made for the purpose of procuring the alien's entry as an immigrant.

**(H)** Waiver authorized for certain misrepresentations

The provisions of this paragraph relating to the deportation of aliens within the United States on the ground that they were excludable at the time of entry as aliens described in section 212(a)(6)(C)(i) [8 U.S.C.A. § 1182(a)(6)(C)(i)], whether willful or innocent, may, in the discretion of the Attorney General, be waived for any alien (other than an alien described in paragraph (6) or (7)) who—

"MAY" —

DISCRE.

(i) is the spouse, parent, son, or daughter of a citizen of the United States or of an alien lawfully admitted to the United States for permanent residence; and

(ii) was in possession of an immigrant visa or equivalent document and was otherwise admissible to the United States at the time of such entry except for those grounds of inadmissibility specified under paragraphs (5)(A) and (7)(A) of section 212(a) [8 U.S.C.A. § 1182(a)] which were a direct result of that fraud or misrepresentation.

A waiver of deportation for fraud or misrepresentation granted under this subparagraph shall also operate to waive deportation based on the grounds of inadmissibility at entry directly resulting from such fraud or misrepresentation.

**(2) Criminal offenses**

**(A)** General crimes

(i) Crimes of moral turpitude

Any alien who—

**(I)** is convicted of a crime involving moral turpitude committed within five years after the date of entry, and

**(II)** either is sentenced to confinement or is confined therefor in a prison or correctional institution for one year or longer,

is deportable.

(ii) Multiple criminal convictions

Any alien who at any time after entry is convicted of two or more crimes involving moral turpitude, not arising out of a single scheme of criminal misconduct, regardless of whether confined therefor and regardless of whether the convictions were in a single trial, is deportable.

**(iii) Aggravated felony**

Any alien who is convicted of an aggravated felony at any time after entry is deportable.

**(iv) Waiver authorized**

Clauses (i), (ii), and (iii) shall not apply in the case of an alien with respect to a criminal conviction if the alien subsequent to the criminal conviction has been granted a full and unconditional pardon by the President of the United States or by the Governor of any of the several States.

**(B) Controlled substances**

**(i) Conviction**

Any alien who at any time after entry has been convicted of a violation of (or a conspiracy or attempt to violate) any law or regulation of a State, the United States, or a foreign country relating to a controlled substance (as defined in section 802 of Title 21); other than a single offense involving possession for one's own use of 30 grams or less of marijuana, is deportable.

**(ii) Drug abusers and addicts**

Any alien who is, or at any time after entry has been, a drug abuser or addict is deportable.

**(C) Certain firearm offenses**

Any alien who at any time after entry is convicted under any law of purchasing, selling, offering for sale, exchanging, using, owning, possessing, or carrying in violation of any law, any weapon, part, or accessory which is a firearm or destructive device (as defined in section 921(a) of Title 18) is deportable.

**(D) Miscellaneous crimes**

Any alien who at any time has been convicted (the judgment on such conviction becoming final) of, or has been so convicted of a conspiracy to violate—

**(i)** any offense under chapter 37 (relating to espionage), chapter 105 (relating to sabotage), or chapter 115 (relating to treason and sedition) of Title 18, for which a term of imprisonment of five or more years may be imposed;

**(ii)** any offense under section 871 or 960 of Title 18;

(iii) a violation of any provision of the Military Selective Service Act (50 U.S.C. App. 451 et seq.) or the Trading With the Enemy Act (50 U.S.C. App. 1 et seq.); or

(iv) a violation of section 215 or 278 [8 U.S.C.A. §§ 1185 or 1328],

is deportable.

### (3) Failure to register and falsification of documents

(A) Change of address

An alien who has failed to comply with the provisions of section 265 [8 U.S.C.A. § 1305] is deportable, unless the alien establishes to the satisfaction of the Attorney General that such failure was reasonably excusable or was not willful.

(B) Failure to register or falsification of documents

Any alien who at any time has been convicted—

(i) under section 266(c) [8 U.S.C.A. § 1306(c)] or under section 36(c) of the Alien Registration Act, 1940,

(ii) of a violation of, or a conspiracy to violate, any provision of the Foreign Agents Registration Act of 1938 (22 U.S.C. 611 et seq.), or

(iii) of a violation of, or a conspiracy to violate, section 1546 of Title 18 (relating to fraud and misuse of visas, permits, and other entry documents),

is deportable.

### (4) Security and related grounds

(A) In general

Any alien who has engaged, is engaged, or at any time after entry has engaged in—

(i) any activity to violate any law of the United States relating to espionage or sabotage or to violate or evade any law prohibiting the export from the United States of goods, technology, or sensitive information,

(ii) any other criminal activity which endangers public safety or national security, or

(iii) any activity a purpose of which is the opposition to, or the control or overthrow of, the Government of the United States by force, violence, or other unlawful means,

is deportable.

(B) Terrorist activities

Any alien who has engaged, is engaged, or at any time after entry has engaged in any terrorist activity (as defined in section 212(a)(3)(B)(iii) [8 U.S.C.A. § 1182(a)(3)(B)(iii)]) is deportable.

(C) Foreign policy

(i) In general

An alien whose presence or activities in the United States the Secretary of State has reasonable ground to believe would have potentially serious adverse foreign policy consequences for the United States is deportable.

(ii) Exceptions

The exceptions described in clauses (ii) and (iii) of section 212(a)(3)(C) [8 U.S.C.A. § 1182(a)(3)(C)(ii) and (iii)] shall apply to deportability under clause (i) in the same manner as they apply to excluability [1] under section 212(a)(3)(C) [8 U.S.C.A. § 1182(a)(3)(C)(i)].

(D) Assisted in Nazi persecution or engaged in genocide

Any alien described in clause (i) or (ii) of section 212(a)(3)(E) [8 U.S.C.A. § 1182(a)(3)(E)(i) or (ii)] is deportable.

### (5) Public charge

Any alien who, within five years after the date of entry, has become a public charge from causes not affirmatively shown to have arisen since entry is deportable.

### (b) Deportation of certain nonimmigrants

An alien, admitted as a nonimmigrant under the provisions of either section 101(a)(15)(A)(i) or 101(a)(15)(G)(i) [8 U.S.C.A. §§ 1101(a)(15)(A)(i) or 1101(a)(15)(G)(i)], and who fails to maintain a status under either of those provisions, shall not be required to depart from the United States without the approval of the Secretary of State, unless such alien is subject to deportation under paragraph (4) of subsection (a) of this section.

### (c) Repealed. Pub.L. 101–649, § 602(b)(1), Nov. 29, 1990, 104 Stat. 5081.

### (d) Applicability to all aliens

Except as otherwise specifically provided in this section, the provisions of this section shall be applicable to all aliens belonging to any of the classes enumerated in subsection (a) of this section, notwithstanding (1) that any such alien entered the United States prior to June 27, 1952, or (2) that the facts, by reason of which any such alien belongs to any of the classes enumerated in subsection (a) of this section, occurred prior to June 27, 1952.

### (e) Redesignated (b)

### (f), (g) Repealed. Pub.L. 101–649, § 602(b)(1), Nov. 29, 1990, 104 Stat. 5081.

### (h) Waiver of grounds for deportation

Paragraphs (1)(A), (1)(B), (1)(C), (1)(D), or (3)(A), of subsection (a) of this section (other than so much of paragraph (1) as relates to a ground of exclusion described in paragraph (2) or (3) of section 212(a) [8 U.S.C.A. § 1182(a)(2) or (3)]) shall not apply to a special immigrant described in section 1101(a)(27)(J) of this title based upon circumstances that exist before the date the alien was provided such special immigrant status.

(June 27, 1952, c. 477, Title II, ch. 5, § 241, 66 Stat. 204; July 18, 1956, c. 629, Title III, § 301(b), (c), 70 Stat. 575; Pub.L. 86–648, § 9, July 14, 1960, 74 Stat. 505; Pub.L. 87–301, § 16, Sept. 26, 1961, 75 Stat. 655; Pub.L. 89–236, § 11(e), Oct. 3, 1965, 79 Stat. 918; Pub.L. 94–571, § 7(e), Oct. 20, 1976, 90 Stat. 2706; Pub.L. 95–549, Title I, § 103, Oct. 30, 1978, 92 Stat. 2065; Pub.L. 97–116, § 8, Dec. 29, 1981, 95 Stat. 1616; Pub.L. 99–570, Title I, § 1751(b), Oct. 27, 1986, 100 Stat. 3207–47; Pub.L. 99–603, Title III, § 303(b), Nov. 6, 1986, 100 Stat. 3431; Pub.L. 99–639, § 2(b), Nov. 10, 1986, 100 Stat. 3541; Pub.L. 99–653, § 7(c), Nov. 14, 1986, 100 Stat. 3657; Pub.L. 100–525, §§ 2(n)(2), 9(m), Oct. 24, 1988, 102 Stat. 2613, 2620; Pub.L. 100–690, Title VII, § 7344(a), 7348(a), Nov. 18, 1988, 102 Stat. 4471, 4473; Nov. 29, 1990, Pub.L. 101–649, Title I, § 153(b), Title V, §§ 505(a), 508(a), 544(b), Title VI, § 602(a), (b), 104 Stat. 5006, 5050, 5051, 5061, 5077–5081.)

**1.** So in original. Probably should be "excludability".

# § 242. Apprehension and deportation of aliens [8 U.S.C.A. § 1252]

**(a) Arrest and custody; review of determination by court; aliens committing aggravated felonies; report to Congressional committees**

(1) Pending a determination of deportability in the case of any alien as provided in subsection (b) of this section, such alien may, upon warrant of the Attorney General, be arrested and taken into custody. Except as provided in paragraph (2), any such alien taken into custody may, in the discretion of the Attorney General and pending such final determination of deportability, (A) be continued in custody; or (B) be released under bond in the amount of not less than $500 with security approved by the Attorney General, containing such conditions as the Attorney General may prescribe; or (C) be released on conditional parole. But such bond or parole, whether heretofore or hereafter authorized, may be revoked at any time by the Attorney General, in his discretion, and the alien may be returned to custody under the warrant which initiated the proceedings against him and detained until final determination of his deportability. Any court of competent jurisdiction shall have authority to review or revise any determination of the Attorney General concerning detention, release on bond, or parole pending final decision of deportability upon a conclusive showing in habeas corpus proceedings that the Attorney General is not proceeding with such reasonable dispatch as may be warranted by the particular facts and circumstances in the case of any alien to determine deportability.

(2)(A) The Attorney General shall take into custody any alien convicted of an aggravated felony upon release of the alien (regardless of whether or not such release is on parole, supervised release, or probation, and regardless of the possibility of rearrest or further confinement in respect of the same offense). Notwithstanding paragraph (1) or subsections (c) and (d) of this section but subject to subparagraph (B), the Attorney General shall not release such felon from custody.

(B) The Attorney General shall release from custody an alien who is lawfully admitted for permanent residence on bond or such other conditions as the Attorney General may prescribe if the Attorney General determines that the alien is not a threat to the community and that the alien is likely to appear before any scheduled hearings.

(3)(A) The Attorney General shall devise and implement a system—

(i) to make available, daily (on a 24-hour basis), to Federal, State, and local authorities the investigative resources of the Service to determine whether individuals arrested by such authorities for aggravated felonies are aliens;

(ii) to designate and train officers and employees of the Service within each district to serve as a liaison to Federal, State, and local law enforcement and correctional agencies and courts with respect to the arrest, conviction, and release of any alien charged with an aggravated felony; and

(iii) which uses computer resources to maintain a current record of aliens who have been convicted of an aggravated felony and who have been deported; such record shall be made available to inspectors at ports of entry and to border patrol agents at sector headquarters for purposes of immediate identification of any such previously deported alien seeking to reenter the United States.

(B) The Attorney General shall submit reports to the Committees on the Judiciary of the House of Representatives and of the Senate at the end of the 6-month period and at the end of the 18-month period beginning on the effective date of this paragraph which describe in detail specific efforts made by the Attorney General to implement this paragraph.

### (b) Proceedings to determine deportability; removal expenses

A special inquiry officer shall conduct proceedings under this section to determine the deportability of any alien, and shall administer oaths, present and receive evidence, interrogate, examine, and cross-examine the alien or witnesses, and, as authorized by the Attorney General, shall make determinations, including orders of deportation. Determination of deportability in any case shall be made only upon a record made in a proceeding before a special inquiry officer, at which the alien shall have reasonable opportunity to be present, unless by reason of the alien's mental incompetency it is impracticable for him to be present, in which case the Attorney General shall prescribe necessary and proper safeguards for the rights and privileges of such alien. If any alien has been given a reasonable opportunity to be present at a proceeding under this section, and without reasonable cause fails or refuses to attend or remain in attendance at such proceeding, the special inquiry officer may proceed to a determination in like manner as if the alien were present. In any case or class of cases in which the Attorney General believes that such procedure would be of aid in making a determination, he may require specifically or by regulation that an additional immigration officer shall be assigned to present the evidence on behalf of the United States and in such case such additional immigration officer shall have authority to present evidence, and to interrogate, examine and cross-examine the alien or other witnesses in the proceedings. Nothing in the preceding sentence shall be construed to diminish the authority conferred upon the special inquiry officer conducting such proceedings. No special inquiry officer shall conduct a proceeding in any case under this section in which he shall have participated in investigative functions or in which he shall have participated (except as provided in this subsection) in prosecuting functions. Proceedings before a special inquiry officer acting under the provisions of this section shall be in accordance with such regulations, not inconsistent with this chapter, as the Attorney General shall prescribe. Such regulations shall include requirements that—

(1) the alien shall be given notice, reasonable under all the circumstances, of the nature of the charges against him and of the time and place at which the proceedings will be held;

(2) the alien shall have the privilege of being represented (at no expense to the Government) by such counsel, authorized to practice in such proceedings, as he shall choose;

(3) the alien shall have a reasonable opportunity to examine the evidence against him, to present evidence in his own behalf, and to cross-examine witnesses presented by the Government; and

(4) no decision of deportability shall be valid unless it is based upon reasonable, substantial, and probative evidence.*

The procedure so prescribed shall be the sole and exclusive procedure for determining the deportability of an alien under this section. In any case in which an alien is ordered deported from the United States under the provisions of this chapter, or of any other law or treaty, the decision of the Attorney General shall be final. In the discretion of the Attorney General, and under such regulations as he may prescribe, deportation proceedings, including issuance of a warrant of arrest, and

*Pub.L. 101–649, Title V, § 545(e), (g)(1)(A), (B), Nov. 29, 1990, 104 Stat. 5066, provided that, effective on the date specified by the Attorney General in the certification to the Congress when the central address file system, described in section 242B(a)(4) [8 U.S.C.A. § 1252b(a)(4)], has been established, which date may not be earlier than 6 months after the date of such certification, the 8th sentence of subsec. (b) is amended to read as follows:

"Such regulations shall include requirements consisent with section 242B [8 U.S.C.A. § 1252b]."

165

a finding of deportability under this section need not be required in the case of any alien who admits to belonging to a class of aliens who are deportable under section 241 [8 U.S.C.A. § 1251] if such alien voluntarily departs from the United States at his own expense, or is removed at Government expense as hereinafter authorized, unless the Attorney General has reason to believe that such alien is deportable under paragraphs (2), (3), or (4) of section 241(a) [8 U.S.C.A. § 1251(a)(2), (3), or (4)]. If any alien who is authorized to depart voluntarily under the preceding sentence is financially unable to depart at his own expense and the Attorney General deems his removal to be in the best interest of the United States, the expense of such removal may be paid from the appropriation for the enforcement of this chapter.

### (c) Final order of deportation; place of detention

When a final order of deportation under administrative processes is made against any alien, the Attorney General shall have a period of six months from the date of such order, or, if judicial review is had, then from the date of the final order of the court, within which to effect the alien's departure from the United States, during which period, at the Attorney General's discretion, the alien may be detained, released on bond in an amount and containing such conditions as the Attorney General may prescribe, or released on such other condition as the Attorney General may prescribe. Any court of competent jurisdiction shall have authority to review or revise any determination of the Attorney General concerning detention, release on bond, or other release during such six-month period upon a conclusive showing in habeas corpus proceedings that the Attorney General is not proceeding with such reasonable dispatch as may be warranted by the particular facts and circumstances in the case of any alien to effect such alien's departure from the United States within such six-month period. If deportation has not been practicable, advisable, or possible, or departure of the alien from the United States under the order of deportation has not been effected, within such six-month period, the alien shall become subject to such further supervision and detention pending eventual deportation as is authorized in this section. The Attorney General is authorized and directed to arrange for appropriate places of detention for those aliens whom he shall take into custody and detain under this section. Where no Federal buildings are available or buildings adapted or suitably located for the purpose are available for rental, the Attorney General is authorized, notwithstanding section 5 of title 41 or section 278a of title 40 to expend, from the appropriation provided for the administration and enforcement of the immigration laws, such amounts as may be necessary for the acquisition of land and the erection, acquisition, maintenance, operation, remodeling, or repair of buildings, sheds, and office quarters (including living quarters for officers where none are otherwise available), and adjunct facilities, necessary for the detention of aliens. For the purposes of this section an order of deportation heretofore or hereafter entered against an alien in legal detention or confinement, other than under an immigration process, shall be considered as being made as of the moment he is released from such detention or confinement, and not prior thereto.

### (d) Supervision of deportable alien; violation by alien

Any alien, against whom a final order of deportation as defined in subsection (c) of this section heretofore or hereafter issued has been outstanding for more than six months, shall, pending eventual deportation, be subject to supervision under regulations prescribed by the Attorney General. Such regulations shall include provisions which will require any alien subject to supervision (1) to appear from time to time before an immigration officer for identification; (2) to submit, if necessary, to medical and psychiatric examination at the expense of the United States; (3) to give information under oath as to his nationality, circumstances, habits, associations, and activities, and such other information, whether or not related to the foregoing, as the Attorney General may deem fit and proper; and (4) to conform to such reasonable written restrictions on his conduct or activities as are prescribed by the Attorney General in his case. Any alien who shall willfully fail to comply with such regulations, or willfully fail to appear or to give information or submit to medical or psychiatric examination if required, or knowingly give false information in relation to the requirements of such regulations, or knowingly violate a reasonable restriction imposed upon his conduct or activity, shall be fined not more than $1,000 or shall be imprisoned not more than one year, or both.

### (e) Penalty for willful failure to depart; suspension of sentence

Any alien against whom a final order of deportation is outstanding by reason of being a member of any of the classes described in paragraph (2), (3), or (4) of section 241(a) [8 U.S.C.A. § 1251(a)(2), (3), or (4)], who shall willfully fail or refuse to depart from the United States within a period of six months from the date of the final order of deportation under administrative processes, or, if judicial review is had, then from the date of the final order of the court, or shall willfully fail or refuse to make timely application in good faith for travel or other documents necessary to his departure, or who shall connive or conspire, or take any other action, designed to prevent or hamper or with the purpose of preventing or hampering his departure pursuant to such order of deportation, or who shall willfully fail or refuse to present himself for deportation at the time and place required by the Attorney General pursuant to such order of deportation, shall upon conviction be guilty of a felony, and shall be imprisoned not more than ten years: *Provided,* That this subsection shall not make it illegal for any alien to take any proper steps for the purpose of securing cancellation of or exemption from such order of deportation or for the purpose of securing his release from incarceration or custody: *Provided further,* That the court may for good cause suspend the sentence of such alien and order his release under such conditions as the court may prescribe. In determining whether good cause has been shown to justify releasing the

167

alien, the court shall take into account such factors as (1) the age, health, and period of detention of the alien; (2) the effect of the alien's release upon the national security and public peace or safety; (3) the likelihood of the alien's resuming or following a course of conduct which made or would make him deportable; (4) the character of the efforts made by such alien himself and by representatives of the country or countries to which his deportation is directed to expedite the alien's departure from the United States; (5) the reason for the inability of the Government of the United States to secure passports, other travel documents, or deportation facilities from the country or countries to which the alien has been ordered deported; and (6) the eligibility of the alien for discretionary relief under the immigration laws.

### (f) Unlawful reentry

Should the Attorney General find that any alien has unlawfully reentered the United States after having previously departed or been deported pursuant to an order of deportation, whether before or after June 27, 1952, on any ground described in any of the paragraphs enumerated in subsection (e) of this section, the previous order of deportation shall be deemed to be reinstated from its original date and such alien shall be deported under such previous order at any time subsequent to such reentry. For the purposes of subsection (e) of this section the date on which the finding is made that such reinstatement is appropriate shall be deemed the date of the final order of deportation.

### (g) Voluntary deportation; payment of expenses

If any alien, subject to supervision or detention under subsections (c) or (d) of this section, is able to depart from the United States under the order of deportation, except that he is financially unable to pay his passage, the Attorney General may in his discretion permit such alien to depart voluntarily, and the expense of such passage to the country to which he is destined may be paid from the appropriation for the enforcement of this chapter, unless such payment is otherwise provided for under this chapter.

### (h) Service of prison sentence prior to deportation

An alien sentenced to imprisonment shall not be deported until such imprisonment has been terminated by the release of the alien from confinement. Parole, supervised release, probation, or possibility of rearrest or further confinement in respect of the same offense shall not be a ground for deferral of deportation.

### (i) Expeditious deportation of convicted aliens

In the case of an alien who is convicted of an offense which makes the alien subject to deportation, the Attorney General shall begin any deportation proceeding as expeditiously as possible after the date of the conviction.

(June 27, 1952, c. 477, Title II, ch. 5, § 242, 66 Stat. 208; Sept. 3, 1954, c. 1263, § 17, 68 Stat. 1232; Pub.L. 97–116, § 18(h)(1), Dec. 29, 1981, 95 Stat. 1620;

Pub.L. 99–473, Title II, § 220(b), Oct. 12, 1984, 98 Stat. 2028; Pub.L. 99–603, Title VII, § 701, Nov. 6, 1986, 100 Stat. 3445; Pub.L. 100–525, § 9(n), Oct. 24, 1988, 102 Stat. 2620; Pub.L. 100–690, Title VII, § 7343(a), Nov. 18, 1988, 102 Stat. 4470; Nov. 29, 1990, Pub.L. 101–649, Title V, §§ 504(a), 545(e), (g)(1)(A), (B), Title VI, § 603(b)(2), 104 Stat. 5049, 5066, 5085.)

## § 242A. Expedited procedures for deportation of aliens convicted of committing aggravated felonies [8 U.S.C.A. § 1252a]

### (a) In general

The Attorney General shall provide for the availability of special deportation proceedings at certain Federal, State, and local correctional facilities for aliens convicted of aggravated felonies (¹ as defined in section 101(a)(43) [8 U.S.C.A. § 1101(a)(43)]. Such proceedings shall be conducted in conformity with section 242 [8 U.S.C.A. § 1252] (except as otherwise provided in this section), and in a manner which eliminates the need for additional detention at any processing center of the Service and in a manner which assures expeditious deportation, where warranted, following the end of the alien's incarceration for the underlying sentence.

### (b) Implementation

With respect to an alien convicted of an aggravated felony who is taken into custody by the Attorney General pursuant to section 242(a)(2) [8 U.S.C.A. § 1252(a)(2)], the Attorney General shall, to the maximum extent practicable, detain any such felon at a facility at which other such aliens are detained. In the selection of such facility, the Attorney General shall make reasonable efforts to ensure that the alien's access to counsel and right to counsel under section 292 [8 U.S.C.A. § 1362] are not impaired.

### (c) Presumption of deportability

An alien convicted of an aggravated felony shall be conclusively presumed to be deportable from the United States.

### (d) Expedited proceedings

(1) Notwithstanding any other provision of law, the Attorney General shall provide for the initiation and, to the extent possible, the completion of deportation proceedings, and any administrative appeals thereof, in the case of any alien convicted of an aggravated felony before the alien's release from incarceration for the underlying aggravated felony.

(2) Nothing in this section shall be construed as requiring the Attorney General to effect the deportation of any alien sentenced to actual incarceration, before release from the penitentiary or correctional institution where such alien is confined.

### (e) Review

(1) The Attorney General shall review and evaluate deportation proceedings conducted under this section. Within 12 months after the effective date of this section, the Attorney General shall submit a report to the Committees on the Judiciary of the House of Representatives and of the Senate concerning the effectiveness of such deportation proceedings in facilitating the deportation of aliens convicted of aggravated felonies.

(2) The Comptroller General shall monitor, review, and evaluate deportation proceedings conducted under this section. Within 18 months after the effective date of this section, the Comptroller General shall submit a report to such Committees concerning the extent to which deportation proceedings conducted under this section may adversely affect the ability of such aliens to contest deportation effectively.[1]

(June 27, 1952, c. 477, Title II, ch. 5, § 242A, as added Nov. 18, 1988, Pub.L. 100–690, Title VII, § 7347(a), 102 Stat. 4471, and amended Nov. 29, 1990, Pub.L. 101–649, Title V, § 506(a), 104 Stat. 5050.)

1. So in original. There is no closing parenthesis.

## 242B. Deportation procedures [8 U.S.C.A. § 1252b]

### (a) Notices

#### (1) Order to show cause

In deportation proceedings under section 242 [8 U.S.C.A. § 1252], written notice (in this section referred to as an "order to show cause") shall be given in person to the alien (or, if personal service is not practicable, such notice shall be given by certified mail to the alien or to the alien's counsel of record, if any) specifying the following:

(A) The nature of the proceedings against the alien.

(B) The legal authority under which the proceedings are conducted.

(C) The acts or conduct alleged to be in violation of law.

(D) The charges against the alien and the statutory provisions alleged to have been violated.

(E) The alien may be represented by counsel and, upon request, the alien will be provided a list of counsel prepared under subsection (b)(2) of this section.

(F)(i) The requirement that the alien must immediately provide (or have provided) the Attorney General with a written record of an address and telephone number (if any) at which the alien may be contacted respecting proceedings under section 242 [8 U.S.C.A. § 1252].

(ii) The requirement that the alien must provide the Attorney General immediately with a written record of any change of the alien's address or telephone number.

(iii) The consequences under subsection (c)(2) of this section of failure to provide address and telephone information pursuant to this subparagraph.

### (2) Notice of time and place of proceedings

In deportation proceedings under section 242 [8 U.S.C.A. § 1252]—

(A) written notice shall be given in person to the alien (or, if personal service is not practicable, written notice shall be given by certified mail to the alien or to the alien's counsel of record, if any), in the order to show cause or otherwise, of—

(i) the time and place at which the proceedings will be held, and

(ii) the consequences under subsection (c) of this section of the failure to appear at such proceedings; and

(B) in the case of any change or postponement in the time and place of such proceedings, written notice shall be given in person to the alien (or, if personal service is not practicable, written notice shall be given by certified mail to the alien or to the alien's counsel of record, if any) of—

(i) the new time or place of the proceedings, and

(ii) the consequences under subsection (c) of this section of failing, except under exceptional circumstances, to attend such proceedings.

### (3) Form of information

Each order to show cause or other notice under this subsection—

(A) shall be in English and Spanish, and

(B) shall specify that the alien may be represented by an attorney in deportation proceedings under section 242 [8 U.S.C.A. § 1252] and will be provided, in accordance with subsection (b)(1) of this section, a period of time in order to obtain counsel and a current list described in subsection (b)(2) of this section.

### (4) Central address files

The Attorney General shall create a system to record and preserve on a timely basis notices of addresses and telephone numbers (and changes) provided under paragraph (1)(F).

### (b) Securing of counsel

### (1) In general

In order that an alien be permitted the opportunity to secure counsel before the first hearing date in proceedings under section 242 [8 U.S.C.A. § 1252], the hearing date shall not be scheduled earlier than 14 days after the service of the order to show cause.

### (2) Current lists of counsel

The Attorney General shall provide for lists (updated not less often than quarterly) of persons who have indicated their availability to represent aliens in proceedings under section 242 [8 U.S.C.A. § 1252].

## (c) Consequences of failure to appear

### (1) In general

Any alien who, after written notice required under subsection (a)(2) of this section has been provided to the alien or the alien's counsel of record, except as provided in paragraph (2), does not attend a proceeding under section 242 [8 U.S.C.A. § 1252], shall be ordered deported under section 242(b)(1) [8 U.S.C.A. § 1252(b)(1)] in absentia if the Service establishes by clear, unequivocal, and convincing evidence that, except as provided in paragraph (2), the written notice was so provided and that the alien is deportable.

### (2) No notice if failure to provide address information

No written notice shall be required under paragraph (1) if the alien has failed to provide the address required under subsection (a)(1)(F) of this section. Such written notice shall be considered sufficient if provided at the most recent address provided under such subsection.

### (3) Rescission of order

Such an order may be rescinded only—

(A) upon a motion to reopen filed within 180 days after the date of the order of deportation if the alien demonstrates that the failure to appear was because of exceptional circumstances (as defined in subsection (f)(2) of this section), or

(B) upon a motion to reopen filed at any time if the alien demonstrates that the alien did not receive notice in accordance with subsection (a)(2) of this section or the alien demonstrates that the alien was in Federal or State custody and did not appear through no fault of the alien.

The filing of the motion to reopen described in subparagraph (A) or (B) shall stay the deportation of the alien pending disposition of the motion.

### (4) Effect on judicial review

Any petition for review under section 106 [8 U.S.C.A. § 1105a] of an order entered in absentia under this subsection shall, notwithstanding such section, be filed not later than 60 days after the date of the final order of deportation and shall (except in cases described in section 106(a)(5) [8 U.S.C.A. § 1105a(a)(5)]) be confined to the issues of the validity of the notice provided to the alien, to the reasons for the alien's not attending the proceeding, and to whether or not clear, convincing, and unequivocal evidence of deportability has been established.

**(d) Treatment of frivolous behavior**

The Attorney General shall, by regulation—

**(1)** define in a proceeding before a special inquiry officer or before an appellate administrative body under this subchapter, frivolous behavior for which attorneys may be sanctioned,

**(2)** specify the circumstances under which an administrative appeal of a decision or ruling will be considered frivolous and will be summarily dismissed, and

**(3)** impose appropriate sanctions (which may include suspension and disbarment) in the case of frivolous behavior.

Nothing in this subsection shall be construed as limiting the authority of the Board to take actions with respect to inappropriate behavior.

**(e) Limitation on discretionary relief for failure to appear**

**(1) At deportation proceedings**

Any alien against whom a final order of deportation is entered in absentia under this section and who, at the time of the notice described in subsection (a)(2) of this section, was provided oral notice, either in the alien's native language or in another language the alien understands, of the time and place of the proceedings and of the consequences under this paragraph of failing, other than because of exceptional circumstances (as defined in subsection (f)(2) of this section) to attend a proceeding under section 242 [8 U.S.C.A. § 1252], shall not be eligible for relief described in paragraph (5) for a period of 5 years after the date of the entry of the final order of deportation.

**(2) Voluntary departure**

**(A)** In general

Subject to subparagraph (B), any alien allowed to depart voluntarily under section 244(e)(1) [8 U.S.C.A. § 1254(e)(1)] or who has agreed to depart voluntarily at his own expense under section 242(b)(1) [8 U.S.C.A. § 1252(b)(1)] who remains in the United States after the scheduled date of departure, other than because of exceptional circumstances, shall not be eligible for relief described in paragraph (5) for a period of 5 years after the scheduled date of departure or the date of unlawful reentry, respectively.

**(B)** Written and oral notice required

Subparagraph (A) shall not apply to an alien allowed to depart voluntarily unless, before such departure, the Attorney

173

General has provided written notice to the alien in English and Spanish and oral notice either in the alien's native language or in another language the alien understands of the consequences under subparagraph (A) of the alien's remaining in the United States after the scheduled date of departure, other than because of exceptional circumstances.

### (3) Failure to appear under deportation order

**(A) In general**

Subject to subparagraph (B), any alien against whom a final order of deportation is entered under this section and who fails, other than because of exceptional circumstances, to appear for deportation at the time and place ordered shall not be eligible for relief described in paragraph (5) for a period of 5 years after the date the alien was required to appear for deportation.

**(B) Written and oral notice required**

Subparagraph (A) shall not apply to an alien against whom a deportation under is entered unless the Attorney General has provided, orally in the alien's native language or in another language the alien understands and in the final order of deportation under this section of the consequences under subparagraph (A) of the alien's failure, other than because of exceptional circumstances, to appear for deportation at the time and place ordered.

### (4) Failure to appear for asylum hearing

**(A) In general**

Subject to subparagraph (B), any alien—

    **(i)** whose period of authorized stay (if any) has expired through the passage of time,

    **(ii)** who has filed an application for asylum, and

    **(iii)** who fails, other than because of exceptional circumstances, to appear at the time and place specified for the asylum hearing,

shall not be eligible for relief described in paragraph (5) for a period of 5 years after the date of the asylum hearing.

**(B) Written and oral notice required**

Subparagraph (A) shall not apply in the case of an alien with respect to failure to be present at a hearing unless—

    **(i)** written notice in English and Spanish, and oral notice either in the alien's native language or in another language the alien understands, was provided to the alien of the time and place at which the asylum hearing will be held, and in the case of any change or postponement in such time or place, written notice in English and Spanish, and oral notice either in the alien's native language or in another language the alien understands, was provided to the alien of the new time or place of the hearing; and

(ii) notices under clause (i) specified the consequences under subparagraph (A) of failing, other than because of exceptional circumstances, to attend such hearing.

### (5) Relief covered

The relief described in this paragraph is—

(A) relief under section 212(c) [8 U.S.C.A. § 1182(c)],

(B) voluntary departure under section 242(b)(1) [8 U.S.C.A. § 1252(b)(1)],

(C) suspension of deportation or voluntary departure under section 244 [8 U.S.C.A. § 1254], and

(D) adjustment or change of status under section 244, 245, 248, or 249 [8 U.S.C.A. §§ 1254, 1255, 1258, or 1259].

### (f) Definitions

In this section:

(1) The term "certified mail" means certified mail, return receipt requested.

(2) The term "exceptional circumstances" refers to exceptional circumstances (such as serious illness of the alien or death of an immediate relative of the alien, but not including less compelling circumstances) beyond the control of the alien.

(Act June 27, 1952, c. 477, Title II, ch. 5, § 242B, as added Nov. 29, 1990, Pub.L. 101–649, Title V, § 545(a), 104 Stat. 5061.)

### Editorial Note

*Effective Date.* Section 545(g) of Pub.L. 101–649 [Immigration Act of 1990] provided that:

*"(1) Notice-related provisions.—*

*"(A) Subsections (a), (b), (c), and (e)(1) of section 242B of the Immigration and Nationality Act (as inserted by the amendment made by subsection (a)) [subsecs. (a), (b), (c), and (e)(1) of this section], and the amendment made by subsection (e) [amending section 242B [8 U.S.C.A. § 1252(b)], shall be effective on a date specified by the Attorney General in the certification described in subparagraph (B), which date may not be earlier than 6 months after the date of such certification.*

*"(B) The Attorney General shall certify to the Congress when the central address file system (described in section 242B(a)(4) of the Immigration and Nationality Act) [subsec. (a)(14) of this section] has been established.*

*"(C) The Comptroller General shall submit to Congress, within 3 months after the date of the Attorney General's certification under subparagraph (B), a report on the adequacy of such system.*

*"(2) Certain limits on discretionary relief; sanctions for frivolous behavior.—Subsections (d), (e)(2), and (e)(3) of section 242B of the Immigration and Nationality Act (as inserted by the amendment made by subsection (a)) [subsecs. (d), (e)(2) and (e)(3) of this section] shall be effective on the date of the enactment of this Act [Nov. 29, 1990].*

*"(3) Limits on discretionary relief for failure to appear in asylum hearing.—Subsection (e)(4) of section 242B of the Immigration and Nationality Act (as inserted by the amendment made by subsection (a)) [subsec. (e)(4) of this section] shall be effective on February 1, 1991.*

"**(4) Consolidation of relief in judicial review.**—The amendments made by subsection (b) [amending section 1105a(a) of this title] shall apply to final orders of deportation entered on or after January 1, 1991."

## § 243. Countries to which aliens shall be deported [8 U.S.C.A. § 1253]

**(a) Acceptance by designated country; deportation upon non-acceptance by country**

The deportation of an alien in the United States provided for in this chapter, or any other Act or treaty, shall be directed by the Attorney General to a country promptly designated by the alien if that country is willing to accept him into its territory, unless the Attorney General, in his discretion, concludes that deportation to such country would be prejudicial to the interests of the United States. No alien shall be permitted to make more than one such designation, nor shall any alien designate, as the place to which he wishes to be deported, any foreign territory contiguous to the United States or any island adjacent thereto or adjacent to the United States unless such alien is a native, citizen, subject, or national of, or had a residence in such designated foreign contiguous territory or adjacent island. If the government of the country designated by the alien fails finally to advise the Attorney General within three months following original inquiry whether that government will or will not accept such alien into its territory, such designation may thereafter be disregarded. Thereupon deportation of such alien shall be directed to any country of which such alien is a subject, national, or citizen if such country is willing to accept him into its territory. If the government of such country fails finally to advise the Attorney General or the alien within three months following the date of original inquiry, or within such other period as the Attorney General shall deem reasonable under the circumstances in a particular case, whether that government will or will not accept such alien into its territory, then such deportation shall be directed by the Attorney General within his discretion and without necessarily giving any priority or preference because of their order as herein set forth either—

(1) to the country from which such alien last entered the United States;

(2) to the country in which is located the foreign port at which such alien embarked for the United States or for foreign contiguous territory;

**(3)** to the country in which he was born;

**(4)** to the country in which the place of his birth is situated at the time he is ordered deported;

**(5)** to any country in which he resided prior to entering the country from which he entered the United States;

**(6)** to the country which had sovereignty over the birthplace of the alien at the time of his birth; or

**(7)** if deportation to any of the foregoing places or countries is impracticable, inadvisable, or impossible, then to any country which is willing to accept such alien into its territory.

### (b) Deportation during war

If the United States is at war and the deportation, in accordance with the provisions of subsection (a) of this section, of any alien who is deportable under any law of the United States shall be found by the Attorney General to be impracticable, inadvisable, inconvenient, or impossible because of enemy occupation of the country from which such alien came or wherein is located the foreign port at which he embarked for the United States or because of reasons connected with the war, such alien may, in the discretion of the Attorney General, be deported as follows:

**(1)** if such alien is a citizen or subject of a country whose recognized government is in exile, to the country in which is located that government in exile if that country will permit him to enter its territory; or

**(2)** if such alien is a citizen or subject of a country whose recognized government is not in exile, then to a country or any political or territorial subdivision thereof which is proximate to the country of which the alien is a citizen or subject, or, with the consent of the country of which the alien is a citizen or subject, to any other country.

### (c) Payment of deportation costs; within five years

If deportation proceedings are instituted at any time within five years after the entry of the alien for causes existing prior to or at the time of entry, the cost of removal to the port of deportation shall be at the expense of the appropriation for the enforcement of this chapter, and the deportation from such port shall be at the expense of the owner or owners of the vessels, aircraft, or other transportation lines by which such alien came to the United States, or if in the opinion of the Attorney General that is not practicable, at the expense of the appropriation for the enforcement of this chapter: *Provided,* That the costs of the deportation of any such alien from such port shall not be assessed against the owner or owners of the vessels, aircraft, or other transportation lines in the case of any alien who arrived in possession of a valid unexpired immigrant visa and who was inspected and admitted to the United States for permanent residence. In the case of an alien crewman, if deportation proceedings are instituted at any time within five years after the granting of the last conditional permit to land temporarily under the provisions of section 252 [8 U.S.C.A. § 1282], the cost of removal to the port of deportation shall be at the expense of the appropriation for the enforcement of this chapter and the deportation from such port shall be at the expense of the owner or owners of the vessels or aircraft by which such alien came to the United States, or if in the opinion of the Attorney General that is not practicable, at the expense of the appropriation for the enforcement of this chapter.

### (d) Cost of deportation, subsequent to five years

If deportation proceedings are instituted later than five years after the entry of the alien, or in the case of an alien crewman later than five years after the granting of the last conditional permit to land temporarily, the cost thereof shall be payable from the appropriation for the enforcement of this chapter.

### (e) Refusal to transport or to pay

A failure or refusal on the part of the master, commanding officer, agent, owner, charterer, or consignee of a vessel, aircraft, or other transportation line to comply with the order of the Attorney General to take on board, guard safely, and transport to the destination specified any alien ordered to be deported under the provisions of this chapter, or a failure or refusal by any such person to comply with an order of the Attorney General to pay deportation expenses in accordance with the requirements of this section, shall be punished by the imposition of a penalty in the sum and manner prescribed in section 237(b) [8 U.S.C.A. § 1227(b)].

### (f) Payment of expenses of physically incapable deportees

When in the opinion of the Attorney General the mental or physical condition of an alien being deported is such as to require personal care and attendance, the Attorney General shall, when necessary, employ a suitable person for that purpose who shall accompany such alien to his final destination, and the expense incident to such service shall be defrayed in the same manner as the expense of deporting the accompanied alien is defrayed, and any failure or refusal to defray such expenses shall be punished in the manner prescribed by subsection (e) of this section.

### (g) Countries delaying acceptance of deportees

Upon the notification by the Attorney General that any country upon request denies or unduly delays acceptance of the return of any alien who is a national, citizen, subject, or resident thereof, the Secretary of State shall instruct consular officers performing their duties in the territory of such country to discontinue the issuance of immigrant visas to nationals, citizens, subjects, or residents of such country, until such time as the Attorney General shall inform the Secretary of State that such country has accepted such alien.

### (h) Withholding of deportation or return

(1) The Attorney General shall not deport or return any alien (other than an alien described in section 241(a)(4)(D) [8 U.S.C.A. § 1251(a)(4)(D)]) to a country if the Attorney General determines that such alien's life or freedom would be threatened in such country on account of race, religion, nationality, membership in a particular social group, or political opinion.

(2) Paragraph (1) shall not apply to any alien if the Attorney General determines that—

(A) the alien ordered, incited, assisted, or otherwise participated in the persecution of any person on account of race, religion, nationality, membership in a particular social group, or political opinion;

(B) the alien, having been convicted by a final judgment of a particularly serious crime, constitutes a danger to the community of the United States;

(C) there are serious reasons for considering that the alien has committed a serious nonpolitical crime outside the United States prior to the arrival of the alien in the United States; or

(D) there are reasonable grounds for regarding the alien as a danger to the security of the United States.

For purposes of subparagraph (B), an alien who has been convicted of an aggravated felony shall be considered to have committed a particularly serious crime.

(June 27, 1952, c. 477, Title II, ch. 5, § 243, 66 Stat. 212; Pub L. 89–236, § 11(f), Oct. 3, 1965, 79 Stat. 918; Pub.L. 95–549, Title I, § 104, Oct. 30, 1978, 92 Stat. 2066; Pub.L. 96–212, Title II, § 203(e), Mar. 17, 1980, 94 St. t. 107; Pub.L. 97–116, § 18(i), Dec. 29, 1981, 95 Stat. 1620; Pub.L. 101–649, Title V, § 515(a)(2), Title VI, § 603(b)(3), Nov. 29, 1990, 104 Stat. 5053, 5085.)

# § 244. Suspension of deportation [8 U.S.C.A. § 1254]

### (a) Adjustment of status for permanent residence; contents

As hereinafter prescribed in this section, the Attorney General may, in his discretion, suspend deportation and adjust the status to that of an alien lawfully admitted for permanent residence, in the case of an alien (other than an alien described in section 241(a)(4)(D) [8 U.S.C.A. § 1251(a)(4)(D)]) who applies to the Attorney General for suspension of deportation and—

(1) is deportable under any law of the United States except the provisions specified in paragraph (2) of this subsection; has been physically present in the United States for a continuous period of not less than seven years immediately preceding the date of such application, and proves that during all of such period he was and is a person of good moral character; and is a person whose deportation would, in the opinion of the Attorney General, result in extreme hardship to the alien or to his spouse, parent, or child, who

is a citizen of the United States or an alien lawfully admitted for permanent residence; or

(2) is deportable under paragraph (2), (3), or (4) of section 241(a) [8 U.S.C.A. § 1251(a)(2), (3), or (4)]; has been physically present in the United States for a continuous period of not less than ten years immediately following the commission of an act, or the assumption of a status, constituting a ground for deportation, and proves that during all of such period he has been and is a person of good moral character; and is a person whose deportation would, in the opinion of the Attorney General, result in exceptional and extremely unusual hardship to the alien or to his spouse, parent, or child, who is a citizen of the United States or an alien lawfully admitted for permanent residence.

**(b) Continuous physical presence not required because of honorable service in Armed Forces and presence upon entry into service**

(1) The requirement of continuous physical presence in the United States specified in paragraphs (1) and (2) of subsection (a) of this section shall not be applicable to an alien who (A) has served for a minimum period of twenty-four months in an active-duty status in the Armed Forces of the United States and, if separated from such service, was separated under honorable conditions, and (B) at the time of his enlistment or induction was in the United States.

(2) An alien shall not be considered to have failed to maintain continuous physical presence in the United States under paragraphs (1) and (2) of subsection (a) if the absence from the United States was brief, casual, and innocent and did not meaningfully interrupt the continuous physical presence.

**(c) Fulfillment of requirements of subsection (a)**

Upon application by any alien who is found by the Attorney General to meet the requirements of subsection (a) of this section the Attorney General may in his discretion suspend deportation of such alien.

**(d) Record of cancellation of deportation**

Upon the cancellation of deportation in the case of any alien under this section, the Attorney General shall record the alien's lawful admission for permanent residence as of the date the cancellation of deportation of such alien is made.

**(e) Voluntary departure; inapplicability to alien deportable for conviction of aggravated felony**

(1) Except as provided in paragraph (2), the Attorney General may, in his discretion, permit any alien under deportation proceedings, other than an alien within the provisions of paragraph (2), (3), or (4) of section 241(a) [8 U.S.C.A. § 1251(a)(2), (3), or (4) ] (and also any alien within the purview of such paragraphs if he is also within the provisions of

paragraph (2) of subsection (a) of this section), to depart voluntarily from the United States at his own expense in lieu of deportation if such alien shall establish to the satisfaction of the Attorney General that he is, and has been, a person of good moral character for at least five years immediately preceding his application for voluntary departure under this subsection.

**(2)** The authority contained in paragraph (1) shall not apply to any alien who is deportable because of a conviction for an aggravated felony.

**(f) Alien crewmen; nonimmigrant exchange aliens admitted to receive graduate medical education or training; other**

The provisions of subsection (a) of this section shall not apply to an alien who—

**(1)** entered the United States as a crewman subsequent to June 30, 1964;

**(2)** was admitted to the United States as a nonimmigrant exchange alien as defined in section 101(a)(15)(J) [8 U.S.C.A. § 1101(a)(15)(J)], or has acquired the status of such a nonimmigrant exchange alien after admission, in order to receive graduate medical education or training, regardless of whether or not the alien is subject to or has fulfilled the two-year foreign residence requirement of section 212(e) [8 U.S.C.A. § 1182(e)]; or

**(3)(A)** was admitted to the United States as a nonimmigrant exchange alien as defined in section 101(a)(15)(J) [8 U.S.C.A. § 1101(a)(15)(J)] or has acquired the status of such a nonimmigrant exchange alien after admission other than to receive graduate medical education or training, **(B)** is subject to the two-year foreign residence requirement of section 212(e) [8 U.S.C.A. § 1182(e)], and **(C)** has not fulfilled that requirement or received a waiver thereof.

(June 27, 1952, c. 477, Title II, ch. 5, § 244, 66 Stat. 214; Pub.L. 87–885, § 4, Oct. 24, 1962, 76 Stat. 1247; Pub.L. 89–236, § 12, Oct. 3, 1965, 79 Stat. 918; Pub.L. 94–571, § 7(f), Oct. 20, 1976, 90 Stat. 2706; Pub.L. 95–549, Title I, § 105, Oct. 30, 1978, 92 Stat. 2066; Pub.L. 96–212, Title II, § 203(d), Mar. 17, 1980, 94 Stat. 107; Pub.L. 97–116, §§ 9, 18(h)(2), (j), Dec. 29, 1981, 95 Stat. 1616, 1620; Pub.L. 99–603, Title III, § 315(b), Nov. 6, 1986, 100 Stat. 3439, amended Pub.L. 100–525, § 2(q)(1), Oct. 24, 1988, 102 Stat. 2613; Pub.L. 100–690, Title VII, § 7343(b), Nov. 18, 1988, 102 Stat. 4470; Pub.L. 101–649, Title I, §§ 161, 162(e)(2), Title VI, § 603(b)(3), (4), Nov. 29, 1990, 104 Stat. 5008, 5011, 5085.)

# § 244a. Temporary protected status [8 U.S.C.A. § 1254a]

## (a) Granting of status

### (1) In general

In the case of an alien who is a national of a foreign state designated under subsection (b) of this section and who meets the requirements of subsection (c) of this section, the Attorney General, in accordance with this section—

(A) may grant the alien temporary protected status in the United States and shall not deport the alien from the United States during the period in which such status is in effect, and

(B) shall authorize the alien to engage in employment in the United States and provide the alien with an "employment authorized" endorsement or other appropriate work permit.

## (2) Duration of work authorization

Work authorization provided under this section shall be effective throughout the period the alien is in temporary protected status under this section.

## (3) Notice

(A) Upon the granting of temporary protected status under this section, the Attorney General shall provide the alien with information concerning such status under this section.

(B) If, at the time of initiation of a deportation proceeding against an alien, the foreign state (of which the alien is a national) is designated under subsection (b) of this section, the Attorney General shall promptly notify the alien of the temporary protected status that may be available under this section.

(C) If, at the time of designation of a foreign state under subsection (b) of this section, an alien (who is a national of such state) is in a deportation proceeding under this subchapter, the Attorney General shall promptly notify the alien of the temporary protected status that may be available under this section.

(D) Notices under this paragraph shall be provided in a form and language that the alien can understand.

## (4) Temporary treatment for eligible aliens

(A) In the case of an alien who can establish a prima facie case of eligibility for benefits under paragraph (1), but for the fact that the period of registration under subsection (c)(1)(A)(iv) of this section has not begun, until the alien has had a reasonable opportunity to register during the first 30 days of such period, the Attorney General shall provide for the benefits of paragraph (1).

(B) In the case of an alien who establishes a prima facie case of eligibility for benefits under paragraph (1), until a final determination with respect to the alien's eligibility for such benefits under paragraph (1) has been made, the alien shall be provided such benefits.

## (5) Clarification

Nothing in this section shall be construed as authorizing the Attorney General to deny temporary protected status to an alien based on the alien's immigration status or to require any alien, as a condition of being granted such status, either to relinquish nonimmigrant or other status the alien may have or to execute any waiver of other rights under this chapter. The granting of temporary protected status under this section shall not be considered to be inconsistent with the granting of nonimmigrant status under this chapter.

## (b) Designations

### (1) In general

The Attorney General, after consultation with appropriate agencies of the Government, may designate any foreign state (or any part of such foreign state) under this subsection only if—

(A) the Attorney General finds that there is an ongoing armed conflict within the state and, due to such conflict, requiring the return of aliens who are nationals of that state to that state (or to the part of the state) would pose a serious threat to their personal safety;

(B) the Attorney General finds that—

(i) there has been an earthquake, flood, drought, epidemic, or other environmental disaster in the state resulting in a substantial, but temporary, disruption of living conditions in the area affected,

(ii) the foreign state is unable, temporarily, to handle adequately the return to the state of aliens who are nationals of the state, and

(iii) the foreign state officially has requested designation under this subparagraph; or

(C) the Attorney General finds that there exist extraordinary and temporary conditions in the foreign state that prevent aliens who are nationals of the state from returning to the state in safety, unless the Attorney General finds that permitting the aliens to remain temporarily in the United States is contrary to the national interest of the United States.

A designation of a foreign state (or part of such foreign state) under this paragraph shall not become effective unless notice of the designation (including a statement of the findings under this paragraph and the effective date of the designation) is published in the Federal Register. In such notice, the Attorney General shall also state an estimate of the number of nationals of the foreign state designated who are (or within the effective period of the designation are likely to become) eligible for temporary protected status under this section and their immigration status in the United States.

### (2) Effective period of designation for foreign states

The designation of a foreign state (or part of such foreign state) under paragraph (1) shall—

**(A)** take effect upon the date of publication of the designation under such paragraph, or such later date as the Attorney General may specify in the notice published under such paragraph, and

**(B)** shall remain in effect until the effective date of the termination of the designation under paragraph (3)(B).

For purposes of this section, the initial period of designation of a foreign state (or part thereof) under paragraph (1) is the period, specified by the Attorney General, of not less than 6 months and not more than 18 months.

**(3) Periodic review, terminations, and extensions of designations**

**(A)** Periodic review

At least 60 days before end of the initial period of designation, and any extended period of designation, of a foreign state (or part thereof) under this section the Attorney General, after consultation with appropriate agencies of the Government, shall review the conditions in the foreign state (or part of such foreign state) for which a designation is in effect under this subsection and shall determine whether the conditions for such designation under this subsection continue to be met. The Attorney General shall provide on a timely basis for the publication of notice of each such determination (including the basis for the determination, and, in the case of an affirmative determination, the period of extension of designation under subparagraph (C)) in the Federal Register.

**(B)** Termination of designation

If the Attorney General determines under subparagraph (A) that a foreign state (or part of such foreign state) no longer continues to meet the conditions for designation under paragraph (1), the Attorney General shall terminate the designation by publishing notice in the Federal Register of the determination under this subparagraph (including the basis for the determination). Such termination is effective in accordance with subsection (d)(3) of this section, but shall not be effective earlier than 60 days after the date the notice is published or, if Later, the expiration of the most recent previous extension under subparagraph (C).

**(C)** Extension of designation

If the Attorney General does not determine under subparagraph (A) that a foreign state (or part of such foreign state) no longer meets the conditions for designation under paragraph (1), the period of designation of the foreign state is extended for an additional period of 6 months (or, in the discretion of the Attorney General, a period of 12 or 18 months).

**(4) Information concerning protected status at time of designations**

At the time of a designation of a foreign state under this subsection, the Attorney General shall make available information respecting the temporary protected status made available to aliens who are nationals of such designated foreign state.

**(5) Review**

**(A)** Designations

There is no judicial review of any determination of the Attorney General with respect to the designation, or termination or extension of a designation, of a foreign state under this subsection.

**(B)** Application to individuals

The Attorney General shall establish an administrative procedure for the review of the denial of benefits to aliens under this subsection. Such procedure shall not prevent an alien from asserting protection under this section in deportation proceedings if the alien demonstrates that the alien is a national of a state designated under paragraph (1).

**(c) Aliens eligible for temporary protected status**

**(1) In general**

**(A)** Nationals of designated foreign states

Subject to paragraph (3), an alien, who is a national of a state designated under subsection (b)(1) of this section, meets the requirements of this paragraph only if—

(i) the alien has been continuously physically present in the United States since the effective date of the most recent designation of that state;

(ii) the alien has continuously resided in the United States since such date as the Attorney General may designate;

(iii) the alien is admissible as an immigrant, except as otherwise provided under paragraph (2)(A), and is not ineligible for temporary protected status under paragraph (2)(B); and

(iv) to the extent and in a manner which the Attorney General establishes, the alien registers for the temporary protected status under this section during a registration period of not less than 180 days.

**(B)** Registration fee

The Attorney General may require payment of a reasonable fee as a condition of registering an alien under subparagraph (A)(iv) (including providing an alien with an "employment authorized" endorsement or other appropriate work permit under this section). The amount of any such fee shall not exceed $50.

## (2) Eligibility standards

**(A)** Waiver of certain grounds for inadmissibility

In the determination of an alien's admissibility for purposes of subparagraph (A)(iii) of paragraph (1)—

(i) the provisions of paragraphs (5) and (7)(A) of section 212(a) [8 U.S.C.A. § 1182(a)(5) and (7)(A)] shall not apply;

(ii) except as provided in clause (iii), the Attorney General may waive any other provision of section 212(a) [8 U.S.C.A. § 1182(a)] in the case of individual aliens for humanitarian purposes, to assure family unity, or when it is otherwise in the public interest; but

(iii) the Attorney General may not waive—

(I) paragraphs (2)(A) and (2)(B) (relating to criminals) of such section,

(II) paragraph (2)(C) of such section (relating to drug offenses), except for so much of such paragraph as relates to a single offense of simple possession of 30 grams or less of marijuana, or

(III) paragraphs[1] (3) (relating to security and related grounds).

(B) Aliens ineligible

An alien shall not be eligible for temporary protected status under this section if the Attorney General finds that—

(i) the alien has been convicted of any felony or 2 or more misdemeanors committed in the United States, or

(ii) the alien is described in section 243(h)(2) [8 U.S. C.A. § 1253(h)(2)].

## (3) Withdrawal of temporary protected status

The Attorney General shall withdraw temporary protected status granted to an alien under this section if—

(A) the Attorney General finds that the alien was not in fact eligible for such status under this section,

(B) except as provided in paragraph (4) and permitted in subsection (f)(3) of this section, the alien has not remained continuously physically present in the United States from the date the alien first was granted temporary protected status under this section, or

(C) the alien fails, without good cause, to register with the Attorney General annually, at the end of each 12–month period after the granting of such status, in a form and manner specified by the Attorney General.

**(4) Treatment of brief, casual, and innocent departures and certain other absences**

(A) For purposes of paragraphs (1)(A)(i) and (3)(B), an alien shall not be considered to have failed to maintain continuous physical presence in the United States by virtue of brief, casual, and innocent absences from the United States, without regard to whether such absences were authorized by the Attorney General.

(B) For purposes of paragraph (1)(A)(ii), an alien shall not be considered to have failed to maintain continuous residence in the United States by reason of a brief, casual, and innocent absence described in subparagraph (A) or due merely to a brief temporary trip abroad required by emergency or extenuating circumstances outside the control of the alien.

**(5) Construction**

Nothing in this section shall be construed as authorizing an alien to apply for admission to, or to be admitted to, the United States in order to apply for temporary protected status under this section.

**(6) Confidentiality of information**

The Attorney General shall establish procedures to protect the confidentiality of information provided by aliens under this section.

**(d) Documentation**

**(1) Initial issuance**

Upon the granting of temporary protected status to an alien under this section, the Attorney General shall provide for the issuance of such temporary documentation and authorization as may be necessary to carry out the purposes of this section.

**(2) Period of validity**

Subject to paragraph (3), such documentation shall be valid during the initial period of designation of the foreign state (or part thereof) involved and any extension of such period. The Attorney General may stagger the periods of validity of the documentation and authorization in order to provide for an orderly renewal of such documentation and authorization and for an orderly transition (under paragraph (3)) upon the termination of a designation of a foreign state (or any part of such foreign state).

**(3) Effective date of terminations**

If the Attorney General terminates the designation of a foreign state (or part of such foreign state) under subsection (b)(3)(B) of this section, such termination shall only apply to documentation and authorization issued or renewed after the effective date of the publication of notice of the determination under that subsection (or, at the Attorney General's option, after such period after the effective date of the determination as the Attorney General determines to be appropriate in order to provide for an orderly transition).

### (4) Detention of the alien

An alien provided temporary protected status under this section shall not be detained by the Attorney General on the basis of the alien's immigration status in the United States.

### (e) Relation of period of temporary protected status to suspension of deportation

With respect to an alien granted temporary protected status under this section, the period of such status shall not be counted as a period of physical presence in the United States for purposes of section 244(a) [8 U.S.C.A. § 1254(a)], unless the Attorney General determines that extreme hardship exists. Such period shall not cause a break in the continuity of residence of the period before and after such period for purposes of such section.

### (f) Benefits and status during period of temporary protected status

During a period in which an alien is granted temporary protected status under this section—

(1) the alien shall not be considered to be permanently residing in the United States under color of law;

(2) the alien may be deemed ineligible for public assistance by a State (as defined in section 101(a)(36) [8 U.S.C.A. § 1101(a)(36)]) or any political subdivision thereof which furnishes such assistance;

(3) the alien may travel abroad with the prior consent of the Attorney General; and

(4) for purposes of adjustment of status under section 245 [8 U.S.C.A. § 1255] and change of status under section 248 [8 U.S.C.A. § 1258], the alien shall be considered as being in, and maintaining, lawful status as a nonimmigrant.

### (g) Exclusive remedy

Except as otherwise specifically provided, this section shall constitute the exclusive authority of the Attorney General under law to permit aliens who are or may become otherwise deportable or have been paroled into the United States to remain in the United States temporarily because of their particular nationality or region of foreign state of nationality.

**(h) Limitation on consideration in the senate of legislation adjusting status**

### (1) In general

Except as provided in paragraph (2), it shall not be in order in the Senate to consider any bill, resolution, or amendment that—

**(A)** provides for adjustment to lawful temporary or permanent resident alien status for any alien receiving temporary protected status under this section, or

**(B)** has the effect of amending this subsection or limiting the application of this subsection.

### (2) Supermajority required

Paragraph (1) may be waived or suspended in the Senate only by the affirmative vote of three-fifths of the Members duly chosen and sworn. An affirmative vote of three-fifths of the Members of the Senate duly chosen and sworn shall be required in the Senate to sustain an appeal of the ruling of the Chair on a point of order raised under paragraph (1).

### (3) Rules

Paragraphs (1) and (2) are enacted—

**(A)** as an exercise of the rulemaking power of the Senate and such they are deemed a part of the rules of the Senate, but applicable only with respect to the matters described in paragraph (1) and supersede other rules of the Senate only to the extent that such paragraphs are inconsistent therewith; and

**(B)** with full recognition of the constitutional right of the Senate to change such rules at any time, in the same manner as in the case of any other rule of the Senate.

**(i) Annual report and review**

### (1) Annual report

Not later than March 1 of each year (beginning with 1992), the Attorney General, after consultation with the appropriate agencies of the Government, shall submit a report to the Committees on the Judiciary of the House of Representatives and of the Senate on the operation of this section during the previous year. Each report shall include—

**(A)** a listing of the foreign states or parts thereof designated under this section,

**(B)** the number of nationals of each such state who have been granted temporary protected status under this section and their immigration status before being granted such status, and

**(C)** an explanation of the reasons why foreign states or parts thereof were designated under subsection (b)(1) of this section and, with respect to foreign states or parts thereof previously designated, why the designation was terminated or extended under subsection (b)(3) of this section.

### (2) Committee report

No later than 180 days after the date of receipt of such a report, the Committee on the Judiciary of each House of Congress shall report to its respective House such oversight findings and legislation as it deems appropriate.

(June 27, 1952, c. 477, Title II, ch. 5, § 244A, as added and amended Nov. 29, 1990, Pub.L. 101–649, Title III, § 302(a), Title VI, § 603(a)(24), 104 Stat. 5030, 5084.)

1. So in original.  Probably should be "paragraph".

## § 245.  Adjustment of status of nonimmigrant inspected and admitted or paroled into United States [8 U.S.C.A. § 1255]

### (a) Status as person admitted for permanent residence upon application and eligibility for immigrant visa

The status of an alien who was inspected and admitted or paroled into the United States may be adjusted by the Attorney General, in his discretion and under such regulations as he may prescribe, to that of an alien lawfully admitted for permanent residence if (1) the alien makes an application for such adjustment, (2) the alien is eligible to receive an immigrant visa and is admissible to the United States for permanent residence, and (3) an immigrant visa is immediately available to him at the time his application is filed.

### (b) Record of lawful admission for permanent residence; reduction of preference or nonpreference visas

Upon the approval of an application for adjustment made under subsection (a) of this section, the Attorney General shall record the alien's lawful admission for permanent residence as of the date the order of the Attorney General approving the application for the adjustment of status is made, and the Secretary of State shall reduce by one the number of the preference visas authorized to be issued under section 201(e) [8 U.S.C.A. § 1151(a)] within the class to which the alien is chargeable for the succeeding fiscal year.

### (c) Alien crewmen, aliens continuing or accepting unauthorized employment, and aliens admitted in transit without visa

Subsection (a) of this section shall not be applicable to (1) an alien crewman; (2) an alien (other than an immediate relative as defined in section 201(b) [8 U.S.C.A. § 1151(b)] or a special immigrant described in section 101(a)(27)(H) or (I) [8 U.S.C.A. § 1101(a)(27)(H) or (I)]) who hereafter continues in or accepts unauthorized employment prior to filing an application for adjustment of status; or who is in unlawful

190

immigration status on the date of filing the application for adjustment of status or who has failed (other than through no fault of his own or for technical reasons) to maintain continuously a lawful status since entry into the United States; or (3) any alien admitted in transit without visa under section 212(d)(4)(C) [8 U.S.C.A. § 1182(d)(4)(C)]; or (4) an alien (other than an immediate relative as defined in section 201(b) [8 U.S.C.A. § 1151(b)]) who was admitted as a nonimmigrant visitor without a visa under section 212(*l*) [8 U.S.C.A. § 1182(*l*)] or section 217 [8 U.S.C.A. § 1187].

### (d) Alien admitted for permanent residence on conditional basis; fiancée or fiancé of citizen

The Attorney General may not adjust, under subsection (a) of this section, the status of an alien lawfully admitted to the United States for permanent residence on a conditional basis under section 216 [8 U.S.C.A. § 1186a]. The Attorney General may not adjust, under subsection (a) of this section, the status of a nonimmigrant alien described in section 101(a)(15)(K) [8 U.S.C.A. § 1101(a)(15)(K)] (relating to an alien fiancee or fiance or the minor child of such alien) except to that of an alien lawfully admitted to the United States on a conditional basis under section 216 [8 U.S.C.A. § 1186a] as a result of the marriage of the nonimmigrant (or, in the case of a minor child, the parent) to the citizen who filed the petition to accord that alien's nonimmigrant status under section 101(a)(15)(K) [8 U.S.C.A. § 1101(a)(15)(K)].

### (e) Restrictions on adjustment of status based on marriages entered while in exclusion or deportation proceedings; bona fide marriage exception

(1) Except as provided in paragraph (3), an alien who is seeking to receive an immigrant visa on the basis of a marriage which was entered into during the period described in paragraph (2) may not have the alien's status adjusted under subsection (a) of this section.

(2) The period described in this paragraph is the period during which administrative or judicial proceedings are pending regarding the alien's right to enter or remain in the United States.

(3) Paragraph (1) and section 204(h) [8 U.S.C.A. § 1154(h)] shall not apply with respect to a marriage if the alien establishes by clear and convincing evidence to the satisfaction of the Attorney General that the marriage was entered into in good faith and in accordance with the laws of the place where the marriage took place and the marriage was not entered into for the purpose of procuring the alien's entry as an immigrant and no fee or other consideration was given (other than a fee or other consideration to an attorney for assistance in preparation of a lawful petition) for the filing of a petition under section 204(a) [8 U.S.C.A. § 1154(a)] or 214(d) [8 U.S.C.A. § 1184(d)] with respect to the alien spouse or alien son or daughter. In accordance with regulations, there shall be only one level of administrative appellate review for each alien under the previous sentence.

191

### (f) Limitation on adjustment of status

The Attorney General may not adjust, under subsection (a) of this section, the status of an alien lawfully admitted to the United States for permanent residence on a conditional basis under section 216A [8 U.S.C.A. § 1186b].

(June 27, 1952, c. 477, Title II, ch. 5, § 245, 66 Stat. 217; Pub.L. 85–700, § 1, Aug. 21, 1958, 72 Stat. 699; Pub.L. 86–648, § 10, July 14, 1960, 74 Stat. 505; Pub.L. 89–236, § 13, Oct. 3, 1965, 79 Stat. 918; Pub.L. 94–571, § 6, Oct. 20, 1976, 90 Stat. 2705; Pub.L. 97–116, § 5(d)(2), Dec. 29, 1981, 95 Stat. 1614; Pub.L. 99–603, Title I, § 117, Title III, § 313(c), Nov. 6, 1986, 100 Stat. 3384, 3438; Pub.L. 99–603, Title III, § 313(c), as amended Pub.L. 100–525, § 2(p)(3), Oct. 24, 1988, 102 Stat. 2613; Pub.L. 99–639, §§ 2(e), 3(b), 5(a), Nov. 10, 1986, 100 Stat. 3542, 3543; Pub.L. 99–639, § 3(b), as amended Pub.L. 100–525, § 7(b), Oct. 24, 1988, 102 Stat. 2616; Pub.L. 100–525, § 2(f)(1), Oct. 24, 1988, 102 Stat. 2611; Pub.L. 101–649, Title I, §§ 121(b)(4), 161, 162(e)(3), Title VII, § 702(a), Nov. 29, 1990, 104 Stat. 4994, 5008, 5011, 5086.)

## § 245A.  Adjustment of status of certain entrants before January 1, 1982, to that of person admitted for lawful residence [8 U.S.C.A. § 1255a]

### (a) Temporary resident status

The Attorney General shall adjust the status of an alien to that of an alien lawfully admitted for temporary residence if the alien meets the following requirements:

#### (1) Timely application

(A) During application period

Except as provided in subparagraph (B), the alien must apply for such adjustment during the 12-month period beginning on a date (not later than 180 days after November 6, 1986) designated by the Attorney General.

(B) Application within 30 days of show-cause order

An alien who, at any time during the first 11 months of the 12-month period described in subparagraph (A), is the subject of an order to show cause issued under section 242 [8 U.S.C.A. § 1252], must make application under this section not later than the end of the 30-day period beginning either on the first day of such 12-month period or on the date of the issuance of such order, whichever day is later.

(C) Information included in application

Each application under this subsection shall contain such information as the Attorney General may require, including information on living relatives of the applicant with respect to whom a petition for preference or other status may be filed by the applicant at any later date under section 204(a) [8 U.S.C.A. § 1154(a)].

## (2) Continuous unlawful residence since 1982

### (A) In general

The alien must establish that he entered the United States before January 1, 1982, and that the has resided continuously in the United States in an unlawful status since such date and through the date the application is filed under this subsection.

### (B) Nonimmigrants

In the case of an alien who entered the United States as a nonimmigrant before January 1, 1982, the alien must establish that the alien's period of authorized stay as a nonimmigrant expired before such date through the passage of time or the alien's unlawful status was known to the Government as of such date.

### (C) Exchange visitors

If the alien was at any time a nonimmigrant exchange alien (as defined in section 101(a)(15)(J) [8 U.S.C.A. § 1101(a)(15)(J)]), the alien must establish that the alien was not subject to the two-year foreign residence requirement of section 212(e) [8 U.S.C.A. § 1182(e)] or has fulfilled that requirement or received a waiver thereof.

## (3) Continuous physical presence since November 6, 1986

### (A) In general

The alien must establish that the alien has been continuously physically present in the United States since November 6, 1986.

### (B) Treatment of brief, casual, and innocent absences

An alien shall not be considered to have failed to maintain continuous physical presence in the United States for purposes of subparagraph (A) by virtue of brief, casual, and innocent absences from the United States.

### (C) Admissions

Nothing in this section shall be construed as authorizing an alien to apply for admission to, or to be admitted to, the United States in order to apply for adjustment of status under this subsection.

## (4) Admissible as immigrant

The alien must establish that he—

(A) is admissible to the United States as an immigrant, except as otherwise provided under subsection (d)(2) of this section,

(B) has not been convicted of any felony or of three or more misdemeanors committed in the United States,

**(C)** has not assisted in the persecution of any person or persons on account of race, religion, nationality, membership in a particular social group, or political opinion, and

**(D)** is registered or registering under the Military Selective Service Act [50 U.S.C.A. App. § 451 et seq.], if the alien is required to be so registered under that Act.

For purposes of this subsection, an alien in the status of a Cuban and Haitian entrant described in paragraph (1) or (2)(A) of section 501(e) of Public Law 96–422 [8 U.S.C.A. § 1522 note] shall be considered to have entered the United States and to be in an unlawful status in the United States.

**(b) Subsequent adjustment to permanent residence and nature of temporary resident status**

**(1) Adjustment to permanent residence**

The Attorney General shall adjust the status of any alien provided lawful temporary resident status under subsection (a) of this section to that of an alien lawfully admitted for permanent residence if the alien meets the following requirements:

**(A)** Timely application after 2 years' residence

The alien must apply for such adjustment during the 2-year period beginning with the nineteenth month that begins after the date the alien was granted such temporary resident status.

**(B)** Continuous residence

**(i)** In general

The alien must establish that he has continuously resided in the United States since the date the alien was granted such temporary resident status.

**(ii)** Treatment of certain absences

An alien shall not be considered to have lost the continuous residence referred to in clause (i) by reason of an absence from the United States permitted under paragraph (3)(A).

**(C)** Admissible as immigrant

The alien must establish that he—

**(i)** is admissible to the United States as an immigrant, except as otherwise provided under subsection (d)(2) of this section, and

**(ii)** has not been convicted of any felony or three or more misdemeanors committed in the United States.

**(D)** Basic citizenship skills

**(i)** In general

The alien must demonstrate that he either—

**(I)** meets the requirements of section 312 [8 U.S.C.A. § 1423] (relating to minimal understanding of ordinary English and a knowledge and understanding of the history and government of the United States), or

**(II)** is satisfactorily pursuing a course of study (recognized by the Attorney General) to achieve such an understanding of English and such a knowledge and understanding of the history and government of the United States.

**(ii) Exception for elderly or developmentally disabled individuals**

The Attorney General may, in his discretion, waive all or part of the requirements of clause (i) in the case of an alien who is 65 years of age or older or who is developmentally disabled.

**(iii) Relation to naturalization examination**

In accordance with regulations of the Attorney General, an alien who has demonstrated under clause (i)(I) that the alien meets the requirements of section 312 [8 U.S.C.A. § 1423] may be considered to have satisfied the requirements of that section for purposes of becoming naturalized as a citizen of the United States under title III.

**(2) Termination of temporary residence**

The Attorney General shall provide for termination of temporary resident status granted an alien under subsection (a) of this section—

**(A)** if it appears to the Attorney General that the alien was in fact not eligible for such status;

**(B)** if the alien commits an act that (i) makes the alien inadmissible to the United States as an immigrant, except as otherwise provided under subsection (d)(2) of this section, or (ii) is convicted of any felony or three or more misdemeanors committed in the United States; or

**(C)** at the end of the 43rd month beginning after the date the alien is granted such status, unless the alien has filed an application for adjustment of such status pursuant to paragraph (1) and such application has not been denied.

**(3) Authorized travel and employment during temporary residence**

During the period an alien is in lawful temporary resident status granted under subsection (a) of this section—

**(A)** Authorization of travel abroad

The Attorney General shall, in accordance with regulations, permit the alien to return to the United States after such brief and casual trips abroad as reflect an intention on the part of the alien to adjust to lawful permanent resident status under paragraph (1) and after brief temporary trips abroad occasioned by a family obligation involving an occurrence such as the illness or death of a close relative or other family need.

**(B)** Authorization of employment

The Attorney General shall grant the alien authorization to engage in employment in the United States and provide to that alien an "employment authorized" endorsement or other appropriate work permit.

## (c) Applications for adjustment of status

### (1) To whom may be made

The Attorney General shall provide that applications for adjustment of status under subsection (a) of this section may be filed—

**(A)** with the Attorney General, or

**(B)** with a qualified designated entity, but only if the applicant consents to the forwarding of the application to the Attorney General.

As used in this section, the term "qualified designated entity" means an organization or person designated under paragraph (2).

### (2) Designation of qualified entities to receive applications

For purposes of assisting in the program of legalization provided under this section, the Attorney General—

**(A)** shall designate qualified voluntary organizations and other qualified State, local, and community organizations, and

**(B)** may designate such other persons as the Attorney General determines are qualified and have substantial experience, demonstrated competence, and traditional long-term involvement in the preparation and submittal of applications for adjustment of status under section 209 or 245, Public Law 89–732 [8 U.S.C.A. § 1255 note], or Public Law 95–145.

### (3) Treatment of applications by designated entities

Each qualified designated entity must agree to forward to the Attorney General applications filed with it in accordance with paragraph (1)(B) but not to forward to the Attorney General applications filed with it unless the applicant has consented to such forwarding. No such entity may make a determination required by this section to be made by the Attorney General.

#### (4) Limitation on access to information

Files and records of qualified designated entities relating to an alien's seeking assistance or information with respect to filing an application under this section are confidential and the Attorney General and the Service shall not have access to such files or records relating to an alien without the consent of the alien.

#### (5) Confidentiality of information

Neither the Attorney General, nor any other official or employee of the Department of Justice, or bureau or agency thereof, may—

**(A)** use the information furnished pursuant to an application filed under this section for any purpose other than to make a determination on the application or for enforcement of paragraph (6) or for the preparation of reports to Congress under section 404 of the Immigration Reform and Control Act of 1986,

**(B)** make any publication whereby the information furnished by any particular individual can be identified, or

**(C)** permit anyone other than the sworn officers and employees of the Department or bureau or agency or, with respect to applications filed with a designated entity, that designated entity, to examine individual applications;

except that the Attorney General may provide, in the Attorney General's discretion, for the furnishing of information furnished under this section in the same manner and circumstances as census information may be disclosed by the Secretary of Commerce under section 8 of Title 13. Anyone who uses, publishes, or permits information to be examined in violation of this paragraph shall be fined in accordance with Title 18, or imprisoned not more than five years, or both.

#### (6) Penalties for false statements in applications

Whoever files an application for adjustment of status under this section and knowingly and willfully falsifies, misrepresents, conceals, or covers up a material fact or makes any false, fictitious, or fraudulent statements or representations, or makes or uses any false writing or document knowing the same to contain any false, fictitious, or fraudulent statement or entry, shall be fined in accordance with Title 18, or imprisoned not more than five years, or both.

#### (7) Application fees

#### (A) Fee schedule

The Attorney General shall provide for a schedule of fees to be charged for the filing of applications for adjustment under subsection (a) or (b)(1) of this section. The Attorney

General shall provide for an additional fee for filing an application for adjustment under subsection (b)(1) of this section after the end of the first year of the 2-year period described in subsection (b)(1)(A) of this section.

**(B)** Use of fees

The Attorney General shall deposit payments received under this paragraph in a separate account and amounts in such account shall be available, without fiscal year limitation, to cover administrative and other expenses incurred in connection with the review of applications filed under this section.

## (d) Waiver of numerical limitations and certain grounds for exclusion

### (1) Numerical limitations do not apply

The numerical limitations of sections 201 and 202 [8 U.S.C.A. §§ 1151 and 1152] shall not apply to the adjustment of aliens to lawful permanent resident status under this section.

### (2) Waiver of grounds for exclusion

In the determination of an alien's admissibility under subsections (a)(4)(A), (b)(1)(C)(i), and (b)(2)(B)—

**(A)** Grounds of exclusion not applicable

The provisions of paragraphs (5) and (7)(A) of section 212(a) [8 U.S.C.A. § 1182(a)(5) and (7)(A)] shall not apply.

**(B)** Waiver of other grounds

(i) In general

Except as provided in clause (ii), the Attorney General may waive any other provision of section 212(a) [8 U.S.C.A. § 1182(a)] in the case of individual aliens for humanitarian purposes, to assure family unity, or when it is otherwise in the public interest.

(ii) Grounds that may not be waived

The following provisions of section 212(a) [8 U.S.C.A. § 1182(a)] may not be waived by the Attorney General under clause (i):

(I) Paragraphs (2)(A) and (2)(B) (relating to criminals).

(II) Paragraph (4) (relating to aliens likely to become public charges) insofar as it relates to an application for adjustment to permanent residence.

(III) Paragraph (2)(C) (relating to drug offenses), except for so much of such paragraph as relates to a single offense of simple possession of 30 grams or less of marihuana.

**(IV)** Paragraphs[1] (3) (relating to security and related grounds), other than subparagraph (E) thereof.

Subclause (II) (prohibiting the waiver of section 212(a)(4) [8 U.S.C.A. § 1182(a)(4)]) shall not apply to an alien who is or was an aged, blind, or disabled individual (as defined in section 1382c(a)(1) of Title 42).

**(iii)** Special rule for determination of public charge

An alien is not ineligible for adjustment of status under this section due to being inadmissible under section 212(a)(4) [8 U.S.C.A. § 1182(a)(4)] if the alien demonstrates a history of employment in the United States evidencing self-support without receipt of public cash assistance.

**(C)** Medical examination

The alien shall be required, at the alien's expense, to undergo such a medical examination (including a determination of immunization status) as is appropriate and conforms to generally accepted professional standards of medical practice.

**(e) Temporary stay of deportation and work authorization for certain applicants**

**(1) Before application period**

The Attorney General shall provide that in the case of an alien who is apprehended before the beginning of the application period described in subsection (a)(1)(A) of this section and who can establish a prima facie case of eligibility to have his status adjusted under subsection (a) of this section (but for the fact that he may not apply for such adjustment until the beginning of such period), until the alien has had the opportunity during the first 30 days of the application period to complete the filing of an application for adjustment, the alien—

**(A)** may not be deported, and

**(B)** shall be granted authorization to engage in employment in the United States and be provided an "employment authorized" endorsement or other appropriate work permit.

**(2) During application period**

The Attorney General shall provide that in the case of an alien who presents a prima facie application for adjustment of status under subsection (a) of this section during the application period, and until a final determination on the application has been made in accordance with this section, the alien—

**(A)** may not be deported, and

**(B)** shall be granted authorization to engage in employment in the United States and be provided an "employment authorized" endorsement or other appropriate work permit.

### (f) Administrative and judicial review

#### (1) Administrative and judicial review

There shall be no administrative or judicial review of a determination respecting an application for adjustment of status under this section except in accordance with this subsection.

#### (2) No review for late filings

No denial of adjustment of status under this section based on a late filing of an application for such adjustment may be reviewed by a court of the United States or of any State or reviewed in any administrative proceeding of the United States Government.

#### (3) Administrative review

**(A)** Single level of administrative appellate review

The Attorney General shall establish an appellate authority to provide for a single level of administrative appellate review of a determination described in paragraph (1).

**(B)** Standard for review

Such administrative appellate review shall be based solely upon the administrative record established at the time of the determination on the application and upon such additional or newly discovered evidence as may not have been available at the time of the determination.

#### (4) Judicial review

**(A)** Limitation to review of deportation

There shall be judicial review of such a denial only in the judicial review of an order of deportation under section 106 [8 U.S.C.A. § 1105a].

**(B)** Standard for judicial review

Such judicial review shall be based solely upon the administrative record established at the time of the review by the appellate authority and the findings of fact and determinations contained in such record shall be conclusive unless the applicant can establish abuse of discretion or that the findings are directly contrary to clear and convincing facts contained in the record considered as a whole.

### (g) Implementation of section

#### (1) Regulations

The Attorney General, after consultation with the Committees on the Judiciary of the House of Representatives and of the Senate, shall prescribe—

**(A)** regulations establishing a definition of the term "resided continuously", as used in this section, and the evidence needed to establish that an alien has resided continuously in the United States for purposes of this section, and

**(B)** such other regulations as may be necessary to carry out this section.

**(2) Considerations**

In prescribing regulations described in paragraph (1)(A)—

**(A)** Periods of continuous residence

The Attorney General shall specify individual periods, and aggregate periods, of absence from the United States which will be considered to break a period of continuous residence in the United States and shall take into account absences due merely to brief and casual trips abroad.

**(B)** Absences caused by deportation or advanced parole

The Attorney General shall provide that—

**(i)** an alien shall not be considered to have resided continuously in the United States, if, during any period for which continuous residence is required, the alien was outside the United States as a result of a departure under an order of deportation, and

**(ii)** any period of time during which an alien is outside the United States pursuant to the advance parole procedures of the Service shall not be considered as part of the period of time during which an alien is outside the United States for purposes of this section.

**(C)** Waivers of certain absences

The Attorney General may provide for a waiver, in the discretion of the Attorney General, of the periods specified under subparagraph (A) in the case of an absence from the United States due merely to a brief temporary trip abroad required by emergency or extenuating circumstances outside the control of the alien.

**(D)** Use of certain documentation

The Attorney General shall require that—

**(i)** continuous residence and physical presence in the United States must be established through documents, together with independent corroboration of the information contained in such documents, and

**(ii)** the documents provided under clause (i) be employment-related if employment-related documents with respect to the alien are available to the applicant.

**(3) Interim final regulations**

Regulations prescribed under this section may be prescribed to take effect on an interim final basis if the Attorney General determines that this is necessary in order to implement this section in a timely manner.

**(h)** Temporary disqualification of newly legalized aliens from receiving certain public welfare assistance

### (1) In general

During the five-year period beginning on the date an alien was granted lawful temporary resident status under subsection (a) of this section, and notwithstanding any other provision of law—

**(A)** except as provided in paragraphs (2) and (3), the alien is not eligible for—

(i) any program of financial assistance furnished under Federal law (whether through grant, loan, guarantee, or otherwise) on the basis of financial need, as such programs are identified by the Attorney General in consultation with other appropriate heads of the various departments and agencies of Government (but in any event including the program of aid to families with dependent children under part A of title IV of the Social Security Act [42 U.S.C.A. § 601 et seq.]),

(ii) medical assistance under a State plan approved under title XIX of the Social Security Act [42 U.S.C.A. § 1390 et seq.], and

(iii) assistance under the Food Stamp Act of 1977 [7 U.S.C.A. § 2011 et seq.]; and

**(B)** a State or political subdivision therein may, to the extent consistent with subparagraph (A) and paragraphs (2) and (3), provide that the alien is not eligible for the programs of financial assistance or for medical assistance described in subparagraph (A)(ii) furnished under the law of that State or political subdivision.

Unless otherwise specifically provided by this section or other law, an alien in temporary lawful residence status granted under subsection (a) of this section shall not be considered (for purposes of any law of a State or political subdivision providing for a program of financial assistance) to be permanently residing in the United States under color of law.

### (2) Exceptions

Paragraph (1) shall not apply—

**(A)** to a Cuban and Haitian entrant (as defined in paragraph (1) or (2)(A) of section 502(e) of Public Law 96–422 [8 U.S.C.A. § 1255 note], as in effect on April 1, 1983), or

**(B)** in the case of assistance (other than aid to families with dependent children) which is furnished to an alien who is an aged, blind, or disabled individual (as defined in section 1614(a)(1) of the Social Security Act [42 U.S.C.A. § 1382c]).

**(3) Restricted Medicaid benefits**

**(A)** Clarification of entitlement

Subject to the restrictions under subparagraph (B), for the purpose of providing aliens with eligibility to receive medical assistance—

(i) paragraph (1) shall not apply,

(ii) aliens who would be eligible for medical assistance but for the provisions of paragraph (1) shall be deemed, for purposes of title XIX of the Social Security Act [42 U.S.C.A. § 1396 et seq.], to be so eligible, and

(iii) aliens lawfully admitted for temporary residence under this section, such status not having changed, shall be considered to be permanently residing in the United States under color of law.

**(B)** Restriction of benefits

(i) Limitation to emergency services and services for pregnant women

Notwithstanding any provision of title XIX of the Social Security Act (including subparagraphs (B) and (C) of section 1902(a)(10) of such Act [42 U.S.C.A. § 1396a(a)(10)]), aliens who, but for subparagraph (A), would be ineligible for medical assistance under paragraph (1), are only eligible for such assistance with respect to—

(I) emergency services (as defined for purposes of section 1916(a)(2)(D) of the Social Security Act [42 U.S.C.A. § 1396o(a)(2)(D)]), and

(II) services described in section 1916(a)(2)(B) of such Act [42 U.S.C.A. § 1396o(a)(2)(B)] (relating to service for pregnant women).

(ii) No restriction for exempt aliens and children

The restrictions of clause (i) shall not apply to aliens who are described in paragraph (2) or who are under 18 years of age.

**(C)** Definition of medical assistance

In this paragraph, the term "medical assistance" refers to medical assistance under a State plan approved under title XIX of the Social Security Act.

**(4) Treatment of certain programs**

Assistance furnished under any of the following provisions of law shall not be construed to be financial assistance described in paragraph (1)(A)(i):

(A) The National School Lunch Act [42 U.S.C.A. § 1751 et seq.].

(B) The Child Nutrition Act of 1966 [42 U.S.C. 1771 et seq.].

(C) The Vocational Education Act of 1963 [20 U.S.C. 2301 et seq.].

(D) Chapter 1 of the Education Consolidation and Improvement Act of 1981 [20 U.S.C. 3801 et seq.].

(E) The Headstart Follow-Through Act.

(F) The Job Training Partnership Act [29 U.S.C. 1501 et seq.].

(G) Title IV of the Higher Education Act of 1965 [20 U.S.C. 1070 et seq.].

(H) The Public Health Service Act [42 U.S.C. 1201 et seq.].

(I) Titles V, XVI, and XX, and parts B, D, and E of title IV, of the Social Security Act [42 U.S.C. 701 et seq., 1381 et seq., 1391 et seq., 620 et seq., 651 et seq., and 670 et seq., respectively] (and titles I, X, XIV, and XVI of such Act [42 U.S.C. 301 et seq., 1201 et seq., 1351 et seq., and 1381 et seq., respectively] as in effect without regard to the amendment made by section 301 of the Social Security Amendments of 1972).

### (5) Adjustment not affecting Fascell-Stone benefits

For the purpose of section 501 of the Refugee Education Assistance Act of 1980 (Public Law 96–122) [2] [8 U.S.C. 1522 note]; assistance shall be continued under such section with respect to an alien without regard to the alien's adjustment of status under this section.

### (i) Dissemination of information on legalization program

Beginning not later than the date designated by the Attorney General under subsection (a)(1)(A) of this section, the Attorney General, in cooperation with qualified designated entities, shall broadly disseminate information respecting the benefits which aliens may receive under this section and the requirements to obtain such benefits.

(June 27, 1952, c. 477, Title II, ch. 5, § 245A, as added Pub.L. 99–603, Title II, § 201(a), Nov. 6, 1986, 100 Stat. 3394, and amended Pub.L. 100–525, § 2(h)(1), Oct. 24, 1988, 102 Stat. 2611; Pub.L. 101–649, Title VI, § 603(a)(13), Title VII, § 703, Nov. 29, 1990, 104 Stat. 5083, 5086.)

1. So in original. Probably should be "Paragraph".

2. So in original. Probably should be "(Public Law 96–422)".

## § 246. Rescission of adjustment of status; report to Congress; effect upon naturalized citizen [8 U.S.C.A. § 1256]

(a) If, at any time within five years after the status of a person has been adjusted under the provisions of section 244 [8 U.S.C.A. § 1254] or under section 19(c) of the Immigration Act of February 5, 1917, to that of an alien lawfully admitted for permanent residence, it shall appear to the satisfaction of the Attorney General that the person was not in fact eligible for such adjustment of status, the Attorney General shall submit to the Congress a complete and detailed statement of the facts and pertinent provisions of law in the case. Such reports shall be submitted on the first and fifteenth day of each calendar month in which Congress is in session. If during the session of the Congress at which a case is reported, or prior to the close of the session of the Congress next following the session at which a case is reported, the Congress passes a concurrent resolution withdrawing suspension of deportation, the person shall thereupon be subject to all provisions of this chapter to the same extent as if the adjustment of status had not been made. If, at any time within five years after the status of a person has been otherwise adjusted under the provisions of section 245 or 249 [8 U.S.C.A. §§ 1255 or 1259] or any other provision of law to that of an alien lawfully admitted for permanent residence, it shall appear to the satisfaction of the Attorney General that the person was not in fact eligible for such adjustment of status, the Attorney General shall rescind the action taken granting an adjustment of status to such person and cancelling deportation in the case of such person if that occurred and the person shall thereupon be subject to all provisions of this chapter to the same extent as if the adjustment of status had not been made.

(b) Any person who has become a naturalized citizen of the United States upon the basis of a record of a lawful admission for permanent residence, created as a result of an adjustment of status for which such person was not in fact eligible, and which is subsequently rescinded under subsection (a) of this section, shall be subject to the provisions of section 340 [8 U.S.C.A. § 1451] as a person whose naturalization was procured by concealment of a material fact or by willful misrepresentation.

(June 27, 1952, c. 477, Title II, ch. 5, § 246, 66 Stat. 217.)

## § 247. Adjustment of status of certain resident aliens to nonimmigrant status; exceptions [8 U.S.C.A. § 1257]

(a) The status of an alien lawfully admitted for permanent residence shall be adjusted by the Attorney General, under such regulations as he may prescribe, to that of a nonimmigrant under paragraph (15)(A), (E), or (G) of section 101(a) [8 U.S.C.A. § 1101(a)(15)(A), (E), or

(G)], if such alien had at the time of entry or subsequently acquires an occupational status which would, if he were seeking admission to the United States, entitle him to a nonimmigrant status under such paragraphs. As of the date of the Attorney General's order making such adjustment of status, the Attorney General shall cancel the record of the alien's admission for permanent residence, and the immigrant status of such alien shall thereby be terminated.

**(b)** The adjustment of status required by subsection (a) of this section shall not be applicable in the case of any alien who requests that he be permitted to retain his status as an immigrant and who, in such form as the Attorney General may require, executes and files with the Attorney General a written waiver of all rights, privileges, exemptions, and immunities under any law or any executive order which would otherwise accrue to him because of the acquisition of an occupational status entitling him to a nonimmigrant status under paragraph (15)(A), (E), or (G) of section 101(a) [8 U.S.C.A. § 1101(a)(15)(A), (E), or (G)].

(June 27, 1952, c. 477, Title II, ch. 5, § 247, 66 Stat. 218.)

## § 248.  Change of nonimmigrant classification [8 U.S. C.A. § 1258]

The Attorney General may, under such conditions as he may prescribe, authorize a change from any nonimmigrant classification to any other nonimmigrant classification in the case of any alien lawfully admitted to the United States as a nonimmigrant who is continuing to maintain that status, except in the case of—

(1) an alien classified as a nonimmigrant under subparagraph (C), (D), or (K) of section 101(a)(15) [8 U.S.C.A. § 1101(a)(15)(C), (D), or (K)],

(2) an alien classified as a nonimmigrant under subparagraph (J) of section 101(a)(15) [8 U.S.C.A. § 1101(a)(15)(J)] who came to the United States or acquired such classification in order to receive graduate medical education or training,

(3) an alien (other than an alien described in paragraph (2)) classified as a nonimmigrant under subparagraph (J) of section 101(a)(15) [8 U.S.C.A. § 1101(a)(15)(J)] who is subject to the two-year foreign residence requirement of section 212(e) [8 U.S.C.A. § 1182(e)] and has not received a waiver thereof, unless such alien applies to have the alien's classification changed from classification under subparagraph (J) of section 101(a)(15) [8 U.S.C.A. § 1101(a)(15)(J)] to a classification under subparagraph (A) or (G) of such section, and

(4) an alien admitted as a nonimmigrant visitor without a visa under section 212(l) [8 U.S.C.A. § 1182(l)] or section 217 [8 U.S.C.A. § 1187].

(June 27, 1952, c. 477, Title II, ch. 5, § 248, 66 Stat. 218; Pub.L. 87–256, § 109(d), Sept. 21, 1961, 75 Stat. 535; Pub.L. 97–116, § 10, Dec. 29, 1981, 95 Stat. 1617; Pub.L. 99–603, Title III, § 313(d), Nov. 6, 1986, 100 Stat. 3439.)

## § 249. Record of admission for permanent residence in the case of certain aliens who entered the United States prior to January 1, 1972 [8 U.S.C.A. § 1259]

A record of lawful admission for permanent residence may, in the discretion of the Attorney General and under such regulations as he may prescribe, be made in the case of any alien, as of the date of the approval of his application or, if entry occurred prior to July 1, 1924, as of the date of such entry, if no such record is otherwise available and such alien shall satisfy the Attorney General that he is not inadmissible under section 212(a)(3)(E) [8 U.S.C.A. § 1182(a)(3)(E)] or under section 212(a) [8 U.S.C.A. § 1182(a)] insofar as it relates to criminals, procurers and other immoral persons, subversives, violators of the narcotic laws or smugglers of aliens, and he establishes that he—

(a) entered the United States prior to January 1, 1972;

(b) has had his residence in the United States continuously since such entry;

(c) is a person of good moral character; and

(d) is not ineligible to citizenship.

(June 27, 1952, c. 477, Title II, ch. 5, § 249, 66 Stat. 219; Pub.L. 85–616, Aug. 8, 1958, 72 Stat. 546; Pub.L. 89–236, § 19, Oct. 3, 1965, 79 Stat. 920; Pub.L. 99–603, Title II, § 203(a), Nov. 6, 1986, 100 Stat. 3405, as amended Pub.L. 100–525, § 2(j), Oct. 24, 1988, 102 Stat. 2612; Pub.L. 101–649, Title VI, § 603(a)(14), Nov. 29, 1990, 104 Stat. 5083.)

## § 250. Removal of aliens falling into distress [8 U.S.C.A. § 1260]

The Attorney General may remove from the United States any alien who falls into distress or who needs public aid from causes arising subsequent to his entry, and is desirous of being so removed, to the native country of such alien, or to the country from which he came, or to the country of which he is a citizen or subject, or to any other country to which he wishes to go and which will receive him, at the expense of the appropriation for the enforcement of this chapter. Any alien so removed shall be ineligible to apply for or receive a visa or other documentation for readmission, or to apply for admission to the United States except with the prior approval of the Attorney General.

(June 27, 1952, c. 477, Title II, ch. 5, § 250, 66 Stat. 219.)

## CHAPTER VI—SPECIAL PROVISIONS RELATING TO ALIEN CREWMEN

# § 251. Alien crewmen [8 U.S.C.A. § 1281]

### (a) Arrival; submission of list; exceptions

Upon arrival of any vessel or aircraft in the United States from any place outside the United States it shall be the duty of the owner, agent, consignee, master, or commanding officer thereof to deliver to an immigration officer at the port of arrival (1) a complete, true, and correct list containing the names of all aliens employed on such vessel or aircraft, the positions they respectively hold in the crew of the vessel or aircraft, when and where they were respectively shipped or engaged, and those to be paid off or discharged in the port of arrival; or (2) in the discretion of the Attorney General, such a list containing so much of such information, or such additional or supplemental information, as the Attorney General shall by regulations prescribe. In the case of a vessel engaged solely in traffic on the Great Lakes, Saint Lawrence River, and connecting waterways, such lists shall be furnished at such times as the Attorney General may require.

### (b) Reports of illegal landings

It shall be the duty of any owner, agent, consignee, master, or commanding officer of any vessel or aircraft to report to an immigration officer, in writing, as soon as discovered, all cases in which any alien crewman has illegally landed in the United States from the vessel or aircraft, together with a description of such alien and any information likely to lead to his apprehension.

### (c) Departure; submission of list; exceptions

Before the departure of any vessel or aircraft from any port in the United States, it shall be the duty of the owner, agent, consignee, master, or commanding officer thereof, to deliver to an immigration officer at that port (1) a list containing the names of all alien employees who were not employed thereon at the time of the arrival at that port but who will leave such port thereon at the time of the departure of such vessel or aircraft and the names of those, if any, who have been paid off or discharged, and of those, if any, who have deserted or landed at that port, or (2) in the discretion of the Attorney General, such a list containing so much of such information, or such additional or supplemental information, as the Attorney General shall by regulations prescribe. In the case of a vessel engaged solely in traffic on the Great Lakes, Saint Lawrence River, and connecting waterways, such lists shall be furnished at such times as the Attorney General may require.

### (d) Violations

In case any owner, agent, consignee, master, or commanding officer shall fail to deliver complete, true, and correct lists or reports of aliens, or to report cases of desertion or landing, as required by subsections (a), (b), and (c) of this section, such owner, agent, consignee, master, or commanding officer, shall, if required by the Attorney General, pay to the Commissioner the sum of $200 for each alien concerning whom such lists are not delivered or such reports are not made as required in the preceding subsections. In the case that any owner, agent, consignee, master, or commanding officer of a vessel shall secure services of an alien crewman described in section 101(a)(15)(D)(i) [8 U.S.C.A. § 1101(a)(15)(D)(i)] to perform longshore work not included in the normal operation and service on board the vessel under section 258 [8 U.S.C.A. § 1288], the owner, agent, charterer, master, or commanding officer shall pay to the Commissioner the sum of $5,000, and such fine shall be a lien against the vessel. No such vessel or aircraft shall be granted clearance from any port at which it arrives pending the determination of the question of the liability to the payment of such fine, and if such fine is imposed, while it remains unpaid. No such fine shall be remitted or refunded. Clearance may be granted prior to the determination of such question upon deposit of a bond or a sum sufficient to cover such fine.

### (e) Regulations

The Attorney General is authorized to prescribe by regulations the circumstances under which a vessel or aircraft shall be deemed to be arriving in, or departing from the United States or any port thereof within the meaning of any provision of this part.

(June 27, 1952, c. 477, Title II, ch. 6, § 251, 66 Stat. 219; Nov. 29, 1990, Pub.L. 101–649, Title II, § 203(b), 104 Stat. 5018.)

## § 252. Conditional permits to land temporarily [8 U.S.C.A. § 1282]

### (a) Period of time

No alien crewman shall be permitted to land temporarily in the United States except as provided in this section and sections 212(d)(3), (5) and 253 [8 U.S.C.A. §§ 1182(d)(3), (5) and 1283]. If an immigration officer finds upon examination that an alien crewman is a nonimmigrant under paragraph (15)(D) of section 101(a) [8 U.S.C.A. § 1101(a)] and is otherwise admissible and has agreed to accept such permit, he may, in his discretion, grant the crewman a conditional permit to land temporarily pursuant to regulations prescribed by the Attorney General, subject to revocation in subsequent proceedings as provided in subsection (b) of this section, and for a period of time, in any event, not to exceed—

(1) the period of time (not exceeding twenty-nine days) during which the vessel or aircraft on which he arrived remains in port, if the immigration officer is satisfied that the crewman intends to depart on the vessel or aircraft on which he arrived; or

(2) twenty-nine days, if the immigration officer is satisfied that the crewman intends to depart, within the period for which he is

permitted to land, on a vessel or aircraft other than the one on which he arrived.

### (b) Revocation; expenses of detention

Pursuant to regulations prescribed by the Attorney General, any immigration officer may, in his discretion, if he determines that an alien is not a bona fide crewman, or does not intend to depart on the vessel or aircraft which brought him, revoke the conditional permit to land which was granted such crewman under the provisions of subsection (a)(1) of this section, take such crewman into custody, and require the master or commanding officer of the vessel or aircraft on which the crewman arrived to receive and detain him on board such vessel or aircraft, if practicable, and such crewman shall be deported from the United States at the expense of the transportation line which brought him to the United States. Until such alien is so deported, any expenses of his detention shall be borne by such transportation company. Nothing in this section shall be construed to require the procedure prescribed in section 242 [8 U.S.C.A. § 1252] to cases falling within the provisions of this subsection.

### (c) Penalties

Any alien crewman who willfully remains in the United States in excess of the number of days allowed in any conditional permit issued under subsection (a) of this section shall be fined not more than $2,000 (or, if greater, the amount provided under Title 18) or imprisoned not more than 6 months, or both.

(June 27, 1952, c. 477, Title II, ch. 6, § 252, 66 Stat. 220; Nov. 29, 1990, Pub.L. 101–649, Title V, § 543(b)(1), 104 Stat. 5059.)

## § 253. Hospital treatment of alien crewmen afflicted with certain diseases [8 U.S.C.A. § 1283]

An alien crewman, including an alien crewman ineligible for a conditional permit to land under section 252(a) [8 U.S.C.A. § 1282(a)], who is found on arrival in a port of the United States to be afflicted with any of the disabilities or diseases mentioned in section 255 [8 U.S.C.A. § 1285], shall be placed in a hospital designated by the immigration officer in charge at the port of arrival and treated, all expenses connected therewith, including burial in the event of death, to be borne by the owner, agent, consignee, commanding officer, or master of the vessel or aircraft, and not to be deducted from the crewman's wages. No such vessel or aircraft shall be granted clearance until such expenses are paid, or their payment appropriately guaranteed, and the collector of customs is so notified by the immigration officer in charge. An alien crewman suspected of being afflicted with any such disability or disease may be removed from the vessel or aircraft on which he arrived to an immigration station, or other appropriate place, for such observation as will enable the examining surgeons to determine definitely whether or not he is so afflicted, all expenses connected therewith to be borne in the manner hereinbefore prescribed. In cases in which it appears to the satisfaction of the immigration officer in charge that it will not be possible within a reasonable time to effect a cure, the return of the alien crewman shall be enforced on, or at the expense of, the transportation line on which he came, upon such conditions as the Attorney General shall prescribe, to insure that the alien shall be properly cared for and protected, and that the spread of contagion shall be guarded against.

(June 27, 1952, c. 477, Title II, ch. 6, § 253, 66 Stat. 221.)

## § 254. Control of alien crewmen [8 U.S.C.A. § 1284]

### (a) Penalties for failure

The owner, agent, consignee, charterer, master, or commanding officer of any vessel or aircraft arriving in the United States from any place outside thereof who fails (1) to detain on board the vessel, or in the case of an aircraft to detain at a place specified by an immigration officer at the expense of the airline, any alien crewman employed thereon until an immigration officer has completely inspected such alien crewman, including a physical examination by the medical examiner, or (2) to detain any alien crewman on board the vessel, or in the case of an aircraft at a place specified by an immigration officer at the expense of the airline, after such inspection unless a conditional permit to land temporarily has been granted such alien crewman under section 252 [8 U.S.C.A. § 1282] or unless an alien crewman has been permitted to land temporarily under section 212(d)(5) or 253 [8 U.S.C.A. §§ 1182(d)(5) or 1283] for medical or hospital treatment, or (3) to deport such alien crewman if required to do so by an immigration officer, whether such deportation requirement is imposed before or after the crewman is permitted to land temporarily under section 212(d)(5), 252, or 253 [8 U.S.C.A. §§ 1182(d)(5), 1282, or 1283], shall pay to the Commissioner the sum of $3000 for each alien crewman in respect to whom any such failure occurs. No such vessel or aircraft shall be granted clearance pending the determination of the liability to the payment of such fine, or while the fine remains unpaid, except that clearance may be granted prior to the determination of such question upon the deposit of a sum sufficient to cover such fine, or of a bond with sufficient surety to secure the payment thereof approved by the collector of customs. The Attorney General may, upon application in writing therefor, mitigate such penalty to not less than $500 for each alien crewman in respect of whom such failure occurs, upon such terms as he shall think proper.

### (b) Prima facie evidence against transportation line

Except as may be otherwise prescribed by regulations issued by the Attorney General, proof that an alien crewman did not appear upon the outgoing manifest of the vessel or aircraft on which he arrived in the United States from any place outside thereof, or that he was reported by the master or commanding officer of such vessel or aircraft as a deserter, shall be prima facie evidence of a failure to detain or deport such alien crewman.

### (c) Deportation on other than arriving vessel or aircraft; expenses

If the Attorney General finds that deportation of an alien crewman under this section on the vessel or aircraft on which he arrived is impracticable or impossible, or would cause undue hardship to such alien crewman, he may cause the alien crewman to be deported from the port of arrival or any other port on another vessel or aircraft of the same transportation line, unless the Attorney General finds this to be impracticable.  All expenses incurred in connection with such deportation, including expenses incurred in transferring an alien crewman from one place in the United States to another under such conditions and safeguards as the Attorney General shall impose, shall be paid by the owner or owners of the vessel or aircraft on which the alien arrived in the United States.  The vessel or aircraft on which the alien arrived shall not be granted clearance until such expenses have been paid or their payment guaranteed to the satisfaction of the Attorney General.  An alien crewman who is transferred within the United States in accordance with this subsection shall not be regarded as having been landed in the United States.

(June 27, 1952, c. 477, Title II, ch. 6, § 254, 66 Stat. 221; Nov. 29, 1990, Pub.L. 101–649, Title V, § 543(a)(4), 104 Stat. 5058.)

## § 255. Employment on passenger vessels of aliens afflicted with certain disabilities [8 U.S. C.A. § 1285]

It shall be unlawful for any vessel or aircraft carrying passengers between a port of the United States and a port outside thereof to have employed on board upon arrival in the United States any alien afflicted with feeble-mindedness, insanity, epilepsy, tuberculosis in any form, leprosy, or any dangerous contagious disease.  If it appears to the satisfaction of the Attorney General, from an examination made by a medical officer of the United States Public Health Service, and is so certified by such officer, that any such alien was so afflicted at the time he was shipped or engaged and taken on board such vessel or aircraft and that the existence of such affliction might have been detected by means of a competent medical examination at such time, the owner, commanding officer, agent, consignee, or master thereof shall pay for each alien so afflicted to the Commissioner the sum of $1,000.  No vessel or aircraft shall be granted clearance pending the determination of the question of the liability to the payment of such sums, or while such sums remain unpaid, except that clearance may be granted prior to the determination of such question upon the deposit of an amount sufficient to cover such sums or of a bond approved by the Commissioner with sufficient surety to secure the payment thereof.  Any such fine may, in the discretion of the Attorney General, be mitigated or remitted.

(June 27, 1952, c. 477, Title II, ch. 6, § 255, 66 Stat. 222; Nov. 29, 1990, Pub.L. 101–649, Title V, § 543(a)(5), 104 Stat. 5058.)

## § 256. Discharge of alien crewmen; penalties [8 U.S.C.A. § 1286]

It shall be unlawful for any person, including the owner, agent, consignee, charterer, master, or commanding officer of any vessel or aircraft, to pay off or discharge any alien crewman, except an alien lawfully admitted for permanent residence, employed on board a vessel or aircraft arriving in the United States without first having obtained the consent of the Attorney General. If it shall appear to the satisfaction of the Attorney General that any alien crewman has been paid off or discharged in the United States in violation of the provisions of this section, such owner, agent, consignee, charterer, master, commanding officer, or other person, shall pay to the Commissioner the sum of $3,000 for each such violation. No vessel or aircraft shall be granted clearance pending the determination of the question of the liability to the payment of such sums, or while such sums remain unpaid, except that clearance may be granted prior to the determination of such question upon the deposit of an amount sufficient to cover such sums, or of a bond approved by the Commissioner with sufficient surety to secure the payment thereof. Such fine may, in the discretion of the Attorney General, be mitigated to not less than $1,500 for each violation, upon such terms as he shall think proper.

(June 27, 1952, c. 477, Title II, ch. 6, § 256, 66 Stat. 223; Nov. 29, 1990, Pub.L. 101–649, Title V, § 543(a)(6), 104 Stat. 5058.)

## § 257. Alien crewmen brought into the United States with intent to evade immigration laws; penalties [8 U.S.C.A. § 1287]

Any person, including the owner, agent, consignee, master, or commanding officer of any vessel or aircraft arriving in the United States from any place outside thereof, who shall knowingly sign on the vessel's articles, or bring to the United States as one of the crew of such vessel or aircraft, any alien, with intent to permit or assist such alien to enter or land in the United States in violation of law, or who shall falsely and knowingly represent to a consular officer at the time of application for visa, or to the immigration officer at the port of arrival in the United States, that such alien is a bona fide member of the crew employed in any capacity regularly required for normal operation and services aboard such vessel or aircraft, shall be liable to a penalty not exceeding $10,000 for each such violation, for which sum such vessel or aircraft shall be liable and may be seized and proceeded against by way of libel in any district court of the United States having jurisdiction of the offense.

(June 27, 1952, c. 477, Title II, ch. 6, § 257, 66 Stat. 223; Nov. 29, 1990, Pub.L. 101–649, Title V, § 543(a)(7), 104 Stat. 5058.)

# § 258. Limitations on performance of longshore work by alien crewmen [8 U.S.C.A. § 1288]

## (a) In general

For purposes of section 101(a)(15)(D)(i) [8 U.S.C.A. § 1101(a)(15)(D)(i)], the term "normal operation and service on board a vessel" does not include any activity that is longshore work (as defined in subsection (b) of this section), except as provided under subsection (c) or subsection (d) of this section.

## (b) Longshore work defined

### (1) In general

In this section, except as provided in paragraph (2), the term "longshore work" means any activity relating to the loading or unloading of cargo, the operation of cargo-related equipment (whether or not integral to the vessel), and the handling of mooring lines on the dock when the vessel is made fast or let go, in the United States or the coastal waters thereof.

### (2) Exception for safety and environmental protection

The term "longshore work" does not include the loading or unloading of any cargo for which the Secretary of Transportation has, under the authority contained in chapter 37 of Title 46 (relating to Carriage of Liquid Bulk Dangerous Cargoes), section 311 of the Federal Water Pollution Control Act (33 U.S.C. 1321), section 4106 of the Oil Pollution Act of 1990, or section 105 or 106 of the Hazardous Materials Transportation Act (49 U.S.C. App. 1804, 1805) prescribed regulations which govern—

(A) the handling or stowage of such cargo,

(B) the manning of vessels and the duties, qualifications, and training of the officers and crew of vessels carrying such cargo, and

(C) the reduction or elimination of discharge during ballasting, tank cleaning, handling of such cargo.

### (3) Construction

Nothing in this section shall be construed as broadening, limiting, or otherwise modifying the meaning or scope of longshore work for purposes of any other law, collective bargaining agreement, or international agreement.

## (c) Prevailing practice exception

(1) Subsection (a) of this section shall not apply to a particular activity of longshore work in and about a local port if—

(A)(i) there is in effect in the local port one or more collective bargaining agreements each covering at least 30 percent of the number of individuals employed in performing longshore work and (ii) each such agreement (covering such percentage of longshore workers) permits the activity to be performed by alien crewmen under the terms of such agreement; or

**(B)** there is no collective bargaining agreement in effect in the local port covering at least 30 percent of the number of individuals employed in performing longshore work, and an employer of alien crewmen (or the employer's designated agent or representative) has filed with the Secretary of Labor at least 14 days before the date of performance of the activity (or later, if necessary due to an unanticipated emergency, but not later than the date of performance of the activity) an attestation setting forth facts and evidence to show that—

**(i)** the performance of the activity by alien crewmen is permitted under the prevailing practice of the particular port as of the date of filing of the attestation and that the use of alien crewmen for such activity—

**(I)** is not during a strike or lockout in the course of a labor dispute, and

**(II)** is not intended or designed to influence an election of a bargaining representative for workers in the local port; and

**(ii)** notice of the attestation has been provided by owner, agent, consignee, master, or commanding officer to the bargaining representative of longshore workers in the local port, or, where there is no such bargaining representative, notice of the attestation has been provided to longshore workers employed at the local port.

In applying subparagraph (B) in the case of a particular activity of longshore work consisting of the use of an automated self-unloading conveyor belt or vacuum-actuated system on a vessel, the attestation shall be required to be filed only if the Secretary of Labor finds, based on a preponderance of the evidence which may be submitted by any interested party, that the performance of such particular activity is not described in clause (i) of such subparagraph.

**(2)** Subject to paragraph (4), an attestation under paragraph (1) shall—

**(A)** expire at the end of the 1-year period beginning on the date of its filing with the Secretary of Labor, and

**(B)** apply to aliens arriving in the United States during such 1-year period if the owner, agent, consignee, master, or commanding officer states in each such list under section 251 [8 U.S.C.A. § 1281] that it continues to comply with the conditions in the attestation.

(3) An owner, agent, consignee, master, or commanding officer may meet the requirements under this subsection with respect to more than one alien crewman in a single list.

(4)(A) The Secretary of Labor shall compile and make available for public examination in a timely manner in Washington, D.C., a list identifying owners, agents, consignees, masters, or commanding officers which have filed lists for nonimmigrants described in section 101(a)(15)(D)(i) [8 U.S.C.A. § 1101(a)(15)(D)(i)] with respect to whom an attestation under paragraph (1) is made and, for each such entity, a copy of the entity's attestation under paragraph (1) (and accompanying documentation) and each such list filed by the entity.

(B)(i) The Secretary of Labor shall establish a process for the receipt, investigation, and disposition of complaints respecting an entity's failure to meet conditions attested to, an entity's misrepresentation of a material fact in an attestation, or, in the case described in the last sentence of paragraph (1), whether the performance of the particular activity is or is not described in paragraph (1)(B)(i).

(ii) Complaints may be filed by any aggrieved person or organization (including bargaining representatives, associations deemed appropriate by the Secretary, and other aggrieved parties as determined under regulations of the Secretary).

(iii) The Secretary shall promptly conduct an investigation under this subparagraph if there is reasonable cause to believe that an entity fails to meet conditions attested to, an entity has misrepresented a material fact in the attestation, or, in the case described in the last sentence of paragraph (1), the performance of the particular activity is not described in paragraph (1)(B)(i).

(C)(i) If the Secretary determines that reasonable cause exists to conduct an investigation with respect to an attestation, a complaining party may request that the activities attested to by the employer cease during the hearing process described in subparagraph (D). If such a request is made, the attesting employer shall be issued notice of such request and shall respond within 14 days to the notice. If the Secretary makes an initial determination that the complaining party's position is supported by a preponderance of the evidence submitted, the Secretary shall require immediately that the employer cease and desist from such activities until completion of the process described in subparagraph (D).

(ii) If the Secretary determines that reasonable cause exists to conduct an investigation with respect to a matter under the last sentence of paragraph (1), a complaining party may request that the activities of the employer cease during the hearing process described in subparagraph (D) unless the employer files with the Secretary of Labor an attestation under paragraph (1). If such a request is made, the employer shall be issued notice of such request and shall respond within 14 days to the notice. If the Secretary makes an initial determination that the complaining party's position is supported by a preponderance of the evidence submitted, the Secretary shall require immediately that the employer cease and desist from such activities until completion of the process described in subparagraph (D) unless the employer files with the Secretary of Labor an attestation under paragraph (1).

**(D)** Under the process established under subparagraph (B), the Secretary shall provide, within 180 days after the date a complaint is filed (or later for good cause shown), for a determination as to whether or not a basis exists to make a finding described in subparagraph (E). The Secretary shall provide notice of such determination to the interested parties and an opportunity for a hearing on the complaint within 60 days of the date of the determination.

**(E)(i)** If the Secretary of Labor finds, after notice and opportunity for a hearing, that an entity has filed to meet a condition attested to or has made a misrepresentation of material fact in the attestation, the Secretary shall notify the Attorney General of such finding and may, in addition, impose such other administrative remedies (including civil monetary penalties in an amount not to exceed $5,000 for each alien crewman performing unauthorized longshore work) as the Secretary determines to be appropriate. Upon receipt of such notice, the Attorney General shall not permit the vessels owned or chartered by such entity to enter any port of the United States during a period of up to 1 year.

**(ii)** If the Secretary of Labor finds, after notice and opportunity for a hearing, that, in the case described in the last sentence of paragraph (1), the performance of the particular activity is not described in subparagraph (B)(i), the Secretary shall notify the Attorney General of such finding and, thereafter, the attestation described in paragraph (1) shall be required of the employer for the performance of the particular activity.

**(F)** A finding by the Secretary of Labor under this paragraph that the performance of an activity by alien crewmen is not permitted under the prevailing practice of a local port shall preclude for one year the filing of a subsequent attestation concerning such activity in the port under paragraph (1).

#### (d) Reciprocity exception

##### (1) In general

Subject to the determination of the Secretary of State pursuant to paragraph (2), the Attorney General shall permit an alien crewman to perform an activity constituting longshore work if—

> **(A)** the vessel is registered in a country that by law, regulation, or in practice does not prohibit such activity by crewmembers aboard United States vessels; and

> **(B)** nationals of a country (or countries) which by law, regulation, or in practice does not prohibit such activity by

crewmembers aboard United States vessels hold a majority of the ownership interest in the vessel.

### (2) Establishment of list

The Secretary of State shall, in accordance with section 553 of Title 5, compile and annually maintain a list, of longshore work by particular activity, of countries where performance of such a particular activity by crewmembers aboard United States vessels is prohibited by law, regulation, or in practice in the country. By not later than 90 days after November 29, 1990, the Secretary shall publish a notice of proposed rulemaking to establish such list. The Secretary shall first establish such list by not later than 180 days after November 29, 1990.

### (3) In practice defined

For purposes of this subsection, the term "in practice" refers to an activity normally performed in such country during the one-year period preceding the arrival of such vessel into the United States or coastal waters thereof.

(June 27, 1952, c. 477, Title II, ch. 6, § 258, as added Nov. 29, 1990, Pub.L. 101–649, Title II, § 203(a)(1), 104 Stat. 5015.)

## Chapter VII—Registration of Aliens

# § 261. Alien seeking entry; contents [8 U.S.C.A. § 1301]

No visa shall be issued to any alien seeking to enter the United States until such alien has been registered in accordance with section 221(b) [8 U.S.C.A. § 1201(b)].

(June 27, 1952, c. 477, Title II, ch. 7, § 261, 66 Stat. 223; Pub.L. 99–653, § 8, Nov. 14, 1986, 100 Stat. 3657, as amended Pub.L. 100–525, § 8(g), Oct. 24, 1988, 102 Stat. 2617.)

# § 262. Registration of aliens [8 U.S.C.A. § 1302]

### (a) In general

It shall be the duty of every alien now or hereafter in the United States, who (1) is fourteen years of age or older, (2) has not been registered and fingerprinted under section 221(b) [8 U.S.C.A. § 1201(b)] or section 30 or 31 of the Alien Registration Act, 1940, and (3) remains in the United States for thirty days or longer, to apply for registration and to be fingerprinted before the expiration of such thirty days.

### (b) Aliens less than fourteen years of age

It shall be the duty of every parent or legal guardian of any alien now or hereafter in the United States, who (1) is less than fourteen years of age, (2) has not been registered under section 221(b) [8 U.S.C.A. § 1201(b)] or section 30 or 31 of the Alien Registration Act, 1940, and (3) remains in the United States for thirty days or longer, to apply for the registration of such alien before the expiration of such thirty days. Whenever any alien attains his fourteenth birthday in the United States he shall, within thirty days thereafter, apply in person for registration and to be fingerprinted.

### (c) Waiver of fingerprinting requirement

The Attorney General may, in his discretion and on the basis of reciprocity pursuant to such regulations as he may prescribe, waive the requirement of fingerprinting specified in subsection (a) and (b) of this section in the case of any nonimmigrant.

(June 27, 1952, c. 477, Title II, ch. 7, § 262, 66 Stat. 224; Pub.L. 99–653, § 9, Nov. 14, 1986, 100 Stat. 3657, as amended Pub.L. 100–525, § 8(h), Oct. 24, 1988, 102 Stat. 2617.)

## § 263. Registration of special groups [8 U.S.C.A. § 1303]

**(a)** Notwithstanding the provisions of sections 261 and 262 [8 U.S.C.A. §§ 1301 and 1302], the Attorney General is authorized to prescribe special regulations and forms for the registration and fingerprinting of (1) alien crewmen, (2) holders of border-crossing identification cards, (3) aliens confined in institutions within the United States, (4) aliens under order of deportation, and (5) aliens of any other class not lawfully admitted to the United States for permanent residence.

**(b)** The provisions of section 262 [8 U.S.C.A. § 1302] and of this section shall not be applicable to any alien who is in the United States as a nonimmigrant under section 101(a)(15)(A) or (a)(15)(G) [8 U.S.C.A. § 1101(a)(15)(A) or (a)(15)(G)] until the alien ceases to be entitled to such a nonimmigrant status.

(June 27, 1952, c. 477, Title II, ch. 7, § 263, 66 Stat. 224.)

## § 264. Forms for registration and fingerprinting [8 U.S.C.A. § 1304]

### (a) Preparation; contents

The Attorney General and the Secretary of State jointly are authorized and directed to prepare forms for the registration of aliens under section 261 [8 U.S.C.A. § 1301], and the Attorney General is authorized and directed to prepare forms for the registration and fingerprinting of aliens under section 1302 of this title. Such forms shall contain inquiries with respect to (1) the date and place of entry of the alien into the United States; (2) activities in which he has been and intends to be engaged; (3) the length of time he expects to remain in the United States; (4) the police and criminal record, if any, of such alien; and (5) such additional matters as may be prescribed.

### (b) Confidential nature

All registration and fingerprint records made under the provisions of this subchapter shall be confidential, and shall be made available only (1) pursuant to section 287(f)(2) [8 U.S.C.A. § 1357(f)(2)], and (2) to such persons or agencies as may be designated by the Attorney General.

### (c) Information under oath

Every person required to apply for the registration of himself or another under this subchapter shall submit under oath the information required for such registration. Any person authorized under regulations issued by the Attorney General to register aliens under this subchapter shall be authorized to administer oaths for such purpose.

### (d) Certificate of alien registration or alien receipt card

Every alien in the United States who has been registered and fingerprinted under the provisions of the Alien Registration Act, 1940, or under the provisions of this chapter shall be issued a certificate of alien registration or an alien registration receipt card in such form and manner and at such time as shall be prescribed under regulations issued by the Attorney General.

### (e) Personal possession of registration or receipt card; penalties

Every alien, eighteen years of age and over, shall at all times carry with him and have in his personal possession any certificate of alien registration or alien registration receipt card issued to him pursuant to subsection (d) of this section. Any alien who fails to comply with the provisions of this subsection shall be guilty of a misdemeanor and shall upon conviction for each offense be fined not to exceed $100 or be imprisoned not more than thirty days, or both.

(June 27, 1952, c. 477, Title II, ch. 7, § 264, 66 Stat. 224; Pub.L. 99–653, § 10, Nov. 14, 1986, 100 Stat. 3657, as amended Pub.L. 100–525, § 8(i), Oct. 24, 1988, 102 Stat. 2617; Pub.L. 101–649, Title V, § 503(b)(2), Nov. 29, 1990, 104 Stat. 5049.)

## § 265. Notices of change of address [8 U.S.C.A. § 1305]

### (a) Notification of change

Each alien required to be registered under this subchapter who is within the United States shall notify the Attorney General in writing of each change of address and new address within ten days from the date of such change and furnish with such notice such additional information as the Attorney General may require by regulation.

### (b) Current address of natives of any one or more foreign states

The Attorney General may in his discretion, upon ten days notice, require the natives of any one or more foreign states, or any class or group thereof, who are within the United States and who are required to be registered under this subchapter, to notify the Attorney General of their current addresses and furnish such additional information as the Attorney General may require.

### (c) Notice to parent or legal guardian

In the case of an alien for whom a parent or legal guardian is required to apply for registration, the notice required by this section shall be given to such parent or legal guardian.

(June 27, 1952, c. 477, Title II, c. 7, § 265, 66 Stat. 225; Pub.L. 97–116, § 11, Dec. 29, 1981, 95 Stat. 1617; Pub.L. 100–525, § 9(o), Oct. 24, 1988, 102 Stat. 2620.)

## § 266. Penalties [8 U.S.C.A. § 1306]

### (a) Willful failure to register

Any alien required to apply for registration and to be fingerprinted in the United States who willfully fails or refuses to make such application or to be fingerprinted, and any parent or legal guardian required to apply for the registration of any alien who willfully fails or refuses to file application for the registration of such alien shall be guilty of a misdemeanor and shall, upon conviction thereof, be fined not to exceed $1,000 or be imprisoned not more than six months, or both.

### (b) Failure to notify change of address

Any alien or any parent or legal guardian in the United States of any alien who fails to give written notice to the Attorney General, as required by section 265 [8 U.S.C.A. § 1305], shall be guilty of a misdemeanor and shall, upon conviction thereof, be fined not to exceed $200 or be imprisoned not more than thirty days, or both. Irrespective of whether an alien is convicted and punished as herein provided, any alien who fails to give written notice to the Attorney General, as required by section 265 [8 U.S.C.A. § 1305], shall be taken into custody and deported in the manner provided by part V of this subchapter, unless such alien establishes to the satisfaction of the Attorney General that such failure was reasonably excusable or was not willful.

### (c) Fraudulent statements

Any alien or any parent or legal guardian of any alien, who files an application for registration containing statements known by him to be false, or who procures or attempts to procure registration of himself or another person through fraud, shall be guilty of a misdemeanor and shall, upon conviction thereof, be fined not to exceed $1,000, or be imprisoned not more than six months, or both; and any alien so convicted shall, upon the warrant of the Attorney General, be taken into custody and be deported in the manner provided in part V of this subchapter.

### (d) Counterfeiting

Any person who with unlawful intent photographs, prints, or in any other manner makes, or executes, any engraving, photograph, print, or impression in the likeness of any certificate of alien registration or an alien registration receipt card or any colorable imitation thereof, except when and as authorized under such rules and regulations as may be prescribed by the Attorney General, shall upon conviction be fined not to exceed $5,000 or be imprisoned not more than five years, or both.

(June 27, 1952, c. 477, Title II, ch. 7, § 266, 66 Stat. 225.)

## CHAPTER VIII—GENERAL PENALTY PROVISIONS

## § 271. Prevention of unauthorized landing of aliens; penalties; failure to report; prima facie evidence; liability of owners and operators of international bridges and toll roads [8 U.S.C.A. § 1321]

(a) It shall be the duty of every person, including the owners, masters, officers, and agents of vessels, aircraft, transportation lines, or international bridges or toll roads, other than transportation lines which may enter into a contract as provided in section 238 [8 U.S.C.A. § 1228], bringing an alien to, or providing a means for an alien to come to, the United States (including an alien crewman whose case is not covered by section 254(a) [8 U.S.C.A. § 1284(a)]) to prevent the landing of such alien in the United States at a port of entry other than as designated by the Attorney General or at any time or place other than as designated by the immigration officers. Any such person, owner, master, officer, or agent who fails to comply with the foregoing requirements shall be liable to a penalty to be imposed by the Attorney General of $3,000 for each such violation, which may, in the discretion of the Attorney General, be remitted or mitigated by him in accordance with such proceedings as he shall by regulation prescribe. Such penalty shall be a lien upon the vessel or aircraft whose owner, master, officer, or agent violates the provisions of this section, and such vessel or aircraft may be libeled therefor in the appropriate United States court.

(b) Proof that the alien failed to present himself at the time and place designated by the immigration officers shall be prima facie evidence that such alien has landed in the United States at a time or place other than as designated by the immigration officers.

(c)(1) Any owner or operator of a railroad line, international bridge, or toll road who establishes to the satisfaction of the Attorney General that the person has acted diligently and reasonably to fulfill the duty imposed by subsection (a) of this section shall not be liable for the penalty described in such subsection, notwithstanding the failure of the person to prevent the unauthorized landing of any alien.

(2)(A) At the request of any person described in paragraph (1), the Attorney General shall inspect any facility established, or any method utilized, at a point of entry into the United States by such person for the purpose of complying with subsection (a) of this section. The Attorney General shall approve any such facility or method (for such period of time as the Attorney General may prescribe) which the Attorney General determines is satisfactory for such purpose.

**(B)** Proof that any person described in paragraph (1) has diligently maintained any facility, or utilized any method, which has been approved by the Attorney General under subparagraph (A) (within the period for which the approval is effective) shall be prima facie evidence that such person acted diligently and reasonably to fulfill the duty imposed by subsection (a) of this section (within the meaning of paragraph (1) of this subsection).

(June 27, 1952, c. 477, Title II, ch. 8, § 271, 66 Stat. 226; Pub.L. 99–603, Title I, § 114, Nov. 6, 1986, 100 Stat. 3383; Pub.L. 101–649, Title V, § 543(a)(8), Nov. 29, 1990, 104 Stat. 5058.)

## § 272. Bringing in aliens subject to exclusion on a health-related ground; persons liable; clearance papers; exceptions; definition [8 U.S.C.A. § 1322]

**(a)** Any person who shall bring to the United States an alien (other than an alien crewman) who is excludable under section 212(a)(1) [8 U.S.C.A. § 1182(a)(1)], shall pay to the Commissioner for each and every alien so afflicted, the sum of $3,000 unless (1) the alien was in possession of a valid, unexpired immigrant visa, or (2) the alien was allowed to land in the United States, or (3) the alien was in possession of a valid unexpired nonimmigrant visa or other document authorizing such alien to apply for temporary admission to the United States or an unexpired reentry permit issued to him, and (A) such application was made within one hundred and twenty days of the date of issuance of the visa or other document, or in the case of an alien in possession of a reentry permit, within one hundred and twenty days of the date on which the alien was last examined and admitted by the Service, or (B) in the event the application was made later than one hundred and twenty days of the date of issuance of the visa or other document or such examination and admission, if such person establishes to the satisfaction of the Attorney General that the existence of the excluding condition could not have been detected by the exercise of due diligence prior to the alien's embarkation.

**(b)** No vessel or aircraft shall be granted clearance papers pending determination of the question of liability to the payment of any fine under this section, or while the fines remain unpaid, nor shall such fines be remitted or refunded; but clearance may be granted prior to the determination of such question upon the deposit of a sum sufficient to cover such fines or of a bond with sufficient surety to secure the payment thereof, approved by the Commissioner.

**(c)** Nothing contained in this section shall be construed to subject transportation companies to a fine for bringing to ports of entry in the United States aliens who are entitled by law to exemption from the excluding provisions of section 212(a) [8 U.S.C.A. § 1182(a)].

(d) As used in this section, the term "person" means the owner, master, agent, commanding officer, charterer, or consignee of any vessel or aircraft.

(June 27, 1952, c. 477, Title II, ch. 8, § 272, 66 Stat. 226; Pub.L. 89–236, § 18, Oct. 3, 1965, 79 Stat. 920; Pub.L. 101–649, Title V, § 543(a)(9), Title VI, § 603(a)(15), Nov. 29, 1990, 104 Stat. 5058, 5084.)

## § 273. Unlawful bringing of aliens into United States [8 U.S.C.A. § 1323]

### (a) Persons liable

It shall be unlawful for any person, including any transportation company, or the owner, master, commanding officer, agent, charterer, or consignee of any vessel or aircraft, to bring to the United States from any place outside thereof (other than from foreign contiguous territory) any alien who does not have a valid passport and an unexpired visa, if a visa was required under this chapter or regulations issued thereunder.

### (b) Evidence

If it appears to the satisfaction of the Attorney General that any alien has been so brought, such person, or transportation company, or the master, commanding officer, agent, owner, charterer, or consignee of any such vessel or aircraft, shall pay to the Commissioner the sum of $3,000 for each alien so brought and, except in the case of any such alien who is admitted, or permitted to land temporarily, in addition, a sum equal to that paid by such alien for his transportation from the initial point of departure, indicated in his ticket, to the port of arrival, such latter sum to be delivered by the collector of customs to the alien on whose account the assessment is made. No vessel or aircraft shall be granted clearance pending the determination of the liability to the payment of such sums or while such sums remain unpaid, except that clearance may be granted prior to the determination of such question upon the deposit of an amount sufficient to cover such sums, or of a bond with sufficient surety to secure the payment thereof approved by the collector of customs.

### (c) Remissions or refund

Such sums shall not be remitted or refunded, unless it appears to the satisfaction of the Attorney General that such person, and the owner, master, commanding officer, agent, charterer, and consignee of the vessel or aircraft, prior to the departure of the vessel or aircraft from the last port outside the United States, did not know, and could not have ascertained by the exercise of reasonable diligence, that the individual transported was an alien and that a valid passport or visa was required.

### (d) Alien stowaways

The owner, charterer, agent, consignee, commanding officer, or master of any vessel or aircraft arriving at the United States from any place outside thereof who fails to detain on board or at such other place as may be designated by an immigration officer any alien stowaway until such stowaway has been inspected by an immigration officer, or who fails to detain such stowaway on board or at such other designated place after inspection if ordered to do so by an immigration officer, or who fails to deport such stowaway on the vessel or aircraft on which he arrived or on another vessel or aircraft at the expense of the vessel or aircraft on which he arrived when required to do so by an immigration officer, shall pay to the Commissioner the sum of $3,000 for each alien stowaway, in respect of whom any such failure occurs. Pending final determination of liability for such fine, no such vessel or aircraft shall be granted clearance, except that clearance may be granted upon the deposit of a sum sufficient to cover such fine, or of a bond with sufficient surety to secure the payment thereof approved by the Commissioner. The provisions of section 235 [8 U.S.C.A. § 1225] for detention of aliens for examination before special inquiry officers and the right of appeal provided for in section 236 [8 U.S.C.A. § 1226] shall not apply to aliens who arrive as stowaways and no such alien shall be permitted to land in the United States, except temporarily for medical treatment, or pursuant to such regulations as the Attorney General may prescribe for the ultimate departure or removal or deportation of such alien from the United States.

(June 27, 1952, c. 477, Title II, ch. 8, § 273, 66 Stat. 227; Nov. 29, 1990, Pub.L. 101–649, Title II, § 201(b), Title V, § 543(a)(10), 104 Stat. 5014, 5058.)

## § 274. Bringing in and harboring certain aliens [8 U.S.C.A. § 1324]

### (a) Criminal penalties

(1) Any person who—

(A) knowing that a person is an alien, brings to or attempts to bring to the United States in any manner whatsoever such person at a place other than a designated port of entry or place other than as designated by the Commissioner, regardless of whether such alien has received prior official authorization to come to, enter, or reside in the United States and regardless of any future official action which may be taken with respect to such alien;

(B) knowing or in reckless disregard of the fact that an alien has come to, entered, or remains in the United States in violation of law, transports, or moves or attempts to transport or move such alien within the United States by means of transportation or otherwise, in furtherance of such violation of law;

(C) knowing or in reckless disregard of the fact that an alien has come to, entered, or remains in the United States in violation of law, conceals, harbors, or shields from detection, or attempts to conceal, harbor, or shield from detection, such alien in any place, including any building or any means of transportation; or

(D) encourages or induces an alien to come to, enter, or reside in the United States, knowing or in reckless disregard of the fact that such coming to, entry, or residence is or will be in violation of law,

shall be fined in accordance with Title 18, or imprisoned not more than five years, or both, for each alien in respect to whom any violation of this paragraph occurs.

(2) Any person who, knowing or in reckless disregard of the fact that an alien has not received prior official authorization to come to, enter, or reside in the United States, brings to or attempts to bring to the United States in any manner whatsoever, such alien, regardless of any official action which may later be taken with respect to such alien shall, for each transaction constituting a violation of this paragraph, regardless of the number of aliens involved—

(A) be fined in accordance with Title 18, or imprisoned not more than one year, or both; or

(B) in the case of—

(i) a second or subsequent offense,

(ii) an offense done for the purpose of commercial advantage or private financial gain, or

(iii) an offense in which the alien is not upon arrival immediately brought and presented to an appropriate immigration officer at a designated port of entry,

be fined in accordance with Title 18, or imprisoned not more than five years, or both.

**(b) Seizure and forfeiture of conveyances; exceptions; officers and authorized persons; disposition of forfeited conveyances; suits and actions**

(1) Any conveyance, including any vessel, vehicle, or aircraft, which has been or is being used in the commission of a violation of subsection (a) of this section shall be seized and subject to forfeiture, except that—

(A) no conveyance used by any person as a common carrier in the transaction of business as a common carrier shall be forfeited under the provisions of this section unless it shall appear that the owner or other person in charge of such conveyance was a consenting party or privy to the illegal act; and

(B) no conveyance shall be forfeited under the provisions of this section by reason of any act or omission established by the owner thereof to have been committed or omitted by any person other than such owner while such conveyance was unlawfully in the possession of a person other than the owner in violation of the criminal laws of the United States or of any State.

(2) Any conveyance subject to seizure under this section may be seized without warrant if there is probable cause to believe the conveyance has been or is being used in a violation of subsection (a) of this

section and circumstances exist where a warrant is not constitutionally required.

(3) All provisions of law relating to the seizure, summary and judicial forfeiture, and condemnation of property for the violation of the customs laws; the disposition of such property or the proceeds from the sale thereof; the remission or mitigation of such forfeitures; and the compromise of claims and the award of compensation to informers in respect of such forfeitures shall apply to seizures and forfeitures incurred, or alleged to have been incurred, under the provisions of this section, insofar as applicable and not inconsistent with the provisions hereof, except that duties imposed on customs officers or other persons regarding the seizure and forfeiture of property under the customs laws shall be performed with respect to seizures and forfeitures carried out under the provisions of this section by such officers or persons authorized for that purpose by the Attorney General.

(4) Whenever a conveyance is forfeited under this section the Attorney General may—

(A) retain the conveyance for official use;

(B) sell the conveyance, in which case the proceeds from any such sale shall be used to pay all proper expenses of the proceedings for forfeiture and sale including expenses of seizure, maintenance of custody, advertising, and court costs;

(C) require that the General Services Administration, or the Maritime Administration if appropriate under section 484(i) of Title 40, take custody of the conveyance and remove it for disposition in accordance with law; or

(D) dispose of the conveyance in accordance with the terms and conditions of any petition of remission or mitigation of forfeiture granted by the Attorney General.

(5) In all suits or actions brought for the forfeiture of any conveyance seized under this section, where the conveyance is claimed by any person, the burden of proof shall lie upon such claimant, except that probable cause shall be first shown for the institution of such suit or action. In determining whether probable cause exists, any of the following shall be prima facie evidence that an alien involved in the alleged violation had not received prior official authorization to come to, enter, or reside in the United States or that such alien had come to, entered or remained in the United States in violation of law:

(A) Records of any judicial or administrative proceeding in which that alien's status was an issue and in which it was determined that the alien was not lawfully entitled to enter, or reside within, the United States.

(B) Official records of the Service or of the Department of State showing that the alien had not received prior official authorization to come to, enter, or reside in the United States or that such alien had come to, entered, or remained in the United States in violation of law.

(C) Testimony, by an immigration officer having personal knowledge of the facts concerning that alien's status, that the alien had not received prior official authorization to come to, enter, or reside in the United States or that such alien had come to, entered, or remained in the United States in violation of law.

### (c) Authority to arrest

No officer or person shall have authority to make any arrests for a violation of any provision of this section except officers and employees of the Service designated by the Attorney General, either individually or as a member of a class, and all other officers whose duty it is to enforce criminal laws.

(June 27, 1952, c. 477, Title II, c. 8, § 274, 66 Stat. 228; Pub.L. 95–582, § 2, Nov. 2, 1978, 92 Stat. 2479; Pub.L. 97–116, § 12, Dec. 29, 1981, 95 Stat. 1617; Pub.L. 99–603, § 112, Nov. 6, 1986, 100 Stat. 3381, as amended Oct. 24, 1988, Pub.L. 100–525, § 2(d)(2), 102 Stat. 2610; Oct. 24, 1988, Pub.L. 100–525, § 2(d)(1), 102 Stat. 2610.)

## § 274A.  Unlawful employment of aliens [8 U.S.C.A. § 1324a]

### (a) Making employment of unauthorized aliens unlawful

#### (1) In general

It is unlawful for a person or other entity—

(A) to hire, or to recruit or refer for a fee, for employment in the United States an alien knowing the alien is an unauthorized alien (as defined in subsection (h)(3) of this section) with respect to such employment, or

(B) (i) to hire for employment in the United States an individual without complying with the requirements of subsection (b) of this section or (ii) if the person or entity is an agricultural association, agricultural employer, or farm labor contractor (as defined in section 1802 of Title 29) to hire, or to recruit or refer for a fee, for employment in the United States an individual without complying with the requirements of subsection (b) of this section.

#### (2) Continuing employment

It is unlawful for a person or other entity, after hiring an alien for employment in accordance with paragraph (1), to continue to employ the alien in the United States knowing the alien is (or has become) an unauthorized alien with respect to such employment.

#### (3) Defense

A person or entity that establishes that it has complied in good faith with the requirements of subsection (b) of this section with respect to the hiring, recruiting, or referral for employment of an alien in the United States has established an affirmative defense that the person or entity has not violated paragraph (1)(A) with respect to such hiring, recruiting, or referral.

### (4) Use of labor through contract

For purposes of this section, a person or other entity who uses a contract, subcontract, or exchange, entered into, renegotiated, or extended after the date of the enactment of this section, to obtain the labor of an alien in the United States knowing that the alien is an unauthorized alien (as defined in subsection (h)(3) of this section) with respect to performing such labor, shall be considered to have hired the alien for employment in the United States in violation of paragraph (1)(A).

### (5) Use of State employment agency documentation

For purposes of paragraphs (1)(B) and (3), a person or entity shall be deemed to have complied with the requirements of subsection (b) of this section with respect to the hiring of an individual who was referred for such employment by a State employment agency (as defined by the Attorney General), if the person or entity has and retains (for the period and in the manner described in subsection (b)(3)) appropriate documentation of such referral by that agency, which documentation certifies that the agency has complied with the procedures specified in subsection (b) of this section with respect to the individual's referral.

### (b) Employment verification system

The requirements referred to in paragraphs (1)(B) and (3) of subsection (a) of this section are, in the case of a person or other entity hiring, recruiting, or referring an individual for employment in the United States, the requirements specified in the following three paragraphs:

### (1) Attestation after examination of documentation

#### (A) In general

The person or entity must attest, under penalty of perjury and on a form designated or established by the Attorney General by regulation, that it has verified that the individual is not an unauthorized alien by examining—

(i) a document described in subparagraph (B), or

(ii) a document described in subparagraph (C) and a document described in subparagraph (D).

A person or entity has complied with the requirement of this paragraph with respect to examination of a document if the document reasonably appears on its face to be genuine. If an individual provides a document or combination of documents that reasonably appears on its face to be genuine and that is sufficient to meet the requirements of the first sentence of this paragraph, nothing in this paragraph shall be construed as requiring the person or entity to solicit the production of any other document or as requiring the individual to produce such another document.

**(B)** Documents establishing both employment authorization and identity

A document described in this subparagraph is an individual's—

(i) United States passport;

(ii) certificate of United States citizenship;

(iii) certificate of naturalization;

(iv) unexpired foreign passport, if the passport has an appropriate, unexpired endorsement of the Attorney General authorizing the individual's employment in the United States; or

(v) resident alien card or other alien registration card, if the card—

(I) contains a photograph of the individual or such other personal identifying information relating to the individual as the Attorney General finds, by regulation, sufficient for purposes of this subsection, and

(II) is evidence of authorization of employment in the United States.

**(C)** Documents evidencing employment authorization

A document described in this subparagraph is an individual's—

(i) social security account number card (other than such a card which specifies on the face that the issuance of the card does not authorize employment in the United States);

(ii) certificate of birth in the United States or establishing United States nationality at birth, which certificate the Attorney General finds, by regulation, to be acceptable for purposes of this section; or

(iii) other documentation evidencing authorization of employment in the United States which the Attorney General finds, by regulation, to be acceptable for purposes of this section.

**(D)** Documents establishing identity of individual

A document described in this subparagraph is an individual's—

(i) driver's license or similar document issued for the purpose of identification by a State, if it contains a photograph of the individual or such other personal identifying information relating to the individual as the Attorney General finds, by regulation, sufficient for purposes of this section; or

(ii) in the case of individuals under 16 years of age or in a State which does not provide for issuance of an identification document (other than a driver's license) referred to in clause (ii), documentation of personal identity of such other type as the Attorney General finds, by regulation, provides a reliable means of identification.

## (2) Individual attestation of employment authorization

The individual must attest, under penalty of perjury on the form designated or established for purposes of paragraph (1), that the individual is a citizen or national of the United States, an alien lawfully admitted for permanent residence, or an alien who is authorized under this chapter or by the Attorney General to be hired, recruited, or referred for such employment.

## (3) Retention of verification form

After completion of such form in accordance with paragraphs (1) and (2), the person or entity must retain the form and make it available for inspection by officers of the Service, the Special Counsel for Immigration-Related Unfair Employment Practices, or the Department of Labor during a period beginning on the date of the hiring, recruiting, or referral of the individual and ending—

(A) in the case of the recruiting or referral for a fee (without hiring) of an individual, three years after the date of the recruiting or referral, and

(B) in the case of the hiring of an individual—

(i) three years after the date of such hiring, or

(ii) one year after the date the individual's employment is terminated,

whichever is later.

## (4) Copying of documentation permitted

Notwithstanding any other provision of law, the person or entity may copy a document presented by an individual pursuant to this subsection and may retain the copy, but only (except as otherwise permitted under law) for the purpose of complying with the requirements of this subsection.

## (5) Limitation on use of attestation form

A form designated or established by the Attorney General under this subsection and any information contained in or appended to such form, may not be used for purposes other than for enforcement of this chapter and sections 1001, 1028, 1546, and 1621 of Title 18.

### (c) No authorization of national identification cards

Nothing in this section shall be construed to authorize, directly or indirectly, the issuance or use of national identification cards or the establishment of a national identification card.

### (d) Evaluation and changes in employment verification system

#### (1) Presidential monitoring and improvements in system

**(A)** Monitoring

The President shall provide for the monitoring and evaluation of the degree to which the employment verification system established under subsection (b) of this section provides a secure system to determine employment eligibility in the United States and shall examine the suitability of existing Federal and State identification systems for use for this purpose.

**(B)** Improvements to establish secure system

To the extent that the system established under subsection (b) of this section is found not to be a secure system to determine employment eligibility in the United States, the President shall, subject to paragraph (3) and taking into account the results of any demonstration projects conducted under paragraph (4), implement such changes in (including additions to) the requirements of subsection (b) of this section as may be necessary to establish a secure system to determine employment eligibility in the United States. Such changes in the system may be implemented only if the changes conform to the requirements of paragraph (2).

#### (2) Restrictions on changes in system

Any change the President proposes to implement under paragraph (1) in the verification system must be designed in a manner so the verification system, as so changed, meets the following requirements:

**(A)** Reliable determination of identity

The system must be capable of reliably determining whether—

> **(i)** a person with the identity claimed by an employee or prospective employee is eligible to work, and

> **(ii)** the employee or prospective employee is claiming the identity of another individual.

**(B)** Using of counterfeit-resistant documents

If the system requires that a document be presented to or examined by an employer, the document must be in a form which is resistant to counterfeiting and tampering.

**(C)** Limited use of system

Any personal information utilized by the system may not be made available to Government agencies, employers, and other persons except to the extent necessary to verify that an individual is not an unauthorized alien.

**(D)** Privacy of information

The system must protect the privacy and security of personal information and identifiers utilized in the system.

**(E)** Limited denial of verification

A verification that an employee or prospective employee is eligible to be employed in the United States may not be withheld or revoked under the system for any reason other than that the employee or prospective employee is an unauthorized alien.

**(F)** Limited use for law enforcement purposes

The system may not be used for law enforcement purposes, other than for enforcement of this chapter or sections 1001, 1028, 1546, and 1621 of Title 18.

**(G)** Restriction on use of new documents

If the system requires individuals to present a new card or other document (designed specifically for use for this purpose) at the time of hiring, recruitment, or referral, then such document may not be required to be presented for any purpose other than under this chapter (or enforcement of sections 1001, 1028, 1546, and 1621 of Title 18) nor to be carried on one's person.

**(3) Notice to Congress before implementing changes**

**(A)** In general

The President may not implement any change under paragraph (1) unless at least—

> **(i)** 60 days,

> **(ii)** one year, in the case of a major change described in subparagraph (D)(iii), or

> **(iii)** two years, in the case of a major change described in clause (i) or (ii) of subparagraph (D),

before the date of implementation of the change, the President has prepared and transmitted to the Committee on the Judiciary of the House of Representatives and to the Committee on the Judiciary of the Senate a written report setting forth the proposed change. If the President proposes to make any change regarding social security account number cards, the President shall transmit to the Committee on Ways and Means of the House of Representatives and to the Committee on Finance of the Senate a written report setting forth the proposed change. The President promptly shall cause to have printed in the Federal Register the substance of any major change (described in subparagraph (D)) proposed and reported to Congress.

**(B)** Contents of report

In any report under subparagraph (A) the President shall include recommendations for the establishment of civil and criminal sanctions for unauthorized use or disclosure of the information or identifiers contained in such system.

**(C)** Congressional review of major changes

    **(i)** Hearings and review

The Committees on the Judiciary of the House of Representatives and of the Senate shall cause to have printed in the Congressional Record the substance of any major change described in subparagraph (D), shall hold hearings respecting the feasibility and desirability of implementing such a change, and, within the two year period before implementation, shall report to their respective Houses findings on whether or not such a change should be implemented.

    **(ii)** Congressional action

No major change may be implemented unless the Congress specifically provides, in an appropriations or other Act, for funds for implementation of the change.

**(D)** Major changes defined

As used in this paragraph, the term "major change" means a change which would—

    **(i)** require an individual to present a new card or other document (designed specifically for use for this purpose) at the time of hiring, recruitment, or referral,

    **(ii)** provide for a telephone verification system under which an employer, recruiter, or referrer must transmit to a Federal official information concerning the immigration status of prospective employees and the official transmits to the person, and the person must record, a verification code, or

    **(iii)** require any change in any card used for accounting purposes under the Social Security Act [42 U.S.C.A. § 301 et seq.]; including any change requiring that the only social security account number cards which may be presented in order to comply with subsection (b)(1)(C)(i) of this section are such cards as are in a counterfeit-resistant form consistent with the second sentence of section

205(c)(2)(D) of the Social Security Act [42 U.S.C.A. § 405(c)(2)(D)].

**(E)** General revenue funding of social security card changes

Any costs incurred in developing and implementing any change described in subparagraph (D)(iii) for purposes of this subsection shall not be paid for out of any trust fund established under the Social Security Act.

**(4) Demonstration projects**

**(A)** Authority

The President may undertake demonstration projects (consistent with paragraph (2)) of different changes in the requirements of subsection (b) of this section. No such project may extend over a period of longer than three years.

**(B)** Reports on projects

The President shall report to the Congress on the results of demonstration projects conducted under this paragraph.

**(e) Compliance**

**(1) Complaints and investigations**

The Attorney General shall establish procedures—

**(A)** for individuals and entities to file written, signed complaints respecting potential violations of subsection (a) or (g)(1) of this section,

**(B)** for the investigation of those complaints which, on their face, have a substantial probability of validity,

**(C)** for the investigation of such other violations of subsection (a) or (g)(1) of this section as the Attorney General determines to be appropriate, and

**(D)** for the designation in the Service of a unit which has, as its primary duty, the prosecution of cases of violations of subsection (a) or (g)(1) of this section under this subsection.

**(2) Authority in investigations**

In conducting investigations and hearings under this subsection—

**(A)** immigration officers and administrative law judges shall have reasonable access to examine evidence of any person or entity being investigated, and

**(B)** administrative law judges may, if necessary, compel by subpoena the attendance of witnesses and the production of evidence at any designated place or hearing.

In case of contumacy or refusal to obey a subpoena lawfully issued under this paragraph and upon application of the Attorney General, an appropriate district court of the United States may issue an order requiring compliance with such subpoena and any failure to obey such order may be punished by such court as a contempt thereof.

### (3) Hearing

#### (A) In general

Before imposing an order described in paragraph (4), (5), or (6) against a person or entity under this subsection for a violation of subsection (a) or (g)(1) of this section, the Attorney General shall provide the person or entity with notice and, upon request made within a reasonable time (of not less than 30 days, as established by the Attorney General) of the date of the notice, a hearing respecting the violation.

#### (B) Conduct of hearing

Any hearing so requested shall be conducted before an administrative law judge. The hearing shall be conducted in accordance with the requirements of section 554 of Title 5. The hearing shall be held at the nearest practicable place to the place where the person or entity resides or of the place where the alleged violation occurred. If no hearing is so requested, the Attorney General's imposition of the order shall constitute a final and unappealable order.

#### (C) Issuance of orders

If the administrative law judge determines, upon the preponderance of the evidence received, that a person or entity named in the complaint has violated subsection (a) or (g)(1) of this section, the administrative law judge shall state his findings of fact and issue and cause to be served on such person or entity an order described in paragraph (4), (5), or (6).

### (4) Cease and desist order with civil money penalty for hiring, recruiting, and referral violations

With respect to a violation of subsection (a)(1)(A) or (a)(2) of this section, the order under this subsection—

(A) shall require the person or entity to cease and desist from such violations and to pay a civil penalty in an amount of—

(i) not less than $250 and not more than $2,000 for each unauthorized alien with respect to whom a violation of either such subsection occurred,

(ii) not less than $2,000 and not more than $5,000 for each such alien in the case of a person or entity previously subject to one order under this paragraph, or

(iii) not less than $3,000 and not more than $10,000 for each such alien in the case of a person or entity previously subject to more than one order under this paragraph; and

**(B)** may require the person or entity—

(i) to comply with the requirements of subsection (b) (or subsection (d) of this section if applicable) with respect to individuals hired (or recruited or referred for employment for a fee) during a period of up to three years, and

(ii) to take such other remedial action as is appropriate.

In applying this subsection in the case of a person or entity composed of distinct, physically separate subdivisions each of which provides separately for the hiring, recruiting, or referring for employment, without reference to the practices of, and not under the control of or common control with, another subdivision, each such subdivision shall be considered a separate person or entity.

**(5) Order for civil money penalty for paperwork violations**

With respect to a violation of subsection (a)(1)(B) of this section, the order under this subsection shall require the person or entity to pay a civil penalty in an amount of not less than $100 and not more than $1,000 for each individual with respect to whom such violation occurred. In determining the amount of the penalty, due consideration shall be given to the size of the business of the employer being charged, the good faith of the employer, the seriousness of the violation, whether or not the individual was an unauthorized alien, and the history of previous violations.

**(6) Order for prohibited indemnity bonds**

With respect to a violation of subsection (g)(1) of this section, the order under this subsection may provide for the remedy described in subsection (g)(2) of this section.

**(7) Administrative appellate review**

The decision and order of an administrative law judge shall become the final agency decision and order of the Attorney General unless, within 30 days, the Attorney General modifies or vacates the decision and order, in which case the decision and order of the Attorney General shall become a final order under this subsection. The Attorney General may not delegate the Attorney General's authority under this paragraph to any entity which has review authority over immigration-related matters.

**(8) Judicial review**

A person or entity adversely affected by a final order respecting an assessment may, within 45 days after the date the final order is issued, file a petition in the Court of Appeals for the appropriate circuit for review of the order.

### (9) Enforcement of orders

If a person or entity fails to comply with a final order issued under this subsection against the person or entity, the Attorney General shall file a suit to seek compliance with the order in any appropriate district court of the United States. In any such suit, the validity and appropriateness of the final order shall not be subject to review.

## (f) Criminal penalties and injunctions for pattern or practice violations

### (1) Criminal penalty

Any person or entity which engages in a pattern or practice of violations of subsection (a)(1)(A) or (a)(2) of this section shall be fined not more than $3,000 for each unauthorized alien with respect to whom such a violation occurs, imprisoned for not more than six months for the entire pattern or practice, or both, notwithstanding the provisions of any other Federal law relating to fine levels.

### (2) Enjoining of pattern or practice violations

Whenever the Attorney General has reasonable cause to believe that a person or entity is engaged in a pattern or practice of employment, recruitment, or referral in violation of paragraph (1)(A) or (2) of subsection (a) of this section, the Attorney General may bring a civil action in the appropriate district court of the United States requesting such relief, including a permanent or temporary injunction, restraining order, or other order against the person or entity, as the Attorney General deems necessary.

## (g) Prohibition of indemnity bonds

### (1) Prohibition

It is unlawful for a person or other entity, in the hiring, recruiting, or referring for employment of any individual, to require the individual to post a bond or security, to pay or agree to pay an amount, or otherwise to provide a financial guarantee or indemnity, against any potential liability arising under this section relating to such hiring, recruiting, or referring of the individual.

### (2) Civil penalty

Any person or entity which is determined, after notice and opportunity for an administrative hearing under subsection (e) of this section, to have violated paragraph (1) shall be subject to a civil penalty of $1,000 for each violation and to an administrative order requiring the return of any amounts received in violation of such paragraph to the employee or, if the employee cannot be located, to the general fund of the Treasury.

### (h) Miscellaneous provisions

#### (1) Documentation

In providing documentation or endorsement of authorization of aliens (other than aliens lawfully admitted for permanent residence) authorized to be employed in the United States, the Attorney General shall provide that any limitations with respect to the period or type of employment or employer shall be conspicuously stated on the documentation or endorsement.

#### (2) Preemption

The provisions of this section preempt any State or local law imposing civil or criminal sanctions (other than through licensing and similar laws) upon those who employ, or recruit or refer for a fee for employment, unauthorized aliens.

#### (3) Definition of unauthorized alien

As used in this section, the term "unauthorized alien" means, with respect to the employment of an alien at a particular time, that the alien is not at that time either (A) an alien lawfully admitted for permanent residence, or (B) authorized to be so employed by this chapter or by the Attorney General.

### (i) Effective Dates

#### (1) 6-month public information period

During the six-month period beginning on the first day of the first month after November 6, 1986—

> **(A)** the Attorney General, in cooperation with the Secretaries of Agriculture, Commerce, Health and Human Services, Labor, and the Treasury and the Administrator of the Small Business Administration, shall disseminate forms and information to employers, employment agencies, and organizations representing employees and provide for public education respecting the requirements of this section, and

> **(B)** the Attorney General shall not conduct any proceeding, nor issue any order, under this section on the basis of any violation alleged to have occurred during the period.

#### (2) 12-month first citation period

In the case of a person or entity, in the first instance in which the Attorney General has reason to believe that the person or entity may have violated subsection (a) of this section during the subsequent 12-month period, the Attorney General shall provide a citation to the person or entity indicating that such a violation or violations may have occurred and shall not conduct any proceeding, nor issue any order, under this section on the basis of such alleged violation or violations.

#### (3) Deferral of enforcement with respect to seasonal agricultural services

**(A)** In general

Except as provided in subparagraph (B), before the end of the application period (as defined in subparagraph (C)(i)), the Attorney General shall not conduct any proceeding, nor impose any penalty, under this section on the basis of any violation alleged to have occurred with respect to employment of an individual in seasonal agricultural services.

**(B)** Prohibition of recruitment outside the United States

**(i)** In general

During the application period, it is unlawful for a person or entity (including a farm labor contractor) or an agent of such a person or entity, to recruit an unauthorized alien (other than an alien described in clause (ii)) who is outside the United States to enter the United States to perform seasonal agricultural services.

**(ii)** Exception

Clause (i) shall not apply to an alien who the person or entity reasonably believes meets the requirements of section 210(a)(2) [8 U.S.C.A. § 1160(a)(2)] (relating to performance of seasonal agricultural services).

**(iii)** Penalty for violation

A person, entity, or agent that violates clause (i) shall be deemed to be subject to an order under this section in the same manner as if it had violated subsection (a)(1)(A) of this section, without regard to paragraph (2) of this subsection.

**(C)** Definitions

In this paragraph:

**(i)** Application period

The term "application period" means the period described in section 210(a)(1) [8 U.S.C.A. § 1160(a)(1)].

**(ii)** Seasonal agricultural services

The term "seasonal agricultural services" has the meaning given such term in section 210(h) [8 U.S.C.A. § 1160(h)].

**(j) General Accounting Office Reports**

**(1) In general**

Beginning one year after November 6, 1986, and at intervals of one year thereafter for a period of three years after such date, the Comptroller General shall prepare and transmit to the Congress and to the taskforce established under subsection (k) of this section a report describing the results of a review of the implementation and enforcement of this section during the preceding twelve-month period, for the purpose of determining if—

(A) such provisions have been carried out satisfactorily;

(B) a pattern of discrimination has resulted against citizens or nationals of the United States or against eligible workers seeking employment; and

(C) an unnecessary regulatory burden has been created for employers hiring such workers.

### (2) Determination on discrimination

In each report, the Comptroller General shall make a specific determination as to whether the implementation of this section has resulted in a pattern of discrimination in employment (against other than unauthorized aliens) on the basis of national origin.

### (3) Recommendations

If the Comptroller General has determined that such a pattern of discrimination has resulted, the report—

(A) shall include a description of the scope of that discrimination, and

(B) may include recommendations for such legislation as may be appropriate to deter or remedy such discrimination.

## (k) Review by taskforce

### (1) Establishment of joint taskforce

The Attorney General, jointly with the Chairman of the Commission on Civil Rights and the Chairman of the Equal Employment Opportunity Commission, shall establish a taskforce to review each report of the Comptroller General transmitted under subsection (j)(1) of this section.

### (2) Recommendations to Congress

If the report transmitted includes a determination that the implementation of this section has resulted in a pattern of discrimination in employment (against other than unauthorized aliens) on the basis of national origin, the taskforce shall, taking into consideration any recommendations in the report, report to Congress recommendations for such legislation as may be appropriate to deter or remedy such discrimination.

### (3) Congressional hearings

The Committees on the Judiciary of the House of Representatives and of the Senate shall hold hearings respecting any report of the taskforce under paragraph (2) within 60 days after the date of receipt of the report.

## (l) Termination date for employer sanctions

### (1) If report of widespread discrimination and congressional approval

The provisions of this section shall terminate 30 calendar days after receipt of the last report required to be transmitted under subsection (j) of this section, if—

(A) the Comptroller General determines, and so reports in such report, that a widespread pattern of discrimination has resulted against citizens or nationals of the United States or against eligible workers seeking employment solely from the implementation of this section; and

(B) there is enacted, within such period of 30 calendar days, a joint resolution stating in substance that the Congress approves the findings of the Comptroller General contained in such report.

### (2) Senate procedures for consideration

Any joint resolution referred to in clause (B) of paragraph (1) shall be considered in the Senate in accordance with subsection (n) of this section.

## (m) Expedited procedures in the House of Representatives

For the purpose of expediting the consideration and adoption of joint resolutions under subsection (l) of this section, a motion to proceed to the consideration of any such joint resolution after it has been reported by the appropriate committee shall be treated as highly privileged in the House of Representatives.

## (n) Expedited procedures in the Senate

### (1) Continuity of session

For purposes of subsection (l) of this section, the continuity of a session of Congress is broken only by an adjournment of the Congress sine die, and the days on which either House is not in session because of an adjournment of more than three days to a day certain are excluded in the computation of the period indicated.

### (2) Rulemaking power

Paragraphs (3) and (4) of this subsection are enacted—

(A) as an exercise of the rulemaking power of the Senate and as such they are deemed a part of the rules of the Senate, but applicable only with respect to the procedure to be followed in the Senate in the case of joint resolutions referred to in subsection (l) of this section and supersede other rules of the Senate only to the extent that such paragraphs are inconsistent therewith; and

(B) with full recognition of the constitutional right of the Senate to change such rules at any time, in the same manner as in the case of any other rule of the Senate.

### (3) Committee consideration

#### (A) Motion to discharge

If the committee of the Senate to which has been referred a joint resolution relating to the report described in subsection (*l*) of this section has not reported such joint resolution at the end of ten calendar days after its introduction, not counting any day which is excluded under paragraph (1) of this subsection, it is in order to move either to discharge the committee from further consideration of the joint resolution or to discharge the committee from further consideration of any other joint resolution introduced with respect to the same report which has been referred to the committee, except that no motion to discharge shall be in order after the committee has reported a joint resolution with respect to the same report.

#### (B) Consideration of motion

A motion to discharge under subparagraph (A) of this paragraph may be made only by a Senator favoring the joint resolution, is privileged, and debate thereon shall be limited to not more than 1 hour, to be divided equally between those favoring and those opposing the joint resolution, the time to be divided equally between, and controlled by, the majority leader and the minority leader or their designees. An amendment to the motion is not in order, and it is not in order to move to reconsider the vote by which the motion is agreed to or disagreed to.

### (4) Motion to proceed to consideration

#### (A) In general

A motion in the Senate to proceed to the consideration of a joint resolution shall be privileged. An amendment to the motion shall not be in order, nor shall it be in order to move to reconsider the vote by which the motion is agreed to or disagreed to.

#### (B) Debate on resolution

Debate in the Senate on a joint resolution, and all debatable motions and appeals in connection therewith, shall be limited to not more than 10 hours, to be equally divided between, and controlled by, the majority leader and the minority leader or their designees.

#### (C) Debate on motion

Debate in the Senate on any debatable motion or appeal in connection with a joint resolution shall be limited to not more than 1 hour, to be equally divided between, and controlled by, the mover and the manager of the joint resolution, except that in the event the manager of the joint resolution is in favor of any such motion or appeal, the time in opposition thereto shall

243

be controlled by the minority leader or his designee. Such leaders, or either of them, may, from time under their control on the passage of a joint resolution, allot additional time to any Senator during the consideration of any debatable motion or appeal.

**(D)** Motions to limit debate

A motion in the Senate to further limit debate on a joint resolution, debatable motion, or appeal is not debatable. No amendment to, or motion to recommit, a joint resolution is in order in the Senate.

(June 27, 1952, c. 477, Title II, ch. 8, § 274A, as added Pub.L. 99–603, Title I, § 101(a)(1), Nov. 6, 1986, 100 Stat. 3360, and amended Pub.L. 100–525, § 2(a)(1), Oct. 24, 1988, 102 Stat. 2609; Pub.L. 101–649, Title V, §§ 521(a), 538(a), Nov. 29, 1990, 104 Stat. 5053, 5056.)

# § 274B. Unfair immigration-related employment practices [8 U.S.C.A. § 1324b]

**(a) Prohibition of discrimination based on national origin or citizenship status**

### (1) General rule

It is an unfair immigration-related employment practice for a person or other entity to discriminate against any individual (other than an unauthorized alien, as defined in section 274A(h)(3) [8 U.S.C.A. § 1324a(h)(3)]) with respect to the hiring, or recruitment or referral for a fee, of the individual for employment or the discharging of the individual from employment—

**(A)** because of such individual's national origin, or

**(B)** in the case of a protected individual (as defined in paragraph (3)), because of such individual's citizenship status.

### (2) Exceptions

Paragraph (1) shall not apply to—

**(A)** a person or other entity that employs three or fewer employees,

**(B)** a person's or entity's discrimination because of an individual's national origin if the discrimination with respect to that person or entity and that individual is covered under section 2000e–2 of Title 42, or

**(C)** discrimination because of citizenship status which is otherwise required in order to comply with law, regulation, or executive order, or required by Federal, State, or local government contract, or which the Attorney General determines to be essential for an employer to do business with an agency or department of the Federal, State, or local government.

### (3) Definition of protected individual

As used in paragraph (1), the term "protected individual" means an individual who—

(**A**) is a citizen or national of the United States, or

(**B**) is an alien who is lawfully admitted for permanent residence, is granted the status of an alien lawfully admitted for temporary residence under section 210(a), 210A, or 245A(a)(1) [8 U.S.C.A. §§ 1160(a), 1161(a), or 1255a(a)(1)], is admitted as a refugee under section 207 [8 U.S.C.A. § 1157], or is granted asylum under section 208 [8 U.S.C.A. § 1158]; but does not include (i) an alien who fails to apply for naturalization within six months of the date the alien first becomes eligible (by virtue of period of lawful permanent residence) to apply for naturalization or, if later, within six months after November 6, 1986 and (ii) an alien who has applied on a timely basis, but has not been naturalized as a citizen within 2 years after the date of the application, unless the alien can establish that the alien is actively pursuing naturalization, except that time consumed in the Service's processing the application shall not be counted toward the 2-year period.

**(4) Additional exception providing right to prefer equally qualified citizens**

Notwithstanding any other provision of this section, it is not an unfair immigration-related employment practice for a person or other entity to prefer to hire, recruit, or refer an individual who is a citizen or national of the United States over another individual who is an alien if the two individuals are equally qualified.

**(5) Prohibition of intimidation or retaliation**

It is also an unfair immigration-related employment practice for a person or other entity to intimidate, threaten, coerce, or retaliate against any individual for the purpose of interfering with any right or privilege secured under this section or because the individual intends to file or has filed a charge or a complaint, testified, assisted, or participated in any manner in an investigation, proceeding, or hearing under this section. An individual so intimidated, threatened, coerced, or retaliated against shall be considered, for purposes of subsections (d) and (g) of this section, to have been discriminated against.

**(6) Treatment of certain documentary practices as employment practices**

For purposes of paragraph (1), a person's or other entity's request, for purposes of satisfying the requirements of section 274A(b) [8 U.S.C.A. § 1324a(b)], for more or different documents than are required under such section or refusing to honor documents tendered that on their face reasonably appear to be genuine shall be treated as an unfair immigration-related employment practice relating to the hiring of individuals.

## (b) Charges of violations

### (1) In general

Except as provided in paragraph (2), any person alleging that the person is adversely affected directly by an unfair immigration-related employment practice (or a person on that person's behalf) or an officer of the Service alleging that an unfair immigration-related employment practice has occurred or is occurring may file a charge respecting such practice or violation with the Special Counsel (appointed under subsection (c) of this section). Charges shall be in writing under oath or affirmation and shall contain such information as the Attorney General requires. The Special Counsel by certified mail shall serve a notice of the charge (including the date, place, and circumstances of the alleged unfair immigration-related employment practice) on the person or entity involved within 10 days.

### (2) No overlap with EEOC complaints

No charge may be filed respecting an unfair immigration-related employment practice described in subsection (a)(1)(A) of this section if a charge with respect to that practice based on the same set of facts has been filed with the Equal Employment Opportunity Commission under title VII of the Civil Rights Act of 1964 [42 U.S.C.A. § 2000e et seq.], unless the charge is dismissed as being outside the scope of such title. No charge respecting an employment practice may be filed with the Equal Employment Opportunity Commission under such title if a charge with respect to such practice based on the same set of facts has been filed under this subsection, unless the charge is dismissed under this section as being outside the scope of this section.

## (c) Special Counsel

### (1) Appointment

The President shall appoint, by and with the advice and consent of the Senate, a Special Counsel for Immigration-Related Unfair Employment Practices (hereinafter in this section referred to as the "Special Counsel") within the Department of Justice to serve for a term of four years. In the case of a vacancy in the office of the Special Counsel the President may designate the officer or employee who shall act as Special Counsel during such vacancy.

### (2) Duties

The Special Counsel shall be responsible for investigation of charges and issuance of complaints under this section and in respect of the prosecution of all such complaints before administrative law judges and the exercise of certain functions under subsection (i)(1) of this section.

### (3) Compensation

The Special Counsel is entitled to receive compensation at a rate not to exceed the rate now or hereafter provided for grade GS–17 of the General Schedule, under section 5332 of Title 5.

### (4) Regional offices

The Special Counsel, in accordance with regulations of the Attorney General, shall establish such regional offices as may be necessary to carry out his duties.

## (d) Investigation of charges

### (1) By Special Counsel

The Special Counsel shall investigate each charge received and, within 120 days of the date of the receipt of the charge, determine whether or not there is reasonable cause to believe that the charge is true and whether or not to bring a complaint with respect to the charge before an administrative law judge. The Special Counsel may, on his own initiative, conduct investigations respecting unfair immigration-related employment practices and, based on such an investigation and subject to paragraph (3), file a complaint before such a judge.

### (2) Private actions

If the Special Counsel, after receiving such a charge respecting an unfair immigration-related employment practice which alleges knowing and intentional discriminatory activity or a pattern or practice of discriminatory activity, has not filed a complaint before an administrative law judge with respect to such charge within such 120-day period, the Special Counsel shall notify the person making the charge of the determination not to file such a complaint during such period and the person making the charge may (subject to paragraph (3)) file a complaint directly before such a judge, within 90 days after the date of receipt of the notice. The Special Counsel's failure to file such a complaint within such 120-day period shall not affect the right of the Special Counsel to investigate the charge or to bring a complaint before an administrative law judge during such 90-day period.

### (3) Time limitations on complaints

No complaint may be filed respecting any unfair immigration-related employment practice occurring more than 180 days prior to the date of the filing of the charge with the Special Counsel. This subparagraph shall not prevent the subsequent amending of a charge or complaint under subsection (e)(1) of this section.

## (e) Hearings

### (1) Notice

Whenever a complaint is made that a person or entity has engaged in or is engaging in any such unfair immigration-related employment practice, an administrative law judge shall have power

247

to issue and cause to be served upon such person or entity a copy of the complaint and a notice of hearing before the judge at a place therein fixed, not less than five days after the serving of the complaint. Any such complaint may be amended by the judge conducting the hearing, upon the motion of the party filing the complaint, in the judge's discretion at any time prior to the issuance of an order based thereon. The person or entity so complained of shall have the right to file an answer to the original or amended complaint and to appear in person or otherwise and give testimony at the place and time fixed in the complaint.

### (2) Judges hearing cases

Hearings on complaints under this subsection shall be considered before administrative law judges who are specially designated by the Attorney General as having special training respecting employment discrimination and, to the extent practicable, before such judges who only consider cases under this section.

### (3) Complainant as party

Any person filing a charge with the Special Counsel respecting an unfair immigration-related employment practice shall be considered a party to any complaint before an administrative law judge respecting such practice and any subsequent appeal respecting that complaint. In the discretion of the judge conducting the hearing, any other person may be allowed to intervene in the proceeding and to present testimony.

## (f) Testimony and authority of hearing officers

### (1) Testimony

The testimony taken by the administrative law judge shall be reduced to writing. Thereafter, the judge, in his discretion, upon notice may provide for the taking of further testimony or hear argument.

### (2) Authority of administrative law judges

In conducting investigations and hearings under this subsection and in accordance with regulations of the Attorney General, the Special Counsel and administrative law judges shall have reasonable access to examine evidence of any person or entity being investigated. The administrative law judges by subpoena may compel the attendance of witnesses and the production of evidence at any designated place or hearing. In case of contumacy or refusal to obey a subpoena lawfully issued under this paragraph and upon application of the administrative law judge, an appropriate district court of the United States may issue an order requiring compliance with such subpoena and any failure to obey such order may be punished by such court as a contempt thereof.

## (g) Determinations

### (1) Order

The administrative law judge shall issue and cause to be served on the parties to the proceeding an order, which shall be final unless appealed as provided under subsection (i) of this section.

### (2) Orders finding violations

**(A) In general**

If, upon the preponderance of the evidence, an administrative law judge determines that any person or entity named in the complaint has engaged in or is engaging in any such unfair immigration-related employment practice, then the judge shall state his findings of fact and shall issue and cause to be served on such person or entity an order which requires such person or entity to cease and desist from such unfair immigration-related employment practice.

**(B)** Contents of order

Such an order also may require the person or entity—

(i) to comply with the requirements of section 274A(b) [8 U.S.C.A. § 1324a(b)] with respect to individuals hired (or recruited or referred for employment for a fee) during a period of up to three years;

(ii) to retain for the period referred to in clause (i) and only for purposes consistent with section 274A(b)(5) [8 U.S.C.A. § 1324a(b)(5)], the name and address of each individual who applies, in person or in writing, for hiring for an existing position, or for recruiting or referring for a fee, for employment in the United States;

(iii) to hire individuals directly and adversely affected, with or without back pay;

(iv)(I) except as provided in subclauses (II) through (IV), to pay a civil penalty of not less than $250 and not more than $2,000 for each individual discriminated against,

(II) except as provided in subclause (IV), in the case of a person or entity previously subject to a single order under this paragraph, to pay a civil penalty of not less than $2,000 and not more than $5,000 for each individual discriminated against,

(III) except as provided in subclause (IV), in the case of a person or entity previously subject to more than one order under this paragraph, to pay a civil penalty of not less than $3,000 and not more than $10,000 for each individual discriminated against, and

(IV) in the case of an unfair immigration-related employment practice described in subsection (a)(6) of this section, to pay a civil penalty of not less than $100 and not more than $1,000 for each individual discriminated against,

(v) to post notices to employees about their rights under this section and employers' obligations under section 274A [8 U.S.C.A. § 1324a],

(vi) to educate all personnel involved in hiring and complying with this section or section 274A [8 U.S.C.A. § 1324a] about the requirements of this section or such section,

(vii) to order (in an appropriate case) the removal of a false performance review or false warning from an employee's personnel file, and

(viii) to order (in an appropriate case) the lifting of any restrictions on an employee's assignments, work shifts, or movements.

**(C)** Limitation on back pay remedy

In providing a remedy under subparagraph (B)(iii), back pay liability shall not accrue from a date more than two years prior to the date of the filing of a charge with an administrative law judge. Interim earnings or amounts earnable with reasonable diligence by the individual or individuals discriminated against shall operate to reduce the back pay otherwise allowable under such subparagraph. No order shall require the hiring of an individual as an employee or the payment to an individual of any back pay, if the individual was refused employment for any reason other than discrimination on account of national origin or citizenship status.

**(D)** Treatment of distinct entities

In applying this subsection in the case of a person or entity composed of distinct, physically separate subdivisions each of which provides separately for the hiring, recruiting, or referring for employment, without reference to the practices of, and not under the control of or common control with, another subdivision, each such subdivision shall be considered a separate person or entity.

**(3) Orders not finding violations**

If upon the preponderance of the evidence an administrative law judge determines that the person or entity named in the complaint has not engaged and is not engaging in any such unfair immigration-related employment practice, then the judge shall state his findings of fact and shall issue an order dismissing the complaint.

## (h) Awarding of attorney's fees

In any complaint respecting an unfair immigration-related employment practice, an administrative law judge, in the judge's discretion, may allow a prevailing party, other than the United States, a reasonable attorney's fee, if the losing party's argument is without reasonable foundation in law and fact.

## (i) Review of final orders

### (1) In general

Not later than 60 days after the entry of such final order, any person aggrieved by such final order may seek a review of such order in the United States court of appeals for the circuit in which the violation is alleged to have occurred or in which the employer resides or transacts business.

### (2) Further review

Upon the filing of the record with the court, the jurisdiction of the court shall be exclusive and its judgment shall be final, except that the same shall be subject to review by the Supreme Court of the United States upon writ of certiorari or certification as provided in section 1254 of Title 28.

## (j) Court enforcement of administrative orders

### (1) In general

If an order of the agency is not appealed under subsection (i)(1) of this section, the Special Counsel (or, if the Special Counsel fails to act, the person filing the charge) may petition the United States district court for the district in which a violation of the order is alleged to have occurred, or in which the respondent resides or transacts business, for the enforcement of the order of the administrative law judge, by filing in such court a written petition praying that such order be enforced.

### (2) Court enforcement order

Upon the filing of such petition, the court shall have jurisdiction to make and enter a decree enforcing the order of the administrative law judge. In such a proceeding, the order of the administrative law judge shall not be subject to review.

### (3) Enforcement decree in original review

If, upon appeal of an order under subsection (i)(1) of this section, the United States court of appeals does not reverse such order, such court shall have the jurisdiction to make and enter a decree enforcing the order of the administrative law judge.

### (4) Awarding of attorney's fees

In any judicial proceeding under subsection (i) of this section or this subsection, the court, in its discretion, may allow a prevailing party, other than the United States, a reasonable attorney's fee as part of costs but only if the losing party's argument is without reasonable foundation in law and fact.

251

### (k) Termination dates

(1) This section shall not apply to discrimination in hiring, recruiting, referring, or discharging of individuals occurring after the date of any termination of the provisions of section 274A [8 U.S.C.A. § 1324a], under subsection (*l*) of that section.

(2) The provisions of this section shall terminate 30 calendar days after receipt of the last report required to be transmitted under section 274A(i) [8 U.S.C.A. § 1324a(i)] if—

(A) the Comptroller General determines, and so reports in such report that—

(i) no significant discrimination has resulted, against citizens or nationals of the United States or against any eligible workers seeking employment, from the implementation of section 274A [8 U.S.C.A. § 1324a], or

(ii) such section has created an unreasonable burden on employers hiring such workers; and

(B) there has been enacted, within such period of 30 calendar days, a joint resolution stating in substance that the Congress approves the findings of the Comptroller General contained in such report.

The provisions of subsections (m) and (n) of section 274A [8 U.S.C.A. § 1324a(m) and (n)] shall apply to any joint resolution under subparagraph (B) in the same manner as they apply to a joint resolution under subsection (*l*) of such section.

### (*l*) Dissemination of information concerning anti-discrimination provisions

(1) Not later than 3 months after November 29, 1990, the Special Counsel, in cooperation with the chairman of the Equal Employment Opportunity Commission, the Secretary of Labor, and the Administrator of the Small Business Administration, shall conduct a campaign to disseminate information respecting the rights and remedies prescribed under this section and under title VII of the Civil Rights Act of 1964 [42 U.S.C.A. § 2000e et seq.] in connection with unfair immigration-related employment practices. Such campaign shall be aimed at increasing the knowledge of employers, employees, and the general public concerning employer and employee rights, responsibilities, and remedies under this section and such title.

(2) In order to carry out the campaign under this subsection, the Special Counsel—

(A) may, to the extent deemed appropriate and subject to the availability of appropriations, contract with public and private organizations for outreach activities under the campaign, and

**(B)** shall consult with the Secretary of Labor, the chairman of the Equal Employment Opportunity Commission, and the heads of such other agencies as may be appropriate.

**(3)** There are authorized to be appropriated to carry out this subsection $10,000,000 for each fiscal year (beginning with fiscal year 1991).

(June 27, 1952, c. 477, Title II, ch. 8, § 274B, as added Pub.L. 99–603, Title I, § 102(a), Nov. 6, 1986, 100 Stat. 3374, and amended Pub.L. 100–525, § 2(b), Oct. 24, 1988, 102 Stat. 2610; Pub.L. 101–649, Title V, §§ 531, 532(a), 533(a), 534(a), 535(a), 536(a), 537(a), 539(a), Nov. 29, 1990, 104 Stat. 5054, 5055, 5056.)

## § 274C. Penalties for document fraud [8 U.S.C.A. § 1324c]

### (a) Activities prohibited

It is unlawful for any person or entity knowingly—

**(1)** to forge, counterfeit, alter, or falsely make any document for the purpose of satisfying a requirement of this chapter,

**(2)** to use, attempt to use, possess, obtain, accept, or receive any forged, counterfeit, altered, or falsely made documents in order to satisfy any requirement of this chapter,

**(3)** to use or attempt to use any document lawfully issued to a person other than the possessor (including a deceased individual) for the purpose of satisfying a requirement of this chapter, or

**(4)** to accept or receive any document lawfully issued to a person other than the possessor (including a deceased individual) for the purpose of complying with section 274A(b) [8 U.S.C.A. § 1324a(b)].

### (b) Exception

This section does not prohibit any lawfully authorized investigative, protective, or intelligence activity of a law enforcement agency of the United States, a State, or a subdivision of a State, or of an intelligence agency of the United States, or any activity authorized under title V of the Organized Crime Control Act of 1970 (18 U.S.C. note prec. 3481).

### (c) Construction

Nothing in this section shall be construed to diminish or qualify any of the penalties available for activities prohibited by this section but proscribed as well in Title 18.

### (d) Enforcement

#### (1) Authority in investigations

In conducting investigations and hearings under this subsection—

253

**(A)** immigration officers and administrative law judges shall have reasonable access to examine evidence of any person or entity being investigated, and

**(B)** administrative law judges, may, if necessary, compel by subpoena the attendance of witnesses and the production of evidence at any designated place or hearing.

In case of contumacy or refusal to obey a subpoena lawfully issued under this paragraph and upon application of the Attorney General, an appropriate district court of the United States may issue an order requiring compliance with such subpoena and any failure to obey such order may be punished by such court as a contempt thereof.

**(2) Hearing**

**(A)** In general

Before imposing an order described in paragraph (3) against a person or entity under this subsection for a violation of subsection (a) of this section, the Attorney General shall provide the person or entity with notice and, upon request made within a reasonable time (of not less than 30 days, as established by the Attorney General) of the date of the notice, a hearing respecting the violation.

**(B)** Conduct of hearing

Any hearing so requested shall be conducted before an administrative law judge. The hearing shall be conducted in accordance with the requirements of section 554 of Title 5. The hearing shall be held at the nearest practicable place to the place where the person or entity resides or of the place where the alleged violation occurred. If no hearing is so requested, the Attorney General's imposition of the order shall constitute a final and unappealable order.

**(C)** Issuance of orders

If the administrative law judge determines, upon the preponderance of the evidence received, that a person or entity has violated subsection (a), the administrative law judge shall state his findings of fact and issue and cause to be served on such person or entity an order described in paragraph (3).

**(3) Cease and desist order with civil money penalty**

With respect to a violation of subsection (a) of this section, the order under this subsection shall require the person or entity to cease and desist from such violations and to pay a civil penalty in an amount of—

**(A)** not less than $250 and not more than $2,000 for each document used, accepted, or created and each instance of use, acceptance, or creation, or

254

**(B)** in the case of a person or entity previously subject to an order under this paragraph, not less than $2,000 and not more than $5,000 for each document used, accepted, or created and each instance of use, acceptance, or creation.

In applying this subsection in the case of a person or entity composed of distinct, physically separate subdivisions each of which provides separately for the hiring, recruiting, or referring for employment, without reference to the practices of, and not under the control of or common control with, another subdivision, each such subdivision shall be considered a separate person or entity.

### (4) Administrative appellate review

The decision and order of an administrative law judge shall become the final agency decision and order of the Attorney General unless, within 30 days, the Attorney General modifies or vacates the decision and order, in which case the decision and order of the Attorney General shall become a final order under this subsection.

### (5) Judicial review

A person or entity adversely affected by a final order under this section may, within 45 days after the date the final order is issued, file a petition in the Court of Appeals for the appropriate circuit for review of the order.

### (6) Enforcement of orders

If a person or entity fails to comply with a final order issued under this section against the person or entity, the Attorney General shall file a suit to seek compliance with the order in any appropriate district court of the United States. In any such suit, the validity and appropriateness of the final order shall not be subject to review.

(June 27, 1952, c. 477, Title II, ch. 8, § 274C, as added Nov. 29, 1990, Pub.L. 101–649, Title V, § 544(a), 104 Stat. 5059.)

## § 275. Improper entry by alien [8 U.S.C.A. § 1325]

### (a) Improper time or place; avoidance of examination or inspection; misrepresentation and concealment of facts

Any alien who (1) enters or attempts to enter the United States at any time or place other than as designated by immigration officers, or (2) eludes examination or inspection by immigration officers, or (3) attempts to enter or obtains entry to the United States by a willfully false or misleading representation or the willful concealment of a material fact, shall, for the first commission of any such offense, be fined not more than $2,000 (or, if greater, the amount provided under Title 18) or imprisoned not more than 6 months, or both, and, for a subsequent commission of any such offense, be fined under Title 18 or imprisoned not more than 2 years or both.

### (b) Marriage fraud

Any individual who knowingly enters into a marriage for the purpose of evading any provision of the immigration laws shall be imprisoned for not more than 5 years, or fined not more than $250,000, or both.

### (c) Immigration-related entrepreneurship fraud

Any individual who knowingly establishes a commercial enterprise for the purpose of evading any provision of the immigration laws shall be imprisoned for not more than 5 years, fined in accordance with Title 18, or both.

(June 27, 1952, c. 477, Title II, ch. 8, § 275, 66 Stat. 229;  Pub.L. 99–639, § 2(d), Nov. 10, 1986, 100 Stat. 3542;  Pub.L. 101–649, Title I, § 121(b)(3), 161, Title V, § 543(b)(2), Nov. 29, 1990, 104 Stat. 4994, 5008, 5059.)

## § 276.  Reentry of deported alien; criminal penalties for reentry of certain deported aliens [8 U.S.C.A. § 1326]

(a) Subject to subsection (b) of this section, any alien who—

(1) has been arrested and deported or excluded and deported, and thereafter

(2) enters, attempts to enter, or is at any time found in, the United States, unless (A) prior to his reembarkation at a place outside the United States or his application for admission from foreign contiguous territory, the Attorney General has expressly consented to such alien's reapplying for admission;  or (B) with respect to an alien previously excluded and deported, unless such alien shall establish that he was not required to obtain such advance consent under this chapter or any prior Act,

shall be fined under Title 18, or imprisoned not more than 2 years, or both.

(b) Notwithstanding subsection (a) of this section, in the case of any alien described in such subsection—

(1) whose deportation was subsequent to a conviction for commission of a felony (other than an aggravated felony), such alien shall be fined under Title 18, imprisoned not more than 5 years, or both;  or

(2) whose deportation was subsequent to a conviction for commission of an aggravated felony, such alien shall be fined under such title, imprisoned not more than 15 years, or both.

(June 27, 1952, c. 477, Title II, ch. 8, § 276, 66 Stat. 229;  Pub.L. 100–690, Title VII, § 7345(a), Nov. 18, 1988, 102 Stat. 4471;  Pub.L. 101–649, Title V, § 543(b)(3), Nov. 29, 1990, 104 Stat. 5059.)

## § 277. Aiding or assisting certain aliens to enter [8 U.S.C.A. § 1327]

Any person who knowingly aids or assists any alien excludable under section 212(a)(2) [8 U.S.C.A. § 1182(a)(2)] (insofar as an alien excludable under such section has been convicted of an aggravated felony) or 212(a)(3) [8 U.S.C.A. § 1182 (a)(3)] (other than subparagraph (E) thereof) to enter the United States, or who connives or conspires with any person or persons to allow, procure, or permit any such alien to enter the United States, shall be fined under Title 18, or imprisoned not more than 10 years, or both.

(June 27, 1952, c. 477, Title II, ch. 8, § 277, 66 Stat. 229; Pub.L. 100–690, Title VII, § 7346(a), (c)(1), Nov. 18, 1988, 102 Stat. 4471; Pub.L. 101–649, Title V, § 543(b)(4), Title VI, § 603(a)(16), 104 Stat. 5059, 5084.)

## § 278. Importation of alien for immoral purpose [8 U.S.C.A. § 1328]

The importation into the United States of any alien for the purpose of prostitution, or for any other immoral purpose, is forbidden. Whoever shall, directly or indirectly, import, or attempt to import into the United States any alien for the purpose of prostitution or for any other immoral purpose, or shall hold or attempt to hold any alien for any such purpose in pursuance of such illegal importation, or shall keep, maintain, control, support, employ, or harbor in any house or other place, for the purpose of prostitution or for any other immoral purpose, any alien, in pursuance of such illegal importation, shall be fined under Title 18, or imprisoned not more than 10 years, or both. The trial and punishment of offenses under this section may be in any district to or into which such alien is brought in pursuance of importation by the person or persons accused, or in any district in which a violation of any of the provisions of this section occurs. In all prosecutions under this section, the testimony of a husband or wife shall be admissible and competent evidence against each other.

(June 27, 1952, c. 477, Title II, ch. 8, § 278, 66 Stat. 230; Nov. 29, 1990, Pub.L. 101–649, Title V, § 543(b)(5), 104 Stat. 5059.)

## § 279. Jurisdiction of district courts [8 U.S.C.A. § 1329]

The district courts of the United States shall have jurisdiction of all causes, civil and criminal, arising under any of the provisions of this subchapter. It shall be the duty of the United States attorney of the proper district to prosecute every such suit when brought by the United States. Notwithstanding any other law, such prosecutions or suits may be instituted at any place in the United States at which the violation may occur or at which the person charged with a violation under section 275 or 276 [8 U.S.C.A. §§ 1325 or 1326] may be apprehended. No suit or proceeding for a violation of any of the provisions of this subchapter shall be settled, compromised, or discontinued without the consent of the court in which it is pending and any such settlement, compromise, or discontinuance shall be entered of record with the reasons therefor.

(June 27, 1952, c. 477, Title II, ch. 8, § 279, 66 Stat. 230.)

## § 280. Collection of penalties and expenses [8 U.S. C.A. § 1330]

(a) Notwithstanding any other provisions of this subchapter, the withholding or denial of clearance of or a lien upon any vessel or aircraft provided for in section 231, 237, 239, 243, 251, 253, 256, 271, 272, or 273 [8 U.S.C.A. §§ 1221, 1227, 1229, 1253, 1281, 1283, 1284, 1285, 1286, 1321, 1322, or 1323] shall not be regarded as the sole and exclusive means or remedy for the enforcement of payments of any fine, penalty or expenses imposed or incurred under such sections, but, in the discretion of the Attorney General, the amount thereof may be recovered by civil suit, in the name of the United States, from any person made liable under any of such sections.

(b) Notwithstanding section 3302 of Title 31, the increase in penalties collected resulting from the amendments made by sections 203(b), 543(a), and 544 of the Immigration Act of 1990 shall be credited to the appropriation—

(1) for the Immigration and Naturalization Service for activities that enhance enforcement of provisions of this subchapter, including—

(A) the identification, investigation, and apprehension of criminal aliens,

(B) the implementation of the system described in section 242(a)(3)(A) [8 U.S.C.A. § 1252(a)(3)(A)], and

(C) for the repair, maintainance, or construction on the United States border, in areas experiencing high levels of apprehensions of illegal aliens, of structures to deter illegal entry into the United States; and

(2) for the Executive Office for Immigration Review in the Department of Justice for the purpose of removing the backlogs in the preparation of transcripts of deportation proceedings conducted under section 242 [8 U.S.C.A. § 1252].

(June 27, 1952, c. 477, Title II, ch. 8, § 280, 66 Stat. 230; Nov. 29, 1990, Pub.L. 101–649, Title V, § 542(a), 104 Stat. 5057.)

## CHAPTER IX.   MISCELLANEOUS

## § 281.   Nonimmigrant visa fees [8 U.S.C.A. § 1351]

The fees for the furnishing and verification of applications for visas by nonimmigrants of each foreign country and for the issuance of visas to nonimmigrants of each foreign country shall be prescribed by the Secretary of State, if practicable, in amounts corresponding to the total of all visa, entry, residence, or other similar fees, taxes, or charges assessed or levied against nationals of the United States by the foreign countries of which such nonimmigrants are nationals or stateless residents: *Provided,* That nonimmigrant visas issued to aliens coming to the United States in transit to and from the headquarters district of the United Nations in accordance with the provisions of the Headquarters Agreement shall be gratis.

(June 27, 1952, c. 477, Title II, ch. 9, § 281, 66 Stat. 230; Oct. 3, 1965, Pub. L. 89–236, § 14, 79 Stat. 919; Oct. 21, 1968, Pub. L. 90–609, § 1, 82 Stat. 1199.)

## § 282. Printing of reentry permits and blank forms of manifest and crew lists; sale to public [8 U.S.C.A. § 1352]

(a) Reentry permits issued under section 223 [8 U.S.C.A. § 1203] shall be printed on distinctive safety paper and shall be prepared and issued under regulations prescribed by the Attorney General.

(b) The Public Printer is authorized to print for sale to the public by the Superintendent of Documents, upon prepayment, copies of blank forms of manifests and crew lists and such other forms as may be prescribed and authorized by the Attorney General to be sold pursuant to the provisions of this subchapter.

(June 27, 1952, c. 477, Title II, ch. 9, § 282, 66 Stat. 231.)

## § 283. Travel expenses and expense of transporting remains of officers and employees dying outside of United States [8 U.S.C.A. § 1353]

When officers, inspectors, or other employees of the Service are ordered to perform duties in a foreign country, or are transferred from one station to another, in the United States or in a foreign country, or while performing duties in any foreign country become eligible for voluntary retirement and return to the United States, they shall be allowed their traveling expenses in accordance with such regulations as the Attorney General may deem advisable, and they may also be allowed, within the discretion and under written orders of the Attorney General, the expenses incurred for the transfer of their wives and dependent children, their household effects and other personal property, including the expenses for packing, crating, freight, unpacking, temporary storage, and drayage thereof in accordance with subchapter II of chapter 57 of Title 5. The expense of transporting the remains of such officers, inspectors, or other employees who die while in, or in transit to, a foreign country in the discharge of their official duties, to their former homes in this country for interment, and the ordinary and necessary expenses of such interment and of preparation for shipment, are authorized to be paid on the written order of the Attorney General.

(June 27, 1952, c. 477, Title II, ch. 9, § 283, 66 Stat. 231; Pub.L. 100–525, § 9(p), Oct. 24, 1988, 102 Stat. 2621.)

## § 284.  Applicability to members of the armed forces
### [8 U.S.C.A. § 1354]

Nothing contained in this subchapter shall be construed so as to limit, restrict, deny, or affect the coming into or departure from the United States of an alien member of the Armed Forces of the United States who is in the uniform of, or who bears documents identifying him as a member of, such Armed Forces, and who is coming to or departing from the United States under official orders or permit of such Armed Forces: *Provided,* That nothing contained in this section shall be construed to give to or confer upon any such alien any other privileges, rights, benefits, exemptions, or immunities under this chapter, which are not otherwise specifically granted by this chapter.

(June 27, 1952, c. 477, Title II, ch. 9, § 284, 66 Stat. 232.)

## § 285.  Disposal of privileges at immigrant stations; rentals; retail sale; disposition of receipts
### [8 U.S.C.A. § 1355]

(a) Subject to such conditions and limitations as the Attorney General shall prescribe, all exclusive privileges of exchanging money, transporting passengers or baggage, keeping eating houses, or other like privileges in connection with any United States immigrant station, shall be disposed of to the lowest responsible and capable bidder (other than an alien) in accordance with the provisions of section 5 of Title 41 and for the use of Government property in connection with the exercise of such exclusive privileges a reasonable rental may be charged. The feeding of aliens, or the furnishing of any other necessary service in connection with any United States immigrant station, may be performed by the Service without regard to the foregoing provisions of this subsection if the Attorney General shall find that it would be advantageous to the Government in terms of economy and efficiency. No intoxicating liquors shall be sold at any immigrant station.

(b) Such articles determined by the Attorney General to be necessary to the health and welfare of aliens detained at any immigrant station, when not otherwise readily procurable by such aliens, may be sold at reasonable prices to such aliens through Government canteens operated by the Service, under such conditions and limitations as the Attorney General shall prescribe.

(c) All rentals or other receipts accruing from the disposal of privileges, and all moneys arising from the sale of articles through Service-operated canteens, authorized by this section, shall be covered into the Treasury to the credit of the appropriation for the enforcement of this subchapter.

(June 27, 1952, c. 477, Title II, ch. 9, § 285, 66 Stat. 232.)

## § 286. Disposition of monies collected under the provisions of this subchapter [8 U.S.C.A. § 1356]

### (a) Detention, transportation, hospitalization, and all other expenses of detained aliens; expenses of landing stations

All moneys paid into the Treasury to reimburse the Service for detention, transportation, hospitalization, and all other expenses of detained aliens paid from the appropriation for the enforcement of this chapter, and all moneys paid into the Treasury to reimburse the Service for expenses of landing stations referred to in section 238(b) [8 U.S.C.A. § 1228(b)] paid by the Service from the appropriation for the enforcement of this chapter, shall be credited to the appropriation for the enforcement of this chapter for the fiscal year in which the expenses were incurred.

### (b) Purchase of evidence

Moneys expended from appropriations for the Service for the purchase of evidence and subsequently recovered shall be reimbursed to the current appropriation for the Service.

### (c) Fees and administrative fines and penalties; exception

Except as otherwise provided in subsection (a) and subsection (b) of this section, or in any other provision of this subchapter, all moneys received in payment of fees and administrative fines and penalties under this subchapter shall be covered into the Treasury as miscellaneous receipts: *Provided, however,* That all fees received from applicants residing in the Virgin Islands of the United States, and in Guam, required to be paid under section 1351 of this title, shall be paid over to the Treasury of the Virgin Islands and to the Treasury of Guam, respectively.

### (d) Schedule of fees

In addition to any other fee authorized by law, the Attorney General shall charge and collect $5 per individual for the immigration inspection of each passenger arriving at a port of entry in the United States, or for the preinspection of a passenger in a place outside of the United States prior to such arrival, aboard a commercial aircraft or commercial vessel.

### (e) Limitations on fees

(1) No fee shall be charged under subsection (d) of this section for immigration inspection or preinspection provided in connection with the arrival of any passenger, other than aircraft passengers, whose journey originated in the following:

(A) Canada,

(B) Mexico,

(C) a territory or possession of the United States, or

**(D)** any adjacent island (within the meaning of section 101(b)(5) [8 U.S.C.A. § 1101(b)(5)]).

**(2)** No fee may be charged under subsection (d) of this section with respect to the arrival of any passenger—

**(A)** who is in transit to a destination outside the United States, and

**(B)** for whom immigration inspection services are not provided.

**(f) Collection**

**(1)** Each person that issues a document or ticket to an individual for transportation by a commercial vessel or commercial aircraft into the United States shall—

**(A)** collect from that individual the fee charged under subsection (d) of this section at the time the document or ticket is issued; and

**(B)** identify on that document or ticket the fee charged under subsection (d) of this section as a Federal inspection fee.

**(2)** If—

**(A)** a document or ticket for transportation of a passenger into the United States is issued in a foreign country; and

**(B)** the fee charged under subsection (d) of this section is not collected at the time such document or ticket is issued;

the person providing transportation to such passenger shall collect such fee at the time such passenger departs from the United States and shall provide such passenger a receipt for the payment of such fee.

**(3)** The person who collects fees under paragraph (1) or (2) shall remit those fees to the Attorney General at any time before the date that is thirty-one days after the close of the calendar quarter in which the fees are collected, except the fourth quarter payment for fees collected from airline passengers shall be made on the date that is ten days before the end of the fiscal year, and the first quarter payment shall include any collections made in the preceding quarter that were not remitted with the previous payment. Regulations issued by the Attorney General under this subsection with respect to the collection of the fees charged under subsection (d) of this section and the remittance of such fees to the Treasury of the United States shall be consistent with the regulations issued by the Secretary of the Treasury for the collection and remittance of the taxes imposed by subchapter C of chapter 33 [§ 4261 et seq.] of Title 26, but only to the extent the regulations issued with respect to such taxes do not conflict with the provisions of this section.

### (g) Provision of immigration inspection and preinspection services

Notwithstanding section 1353b of this title, or any other provision of law, the immigration services required to be provided to passengers upon arrival in the United States on scheduled airline flights shall be adequately provided, within forty-five minutes of their presentation for inspection, when needed and at no cost (other than the fees imposed under subsection (d) of this section) to airlines and airline passengers at:

(1) immigration serviced airports, and

(2) places located outside of the United States at which an immigration officer is stationed for the purpose of providing such immigration services.

### (h) Disposition of receipts

(1)(A) There is established in the general fund of the Treasury a separate account which shall be known as the "Immigration User Fee Account". Notwithstanding any other section of this title, there shall be deposited as offsetting receipts into the Immigration User Fee Account all fees collected under subsection (d) of this section, to remain available until expended. At the end of each 2-year period, beginning with the creation of this account, the Attorney General, following a public rulemaking with opportunity for notice and comment, shall submit a report to the Congress concerning the status of the account, including any balances therein, and recommend any adjustment in the prescribed fee that may be required to ensure that the receipts collected from the fee charged for the succeeding two years equal, as closely as possible, the cost of providing these services.

(B) Notwithstanding any other provisions of law, all civil fines or penalties collected pursuant to sections 271 and 273 [8 U.S.C.A. §§ 1321 and 1323] and all liquidated damages and expenses collected pursuant to this chapter shall be deposited in the Immigration User Fee Account.

(2)(A) The Secretary of the Treasury shall refund out of the Immigration User Fee Account to any appropriation the amount paid out of such appropriation for expenses incurred by the Attorney General in providing immigration inspection and preinspection services for commercial aircraft or vessels and in—

(i) providing overtime immigration inspection services for commercial aircraft or vessels;

(ii) administration of debt recovery, including the establishment and operation of a national collections office;

(iii) expansion, operation and maintenance of information systems for nonimmigrant control and debt collection;

(iv) detection of fraudulent documents used by passengers traveling to the United States; and

(v) providing detention and deportation services for excludable aliens arriving on commercial aircraft and vessels.

**(B)** The amounts which are required to be refunded under subparagraph (A) shall be refunded at least quarterly on the basis of estimates made by the Attorney General of the expenses referred to in subparagraph (A). Proper adjustments shall be made in the amounts subsequently refunded under subparagraph (A) to the extent prior estimates were in excess of, or less than, the amount required to be refunded under subparagraph (A).

### (i) Reimbursement

Notwithstanding any other provision of law, the Attorney General is authorized to receive reimbursement from the owner, operator, or agent of a private or commercial aircraft or vessel, or from any airport or seaport authority for expenses incurred by the Attorney General in providing immigration inspection services which are rendered at the request of such person or authority (including the salary and expenses of individuals employed by the Attorney General to provide such immigration inspection services). The Attorney General's authority to receive such reimbursement shall terminate immediately upon the provision for such services by appropriation.

### (j) Regulations

The Attorney General may prescribe such rules and regulations as may be necessary to carry out the provisions of this section.

### (k) Advisory committee

In accordance with the provisions of the Federal Advisory Committee Act [5 U.S.C.A. App. § 1 et seq.], the Attorney General shall establish an advisory committee, whose membership shall consist of representatives from the airline and other transportation industries who may be subject to any fee or charge authorized by law or proposed by the Immigration and Naturalization Service for the purpose of covering expenses incurred by the Immigration and Naturalization Service. The advisory committee shall meet on a periodic basis and shall advise the Attorney General on issues related to the performance of the inspectional services of the Immigration and Naturalization Service. This advice shall include, but not be limited to, such issues as the time periods during which such services should be performed, the proper number and deployment of inspection officers, the level of fees, and the appropriateness of any proposed fee. The Attorney General shall give substantial consideration to the views of the advisory committee in the exercise of his duties.

### (l) Report to Congress

In addition to the reporting requirements established pursuant to subsection (h) of this section, the Attorney General shall prepare and submit annually to the Congress, not later than March 31st of each year, a statement of the financial condition of the "Immigration User Fee Account" including beginning account balance, revenues, withdrawals and their purpose, ending balance, projections for the ensuing fiscal year and a full and complete workload analysis showing on a port by port basis the current and projected need for inspectors. The statement shall indicate the success rate of the Immigration and Naturalization Service in meeting the forty-five minute inspection standard and shall provide detailed statistics regarding the number of passengers inspected within the standard, progress that is being made to expand the utilization of United States citizen by-pass, the number of passengers for whom the standard is not met and the length of their delay, locational breakdown of these statistics and the steps being taken to correct any nonconformity.

### (m) Immigration Examinations Fee Account

Notwithstanding any other provisions of law, all adjudication fees as are designated by the Attorney General in regulations shall be deposited as offsetting receipts into a separate account entitled "Immigration Examinations Fee Account" in the Treasury of the United States, whether collected directly by the Attorney General or through clerks of courts: *Provided, however,* That all fees received by the Attorney General from applicants residing in the Virgin Islands of the United States, and in Guam, under this subsection shall be paid over to the treasury of the Virgin Islands and to the treasury of Guam: *Provided further,* That fees for providing adjudication and naturalization services may be set at a level that will ensure recovery of the full costs of providing all such services, including the costs of similar services provided without charge to asylum applicants or other immigrants. Such fees may also be set at a level that will recover any additional costs associated with the administration of the fees collected.

### (n) Reimbursement of administrative expenses; transfer of deposits to General Fund of United States Treasury

All deposits into the "Immigration Examinations Fee Account" shall remain available until expended to the Attorney General to reimburse any appropriation the amount paid out of such appropriation for expenses in providing immigration adjudication and naturalization services and the collection, safeguarding and accounting for fees deposited in and funds reimbursed from the "Immigration Examinations Fee Account".

### (o) Annual financial reports to Congress

The Attorney General will prepare and submit annually to Congress statements of financial condition of the "Immigration Examinations Fee Account", including beginning account balance, revenues, withdrawals, and ending account balance and projections for the ensuing fiscal year.

### (p) Additional effective dates

The provisions set forth in subsections (m), (n), and (o) of this section apply to adjudication and naturalization services performed and to related fees collected on or after October 1, 1988.

## (q) Land border inspection fee account

(1) Notwithstanding any other provision of law, the Attorney General is authorized to establish, by regulation, a project under which a fee may be charged and collected for inspection services provided at one or more land border points of entry. Such project may include the establishment of commuter lanes to be made available to qualified United States citizens and aliens, as determined by the Attorney General.

(2) All of the fees collected under this subsection shall be deposited as offsetting receipts in a separate account within the general fund of the Treasury of the United States, to remain available until expended. Such account shall be known as the Land Border Inspection Fee Account.

(3)(A) The Secretary of Treasury shall refund, at least on a quarterly basis amounts to any appropriations for expenses incurred in providing inspection services at land border points of entry. Such expenses shall include—

(i) the providing of overtime inspection services;

(ii) the expansion, operation and maintenance of information systems for nonimmigrant control;

(iii) the hire of additional permanent and temporary inspectors;

(iv) the minor construction costs associated with the addition of new traffic lanes (with the concurrence of the General Services Administration);

(v) the detection of fraudulent documents used by passengers travelling to the United States;

(vi) providing for the administration of said account.

(B) The amounts required to be refunded from the Land Border Inspection Fee Account for fiscal years 1992 and thereafter shall be refunded in accordance with estimates made in the budget request of the Attorney General for those fiscal years: *Provided,* That any proposed changes in the amounts designated in said budget requests shall only be made after notification to the Committees on Appropriations of the House of Representatives and the Senate in accordance with section 606 of Public Law 101–162.

(4) The Attorney General will prepare and submit annually to the Congress statements of financial condition of the Land Border Immigration Fee Account, including beginning account balance, revenues, withdrawals, and ending account balance and projection for the ensuing fiscal year.

(5)(A) The program authorized in this subsection shall terminate on September 30, 1993, unless further authorized by an Act of Congress.

(B) The provisions set forth in this subsection shall take effect 30 days after submission of a written plan by the Attorney General detailing the proposed implementation of the project specified in subsection (q)(1) of this section.

**(C)** If implemented, the Attorney General shall prepare and submit on a quarterly basis, until September 30, 1993, a status report on the land border inspection project.

(June 27, 1952, c. 477, Title II, ch. 9, § 286, 66 Stat. 232; Pub.L. 97–116, § 13, Dec. 29, 1981, 95 Stat. 1618; Pub.L. 99–500, Title I, § 101(b) [Title II § 205(a), formerly § 205], Oct. 18, 1986, 100 Stat. 1783–53, as renumbered Pub.L. 100–525, § 4(a)(2)(A), Oct. 24, 1988, 102 Stat. 2615; Pub.L. 99–653, § 7(d)(1), as added Pub.L. 100–525, § 8(f), Oct. 24, 1988, 102 Stat. 2617; Pub.L. 100–71, Title I, § 1, July 11, 1987, 100 Stat. 394; Pub.L. 100–459, § 209(a), Oct. 1, 1988, 102 Stat. 2203; Pub.L. 100–525, § 4(a)(1), Oct. 24, 1988, 102 Stat. 2614; Nov. 21, 1989, Pub.L. 101–162, Title II, 103 Stat. 1000; Pub.L. 101–515, Title II, § 210(a), (d), Nov. 5, 1990, 104 Stat. 2120, 2121.)

## § 287. Powers of immigration officers and employees [8 U.S.C.A. § 1357]

### (a) Powers without warrant

Any officer or employee of the Service authorized under regulations prescribed by the Attorney General shall have power without warrant—

**(1)** to interrogate any alien or person believed to be an alien as to his right to be or to remain in the United States;

**(2)** to arrest any alien who in his presence or view is entering or attempting to enter the United States in violation of any law or regulation made in pursuance of law regulating the admission, exclusion, or expulsion of aliens, or to arrest any alien in the United States, if he has reason to believe that the alien so arrested is in the United States in violation of any such law or regulation and is likely to escape before a warrant can be obtained for his arrest, but the alien arrested shall be taken without unnecessary delay for examination before an officer of the Service having authority to examine aliens as to their right to enter or remain in the United States;

**(3)** within a reasonable distance from any external boundary of the United States, to board and search for aliens any vessel within the territorial waters of the United States and any railway car, aircraft, conveyance, or vehicle, and within a distance of twenty-five miles from any such external boundary to have access to private lands, but not dwellings, for the purpose of patrolling the border to prevent the illegal entry of aliens into the United States;

**(4)** to make arrests for felonies which have been committed and which are cognizable under any law of the United States regulating the admission, exclusion, or expulsion of aliens, if he has reason to believe that the person so arrested is guilty of such felony and if there is likelihood of the person escaping before a warrant can be obtained for his arrest, but the person arrested shall be taken without unnecessary delay before the nearest available officer empowered to commit persons charged with offenses against the laws of the United States, and

(5) to make arrests—

(A) for any offense against the United States, if the offense is committed in the officer's or employee's presence, or

(B) for any felony cognizable under the laws of the United States, if the officer or employee has reasonable grounds to believe that the person to be arrested has committed or is committing such a felony,

if the officer or employee is performing duties relating to the enforcement of the immigration laws at the time of the arrest and if there is a likelihood of the person escaping before a warrant can be obtained for his arrest.

Under regulations prescribed by the Attorney General, an officer or employee of the Service may carry a firearm and may execute and serve any order, warrant, subpoena, summons, or other process issued under the authority of the United States. The authority to make arrests under paragraph (5)(B) shall only be effective on and after the date on which the Attorney General publishes final regulations which (i) prescribe the categories of officers and employees of the Service who may use force (including deadly force) and the circumstances under which such force may be used, (ii) establish standards with respect to enforcement activities of the Service, (iii) require that any officer or employee of the Service is not authorized to make arrests under paragraph (5)(B) unless the officer or employee has received certification as having completed a training program which covers such arrests and standards described in clause (ii), and (iv) establish an expedited, internal review process for violations of such standards, which process is consistent with standard agency procedure regarding confidentiality of matters related to internal investigations.

### (b) Administration of oath; taking of evidence

Any officer or employee of the Service designated by the Attorney General, whether individually or as one of a class, shall have power and authority to administer oaths and to take and consider evidence concerning the privilege of any person to enter, reenter, pass through, or reside in the United States, or concerning any matter which is material or relevant to the enforcement of this chapter and the administration of the Service; and any person to whom such oath has been administered, (or who has executed an unsworn declaration, certificate, verification, or statement under penalty of perjury as permitted under section 1746 of Title 28), under the provisions of this chapter, who shall knowingly or willfully give false evidence or swear (or subscribe under penalty of perjury as permitted under section 1746 of Title 28) to any false statement concerning any matter referred to in this subsection shall be guilty of perjury and shall be punished as provided by section 1621 of Title 18.

### (c) Search without warrant

Any officer or employee of the Service authorized and designated under regulations prescribed by the Attorney General, whether individually or as one of a class, shall have power to conduct a search, without warrant, of the person, and of the personal effects in the possession of any person seeking admission to the United States, concerning whom such officer or employee may have reasonable cause to suspect that grounds exist for exclusion from the United States under this chapter which would be disclosed by such search.

### (d) Detainer of aliens for violation of controlled substances laws

In the case of an alien who is arrested by a Federal, State, or local law enforcement official for a violation of any law relating to controlled substances, if the official (or another official)—

(1) has reason to believe that the alien may not have been lawfully admitted to the United States or otherwise is not lawfully present in the United States,

(2) expeditiously informs an appropriate officer or employee of the Service authorized and designated by the Attorney General of the arrest and of facts concerning the status of the alien, and

(3) requests the Service to determine promptly whether or not to issue a detainer to detain the alien,

the officer or employee of the Service shall promptly determine whether or not to issue such a detainer. If such a detainer is issued and the alien is not otherwise detained by Federal, State, or local officials, the Attorney General shall effectively and expeditiously take custody of the alien.

### (e) Restricting warrantless entry in case of outdoor agricultural operations

Notwithstanding any other provision of this section other than paragraph (3) of subsection (a) of this section an officer or employee of the Service may not enter without the consent of the owner (or agent thereof) or a properly executed warrant onto the premises of a farm or other outdoor agricultural operation for the purpose of interrogating a person believed to be an alien as to the person's right to be or to remain in the United States.

### (f) Fingerprinting and photographing of certain aliens

(1) Under regulations of the Attorney General, the Commissioner shall provide for the fingerprinting and photographing of each alien 14 years of age or older against whom a proceeding is commenced under section 242 [8 U.S.C.A. § 1252].

(2) Such fingerprints and photographs shall be made available to Federal, State, and local law enforcement agencies, upon request.

(June 27, 1952, c. 477, Title II, ch. 9, § 287, 66 Stat. 233; Pub.L. 94–550, § 7, Oct. 18, 1976, 90 Stat. 2535; Pub.L. 99–570, Title I, § 1751(d), Oct. 27, 1986, 100 Stat. 3207–47; Pub.L. 99–603, Title I, § 116, Nov. 6, 1986, 100 Stat. 3384, as amended Pub.L. 100–525, § 2(e), Oct. 24, 1988, 102 Stat. 2610; Pub.L. 100–525, § 5, Oct. 24, 1988, 102 Stat. 2615; Pub.L. 101–649, Title V, § 503(a), (b)(1), Nov. 29, 1990, 104 Stat. 5048.)

## § 288.   Local jurisdiction over immigrant stations [8 U.S.C.A. § 1358]

The officers in charge of the various immigrant stations shall admit therein the proper State and local officers charged with the enforcement of the laws of the State or Territory of the United States in which any such immigrant station is located in order that such State and local officers may preserve the peace and make arrests for crimes under the laws of the States and Territories. For the purpose of this section the jurisdiction of such State and local officers and of the State and local courts shall extend over such immigrant stations.

(June 27, 1952, c. 477, Title II, ch. 9, § 288, 66 Stat. 234.)

## § 289.   Application to American Indians born in Canada [8 U.S.C.A. § 1359]

Nothing in this subchapter shall be construed to affect the right of American Indians born in Canada to pass the borders of the United States, but such right shall extend only to persons who possess at least 50 per centum of blood of the American Indian race.

(June 27, 1952, c. 477, Title II, ch. 9, § 289, 66 Stat. 234.)

## § 290.   Establishment of central file; information from other departments and agencies [8 U.S.C.A. § 1360]

(a) There shall be established in the office of the Commissioner, for the use of security and enforcement agencies of the Government of the United States, a central index, which shall contain the names of all aliens heretofore admitted to the United States, or excluded therefrom, insofar as such information is available from the existing records of the Service, and the names of all aliens hereafter admitted to the United States, or excluded therefrom, the names of their sponsors of record, if any, and such other relevant information as the Attorney General shall require as an aid to the proper enforcement of this chapter.

(b) Any information in any records kept by any department or agency of the Government as to the identity and location of aliens in the United States shall be made available to the Service upon request made by the Attorney General to the head of any such department or agency.

**(c)** The Secretary of Health and Human Services shall notify the Attorney General upon request whenever any alien is issued a social security account number and social security card. The Secretary shall also furnish such available information as may be requested by the Attorney General regarding the identity and location of aliens in the United States.

**(d)** A written certification signed by the Attorney General or by any officer of the Service designated by the Attorney General to make such certification, that after diligent search no record or entry of a specified nature is found to exist in the records of the Service, shall be admissible as evidence in any proceeding as evidence that the records of the Service contain no such record or entry, and shall have the same effect as the testimony of a witness given in open court.

(June 27, 1952, c. 477, Title II, ch. 9, § 290, 66 Stat. 234; 1953 Reorg. Plan No. 1, §§ 5, 8, eff. Apr. 11, 1953, 18 F.R. 2053, 67 Stat. 631; Oct. 17, 1979, Pub.L. 96–88, Title V, § 509(b), 93 Stat. 695; Oct. 24, 1988, Pub.L. 100–525, § 9(q), 102 Stat. 2621.)

## § 291.  Burden of proof upon alien [8 U.S.C.A. § 1361]

Whenever any person makes application for a visa or any other document required for entry, or makes application for admission, or otherwise attempts to enter the United States, the burden of proof shall be upon such person to establish that he is eligible to receive such visa or such document, or is not subject to exclusion under any provision of this chapter, and, if an alien, that he is entitled to the nonimmigrant, immigrant, special immigrant, immediate relative, or refugee status claimed, as the case may be. If such person fails to establish to the satisfaction of the consular officer that he is eligible to receive a visa or other document required for entry, no visa or other document required for entry shall be issued to such person, nor shall such person be admitted to the United States unless he establishes to the satisfaction of the Attorney General that he is not subject to exclusion under any provision of this chapter. In any deportation proceeding under part V of this subchapter against any person, the burden of proof shall be upon such person to show the time, place, and manner of his entry into the United States, but in presenting such proof he shall be entitled to the production of his visa or other entry document, if any, and of any other documents and records, not considered by the Attorney General to be confidential, pertaining to such entry in the custody of the Service. If such burden of proof is not sustained, such person shall be presumed to be in the United States in violation of law.

(June 27, 1952, c. 477, Title II, ch. 9, § 291, 66 Stat. 234; Pub.L. 97–116, § 18(k)(1), Dec. 29, 1981, 95 Stat. 1620.)

## § 292.  Right to counsel [8 U.S.C.A. § 1362]

In any exclusion or deportation proceedings before a special inquiry officer and in any appeal proceedings before the Attorney General from any such exclusion or deportation proceedings, the person concerned shall have the privilege of being represented (at no expense to the Government) by such counsel, authorized to practice in such proceedings, as he shall choose.

(June 27, 1952, c. 477, Title II, ch. 9, § 292, 66 Stat. 235.)

## § 293. Deposit of and interest on cash received to secure immigration bonds [8 U.S.C.A. § 1363]

(a) Cash received by the Attorney General as security on an immigration bond shall be deposited in the Treasury of the United States in trust for the obligor on the bond, and shall bear interest payable at a rate determined by the Secretary of the Treasury, except that in no case shall the interest rate exceed 3 per centum per annum. Such interest shall accrue from date of deposit occurring after April 27, 1966, to and including date of withdrawal or date of breach of the immigration bond, whichever occurs first: *Provided*, That cash received by the Attorney General as security on an immigration bond, and deposited by him in the postal savings system prior to discontinuance of the system, shall accrue interest as provided in this section from the date such cash ceased to accrue interest under the system. Appropriations to the Treasury Department for interest on uninvested funds shall be available for payment of said interest.

(b) The interest accruing on cash received by the Attorney General as security on an immigration bond shall be subject to the same disposition as prescribed for the principal cash, except that interest accruing to the date of breach of the immigration bond shall be paid to the obligor on the bond.

(June 27, 1952, c. 477, Title II, ch. 9, § 293; as added Pub.L. 91–313, § 2, July 10, 1970, 84 Stat. 413.)

# TITLE III

# NATIONALITY AND NATURALIZATION

## CHAPTER I—NATIONALITY AT BIRTH AND COLLECTIVE NATURALIZATION

## § 301. Nationals and citizens of United States at birth [8 U.S.C.A. § 1401]

The following shall be nationals and citizens of the United States at birth:

(a) a person born in the United States, and subject to the jurisdiction thereof;

(b) a person born in the United States to a member of an Indian, Eskimo, Aleutian, or other aboriginal tribe: *Provided,* That the granting of citizenship under this subsection shall not in any manner impair or otherwise affect the right of such person to tribal or other property;

(c) a person born outside of the United States and its outlying possessions of parents both of whom are citizens of the United States and one of whom has had a residence in the United States or one of its outlying possessions, prior to the birth of such person;

(d) a person born outside of the United States and its outlying possessions of parents one of whom is a citizen of the United States who has been physically present in the United States or one of its outlying possessions for a continuous period of one year prior to the birth of such person, and the other of whom is a national, but not a citizen of the United States;

(e) a person born in an outlying possession of the United States of parents one of whom is a citizen of the United States who has been physically present in the United States or one of its outlying possessions for a continuous period of one year at any time prior to the birth of such person;

(f) a person of unknown parentage found in the United States while under the age of five years, until shown, prior to his attaining the age of twenty-one years, not to have been born in the United States;

(g) a person born outside the geographical limits of the United States and its outlying possessions of parents one of whom is an alien, and the other a citizen of the United States who, prior to the birth of such person, was physically present in the United States or its outlying possessions for a period or periods totaling not less than five years, at least two of which were after attaining the age of fourteen years: *Provided,* That any periods of honorable service in the Armed Forces of the United States, or periods of employment with the United States Government or with an international organization as that term is defined in section 288 of Title 22 by such citizen parent, or any periods during which such citizen parent is physically present abroad as the dependent unmarried son or daughter and a member of the household of a person (A) honorably serving with the Armed Forces of the United States, or (B) employed by the United States Government or an international organization as defined in section 288 of Title 22, may be included in order to satisfy the physical-presence requirement of this paragraph. This proviso shall be applicable to persons born on or after December 24, 1952, to the same extent as if it had become effective in its present form on that date.

(June 27, 1952, c. 477, Title III, ch. 1, § 301, 66 Stat. 235; Pub. L. 89–770, Nov. 6, 1966, 80 Stat. 1322; Pub. L. 92–584, §§ 1, 3, Oct. 27, 1972, 86 Stat. 1289; Pub. L. 95–432, §§ 1, 3, Oct. 10, 1978, 92 Stat. 1046; Pub.L. 99–653, § 12, Nov. 14, 1986, 100 Stat. 3657.)

## § 302. Persons born in Puerto Rico on or after April 11, 1899 [8 U.S.C.A. § 1402]

All persons born in Puerto Rico on or after April 11, 1899, and prior to January 13, 1941, subject to the jurisdiction of the United States, residing on January 13, 1941, in Puerto Rico or other territory over which the United States exercises rights of sovereignty and not citizens of the United States under any other Act, are declared to be citizens of the United States as of January 13, 1941. All persons born in Puerto Rico on or after January 13, 1941, and subject to the jurisdiction of the United States, are citizens of the United States at birth.

(June 27, 1952, c. 477, Title III, ch. 1, § 302, 66 Stat. 236.)

## § 303. Persons born in the Canal Zone or Republic of Panama on or after February 26, 1904 [8 U.S.C.A. § 1403]

(a) Any person born in the Canal Zone on or after February 26, 1904, and whether before or after the effective date of this chapter, whose father or mother or both at the time of the birth of such person was or is a citizen of the United States, is declared to be a citizen of the United States.

(b) Any person born in the Republic of Panama on or after February 26, 1904, and whether before or after the effective date of this chapter, whose father or mother or both at the time of the birth of such person was or is a citizen of the United States employed by the Government of the United States or by the Panama Railroad Company, or its successor in title, is declared to be a citizen of the United States.

(June 27, 1952, c. 477, Title III, ch. 1, § 303, 66 Stat. 236.)

## § 304. Persons born in Alaska on or after March 30, 1867 [8 U.S.C.A. § 1404]

A person born in Alaska on or after March 30, 1867, except a noncitizen Indian, is a citizen of the United States at birth. A noncitizen Indian born in Alaska on or after March 30, 1867, and prior to June 2, 1924, is declared to be a citizen of the United States as of June 2, 1924. An Indian born in Alaska on or after June 2, 1924, is a citizen of the United States at birth.

(June 27, 1952, c. 477, Title III, ch. 1, § 304, 66 Stat. 237.)

## § 305. Persons born in Hawaii [8 U.S.C.A. § 1405]

A person born in Hawaii on or after August 12, 1898, and before April 30, 1900, is declared to be a citizen of the United States as of April 30, 1900. A person born in Hawaii on or after April 30, 1900, is a citizen of the United States at birth. A person who was a citizen of the Republic of Hawaii on August 12, 1898, is declared to be a citizen of the United States as of April 30, 1900.

(June 27, 1952, c. 477, Title III, ch. 1, § 305, 66 Stat. 237.)

## § 306. Persons living in and born in the Virgin Islands [8 U.S.C.A. § 1406]

(a) The following persons and their children born subsequent to January 17, 1917, and prior to February 25, 1927, are declared to be citizens of the United States as of February 25, 1927:

(1) All former Danish citizens who, on January 17, 1917, resided in the Virgin Islands of the United States, and were residing in those islands or in the United States or Puerto Rico on February 25, 1927, and who did not make the declaration required to preserve their Danish citizenship by article 6 of the treaty entered into on August 4, 1916, between the United States and Denmark, or who, having made such a declaration have heretofore renounced or may hereafter renounce it by a declaration before a court of record;

(2) All natives of the Virgin Islands of the United States who, on January 17, 1917, resided in those islands, and were residing in those islands or in the United States or Puerto Rico on February 25, 1927, and who were not on February 25, 1927, citizens or subjects of any foreign country;

(3) All natives of the Virgin Islands of the United States who, on January 17, 1917, resided in the United States, and were residing in those islands on February 25, 1927, and who were not on February 25, 1927, citizens or subjects of any foreign country; and

(4) All natives of the Virgin Islands of the United States who, on June 28, 1932, were residing in continental United States, the Virgin Islands of the United States, Puerto Rico, the Canal Zone, or

any other insular possession or territory of the United States, and who, on June 28, 1932, were not citizens or subjects of any foreign country, regardless of their place of residence on January 17, 1917.

**(b)** All persons born in the Virgin Islands of the United States on or after January 17, 1917, and prior to February 25, 1927, and subject to the jurisdiction of the United States are declared to be citizens of the United States as of February 25, 1927; and all persons born in those islands on or after February 25, 1927, and subject to the jurisdiction of the United States, are declared to be citizens of the United States at birth.

(June 27, 1952, c. 477, Title III, ch. 1, § 306, 66 Stat. 237.)

## § 307. Persons living in and born in Guam [8 U.S. C.A. § 1407]

**(a)** The following persons, and their children born after April 11, 1899, are declared to be citizens of the United States as of August 1, 1950, if they were residing on August 1, 1950, on the island of Guam or other territory over which the United States exercises rights of sovereignty:

**(1)** All inhabitants of the island of Guam on April 11, 1899, including those temporarily absent from the island on that date, who were Spanish subjects, who after that date continued to reside in Guam or other territory over which the United States exercises sovereignty, and who have taken no affirmative steps to preserve or acquire foreign nationality; and

**(2)** All persons born in the island of Guam who resided in Guam on April 11, 1899, including those temporarily absent from the island on that date, who after that date continued to reside in Guam or other territory over which the United States exercises sovereignty, and who have taken no affirmative steps to preserve or acquire foreign nationality.

**(b)** All persons born in the island of Guam on or after April 11, 1899 (whether before or after August 1, 1950) subject to the jurisdiction of the United States, are declared to be citizens of the United States: *Provided,* That in the case of any person born before August 1, 1950, he has taken no affirmative steps to preserve or acquire foreign nationality.

**(c)** Any person hereinbefore described who is a citizen or national of a country other than the United States and desires to retain his present political status shall have made, prior to August 1, 1952, a declaration under oath of such desire, said declaration to be in form and executed in the manner prescribed by regulations. From and after the making of such a declaration any such person shall be held not to be a national of the United States by virtue of this chapter.

(June 27, 1952, c. 477, Title III, ch. 1, § 307, 66 Stat. 237.)

## § 308. Nationals but not citizens of the United States at birth [8 U.S.C.A. § 1408]

Unless otherwise provided in section 301 [8 U.S.C.A. § 1401], the following shall be nationals, but not citizens, of the United States at birth:

(1) A person born in an outlying possession of the United States on or after the date of formal acquisition of such possession;

(2) A person born outside the United States and its outlying possessions of parents both of whom are nationals, but not citizens, of the United States, and have had a residence in the United States, or one of its outlying possessions prior to the birth of such person;

(3) A person of unknown parentage found in an outlying possession of the United States while under the age of five years, until shown, prior to his attaining the age of twenty-one years, not to have been born in such outlying possession; and

(4) A person born outside the United States and its outlying possessions of parents one of whom is an alien, and the other a national, but not a citizen, of the United States who, prior to the birth of such person, was physically present in the United States or its outlying possessions for a period or periods totaling not less than seven years in any continuous period of ten years—

(A) during which the national parent was not outside the United States or its outlying possessions for a continuous period of more than one year, and

(B) at least five years of which were after attaining the age of fourteen years.

The proviso of section 301(g) [8 U.S.C.A. § 1401(g)] shall apply to the national parent under this paragraph in the same manner as it applies to the citizen parent under that section.

(June 27, 1952, c. 477, Title III, ch. 1, § 308, 66 Stat. 238; Pub. L. 99–396, § 15(a), Aug. 27, 1986, 100 Stat. 842, as amended Pub.L. 100–525, § 3(2), Oct. 24, 1988, 102 Stat. 2614.)

## § 309. Children born out of wedlock [8 U.S.C.A. § 1409]

(a) The provisions of paragraphs (c), (d), (e), and (g) of section 301 [8 U.S.C.A. § 1401(c), (d), (e), and (g)], and of paragraph (2) of section 308 [8 U.S.C.A. § 1408], shall apply as of the date of birth to a person born out of wedlock if—

(1) a blood relationship between the person and the father is established by clear and convincing evidence,

(2) the father had the nationality of the United States at the time of the person's birth,

(3) the father (unless deceased) has agreed in writing to provide financial support for the person until the person reaches the age of 18 years, and

(4) while the person is under the age of 18 years—

(A) the person is legitimated under the law of the person's residence or domicile,

(B) the father acknowledges paternity of the person in writing under oath, or

(C) the paternity of the person is established by adjudication of a competent court.

(b) Except as otherwise provided in section 405 of this Act, the provisions of section 301(g) [8 U.S.C.A. § 1401(g)] shall apply to a child born out of wedlock on or after January 13, 1941, and before December 24, 1952, as of the date of birth, if the paternity of such child is established at any time and while such child is under the age of twenty-one years by legitimation.

(c) Notwithstanding the provision of subsection (a) of this section, a person born after December 23, 1952, outside the United States and out of wedlock shall be held to have acquired at birth the nationality status of his mother, if the mother had the nationality of the United States at the time of such person's birth, and if the mother had previously been physically present in the United States or one of its outlying possessions for a continuous period of one year.

(June 27, 1952, c. 477, Title III, ch. 1, § 309, 66 Stat. 238; Pub. L. 97–116, § 18(*l*), Dec. 29, 1981, 95 Stat. 1620; Pub.L. 99–653, § 13, Nov. 14, 1986, 100 Stat. 3657, as amended Pub.L. 100–525, § 8(k), Oct. 24, 1988, 102 Stat. 2617; Pub.L. 100–525, § 9(r), Oct. 24, 1988, 102 Stat. 2621.)

## CHAPTER II—NATIONALITY THROUGH NATURALIZATION

## § 310. Naturalization authority [8 U.S.C.A. § 1421]

### (a) Authority in Attorney General

The sole authority to naturalize persons as citizens of the United States is conferred upon the Attorney General.

### (b) Administration of oaths.

An applicant for naturalization may choose to have the oath of allegiance under section 337(a) [8 U.S.C.A. § 1448(a)] administered by the Attorney General or by any District Court of the United States for any State or by any court of record in any State having a seal, a clerk, and jurisdiction in actions in law or equity, or law and equity, in which the amount in controversy is unlimited. The jurisdiction of all courts in this subsection specified to administer the oath of allegiance shall extend only to persons resident within the respective jurisdiction of such courts.

### (c) Judicial review

A person whose application for naturalization under this subchapter is denied, after a hearing before an immigration officer under section 336(a) [8 U.S.C.A. § 1447(a)], may seek review of such denial before the United States district court for the district in which such person resides in accordance with chapter 7 of Title 5. Such review shall be de novo, and the court shall make its own findings of fact and conclusions of law and shall, at the request of the petitioner, conduct a hearing de novo on the application.

### (d) Sole procedure

A person may only be naturalized as a citizen of the United States in the manner and under the conditions prescribed in this subchapter and not otherwise.

(June 27, 1952, c. 477, Title III, ch. 2, § 310, 66 Stat. 239; Pub. L. 85–508, § 25, July 7, 1958, 72 Stat. 351; Pub. L. 86–3, § 20(c), Mar. 18, 1959, 73 Stat. 13; Pub. L. 87–301, § 17, Sept. 26, 1961, 75 Stat. 656; Pub.L. 100–525, § 9(s), Oct. 24, 1988, 102 Stat. 2621; Pub.L. 101–649, Title IV, § 401(a), Nov. 29, 1990, 104 Stat. 5038.)

## § 311. Eligibility for naturalization [8 U.S.C.A. § 1422]

The right of a person to become a naturalized citizen of the United States shall not be denied or abridged because of race or sex or because such person is married.

(June 27, 1952, c. 477, Title III, ch. 2, § 311, 66 Stat. 239; Pub.L. 100–525, § 9(t), Oct. 24, 1988, 102 Stat. 2621.)

## § 312. Requirements as to understanding the English language, history, principles and form of government of the United States [8 U.S.C.A. § 1423]

No person except as otherwise provided in this subchapter shall hereafter be naturalized as a citizen of the United States upon his own petition who cannot demonstrate—

(1) an understanding of the English language, including an ability to read, write, and speak words in ordinary usage in the English language: *Provided*, That this requirement shall not apply to any person physically unable to comply therewith, if otherwise qualified to be naturalized, or to any person who, on the date of the filing of his petition for naturalization as provided in section 1445 of this title, either (A) is over 50 years of age and has been living in the United States for periods totaling at least 20 years subsequent to a lawful admission for permanent residence, or (B) is over 55 years of age and has been living in the United States for periods totaling at least 15 years subsequent to a lawful admission for permanent residence: *Provided further*, That the requirements of this section relating to ability to read and write shall be met if the applicant can read or write simple words and phrases to the end

that a reasonable test of his literacy shall be made and that no extraordinary or unreasonable condition shall be imposed upon the applicant; and

(2) a knowledge and understanding of the fundamentals of the history, and of the principles and form of government, of the United States.

(June 27, 1952, c. 477, Title III, ch. 2, § 312, 66 Stat. 239; Pub. L. 95–579, § 3, Nov. 2, 1978, 92 Stat. 2474; Pub.L. 101–649, Title IV, § 403, Nov. 29, 1990, 104 Stat. 5039.)

## § 313. Prohibition upon the naturalization of persons opposed to government or law, or who favor totalitarian forms of government [8 U.S.C.A. § 1424]

(a) Notwithstanding the provisions of section 405(b) of this Act, no person shall hereafter be naturalized as a citizen of the United States—

(1) who advocates or teaches, or who is a member of or affiliated with any organization that advocates or teaches, opposition to all organized government; or

(2) who is a member of or affiliated with (A) the Communist Party of the United States; (B) any other totalitarian party of the United States; (C) the Communist Political Association; (D) the Communist or other totalitarian party of any State of the United States, of any foreign state, or of any political or geographical subdivision of any foreign state; (E) any section, subsidiary, branch, affiliate, or subdivision of any such association or party; (F) the direct predecessors or successors of any such association or party, regardless of what name such group or organization may have used, may now bear, or may hereafter adopt; (G) who, regardless of whether he is within any of the other provisions of this section, is a member of or affiliated with any Communist-action organization during the time it is registered or required to be registered under the provisions of section 786 of Title 50; or (H) who, regardless of whether he is within any of the other provisions of this section, is a member of or affiliated with any Communist-front organization during the time it is registered or required to be registered under section 786 of Title 50, unless such alien establishes that he did not have knowledge or reason to believe at the time he became a member of or affiliated with such an organization (and did not thereafter and prior to the date upon which such organization was so registered or so required to be registered have such knowledge or reason to believe) that such organization was a Communist-front organization; or

(3) who, although not within any of the other provisions of this section, advocates the economic, international, and governmental doctrines of world communism or the establishment in the United States of a totalitarian dictatorship, or who is a member of or

affiliated with any organization that advocates the economic, international, and governmental doctrines of world communism or the establishment in the United States of a totalitarian dictatorship, either through its own utterances or through any written or printed publications issued or published by or with the permission or consent of or under authority of such organization or paid for by the funds of such organization; or

(4) who advocates or teaches or who is a member of or affiliated with any organization that advocates or teaches (A) the overthrow by force or violence or other unconstitutional means of the Government of the United States or of all forms of law; or (B) the duty, necessity, or propriety of the unlawful assaulting or killing of any officer or officers (either of specific individuals or of officers generally) of the Government of the United States or of any other organized government because of his or their official character; or (C) the unlawful damage, injury, or destruction of property; or (D) sabotage; or

(5) who writes or publishes or causes to be written or published, or who knowingly circulates, distributes, prints, or displays, or knowingly causes to be circulated, distributed, printed, published, or displayed, or who knowingly has in his possession for the purpose of circulation, publication, distribution, or display, any written or printed matter, advocating or teaching opposition to all organized government, or advocating (A) the overthrow by force, violence, or other unconstitutional means of the Government of the United States or of all forms of law; or (B) the duty, necessity, or propriety of the unlawful assaulting or killing of any officer or officers (either of specific individuals or of officers generally) of the Government of the United States or of any other organized government, because of his or their official character; or (C) the unlawful damage, injury, or destruction of property; or (D) sabotage; or (E) the economic, international, and governmental doctrines of world communism or the establishment in the United States of a totalitarian dictatorship; or

(6) who is a member of or affiliated with any organization that writes, circulates, distributes, prints, publishes, or displays, or causes to be written, circulated, distributed, printed, published, or displayed, or that has in its possession for the purpose of circulation, distribution, publication, issue, or display, any written or printed matter of the character described in subparagraph (5) of this subsection.

(b) The provisions of this section or of any other section of this title shall not be construed as declaring that any of the organizations referred to in this section or in any other section of this title do not advocate the overthrow of the Government of the United States by force, violence, or other unconstitutional means.

(c) The provisions of this section shall be applicable to any applicant for naturalization who at any time within a period of ten years immediately preceding the filing of the application for naturalization or after such filing and before taking the final oath of citizenship is, or has been found to be within any of the classes enumerated within this section, notwithstanding that at the time the application is filed he may not be included within such classes.

(d) Any person who is within any of the classes described in subsection (a) of this section solely because of past membership in, or past affiliation with, a party or organization may be naturalized without regard to the provisions of subsection (c) of this section if such person establishes that such membership or affiliation is or was involuntary, or occurred and terminated prior to the attainment by such alien of the age of sixteen years, or that such membership or affiliation is or was by operation of law, or was for purposes of obtaining employment, food rations, or other essentials of living and where necessary for such purposes.

(June 27, 1952, c. 477, Title III, ch. 2, § 313, 66 Stat. 240; Pub.L. 100–525, § 9(u), Oct. 24, 1988, 102 Stat. 2621; Pub.L. 101–649, Title IV, § 407(c), Nov. 29, 1990, 104 Stat. 5041.)

## § 314. Ineligibility to naturalization of deserters from the armed forces [8 U.S.C.A. § 1425]

A person who, at any time during which the United States has been or shall be at war, deserted or shall desert the military, air, or naval forces of the United States, or who, having been duly enrolled, departed, or shall depart from the jurisdiction of the district in which enrolled, or who, whether or not having been duly enrolled, went or shall go beyond the limits of the United States, with intent to avoid any draft into the military, air, or naval service, lawfully ordered, shall, upon conviction thereof by a court martial or a court of competent jurisdiction, be permanently ineligible to become a citizen of the United States; and such deserters and evaders shall be forever incapable of holding any office of trust or of profit under the United States, or of exercising any rights of citizens thereof.

(June 27, 1952, c. 477, Title III, ch. 2, § 314, 66 Stat. 241.)

## § 315. Citizenship denied alien relieved of service in armed forces because of alienage [8 U.S.C.A. § 1426]

### (a) Permanent ineligibility

Notwithstanding the provisions of section 405(b) of this Act but subject to subsection (c) of this section, any alien who applies or has applied for exemption or discharge from training or service in the Armed Forces or in the National Security Training Corps of the United States on the ground that he is an alien, and is or was relieved or discharged from such training or service on such ground, shall be permanently ineligible to become a citizen of the United States.

### (b) Conclusiveness of records

The records of the Selective Service System or of the Department of Defense shall be conclusive as to whether an alien was relieved or discharged from such liability for training or service because he was an alien.

### (c) Service in armed forces of a foreign country

An alien shall not be ineligible for citizenship under this section or otherwise because of an exemption from training or service in the Armed Forces of the United States pursuant to the exercise of rights under a treaty, if before the time of the exercise of such rights the alien served in the Armed Forces of a foreign country of which the alien was a national.

(June 27, 1952, c. 477, Title III, ch. 2, § 315, 66 Stat. 242; Pub.L. 100–525, § 9(v), Oct. 24, 1988, 102 Stat. 2621; Pub.L. 101–649, Title IV, § 404, Nov. 29, 1990, 104 Stat. 5039.)

## § 316. Requirements of naturalization [8 U.S.C.A. § 1427]

### (a) Residence

No person, except as otherwise provided in this subchapter, shall be naturalized unless such applicant, (1) immediately preceding the date of filing his application for naturalization has resided continuously, after being lawfully admitted for permanent residence, within the United States for at least five years and during the five years immediately preceding the date of filing his application has been physically present therein for periods totaling at least half of that time, and who has resided within the State or within the district of the Service in the United States in which the applicant filed the application for at least three months (2) has resided continuously within the United States from the date of the application up to the time of admission to citizenship, and (3) during all the period referred to in this subsection has been and still is a person of good moral character, attached to the principles of the Constitution of the United States, and well disposed to the good order and happiness of the United States.

### (b) Absences

Absence from the United States of more than six months but less than one year during the period for which continuous residence is required for admission to citizenship, immediately preceding the date of filing the petition for naturalization, or during the period between the date of filing the petition and the date of any hearing under section 336(a) [8 U.S.C.A. § 1447(a)] shall break the continuity of such residence, unless the petitioner shall establish to the satisfaction of the Attorney General that he did not in fact abandon his residence in the United States during such period.

Absence from the United States for a continuous period of one year or more during the period for which continuous residence is required for admission to citizenship (whether preceding or subsequent to the filing of the application for naturalization) shall break the continuity of such residence, except that in the case of a person who has been physically present and residing in the United States, after being lawfully admitted for permanent residence, for an uninterrupted period of at least one year, and who thereafter is employed by or under contract with the Government of the United States or an American institution of research recognized as such by the Attorney General, or is employed by an American firm or corporation engaged in whole or in part in the development of foreign trade and commerce of the United States, or a subsidiary thereof more than 50 per centum of whose stock is owned by an American firm or corporation, or is employed by a public international organization of which the United States is a member by treaty or statute and by which the alien was not employed until after being lawfully admitted for permanent residence, no period of absence from the United States shall break the continuity of residence if—

(1) prior to the beginning of such period of employment (whether such period begins before or after his departure from the United States), but prior to the expiration of one year of continuous absence from the United States, the person has established to the satisfaction of the Attorney General that his absence from the United States for such period is to be on behalf of such Government, or for the purpose of carrying on scientific research on behalf of such institution, or to be engaged in the development of such foreign trade and commerce or whose residence abroad is necessary to the protection of the property rights in such countries in such firm or corporation, or to be employed by a public international organization of which the United States is a member by treaty or statute and by which the alien was not employed until after being lawfully admitted for permanent residence; and

(2) such person proves to the satisfaction of the Attorney General that his absence from the United States for such period has been for such purpose.

The spouse and dependent unmarried sons and daughters who are members of the household of a person who qualifies for the benefits of this subsection shall also be entitled to such benefits during the period for which they were residing abroad as dependent members of the household of the person.

### (c) Physical presence

The granting of the benefits of subsection (b) of this section shall not relieve the applicant from the requirement of physical presence within the United States for the period specified in subsection (a) of this section, except in the case of those persons who are employed by, or under contract with, the Government of the United States. In the case of a person employed by or under contract with Central Intelligence

Agency, the requirement in subsection (b) of this section of an uninterrupted period of at least one year of physical presence in the United States may be complied with by such person at any time prior to filing an application for naturalization.

**(d) Moral character**

No finding by the Attorney General that the applicant is not deportable shall be accepted as conclusive evidence of good moral character.

**(e) Determination**

In determining whether the applicant has sustained the burden of establishing good moral character and the other qualifications for citizenship specified in subsection (a) of this section, the Attorney General shall not be limited to the applicant's conduct during the five years preceding the filing of the application, but may take into consideration as a basis for such determination the applicant's conduct and acts at any time prior to that period.

**(f) Persons making extraordinary contributions to national security**

(1) Whenever the Director of Central Intelligence, the Attorney General and the Commissioner of Immigration determine that an applicant otherwise eligible for naturalization has made an extraordinary contribution to the national security of the United States or to the conduct of United States intelligence activities, the applicant may be naturalized without regard to the residence and physical presence requirements of this section, or to the prohibitions of section 313 [8 U.S.C.A. § 1424], and no residence within a particular State or district of the Service in the United States shall be required: *Provided*, That the applicant has continuously resided in the United States for at least one year prior to naturalization: *Provided further*, That the provisions of this subsection shall not apply to any alien described in subparagraphs (A) through (D) of section 243(h)(2) [8 U.S.C.A. § 1253(h)(2)(A) through (D)].

(2) An applicant for naturalization under this subsection may be administered the oath of allegiance under section 337(a) [8 U.S.C.A. § 1448(a)] by any district court of the United States, without regard to the residence of the applicant. Proceedings under this subsection shall be conducted in a manner consistent with the protection of intelligence sources, methods and activities.

(3) The number of aliens naturalized pursuant to this subsection in any fiscal year shall not exceed five. The Director of Central Intelligence shall inform the Select Committee on Intelligence and the Committee on the Judiciary of the Senate and the Permanent Select Committee on Intelligence and the Committee on the Judiciary of the House of Representatives within a reasonable time prior to the filing of each application under the provisions of this subsection.

(June 27, 1952, c. 477, Title III, ch. 2, § 316, 66 Stat. 242; Pub. L. 97–116, § 14, Dec. 29, 1981, 95 Stat. 1619; Pub.L. 99–169, Title VI, § 601, Dec. 4, 1985, 99 Stat. 1007; Pub.L. 101–649, Title IV, §§ 402, 407(c), (d)(1), (e)(1), 104 Stat. 5038, 5041, 5046.)

## § 317. Temporary absence of persons performing religious duties [8 U.S.C.A. § 1428]

Any person who is authorized to perform the ministerial or priestly functions of a religious denomination having a bona fide organization within the United States, or any person who is engaged solely by a religious denomination or by an interdenominational mission organization having a bona fide organization within the United States as a missionary, brother, nun, or sister, who (1) has been lawfully admitted to the United States for permanent residence, (2) has at any time thereafter and before filing an application for naturalization been physically present and residing within the United States for an uninterrupted period of at least one year, and (3) has heretofore been or may hereafter be absent temporarily from the United States in connection with or for the purpose of performing the ministerial or priestly functions of such religious denomination, or serving as a missionary, brother, nun, or sister, shall be considered as being physically present and residing in the United States for the purpose of naturalization within the meaning of section 316(a) [8 U.S.C.A. § 1427(a)], notwithstanding any such absence from the United States, if he shall in all other respects comply with the requirements of the naturalization law. Such person shall prove to the satisfaction of the Attorney General that his absence from the United States has been solely for the purpose of performing the ministerial or priestly functions of such religious denomination, or of serving as a missionary, brother, nun, or sister.

(June 27, 1952, c. 477, Title III, ch. 2, § 317, 66 Stat. 243; Nov. 29, 1990, Pub.L. 101–649, Title IV, § 407(c), (d)(2), 104 Stat. 5041.)

## § 318. Prerequisite to naturalization; burden of proof [8 U.S.C.A. § 1429]

Except as otherwise provided in this subchapter, no person shall be naturalized unless he has been lawfully admitted to the United States for permanent residence in accordance with all applicable provisions of this chapter. The burden of proof shall be upon such person to show that he entered the United States lawfully, and the time, place, and manner of such entry into the United States, but in presenting such proof he shall be entitled to the production of his immigrant visa, if any, or of other entry document, if any, and of any other documents and records, not considered by the Attorney General to be confidential, pertaining to such entry, in the custody of the Service. Notwithstanding the provisions of section 405(b) of this Act, and except as provided in sections 328 and 329 [8 U.S.C.A. §§ 1439 and 1440] no person shall be naturalized against whom there is outstanding a final finding of deportability pursuant to a warrant of arrest issued under the provisions of this chapter or any other Act; and no application for naturalization shall be considered by the Attorney General if there is pending against the applicant a deportation proceeding pursuant to a warrant of arrest issued under the provisions of this chapter or any other Act: *Provided,* That the findings of the Attorney General in terminating deportation proceedings or in suspending the deportation of an alien pursuant to the provisions of this chapter, shall not be deemed binding in any way upon the naturalization court with respect to the question of whether such person has established his eligibility for naturalization as required by this subchapter.

(June 27, 1952, c. 477, Title III, ch. 2, § 318, 66 Stat. 244; Oct. 24, 1968, Pub. L. 90–633, § 4, 82 Stat. 1344; Nov. 29, 1990, Pub.L. 101–649, Title IV, § 407(c), (d)(3), 104 Stat. 5041.)

## § 319. Married persons and employees of certain nonprofit organizations [8 U.S.C.A. § 1430]

(a) Any person whose spouse is a citizen of the United States may be naturalized upon compliance with all the requirements of this subchapter except the provisions of paragraph (1) of section 316(a) [8 U.S.C.A. § 1427(a)(1)] if such person immediately preceding the date of filing his application for naturalization has resided continuously, after being lawfully admitted for permanent residence, within the United States for at least three years, and during the three years immediately preceding the date of filing his application has been living in marital union with the citizen spouse, who has been a United States citizen during all of such period, and has been physically present in the United States for periods totaling at least half of that time and has resided within the State or the district of the Service in the United States in which the applicant filed his application for at least three months.

(b) Any person, (1) whose spouse is (A) a citizen of the United States, (B) in the employment of the Government of the United States, or of an American institution of research recognized as such by the Attorney General, or of an American firm or corporation engaged in whole or in part in the development of foreign trade and commerce of the United States, or a subsidiary thereof, or of a public international organization in which the United States participates by treaty or statute, or is authorized to perform the ministerial or priestly functions of a religious denomination having a bona fide organization within the United States, or is engaged solely as a missionary by a religious denomination or by an interdenominational mission organization having a bona fide organization within the United States, and (C) regularly stationed abroad in such employment, and (2) who is in the United States at the time of naturalization, and (3) who declares before the Attorney General in good faith an intention to take up residence within the United States immediately upon the termination of such employment abroad of the citizen spouse, may be naturalized upon compliance with all the requirements of the naturalization laws, except that no prior residence or specified period of physical presence within the

United States or within a State or a district of the Service in the United States or proof thereof shall be required.

(c) Any person who (1) is employed by a bona fide United States incorporated nonprofit organization which is principally engaged in conducting abroad through communications media the dissemination of information which significantly promotes United States interests abroad and which is recognized as such by the Attorney General, and (2) has been so employed continuously for a period of not less than five years after a lawful admission for permanent residence, and (3) who files his application for naturalization while so employed or within six months following the termination thereof, and (4) who is in the United States at the time of naturalization, and (5) who declares before the Attorney General in good faith an intention to take up residence within the United States immediately upon termination of such employment, may be naturalized upon compliance with all the requirements of this subchapter except that no prior residence or specified period of physical presence within the United States or any State or district of the Service in the United States, or proof thereof, shall be required.

(d) Any person who is the surviving spouse of a United States citizen, whose citizen spouse dies during a period of honorable service in an active duty status in the Armed Forces of the United States and who was living in marital union with the citizen spouse at the time of his death, may be naturalized upon compliance with all the requirements of this subchapter except that no prior residence or specified physical presence within the United States, or within a State or a district of the Service in the United States shall be required.

(June 27, 1952, c. 477, Title III, ch. 2, § 319, 66 Stat. 244; Pub. L. 85–697, § 2, Aug. 20, 1958, 72 Stat. 687; Pub. L. 90–215, § 1(a), Dec. 18, 1967, 81 Stat. 661; Pub. L. 90–369, June 29, 1968, 82 Stat. 279; Pub.L. 101–649, Title IV, § 407(b)(1), (c), (d)(4), 104 Stat. 5040, 5041.)

## § 320.   Children born outside United States of one alien and one citizen parent; conditions for automatic citizenship [8 U.S.C.A. § 1431]

(a) A child born outside of the United States, one of whose parents at the time of the child's birth was an alien and the other of whose parents then was and never thereafter ceased to be a citizen of the United States, shall, if such alien parent is naturalized, become a citizen of the United States, when—

(1) such naturalization takes place while such child is under the age of eighteen years; and

(2) such child is residing in the United States pursuant to a lawful admission for permanent residence at the time of naturalization or thereafter and begins to reside permanently in the United States while under the age of eighteen years.

**(b)** Subsection (a) of this section shall apply to an adopted child only if the child is residing in the United States at the time of naturalization of such adoptive parent, in the custody of his adoptive parents, pursuant to a lawful admission for permanent residence.

(June 27, 1952, c. 477, Title III, ch. 2, § 320, 66 Stat. 245; Pub. L. 95–417, § 4, Oct. 5, 1978, 92 Stat. 917; Pub. L. 97–116, § 18(m), Dec. 29, 1981, 95 Stat. 1620; Pub.L. 99–653, § 14, Nov. 14, 1986, 100 Stat. 3658; Pub.L. 100–525, §§ 8(*l*), 9(w), Oct. 24, 1988, 102 Stat. 2618, 2621.)

## § 321. Children born outside of United States of alien parents; conditions for automatic citizenship [8 U.S.C.A. § 1432]

**(a)** A child born outside of the United States of alien parents, or of an alien parent and a citizen parent who has subsequently lost citizenship of the United States, becomes a citizen of the United States upon fulfillment of the following conditions:

**(1)** The naturalization of both parents; or

**(2)** The naturalization of the surviving parent if one of the parents is deceased; or

**(3)** The naturalization of the parent having legal custody of the child when there has been a legal separation of the parents or the naturalization of the mother if the child was born out of wedlock and the paternity of the child has not been established by legitimation; and if

**(4)** Such naturalization takes place while such child is under the age of eighteen years; and

**(5)** Such child is residing in the United States pursuant to a lawful admission for permanent residence at the time of the naturalization of the parent last naturalized under clause (1) of this subsection, or the parent naturalized under clause (2) or (3) of this subsection, or thereafter begins to reside permanently in the United States while under the age of eighteen years.

**(b)** Subsection (a) of this section shall apply to an adopted child only if the child is residing in the United States at the time of naturalization of such adoptive parent or parents, in the custody of his adoptive parent or parents, pursuant to a lawful admission for permanent residence.

(June 27, 1952, c. 477, Title III, ch. 2, § 321, 66 Stat. 245; Pub. L. 95–417, § 5, Oct. 5, 1978, 92 Stat. 918; Pub. L. 97–116, § 18(m), Dec. 29, 1981, 95 Stat. 1620; Pub.L. 99–653, § 15, Nov. 14, 1986, 100 Stat. 3658; Pub.L. 100–525, § 8(*l*), Oct. 24, 1988, 102 Stat. 2618.)

## § 322. Children born outside United States [8 U.S. C.A. § 1433]

**(a) Naturalization on petition of citizen parents; requirements**

A child born outside of the United States, one or both of whose parents is at the time of applying for the naturalization of the child, a citizen of the United States, either by birth or naturalization, may be naturalized if under the age of eighteen years and not otherwise disqualified from becoming a citizen by reason of section 313, 314, 315, or 318 [8 U.S.C.A. §§ 1424, 1425, 1426, or 1429], and if residing permanently in the United States, with the citizen parent, pursuant to a lawful admission for permanent residence, on the application of such citizen parent, upon compliance with all the provisions of this subchapter, except that no particular period of residence or physical presence in the United States shall be required. If the child is of tender years he may be presumed to be of good moral character, attached to the principles of the Constitution, and well disposed to the good order and happiness of the United States.

### (b) Adopted children

Subsection (a) of this section shall apply to an adopted child only if the child is residing in the United States, in the custody of the adoptive parent or parents, pursuant to a lawful admission for permanent residence.

### (c) Specified period of residence for adopted children; waiver of proof; requirements

In the case of an adopted child (1) who is in the United States at the time of naturalization, and (2) one of whose adoptive parents (A) applications for naturalization of the child under this section, (B) meets the criteria of clauses (A), (B), and (C) of section 319(b)(1) [8 U.S.C.A. § 1430(b)(1)(A), (B), and (C)], and (C) declares before the Attorney General in good faith an intention to take up residence within the United States immediately upon the termination of the employment described in section 319(b)(1)(B) [8 U.S.C.A. § 1430(b)(1)(B)], no specified period of residence within a State or a district of the Service of the United States or proof thereof shall be required.

(June 27, 1952, c. 477, Title III, ch. 2, § 322, 66 Stat. 246; Pub. L. 95–417, § 6, Oct. 5, 1978, 92 Stat. 918; Pub. L. 97–116, § 18(m), (n), Dec. 29, 1981, 95 Stat. 1620, 1621; Pub.L. 99–653, § 16, Nov. 14, 1986, 100 Stat. 3658; Pub.L. 100–525, § 8(*l*), Oct. 24, 1988, 102 Stat. 2618; Pub.L. 101–649, Title IV, § 407(b)(2), (c), (d)(5), 104 Stat. 5040, 5041, 5042.)

## § 323. Repealed. Pub. L. 95–417, § 7, Oct. 5, 1978, 92 Stat. 918 [8 U.S.C.A. § 1434]

## § 324. Former citizens regaining citizenship [8 U.S.C.A. § 1435]

### (a) Requirements

Any person formerly a citizen of the United States who (1) prior to September 22, 1922, lost United States citizenship by marriage to an alien, or by the loss of United States citizenship of such person's spouse, or (2) on or after September 22, 1922, lost United States citizenship by marriage to an alien ineligible to citizenship, may if no other nationality was acquired by an affirmative act of such person other than by marriage be naturalized upon compliance with all requirements of this subchapter, except—

(1) no period of residence or specified period of physical presence within the United States or within the State or district of the Service in the United States where the application is filed shall be required; and

(2) the application need not set forth that it is the intention of the applicant to reside permanently within the United States.

(3), (4) **Repealed.** Pub.L. 101–649, Title IV, § 407(d)(6)(A)(iii), Nov. 29, 1990, 104 Stat. 5042.

Such person, or any person who was naturalized in accordance with the provisions of section 317(a) of the Nationality Act of 1940, shall have, from and after her naturalization, the status of a native-born or naturalized citizen of the United States, whichever status existed in the case of such person prior to the loss of citizenship: *Provided,* That nothing contained herein or in any other provision of law shall be construed as conferring United States citizenship retroactively upon such person, or upon any person who was naturalized in accordance with the provisions of section 317(a) of the Nationality Act of 1940, during any period in which such person was not a citizen.

### (b) Additional requirements

No person who is otherwise eligible for naturalization in accordance with the provisions of subsection (a) of this section shall be naturalized unless such person shall establish to the satisfaction of the Attorney General that she has been a person of good moral character, attached to the principles of the Constitution of the United States, and well disposed to the good order and happiness of the United States for a period of not less than five years immediately preceding the date of filing an application for naturalization and up to the time of admission to citizenship, and, unless she has resided continuously in the United States since the date of her marriage, has been lawfully admitted for permanent residence prior to filing her application for naturalization.

### (c) Oath of allegiance

(1) A woman who was a citizen of the United States at birth and (A) who has or is believed to have lost her United States citizenship solely by reason of her marriage prior to September 22, 1922, to an alien, or by her marriage on or after such date to an alien ineligible to citizenship, (B) whose marriage to such alien shall have terminated subsequent to January 12, 1941, and (C) who has not acquired by an affirmative act other than by marriage any other nationality, shall, from and after taking the oath of allegiance required by section 337 [8 U.S.C.A. § 1448], be a citizen of the United States and have the status of a citizen of the United States by birth, without filing an application for naturalization, and notwithstanding any of the other provisions of

this subchapter except the provisions of section 313 [8 U.S.C.A. § 1424]: *Provided,* That nothing contained herein or in any other provision of law shall be construed as conferring United States citizenship retroactively upon such person, or upon any person who was naturalized in accordance with the provisions of section 317(b) of the Nationality Act of 1940, during any period in which such person was not a citizen.

(2) Such oath of allegiance may be taken abroad before a diplomatic or consular officer of the United States, or in the United States before the Attorney General or the judge or clerk of a court described in section 310(b) [8 U.S.C.A. § 1421(b)].

(3) Such oath of allegiance shall be entered in the records of the appropriate embassy, legation, consulate, court, or the Attorney General and, upon demand, a certified copy of the proceedings, including a copy of the oath administered, under the seal of the embassy, legation, consulate, court, or the Attorney General shall be delivered to such woman at a cost not exceeding $5, which certified copy shall be evidence of the facts stated therein before any court of record or judicial tribunal and in any department or agency of the Government of the United States.

(June 27, 1952, c. 477, Title III, ch. 2, § 324, 66 Stat. 246; Pub.L. 100–525, § 9(x), Oct. 24, 1988, 102 Stat. 2621; Pub.L. 101–649, Title IV, § 407(b)(3), (c)(7), (d)(6), Nov. 29, 1990, 104 Stat. 5040, 5041, 5042.)

## § 325. Nationals but not citizens; residence within outlying possessions [8 U.S.C.A. § 1436]

A person not a citizen who owes permanent allegiance to the United States, and who is otherwise qualified, may, if he becomes a resident of any State, be naturalized upon compliance with the applicable requirements of this subchapter, except that in applications for naturalization filed under the provisions of this section residence and physical presence within the United States within the meaning of this subchapter shall include residence and physical presence within any of the outlying possessions of the United States.

(June 27, 1952, c. 477, Title III, ch. 2, § 325, 66 Stat. 248; Nov. 29, 1990, Pub.L. 101–649, Title IV, § 407(c)(8), 104 Stat. 5041.)

## § 326. Resident Philippine citizens excepted from certain requirements [8 U.S.C.A. § 1437]

Any person who (1) was a citizen of the Commonwealth of the Philippines on July 2, 1946, (2) entered the United States prior to May 1, 1934, and (3) has, since such entry, resided continuously in the United States shall be regarded as having been lawfully admitted to the United States for permanent residence for the purpose of applying for naturalization under this subchapter.

(June 27, 1952, c. 477, Title III, ch. 2, § 326, 66 Stat. 248; Nov. 29, 1990, Pub.L. 101–649, Title IV, § 407(c)(9), 104 Stat. 5041.)

## § 327. Former citizens losing citizenship by entering armed forces of foreign countries during World War II [8 U.S.C.A. § 1438]

### (a) Requirements; oath; certified copies of oath

Any person who, (1) during World War II and while a citizen of the United States, served in the military, air, or naval forces of any country at war with a country with which the United States was at war after December 7, 1941, and before September 2, 1945, and (2) has lost United States citizenship by reason of entering or serving in such forces, or taking an oath or obligation for the purpose of entering such forces, may, upon compliance with all the provisions of subchapter III of this chapter, except section 316(a) [8 U.S.C.A. § 1427(a)], and except as otherwise provided in subsection (b) of this section, be naturalized by taking before the Attorney General or before a court described in section 310(b) [8 U.S.C.A. § 1421(b)] the oath required by section 337 [8 U.S.C.A. § 1448]. Certified copies of such oath shall be sent by such court to the Department of State and to the Department of Justice and by the Attorney General to the Secretary of State.

### (b) Exceptions

No person shall be naturalized under subsection (a) of this section unless he—

(1) is, and has been for a period of at least five years immediately preceding taking the oath required in subsection (a) of this section, a person of good moral character, attached to the principles of the Constitution of the United States and well disposed to the good order and happiness of the United States; and

(2) has been lawfully admitted to the United States for permanent residence and intends to reside permanently in the United States.

### (c) Status

Any person naturalized in accordance with the provisions of this section, or any person who was naturalized in accordance with the provisions of section 323 of the Nationality Act of 1940, shall have, from and after such naturalization, the status of a native-born, or naturalized, citizen of the United States, whichever status existed in the case of such person prior to the loss of citizenship: *Provided*, That nothing contained herein, or in any other provision of law, shall be construed as conferring United States citizenship retroactively upon any such person during any period in which such person was not a citizen.

### (d) Span of World War II

For the purposes of this section, World War II shall be deemed to have begun on September 1, 1939, and to have terminated on September 2, 1945.

### (e) Inapplicability to certain persons

This section shall not apply to any person who during World War II served in the armed forces of a country while such country was at war with the United States.

(June 27, 1952, c. 477, Title III, ch. 2, § 327, 66 Stat. 248; Nov. 29, 1990, Pub.L. 101–649, Title IV, § 407(d)(7), 104 Stat. 5042.)

## § 328. Naturalization through service in the armed forces [8 U.S.C.A. § 1439]

### (a) Requirements

A person who has served honorably at any time in the armed forces of the United States for a period or periods aggregating three years, and, who, if separated from such service, was never separated except under honorable conditions, may be naturalized without having resided, continuously immediately preceding the date of filing such person's application, in the United States for at least five years, and in the State or district of the Service in the United States in which the application for naturalization is filed for at least three months, and without having been physically present in the United States for any specified period, if such application is filed while the applicant is still in the service or within six months after the termination of such service.

### (b) Exceptions

A person filing an application under subsection (a) of this section shall comply in all other respects with the requirements of this subchapter, except that—

(1) no residence within a State or district of the Service in the United States shall be required;

(2) notwithstanding section 318 [8 U.S.C.A. § 1429] insofar as it relates to deportability, such applicant may be naturalized immediately if the applicant be then actually in the Armed Forces of the United States, and if prior to the filing of the application, the applicant shall have appeared before and been examined by a representative of the Service;

(3) the applicant shall furnish to the Attorney General, prior to the final hearing upon his application, a certified statement from the proper executive department for each period of his service upon which he relies for the benefits of this section, clearly showing that such service was honorable and that no discharges from service, including periods of service not relied upon by him for the benefits of this section, were other than honorable. The certificate or certificates herein provided for shall be conclusive evidence of such service and discharge.

### (c) When service not continuous

In the case such applicant's service was not continuous, the applicant's residence in the United States and State or district of the Service in the United States, good moral character, attachment to the principles of the Constitution of the United States, and favorable disposition toward the good order and happiness of the United States, during any period within five years immediately preceding the date of filing such application between the periods of applicant's service in the Armed Forces, shall be alleged in the application filed under the provisions of subsection (a) of this section, and proved at any hearing thereon. Such allegation and proof shall also be made as to any period between the termination of applicant's service and the filing of the application for naturalization.

### (d) Residence requirements

The applicant shall comply with the requirements of section 316(a) [8 U.S.C.A. § 1427(a)], if the termination of such service has been more than six months preceding the date of filing the application for naturalization, except that such service within five years immediately preceding the date of filing such application shall be considered as residence and physical presence within the United States.

### (e) Moral character

Any such period or periods of service under honorable conditions, and good moral character, attachment to the principles of the Constitution of the United States, and favorable disposition toward the good order and happiness of the United States, during such service, shall be proved by duly authenticated copies of the records of the executive departments having custody of the records of such service, and such authenticated copies of records shall be accepted in lieu of compliance with the provisions of section 316(a) [8 U.S.C.A. § 1427(a)].

(June 27, 1952, c. 477, Title III, ch. 2, § 328, 66 Stat. 249; Pub. L. 90–633, § 5, Oct. 24, 1968, 82 Stat. 1344; Pub. L. 97–116, § 15(e), Dec. 29, 1981, 95 Stat. 1619; Pub.L. 101–649, Title IV, § 407(b)(4), (c)(10), (d)(8), Nov. 29, 1990, 104 Stat. 5040, 5041, 5042.)

## § 329. Naturalization through active-duty service in the armed forces during World War I, World War II, Korean hostilities, Vietnam hostilities, or other periods of military hostilities [8 U.S.C.A. § 1440]

### (a) Requirements

Any person who, while an alien or a noncitizen national of the United States, has served honorably in an active-duty status in the military, air, or naval forces of the United States during either World War I or during a period beginning September 1, 1939, and ending December 31, 1946, or during a period beginning June 25, 1950, and ending July 1, 1955, or during a period beginning February 28, 1961, and ending on a date designated by the President by Executive order as of the date of termination of the Vietnam hostilities, or thereafter during any other period which the President by Executive order shall designate as a period in which Armed Forces of the United States are or were engaged in military operations involving armed conflict with a hostile foreign force, and who, if separated from such service, was separated under honorable conditions, may be naturalized as provided in this section if (1) at the time of enlistment or induction such person shall have been in the United States, the Canal Zone, American Samoa, or Swains Island, whether or not he has been lawfully admitted to the United States for permanent residence, or (2) at any time subsequent to enlistment or induction such person shall have been lawfully admitted to the United States for permanent residence. The executive department under which such person served shall determine whether persons have served honorably in an active-duty status, and whether separation from such service was under honorable conditions: *Provided, however,* That no person who is or has been separated from such service on account of alienage, or who was a conscientious objector who performed no military, air, or naval duty whatever or refused to wear the uniform, shall be regarded as having served honorably or having been separated under honorable conditions for the purposes of this section. No period of service in the Armed Forces shall be made the basis of an application for naturalization under this section if the applicant has previously been naturalized on the basis of the same period of service.

### (b) Exceptions

A person filing an application under subsection (a) of this section shall comply in all other respects with the requirements of this subchapter, except that—

(1) he may be naturalized regardless of age, and notwithstanding the provisions of section 318 [8 U.S.C.A. § 1429] as they relate to deportability and the provisions of section 331 [8 U.S.C.A. § 1442];

(2) no period of residence or specified period of physical presence within the United States or any State or district of the Service in the United States shall be required; and

(3) service in the military, air, or naval forces of the United States shall be proved by a duly authenticated certification from the executive department under which the applicant served or is serving, which shall state whether the applicant served honorably in an active-duty status during either World War I or during a period beginning September 1, 1939, and ending December 31, 1946, or during a period beginning June 25, 1950, and ending July 1, 1955, or during a period beginning February 28, 1961, and ending on a date designated by the President by Executive order as the date of termination of the Vietnam hostilities, or thereafter during any other period which the President by Executive order shall designate as a period in which Armed Forces of the United States are or were engaged in military operations involving armed conflict with a hostile foreign force, and was separated from such service under honorable conditions.

**(4) Redesignated (3).**

**(5) Repealed.** Pub. L. 97–116, § 15(a), Dec. 29, 1981, 95 Stat. 1619.

### (c) Revocation

Citizenship granted pursuant to this section may be revoked in accordance with section 340 [8 U.S.C.A. § 1451] if at any time subsequent to naturalization the person is separated from the military, air, or naval forces under other than honorable conditions, and such ground for revocation shall be in addition to any other provided by law. The fact that the naturalized person was separated from the service under other than honorable conditions shall be proved by a duly authenticated certification from the executive department under which the person was serving at the time of separation.

**(d) Repealed.** Pub.L. 100–525, § 9(y), Oct. 24, 1988, 102 Stat. 2621.

(June 27, 1952, c. 477, Title III, ch. 2, § 329, 66 Stat. 250; Pub. L. 87–301, § 8, Sept. 26, 1961, 75 Stat. 654; Pub. L. 90–633, §§ 1, 2, 6, Oct. 24, 1968, 82 Stat. 1343, 1344; Pub. L. 97–116, § 15(a), Dec. 29, 1981, 95 Stat. 1619; Pub.L. 100–525, § 9(y), Oct. 24, 1988, 102 Stat. 2621; Pub.L. 101–649, Title IV, § 407(b)(5), (c)(11), Nov. 29, 1990, 104 Stat. 5040, 5041.)

## § 329A. Posthumous citizenship through death while on active-duty service in the armed forces during World War I, World War II, the Korean hostilities, the Vietnam hostilities, or in other periods of military hostilities [8 U.S.C.A. § 1440–1]

**(a) Permitting granting of posthumous citizenship.**—Notwithstanding any other provision of this subchapter, the Attorney General shall provide, in accordance with this section, for the granting of posthumous citizenship at the time of death to a person described in subsection (b) of this section if the Attorney General approves an application for that posthumous citizenship under subsection (c) of this section.

**(b) Noncitizens eligible for posthumous citizenship.**—A person referred to in subsection (a) of this section is a person who, while an alien or a noncitizen national of the United States—

**(1)** served honorably in an active-duty status in the military, air, or naval forces of the United States during any period described in the first sentence of section 329(a) [8 U.S.C.A. § 1440(a)],

**(2)** died as a result of injury or disease incurred in or aggravated by that service, and

**(3)** satisfied the requirements of clause (1) or (2) of the first sentence of section 329(a) [8 U.S.C.A. § 1440(a)(1) or (2)].

The executive department under which the person so served shall determine whether the person satisfied the requirements of paragraphs (1) and (2).

**(c) Requests for posthumous citizenship.**—A request for the granting of posthumous citizenship to a person described in subsection (b) of this section may be filed on behalf of the person only by the next-of-kin (as defined by the Attorney General) or another representative (as defined by the Attorney General). The Attorney General shall approve such a request respecting a person if—

(1) the request is filed not later than 2 years after—

**(A)** March 6, 1990, or

**(B)** the date of the person's death, whichever date is later;

(2) the request is accompanied by a duly authenticated certificate from the executive department under which the person served which states that the person satisfied the requirements of paragraphs (1) and (2) of subsection (b) of this section; and

(3) the Attorney General finds that the person satisfied the requirement of subsection (b)(3) of this section.

**(d) Documentation of posthumous citizenship.**—If the Attorney General approves such a request to grant a person posthumous citizenship, the Attorney General shall send to the individual who filed the request a suitable document which states that the United States considers the person to have been a citizen of the United States at the time of the person's death.

**(e) No benefits to survivors.**—Nothing in this section or section 319(d) [8 U.S.C.A. § 1430(d)] shall be construed as providing for any benefits under this chapter for any spouse, son, daughter, or other relative of a person granted posthumous citizenship under this section.

(June 27, 1952, c. 477, Title III, ch. 2, § 329A, as added Mar. 6, 1990, Pub.L. 101–249, § 2(a), 104 Stat. 94.)

## § 330. Constructive residence through service on certain United States vessels [8 U.S.C.A. § 1441]

Any periods of time during all of which a person who was previously lawfully admitted for permanent residence has served honorably or with good conduct, in any capacity other than as a member of the Armed Forces of the United States, (A) on board a vessel operated by the United States, or an agency thereof, the full legal and equitable title to which is in the United States; or (B) on board a vessel whose home port is in the United States, and (i) which is registered under the laws of the United States, or (ii) the full legal and equitable title to which is in a citizen of the United States, or a corporation organized under the laws of any of the several States of the United States, shall be deemed residence and physical presence within the United States within the meaning of section 316(a) [8 U.S.C.A. § 1427(a)], if such service occurred within five years immediately preceding the date such person shall file an application for naturalization. Service on vessels described in clause (A) of this subsection shall be proved by duly authenticated copies of the records of the executive departments or agency having custody of the records of such service. Service on vessels described in clause (B) of this subsection may be proved by certificates from the masters of such vessels.

(June 27, 1952, c. 477, Title III, ch. 2, § 330, 66 Stat. 251; Pub.L. 100–525, § 9(z), Oct. 24, 1988, 102 Stat. 2621; Pub.L. 101–649, Title IV, § 407(c)(12), Nov. 29, 1990, 104 Stat. 5041.)

## § 331. Alien enemies [8 U.S.C.A. § 1442]

### (a) Naturalization under specified conditions

An alien who is a native, citizen, subject, or denizen of any country, state, or sovereignty with which the United States is at war may, after his loyalty has been fully established upon investigation by the Attorney General, be naturalized as a citizen of the United States if such alien's application for naturalization shall be pending at the beginning of the state of war and the applicant is otherwise entitled to admission to citizenship.

### (b) Procedure

An alien embraced within this section shall not have his application for naturalization considered or heard except after 90 days' notice to the Attorney General to be considered at the examination or hearing, and the Attorney General's objection to such consideration shall cause the application to be continued from time to time for so long as the Attorney General may require.

### (c) Exceptions from classification

The Attorney General may, in his discretion, upon investigation fully establishing the loyalty of any alien enemy who did not have an application for naturalization pending at the beginning of the state of war, except such alien enemy from the classification of alien enemy for the purposes of this subchapter, and thereupon such alien shall have the privilege of filing an application for naturalization.

### (d) Effect of cessation of hostilities

An alien who is a native, citizen, subject, or denizen of any country, state, or sovereignty with which the United States is at war shall cease to be an alien enemy within the meaning of this section upon the determination by proclamation of the President, or by concurrent resolution of the Congress, that hostilities between the United States and such country, state, or sovereignty have ended.

### (e) Apprehension and removal

Nothing contained herein shall be taken or construed to interfere with or prevent the apprehension and removal, consistent with law, of any alien enemy at any time prior to the actual naturalization of such alien.

(June 27, 1952, c. 477, Title III, ch. 2, § 331, 66 Stat. 252; Nov. 29, 1990, Pub.L. 101–649, Title IV, § 407(c)(13), (d)(9), (e)(2), 104 Stat. 5041, 5042, 5046.)

# § 332. Administration [8 U.S.C.A. § 1443]

### (a) Rules and regulations governing examination of petitioners

The Attorney General shall make such rules and regulations as may be necessary to carry into effect the provisions of this part and is authorized to prescribe the scope and nature of the examination of petitioners for naturalization as to their admissibility to citizenship. Such examination shall be limited to inquiry concerning the applicant's residence, physical presence in the United States, good moral character, understanding of and attachment to the fundamental principles of the Constitution of the United States, ability to read, write, and speak English, and other qualifications to become a naturalized citizen as required by law, and shall be uniform throughout the United States.

### (b) Instruction in citizenship

The Attorney General is authorized to promote instruction and training in citizenship responsibilities of applicants for naturalization including the sending of names of candidates for naturalization to the public schools, preparing and distributing citizenship textbooks to such candidates as are receiving instruction in preparation for citizenship within or under the supervision of the public schools, preparing and distributing monthly an immigration and naturalization bulletin and securing the aid of and cooperating with official State and national organizations, including those concerned with vocational education.

### (c) Prescription of forms

The Attorney General shall prescribe and furnish such forms as may be required to give effect to the provisions of this part, and only such forms as may be so provided shall be legal. All certificates of naturalization and of citizenship shall be printed on safety paper and shall be consecutively numbered in separate series.

### (d) Administration of oaths and depositions

Employees of the Service may be designated by the Attorney General to administer oaths and to take depositions without charge in matters relating to the administration of the naturalization and citizenship laws. In cases where there is a likelihood of unusual delay or of hardship, the Attorney General may, in his discretion, authorize such depositions to be taken before a postmaster without charge, or before a notary public or other person authorized to administer oaths for general purposes.

### (e) Issuance of certificate of naturalization or citizenship

A certificate of naturalization or of citizenship issued by the Attorney General under the authority of this subchapter shall have the same effect in all courts, tribunals, and public offices of the United States, at home and abroad, of the District of Columbia, and of each State, Territory, and outlying possession of the United States, as a certificate of naturalization or of citizenship issued by a court having naturalization jurisdiction.

### (f) Copies of records

Certifications and certified copies of all papers, documents, certificates, and records required or authorized to be issued, used, filed, recorded, or kept under any and all provisions of this chapter shall be admitted in evidence equally with the originals in any and all cases and proceedings under this chapter and in all cases and proceedings in which the originals thereof might be admissible as evidence.

### (g) Furnished quarters for photographic studios

The officers in charge of property owned or leased by the Government are authorized, upon the recommendation of the Attorney General, to provide quarters, without payment of rent, in any building occupied by the Service, for a photographic studio, operated by welfare organizations without profit and solely for the benefit of persons seeking to comply with requirements under the immigration and nationality laws. Such studio shall be under the supervision of the Attorney General.

### (h) Public education regarding naturalization benefits

In order to promote the opportunities and responsibilities of United States citizenship, the Attorney General shall broadly distribute information concerning the benefits which persons may receive under this subchapter and the requirements to obtain such benefits. In carrying out this subsection, the Attorney General shall seek the assistance of appropriate community groups, private voluntary agencies, and other relevant organizations. There are authorized to be appropriated (for each fiscal year beginning with fiscal year 1991) such sums as may be necessary to carry out this subsection.

(June 27, 1952, c. 477, Title III, ch. 2, § 332, 66 Stat. 252; Nov. 29, 1990, Pub.L. 101–649, Title IV, §§ 406, 407(d)(10), 104 Stat. 5040, 5042.)

## § 333. Photographs; number [8 U.S.C.A. § 1444]

(a) Three identical photographs of the applicant shall be signed by and furnished by each applicant for naturalization or citizenship. One of such photographs shall be affixed by the Attorney General to the original certificate of naturalization issued to the naturalized citizen and one to the duplicate certificate of naturalization required to be forwarded to the Service.

(b) Three identical photographs of the applicant shall be furnished by each applicant for—

(1) a record of lawful admission for permanent residence to be made under section 249(a) [8 U.S.C.A. § 1259(a)];

(2) a certificate of derivative citizenship;

(3) a certificate of naturalization or of citizenship;

(4) a special certificate of naturalization;

(5) a certificate of naturalization or of citizenship, in lieu of one lost, mutilated, or destroyed;

(6) a new certificate of citizenship in the new name of any naturalized citizen who, subsequent to naturalization, has had his name changed by order of a court of competent jurisdiction or by marriage;  and

(7) a declaration of intention.

One such photograph shall be affixed to each such certificate issued by the Attorney General and one shall be affixed to the copy of such certificate retained by the Service.

(June 27, 1952, c. 477, Title III, ch. 2, § 333, 66 Stat. 253; Nov. 29, 1990, Pub.L. 101–649, § 407(c)(14), (d)(11), 104 Stat. 5041, 5042.)

## § 334.  Application for naturalization; declaration of intention [8 U.S.C.A. § 1445]

### (a) Evidence and form

An applicant for naturalization shall make and file with the Attorney General in duplicate, a sworn application in writing, signed by the applicant in the applicant's own handwriting if physically able to write, which application shall be on a form prescribed by the Attorney General and shall include averments of all facts which in the opinion of the Attorney General may be material to the applicant's naturalization, and required to be proved under this subchapter.  In the case of an applicant subject to a requirement of continuous residence under section 316(a) or 319(a) [8 U.S.C.A. §§ 1427(a) or 1430(a)], the application for naturalization may be filed up to 3 months before the date the applicant would first otherwise meet such continuous residence requirement.

### (b) Who may file

No person shall file a valid application for naturalization unless he shall have attained the age of eighteen years.  An application for naturalization by an alien shall contain an averment of lawful admission for permanent residence.

### (c) Hearings

Hearings under section 336(a) [8 U.S.C.A. § 1447(a)] on applications for naturalization shall be held at regular intervals specified by the Attorney General.

### (d) Filing of application

Except as provided in subsection (e) of this section, an application for naturalization shall be filed in the office of the Attorney General.

### (e) Substitute filing place and administering oath other than before Attorney General

A person may file an application for naturalization other than in the office of the Attorney General, and an oath of allegiance administered other than in a public ceremony before the Attorney General or a court, if the Attorney General determines that the person has an illness or other disability which—

(1) is of a permanent nature and is sufficiently serious to prevent the person's personal appearance, or

(2) is of a nature which so incapacitates the person as to prevent him from personally appearing.

### (f) Redesignated (g)

### (g) Declaration of intention

An alien over 18 years of age who is residing in the United States pursuant to a lawful admission for permanent residence may file with the Attorney General a declaration of intention to become a citizen of the United States. Such a declaration shall be filed in duplicate and in a form prescribed by the Attorney General and shall be accompanied by an application prescribed and approved by the Attorney General. Nothing in this subsection shall be construed as requiring any such alien to make and file a declaration of intention as a condition precedent to filing an application for naturalization nor shall any such declaration of intention be regarded as conferring or having conferred upon any such alien United States citizenship or nationality or the right to United States citizenship or nationality, nor shall such declaration be regarded as evidence of such alien's lawful admission for permanent residence in any proceeding, action, or matter arising under this chapter or any other Act.

(June 27, 1952, c. 477, Title III, ch. 2, § 334, 66 Stat. 254; Pub. L. 97–116, § 15(b), Dec. 29, 1981, 95 Stat. 1619; Pub.L. 101–649, Title IV, §§ 401(b), 407(c)(15), (d)(12), Nov. 29, 1990, 104 Stat. 5038, 5041, 5042.)

## § 335. Investigation of applicants; examination of applications [8 U.S.C.A. § 1446]

### (a) Waiver

Before a person may be naturalized, an employee of the Service, or of the United States designated by the Attorney General, shall conduct a personal investigation of the person applying for naturalization in the vicinity or vicinities in which such person has maintained his actual place of abode and in the vicinity or vicinities in which such person has been employed or has engaged in business or work for at least five years immediately preceding the filing of his application for naturalization. The Attorney General may, in his discretion, waive a personal investigation in an individual case or in such cases or classes of cases as may be designated by him.

### (b) Conduct of examinations; authority of designees; record

The Attorney General shall designate employees of the Service to conduct examinations upon petitions for naturalization. For such purposes any such employee so designated is authorized to take testimony concerning any matter touching or in any way affecting the admissibility of any applicant for naturalization, to administer oaths, including the oath of the applicant for naturalization, and to require by subpena the attendance and testimony of witnesses, including applicant, before such employee so designated and the production of relevant books, papers, and documents, and to that end may invoke the aid of any District Court of the United States; and any such court may, in the event of neglect or refusal to respond to a subpena issued by any such employee so designated or refusal to testify before such employee so designated issue an order requiring such person to appear before such employee so designated, produce relevant books, papers, and documents if demanded, and testify; and any failure to obey such order of the court may be punished by the court as a contempt thereof. The record of the examination authorized by this subsection shall be admissible as evidence in any hearing conducted by an immigration officer under section 336(a) [8 U.S.C.A. § 1447(a)]. Any such employee shall, at the examination, inform the petitioner of the remedies available to the petitioner under section 336 [8 U.S.C.A. § 1447].

### (c) Transmittal of record of examination

The record of the examination upon any application for naturalization may, in the discretion of the Attorney General be transmitted to the Attorney General and the determination with respect thereto of the employee designated to conduct such examination shall when made also be transmitted to the Attorney General.

### (d) Determination to grant or deny application

The employee designated to conduct any such examination shall make a determination as to whether the application should be granted or denied, with reasons therefor.

### (e) Withdrawal of application

After an application for naturalization has been filed with the Attorney General, the applicant shall not be permitted to withdraw his application, except with the consent of the Attorney General. In cases where the Attorney General does not consent to the withdrawal of the application, the application shall be determined on its merits and a final order determination made accordingly. In cases where the applicant fails to prosecute his application, the application shall be decided on the merits unless the Attorney General dismisses it for lack of prosecution.

## (f) Transfer of application

An applicant for naturalization who moves from the district of the Service in the United States in which the application is pending may, at any time thereafter, request the Service to transfer the application to any district of the Service in the United States which may act on the application. The transfer shall not be made without the consent of the Attorney General. In the case of such a transfer, the proceedings on the application shall continue as though the application had originally been filed in the district of the Service to which the application is transferred.

**(g), (h) Repealed. Pub. L. 97–116, § 15(c)(2), Dec. 29, 1981, 95 Stat. 1619**

## (i) Redesignated (f).

(June 27, 1952, c. 477, Title III, ch. 2, § 335, 66 Stat. 255; Pub. L. 97–116, § 15(c), Dec. 29, 1981, 95 Stat. 1619; Pub.L. 100–525, § 9(aa), (bb), Oct. 24, 1988, 102 Stat. 2621; Pub.L. 101–649, Title IV, §§ 401(c), 407(c)(16), (d)(13), Nov. 29, 1990, 104 Stat. 5038, 5041, 5043.)

# § 336. Hearings on denials of applications for naturalization [8 U.S.C.A. § 1447]

## (a) Request for hearing before immigration officer

If, after an examination under section 335 [8 U.S.C.A. § 1446], an application for naturalization is denied, the applicant may request a hearing before an immigration officer.

## (b) Request for hearing before district court

If there is a failure to make a determination under section 335 [8 U.S.C.A. § 1446] before the end of the 120–day period after the date on which the examination is conducted under such section, the applicant may apply to the United States district court for the district in which the applicant resides for a hearing on the matter. Such court has jurisdiction over the matter and may either determine the matter or remand the matter, with appropriate instructions, to the Service to determine the matter.

## (c) Appearance of Attorney General

The Attorney General shall have the right to appear before any immigration officer in any naturalization proceedings for the purpose of cross-examining the applicant and the witnesses produced in support of the application concerning any matter touching or in any way affecting the applicant's right to admission to citizenship, and shall have the right to call witnesses, including the applicant, produce evidence, and be heard in opposition to, or in favor of, the granting of any application in naturalization proceedings.

## (d) Subpena of witness

The immigration officer shall, if the applicant requests it at the time of filing the request for the hearing, issue a subpena for the witnesses named by such applicant to appear upon the day set for the hearing, but in case such witnesses cannot be produced upon the hearing other witnesses may be summoned upon notice to the Attorney General, in such manner and at such time as the Attorney General may by regulation prescribe.  Such subpenas may be enforced in the same manner as subpenas under section 335(b) [8 U.S.C.A. § 1446(b)] may be enforced.

### (e) Change of name of applicant

It shall be lawful at the time and as a part of the administration by a court of the oath of allegiance under section 337(a) [8 U.S.C.A. § 1448(a)] for the court, in its discretion, upon the bona fide prayer of the applicant included in an appropriate petition to the court, to make a decree changing the name of said person, and the certificate of naturalization shall be issued in accordance therewith.

### (f) Redesignated (e)

(June 27, 1952, c. 477, Title III, ch. 2, § 336, 66 Stat. 257;  Pub. L. 91–136, Dec. 5, 1969, 83 Stat. 283;  Pub. L. 97–116, § 15(d), Dec. 29, 1981, 95 Stat. 1619; Pub.L. 100–525, § 9(cc), Oct. 24, 1988, 102 Stat. 2621;  Pub.L. 101–649, Title IV, § 407(c)(17), (d)(14), Nov. 29, 1990, 104 Stat. 5041, 5044.)

## § 337.  Oath of renunciation and allegiance [8 U.S. C.A. § 1448]

### (a) Public ceremony

A person who has applied for naturalization shall, in order to be and before being admitted to citizenship, take in a public ceremony before the Attorney General or a court with jurisdiction under section 310(b) [8 U.S.C.A. § 1421(b)] an oath (1) to support the Constitution of the United States; (2) to renounce and abjure absolutely and entirely all allegiance and fidelity to any foreign prince, potentate, state, or sovereignty of whom or which the applicant was before a subject or citizen; (3) to support and defend the Constitution and the laws of the United States against all enemies, foreign and domestic; (4) to bear true faith and allegiance to the same; and (5)(A) to bear arms on behalf of the United States when required by the law, or (B) to perform noncombatant service in the Armed Forces of the United States when required by the law, or (C) to perform work of national importance under civilian direction when required by the law.  Any such person shall be required to take an oath containing the substance of clauses (1) to (5) of the preceding sentence, except that a person who shows by clear and convincing evidence to the satisfaction of the Attorney General that he is opposed to the bearing of arms in the Armed Forces of the United States by reason of religious training and belief shall be required to take an oath containing the substance of clauses (1) to (4) and clauses (5)(B) and (5)(C) of this subsection, and a person who shows by clear and convincing evidence to the satisfaction of the Attorney General that he is opposed to any type of service in the Armed Forces of the United States by reason of religious training and belief shall be required to take an oath containing the substance of said clauses (1) to

(4) and clause (5)(C). The term "religious training and belief" as used in this section shall mean an individual's belief in a relation to a Supreme Being involving duties superior to those arising from any human relation, but does not include essentially political, sociological, or philosophical views or a merely personal moral code. In the case of the naturalization of a child under the provisions of section 322 [8 U.S.C.A. § 1433] the Attorney General may waive the taking of the oath if in the opinion of the Attorney General the child is unable to understand its meaning.

### (b) Hereditary titles or orders of nobility

In case the person applying for naturalization has borne any hereditary title, or has been of any of the orders of nobility in any foreign state, the applicant shall in addition to complying with the requirements of subsection (a) of this section, make under oath in the same public ceremony in which the oath of allegiance is administered, an express renunciation of such title or order of nobility, and such renunciation shall be recorded as a part of such proceedings.

### (c) Other than public ceremony

If the applicant is prevented by sickness or other disability from attending a public ceremony, the oath required to be taken by subsection (a) of this section may be taken before [1] at such place as the Attorney General may designate under section 334(e) [8 U.S.C.A. § 1445(e)].

### (d) Rules and regulations

The Attorney General shall prescribe rules and procedures to ensure that the ceremonies conducted by the Attorney General for the administration of oaths of allegiance under this section are public, conducted frequently and at regular intervals, and are in keeping with the dignity of the occasion.

(June 27, 1952, c. 477, Title III, ch. 2, § 337, 66 Stat. 258; Pub. L. 97–116, § 18(*o*), Dec. 29, 1981, 95 Stat. 1621; Pub.L. 101–649, Title IV, § 407(c)(18), (d)(15), Nov. 29, 1990, 104 Stat. 5041, 5044.)

1. So in original.

## § 338. Certificate of naturalization; contents [8 U.S.C.A. § 1449]

A person admitted to citizenship in conformity with the provisions of this subchapter shall be entitled upon such admission to receive from the Attorney General a certificate of naturalization, which shall contain substantially the following information: Number of application for naturalization; number of certificate of naturalization; date of naturalization; name, signature, place of residence, autographed photograph, and personal description of the naturalized person, including age, sex, marital status, and country of former nationality; location of the District office of the Service in which the application was filed and the title, authority, and location of the official or court administering the oath of allegiance; statement that the Attorney General, having found that the applicant intends to reside permanently in the United States, except in cases falling within the provisions of section 324(a) [8 U.S.C.A. § 1435(a)], had complied in all respects with all of the applicable provisions of the naturalization laws of the United States, and was entitled to be admitted a citizen of the United States of America, thereupon ordered that the applicant be admitted as a citizen of the United States of America; attestation of an immigration officer; and the seal of the Department of Justice.

(June 27, 1952, c. 477, Title III, ch. 2, § 338, 66 Stat. 259; Nov. 29, 1990, Pub.L. 101–649, Title IV, § 407(c)(19), (d)(16), 104 Stat. 5041, 5045.)

## § 339. Functions and duties of clerks and records of declarations of intention and applications for naturalization [8 U.S.C.A. § 1450]

(a) The clerk of each court that administers oaths of allegiance under section 337 [8 U.S.C.A. § 1448] shall—

(1) issue to each person to whom such an oath is administered a document evidencing that such an oath was administered,

(2) forward to the Attorney General information concerning each person to whom such an oath is administered by the court, within 30 days after the close of the month in which the oath was administered,

(3) make and keep on file evidence for each such document issued, and

(4) forward to the Attorney General certified copies of such other proceedings and orders instituted in or issued out of the court affecting or relating to the naturalization of persons as may be required from time to time by the Attorney General.

(b) Each district office of the Service in the United States shall maintain, in chronological order, indexed, and consecutively numbered, as part of its permanent records, all declarations of intention and applications for naturalization filed with the office.

(June 27, 1952, c. 477, Title III, ch. 2, § 339, 66 Stat. 259; Nov. 29, 1990, Pub.L. 101–649, Title IV, § 407(d)(17), 104 Stat. 5045.)

## § 340. Revocation of naturalization [8 U.S.C.A. § 1451]

### (a) Concealment of material evidence; refusal to testify

It shall be the duty of the United States attorneys for the respective districts, upon affidavit showing good cause therefor, to institute proceedings in any District Court of the United States in the judicial district in which the naturalized citizen may reside at the time of bringing suit, for the purpose of revoking and setting aside the order admitting such person to citizenship and canceling the certificate of naturalization on the ground that such order and certificate of naturalization were illegally procured or were procured by concealment of a material fact or by willful misrepresentation, and such revocation and setting aside of the order admitting such person to citizenship and such canceling of certificate of naturalization shall be effective as of the original date of the order and certificate, respectively: *Provided,* That refusal on the part of a naturalized citizen within a period of ten years following his naturalization to testify as a witness in any proceeding before a congressional committee concerning his subversive activities, in a case where such person has been convicted of contempt for such refusal, shall be held to constitute a ground for revocation of such person's naturalization under this subsection as having been procured by concealment of a material fact or by willful misrepresentation. If the naturalized citizen does not reside in any judicial district in the United States at the time of bringing such suit, the proceedings may be instituted in the United States District Court for the District of Columbia or in the United States district court in the judicial district in which such person last had his residence.

### (b) Notice to party

The party to whom was granted the naturalization alleged to have been illegally procured or procured by concealment of a material fact or by willful misrepresentation shall, in any such proceedings under subsection (a) of this section, have sixty days' personal notice, unless waived by such party, in which to make answers to the petition of the United States; and if such naturalized person be absent from the United States or from the judicial district in which such person last had his residence, such notice shall be given either by personal service upon him or by publication in the manner provided for the service of summons by publication or upon absentees by the laws of the State or the place where such suit is brought.

### (c) Membership in certain organizations; prima facie evidence

If a person who shall have been naturalized after December 24, 1952, shall within five years next following such naturalization become a member of or affiliated with any organization, membership in or affiliation with which at the time of naturalization would have precluded such person from naturalization under the provisions of section 313 [8 U.S.C.A. § 1424], it shall be considered prima facie evidence that such person was not attached to the principles of the Constitution of the United States and was not well disposed to the good order and happiness of the United States at the time of naturalization, and, in the absence of countervailing evidence, it shall be sufficient in the proper proceeding to authorize the revocation and setting aside of the order admitting such person to citizenship and the cancellation of the certificate of naturalization as having been obtained by concealment of a material fact or by willful misrepresentation, and such revocation and setting aside of the order admitting such person to citizenship and such canceling of certificate of naturalization shall be effective as of the original date of the order and certificate, respectively.

### (d) Foreign residence

If a person who shall have been naturalized shall, within one year after such naturalization, return to the country of his nativity, or go to any other foreign country, and take permanent residence therein, it shall be considered prima facie evidence of a lack of intention on the part of such person to reside permanently in the United States at the time of filing his petition for naturalization, and, in the absence of countervailing evidence, it shall be sufficient in the proper proceeding to authorize the revocation and setting aside of the order admitting such person to citizenship and the cancellation of the certificate of naturalization as having been obtained by concealment of a material fact or by willful misrepresentation, and such revocation and setting aside of the order admitting such person to citizenship and such canceling of certificate of naturalization shall be effective as of the original date of the order and certificate, respectively.  The diplomatic and consular officers of the United States in foreign countries shall from time to time, through the Department of State, furnish the Department of Justice with statements of the names of those persons within their respective jurisdictions who have been so naturalized and who have taken permanent residence in the country of their nativity, or in any other foreign country, and such statements, duly certified, shall be admissible in evidence in all courts in proceedings to revoke and set aside the order admitting to citizenship and to cancel the certificate of naturalization.

### (e) Applicability to citizenship through naturalization of parent or spouse

Any person who claims United States citizenship through the naturalization of a parent or spouse in whose case there is a revocation and setting aside of the order admitting such parent or spouse to citizenship under the provisions of subsection (a) of this section on the ground that the order and certificate of naturalization were procured by concealment of a material fact or by willful misrepresentation shall be deemed to have lost and to lose his citizenship and any right or privilege of citizenship which he may have, now has, or may hereafter acquire under and by virtue of such naturalization of such parent or spouse, regardless of whether such person is residing within or without the United States at the time of the revocation and setting aside of the order admitting such parent or spouse to citizenship.  Any person who claims United States citizenship through the naturalization of a parent or spouse in whose case there is a revocation and setting aside of the order admitting such parent or spouse to citizenship and the cancellation of the certificate of naturalization under the provisions of subsections (c) or (d) of this section, or under the provisions of section 329(c) [8 U.S.C.A. § 1440(c)] on any ground other than that the order and certificate of naturalization were procured by concealment of a material fact or by willful misrepresentation, shall be deemed to have lost and to lose his citizenship and any right or privilege of citizenship which would have been enjoyed by such person had there not been a revocation and setting aside of the order admitting such parent or spouse to citizenship and the cancellation of the certificate of naturalization, unless such person is residing in the United States at the time of the revocation and setting aside of the order admitting such parent or spouse to citizenship and the cancellation of the certificate of naturalization.

### (f) Citizenship unlawfully procured

When a person shall be convicted under section 1425 of title 18 of knowingly procuring naturalization in violation of law, the court in which such conviction is had shall thereupon revoke, set aside, and declare void the final order admitting such person to citizenship, and shall declare the certificate of naturalization of such person to be canceled. Jurisdiction is conferred on the courts having jurisdiction of the trial of such offense to make such adjudication.

### (g) Cancellation of certificate of naturalization

Whenever an order admitting an alien to citizenship shall be revoked and set aside or a certificate of naturalization shall be canceled, or both, as provided in this section, the court in which such judgment or decree is rendered shall make an order canceling such certificate and shall send a certified copy of such order to the Attorney General. The clerk of the court shall transmit a copy of such order and judgment to the Attorney General. A person holding a certificate of naturalization or citizenship which has been canceled as provided by this section shall upon notice by the court by which the decree of cancellation was made, or by the Attorney General, surrender the same to the Attorney General.

### (h) Applicability to certificates of naturalization and citizenship

The provisions of this section shall apply not only to any naturalization granted and to certificates of naturalization and citizenship issued under the provisions of this subchapter, but to any naturalization heretofore granted by any court, and to all certificates of naturalization and citizenship which may have been issued heretofore by any court or by the Commissioner based upon naturalization granted by any court, or by a designated representative of the Commissioner under the provisions of section 702 of the Nationality Act of 1940, as amended, or by such designated representative under any other act.

### (i) Power to correct, reopen, alter, modify or vacate order

Nothing contained in this section shall be regarded as limiting, denying, or restricting the power of the Attorney General to correct, reopen, alter, modify, or vacate an order naturalizing the person.

(June 27, 1952, c. 477, Title III, ch. 2, § 340, 66 Stat. 260; Sept. 3, 1954, c. 1263, § 18, 68 Stat. 1232; Pub. L. 87–301, Sept. 26, 1961, § 18, 75 Stat. 656;

Pub.L. 99–653, § 17, Nov. 14, 1986, 100 Stat. 3658; Pub.L. 100–525, § 9(dd), Oct. 24, 1988, 102 Stat. 2621; Pub.L. 101–649, Title IV, § 407(d)(18), Nov. 29, 1990, 104 Stat. 5046.)

## § 341. Certificates of citizenship or U.S. non-citizen national status; procedure [8 U.S.C.A. § 1452]

(a) A person who claims to have derived United States citizenship through the naturalization of a parent or through the naturalization or citizenship of a husband, or who is a citizen of the United States by virtue of the provisions of section 1993 of the United States Revised Statutes, or of section 1993 of the United States Revised Statutes, as amended by section 1 of the Act of May 24, 1934 (48 Stat. 797), or who is a citizen of the United States by virtue of the provisions of subsection (c), (d), (e), (g), or (i) of section 201 of the Nationality Act of 1940, as amended (54 Stat. 1138), or of the Act of May 7, 1934 (48 Stat. 667), or of paragraph (c), (d), (e), or (g) of section 1401 of this title, or under the provisions of the Act of August 4, 1937 (50 Stat. 558), or under the provisions of section 203 or 205 of the Nationality Act of 1940 (54 Stat. 1139), or under the provisions of section 303 [8 U.S.C.A. § 1403], may apply to the Attorney General for a certificate of citizenship. Upon proof to the satisfaction of the Attorney General that the applicant is a citizen, and that the applicant's alleged citizenship was derived as claimed, or acquired, as the case may be, and upon taking and subscribing before a member of the Service within the United States to the oath of allegiance required by this chapter of a petitioner for naturalization, such individual shall be furnished by the Attorney General with a certificate of citizenship, but only if such individual is at the time within the United States.

(b) A person who claims to be a national, but not a citizen, of the United States may apply to the Secretary of State for a certificate of non-citizen national status. Upon—

(1) proof to the satisfaction of the Secretary of State that the applicant is a national, but not a citizen, of the United States, and

(2) in the case of such a person born outside of the United States or its outlying possessions, taking and subscribing, before an immigration officer within the United States or its outlying possessions, to the oath of allegiance required by this chapter of a petitioner for naturalization,

the individual shall be furnished by the Secretary of State with a certificate of non-citizen national status, but only if the individual is at the time within the United States or its outlying possessions.

(c)(1) The adoptive citizen parent or parents of a child described in paragraph (2) may apply to the Attorney General for a certificate of citizenship for the child. Upon proof to the satisfaction of the Attorney General that the applicant and spouse, if married, are citizens of the United States, whether by birth or by naturalization, and that the child is described in paragraph (2), the child shall become a citizen of the United States and shall be furnished by the Attorney General with a certificate of citizenship, but only if the child is at the time within the United States.

(2) A child described in this paragraph is a child born outside of the United States who—

(A) is under the age of 18 years,

(B) is adopted before the child reached the age of 16 years by a parent who is a citizen of the United States, either by birth or naturalization, and

(C) is residing in the United States in the custody of the adopting citizen parent, pursuant to a lawful admission for permanent residence.

(June 27, 1952, c. 477, Title III, ch. 2, § 341, 66 Stat. 263; Pub. L. 97–116, § 18(p), Dec. 29, 1981, 95 Stat. 1621; Pub. L. 99–396, § 16(a), Aug. 27, 1986, 100 Stat. 843; Pub.L. 99–653, § 22, Nov. 14, 1986, 100 Stat. 3658, as amended Pub.L. 100–525, § 8(q), Oct. 24, 1988, 102 Stat. 2618.)

## § 342. Cancellation of certificates issued by Attorney General, the Commissioner or a Deputy Commissioner; action not to affect citizenship status [8 U.S.C.A. § 1453]

The Attorney General is authorized to cancel any certificate of citizenship, certificate of naturalization, copy of a declaration of intention, or other certificate, document or record heretofore issued or made by the Commissioner or a Deputy Commissioner or hereafter made by the Attorney General if it shall appear to the Attorney General's satisfaction that such document or record was illegally or fraudulently obtained from, or was created through illegality or by fraud practiced upon, him or the Commissioner or a Deputy Commissioner; but the person for or to whom such document or record has been issued or made shall be given at such person's last-known place of address written notice of the intention to cancel such document or record with the reasons therefor and shall be given at least sixty days in which to show cause why such document or record should not be canceled. The cancellation under this section of any document purporting to show the citizenship status of the person to whom it was issued shall affect only the document and not the citizenship status of the person in whose name the document was issued.

(June 27, 1952, c. 477, Title III, ch. 2, § 342, 66 Stat. 263.)

## § 343. Documents and copies issued by Attorney General [8 U.S.C.A. § 1454]

(a) If any certificate of naturalization or citizenship issued to any citizen or any declaration of intention furnished to any declarant is lost, mutilated, or destroyed, the citizen or declarant may make application to the Attorney General for a new certificate or declaration. If the Attorney General finds that the certificate or declaration is lost, mutilated, or destroyed, he shall issue to the applicant a new certificate or declaration. If the certificate or declaration has been mutilated, it shall be surrendered to the Attorney General before the applicant may receive such new certificate or declaration. If the certificate or declaration has been lost, the applicant or any other person who shall have, or may come into possession of it is required to surrender it to the Attorney General.

(b) The Attorney General shall issue for any naturalized citizen, on such citizen's application therefor, a special certificate of naturalization for use by such citizen only for the purpose of obtaining recognition as a citizen of the United States by a foreign state. Such certificate when issued shall be furnished to the Secretary of State for transmission to the proper authority in such foreign state.

(c) If the name of any naturalized citizen has, subsequent to naturalization, been changed by order of any court of competent jurisdiction, or by marriage, the citizen may make application for a new certificate of naturalization in the new name of such citizen. If the Attorney General finds the name of the applicant to have been changed as claimed, the Attorney General shall issue to the applicant a new certificate and shall notify the naturalization court of such action.

(d) The Attorney General is authorized to make and issue certifications of any part of the naturalization records of any court, or of any certificate of naturalization or citizenship, for use in complying with any statute, State or Federal, or in any judicial proceeding. No such certification shall be made by any clerk of court except upon order of the court.

(June 27, 1952, c. 477, Title III, ch. 2, § 343, 66 Stat. 263; Pub.L. 100–525, § 9(ee), Oct. 24, 1988, 102 Stat. 2621.)

## § 344.   Fiscal provisions [8 U.S.C.A. § 1455]

(a) The Attorney General shall charge, collect, and account for fees prescribed by the Attorney General pursuant to section 9701 of Title 31 for the following:

(1) Making, filing, and docketing an application for naturalization, including the hearing on such application, if such hearing be held, and a certificate of naturalization, if the issuance of such certificate is authorized by the Attorney General.

(2) Receiving and filing a declaration of intention, and issuing a duplicate thereof.

(b) Notwithstanding the provisions of this chapter or any other law, no fee shall be charged or collected for an application for declaration of intention or a certificate of naturalization in lieu of a declaration or a certificate alleged to have been lost, mutilated, or destroyed, submitted by a person who was a member of the military or naval forces of the United States at any time after April 20, 1898, and before July 5, 1902; or at any time after April 5, 1917, and before November

12, 1918; or who served on the Mexican border as a member of the Regular Army or National Guard between June 1916 and April 1917; or who has served or hereafter serves in the military, air, or naval forces of the United States after September 16, 1940, and who was not at any time during such period or thereafter separated from such forces under other than honorable conditions, who was not a conscientious objector who performed no military duty whatever or refused to wear the uniform, or who was not at any time during such period or thereafter discharged from such military, air, or naval forces on account of alienage.

(c) All fees collected by the Attorney General shall be deposited by the Attorney General in the Treasury of the United States except that all fees collected by the Attorney General on or after October 1, 1988, under the provisions of this subchapter, shall be deposited in the "Immigration Examinations Fee Account" in the Treasury of the United States established pursuant to the provisions of section 286(m), (n), (o), & (p) [8 U.S.C.A. § 1356(m), (n), (o), and (p)]: *Provided, however,* That all fees received by the Attorney General from applicants residing in the Virgin Islands of the United States, and in Guam, under this subchapter, shall be paid over to the treasury of the Virgin Islands and to the treasury of Guam, respectively.

(d) During the time when the United States is at war the Attorney General may not charge or collect a naturalization fee from an alien in the military, air, or naval service of the United States for filing an application for naturalization or issuing a certificate of naturalization upon admission to citizenship.

(e) In addition to the other fees required by this subchapter, the applicant for naturalization shall, upon the filing of an application for naturalization, deposit with and pay to the Attorney General a sum of money sufficient to cover the expenses of subpenaing and paying the legal fees of any witnesses for whom such applicant may request a subpena, and upon the final discharge of such witnesses, they shall receive, if they demand the same from the Attorney General, the customary and usual witness fees from the moneys which the applicant shall have paid to the Attorney General for such purpose, and the residue, if any, shall be returned by the Attorney General to the applicant.

(f) **Repealed.** Pub.L. 101–649, Title IV, § 407(d)(19)(B), Nov. 29, 1990, 104 Stat. 5046.

(g) to (i) redesignated (c) to (e).

(June 27, 1952, c. 477, Title III, ch. 2, § 344, 66 Stat. 264; Pub. L. 85–508, § 26, July 7, 1958, 72 Stat. 351; Pub. L. 90–609, § 3, Oct. 21, 1968, 82 Stat. 1200; Pub. L. 97–116, § 16, Dec. 29, 1981, 95 Stat. 1619; Pub.L. 100–459, Title II, § 209(b), Oct. 1, 1988, 102 Stat. 2203; Pub.L. 100–525, § 9(ff), Oct. 24, 1988, 102 Stat. 2621; Pub.L. 101–649, Title IV, § 407(c)(20), (d)(19), Nov. 29, 1990, 104 Stat. 5041, 5046.)

## § 345. Repealed. Pub. L. 86–682, § 12(c), Sept. 2, 1960, 74 Stat. 708, eff. Sept. 1, 1960 [8 U.S.C.A. § 1456]

## § 346. Publication and distribution of citizenship textbooks; use of naturalization fees [8 U.S.C.A. § 1457]

Authorization is granted for the publication and distribution of the citizenship textbook described in subsection (b) of section 332 [8 U.S.C.A. § 1443(b)] and for the reimbursement of the appropriation of the Department of Justice upon the records of the Treasury Department from the naturalization fees deposited in the Treasury through the Service for the cost of such publication and distribution, such reimbursement to be made upon statements by the Attorney General of books so published and distributed.

(June 27, 1952, c. 477, Title III, ch. 2, § 346, 66 Stat. 266.)

## § 347. Compilation of naturalization statistics and payment for equipment [8 U.S.C.A. § 1458]

The Attorney General is authorized and directed to prepare from the records in the custody of the Service a report upon those heretofore seeking citizenship to show by nationalities their relation to the numbers of aliens annually arriving and to the prevailing census populations of the foreign-born, their economic, vocational, and other classification, in statistical form, with analytical comment thereon, and to prepare such report annually hereafter. Payment for the equipment used in preparing such compilation shall be made from the appropriation for the enforcement of this chapter by the Service.

(June 27, 1952, c. 477, Title III, ch. 2, § 347, 66 Stat. 266.)

## § 348. [8 U.S.C.A. § 1459] Repealed.

### CHAPTER III—LOSS OF NATIONALITY

## § 349. Loss of nationality by native-born or naturalized citizen; voluntary action; burden of proof; presumptions [8 U.S.C.A. § 1481]

(a) A person who is a national of the United States whether by birth or naturalization, shall lose his nationality by voluntarily performing any of the following acts with the intention of relinquishing United States nationality—

(1) obtaining naturalization in a foreign state upon his own application, or upon an application filed by a duly authorized agent, after having attained the age of eighteen years; or

(2) taking an oath or making an affirmation or other formal declaration of allegiance to a foreign state or a political subdivision thereof, after having attained the age of eighteen years; or

(3) entering, or serving in, the armed forces of a foreign state if (A) such armed forces are engaged in hostilities against the United States, or (B) such persons serve as a commissioned or noncommissioned officer; or

(4)(A) accepting, serving in, or performing the duties of any office, post, or employment under the government of a foreign state or a political subdivision thereof, after attaining the age of eighteen years, if he has or acquires the nationality of such foreign state; or

(B) accepting, serving in, or performing the duties of any office, post, or employment under the government of a foreign state or a political subdivision thereof, after attaining the age of eighteen years for which office, post, or employment an oath, affirmation, or declaration of allegiance is required; or

(5) making a formal renunciation of nationality before a diplomatic or consular officer of the United States in a foreign state, in such form as may be prescribed by the Secretary of State; or

(6) making in the United States a formal written renunciation of nationality in such form as may be prescribed by, and before such officer as may be designated by, the Attorney General, whenever the United States shall be in a state of war and the Attorney General shall approve such renunciation as not contrary to the interests of national defense; or

(7) committing any act of treason against, or attempting by force to overthrow, or bearing arms against, the United States, violating or conspiring to violate any of the provisions of section 2383 of Title 18, or willfully performing any act in violation of section 2385 of Title 18, or violating section 2384 of Title 18 by engaging in a conspiracy to overthrow, put down, or to destroy by force the Government of the United States, or to levy war against them, if and when he is convicted thereof by a court martial or by a court of competent jurisdiction.

(b) Whenever the loss of United States nationality is put in issue in any action or proceeding commenced on or after September 26, 1961 under, or by virtue of, the provisions of this chapter or any other Act, the burden shall be upon the person or party claiming that such loss occurred, to establish such claim by a preponderance of the evidence. Any person who commits or performs, or who has committed or performed, any act of expatriation under the provisions of this chapter or any other Act shall be presumed to have done so voluntarily, but such presumption may be rebutted upon a showing, by a preponderance of the evidence, that the act or acts committed or performed were not done voluntarily.

(June 27, 1952, c. 477, Title III, ch. 3, § 349, 66 Stat. 267; Sept. 3, 1954, c. 1256, § 2, 68 Stat. 1146; Pub.L. 87–301, § 19, Sept. 26, 1961, 75 Stat. 656; Pub.L. 94–412, Title V, § 501(a), Sept. 14, 1976, 90 Stat. 1258; Pub.L. 95–432, §§ 2, 4, Oct. 10, 1978, 92 Stat. 1046; Pub.L. 97–116, § 18(k)(2), (q), Dec. 29, 1981,

95 Stat. 1620, 1621; Pub.L. 99–653, §§ 18, 19, Nov. 14, 1986, 100 Stat. 3658, as amended Pub.L. 100–525, § 8(m), (n), Oct. 24, 1988, 102 Stat. 2618; Pub.L. 100–525, § 9(hh), Oct. 24, 1988, 102 Stat. 2618.)

## § 350. Repealed. Pub. L. 95–432, § 1, Oct. 10, 1978, 92 Stat. 1046 [8 U.S.C.A. § 1482]

## § 351. Restrictions on expatriation [8 U.S.C.A. § 1483]

(a) Except as provided in paragraphs (6) and (7) of section 349(a) [8 U.S.C.A. § 1481(a)(6) and (7)], no national of the United States can expatriate himself, or be expatriated, under this chapter while within the United States or any of its outlying possessions, but expatriation shall result from the performance within the United States or any of its outlying possessions of any of the acts or the fulfillment of any of the conditions specified in this part if and when the national thereafter takes up a residence outside the United States and its outlying possessions.

(b) A national who within six months after attaining the age of eighteen years asserts his claim to United States nationality, in such manner as the Secretary of State shall by regulation prescribe, shall not be deemed to have expatriated himself by the commission, prior to his eighteenth birthday, of any of the acts specified in paragraphs (3) and (5) of section 349(a) [8 U.S.C.A. § 1481(a)(3) and (5)].

(June 27, 1952, c. 477, Title III, ch. 3, § 351, 66 Stat. 269; Pub.L. 97–116, § 18(r), Dec. 29, 1981, 95 Stat. 1621; Pub.L. 99–653, § 20, Nov. 20, 1986, 100 Stat. 3658, as amended Pub.L. 100–525, § 8(o), Oct. 24, 1988, 102 Stat. 2618.)

## §§ 352 to 355. Repealed. Pub. L. 95–432, § 2, Oct. 10, 1978, 92 Stat. 1046 [8 U.S.C.A. §§ 1484 to 1487]

## § 356. Nationality lost solely from performance of acts or fulfillment of conditions [8 U.S.C.A. § 1488]

The loss of nationality under this part shall result solely from the performance by a national of the acts or fulfillment of the conditions specified in this Part.

(June 27, 1952, c. 477, Title III, ch. 3, § 356, 66 Stat. 272.)

## § 357. Application of treaties; exceptions [8 U.S.C.A. § 1489]

Nothing in this subchapter shall be applied in contravention of the provisions of any treaty or convention to which the United States is a party and which has been ratified by the Senate before December 25, 1952: *Provided, however,* That no woman who was a national of the United States shall be deemed to have lost her nationality solely by reason of her marriage to an alien on or after September 22, 1922, or to an alien racially ineligible to citizenship on or after March 3, 1931, or, in the case of a woman who was a United States citizen at birth, through residence abroad following such marriage, notwithstanding the provisions of any existing treaty or convention.

(June 27, 1952, c. 477, Title III, ch. 3, § 357, 66 Stat. 272; Pub.L. 100–525, § 9(ii), Oct. 24, 1988, 102 Stat. 2622.)

## CHAPTER IV—MISCELLANEOUS

## § 358. Certificate of diplomatic or consular officer of United States as to loss of American nationality [8 U.S.C.A. § 1501]

Whenever a diplomatic or consular officer of the United States has reason to believe that a person while in a foreign state has lost his United States nationality under any provision of part III of this subchapter, or under any provision of chapter IV of the Nationality Act of 1940, as amended, he shall certify the facts upon which such belief is based to the Department of State, in writing, under regulations prescribed by the Secretary of State. If the report of the diplomatic or consular officer is approved by the Secretary of State, a copy of the certificate shall be forwarded to the Attorney General, for his information, and the diplomatic or consular office in which the report was made shall be directed to forward a copy of the certificate to the person to whom it relates.

(June 27, 1952, c. 477, Title III, ch. 4, § 358, 66 Stat. 272.)

## § 359. Certificate of nationality issued by Secretary of State for person not a naturalized citizen of United States for use in proceedings of a foreign state [8 U.S.C.A. § 1502]

The Secretary of State is authorized to issue, in his discretion and in accordance with rules and regulations prescribed by him, a certificate of nationality for any person not a naturalized citizen of the United States who presents satisfactory evidence that he is an American national and that such certificate is needed for use in judicial or administrative proceedings in a foreign state. Such certificate shall be solely for use in the case for which it was issued and shall be transmitted by the Secretary of State through appropriate official channels to the judicial or administrative officers of the foreign state in which it is to be used.

(June 27, 1952, c. 477, Title III, ch. 4, § 359, 66 Stat. 273.)

## § 360. Denial of rights and privileges as national [8 U.S.C.A. § 1503]

### (a) Proceedings for declaration of United States nationality

If any person who is within the United States claims a right or privilege as a national of the United States and is denied such right or privilege by any department or independent agency, or official thereof, upon the ground that he is not a national of the United States, such person may institute an action under the provisions of section 2201 of Title 28 against the head of such department or independent agency for a judgment declaring him to be a national of the United States, except that no such action may be instituted in any case if the issue of such person's status as a national of the United States (1) arose by reason of, or in connection with any exclusion proceeding under the provisions of this chapter or any other act, or (2) is in issue in any such exclusion proceeding. An action under this subsection may be instituted only within five years after the final administrative denial of such right or privilege and shall be filed in the district court of the United States for the district in which such person resides or claims a residence, and jurisdiction over such officials in such cases is conferred upon those courts.

### (b) Application for certificate of identity; appeal

If any person who is not within the United States claims a right or privilege as a national of the United States and is denied such right or privilege by any department or independent agency, or official thereof, upon the ground that he is not a national of the United States, such person may make application to a diplomatic or consular officer of the United States in the foreign country in which he is residing for a certificate of identity for the purpose of traveling to a port of entry in the United States and applying for admission. Upon proof to the satisfaction of such diplomatic or consular officer that such application is made in good faith and has a substantial basis, he shall issue to such person a certificate of identity. From any denial of an application for such certificate the applicant shall be entitled to an appeal to the Secretary of State, who, if he approves the denial, shall state in writing his reasons for his decision. The Secretary of State shall prescribe rules and regulations for the issuance of certificates of identity as above provided. The provisions of this subsection shall be applicable only to a person who at some time prior to his application for the certificate of identity has been physically present in the United States, or to a person under sixteen years of age who was born abroad of a United States citizen parent.

### (c) Application for admission to United States under certificate of identity; revision of determination

A person who has been issued a certificate of identity under the provisions of subsection (b) of this section, and while in possession thereof, may apply for admission to the United States at any port of entry, and shall be subject to all the provisions of this chapter relating to the conduct of proceedings involving aliens seeking admission to the United States. A final determination by the Attorney General that any such person is not entitled to admission to the United States shall be subject to review by any court of competent jurisdiction in habeas corpus proceedings and not otherwise. Any person described in this section who is finally excluded from admission to the United States shall be subject to all the provisions of this chapter relating to aliens seeking admission to the United States.

(June 27, 1952, c. 477, Title III, ch. 4, § 360, 66 Stat. 273.)

# TITLE IV

## REFUGEE ASSISTANCE

## § 411. Office of Refugee Resettlement; establishment; appointment of Director; functions [8 U.S. C.A. § 1521]

(a) There is established, within the Department of Health and Human Services, an office to be known as the Office of Refugee Resettlement (hereinafter in this subchapter referred to as the "Office"). The head of the Office shall be a Director (hereinafter in this subchapter referred to as the "Director"), to be appointed by the Secretary of Health and Human Services (hereinafter in this subchapter referred to as the "Secretary").

(b) The function of the Office and its Director is to fund and administer (directly or through arrangements with other Federal agencies), in consultation with and under the general policy guidance of the United States Coordinator for Refugee Affairs (hereinafter in this subchapter referred to as the "Coordinator"), programs of the Federal Government under this subchapter.

(June 27, 1952, c. 477, Title IV, ch. 2, § 411, as added Pub. L. 96–212, Title III, § 311(a)(2), Mar. 17, 1980, 94 Stat. 110.)

## § 412. Authorization for programs for domestic resettlement of and assistance to refugees [8 U.S.C.A. § 1522]

### (a) Conditions and considerations

(1) (A) In providing assistance under this section, the Director shall, to the extent of available appropriations, (i) make available sufficient resources for employment training and placement in order to achieve economic self-sufficiency among refugees as quickly as possible, (ii) provide refugees with the opportunity to acquire sufficient English language training to enable them to become effectively resettled as quickly as possible, (iii) insure that cash assistance is made available to refugees in such a manner as not to discourage their economic self-sufficiency, in accordance with subsection (e)(2) of this section, and (iv) insure that women have the same opportunities as men to participate in training and instruction.

(B) It is the intent of Congress that in providing refugee assistance under this section—

(i) employable refugees should be placed on jobs as soon as possible after their arrival in the United States;

(ii) social service funds should be focused on employment-related services, English-as-a-second-language training (in nonwork hours where possible), and case-management services; and

(iii) local voluntary agency activities should be conducted in close cooperation and advance consultation with State and local governments.

(2)(A) The Director and the Federal agency administering subsection (b)(1) of this section, together with the Coordinator, shall consult regularly (not less often than quarterly) with State and local governments and private nonprofit voluntary agencies concerning the sponsorship process and the intended distribution of refugees among the States and localities before their placement in those States and localities.

(B) The Director shall develop and implement, in consultation with representatives of voluntary agencies and State and local governments, policies and strategies for the placement and resettlement of refugees within the United States.

(C) Such policies and strategies, to the extent practicable and except under such unusual circumstances as the Director may recognize, shall—

(i) insure that a refugee is not initially placed or resettled in an area highly impacted (as determined under regulations prescribed by the Director after consultation with such agencies and governments) by the presence of refugees or comparable populations unless the refugee has a spouse, parent, sibling, son, or daughter residing in that area,

(ii) provide for a mechanism whereby representatives of local affiliates of voluntary agencies regularly (not less often than quarterly) meet with representatives of State and local governments to plan and coordinate in advance of their arrival the appropriate placement of refugees among the various States and localities, and

(iii) take into account—

(I) the proportion of refugees and comparable entrants in the population in the area,

(II) the availability of employment opportunities, affordable housing, and public and private resources (including educational, health care, and mental health services) for refugees in the area,

(III) the likelihood of refugees placed in the area becoming self-sufficient and free from long-term dependence on public assistance, and

(IV) the secondary migration of refugees to and from the area that is likely to occur.

(D) With respect to the location of placement of refugees within a State, the Federal agency administering subsection (b)(1) of this section shall, consistent with such policies and strategies and to the maximum extent possible, take into account recommendations of the State.

(3) In the provision of domestic assistance under this section, the Director shall make a periodic assessment, based on refugee population and other relevant factors, of the relative needs of refugees for assistance and services under this subchapter and the resources available to meet such needs. The Director shall compile and maintain data on secondary migration of refugees within the United States and, by State of residence and nationality, on the proportion of refugees receiving cash or medical assistance described in subsection (e) of this section. In allocating resources, the Director shall avoid duplication of services and provide for maximum coordination between agencies providing related services.

(4)(A) No grant or contract may be awarded under this section unless an appropriate proposal and application (including a description of the agency's ability to perform the services specified in the proposal) are submitted to, and approved by, the appropriate administering official. Grants and contracts under this section shall be made to those agencies which the appropriate administering official determines can best perform the services. Payments may be made for activities authorized under this subchapter in advance or by way of reimbursement. In carrying out this section, the Director, the Secretary of State, and any such other appropriate administering official are authorized—

(i) to make loans, and

(ii) to accept and use money, funds, property, and services of any kind made available by gift, devise, bequest, grant, or otherwise for the purpose of carrying out this section.

(B) No funds may be made available under this subchapter (other than under subsection (b)(1) of this section) to States or political subdivisions in the form of block grants, per capita grants, or similar consolidated grants or contracts. Such funds shall be made available under separate grants or contracts—

(i) for medical screening and initial medical treatment under subsection (b)(5) of this section,

(ii) for services for refugees under subsection (c)(1) of this section,

(iii) for targeted assistance project grants under subsection (c)(2) of this section, and

(iv) for assistance for refugee children under subsection (d)(2) of this section.

(C) The Director may not delegate to a State or political subdivision his authority to review or approve grants or contracts under this subchapter or the terms under which such grants or contracts are made.

**(5)** Assistance and services funded under this section shall be provided to refugees without regard to race, religion, nationality, sex, or political opinion.

**(6)** As a condition for receiving assistance under this section, a State must—

(**A**) submit to the Director a plan which provides—

(**i**) a description of how the State intends to encourage effective refugee resettlement and to promote economic self-sufficiency as quickly as possible,

(**ii**) a description of how the State will insure that language training and employment services are made available to refugees receiving cash assistance,

(**iii**) for the designation of an individual, employed by the State, who will be responsible for insuring coordination of public and private resources in refugee resettlement,

(**iv**) for the care and supervision of and legal responsibility for unaccompanied refugee children in the State, and

(**v**) for the identification of refugees who at the time of resettlement in the State are determined to have medical conditions requiring, or medical histories indicating a need for, treatment or observation and such monitoring of such treatment or observation as may be necessary;

(**B**) meet standards, goals, and priorities, developed by the Director, which assure the effective resettlement of refugees and which promote their economic self-sufficiency as quickly as possible and the efficient provision of services; and

(**C**) submit to the Director, within a reasonable period of time after the end of each fiscal year, a report on the uses of funds provided under this subchapter which the State is responsible for administering.

**(7)** The Secretary, together with the Secretary of State with respect to assistance provided by the Secretary of State under subsection (b) of this section, shall develop a system of monitoring the assistance provided under this section. This system shall include—

(**A**) evaluations of the effectiveness of the programs funded under this section and the performance of States, grantees, and contractors;

(**B**) financial auditing and other appropriate monitoring to detect any fraud, abuse, or mismanagement in the operation of such programs; and

(**C**) data collection on the services provided and the results achieved.

**(8)** The Attorney General shall provide the Director with information supplied by refugees in conjunction with their applications to the

Attorney General for adjustment of status, and the Director shall compile, summarize, and evaluate such information.

(9) The Secretary, the Secretary of Education, the Attorney General, and the Secretary of State may issue such regulations as each deems appropriate to carry out this subchapter.

(10) For purposes of this subchapter, the term "refugee" includes any alien described in section 207(c)(2) [8 U.S.C.A. § 1157(c)(2)].

**(b) Program of initial resettlement**

(1)(A) For—

(i) fiscal years 1980 and 1981, the Secretary of State is authorized, and

(ii) fiscal year 1982 and succeeding fiscal years, the Director (except as provided in subparagraph (B)) is authorized,

to make grants to, and contracts with, public or private nonprofit agencies for initial resettlement (including initial reception and placement with sponsors) of refugees in the United States. Grants to, or contracts with, private nonprofit voluntary agencies under this paragraph shall be made consistent with the objectives of this subchapter, taking into account the different resettlement approaches and practices of such agencies. Resettlement assistance under this paragraph shall be provided in coordination with the Director's provision of other assistance under this subchapter. Funds provided to agencies under such grants and contracts may only be obligated or expended during the fiscal year in which they are provided (or the subsequent fiscal year or such subsequent fiscal period as the Federal contracting agency may approve) to carry out the purposes of this subsection.

**(B)** If the President determines that the Director should not administer the program under this paragraph, the authority of the Director under the first sentence of subparagraph (A) shall be exercised by such officer as the President shall from time to time specify.

(2) The Director is authorized to develop programs for such orientation, instruction in English, and job training for refugees, and such other education and training of refugees, as facilitates their resettlement in the United States. The Director is authorized to implement such programs, in accordance with the provisions of this section, with respect to refugees in the United States. The Secretary of State is authorized to implement such programs with respect to refugees awaiting entry into the United States.

(3) The Secretary is authorized, in consultation with the Coordinator, to make arrangements (including cooperative arrangements with other Federal agencies) for the temporary care of refugees in the United States in emergency circumstances, including the establishment of processing centers, if necessary, without regard to such provisions of law (other than the Renegotiation Act of 1951 [50 App. U.S.C.A. § 1211 et seq.] and section 414(b) [8 U.S.C.A. § 1524(b)]) regulating the making,

performance, amendment, or modification of contracts and the expenditure of funds of the United States Government as the Secretary may specify.

(4) The Secretary, in consultation with the Coordinator, shall—

(A) assure that an adequate number of trained staff are available at the location at which the refugees enter the United States to assure that all necessary medical records are available and in proper order;

(B) provide for the identification of refugees who have been determined to have medical conditions affecting the public health and requiring treatment;

(C) assure that State or local health officials at the resettlement destination within the United States of each refugee are promptly notified of the refugee's arrival and provided with all applicable medical records; and

(D) provide for such monitoring of refugees identified under subparagraph (B) as will insure that they receive appropriate and timely treatment.

The Secretary shall develop and implement methods for monitoring and assessing the quality of medical screening and related health services provided to refugees awaiting resettlement in the United States.

(5) The Director is authorized to make grants to, and enter into contracts with, State and local health agencies for payments to meet their costs of providing medical screening and initial medical treatment to refugees.

(6) The Comptroller General shall directly conduct an annual financial audit of funds expended under each grant or contract made under paragraph (1) for fiscal year 1986 and for fiscal year 1987.

(7) Each grant or contract with an agency under paragraph (1) shall require the agency to do the following:

(A) To provide quarterly performance and financial status reports to the Federal agency administering paragraph (1).

(B)(i) To provide, directly or through its local affiliate, notice to the appropriate county or other local welfare office at the time that the agency becomes aware that a refugee is offered employment and to provide notice to the refugee that such notice has been provided, and

(ii) upon request of such a welfare office to which a refugee has applied for cash assistance, to furnish that office with documentation respecting any cash or other resources provided directly by the agency to the refugee under this subsection.

(C) To assure that refugees, known to the agency as having been identified pursuant to paragraph (4)(B) as having medical conditions affecting the public health and requiring treatment, report to the appropriate county or other health agency upon their resettlement in an area.

**(D)** To fulfill its responsibility to provide for the basic needs (including food, clothing, shelter, and transportation for job interviews and training) of each refugee resettled and to develop and implement a resettlement plan including the early employment of each refugee resettled and to monitor the implementation of such plan.

**(E)** To transmit to the Federal agency administering paragraph (1) an annual report describing the following:

**(i)** The number of refugees placed (by county of placement) and the expenditures made in the year under the grant or contract, including the proportion of such expenditures used for administrative purposes and for provision of services.

**(ii)** The proportion of refugees placed by the agency in the previous year who are receiving cash or medical assistance described in subsection (e) of this section.

**(iii)** The efforts made by the agency to monitor placement of the refugees and the activities of local affiliates of the agency.

**(iv)** The extent to which the agency has coordinated its activities with local social service providers in a manner which avoids duplication of activities and has provided notices to local welfare offices and the reporting of medical conditions of certain aliens to local health departments in accordance with subparagraphs (B)(i) and (C).

**(v)** Such other information as the agency administering paragraph (1) deems to be appropriate in monitoring the effectiveness of agencies in carrying out their functions under such grants and contracts.

The agency administering paragraph (1) shall promptly forward a copy of each annual report transmitted under subparagraph (E) to the Committees on the Judiciary of the House of Representatives and of the Senate.

**(8)** The Federal agency administering paragraph (1) shall establish criteria for the performance of agencies under grants and contracts under that paragraph, and shall include criteria relating to an agency's—

**(A)** efforts to reduce welfare dependency among refugees resettled by that agency,

**(B)** collection of travel loans made to refugees resettled by that agency for travel to the United States,

(C) arranging for effective local sponsorship and other nonpublic assistance for refugees resettled by that agency,

(D) cooperation with refugee mutual assistance associations, local social service providers, health agencies, and welfare offices,

(E) compliance with the guidelines established by the Director for the placement and resettlement of refugees within the United States, and

(F) compliance with other requirements contained in the grant or contract, including the reporting and other requirements under subsection (b)(7).

The Federal administering agency shall use the criteria in the process of awarding or renewing grants and contracts under paragraph (1).

### (c) Project grants and contracts for services for refugees

(1) (A) The Director is authorized to make grants to, and enter into contracts with, public or private nonprofit agencies for projects specifically designed—

(i) to assist refugees in obtaining the skills which are necessary for economic self-sufficiency, including projects for job training, employment services, day care, professional refresher training, and other recertification services;

(ii) to provide training in English where necessary (regardless of whether the refugees are employed or receiving cash or other assistance); and

(iii) to provide where specific needs have been shown and recognized by the Director, health (including mental health) services, social services, educational and other services.

(B) The funds available for a fiscal year for grants and contracts under subparagraph (A) shall be allocated among the States based on the total number of refugees (including children and adults) who arrived in the United States not more than 36 months before the beginning of such fiscal year and who are actually residing in each State (taking into account secondary migration) as of the beginning of the fiscal year.

(C) Any limitation which the Director establishes on the proportion of funds allocated to a State under this paragraph that the State may use for services other than those described in subsection (a)(1)(B)(ii) of this section shall not apply if the Director receives a plan (established by or in consultation with local governments) and determines that the plan provides for the maximum appropriate provision of employment-related services for, and the maximum placement of, employable refugees consistent with performance standards established under section 1516 of Title 29.

(2)(A) The Director is authorized to make grants to States for assistance to counties and similar areas in the States where, because of factors such as unusually large refugee populations (including secondary migration), high refugee concentrations, and high use of public assistance by refugees, there exists and can be demonstrated a specific need for supplementation of available resources for services to refugees.

**(B)** Grants shall be made available under this paragraph—

**(i)** primarily for the purpose of facilitating refugee employment and achievement of self-sufficiency,

**(ii)** in a manner that does not supplant other refugee program funds and that assures that not less than 95 percent of the amount of the grant award is made available to the county or other local entity.

### (d) Assistance for refugee children

**(1)** The Secretary of Education is authorized to make grants, and enter into contracts, for payments for projects to provide special educational services (including English language training) to refugee children in elementary and secondary schools where a demonstrated need has been shown.

**(2)(A)** The Director is authorized to provide assistance, reimbursement to States, and grants to and contracts with public and private nonprofit agencies, for the provision of child welfare services, including foster care maintenance payments and services and health care, furnished to any refugee child (except as provided in subparagraph (B)) during the thirty-six month period beginning with the first month in which such refugee child is in the United States.

**(B)(i)** In the case of a refugee child who is unaccompanied by a parent or other close adult relative (as defined by the Director), the services described in subparagraph (A) may be furnished until the month after the child attains eighteen years of age (or such higher age as the State's child welfare services plan under part B of title IV of the Social Security Act [42 U.S.C.A. § 620 et seq.] prescribes for the availability of such services to any other child in that State).

**(ii)** The Director shall attempt to arrange for the placement under the laws of the States of such unaccompanied refugee children, who have been accepted for admission to the United States, before (or as soon as possible after) their arrival in the United States. During any interim period while such a child is in the United States or in transit to the United States but before the child is so placed, the Director shall assume legal responsibility (including financial responsibility) for the child, if necessary, and is authorized to make necessary decisions to provide for the child's immediate care.

**(iii)** In carrying out the Director's responsibilities under clause (ii), the Director is authorized to enter into contracts with appropriate public or private nonprofit agencies under such conditions as the Director determines to be appropriate.

**(iv)** The Director shall prepare and maintain a list of (I) all such unaccompanied children who have entered the United States after April 1, 1975, (II) the names and last known residences of their parents (if living) at the time of arrival, and (III) the children's location, status, and progress.

### (e) Cash assistance and medical assistance for refugees

**(1)** The Director is authorized to provide assistance, reimbursement to States, and grants to, and contracts with, public or private nonprofit agencies for 100 per centum of the cash assistance and medical assistance provided to any refugee during the thirty-six month period beginning with the first month in which such refugee has entered the United States and for the identifiable and reasonable administrative costs of providing this assistance.

**(2)(A)** Cash assistance provided under this subsection to an employable refugee is conditioned, except for good cause shown—

    **(i)** on the refugee's registration with an appropriate agency providing employment services described in subsection (c)(1)(A)(i) of this section, or, if there is no such agency available, with an appropriate State or local employment service;

    **(ii)** on the refugee's participation in any available and appropriate social service or targeted assistance program (funded under subsection (c) of this section) providing job or language training in the area in which the refugee resides; and

    **(iii)** on the refugee's acceptance of appropriate offers of employment.

**(B)** Cash assistance shall not be made available to refugees who are full-time students in institutions of higher education (as defined by the Director after consultation with the Secretary of Education).

**(C)** In the case of a refugee who—

    **(i)** refuses an offer of employment which has been determined to be appropriate either by the agency responsible for the initial resettlement of the refugee under subsection (b) of this section or by the appropriate State or local employment service,

    **(ii)** refuses to go to a job interview which has been arranged through such agency or service, or

    **(iii)** refuses to participate in a social service or targeted assistance program referred to in subparagraph (A)(ii) which such agency or service determines to be available and appropriate,

cash assistance to the refugee shall be terminated (after opportunity for an administrative hearing) for a period of three months (for the first such refusal) or for a period of six months (for any subsequent refusal).

**(3)** The Director shall develop plans to provide English training and other appropriate services and training to refugees receiving cash assistance.

**(4)** If a refugee is eligible for aid or assistance under a State plan approved under part A of title IV or under title XIX of the Social Security Act [42 U.S.C.A. §§ 601 et seq., 1396 et seq.], or for supplemental security income benefits (including State supplementary payments) under the program established under title XVI of that Act [42 U.S.C.A. § 1381 et seq.], funds authorized under this subsection shall only be used for the non-Federal share of such aid or assistance, or for such supplementary payments, with respect to cash and medical assistance provided with respect to such refugee under this paragraph.

**(5)** The Director is authorized to allow for the provision of medical assistance under paragraph (1) to any refugee, during the one-year period after entry, who does not qualify for assistance under a State plan approved under title XIX of the Social Security Act [42 U.S.C.A. § 1396 et seq.] on account of any resources or income requirement of such plan, but only if the Director determines that—

    **(A)** this will (i) encourage economic self-sufficiency, or (ii) avoid a significant burden on State and local governments; and

    **(B)** the refugee meets such alternative financial resources and income requirements as the Director shall establish.

**(6)** As a condition for receiving assistance, reimbursement, or a contract under this subsection and notwithstanding any other provision of law, a State or agency must provide assurances that whenever a refugee applies for cash or medical assistance for which assistance or reimbursement is provided under this subsection, the State or agency must notify promptly the agency (or local affiliate) which provided for the initial resettlement of the refugee under subsection (b) of this section of the fact that the refugee has so applied.

**(7)(A)** The Secretary shall develop and implement alternative projects for refugees who have been in the United States less than thirty-six months, under which refugees are provided interim support, medical services, support services, and case management, as needed, in a manner that encourages self-sufficiency, reduces welfare dependency, and fosters greater coordination among the resettlement agencies and service providers. The Secretary may permit alternative projects to cover specific groups of refugees who have been in the United States 36 months or longer if the Secretary determines that refugees in the group have been significantly and disproportionately dependent on welfare and need the services provided under the project in order to become self-sufficient and that their coverage under the projects would be cost-effective.

    **(B)** Refugees covered under such alternative projects shall be precluded from receiving cash or medical assistance under any other paragraph of this subsection or under title XIX [42 U.S.C.A. § 1396 et seq.] or part A of title IV of the Social Security Act [42 U.S.C.A. § 601 et seq.].

(C) The Secretary, in consultation with the United States Coordinator for Refugee Affairs, shall report to Congress not later than October 31, 1985, on the results of these projects and on any recommendations respecting changes in the refugee assistance program under this section to take into account such results.

(D) To the extent that the use of such funds is consistent with the purposes of such provisions, funds appropriated under paragraph (1) or (2) of section 414(a) [8 U.S.C.A. § 1524(a)(1) or (2)], part A of title IV of the Social Security Act [42 U.S.C.A. § 601 et seq.] or title XIX of such Act [42 U.S.C.A. § 1396 et seq.], may be used for the purpose of implementing and evaluating alternative projects under this paragraph.

(8) In its provision of assistance to refugees, a State or political subdivision shall consider the recommendations of, and assistance provided by, agencies with grants or contracts under subsection (b)(1) of this section.

**(f) Assistance to States and counties for incarceration of certain Cuban nationals; expeditious removal and return to Cuba**

(1) The Attorney General shall pay compensation to States and to counties for costs incurred by the States and counties to confine in prisons, during the fiscal year for which such payment is made, nationals of Cuba who—

(A) were paroled into the United States in 1980 by the Attorney General,

(B) after such parole committed any violation of State or county law for which a term of imprisonment was imposed, and

(C) at the time of such parole and such violation were not aliens lawfully admitted to the United States—

(i) for permanent residence, or

(ii) under the terms of an immigrant or a nonimmigrant visa issued,

under this chapter.

(2) For a State or county to be eligible to receive compensation under this subsection, the chief executive officer of the State or county shall submit to the Attorney General, in accordance with rules to be issued by the Attorney General, an application containing—

(A) the number and names of the Cuban nationals with respect to whom the State or county is entitled to such compensation, and

(B) such other information as the Attorney General may require.

(3) For a fiscal year the Attorney General shall pay the costs described in paragraph (1) to each State and county determined by the Attorney General to be eligible under paragraph (2); except that if the

amounts appropriated for the fiscal year to carry out this subsection are insufficient to cover all such payments, each of such payments shall be ratably reduced so that the total of such payments equals the amounts so appropriated.

(4) The authority of the Attorney General to pay compensation under this subsection shall be effective for any fiscal year only to the extent and in such amounts as may be provided in advance in appropriation Acts.

(5) It shall be the policy of the United States Government that the President, in consultation with the Attorney General and all other appropriate Federal officials and all appropriate State and county officials referred to in paragraph (2), shall place top priority on seeking the expeditious removal from this country and the return to Cuba of Cuban nationals described in paragraph (1) by any reasonable and responsible means, and to this end the Attorney General may use the funds authorized to carry out this subsection to conduct such policy.

(June 27, 1952, c. 477, Title IV, ch. 2, § 412, as added Pub.L. 96–212, Title III, § 311(a)(2), Mar. 17, 1980, 94 Stat. 111, and amended Pub. L. 97–363, §§ 3(a), 4–6, Oct. 25, 1982, 96 Stat. 1734–1736; Pub.L. 98–164, Title X, § 1011(b), Nov. 22, 1983, 97 Stat. 1061; Pub.L. 98–473, Title I, § 101(d), 98 Stat. 1877; Pub.L. 99–605, §§ 3, 4, 5(a), (b), (c), 6(a), (b), (d), 8, 9(a), (b), 10, 12, 13, Nov. 6, 1986, 100 Stat. 3449 to 3451, 3453 to 3455; Pub.L. 100–525, § 6(b), Oct. 24, 1988, 102 Stat. 2616.)

# § 413.  Congressional reports [8 U.S.C.A. § 1523]

(a) The Secretary, in consultation with the Coordinator, shall submit a report on activities under this subchapter to the Committees on the Judiciary of the House of Representatives and of the Senate not later than the January 31 following the end of each fiscal year, beginning with fiscal year 1980.

(b) Each such report shall contain–

(1) an updated profile of the employment and labor force statistics for refugees who have entered the United States within the five-fiscal-year period immediately preceding the fiscal year within which the report is to be made and for refugees who entered earlier and who have shown themselves to be significantly and disproportionately dependent on welfare, as well as a description of the extent to which refugees received the forms of assistance or services under this subchapter during that period;

(2) a description of the geographic location of refugees;

(3) a summary of the results of the monitoring and evaluation conducted under section 412(a)(7) [8 U.S.C.A. § 1522(a)(7)] during the period for which the report is submitted;

(4) a description of (A) the activities, expenditures, and policies of the Office under this subchapter and of the activities of States, voluntary agencies, and sponsors, and (B) the Director's plans for improvement of refugee resettlement;

(5) evaluations of the extent to which (A) the services provided under this subchapter are assisting refugees in achieving economic self-sufficiency, achieving ability in English, and achieving employment commensurate with their skills and abilities, and (B) any fraud, abuse, or mismanagement has been reported in the provisions of services or assistance;

(6) a description of any assistance provided by the Director pursuant to section 412(e)(5) [8 U.S.C.A. § 1522(e)(5)];

(7) a summary of the location and status of unaccompanied refugee children admitted to the United States; and

(8) a summary of the information compiled and evaluation made under section 412(a)(8) [8 U.S.C.A. § 1522(a)(8)].

(June 27, 1952, c. 477, Title IV, ch. 2, § 413, as added Pub. L. 96–212, Title III, § 311(a)(2), Mar. 17, 1980, 94 Stat. 115, and amended Pub. L. 97–363, §§ 3(b), 7, Oct. 25, 1982, 96 Stat. 1734, 1737; Pub.L. 99–605, § 11, Nov. 6, 1986, 100 Stat. 3455; Pub.L. 100–525, § 9(jj), Oct. 24, 1988, 102 Stat. 2622.)

## § 414. Authorization of appropriations [8 U.S.C.A. § 1524]

(a)(1) There are hereby authorized to be appropriated for each of fiscal years 1987 and 1988 such sums as may be necessary for the purpose of carrying out the provisions (other than those described in paragraphs (2) through (4)) of this chapter.

(2) There are hereby authorized to be appropriated for fiscal year 1987 $74,783,000 and for fiscal year 1988 $77,924,000 for the purpose of providing services with respect to refugees under section 412(c)(1) [8 U.S.C.A. § 1522(c)(1)].

(3) There are hereby authorized to be appropriated for fiscal year 1987 $8,761,000 and for fiscal year 1988 $9,125,000 for the purpose of carrying out section 412(b)(5) [8 U.S.C.A. § 1522(b)(5)].

(4) There are authorized to be appropriated for fiscal year 1987 $5,215,000 and for fiscal year 1988 $5,434,000 for the purpose of carrying out the provisions of section 412(f) [8 U.S.C.A. § 1522(f)].

(b) The authority to enter into contracts under this subchapter shall be effective for any fiscal year only to such extent or in such amounts as are provided in advance in appropriation Acts.

(June 27, 1952, c. 477, Title IV, ch. 2, § 414, as added Pub. L. 96–212, Title III, § 311(a)(2), Mar. 17, 1980, 94 Stat. 116, and amended Pub. L. 97–363, § 2, Oct. 25, 1982, 96 Stat. 1734; Pub.L. 99–605, § 2, Nov. 6, 1986, 100 Stat. 3449; Pub.L. 100–525, § 6(a), Oct. 24, 1988, 102 Stat. 2616.)

\*

# ADDITIONAL IMMIGRATION STATUTES

## TITLE 5. GOVERNMENT ORGANIZATION AND EMPLOYEES

### [The Administrative Procedure Act]

## TITLE 8. ALIENS AND NATIONALITY

## TITLE 50. WAR AND NATIONAL DEFENSE

### UNCODIFIED IMMIGRATION STATUTORY PROVISIONS

**Amerasian Immigration.**

**Adjustment to Lawful Resident Status of Certain Nationals of Countries for Which Extended Voluntary Departure Has Been Made Available.**

**Immigration Nursing Relief Act of 1989.**

**Designation and Adjustment of Soviet and Indochinese Refugees.**

**Immigration Act of 1990**

---

# TITLE 5

# GOVERNMENT ORGANIZATION AND EMPLOYEES

## [Excerpts from the Administrative Procedure Act]

## § 551. Definitions

For the purpose of this subchapter—

(1) "agency" means each authority of the Government of the United States, whether or not it is within or subject to review by another agency, but does not include—

(A) the Congress;

(B) the courts of the United States;

(C) the governments of the territories or possessions of the United States;

(D) the government of the District of Columbia;

or except as to the requirements of section 552 of this title—

(E) agencies composed of representatives of the parties or of representatives of organizations of the parties to the disputes determined by them;

(F) courts martial and military commissions;

(G) military authority exercised in the field in time of war or in occupied territory; or

(H) functions conferred by sections 1738, 1739, 1743, and 1744 of title 12; chapter 2 of title 41; or sections 1622, 1884, 1891–1902, and former section 1641(b)(2), of title 50, appendix;

(2) "person" includes an individual, partnership, corporation, association, or public or private organization other than an agency;

(3) "party" includes a person or agency named or admitted as a party, or properly seeking and entitled as of right to be admitted as a party, in an agency proceeding, and a person or agency admitted by an agency as a party for limited purposes;

(4) "rule" means the whole or a part of an agency statement of general or particular applicability and future effect designed to implement, interpret, or prescribe law or policy or describing the organization, procedure, or practice requirements of an agency and includes the approval or prescription for the future of rates, wages, corporate or financial structures or reorganizations thereof, prices, facilities, appliances, services or allowances therefor or of valuations, costs, or accounting, or practices bearing on any of the foregoing;

(5) "rule making" means agency process for formulating, amending, or repealing a rule;

(6) "order" means the whole or a part of a final disposition, whether affirmative, negative, injunctive, or declaratory in form, of an agency in a matter other than rule making but including licensing;

(7) "adjudication" means agency process for the formulation of an order;

(8) "license" includes the whole or a part of an agency permit, certificate, approval, registration, charter, membership, statutory exemption or other form of permission;

(9) "licensing" includes agency process respecting the grant, renewal, denial, revocation, suspension, annulment, withdrawal, limitation, amendment, modification, or conditioning of a license;

(10) "sanction" includes the whole or a part of an agency—

(A) prohibition, requirement, limitation, or other condition affecting the freedom of a person;

(B) withholding of relief;

(C) imposition of penalty or fine;

(D) destruction, taking, seizure, or withholding of property;

(E) assessment of damages, reimbursement, restitution, compensation, costs, charges, or fees;

(F) requirement, revocation, or suspension of a license; or

(G) taking other compulsory or restrictive action;

(11) "relief" includes the whole or a part of an agency—

(A) grant of money, assistance, license, authority, exemption, exception, privilege, or remedy;

(B) recognition of a claim, right, immunity, privilege, exemption, or exception; or

(C) taking of other action on the application or petition of, and beneficial to, a person;

(12) "agency proceeding" means an agency process as defined by paragraphs (5), (7), and (9) of this section;

(13) "agency action" includes the whole or a part of an agency rule, order, license, sanction, relief, or the equivalent or denial thereof, or failure to act; and

(14) "ex parte communication" means an oral or written communication not on the public record with respect to which reasonable prior notice to all parties is not given, but it shall not include requests for status reports on any matter or proceeding covered by this subchapter.

(Pub.L. 89–554, Sept. 6, 1966, 80 Stat. 381; Pub.L. 94–409, § 4(b), Sept. 13, 1976, 90 Stat. 1247.)

## § 553. Rule making

(a) This section applies, according to the provisions thereof, except to the extent that there is involved—

(1) a military or foreign affairs function of the United States; or

(2) a matter relating to agency management or personnel or to public property, loans, grants, benefits, or contracts.

(b) General notice of proposed rule making shall be published in the Federal Register, unless persons subject thereto are named and either personally served or otherwise have actual notice thereof in accordance with law. The notice shall include—

> (1) a statement of the time, place, and nature of public rule making proceedings;

> (2) reference to the legal authority under which the rule is proposed; and

> (3) either the terms or substance of the proposed rule or a description of the subjects and issues involved.

Except when notice or hearing is required by statute, this subsection does not apply—

> (A) to interpretative rules, general statements of policy, or rules of agency organization, procedure, or practice; or

> (B) when the agency for good cause finds (and incorporates the finding and a brief statement of reasons therefor in the rules issued) that notice and public procedure thereon are impracticable, unnecessary, or contrary to the public interest.

(c) After notice required by this section, the agency shall give interested persons an opportunity to participate in the rule making through submission of written data, views, or arguments with or without opportunity for oral presentation. After consideration of the relevant matter presented, the agency shall incorporate in the rules adopted a concise general statement of their basis and purpose. When rules are required by statute to be made on the record after opportunity for an agency hearing, sections 556 and 557 of this title apply instead of this subsection.

(d) The required publication or service of a substantive rule shall be made not less than 30 days before its effective date, except—

> (1) a substantive rule which grants or recognizes an exemption or relieves a restriction;

> (2) interpretative rules and statements of policy; or

> (3) as otherwise provided by the agency for good cause found and published with the rule.

(e) Each agency shall give an interested person the right to petition for the issuance, amendment, or repeal of a rule.

(Pub.L. 89–554, Sept. 6, 1966, 80 Stat. 383.)

# § 701. Application; definitions

(a) This chapter applies, according to the provisions thereof, except to the extent that—

> (1) statutes preclude judicial review; or

> (2) agency action is committed to agency discretion by law.

(b) For the purpose of this chapter—

(1) "agency" means each authority of the Government of the United States, whether or not it is within or subject to review by another agency, but does not include—

(A) the Congress;

(B) the courts of the United States;

(C) the governments of the territories or possessions of the United States;

(D) the government of the District of Columbia;

(E) agencies composed of representatives of the parties or of representatives of organizations of the parties to the disputes determined by them;

(F) courts martial and military commissions;

(G) military authority exercised in the field in time of war or in occupied territory; or

(H) functions conferred by sections 1738, 1739, 1743, and 1744 of title 12; chapter 2 of title 41; or sections 1622, 1884, 1891–1902, and former section 1641(b)(2), of title 50, appendix; and

(2) "person", "rule", "order", "license", "sanction", "relief", and "agency action" have the meanings given them by section 551 of this title.

(Pub.L. 89–554, Sept. 6, 1966, 80 Stat. 392.)

## § 702. Right of review

A person suffering legal wrong because of agency action, or adversely affected or aggrieved by agency action within the meaning of a relevant statute, is entitled to judicial review thereof. An action in a court of the United States seeking relief other than money damages and stating a claim that an agency or an officer or employee thereof acted or failed to act in an official capacity or under color of legal authority shall not be dismissed nor relief therein be denied on the ground that it is against the United States or that the United States is an indispensable party. The United States may be named as a defendant in any such action, and a judgment or decree may be entered against the United States: *Provided,* That any mandatory or injunctive decree shall specify the Federal officer or officers (by name or by title), and their successors in office, personally responsible for compliance. Nothing herein (1) affects other limitations on judicial review or the power or duty of the court to dismiss any action or deny relief on any other appropriate legal or equitable ground; or (2) confers authority to grant relief if any other statute that grants consent to suit expressly or impliedly forbids the relief which is sought.

(Pub.L. 89–554, Sept. 6, 1966, 80 Stat. 392; Pub.L. 94–574, § 1, Oct. 21, 1976, 90 Stat. 2721.)

## § 703.  Form and venue of proceeding

The form of proceeding for judicial review is the special statutory review proceeding relevant to the subject matter in a court specified by statute or, in the absence or inadequacy thereof, any applicable form of legal action, including actions for declaratory judgments or writs of prohibitory or mandatory injunction or habeas corpus, in a court of competent jurisdiction.  If no special statutory review proceeding is applicable, the action for judicial review may be brought against the United States, the agency by its official title, or the appropriate officer. Except to the extent that prior, adequate, and exclusive opportunity for judicial review is provided by law, agency action is subject to judicial review in civil or criminal proceedings for judicial enforcement.

(Pub.L. 89–554, Sept. 6, 1966, 80 Stat. 392;  Pub.L. 94–574, § 1, Oct. 21, 1976, 90 Stat. 2721.)

## § 704.  Actions reviewable

Agency action made reviewable by statute and final agency action for which there is no other adequate remedy in a court are subject to judicial review.  A preliminary, procedural, or intermediate agency action or ruling not directly reviewable is subject to review on the review of the final agency action.  Except as otherwise expressly required by statute, agency action otherwise final is final for the purposes of this section whether or not there has been presented or determined an application for a declaratory order, for any form of reconsiderations, or, unless the agency otherwise requires by rule and provides that the action meanwhile is inoperative, for an appeal to superior agency authority.

(Pub.L. 89–554, Sept. 6, 1966, 80 Stat. 392.)

## § 705.  Relief pending review

When an agency finds that justice so requires, it may postpone the effective date of action taken by it, pending judicial review.  On such conditions as may be required and to the extent necessary to prevent irreparable injury, the reviewing court, including the court to which a case may be taken on appeal from or on application for certiorari or other writ to a reviewing court, may issue all necessary and appropriate process to postpone the effective date of an agency action or to preserve status or rights pending conclusion of the review proceedings.

(Pub.L. 89–554, Sept. 6, 1966, 80 Stat. 393.)

## § 706.  Scope of review

To the extent necessary to decision and when presented, the reviewing court shall decide all relevant questions of law, interpret constitutional and statutory provisions, and determine the meaning or applicability of the terms of an agency action.  The reviewing court shall—

(1) compel agency action unlawfully withheld or unreasonably delayed; and

(2) hold unlawful and set aside agency action, findings, and conclusions found to be—

    (A) arbitrary, capricious, an abuse of discretion, or otherwise not in accordance with law;

    (B) contrary to constitutional right, power, privilege, or immunity;

    (C) in excess of statutory jurisdiction, authority, or limitations, or short of statutory right;

    (D) without observance of procedure required by law;

    (E) unsupported by substantial evidence in a case subject to sections 556 and 557 of this title or otherwise reviewed on the record of an agency hearing provided by statute; or

    (F) unwarranted by the facts to the extent that the facts are subject to trial de novo by the reviewing court.

In making the foregoing determinations, the court shall review the whole record or those parts of it cited by a party, and due account shall be taken of the rule of prejudicial error.

(Pub.L. 89–554, Sept. 6, 1966, 80 Stat. 393.)

# TITLE 8

## ALIENS AND NATIONALITY

## § 1255b. Adjustment of status of certain nonimmigrants to that of persons admitted for permanent residence

Notwithstanding any other provision of law—

### (a) Application

Any alien admitted to the United States as a nonimmigrant under the provisions of either section 101(a)(15)(A)(i) or (ii) or 101(a)(15)(G)(i) or (ii) [of the Immigration and Nationality Act, as amended,] who has failed to maintain a status under any of those provisions, may apply to the Attorney General for adjustment of his status to that of an alien lawfully admitted for permanent residence.

### (b) Record of admission

If, after consultation with the Secretary of State, it shall appear to the satisfaction of the Attorney General that the alien has shown compelling reasons demonstrating both that the alien is unable to return to the country represented by the government which accredited the alien or the member of the alien's immediate family and that adjustment of the alien's status to that of an alien lawfully admitted for permanent residence would be in the national interest, that the alien is a person of good moral character, that he is admissible for permanent residence under the Act, and that such action would not be contrary to the national welfare, safety, or security, the Attorney General, in his discretion, may record the alien's lawful admission for permanent residence as of the date the order of the Attorney General approving the application for adjustment of status is made.

### (c) Report to the Congress; resolution not favoring adjustment of status; reduction of quota

A complete and detailed statement of the facts and pertinent provisions of law in the case shall be reported to the Congress with the reasons for such adjustment of status. Such reports shall be submitted on the first day of each calendar month in which Congress is in session. If, during the session of the Congress at which a case is reported, or prior to the close of the session of Congress next following the session at which a case is reported, either the Senate or the House of Representatives passes a resolution stating in substance that it does not favor the adjustment of status of such alien, the Attorney General shall thereupon require the departure of such alien in the manner provided by law. If neither the Senate nor the House of Representatives passes such a resolution within the time above specified, the Secretary of State shall, if the alien was classifiable as a quota immigrant at the time of his entry, reduce by one the quota of the quota area to which the alien is chargeable under section 202 of the Act for the fiscal year then current or the next following year in which a quota is available. No quota shall be so reduced by more than 50 per centum in any fiscal year.

### (d) Limitations

The number of aliens who may be granted the status of aliens lawfully admitted for permanent residence in any fiscal year, pursuant to this section, shall not exceed fifty.

(Pub.L. 85–316, § 13, Sept. 11, 1957, 71 Stat. 642; Pub.L. 97–116, § 17, Dec. 29, 1981, 95 Stat. 1619; Pub.L. 100–525, § 9(kk), Oct. 24, 1988, 102 Stat. 2622.)

\* \* \*

## § 1401a. Birth abroad before 1952 to service parent

Section 301(g) of the Immigration and Nationality Act [8 U.S.C.A. § 1401(g)] shall be considered to have been and to be applicable to a child born outside of the United States and its outlying possessions after January 12, 1941, and before December 24, 1952, of parents one of whom is a citizen of the United States who has served in the Armed Forces of the United States after December 31, 1946, and before December 24, 1952, and whose case does not come within the provisions of section 201(g) or (i) of the Nationality Act of 1940.

(Mar. 16, 1956, c. 85, 70 Stat. 50; Pub. L. 97–116, § 18(u)(2), Dec. 29, 1981, 95 Stat. 1621.)

\* \* \*

## § 1525. United States Coordinator for Refugee Affairs

### (a) Appointment; rank

The President shall appoint, by and with the advice and consent of the Senate, a United States Coordinator for Refugee Affairs (hereinafter in this section referred to as the "Coordinator"). The Coordinator shall have the rank of Ambassador-at-Large.

### (b) Duties and functions

The Coordinator shall be responsible to the President for—

(1) the development of overall United States refugee admission and resettlement policy;

(2) the coordination of all United States domestic and international refugee admission and resettlement programs in a manner that assures that policy objectives are met in a timely fashion;

(3) the design of an overall budget strategy to provide individual agencies with policy guidance on refugee matters in the preparation of their budget requests, and to provide the Office of Management and Budget with an overview of all refugee-related budget requests;

(4) the presentation to the Congress of the Administration's overall refugee policy and the relationship of individual agency refugee budgets to that overall policy;

(5) advising the President, Secretary of State, Attorney General, and the Secretary of Health and Human Services on the relationship of overall United States refugee policy to the admission of refugees to, and the resettlement of refugees in, the United States;

(6) under the direction of the Secretary of State, representation and negotiation on behalf of the United States with foreign governments and international organizations in discussions on refugee matters and, when appropriate, submitting refugee issues for inclusion in other international negotiations;

(7) development of an effective and responsive liaison between the Federal Government and voluntary organizations, Governors and mayors, and others involved in refugee relief and resettlement work to reflect overall United States Government policy;

(8) making recommendations to the President and to the Congress with respect to policies for, objectives of, and establishment of priorities for, Federal functions relating to refugee admission and resettlement in the United States; and

(9) reviewing the regulations, guidelines, requirements, criteria, and procedures of Federal departments and agencies applicable to the performance of functions relating to refugee admission and resettlement in the United States.

**(c) Consultations with States, localities, etc.; reports by Secretaries of Labor and Education and inclusion of information in report of Coordinator**

(1) In the conduct of the Coordinator's duties, the Coordinator shall consult regularly with States, localities, and private nonprofit voluntary agencies concerning the sponsorship process and the intended distribution of refugees.

(2) The Secretary of Labor and the Secretary of Education shall provide the Coordinator with regular reports describing the efforts of their respective departments to increase refugee access to programs within their jurisdiction, and the Coordinator shall include information on such programs in reports submitted under INA § 413(a)(1) [8 U.S.C.A. § 1523(a)(1)].

(Pub.L. 96–212, Title III, § 301, Mar. 17, 1980, 94 Stat. 109.)

# TITLE 50

# WAR AND NATIONAL DEFENSE

## Alien Enemies

---

## § 21.  Restraint, regulation, and removal

Whenever there is a declared war between the United States and any foreign nation or government, or any invasion or predatory incursion is perpetrated, attempted or threatened against the territory of the United States by any foreign nation or government, and the President makes public proclamation of the event, all natives, citizens, denizens, or subjects of the hostile nation or government, being of the age of fourteen years and upward, who shall be within the United States and not actually naturalized, shall be liable to be apprehended, restrained, secured, and removed as alien enemies.  The President is authorized in any such event, by his proclamation thereof, or other public act, to direct the conduct to be observed on the part of the United States, toward the aliens who become so liable; the manner and degree of the restraint to which they shall be subject and in what cases, and upon what security their residence shall be permitted, and to provide for the removal of those who, not being permitted to reside within the United States, refuse or neglect to depart therefrom; and to establish any other regulations which are found necessary in the premises and for the public safety.

(R.S. § 4067;  Apr. 16, 1918, ch. 55, 40 Stat. 531.)

## § 22.  Time allowed to settle affairs and depart

When an alien who becomes liable as an enemy, in the manner prescribed in section 21 of this title, is not chargeable with actual hostility, or other crime against the public safety, he shall be allowed, for the recovery, disposal, and removal of his goods and effects, and for his departure, the full time which is or shall be stipulated by any treaty then in force between the United States and the hostile nation or government of which he is a native citizen, denizen, or subject; and where no such treaty exists, or is in force, the President may ascertain and declare such reasonable time as may be consistent with the public safety, and according to the dictates of humanity and national hospitality.

(R.S. § 4068.)

## § 23.  Jurisdiction of United States courts and judges

After any such proclamation has been made, the several courts of the United States, having criminal jurisdiction, and the several justices

347

and judges of the courts of the United States, are authorized and it shall be their duty, upon complaint against any alien enemy resident and at large within such jurisdiction or district, to the danger of the public peace or safety, and contrary to the tenor or intent of such proclamation, or other regulations which the President may have established, to cause such alien to be duly apprehended and conveyed before such court, judge, or justice; and after a full examination and hearing on such complaint, and sufficient cause appearing, to order such alien to be removed out of the territory of the United States, or to give sureties for his good behavior, or to be otherwise restrained, conformably to the proclamation or regulations established as aforesaid, and to imprison, or otherwise secure such alien, until the order which may be so made shall be performed.

(R.S. § 4069.)

## § 24. Duties of marshals

When an alien enemy is required by the President, or by order of any court, judge, or justice, to depart and to be removed, it shall be the duty of the marshal of the district in which he shall be apprehended to provide therefor and to execute such order in person, or by his deputy or other discreet person to be employed by him, by causing a removal of such alien out of the territory of the United States; and for such removal the marshal shall have the warrant of the President, or of the court, judge, or justice ordering the same, as the case may be.

(R.S. § 4070.)

\* \* \*

## § 403h. Admission of essential aliens; limitation on number

Whenever the Director, the Attorney General, and the Commissioner of Immigration and Naturalization shall determine that the entry of a particular alien into the United States for permanent residence is in the interest of national security or essential to the furtherance of the national intelligence mission, such alien and his immediate family shall be given entry into the United States for permanent residence without regard to their inadmissibility under the immigration or any other laws and regulations, or to the failure to comply with such laws and regulations pertaining to admissibility: Provided, That the number of aliens and members of their immediate families entering the United States under the authority of this section shall in no case exceed one hundred persons in any one fiscal year.

(June 20, 1949, c. 227, § 7, formerly § 8, 63 Stat. 212, renumbered July 7, 1958, Pub.L. 85–507, § 21(b)(2), 72 Stat. 337.)

# UNCODIFIED IMMIGRATION STATUTORY PROVISIONS

---

## AMERASIAN IMMIGRATION

### [Title 8, U.S.C.A. § 1101, Note]

Section 584 of the Foreign Operations, Export Financing and Related Programs Appropriations Act, 1988 [§ 101(e) of Pub.L. No. 100–202]:

**(a)(1)** Notwithstanding any numerical limitations specified in the Immigration and Nationality Act, the Attorney General may admit aliens described in subsection (b) to the United States as immigrants if—

**(A)** they are admissible (except as otherwise provided in paragraph (2)) as immigrants, and

**(B)** they are issued an immigrant visa and depart from Vietnam on or after March 22, 1988.

**(2)** The provisions of paragraphs (4), (5) and (7)(A) of section 212(a) of the Immigration and Nationality Act shall not be applicable to any alien seeking admission to the United States under this section, and the Attorney General on the recommendation of a consular officer may waive any other provision of such section (other than paragraph (2)(C) or subparagraph (A), (B), (C), or (D) of paragraph (3)) with respect to such an alien for humanitarian purposes, to assure family unity, or when it is otherwise in the public interest. Any such waiver by the Attorney General shall be in writing and shall be granted only on an individual basis following an investigation by a consular officer.

**(3)** Notwithstanding section 221(c) of the Immigration and Nationality Act, immigrant visas issued to aliens under this section shall be valid for a period of one year.

**(b)(1)** An alien described in this section is an alien who, as of the date of the enactment of this Act [Dec. 22, 1987], is residing in Vietnam and who establishes to the satisfaction of a consular officer or an officer of the Immigration and Naturalization Service after a face-to-face interview, that the alien—

**(A)(i)** was born in Vietnam after January 1, 1962, and before January 1, 1976, and (ii) was fathered by a citizen of the United States (such an alien in this section referred to as a "principal alien");

**(B)** is the spouse or child of a principal alien and is accompanying, or following to join, the principal alien; or

(C) subject to paragraph (2), either (i) is the principal alien's natural mother (or is the spouse or child of such mother), or (ii) has acted in effect as the principal alien's mother, father, or next-of-kin (or is the spouse or child of such an alien), and is accompanying, or following to join, the principal alien.

(2) An immigrant visa may not be issued to an alien under paragraph (1)(C) unless the principal alien involved is unmarried and the officer referred to in paragraph (1) has determined, in the officer's discretion, that (A) such an alien has a bona fide relationship with the principal alien similar to that which exists between close family members and (B) the admission of such an alien is necessary for humanitarian purposes or to assure family unity. If an alien described in paragraph (1)(C)(ii) is admitted to the United States, the natural mother of the principal alien involved shall not, thereafter, be accorded any right, privilege, or status under the Immigration and Nationality Act [this chapter] by virtue of such parentage.

(3) For purposes of this section, the term "child" has the meaning given such term in section 101(b)(1)(A), (B), (C), (D), and (E) of the Immigration and Nationality Act.

(c) Any alien admitted (or awaiting admission) to the United States under this section shall be eligible for benefits under chapter 2 of title IV of the Immigration and Nationality Act to the same extent as individuals admitted (or awaiting admission) to the United States under section 207 of such Act are eligible for benefits under such chapter.

(d) The Attorney General, in cooperation with the Secretary of State, shall report to Congress 1 year, 2 years, and 3 years, after the date of the enactment of this Act [Dec. 22, 1987] on the implementation of this section. Each such report shall include the number of aliens who are issued immigrant visas and who are admitted to the United States under this section and number of waivers granted under subsection (a)(2) and the reasons for granting such waivers.

(e) Except as otherwise specifically provided in this section, the definitions contained in the Immigration and Nationality Act shall apply in the administration of this section and nothing contained in this section shall be held to repeal, amend, alter, modify, effect, or restrict the powers, duties, functions, or authority of the Attorney General in the administration and enforcement of such Act or any other law relating to immigration, nationality, or naturalization. The fact that an alien may be eligible to be granted the status of having been lawfully admitted for permanent residence under this section shall not preclude the alien from seeking such status under any other provision of law for which the alien may be eligible.

(Pub.L. 100–202, § 101(e) [Title V, § 584], Dec. 22, 1987, 101 Stat. 1329–183, as amended Pub.L. 101–167, Title II, Nov. 21, 1989, 103 Stat. 1211; Pub.L. 101–302, Title II, May 25, 1990, 104 Stat. 228; Pub.L. 101–513, Title II, Nov. 5, 1990, 104 Stat. 1996; Pub.L. 101–649, Title VI, § 603(a)(20), Nov. 29, 1990, 104 Stat. 5084.)

# ADJUSTMENT TO LAWFUL RESIDENT STATUS OF CERTAIN NATIONALS OF COUNTRIES FOR WHICH EXTENDED VOLUNTARY DEPARTURE HAS BEEN MADE AVAILABLE

### [Title 8, U.S.C.A. § 1255a, Note]

Section 902 of the Foreign Relations Authorization Act, Fiscal Years 1988 and 1989:

(a) **Adjustment of Status.**—The status of any alien who is a national of a foreign country the nationals of which were provided (or allowed to continue in) "extended voluntary departure" by the Attorney General on the basis of a nationality group determination at any time during the 5–year period ending on November 1, 1987, shall be adjusted by the Attorney General to that of an alien lawfully admitted for temporary residence if the alien—

(1) applies for such adjustment within two years after the date of the enactment of this Act [Dec. 22, 1987];

(2) establishes that (A) the alien entered the United States before July 21, 1984, and (B) has resided continuously in the United States since such date and through the date of the enactment of this Act;

(3) establishes continuous physical presence in the United States (other than brief, casual, and innocent absences) since the date of the enactment of this Act;

(4) in the case of an alien who entered the United States as a nonimmigrant before July 21, 1984, establishes that (A) the alien's period of authorized stay as a nonimmigrant expired not later than six months after such date through the passage of time or (B) the alien applied for asylum before July 21, 1984; and

(5) meets the requirements of section 245A(a)(4) of the Immigration and Nationality Act.

The Attorney General shall provide for the acceptance and processing of applications under this subsection by not later than 90 days after the date of the enactment of this Act [Dec. 22, 1987].

(b) **Status and Adjustment of Status.**—The provisions of subsections (b), (c)(6), (d), (f), (g), (h), and (i) of section 245A of the Immigration and Nationality Act shall apply to aliens provided temporary residence under subsection (a) in the same manner as they apply to aliens provided lawful temporary residence status under section 245A(a) of such Act.

(Pub.L. 100–204, § 902, Dec. 22, 1987, 100 Stat. 1400.)

# IMMIGRATION NURSING RELIEF ACT OF 1989

[Title 8, U.S.C.A. § 1255, Note]

### Adjustment of Status for Certain H-1 Nonimmigrant Nurses:

(a) **In general.**—The numerical limitations of sections 201 and 202 of the Immigration and Nationality Act [sections 1151 and 1152 of this title] shall not apply to the adjustment of status under section 245 of such Act of an immigrant, and the immigrant's accompanying spouse and children—

(1) who, as of September 1, 1989, has the status of a nonimmigrant under paragraph (15)(H)(i) of section 101(a) of such Act [section 1101(a)(15)(H)(i) of this title] to perform services as a registered nurse,

(2) who, for at least 3 years before the date of application for adjustment of status (whether or not before, on, or after, the date of the enactment of this Act) [Dec. 18, 1989], has been employed as a registered nurse in the United States, and

(3) whose continued employment as a registered nurse in the United States meets the standards established for the certification described in section 212(a)(14)* of such Act.

The Attorney General shall promulgate regulations to carry out this subsection by not later than 90 days after the date of the enactment of this Act [Dec. 18, 1989].

(b) **Transition.**—For purposes of adjustment of status under section 245 of the Immigration and Nationality Act [this section] in the case of an alien who, as of September 1, 1989, is present in the United States in the status of a nonimmigrant under section 101(a)(15)(H)(i) of such Act [section 1101(a)(15)(H)(i) of this title] to perform services as a registered nurse, or who is the spouse or child of such an alien, unauthorized employment performed before the date of the enactment of the Immigration Act of 1990 [Nov. 29, 1990] shall not be taken into account in applying section 245(c)(2) of the Immigration and Nationality Act [subsec. (c)(2) of this section] and such an alien shall be considered as having continued to maintain lawful status throughout his or her stay in the United States as a nonimmigrant until the end of the 120-day period beginning on the date the Attorney General promulgates regulations carrying out the amendments made by section 162(f)(1) of the Immigration Act of 1990 [section 162(f)(1) of Pub.L. 101-649].

(c) **Application of Immigration and Nationality Act provisions.**—The definitions contained in the Immigration and Nationality Act shall apply in the administration of this section. The fact that an alien may be eligible to be granted the status of having been lawfully

---

* Probably should read: "212(a)(5)(A)."—   eds.

352

admitted for permanent residence under this section shall not preclude the alien from seeking such status under any other provision of law for which the alien may be eligible.

**(d) Application period.**—The alien, and accompanying spouse and children, must apply for such adjustment within the 5-year period beginning on the date the Attorney General promulgates regulations required under subsection (a).

(Pub.L. 101–238, § 2, Dec. 18, 1989, 103 Stat. 2099, as amended Pub.L. 101–649, Title I, § 162(f)(1), Nov. 29, 1990, 104 Stat. 5011).

# DESIGNATION AND ADJUSTMENT OF SOVIET AND INDOCHINESE REFUGEES

**Foreign Operations, Export Financing, and Related Programs Appropriations Act, 1990:**

**Sec. 599D.   Establishing Categories of Aliens for Purposes of Refugee Determinations [Title 8, U.S.C.A. § 207, Note.]**

(a) **In General.**—In the case of an alien who is within a category of aliens established under subsection (b), the alien may establish, for purposes of admission as a refugee under section 207 of the Immigration and Nationality Act, that the alien has a well-founded fear of persecution on account of race, religion, nationality, membership in a particular social group, or political opinion by asserting such a fear and asserting a credible basis for concern about the possibility of such persecution.

(b) **Establishment of Categories.**—

(1) For purposes of subsection (a), the Attorney General, in consultation with the Secretary of State and the Coordinator for Refugee Affairs, shall establish—

(A) one or more categories of aliens who are or were nationals and residents of the Soviet Union and who share common characteristics that identify them as targets of persecution in the Soviet Union on account of race, religion, nationality, membership in a particular social group, or political opinion, and

(B) one or more categories of aliens who are or were nationals and residents of Vietnam, Laos, or Cambodia and who share common characteristics that identify them as targets of persecution in such respective foreign state on such an account.

(2)(A) Aliens who are (or were) nationals and residents of the Soviet Union and who are Jews or Evangelical Christians shall be deemed a category of alien established under paragraph (1)(A).

(B) Aliens who are (or were) nationals of the Soviet Union and who are current members of, and demonstrate public, active, and continuous participation (or attempted participation) in the religious activities of, the Ukrainian Catholic Church or the Ukrainian Orthodox Church, shall be deemed a category of alien established under paragraph (1)(A).

(C) Aliens who are (or were) nationals and residents of Vietnam, Laos, or Cambodia and who are members of categories of individuals determined, by the Attorney General in accordance with "Immigration and Naturalization Service Worldwide Guidelines for Overseas Refugee Processing" (issued by the Immigra-

354

and Naturalization Service in August 1983) shall be deemed a category of alien established under paragraph (1)(B).

(3) Within the number of admissions of refugees allocated for each of fiscal years 1990, 1991, and 1992 for refugees who are nationals of the Soviet Union under section 207(a)(3) of the Immigration and Nationality Act, notwithstanding any other provision of law, the President shall allocate one thousand of such admissions for such fiscal year to refugees who are within the category of aliens described in paragraph (2)(B).

(c) **Written Reasons for Denials of Refugee Status.**—Each decision to deny an application for refugee status of an alien who is within a category established under this section shall be in writing and shall state, to the maximum extent feasible, the reason for the denial.

(d) **Permitting Certain Aliens Within Categories to Reapply for Refugee Status.**—Each alien who is within a category established under this section and who (after August 14, 1988, and before the date of the enactment of this Act [Nov. 21, 1989]) was denied refugee status shall be permitted to reapply for such status. Such an application shall be determined taking into account the application of this section.

(e) **Period of Application.**—

(1) Subsections (a) and (b) shall take effect on the date of the enactment of this Act [Nov. 21, 1989] and shall only apply to applications for refugee status submitted before October 1, 1992.

(2) Subsection (c) shall apply to decisions made after the date of the enactment of this Act [Nov. 21, 1989] and before October 1, 1992.

(3) Subsection (d) shall take effect on the date of the enactment of this Act [Nov. 21, 1989] and shall only apply to reapplications for refugee status submitted before October 1, 1992.

(f) **GAO Reports on Soviet Refugee Processing.**—

(1) The Comptroller General shall submit to the Committees on the Judiciary of the Senate and of the House of Representatives reports on the implementation of this section in Italy and the Soviet Union. Such reports shall include a review of—

(A) the timeliness and length of individual interviews,

(B) the adequacy of staffing and funding by the Department of State, the Immigration and Naturalization Service, and voluntary agencies, including the adequacy of staffing, computerization, and administration of the processing center in Washington,

(C) the sufficiency of the proposed Soviet refugee processing system within the United States,

(D) backlogs (if any) by ethnic or religious groups and the reasons any such backlogs exist,

(E) the sufficiency of the means of distributing and receiving applications for refugee status in Moscow,

(F) to the extent possible, a comparison of the cost of conducting refugee processing only in Moscow and such cost of processing in both Moscow and in Italy, and

(G) an evaluation of efforts to phase out Soviet refugee processing in Italy.

(2) The Comptroller shall submit a preliminary report under paragraph (1) by December 31, 1989, and a final report by March 31, 1990. The final report shall include any recommendations which the Comptroller General may have regarding the need, if any, to revise or extend the application of this section.

(Pub.L. 101–167, Title V, § 599D, Nov. 21, 1989, 103 Stat. 1261, as amended Pub.L. 101–513, Title V, § 598(a), Nov. 5, 1990, 104 Stat. 2063.)

**Sec. 599E. Adjustment of Status for Certain Soviet and Indochinese Parolees [Title 8, U.S.C.A. § 1255, Note.]**

(a) **In General.**—The Attorney General shall adjust the status of an alien described in subsection (b) to that of an alien lawfully admitted for permanent residence if the alien—

(1) applies for such adjustment,

(2) has been physically present in the United States for at least 1 year and is physically present in the United States on the date the application for such adjustment is filed,

(3) is admissible to the United States as an immigrant, except as provided in subsection (c), and

(4) pays a fee (determined by the Attorney General) for the processing of such application.

(b) **Aliens Eligible for Adjustment of Status.**—The benefits provided in subsection (a) shall only apply to an alien who—

(1) was a national of the Soviet Union, Vietnam, Laos, or Cambodia, and

(2) was inspected and granted parole into the United States during the period beginning on August 15, 1988, and ending on September 30, 1992, after being denied refugee status.

(c) **Waiver of Certain Grounds for Inadmissiblity.**—The provisions of paragraphs (4), (5), and (7)(A) of section 212(a) of the Immigration and Nationality Act shall not apply to adjustment of status under this section and the Attorney General may waive any other provision of such section (other than paragraph (23)(B), (27), (29), or (33)*) with respect to such an adjustment for humanitarian purposes, to assure family unity, or when it is otherwise in the public interest.

* Probably should read: "other than of paragraph (3)"—eds.
(2)(C) and subparagraph (A), (B), (C), or (E)

**(d) Date of Approval.**—Upon the approval of such an application for adjustment of status, the Attorney General shall create a record of the alien's admission as a lawful permanent resident as of the date of the alien's inspection and parole described in subsection (b)(2).

**(e) No Offset in Number of Visas Available.**—When an alien is granted the status of having been lawfully admitted for permanent residence under this section, the Secretary of State shall not be required to reduce the number of immigrant visas authorized to be issued under the Immigration and Nationality Act.

(Pub.L. 101–167, tit. V, § 599E, Nov. 21, 1989, 103 Stat. 1263, as amended Pub.L. 101–513, Title V, § 598(b), Nov. 5, 1990, 104 Stat. 2063; Pub.L. 101–649, Title VI, § 603(a)(22), Nov. 29, 1990, 104 Stat. 5084.)

# IMMIGRATION ACT OF 1990

## § 112. Transition for Spouses and Minor Children of Legalized Aliens [Title 8, U.S.C.A. § 1153, Note]

**(a) Additional Visa Numbers.—**

(1) **In general.**—In addition to any immigrant visas otherwise available, immigrant visa numbers shall be available in each of fiscal years 1992, 1993, and 1994 for spouses and children of eligible, legalized aliens (as defined in subsection (c)) in a number equal to 55,000 minus the number (if any) computed under paragraph (2) for the fiscal year.

(2) **Offset.**—The number computed under this paragraph for a fiscal year is the number (if any) by which—

(A) the sum of the number of aliens described in subparagraphs (A) and (B) of section 201(b)(2) of the Immigration and Nationality Act (or, for fiscal year 1992, section 201(b) of such Act) who were issued immigrant visas or otherwise acquired the status of aliens lawfully admitted to the United States for permanent residence in the previous fiscal year, exceeds

(B) 239,000.

**(b) Order.**—Visa numbers under this section shall be made available in the order in which a petition, in behalf of each such immigrant for classification under section 203(a)(2) of the Immigration and Nationality Act, is filed with the Attorney General under section 204 of such Act.

**(c) Legalized Alien Defined.**—In this section, the term "legalized alien" means an alien lawfully admitted for temporary or permanent residence who was provided—

(1) temporary or permanent residence status under section 210 of the Immigration and Nationality Act,

(2) temporary or permanent residence status under section 245A of the Immigration and Nationality Act, or

(3) permanent residence status under section 202 of the Immigration Reform and Control Act of 1986.

## § 132. Diversity Transition for Aliens Who are Natives of Certain Adversely Affected Foreign States [Title 8, U.S.C.A. § 1153, Note]

**(a) In General.**—Notwithstanding the numerical limitations in sections 201 and 202 of the Immigration and Nationality Act, there shall be made available to qualified immigrants described in subsection (b) 40,000 immigrant visas in each of fiscal years 1992, 1993, and 1994.

**(b) Qualified Alien Described.**—An alien described in this subsection is an alien who—

(1) is a native of a foreign state that is not contiguous to the United States and that was identified as an adversely affected foreign state for purposes of section 314 of the Immigration Reform and Control Act of 1986,

(2) has a firm commitment for employment in the United States for a period of at least 1 year (beginning on the date of admission under this section), and

(3) except as provided in subsection (c), is admissible as an immigrant.

**(c) Distribution of Visa Numbers.**—The Secretary of State shall provide for making immigrant visas provided under subsection (a) available in the chronological order in which aliens apply for each fiscal year, except that at least 40 percent of the number of such visas in each fiscal year shall be made available to natives of the foreign state the natives of which received the greatest number of visas issued under section 314 of the Immigration Reform and Control Act (or to aliens described in subsection (d) who are the spouses or children of such natives).

**(d) Derivative Status for Spouses and Children.**—A spouse or child (as defined in section 101(b)(1)(A), (B), (C), (D), or (E) of the Immigration and Nationality Act) shall, if not otherwise entitled to an immigrant status and the immediate issuance of a visa under this section, be entitled to the same status, and the same order of consideration, provided under this section, if accompanying, or following to join, his spouse or parent.

**(e) Waivers of Grounds of Exclusion.**—In determining the admissibility of an alien provided a visa number under this section, the grounds of exclusion specified in paragraphs (5)(B) and (7)(A) of section 212(a) of the Immigration and Nationality Act shall not apply, and the Attorney General shall waive the ground of exclusion specified in paragraph (6)(C) of such section, unless the Attorney General finds that such a waiver is not in the national interest.

**(f) Application fee.**—The Secretary of State shall require payment of a reasonable fee for the filing of an application under this section in order to cover the costs of processing applications under this section.

# § 204. Treaty Traders (E Nonimmigrants) [Title 8, U.S.C.A. § 1101, Note]

* * *

**(b) Application of Treaty Trader for Certain Foreign States.—** Each of the following foreign states shall be considered, for purposes of section 101(a)(15)(E) of the Immigration and Nationality Act, to be a foreign state described in such section if the foreign state extends reciprocal nonimmigrant treatment to nationals of the United States:

(1) The largest foreign state in each region (as defined in section 203(c)(1) of the Immigration and Nationality Act) which (A) has 1 or more dependent areas (ad determined for purposes of section 202 of such Act) and (B) does not have a treaty of commerce and navigation with the United States.

(2) The foreign state which (A) was identified as an adversely affected foreign state for purposes of section 314 of the Immigration Reform and Control Act of 1986 and (B) does not have a treaty of commerce and navigation with the United States, but (C) had such a treaty with the United States before 1925.

\* \* \*

# § 301. Family Unity [Title 8, U.S.C.A. § 1255a, Note]

**(a) Temporary stay of deportation and work authorization for certain eligible immigrants.—**The Attorney General shall provide that in the case of an alien who is an eligible immigrant (as defined in subsection (b)(1)) as of May 5, 1988, who has entered the United States before such date, who resided in the United States on such date, and who is not lawfully admitted for permanent residence, the alien—

(1) may not be deported or otherwise required to depart from the United States on a ground specified in paragraph (1)(A), (1)(B), (1)(C), (3)(A), of section 241(a) of the Immigration and Nationality Act (other than so much of section 241(a)(1)(A) of such Act as relates to a ground of exclusion described in paragraph (2) or (3) of section 212(a) of such Act) and

(2) shall be granted authorization to engage in employment in the United States, and be provided an "employment authorized" endorsement or other appropriate work permit.

**(b) Eligible immigrant and legalized alien defined.—**

In this section:

(1) The term "eligible immigrant" means a qualified immigrant who is the spouse or unmarried child of a legalized alien.

(2) The term "legalized alien" means an alien lawfully admitted for temporary or permanent residence who was provided—

(A) temporary or permanent residence status under section 210 of the Immigration and Nationality Act [section 1160 of this title],

(B) temporary or permanent residence status under section 245A of the Immigration and Nationality Act [this section], or

(C) permanent residence status under section 202 of the Immigration Reform and Control Act of 1986 [section 202 of Pub.L. 99–603].

(c) **Application of definitions.**—Except as otherwise specifically provided in this section, the definitions contained in the Immigration and Nationality Act [this chapter] shall apply in the administration of this section.

(d) **Temporary disqualification from certain public welfare assistance.**—Aliens provided the benefits of this section by virtue of their relation to a legalized alien described in subsection (b)(2)(A) or (b)(2)(B) shall be ineligible for public welfare assistance in the same manner and for the same period as the legalized alien is ineligible for such assistance under section 245A(h) or 210(f), respectively, of the Immigration and Nationality Act [subsec. (h) of this section or 1160(f) respectively of this title].

(e) **Exception for certain aliens.**—An alien is not eligible for the benefits of this section if the Attorney General finds that—

(1) the alien has been convicted of a felony or 3 or more misdemeanors in the United States, or

(2) the alien is described in section 243(h)(2) of the Immigration and Nationality Act [section 1253(h)(2) of this title].

(f) **Construction.**—Nothing in this section shall be construed as authorizing an alien to apply for admission to, or to be admitted to, the United States in order to obtain benefits under this section.

(g) **Effective date.**—This section shall take effect on October 1, 1991; except that the delay in effectiveness of this section shall not be construed as reflecting a Congressional belief that the existing family fairness program should be modified in any way before such date.

## § 303. Special Temporary Protected Status for Salvadorans [Title 8, U.S.C.A. § 244A, Note]

(a) **Designation.**—

(1) **In general.**—El Salvador is hereby designated under section 244A(b) of the Immigration and Nationality Act, subject to the provisions of this section.

(2) **Period of designation.**—Such designation shall take effect on the date of the enactment of this section and shall remain in effect until the end of the 18-month period beginning January 1, 1991.

**(b) Aliens Eligible.—**

(1) **In general.**—In applying section 244A of the Immigration and Nationality Act pursuant to the designation under this section, subject to section 244A(c)(3) of such Act, an alien who is a national of El Salvador meets the requirements of section 244A(c)(1) of such Act only if—

(A) the alien has been continuously physically present in the United States since September 19, 1990;

(B) the alien is admissible as an immigrant, except as otherwise provided under section 244A(c)(2)(A) of such Act, and is not ineligible for temporary protected status under section 244A(c)(2)(B) of such Act; and

(C) in a manner which the Attorney General shall establish, the alien registers for temporary protected status under this section during the registration period beginning January 1, 1991, and ending June 30, 1991.

(2) **Registration fee.**—The Attorney General shall require payment of a reasonable fee as a condition of registering an alien under paragraph (1)(C) (including providing an alien with an "employment authorized" endorsement or other appropriate work permit under this section). The amount of the fee shall be sufficient to cover the costs of administration of this section. Notwithstanding section 3302 of title 31, United States Code, all such registration fees collected shall be credited to the appropriation to be used in carrying out this section.

**(c) Application of Certain Provisions.—**

(1) **In general.**—Except as provided in this subsection, the provisions of section 244A of the Immigration and Nationality Act (including subsection (h) thereof) shall apply to El Salvador (and aliens provided temporary protected status) under this section in the same manner as they apply to a foreign state designated (and aliens provided temporary protected status) under such section.

(2) **Provisions not applicable.**—Subsections (b)(1), (b)(2), (b)(3), (c)(1), (c)(4), (d)(3), and (i) of such section 244A shall not apply under this section.

(3) **6-Month period of registration and work authorization.**—Notwithstanding section 244A(a)(2) of the Immigration and Nationality Act, the work authorization provided under this section shall be effective for periods of 6 months. In applying section 244A(c)(3)(C) of such Act under this section, "semiannually, at the end of each 6-month period" shall be substituted for "annually, at the end of each 12-month period" and, notwithstanding section 244A(d)(2) of such Act, the period of validity of documentation under this section shall be 6 months.

(4) **Reentry permitted after departure for emergency circumstances.**—In applying section 244A(f)(3) of the Immigration

and Nationality Act under this section, the Attorney General shall provide for advance parole in the case of an alien provided special temporary protected status under this section if the alien establishes to the satisfaction of the Attorney General that emergency and extenuating circumstances beyond the control of the alien requires the alien to depart for a brief, temporary trip abroad.

**(d) Enforcement of Requirement to Depart at Time of Termination of Designation.—**

(1) **Show cause order at time of final registration.**—At the registration occurring under this section closest to the date of termination of the designation of El Salvador under subsection (a), the Immigration and Naturalization Service shall serve on the alien granted temporary protected status an order to show cause that establishes a date for deportation proceedings which is after the date of such termination of designation. If El Salvador is subsequently designated under section 244A(b) of the Immigration and Nationality Act, the Service shall cancel such orders.

(2) **Sanction for failure to appear.**—If an alien is provided an order to show cause under paragraph (1) and fails to appear at such proceedings, except for exceptional circumstances, the alien may be deported in absentia under section 242B of the Immigration and Nationality Act (inserted by section 545(a) of this Act) and certain discretionary forms of relief are no longer available to the alien pursuant to such section.

(Pub.L. No. 101–649, Nov. 29, 1990, 104 Stat. 4978).

\*

# EXCERPTS FROM
# CODE OF FEDERAL REGULATIONS

## TITLE 8

## ALIENS AND NATIONALITY

# PART 208—ASYLUM PROCEDURES

## § 208.1  General.

(a) This part shall apply to all applications for asylum or withholding of deportation that are filed on or after October 1, 1990.  No application for asylum or withholding of deportation that has been filed with a District Director or Immigration Judge prior to October 1, 1990, may be reopened or otherwise reconsidered under the provisions of this part except by motion granted in the exercise of discretion by the Board of Immigration Appeals, an Immigration Judge or an Asylum Officer for proper cause shown.  Motions to reopen or reconsider must meet the requirements of 8 CFR 3.2, 3.8, 3.22, 103.5, and 242.22 where applicable.  The provisions of this part shall not affect the finality or validity of any decision made by District Directors, Immigration Judges, or the Board of Immigration Appeals in any asylum or withholding of deportation case prior to October 1, 1990.

(b) There shall be attached to the Office of Refugees, Asylum, and Parole such number of employees as the Commissioner, upon recommendation from the Assistant Commissioner, shall direct.  These shall include a corps of professional Asylum Officers who are to receive special training in international relations and international law under the joint direction of the Assistant Commissioner, Office of Refugees, Asylum, and Parole and the Director of the Asylum Policy and Review Unit of the Office of Policy Development of the Department of Justice. The Assistant Commissioner shall be further responsible for general supervision and direction in the conduct of the asylum program, including evaluation of the performance of the employees attached to the Office.

(c) As an ongoing component of the training required by paragraph (b) of this section, the Assistant Commissioner, Office of Refugees, Asylum and Parole, shall assist the Deputy Attorney General and the Director of the Asylum Policy and Review Unit, in coordination with the Department of State, and in cooperation with other appropriate sources, to compile and disseminate to Asylum Officers information concerning the persecution of persons in other countries on account of race, religion, nationality, membership in a particular social group, or political opinion, as well as other information relevant to asylum determinations, and shall maintain a documentation center with information on human rights conditions.

[55 FR 30680, July 27, 1990]

## § 208.2 Jurisdiction.

(a) Except as provided in paragraph (b) of this section, the Office of Refugees, Asylum, and Parole shall have initial jurisdiction over applications for asylum and withholding of deportation filed by an alien physically present in the United States or seeking admission at a port of entry. All such applications shall be decided in the first instance by Asylum Officers under this part.

(b) Immigration Judges shall have exclusive jurisdiction over asylum applications filed by an alien who has been served notice of referral to exclusion proceedings under part 236 of this chapter, or served an order to show cause under part 242 of this chapter, after a copy of the charging document has been filed with the Office of the Immigration Judge. The Immigration Judge shall make a determination on such claims *de novo* regardless of whether or not a previous application was filed and adjudicated by an Asylum Officer prior to the initiation of exclusion or deportation proceedings. Any previously filed but unadjudicated asylum application must be resubmitted by the alien to the Immigration Judge.

[55 FR 30680, July 27, 1990]

## § 208.3 Form of application.

(a) An application for asylum or withholding of deportation shall be made in quadruplicate on Form I–589 (Request for Asylum in the United States). The applicant's spouse and children as defined in section 101 of the Act may be included on the application if they are in the United States. An application shall be accompanied by one completed Form G–325A (Biographical Information) and one completed Form FD–258 (Fingerprint Card) for every individual included on the application who is fourteen years of age or older; additional supporting material may also accompany the application and, if so, must be provided in quadruplicate. Forms I–589, G–325A, and FD–258 shall be available from the Office of Refugees, Asylum, and Parole, each District Director, and the Offices of Immigration Judges.

(b) An application for asylum shall be deemed to constitute at the same time an application for withholding of deportation, pursuant to §§ 208.16, 236.3, and 242.17 of this chapter.

[55 FR 30681, July 27, 1990]

## § 208.4 Filing the application.

If no prior application for asylum or withholding of deportation has been filed, an applicant shall file any initial application according to the following procedures:

**(a) With the District Director.** Except as provided in paragraph (b) of this section, applications for asylum or withholding of deportation shall be filed with the District Director having jurisdiction over the place of the applicant's residence or over the port of entry from which the applicant seeks admission to the United States. The District Director shall immediately forward the application to an Asylum Officer with jurisdiction in his district. The Asylum Officer shall notify the Asylum Policy and Review Unit of the Department of Justice and shall forward a copy of the completed application, including any supporting material subsequently received pursuant to § 208.9(e), to the Office of Refugees, Asylum and Parole and the Bureau of Human Rights and Humanitarian Affairs of the Department of State.

**(b) With the Immigration Judge.** Initial applications for asylum or withholding of deportation are to be filed with the Office of the Immigration Judge in the following circumstances (and shall be treated as provided in part 236 or 242 of this chapter):

**(1) During exclusion or deportation proceedings.** If exclusion or deportation proceedings have been commenced against an alien pursuant to part 236 or 242 of this chapter, an initial application for asylum or withholding of deportation from that alien shall be filed thereafter with the Office of the Immigration Judge.

**(2) After completion of exclusion or deportation proceedings.** If exclusion or deportation proceedings have been completed, an initial application for asylum or withholding of deportation shall be filed with the Office of the Immigration Judge having jurisdiction over the prior proceeding in conjunction with a motion to reopen pursuant to 8 CFR 3.8, 3.22 and 242.22 where applicable.

**(3) Pursuant to appeal to the Board of Immigration Appeals.** If jurisdiction over the proceedings is vested in the Board of Immigration Appeals under part 3 of this chapter, an initial application for asylum or withholding of deportation shall be filed with the Office of the Immigration Judge having jurisdiction over the prior proceeding in conjunction with a motion to remand or reopen pursuant to 8 CFR 3.2 and 3.8 where applicable.

**(4)** Any motion to reopen or remand accompanied by an initial application for asylum filed under paragraph (b) of this section must reasonably explain the failure to request asylum prior to the completion of the exclusion or deportation proceeding.

[55 FR 30681, July 27, 1990]

## § 208.5 Special duties toward aliens in custody of the Service.

(a) When an alien in the custody of the Service requests asylum or withholding of deportation or expresses fear of persecution or harm upon return to his country of origin or to agents thereof, the Service shall make available the appropriate application forms for asylum and withholding of deportation and shall provide the applicant with a list, if available, of persons or private agencies that can assist in preparation of the application.

(b) Where possible, expedited consideration shall be given to applications of aliens detained under 8 CFR part 235 or 242. Except as provided in paragraph (c) of this section, such alien shall not be deported or excluded before a decision is rendered on his initial asylum or withholding of deportation application.

(c) A motion to reopen or an order to remand accompanied by an application for asylum or withholding of deportation pursuant to § 208.4(b) shall not stay execution of a final order of exclusion or deportation unless such a stay is specifically granted by the Board or the Immigration Judge having jurisdiction over the motion.

[55 FR 30681, July 27, 1990]

## § 208.6 Disclosure to third parties.

(a) An application for asylum or withholding of deportation shall not be disclosed, except as permitted by this section, or at the discretion of the Attorney General, without the written consent of the applicant. Names and other identifying details shall be deleted from copies of asylum or withholding of deportation decisions maintained in public reading rooms under § 103.9 of this chapter.

(b) The confidentiality of other records kept by the Service (including G–325A forms) that indicate that a specific alien has applied for asylum or withholding of deportation shall also be protected from disclosure. The Service will coordinate with the Department of State to ensure that the confidentiality of these records is maintained when they are transmitted to State Department offices in other countries.

(c) This section shall not apply to any disclosure to:

(1) Any United States Government official or contractor having a need to examine information in connection with:

(i) Adjudication of asylum or withholding of deportation applications;

(ii) The defense of any legal action arising from the adjudication of or failure to adjudicate the asylum or withholding of deportation application;

(iii) The defense of any legal action of which the asylum or withholding of deportation application is a part; or

(iv) Any United States Government investigation concerning any criminal or civil matter; or

(2) Any Federal, state, or local court in the United States considering any legal action:

(i) Arising from the adjudication of or failure to adjudicate the asylum or withholding of deportation application; or

(ii) Arising from the proceedings of which the asylum or withholding of deportation application is a part.

[55 FR 30681, July 27, 1990]

## § 208.7 Interim employment authorization.

(a) The Asylum Officer to whom an initial application for employment authorization (Form I–765) accompanying an application for asylum or withholding of deportation is referred shall authorize employment for a period not to exceed one year to aliens who are not in detention and whose applications for asylum or withholding of deportation the Asylum Officer determines are not frivolous. "Frivolous" is defined as manifestly unfounded or abusive.

(b) Employment authorization shall be renewable, in increments not to exceed one year, for the continuous period of time necessary for the Asylum Officer or Immigration Judge to decide the asylum application and, if necessary, for final adjudication of any administrative or judicial review.

(1) If the asylum application is denied by the Asylum Officer, the employment authorization shall terminate at the expiration of the employment authorization document or sixty days after the denial of asylum, whichever is longer.

(2) If the application is denied by the Immigration Judge, the Board of Immigration Appeals, or upon judicial review of the asylum denial, the employment authorization terminates upon the expiration of the employment authorization document.

(c) In order for employment authorization to be renewed under this section, the alien must provide the Asylum Officer, or District Director where appropriate, with a Form I–765 and proof that he has continued to pursue his application for asylum before an Immigration Judge or sought administrative or judicial review. Pursuit of an application for asylum, for purposes of employment authorization is established by presenting to the Asylum Officer one of the following, depending on the stage of the alien's immigration proceedings:

(1) If the alien's case is pending before the Immigration Judge, and the alien wishes to pursue an application for asylum, a copy of the asylum denial and the Order to Show Cause (Form I–221/I–221S) or Notice to Applicant for Admission Detained for Hearing before Immigration Judge (Form I–122) placing the alien in proceedings after asylum has been denied;

(2) If the immigration judge has denied asylum a copy of the Notice of Appeal (EOIR–26) date stamped by the Office of the Immigration Judge to show that a timely appeal has been filed from a denial of the asylum application by the Immigration Judge; or

(3) If the Board has dismissed the alien's appeal of the denial of asylum, a copy of the petition for judicial review or for habeas corpus pursuant to section 106 of the Immigration and Nationality Act, date stamped by the appropriate court.

(d) In order for employment authorization to be renewed before its expiration, applications for renewal must be received by the Service sixty days prior to expiration of the employment authorization.

(e) Upon the denied applicant's request, the District Director, in his discretion, may grant further employment authorization pursuant to 8 CFR 274a.12(c)(12).

[55 FR 30681, July 27, 1990]

## § 208.8 Limitations on travel outside the United States.

An applicant who leaves the United States pursuant to advance parole granted under 8 CFR 212.5(e) shall be presumed to have abandoned his application under this section if he returns to the country of claimed persecution unless he is able to establish compelling reasons for having assumed the risk of persecution in so returning.

[55 FR 30682, July 27, 1990]

## § 208.9 Interview and procedure.

(a) For each application for asylum or withholding of deportation within the jurisdiction of an Asylum Officer, an interview shall be conducted by that Officer, either at the time of application or at a later date to be determined by the Officer in consultation with the applicant. Applications within the jurisdiction of an Immigration Judge are to be adjudicated under the rules of procedure established by the Executive Office for Immigration Review in parts 3, 236, and 242 of this chapter.

(b) The Asylum Officer shall conduct the interview in a nonadversarial manner and, at the request of the applicant, separate and apart from the general public. The purpose of the interview shall be to elicit all relevant and useful information bearing on the applicant's eligibility for the form of relief sought. The applicant may have counsel or a representative present and may submit affidavits of witnesses.

(c) The Asylum Officer shall have authority to administer oaths, present and receive evidence, and question the applicant and any witnesses, if necessary.

(d) Upon completion of the interview, the applicant or his representative shall have an opportunity to make a statement or comment on the evidence presented. The Asylum Officer, in his discretion, may limit the length of such comments or statement and may require their submission in writing.

(e) Following the interview the applicant may be given a period not to exceed 30 days to submit evidence in support of his application, unless, in the discretion of the Asylum Officer, a longer period is required.

(f) The application, all supporting information provided by the applicant, any comments submitted by the Bureau of Human Rights and Humanitarian Affairs of the Department of State, the Asylum Policy and Review Unit of the Department of Justice, or by the Service, and any other information considered by the Asylum Officer shall comprise the record.

[55 FR 30862, July 27, 1990]

## § 208.10   Failure to appear.

The unexcused failure of an applicant to appear for a scheduled interview may be presumed an abandonment of the application. Failure to appear shall be excused if the notice of the interview was not mailed to the applicant's current address and such address had been provided to the Office of Refugees, Asylum, and Parole by the applicant prior to the date of mailing in accordance with section 265 of the Act and regulations promulgated thereunder, unless the Asylum Officer determines that the applicant received reasonable notice of the interview. Such failure to appear may be excused for other serious reasons in the discretion of the Asylum Officer.

[55 FR 30682, July 27, 1990]

## § 208.11   Comments from the Bureau of Human Rights and Humanitarian Affairs.

(a) At its option, the Bureau of Human Rights and Humanitarian Affairs (BHRHA) of the Department of State may comment on an application it receives pursuant to §§ 208.4(a), 236.3 or 242.17 of this chapter by providing:

(1) An assessment of the accuracy of the applicant's assertions about conditions in his country of nationality or habitual residence and his own experiences;

(2) An assessment of his likely treatment were he to return to his country of nationality or habitual residence;

(3) Information about whether persons who are similarly-situated to the applicant are persecuted in his country of nationality or habitual residence and the frequency of such persecution;

(4) Information about whether one of the grounds for denial specified in § 208.14 may apply; or

(5) Such other information or views as it deems relevant to deciding whether to grant or deny the application.

(b) In all cases, BHRHA shall respond within 45 days of receiving a completed application by either providing comments, requesting additional time in which to comment, or indicating that it does not wish to comment. If BHRHA requests additional time in which to provide comments, the Asylum Officer or Immigration Judge may grant BHRHA up to 30 additional days when necessary to gather information pertinent to the application or may proceed without BHRHA's comments. Failure to receive BHRHA's response shall not preclude final decision by the Asylum Officer or Immigration Judge if at least 60 days have elapsed since mailing the completed application to BHRHA. If the Deputy Attorney General determines that an expedited decision is necessary or appropriate, BHRHA shall provide its comments immediately.

(c) Any Department of State comments provided under this section shall be made a part of the asylum record. Unless the comments are classified under E.O. 12356 (3 CFR, 1982 Comp., p. 166), the applicant shall be given a copy of such comments and be provided an opportunity to respond prior to the issuance of an adverse decision.

[55 FR 30682, July 27, 1990]

## § 208.12 Reliance on information compiled by other sources.

(a) In deciding applications for asylum or withholding of deportation, the Asylum Officer may rely on material provided by the Department of State, the Asylum Policy and Review Unit, the Office of Refugees, Asylum, and Parole, the District Director having jurisdiction over the place of the applicant's residence or the port of entry from which the applicant seeks admission to the United States, or other credible sources, such as international organizations, private voluntary agencies, or academic institutions. Prior to the issuance of an adverse decision made in reliance upon such material, that material must be identified and the applicant must be provided with an opportunity to inspect, explain, and rebut the material, unless the material is classified under E.O. 12356.

(b) Nothing in this part shall be construed to entitle the applicant to conduct discovery directed toward the records, officers, agents, or employees of the Service, the Department of Justice, or the Department of State.

[55 FR 30683, July 27, 1990]

## § 208.13 Establishing refugee status; burden of proof.

(a) The burden of proof is on the applicant for asylum to establish that he is a refugee as defined in section 101(a)(42) of the Act. The testimony of the applicant, if credible in light of general conditions in the applicant's country of nationality or last habitual residence, may be sufficient to sustain the burden of proof without corroboration.

**(b)** The applicant may qualify as a refugee either because he has suffered actual past persecution or because he has a well-founded fear of future persecution.

**(1) Past persecution.** An applicant shall be found to be a refugee on the basis of past persecution if he can establish that he has suffered persecution in the past in his country of nationality or last habitual residence on account of race, religion, nationality, membership in a particular social group, or political opinion, and that he is unable or unwilling to return to or avail himself of the protection of that country owing to such persecution.

**(i)** If it is determined that the applicant has established past persecution, he shall be presumed also to have a well-founded fear of persecution unless a preponderance of the evidence establishes that since the time the persecution occurred conditions in the applicant's country of nationality or last habitual residence have changed to such an extent that the applicant no longer has a well-founded fear of being persecuted if he were to return.

**(ii)** An application for asylum shall be denied if the applicant establishes past persecution under this paragraph but is determined not also to have a well-founded fear of future persecution under paragraph (b)(2) of this section, unless it is determined that the applicant has demonstrated compelling reasons for being unwilling to return to his country of nationality or last habitual residence arising out of the severity of the past persecution. If the applicant demonstrates such compelling reasons, he may be granted asylum unless such a grant is barred by paragraph (c) of this section or § 208.14(c).

**(2) Well-founded fear of persecution.** An applicant shall be found to have a well-founded fear of persecution if he can establish first, that he has a fear of persecution in his country of nationality or last habitual residence on account of race, religion, nationality, membership in a particular social group, or political opinion, second, that there is a reasonable possibility of actually suffering such persecution if he were to return to that country, and third, that he is unable or unwilling to return to or avail himself of the protection of that country because of such fear.

**(i)** In evaluating whether the applicant has sustained his burden of proving that he has a well-founded fear of persecution, the Asylum Officer or Immigration Judge shall not require the applicant to provide evidence that he would be singled out individually for persecution if:

**(A)** He establishes that there is a pattern or practice in his country of nationality or last habitual residence of persecution of groups of persons similarly situated to the applicant on account of race, religion, nationality, membership in a particular social group, or political opinion; and

**(B)** He establishes his own inclusion in and identification with such group of persons such that his fear of persecution upon return is reasonable.

**(ii)** The Asylum Officer or Immigration Judge shall give due consideration to evidence that the government of the applicant's country of nationality or last habitual residence persecutes its nationals or residents if they leave the country without authorization or seek asylum in another country.

**(c)** An applicant shall not qualify as a refugee if he ordered, incited, assisted, or otherwise participated in the persecution of any person on account of race, religion, nationality, membership in a particular social group, or political opinion. If the evidence indicates that the applicant engaged in such conduct, he shall have the burden of proving by a preponderance of the evidence that he did not so act.

[55 FR 30683, July 27, 1990]

## § 208.14 Approval or denial of application.

**(a)** An Immigration Judge or Asylum Officer may grant or deny asylum in the exercise of discretion to an applicant who qualifies as a refugee under section 101(a)(42) of the Act unless otherwise prohibited by paragraph (c) of this section.

**(b)** If the evidence indicates that one or more of the grounds for denial of asylum enumerated in paragraph (c) of this section may apply, the applicant shall have the burden of proving by a preponderance of the evidence that such grounds do not apply.

**(c) Mandatory denials.** An application for asylum shall be denied if:

**(1)** The alien, having been convicted by a final judgment of a particularly serious crime in the United States, constitutes a danger to the community;

**(2)** The applicant has been firmly resettled within the meaning of § 208.15; or

**(3)** There are reasonable grounds for regarding the alien as a danger to the security of the United States.

[55 FR 30683, July 27, 1990]

## § 208.15 Definition of "firm resettlement."

An alien is considered to be firmly resettled if, prior to arrival in the United States, he entered into another nation with, or while in that nation received, an offer of permanent resident status, citizenship, or some other type of permanent resettlement unless he establishes:

**(a)** That his entry into that nation was a necessary consequence of his flight from persecution, that he remained in that nation only as long as was necessary to arrange onward travel, and that he did not establish significant ties in that nation; or

(b) That the conditions of his residence in that nation were so substantially and consciously restricted by the authority of the country of refuge that he was not in fact resettled. In making his determination, the Asylum Officer or Immigration Judge shall consider the conditions under which other residents of the country live, the type of housing made available to the refugee, whether permanent or temporary, the types and extent of employment available to the refugee, and the extent to which the refugee received permission to hold property and to enjoy other rights and privileges, such as travel documentation including a right of entry and/or reentry, education, public relief, or naturalization, ordinarily available to others resident in the country.

[55 FR 30683, July 27, 1990]

## § 208.16   Entitlement to withholding of deportation.

(a) **Consideration of application for withholding of deportation.** If the Asylum Officer denies an alien's application for asylum, he shall also decide whether the alien is entitled to withholding of deportation under section 243(h) of the Act. If the application for asylum is granted, no decision on withholding of deportation will be made unless and until the grant of asylum is later revoked or terminated and deportation proceedings at which a new request for withholding of deportation is made are commenced. In such proceedings, an Immigration Judge may adjudicate both a renewed asylum claim and a request for withholding of deportation simultaneously whether or not asylum is granted.

(b) **Eligibility for withholding of deportation; burden of proof.** The burden of proof is on the applicant for withholding of deportation to establish that his life or freedom would be threatened in the proposed country of deportation on account of race, religion, nationality, membership in a particular social group, or political opinion. The testimony of the applicant, if credible in light of general conditions in the applicant's country of nationality or last habitual residence, may be sufficient to sustain the burden of proof without corroboration. The evidence shall be evaluated as follows:

(1) The applicant's life or freedom shall be found to be threatened if it is more likely than not that he would be persecuted on account of race, religion, nationality, membership in a particular social group, or political opinion.

(2) If the applicant is determined to have suffered persecution in the past such that his life or freedom was threatened in the proposed country of deportation on account of race, religion, nationality, membership in a particular social group, or political opinion, it shall be presumed that his life or freedom would be threatened on return to that country unless a preponderance of the

evidence establishes that conditions in the country have changed to such an extent that it is no longer more likely than not that the applicant would be so persecuted there.

(3) In evaluating whether the applicant has sustained the burden of proving that his life or freedom would be threatened in a particular country on account of race, religion, nationality, membership in a particular social group, or political opinion, the Asylum Officer or Immigration Judge shall not require the applicant to provide evidence that he would be singled out individually for such persecution if:

(i) He establishes that there is a pattern or practice in the country of proposed deportation of persecution of groups of persons similarly situated to the applicant on account of race, religion, nationality, membership in a particular social group, or political opinion; and

(ii) He establishes his own inclusion in and identification with such group of persons such that it is more likely than not that his life or freedom would be threatened upon return.

(4) In addition, the Asylum Officer or Immigration Judge shall give due consideration to evidence that the life or freedom of nationals or residents of the country of claimed persecution is threatened if they leave the country without authorization or seek asylum in another country.

(c) **Approval or denial of application.** The following standards shall govern approval or denial of applications for withholding of deportation:

(1) Subject to paragraph (c)(2) of this section, an application for withholding of deportation to a country of proposed deportation shall be granted if the applicant's eligibility for withholding is established pursuant to paragraph (b) of this section.

(2) An application for withholding of deportation shall be denied if:

(i) The alien ordered, incited, assisted, or otherwise participated in the persecution of any person on account of race, religion, nationality, membership in a particular social group, or political opinion;

(ii) The alien, having been convicted by a final judgment of a particularly serious crime, constitutes a danger to the community of the United States;

(iii) There are serious reasons for considering that the alien has committed a serious nonpolitical crime outside the United States prior to arrival in the United States; or

(iv) There are reasonable grounds for regarding the alien as a danger to the security of the United States.

(3) If the evidence indicates that one or more of the grounds for denial of withholding of deportation enumerated in paragraph (c)(2) of this section apply, the applicant shall have the burden of proving by a preponderance of the evidence that such grounds do not apply.

(4) In the event that an applicant is denied asylum solely in the exercise of discretion, and the applicant is subsequently granted withholding of deportation under this section, thereby effectively precluding admission of the applicant's spouse or minor children following to join him, the denial of asylum shall be reconsidered. Factors to be so considered will include the reasons for the denial and reasonable alternatives available to the applicant such as reunification with his spouse or minor children in a third country.

[55 FR 30684, July 27, 1990]

## § 208.17   Decision.

The decision of an Asylum Officer to grant or deny asylum or withholding of deportation shall be communicated in writing to the applicant, the District Director having jurisdiction over the place of the applicant's residence or over the port of entry from which he sought admission to the United States, the Assistant Commissioner, Refugees, Asylum, and Parole, and the Director of the Asylum Policy and Review Unit of the Department of Justice. An adverse decision will state why asylum or withholding of deportation was denied and will contain an assessment of the applicant's credibility.

[55 FR 30684, July 27, 1990]

## § 208.18   Review of decisions and appeal.

(a) The Assistant Commissioner, Office of Refugees, Asylum, and Parole, shall have authority to review decisions by Asylum Officers, before they become effective, in any cases he shall designate. The Office of the Deputy Attorney General, assisted by the Asylum Policy and Review Unit, shall have authority to review decisions by Asylum Officers, before they become effective, in any cases designated pursuant to 28 CFR 0.15(f)(3). There shall be no right of appeal to the Office of Refugees, Asylum, and Parole, to the Office of the Deputy Attorney General, or to the Asylum Policy and Review Unit, and parties shall have no right to appear before such offices in the course of such review.

(b) Except as provided in § 253.1(f) of this chapter, there shall be no appeal from a decision of an Asylum Officer. However, an application for asylum or withholding of deportation may be renewed before an Immigration Judge in exclusion or deportation proceedings. If exclusion or deportation proceedings have not been instituted against an applicant within 30 days of the Asylum Officer's final decision, the applicant may request in writing that the District Director having jurisdiction over the applicant's place of residence commence such proceedings. Absent exceptional circumstances, the District Director shall thereafter promptly institute proceedings against the applicant.

(c) A denial of asylum or withholding of deportation may only be reviewed by the Board of Immigration Appeals in conjunction with an appeal taken under 8 CFR part 3.

[55 FR 30684, July 27, 1990]

## § 208.19 Motion to reopen or reconsider.

(a) A proceeding in which asylum or withholding of deportation was denied may be reopened or a decision from such a proceeding reconsidered for proper cause upon motion pursuant to the requirements of 8 CFR 3.2, 3.8, 3.22, 103.5, and 242.17 where applicable.

(b) A motion to reopen or reconsider shall be filed:

(1) With the District Director having jurisdiction over the location at which the prior determination was made who shall forward the motion immediately to an Asylum Officer; or

(2) With the Office of the Immigration Judge having jurisdiction over the prior proceeding.

[55 FR 30685, July 27, 1990]

## § 208.20 Approval and employment authorization.

When an alien's application for asylum is granted, he is granted asylum status for an indefinite period. Employment authorization is automatically granted or continued for persons granted asylum or withholding of deportation unless the alien is detained pending removal to a third country. Appropriate documentation showing employment authorization shall be provided by the INS.

[55 FR 30685, July 27, 1990]

## § 208.21 Admission of asylee's spouse and children.

(a) **Eligibility.** A spouse, as defined in section 101(a)(35) of the Act, or child, as defined in section 101(b)(1)(A), (B), (C), (D), or (E) of the Act, may also be granted asylum if accompanying or following to join the principal alien, unless it is determined that:

(1) The spouse or child ordered, incited, assisted, or otherwise participated in the persecution of any persons on account of race, religion, nationality, membership in a particular social group, or political opinion;

(2) The spouse or child, having been convicted by a final judgment of a particularly serious crime in the United States, constitutes a danger to the community of the United States; or

(3) There are reasonable grounds for regarding the spouse or child a danger to the security of the United States.

(b) **Relationship.** The relationship of spouse and child as defined in section 101(b)(1) of the Act must have existed at the time the principal alien's asylum application was approved, except for children born to or legally adopted by the principal alien and spouse after approval of the principal alien's asylum application.

(c) **Spouse or child in the United States.** When a spouse or child of an alien granted asylum is in the United States but was not included in the principal alien's application, the principal alien may request asylum for the spouse or child by filing Form I–730 with the District Director having jurisdiction over his place of residence, regardless of the status of that spouse or child in the United States.

(d) **Spouse or child outside the United States.** When a spouse or child of an alien granted asylum is outside the United States, the principal alien may request asylum for the spouse or child by filing form I–730 with the District Director, setting forth the full name, relationship, date and place of birth, and current location of each such person. Upon approval of the request, the District Director shall notify the Department of State, which will send an authorization cable to the American Embassy or Consulate having jurisdiction over the area in which the asylee's spouse or child is located.

(e) **Denial.** If the spouse or child is found to be ineligible for the status accorded under section 208(c) of the Act, a written notice explaining the basis for denial shall be forwarded to the principal alien. No appeal shall lie from this decision.

(f) **Burden of proof.** To establish the claim of relationship of spouse or child as defined in section 101(b)(1) of the Act, evidence must be submitted with the request as set forth in part 204 of this chapter. Where possible this will consist of the documents specified in 8 CFR 204.2(c)(2) and (c)(3). The burden of proof is on the principal alien to establish by a preponderance of the evidence that any person on whose behalf he is making a request under this section is an eligible spouse or child.

(g) **Duration.** The spouse or child qualifying under section 208(c) of the Act shall be granted asylum for an indefinite period unless the principal's status is revoked.

[55 FR 30685, July 27, 1990]

## § 208.22  Effect on deportation proceedings.

(a) An alien who has been granted asylum may not be excluded or deported unless his asylum status is revoked pursuant to § 208.24. An alien in exclusion or deportation proceedings who is granted withholding of deportation may not be deported to the country as to which his deportation is ordered withheld unless withholding of deportation is revoked pursuant to § 208.24.

(b) When an alien's asylum status or withholding of deportation is revoked under this chapter, he shall be placed in exclusion or deportation proceedings. Exclusion or deportation proceedings may be conducted concurrently with a revocation hearing scheduled under § 208.24.

[55 FR 30685, July 27, 1990]

## § 208.23  Restoration of status.

An alien who was maintaining his nonimmigrant status at the time of filing an application for asylum or withholding of deportation may continue or be restored to that status, if it has not expired, notwithstanding the denial of asylum or withholding of deportation.

[55 FR 30685, July 27, 1990]

## § 208.24  Revocation of asylum or withholding of deportation.

(a) **Revocation of asylum by the Assistant Commissioner, Office of Refugees, Asylum, and Parole.**  Upon motion by the Assistant Commissioner and following a hearing before an Asylum Officer, the grant to an alien of asylum made under the jurisdiction of an Asylum Officer may be revoked if, by a preponderance of the evidence, the Service establishes that:

(1) The alien no longer has a well-founded fear of persecution upon return due to a change of conditions in the alien's country of nationality or habitual residence;

(2) There is a showing of fraud in the alien's application such that he was not eligible for asylum at the time it was granted; or

(3) The alien has committed any act that would have been grounds for denial of asylum under § 208.14(c).

(b) **Revocation of withholding of deportation by the Assistant Commissioner, Office of Refugees, Asylum, and Parole.**  Upon motion by the Assistant Commissioner, and following a hearing before an Asylum Officer, the grant to an alien of withholding of deportation made under the jurisdiction of an Asylum Officer may be revoked if, by clear and convincing evidence, the Service establishes that:

(1) The alien is no longer entitled to withholding of deportation due to a change of conditions in the country to which deportation was withheld;

(2) There is a showing of fraud in the alien's application such that he was not eligible for withholding of deportation at the time it was granted;

(3) The alien has committed any other act that would have been grounds for denial of withholding of deportation under § 208.16(c)(2).

(c) **Notice to applicant.**  Upon motion by the Assistant Commissioner to revoke asylum status or withholding of deportation, the alien shall be given notice of intent to revoke, with the reason therefore, at least thirty days before the hearing by the Asylum Officer.  The alien shall be provided the opportunity to present evidence tending to show that he is still eligible for asylum or withholding of deportation.  If the Asylum Officer determines that the alien is no longer eligible for asylum or withholding of deportation, the alien shall be given written notice that asylum status or withholding of deportation along with employment authorization are revoked.

**(d) Revocation of derivative status.** The termination of asylum status for a person who was the principal applicant shall result in termination of the asylum status of a spouse or child whose status was based on the asylum application of the principal.

**(e) Reassertion of asylum claim.** A revocation of asylum or withholding of deportation pursuant to paragraphs (a) or (b) of this section shall not preclude an applicant from reasserting an asylum or withholding of deportation claim in any subsequent exclusion or deportation proceeding.

**(f) Review.** The Office of the Deputy Attorney General, assisted by the Asylum Policy and Review Unit, shall have authority to review decisions to revoke asylum or withholding of deportation, before they become effective, in any cases designated pursuant to 28 CFR 0.15(f)(3). There shall be no right of appeal to the Office of the Deputy Attorney General or to the Asylum Policy and Review Unit and parties shall have no right to appear before such offices in the course of such review.

**(g) Revocation of asylum or withholding of deportation by the Executive Office for Immigration Review.** An Immigration Judge or the Board of Immigration Appeals may reopen a case pursuant to § 3.2 or § 242.22 of this chapter for the purpose of revoking a grant of asylum or withholding of deportation made under the exclusive jurisdiction of an Immigration Judge. In such a reopened proceeding, the Service must similarly establish by the appropriate standard of evidence one or more of the grounds set forth in paragraphs (a) or (b) of this section. Any revocation under this paragraph may occur in conjunction with an exclusion or deportation proceeding.

[55 FR 30685, July 27, 1990]

# PART 216—CONDITIONAL BASIS OF LAWFUL PERMANENT RESIDENCE STATUS FOR CERTAIN ALIEN SPOUSES AND SONS AND DAUGHTERS

## § 216.1  Definition of conditional permanent resident.

A conditional permanent resident is an alien who has been lawfully admitted for permanent residence within the meaning of section 101(a)(20) of the Act, except that a conditional permanent resident is also subject to the conditions and responsibilities set forth in section 216 of the Act and Part 216 of this chapter. Unless otherwise specified, the rights, privileges, responsibilities and duties which apply to all other lawful permanent residents apply equally to conditional permanent residents, including but not limited to the right to apply for naturalization (if otherwise eligible), the right to file petitions on behalf of qualifying relatives, the privilege of residing permanently in the

United States as an immigrant in accordance with the immigration laws, such status not having changed; the duty to register with the Selective Service System, when required; and the responsibility for complying with all laws and regulations of the United States. All references within this chapter to lawful permanent residents apply equally to conditional permanent residents, unless otherwise specified.

## § 216.2 Notification requirements.

(a) **When alien acquires status of conditional permanent resident.** At the time an alien acquires conditional permanent residence through admission to the United States with an immigrant visa or adjustment of status under section 245 of the Act, the Service shall notify the alien of the conditional basis of the alien's status, of the requirement that the alien apply for removal of the conditions within the ninety days immediately preceding the second anniversary of the alien's having been granted such status, and that failure to apply for removal of the conditions will result in automatic termination of the alien's lawful status in the United States.

(b) **When alien is required to apply for removal of the conditional basis of lawful permanent resident status.** Approximately 90 days before the second anniversary of the date on which the alien obtained conditional permanent residence, the Service should notify the alien a second time of the requirement that the alien and the petitioning spouse must file a petition to remove the conditional basis of the alien's lawful permanent residence. Such notification shall be mailed to the alien's last known address.

(c) **Effect of failure to provide notification.** Failure of the Service to provide notification as required by either paragraph (a) or (b) of this section does not relieve the alien and the petitioning spouse of the requirement to file a joint petition to remove conditions within the 90 days immediately preceding the second anniversary of the date on which the alien obtained permanent residence.

## § 216.3 Termination of conditional resident status.

(a) **During the two-year conditional period.** The director shall send a formal written notice to the conditional permanent resident of the termination of the alien's permanent resident status if the director determines that any of the conditions set forth in section 216(b)(1) of the Act are true. Prior to issuing the Notice of Termination, the director shall provide the alien with an opportunity to review and rebut the evidence upon which the decision is to be based, in accordance with § 103.2(b)(2) of this chapter. The termination of status, and of all rights and privileges concomitant thereto (including authorization to accept or continue in employment in this country), shall take effect as of the date of such determination by the district director, although the alien may request a review of such determination in deportation proceedings. In addition to the notice of termination, the district director shall issue an order to show cause why the alien should not be deported from the United States, in accordance with Part 242 of this chapter.  During the ensuing deportation proceedings, the alien may submit evidence to rebut the determination of the district director. The burden of proof shall be on the Service to establish, by a preponderance of the evidence, that one or more of the conditions in section 216(b)(1) of the Act are true.

**(b) Determination of fraud after two years.**  If, subsequent to the removal of the conditional basis of an alien's permanent resident status, the district director determines that the alien obtained permanent resident status through a marriage which was entered into for the purpose of evading the immigration laws, the director may institute rescission proceedings pursuant to section 246 of the Act (if otherwise appropriate) or deportation proceedings under section 242 of the Act.

## § 216.4  Petition to remove conditional basis of lawful permanent resident status.

**(a) Filing the petition—(1) General procedures.**  Within the 90–day period immediately preceding the second anniversary of the date on which the alien obtained permanent residence, the alien and the alien's spouse who filed the original immigrant visa petition or fiance/fiancee petition through which the alien obtained permanent residence must file a Joint Petition to Remove the Conditional Basis of Alien's Permanent Resident Status (Form I–751) with the Service.  The petition shall be filed within this time period regardless of the amount of physical presence which the alien has accumulated in the United States.  Before Form I–751 may be considered as properly filed, it must be accompanied by the fee required under § 103.7(b) of this chapter and by documentation as described in paragraph (a)(5) of this section, and it must be properly signed by the alien and the alien's spouse.  If the joint petition cannot be filed due to the termination of the marriage through annulment, divorce, or the death of the petitioning spouse, or if the petitioning spouse refuses to join in the filing of the petition, the conditional permanent resident may apply for a waiver of the requirement to file the joint petition in accordance with the provisions of § 216.5 of this part.

**(2) Dependent children.**  Dependent children of a conditional permanent resident who acquired conditional permanent resident status concurrently with the parent may be included in the joint petition filed by the parent and the parent's petitioning spouse.  A child shall be deemed to have acquired conditional residence status concurrently with the parent if the child's residence was acquired on the same date or within 90 days thereafter.  Children who cannot be included in a joint petition filed by the parent and parent's petitioning spouse due to the child's not having acquired conditional resident status concurrently with the parent, the death of the parent, or other reasons may file an

Application for Waiver of Requirement to File Joint Petition for Removal of Conditions (Form I–752).

**(3) Jurisdiction.** Form I–751 shall be filed with the director of the regional service center having jurisdiction over the alien's place of residence.

**(4) Physical presence at time of filing.** A petition may be filed regardless of whether the alien is physically present in the United States. However, if the alien is outside the United States at the time of filing, he or she must return to the United States, with his or her spouse and dependent children, to comply with the interview requirements contained in the Act. Furthermore, if the documentation submitted in support of the petition includes affidavits of third parties having knowledge of the bona fides of the marital relationship, the petitioner must arrange for the affiants to be present at the interview, at no expense to the government. Once the petition has been properly filed, the alien may travel outside the United States and return if in possession of documentation as set forth in § 211.1(b)(1) of this chapter, provided the alien and the petitioning spouse comply with the interview requirements described in § 216.4(b). An alien who is not physically present in the United States during the filing period but subsequently applies for admission to the United States shall be processed in accordance with § 235.11 of this chapter.

**(5) Documentation.** Form I–751 shall be accompanied by evidence that the marriage was not entered into for the purpose of evading the immigration laws of the United States. Such evidence may include:

**(i)** Documentation showing joint ownership of property;

**(ii)** Lease showing joint tenancy of a common residence;

**(iii)** Documentation showing commingling of financial resources;

**(iv)** Birth certificates of children born to the marriage;

**(v)** Affidavits of third parties having knowledge of the bona fides of the marital relationship, or

**(vi)** Other documentation establishing that the marriage was not entered into in order to evade the immigration laws of the United States.

**(6) Termination of status for failure to file petition.** Failure to properly file Form I–751 or Form I–752 within the 90–day period immediately preceding the second anniversary of the date on which the alien obtained lawful permanent residence on a conditional basis shall result in the automatic termination of the alien's permanent residence status and the initiation of proceedings to remove the alien from the United States. In such proceedings the burden shall be on the alien to establish that he or she complied with the requirement to file the joint petition within the designated period. Form I–751 may be filed after the expiration of the 90–day period only if the alien establishes to the satisfaction of the director, in writing, that there was good cause for the failure to file Form I–751 within the required time period. If the joint petition is filed prior to the jurisdiction vesting with the immigration judge in deportation proceedings and the director excuses the late filing and approves the petition, he or she shall restore the alien's permanent resident status, remove the conditional basis of such status and cancel any outstanding order to show cause in accordance with § 242.7 of this chapter. If the joint petition is not filed until after jurisdiction vests with the immigration judge, the immigration judge may terminate the matter upon joint motion by the alien and the Service.

(b) **Interview—(1) Authority to waive interview.** The director of the regional service center shall review the Form I–751 filed by the alien and the alien's spouse to determine whether to waive the interview required by the Act. If satisfied that the marriage was not for the purpose of evading the immigration laws, the regional service center director may waive the interview and approve the petition. If not so satisfied, then the regional service center director shall forward the petition to the district director having jurisdiction over the place of the alien's residence so that an interview of both the alien and the alien's spouse may be conducted. The director must either waive the requirement for an interview and adjudicate the petition or arrange for an interview within 90 days of the date on which the petition was properly filed.

(2) **Location of interview.** Unless waived, an interview on the Form I–751 shall be conducted by an immigration examiner or other officer so designated by the district director at the district office, files control office or suboffice having jurisdiction over the residence of the joint petitioners.

(3) **Termination of status for failure to appear for interview.** If the conditional resident alien and/or the petitioning spouse fail to appear for an interview in connection with the joint petition required by section 216(c) of the Act, the alien's permanent residence status will be automatically terminated as of the second anniversary of the date on which the alien obtained permanent residence. The alien shall be provided with written notification of the termination and the reasons therefor, and an order to show cause shall be issued placing the alien under deportation proceedings. The alien may seek review of the decision to terminate his or her status in such proceedings, but the burden shall be on the alien to establish compliance with the interview requirements. If the alien submits a written request that the interview be rescheduled or that the interview be waived, and the director determines that there is good cause for granting the request, the interview may be rescheduled or waived, as appropriate. If the interview is rescheduled at the request of the petitioners, the Service shall not be required to conduct the interview within the 90–day period following the filing of the petition.

(c) **Adjudication of petition.** The director shall adjudicate the petition within 90 days of the date of the interview, unless the interview is waived in accordance with paragraphs (b)(1) of this section. In adjudicating the petition the director shall determine whether—

(1) The qualifying marriage was entered into in accordance with the laws of the place where the marriage took place;

(2) The qualifying marriage has been judicially annulled or terminated, other than through the death of a spouse;

(3) The qualifying marriage was entered into for the purpose of procuring permanent residence status for the alien; or

(4) A fee or other consideration was given (other than a fee or other consideration to an attorney for assistance in preparation of a lawful petition) in connection with the filing of the petition through which the alien obtained conditional permanent residence.

If derogatory information is determined regarding any of these issues, the director shall offer the petitioners the opportunity to rebut such information. If the petitioners fail to overcome such derogatory information the director may deny the joint petition, terminate the alien's permanent residence and issue an order to show cause to initiate deportation proceedings. If derogatory information not relating to any of these issues is determined during the course of the interview, such information shall be forwarded to the investigations unit for appropriate action. If no unresolved derogatory information is determined relating to these issues, the petition shall be approved and the conditional basis of the alien's permanent residence status removed, regardless of any action taken or contemplated regarding other possible grounds for deportation.

(d) **Decision—(1) Approval.** If the director approves the joint petition he or she shall shall provide written notice of the decision to the alien and shall require the alien to report to the appropriate office of the Service for processing for a new Alien Registration Receipt Card (if necessary), at which time the alien shall surrender any Alien Registration Receipt Card previously issued.

(2) **Denial.** If the director denies the joint petition, he or she shall provide written notice to the alien of the decision and the reason(s) therefor and shall issue an order to show cause why the alien should not be deported from the United States. The alien's lawful permanent resident status shall be terminated as of the date of the director's written decision. The alien shall also be instructed to surrender any Alien Registration Receipt Card previously issued by the Service. No appeal shall lie from the decision of the director; however, the alien may seek review of the decision in deportation proceedings. In such proceedings the burden of proof shall be on the Service to establish, by a preponderance of the evidence, that the facts and information set forth by the petitioners are not true and that the petition was properly denied.

## § 216.5   Waiver of requirement to file petition to remove conditions.

(a) **General.** A conditional resident alien who is unable to meet the requirements for removal of the conditional basis of his or her permanent residence status may file an Application for Waiver of Requirement to File Joint Petition for Removal of Conditions (Form I–752), if the alien was not at fault in failing to meet the filing requirement and the conditional resident alien is able to establish that:

(1) Deportation from the United States would result in extreme hardship, or

(2) The marriage upon which his or her status was based was entered into in good faith on the conditional resident alien's part, but the conditional resident sought termination of the marriage for good cause.

(b) **Fee.** Form I–752 shall be accompanied by the appropriate fee required under § 103.7(b) of this Chapter.

(c) **Jurisdiction.** Form I–752 shall be filed with the regional service center director having jurisdiction over the alien's place of residence.

(d) **Interview.** The regional service center director may refer the application to the appropriate district, files control office or suboffice and require that the alien appear for an interview in connection with the application for a waiver. The director shall deny the application and initiate deportation proceedings if the alien fails to appear for the interview as required, unless the alien establishes good cause for such failure and the interview is rescheduled.

(e) **Adjudication of waiver application—(1) Application based on claim of hardship.** In considering an application for a waiver based upon an alien's claim that extreme hardship would result from the alien's deportation from the United States, the director shall take into account only those factors which arose subsequent to the alien's entry as a conditional permanent resident. The director shall bear in mind that any deportation from the United States is likely to result in a certain degree of hardship, and that only in those cases where the hardship is extreme should the application for a waiver be granted. The burden of establishing that extreme hardship exists rests solely with the applicant.

(2) **Application for waiver based upon the alien's claim that the marriage was entered into in good faith.** In considering whether an alien entered into a qualifying marriage in good faith, the director shall consider evidence relating to the amount of commitment by both parties to the marital relationship. Such evidence may include—

(i) Documentation relating to the degree to which the financial assets and liabilities of the parties were combined;

(ii) The length of time during which the parties cohabited after the marriage and after the alien obtained permanent residence;

(iii) The grounds for which the marriage was terminated, except that a finding by the court that the petitioning spouse was at fault shall not be deemed to be conclusive evidence that the alien spouse sought termination of the marriage for good cause, nor shall a divorce obtained in an area which does not require the determination of fault be deemed to be evidence that the alien spouse sought termination of the marriage for good cause; or

(iv) Other evidence deemed pertinent by the director.

(f) **Decision.** The director shall provide the alien with written notice of the decision on the application for waiver. If the decision is adverse, the director shall advise the alien of the reasons therefor, notify the alien of the termination of his or her permanent residence status, instruct the alien to surrender any Alien Registration Receipt Card issued by the Service and issue an order to show cause placing the alien under deportation proceedings. No appeal shall lie from the decision of the director; however, the alien may seek review of such decision in deportation proceedings.

## PART 274a—CONTROL OF EMPLOYMENT OF ALIENS

### SUBPART A—EMPLOYER REQUIREMENTS

## § 274a.1 Definitions.

For the purpose of this part—

(a) The term "unauthorized alien" means, with respect to employment of an alien at a particular time, that the alien is not at that time either: (1) Lawfully admitted for permanent residence, or (2) authorized to be so employed by this Act or by the Attorney General;

(b) The term "entity" means any legal entity, including but not limited to, a corporation, partnership, joint venture, governmental body, agency, proprietorship, or association;

(c) The term "hire" means the actual commencement of employment of an employee for wages or other remuneration. For the purpose of section 274A(a)(4) of the Act and 274a.5 of this part, a hire occurs when a person or entity uses a contract, subcontract or exchange entered into, renegotiated or extended after November 6, 1986 to obtain the labor of an alien in the United States, knowing that the alien is an unauthorized alien;

(d) The term "refer for a fee" means the act of sending or directing a person or transmitting documentation or information to another, directly or indirectly, with the intent of obtaining employment in the

United States for such person, for remuneration whether on a retainer or contingency basis; however, this term does not include union hiring halls that refer union members or non-union individuals who pay union membership dues;

(e) The term "recruit for a fee" means the act of soliciting a person, directly or indirectly, and referring that person to another with the intent of obtaining employment for that person, for remuneration whether on a retainer or contingency basis; however, this term does not include union hiring halls that refer union members or non-union individuals who pay union membership dues;

(f) The term "employee" means an individual who provides services or labor for an employer for wages or other remuneration but does not mean independent contractors as defined in paragraph (j) of this section or those engaged in casual domestic employment as stated in paragraph (h) of this section;

(g) The term "employer" means a person or entity, including an agent or anyone acting directly or indirectly in the interest thereof, who engages the services or labor of an employee to be performed in the United States for wages or other remuneration. In the case of an independent contractor or contract labor or services, the term "employer" shall mean the independent contractor or contractor and not the person or entity using the contract labor;

(h) The term "employment" means any service or labor performed by an employee for an employer within the United States, including service or labor performed on a vessel or aircraft that has arrived in the United States and has been inspected, or otherwise included within the provisions of the Anti-Reflagging Act codified at 46 U.S.C. 8704, but not including duties performed by nonimmigrant crewmen defined in sections 101(a)(10) and (a)(15)(D) of the Act. However, employment does not include casual employment by individuals who provide domestic service in a private home that is sporadic, irregular or intermittent;

(i) The term "State employment agency" means any State government unit designated to cooperate with the United States Employment Service in the operation of the public employment service system;

(j) The term "independent contractor" includes individuals or entities who carry on independent business, contract to do a piece of work according to their own means and methods, and are subject to control only as to results. Whether an individual or entity is an independent contractor, regardless of what the individual or entity calls itself, will be determined on a case-by-case basis. Factors to be considered in that determination include, but are not limited to, whether the individual or entity: Supplies the tools or materials; makes services available to the general public; works for a number of clients at the same time; has an opportunity for profit or loss as a result of labor or services provided; invests in the facilities for work; directs the order or sequence in which the work is to be done and determines the hours during which the work is to be done. The use of labor or services of an independent contractor are subject to the restrictions in section 274A(a)(4) of the Act and § 274a.5;

(k) The term "pattern or practice" means regular, repeated, or intentional activities, but does not include isolated, sporadic, or accidental acts;

(*l*) The term "knowing" includes not only actual knowledge but also knowledge which may fairly be inferred through notice of certain facts and circumstances which would lead a person, through the exercise of reasonable care, to know about a certain condition.

[52 FR 16221, May 1, 1987, as amended at 53 FR 8612, March 16, 1988; 55 FR 25931, June 25, 1990]

# § 274a.2  Verification of employment eligibility.

(a) **General.** This section states the requirements and procedures persons or entities must comply with when hiring, or when recruiting or referring for a fee, or when continuing to employ individuals in the United States. The Form I–9, Employment Eligibility Verification Form, has been designated by the Service as the form to be used in complying with the requirements of this section. The Form I–9 may be obtained in limited quantities at INS District Offices, or ordered from the Superintendent of Documents, Washington, DC 20402. A blank Form I–9 must be photocopied or printed in accordance with the restrictions set forth in § 299.4 of this chapter, with the exception of the black ink or dye requirements contained therein. When photocopying or printing the Form I–9, both sides must be photocopied or printed. Employers need only complete the Form I–9 for individuals who are hired after November 6, 1986 and continue to be employed after May 31, 1987. Employers shall have until September 1, 1987 to complete the Form I–9 for individuals hired from November 7, 1986 through May 31, 1987. Recruiters and referrers for a fee need complete the Form I–9 only for those individuals who are recruited or referred after May 31, 1987. In conjunction with completing the Form I–9, an employer or recruiter or referrer for a fee must examine documents that evidence the identity and employment eligibility of the individual. The employer or recruiter or referrer for a fee and the individual must each complete an attestation on the Form I–9 under penalty of perjury.

(b) **Employment verification requirements—**

(1) **Examination of documents and completion of Form I–9.**

(i) A person or entity that hires or recruits or refers for a fee an individual for employment must ensure that the individual properly:

(A) Complete section 1—"Employee Information and Verification"—on the Form I–9 at the time of hiring; or if an individual is unable to complete the Form I–9 or needs it translated, someone may assist him or her. The preparer or translator must read the Form to the individual, assist him or her in completing Section 1—"Employee Information and Verification," and have the individual sign or mark the Form in the appropriate place. The preparer or translator must then complete the "Preparer/Translator Certification" portion of the Form I-9; and

(B) Present to the employer or the recruiter or referrer for a fee documentation as set forth in paragraph (b)(1)(v) of this section establishing his or her identity and employment eligibility within the time limits set forth in paragraphs (b)(1)(ii) through (b)(1)(v) of this section.

(ii) Except as provided in paragraph (b)(1)(viii) of this section, an employer, his or her agent, or any9one acting directly or indirectly in the interest thereof, must within three business days of the hire:

(A) Physically examine the documentation presented by the individual establishing identity and employment eligibility as set forth in paragraph (b)(1)(v) of this section and ensure that the documents presented appear to be genuine and to relate to the individual; and

(B) Complete section 2—"Employer Review and Verification"—of the Form I-9.

(iii) An employer, his or her agent, or anyone acting directly or indirectly in the interest thereof, who hires an individual for employment for duration of less than three business days must comply with paragraphs (b)(1)(ii)(A) and (b)(1)(ii)(B) of this section at the time of the hire. A receipt for the application of such documentation, as described in paragraph (b)(1)(vi) of this section, may not be accepted by the employer.

(iv) A recruiter or referrer for a fee for employment must comply with paragraphs (b)(1)(ii)(A) and (b)(1)(ii)(B) of this section within three business days of the date the referred individual is hired by the employer. Recruiters and referrers may designate agents to complete the employment verification procedures on their behalf including but not limited to notaries, national associations, or employers. If a recruiter or referrer designates an employer to complete the employment verification procedures, the employer need only provide the recruiter or referrer with a photocopy of the Form I-9.

(v) The individual may present either an original document which establishes both employment authorization and identity, or an original document which establishes employment authorization and a separate original document which establishes identity. The document identification number and expiration date (if any) must be noted in the appropriate space provided on the Form I-9. An employer or a recruiter or referrer for a fee may not specify which document or documents an individual is to present.

**(A)** The following documents, so long as they appear to relate to the individual presenting the document, are acceptable to evidence both identity and employment eligibility:

**(1)** United States passport (Unexpired or expired);

**(2)** Certificate of United States Citizenship, INS Form N–560 or N–561;

**(3)** Certificate of Naturalization, INS Form N–550 or N–570;

**(4)** An unexpired foreign passport which:

**(i)** contains an unexpired stamp therein which reads, "Processed for I–551. Temporary Evidence of Lawful Admission for permanent residence. Valid until _____. Employment authorized." or

**(ii)** has attached thereto a Form I–94 bearing the same name as the passport and contains an employment authorization stamp, so long as the period of endorsement has not yet expired and the proposed employment is not in conflict with any restrictions or limitations identified on the Form I–94.

**(5)** Alien Registration Receipt Card, INS Form I–151 or Resident Alien INS Form I–551, provided that it contains a photograph of the bearer;

**(6)** An unexpired Temporary Resident Card, INS Form 688;

**(7)** An unexpired Employment Authorization Card, INS Form I–688A;

**(8)** An unexpired reentry permit, INS Form I–327;

**(9)** An unexpired Refugee Travel document, INS Form I–571;

**(10)** An unexpired employment authorization document issued by the Immigration and Naturalization Service which contains a photograph, INS Form I–688B.

**(B)** The following documents are acceptable to establish identity only:

**(1)** For individuals 16 years of age or older:

**(i)** A driver's license or identification card containing a photograph, issued by a state (as defined in section 101(a)(36) of the Act) or an outlying possession of the United States (as defined by section 101(a)(29) of the Act). If the drivers's license or identification card does not contain a photograph, identifying information should be included such as: name, date of birth, sex, height, color of eyes, and address;

(ii) School identification card with a photograph;

(iii) U.S. military card or draft record;

(iv) Identification card issued by federal, state, or local government agencies or entities;

(v) Military dependent's identification card;

(vi) Native American tribal documents;

(vii) United States Coast Guard Merchant Mariner Card;

(viii) Driver's license issued by a Canadian government authority;

(2) For individuals under age 18 who are unable to produce a document listed in paragraph (b)(1)(v)(B)(1) of this section, the following documents are acceptable to establish identity only:

(i) School record or report card;

(ii) Clinic doctor or hospital record;

(iii) Daycare or nursery school record.

(3) Minors under the age of 18 who are unable to produce one of the identity documents listed in paragraph (b)(1)(v)(B)(1) or (2) of this section are exempt from producing one of the enumerated identity documents if the following procedures are followed:

(i) The minor's parent or legal guardian completes on the Form I-9 Section 1—"Employee Information and Verification" and in the space for the minor's signature, the parent or legal guardian writes the words, "minor under age 18."

(ii) The minor's parent or legal guardian completes on the Form I-9 the "Preparer/Translator certification."

(iii) The employer or the recruiter or referrer for a fee writes in Section 2—"Employer Review and Verification" under List B in the space after the words "Document Identification #" the words, "minor under age 18."

(4) Individuals with handicaps, who are unable to produce one of the identity documents listed in paragraph (b)(1)(v)(B)(1) or (2) of this section, who are being placed into employment by a nonprofit organization, association or as part of a rehabilitation program, may follow the procedures for establishing identity provided in this section for minors under the age of 18, substituting where appropriate, the term "special placement" for "minor un-

der age 18", and permitting, in addition to a parent or legal guardian, a representative from the nonprofit organization, association or rehabilitation program placing the individual into a position of employment, to fill out and sign in the appropriate section, the Form I-9. For purposes of this section the term "individual with handicaps" means any person who

(i) Has a physical or mental impairment which substantially limits one or more of such person's major life activities,

(ii) Has a record of such impairment, or

(iii) Is regarded as having such impairment.

(C) The following are acceptable documents to establish employment authorization only:

(1) A social security number card other than one which has printed on its face "not valid for employment purposes";

(2) A Certification of Birth Abroad issued by the Department of State, Form FS-545;

(3) A Certification of Birth Abroad issued by the Department of State, Form DS-1350;

(4) An original or certified copy of a birth certificate issued by a State, county, or municipal authority bearing a seal;

(5) Native American tribal document;

(6) United States Citizen Identification Card, INS Form I-197;

(7) Identification card for use of resident citizen in the United States, INS Form I-179;

(8) An employment authorization document issued by the Immigration and Naturalization Service;

(vi) If an individual is unable to provide the required document or documents within the time periods specified in paragraphs (b)(1)(ii) and (b)(1)(iv) of this section, the individual must present a receipt for the application of the document or documents within three business days of the hire and present the required document or documents within 21 business days of the hire. This section is not applicable to an alien who does not have work authorization at the time of hire.

(vii) If an individual's employment authorization expires, or the Service informs the employer, recruiter, or referrer for a fee, in writing, that the employment authorization document presented is insufficient to establish employment authorization, the employer, recruiter or referrer for a fee must complete a new Form I–9 pursuant to the requirements of paragraph 274a.2(b) of this section. In completing the new Form I–9, the employee or referred individual must present a document that either shows continuing employment eligibility or is a new grant of work authorization. The employer or the recruiter or referrer for a fee must review this document and, if it appears to be genuine and to relate to the individual, note the document's identification number and expiration date on the new Form I–9. The new Form I–9 must be maintained along with the previous completed Form I–9 in accordance with paragraph 274a.2(b)(2) of this section.

(viii) An employer is not required to reverify an employee's employment eligibility as set forth in paragraphs (b)(1)(i) through (b)(1)(v) of this section if the employee is continuing his or her employment.

(A) An individual is continuing his or her employment if the employee at all times has reasonable expectation of employment. The person or entity (hereafter the claimant) who is claiming that an employee is a continuing employee must prove at all times that the employee expected to resume employment and that the employee's expectation is reasonable. Whether an employee's expectation is reasonable will be determined on a case-by-case basis taking into consideration several factors. Factors which would indicate that an individual is a continuing employee include, but are not limited to:

(1) The employee in question was employed by claimant on a regular and substantial basis rather than on a sporadic, irregular or intermittent basis. A determination of a regular and substantial basis is based on a comparison of other workers who are similarly employed by the claimant;

(2) The employee in question complied with the claimant's established and published policy regarding his or her absence;

(3) The claimant's past history of recalling absent employees for employment indicates a likelihood that the employee in question will resume employment with claimant within a reasonable time in the future;

(4) The former position held by the employee in question has not been taken by a replacement worker;

(5) The employee in question has not sought or obtained regular and substantial employment with another new employer during his or her absence from employment with claimant (prior employer). A determination of regu-

lar and substantial employment is based on a comparison of other workers who are similarly employed by the new employer;

(6) The employee in question has not sought or obtained benefits during his or her absence from employment with claimant that are inconsistent with an expectation of resuming employment with claimant within a reasonable time in the future;

(7) The financial condition of the claimant indicates a likelihood that the employee in question will resume employment with claimant within a reasonable time in the future;

(8) The oral and/or written communication between claimant, claimant's supervisory employees and the employee in question indicates a likelihood that the employee in question will resume employment with claimant within a reasonable time in the future;

(9) The employment is not seasonal in nature.

(B) "Continuing employment" includes but is not limited to situations where:

(1) An employee takes approved paid or unpaid leave on account of study, illness or disability of a family member, illness or pregnancy, maternity or paternity leave vacation, union business, or other temporary leave approved by the employer;

(2) An employee is promoted, demoted, or gets a pay raise;

(3) An employee is temporarily laid off for lack of work;

(4) An employee is on strike or in a labor dispute;

(5) An employee is reinstated after disciplinary suspension for wrongful termination, found unjustified by any court, arbitrator, or administrative body, or otherwise resolved through reinstatement or settlement;

(6) An employee transfers from one distinct unit of an employer to another distinct unit of the same employer; the employer may transfer the employee's Form I–9 to the receiving unit; or

(7) An employee continues his or her employment with a related, successor, or reorganized employer, provided that the employer obtains and maintains from the previous employer records and Forms I–9 where applicable. For this purpose, a related, successor, or reorganized employer includes:

(i) The same employer at another location;

(ii) An employer who continues to employ some or all of a previous employer's workforce in cases involving a corporate reorganization, merger, or sale of stock or assets.

(2) **Retention and Inspection of Form I-9.** (i) Form I-9 must be retained by an employer or a recruiter or referrer for a fee for the following time periods:

(A) In the case of an employer, three years after the date of the hire or one year after the date the individual's employment is terminated, whichever is later; or

(B) In the case of a recruiter or referrer for a fee, three years after the date of the hire.

(ii) Any person or entity required to retain Form I-9 in accordance with this section shall be provided with at least three days notice prior to an inspection of the Forms I-9 by an authorized Department of Labor or Service officer. At the time of inspection, Forms I-9 must be made available in their original form or on microfilm or microfiche at the location where the request for production was made. If Forms I-9 are kept at another location, the person or entity must inform the Department of Labor or Service officer of the location where the forms are kept and make arrangements for the inspection. Inspections may be performed at an INS office. A recruiter or referrer for a fee who has designated an employer to complete the employment verification procedures may present a photocopy of the Form I-9 in lieu of presenting the Form I-9 in its original form or on microfilm, as set forth in paragraph (b)(1)(iv) of this section. No subpoena or warrant shall be required for such inspection. Any refusal or delay in presentation of the Forms I-9 for inspection is a violation of the retention requirements as set forth in section 274A(b)(3) of the Act. In addition, if the person or entity has not complied with a request to present the Forms I-9, any Service officer listed in § 287.4 of this chapter may compel production of the Forms I-9 by issuing a subpoena.

(iii) The following standards shall apply to Forms I-9 presented on microfilm (or microfiche) submitted to the Service or Department of Labor: Microfilm, when displayed on a microfilm reader (viewer) or reproduced on paper must exhibit a high degree of legibility and readability. For this purpose, legibility is defined as the quality of a letter or numeral which enables the observer to positively and quickly identify it to the exclusion of all other letters or numerals. Readability is defined as the quality of a group of letters or numerals being recognizable as words or whole numbers. A detailed index of all microfilmed data shall be maintained and arranged in such a manner as to permit the immediate location of any particular record. It is the responsibility of the employer, recruiter or referrer for a fee.

(A) To provide for the processing, storage and maintenance of all microfilm and

(B) To be able to make the contents thereof available as required by law. The person or entity presenting the microfilm will make available a reader-printer at the examination site for the ready reading, location and reproduction of any record or records being retained on microfilm. Readers-printers made available to DOL or Service officers shall provide safety features and be in clean condition, properly maintained and in good working order. The readers-printers must have the capacity to display and print a complete page of information. A person or entity who is determined to have failed to comply with the criteria established by this regulation for the presentation of microfilm or microfiche to the Service and at the time of the inspection does not present a properly completed Form I–9 for the employee, is in violation of section 274A(a)(1)(B) of the Act and 8 CFR 274a.2(b)(2).

(3) **Copying of documentation.** An employer, or a recruiter or referrer for a fee may, but is not required to, copy a document presented by an individual solely for the purpose of complying with the verification requirements of this section. If such copy is made, it must be retained with the Form I–9. The retention requirements in paragraph (b)(2) of this section do not apply to the photocopies. The copying and retention of any such document does not relieve the employer from the requirement to fully complete section 2 of the Form I–9.

(4) **Limitation on use of Form I–9.** Any information contained in or appended to the Form I–9, including copies of documents listed in paragraph (c) of this section used to verify an individual's identity or employment eligibility, may be used only for enforcement of the Act and Sections 1001, 1028, 1546, or 1621 of Title 18, United States Code.

(c) **Employment verification requirements in the case of hiring an individual who was previously employed.** (1) When an employer hires an individual whom that person or entity has previously employed, if the employer has previously completed the Form I–9 and complied with the verification requirements set forth in paragraph (b) of this section with regard to the individual, the employer may (in lieu of completing a new Form I–9) inspect the previously completed Form I–9 and:

(i) If upon inspection of the Form I–9 relating to the individual, the employer determines that the Form I–9 relates to such individual and that the individual is eligible to work, no additional verification or new Form I–9 need be completed if the employer reverifies the individual's employment eligibility on the Form I–9 and the individual is hired within three years of the date of the initial execution of the Form I–9, or

(ii) If upon inspection of the Form I–9, the employer determines that the individual's employment authorization has expired, or the Service informs the employer that the employment eligibility document presented is insufficient to establish employment authorization, the employer shall not rehire the individual unless the employer completes a new Form I–9 pursuant to the requirements of 274a.2(b) of this section.

(2) For purposes of retention of the Form I–9 by an employer for a previously employed individual hired pursuant to paragraph (c)(1) of this section, the employer shall retain the Form I–9 for a period of three years commencing from the date of the initial execution of the Form I–9 or one .year after the individual's employment is terminated, whichever is later.

(d) **Employment verification requirements in the case of recruiting or referring for a fee an individual who was previously recruited or referred.** (1) When a recruiter or referrer for a fee refers an individual for whom that recruiter or referrer for a fee has previously completed a Form I–9, and the recruiter or referrer has completed the Form I–9 and complied with the verification requirements set forth in paragraph (b) of this section with regard to the individual, the recruiter or referrer may (in lieu of completing a new Form I–9) inspect the previously completed Form I–9 and:

(i) If upon inspection of the Form I–9 relating to the individual, the recruiter or referrer determines that the Form I–9 relates to the individual and that the individual is authorized to work, no additional verification or new Form I–9 need be completed if the recruiter or referrer for a fee reverifies the individual's employment eligibility on the Form I–9 and the individual is referred within three years of the date of the initial execution of the Form I–9: or

(ii) If upon inspection of the Form I–9, the recruiter or referrer determines that the individual's employment authorization has expired, or the Service informs the employer that the employment eligibility document presented is insufficient to establish employment authorization, the recruiter or referrer shall not refer the individual unless the recruiter or referrer for a fee completes a new Form I–9 pursuant to the requirements of paragraph (b) of this section.

(2) For purposes of retention of the Form I–9 by a recruiter or referrer for a previously recruited or referred individual pursuant to paragraph (d)(1) of this section, the recruiter or referrer shall retain the Form I–9 for a period of three years commencing from the date of the initial execution of the Form I–9.

[52 FR 16221, May 1, 1987, as amended at 53 FR 8612, 8613, March 16, 1988; 55 FR 25932, June 25, 1990]

## § 274a.3 Continuing employment of unauthorized aliens.

An employer who continues the employment of an employee hired after November 6, 1986, knowing that the employee is or has become an unauthorized alien with respect to that employment, is in violation of section 274A(a)(2) of the Act.

[52 FR 16224, May 1, 1987, as amended at 53 FR 8613, March 16, 1988]

## § 274a.4 Good faith defense.

An employer or a recruiter or referrer for a fee for employment who shows good faith compliance with the employment verification requirements of § 274a.2(b) of this part shall have established a rebuttable affirmative defense that the person or entity has not violated section 274A(a)(1)(A) of the Act with respect to such hiring, recruiting, or referral.

[52 FR 16224, May 1, 1987]

## § 274a.5 Use of labor through contract.

Any person or entity who uses a contract, subcontract, or exchange entered into, renegotiated, or extended after November 6, 1986, to obtain the labor or services of an alien in the United States knowing that the alien is an unauthorized alien with respect to performing such labor or services, shall be considered to have hired the alien for employment in the United States in violation of section 274A(a)(1)(A) of the Act.

[52 FR 16224, May 1, 1987; 55 FR 25934, June 25, 1990]

## § 274a.6 State employment agencies.

(a) **General.** Pursuant to sections 274A(a)(5) and 274A(b) of the Act, a state employment agency as defined in § 274a.1 of this part may, but is not required to, verify identity and employment eligibility of individuals referred for employment by the agency. However, should a state employment agency choose to do so, it must:

(1) Complete the verification process in accordance with the requirements of § 274a.2(b) of this part *provided* that the individual may not present receipts in lieu of documents in order to complete the verification process as otherwise permitted by § 274a.2(b)(1)(vi) of this part; and

(2) Complete the verification process prior to referral for all individuals for whom a certification is required to be issued pursuant to paragraph (c) of this section.

(b) **Compliance with the provisions of section 274A of the Act.** A state employment agency which chooses to verify employment eligibility of individuals pursuant to § 274a.2(b) of this part shall comply with all provisions of section 274A of the Act and the regulations issued thereunder.

(c) **State employment agency certification.** (1) A state employment agency which chooses to verify employment eligibility pursuant to paragraph (a) of this section shall issue to an employer who hires an individual referred for employment by the agency, a certification as set forth in paragraph (d) of this section. The certification shall be transmitted by the state employment agency directly to the employer, personally by an agency official, or by mail, so that it will be received by the employer within 21 business days of the date that the referred individual is hired. In no case shall the certification be transmitted to the employer from the state employment agency by the individual referred. During this period:

(i) The job order or other appropriate referral form issued by the state employment agency to the employer, on behalf of the individual who is referred and hired, shall serve as evidence, with respect to that individual, of the employer's compliance with the provisions of section 274A(a)(1)(B) of the Act and the regulations issued thereunder.

(ii) In the case of a telephonically authorized job referral by the state employment agency to the employer, an appropriate annotation by the employer shall be made and shall serve as evidence of the job order. The employer should retain the document containing the annotation where the employer retains Forms I-9.

(2) Job orders or other referrals, including telephonic authorizations, which are used as evidence of compliance pursuant to paragraph (c)(1)(i) of this section shall contain:

(i) The name of the referred individual;

(ii) The date of the referral;

(iii) The job order number or other applicable identifying number relating to the referral;

(iv) The name and title of the referring state employment agency official; and

(v) The telephone number and address of the state employment agency.

(3) A state employment agency shall not be required to verify employment eligibility or to issue a certification to an employer to whom the agency referred an individual if the individual is hired

for a period of employment not to exceed 3 days in duration. Should a state agency choose to verify employment eligibility and to issue a certification to an employer relating to an individual who is hired for a period of employment not to exceed 3 days in duration, it must verify employment eligibility and issue certifications relating to *all* such individuals. Should a state employment agency choose not to verify employment eligibility or issue certifications to employers who hire, for a period not to exceed 3 days in duration, agency-referred individuals, the agency shall notify employers that, as a matter of policy, it does not perform verifications for individuals hired for that length of time, and that the employers must complete the identity and employment eligibility requirements pursuant to § 274a.2(b) of this part. Such notification may be incorporated into the job order or other referral form utilized by the state employment agency as appropriate.

(4) An employer to whom a state employment agency issues a certification relating to an individual referred by the agency and hired by the employer, shall be deemed to have complied with the verification requirements of § 274a.2(b) of this part provided that the employer:

(i) Reviews the identifying information contained in the certification to ensure that it pertains to the individual hired;

(ii) Observes the signing of the certification by the individual at the time of its receipt by the employer as provided for in paragraph (d)(13) of this section;

(iii) Complies with the provisions of § 274a.2(b)(1)(vii) of this part by either:

(A) Updating the state employment agency certification in lieu of Form I–9, upon expiration of the employment authorization date, if any, which was noted on the certification issued by the state employment agency pursuant to paragraph (d)(11) of this section; or

(B) By no longer employing an individual upon expiration of his or her employment authorization date noted on the certification;

(iv) Retains the certification in the same manner prescribed for Form I–9 in § 274a.2(b)(2) of this part, to wit, three years after the date of the hire or one year after the date the individual's employment is terminated, whichever is later; and

(v) Makes it available for inspection to officers of the Service or the Department of Labor, pursuant to the provisions of section 274A(b)(3) of the Act, and § 274a.2(b)(2) of this part.

(5) Failure by an employer to comply with the provisions of paragraph (c)(4)(iii) of this section shall constitute a violation of section 274A(a)(2) of the Act and shall subject the employer to the penalties contained in section 274A(e)(4) of the Act, and § 274a.10 of this part.

(d) **Standards for state employment agency certifications.** All certifications issued by a state employment agency pursuant to paragraph (c) of this section shall conform to the following standards. They must:

(1) Be issued on official agency letterhead;

(2) Be signed by an appropriately designated official of the agency;

(3) Bear a date of issuance;

(4) Contain the employer's name and address;

(5) State the name and date of birth of the individual referred;

(6) Identify the position or type of employment for which the individual is referred;

(7) Bear a job order number relating to the position or type of employment for which the individual is referred;

(8) Identify the document or documents presented by the individual to the state employment agency for the purposes of identity and employment eligibility verification;

(9) State the identifying number or numbers of the document or documents described in paragraph (d)(8) of this section;

(10) Certify that the agency has complied with the requirements of section 274A(b) of the Act concerning verification of the identity and employment eligibility of the individual referred, and has determined that, to the best of the agency's knowledge, the individual is authorized to work in the United States;

(11) Clearly state any restrictions, conditions, expiration dates or other limitations which relate to the individual's employment eligibility in the United States, or contain an affirmative statement that the employment authorization of the referred individual is not restricted;

(12) State that the employer is not required to verify the individual's identity or employment eligibility, but must retain the certification in lieu of Form I–9;

(13) Contain a space or a line for the signature of the referred individual, requiring the individual under penalty of perjury to sign his or her name before the employer at the time of receipt of the certification by the employer; and

(14) State that counterfeiting, falsification, unauthorized issuance or alteration of the certification constitutes a violation of federal law pursuant to Title 18, U.S.C. 1546.

(e) **Retention of Form I–9 by state employment agencies.** A Form I–9 utilized by a state employment agency in verifying the identity and employment eligibility of an individual pursuant to § 274a.2(b) of this part must be retained by a state employment agency for a period of three years from the date that the individual was last referred by the agency and hired by an employer. A state employment agency may retain a Form I–9 either in its original form, or on microfilm or microfiche.

(f) **Retention of state employment agency certifications.** A certification issued by a state employment agency pursuant to this section shall be retained:

(1) By a state employment agency, for a period of three years from the date that the individual was last referred by the agency and hired by an employer, and in a manner to be determined by the agency which will enable the prompt retrieval of the information contained on the original certification for comparison with the relating Form I–9;

(2) By the employer, in the original form, and in the same manner and location as the employer has designated for retention of Forms I–9, and for the period of time provided in paragraph (c)(4)(iv) of this section.

(g) **State employment agency verification requirements in the case of an individual who was previously referred and certified.** When a state employment agency refers an individual for whom the verification requirements have been previously complied with and a Form I–9 completed, the agency shall inspect the previously completed Form I–9:

(1) If, upon inspection of the Form, the agency determines that the Form I–9 pertains to the individual and that the individual remains authorized to be employed in the United States, no additional verification need be conducted and no new Form I–9 need be completed prior to issuance of a new certification *provided* that the individual is referred by the agency within 3 years of the execution of the initial Form I–9.

(2) If, upon inspection of the Form, the agency determines that the Form I–9 pertains to the individual but that the individual does not appear to be authorized to be employed in the United States based on restrictions, expiration dates or other conditions annotated on the Form I–9, the agency shall not issue a certification unless the agency follows the updating procedures pursuant to § 274a.2(b)(1)(vii) of this part; otherwise the individual may no longer be referred for employment by the state employment agency.

(3) For the purposes of retention of the Form I–9 by a state employment agency pursuant to paragraph (e) of this section, for an individual previously referred and certified, the state employment agency shall retain the Form for a period of 3 years from the date that the individual is last referred and hired.

(h) **Employer verification requirements in the case of an individual who was previously referred and certified.** When an employer rehires an individual for whom the verification and certification requirements have been previously complied with by a state employment agency, the employer shall inspect the previously issued certification.

(1) If, upon inspection of the certification, the employer determines that the certification pertains to the individual and that the individual remains authorized to be employed in the United States, no additional verification need be conducted and no new Form I–9 or certification need be completed *provided* that the individual is rehired by the employer within 3 years of the issuance of the initial certification, and that the employer follows the same procedures for the certification which pertain to Form I–9, as specified in § 274a.2(c)(1)(i) of this part.

(2) If, upon inspection of the certification, the employer determines that the certification pertains to the individual but that the certification reflects restrictions, expiration dates or other conditions which indicate that the individual no longer appears authorized to be employed in the United States, the employer shall verify that the individual remains authorized to be employed and shall follow the updating procedures for the certification which pertain to Form I–9, as specified in § 274a.2(c)(1)(ii) of this part; otherwise the individual may no longer be employed.

(3) For the purposes of retention of the certification by an employer pursuant to this paragraph for an individual previously referred and certified by a state employment agency and rehired by the employer, the employer shall retain the certification for a period of 3 years after the date that the individual is last hired, or one year after the date the individual's employment is terminated, whichever is later.

[52 FR 16224, May 1, 1987, as amended to 52 FR 43052, Nov. 9, 1987]

## § 274a.7 Pre-enactment provisions for employees hired prior to November 7, 1986.

(a) The penalties provisions as set forth in section 274A(e) and (f) of the Act for violations of section 274A(a)(2) and (b) of the Act shall not apply to an employee who was hired prior to November 7, 1986.

(b) For purposes of this section, an employee who was hired prior to November 7, 1986 shall lose his or her pre-enactment status if the employee:

(1) Quits; or

(2) Is terminated by the employer; the term termination shall include, but is not limited to, situations in which an employee is subject to seasonal employment; or

(3) Is excluded or deported from the United States or departs the United States under a grant of voluntary departure; or

(4) Is no longer continuing his or her employment (or does not have a reasonable expectation of employment at all times) as set forth in § 274a.2(b)(1)(viii).

[52 FR 16224, May 1, 1987, as amended at 53 FR 8613, March 16, 1988; 55 FR 25935, July 25, 1990]

## § 274a.8  Prohibition of indemnity bonds.

(a) **General.** It is unlawful for a person or other entity, in hiring or recruiting or referring for a fee for employment of an individual, to require the individual to post a bond or security, to pay or agree to pay an amount, or otherwise to provide a financial guarantee or indemnity, against any potential liability arising under this part relating to such hiring, recruiting, or referring of the individual. However, this prohibition does not apply to performance clauses which are stipulated by agreement between contracting parties.

(b) **Penalty.** Any person or other entity who requires any individual to post a bond or security as stated in this section shall, after notice and opportunity for an administrative hearing in accordance with section 274A(e)(3)(B) of the Act, be subject to a civil fine of $1,000 for each violation and to an administrative order requiring the return to the individual of any amounts received in violation of this section or, if the individual cannot be located, to the general fund of the Treasury.

[52 FR 16224, May 1, 1987]

## § 274a.9  Enforcement procedures.

(a) **Procedures for the filing of complaints.** Any person or entity having knowledge of a violation or potential violation of section 274A of the Act may submit a signed, written complaint in person or by mail to the Service office having jurisdiction over the business or residence of the potential violator. The signed, written complaint must contain sufficient information to identify both the complainant and the potential violator, including their names and addresses. The complaint should also contain detailed factual allegations relating to the potential violation including the date, time and place of the alleged violation and the specific act or conduct alleged to constitute a violation of the Act. Written complaints may be delivered either by mail to the appropriate Service office or by personally appearing before any immigration officer at a Service office.

(b) **Investigation.** The Service may conduct investigations for violations on its own initiative and without having received a written complaint. When the Service receives a complaint from a third party, it shall investigate only those complaints which have a reasonable probability of validity. If it is determined after investigation that the person or entity has violated section 274A of the Act, the Service shall issue and serve upon the alleged violator a citation or a Notice of Intent to Fine. Service officers shall have reasonable access to examine any relevant evidence of any person or entity being investigated.

**(c) Citation and Notice of Intent to Fine.** If after investigation the Service determines that a person or entity has violated section 274A of the Act for the first time during the citation period (June 1, 1987 through May 31, 1988) the Service shall issue a citation. If after investigation the Service determines that a person or entity has violated section 274A of the Act for the second time during the citation period or for the first time after May 31, 1988, the proceeding to assess administrative penalties under section 274A of the Act is commenced by the Service by issuing a Notice of Intent to Fine on Form I–763. Service of this Notice shall be accomplished pursuant to Part 103 of this chapter. The person or entity identified in the Notice of Intent to Fine shall be known as the respondent. The Notice of Intent to Fine may be issued by an officer defined in § 242.1 of this chapter with concurrence of the District Counsel or his or her designee or Sector Counsel.

**(1) Contents of the Notice of Intent to Fine.** (i) The Notice of Intent to Fine will contain the basis for the Notice of Intent to Fine, a designation of the charge(s) against the respondent, the statutory provisions alleged to have been violated, and the penalty that will be imposed.

**(ii)** The Notice of Intent to Fine will provide the following advisals to the respondent;

**(A)** That the person or entity has the right to representation by counsel of his or her own choice at no expense to the government;

**(B)** That any statement given may be used against the person or entity;

**(C)** That the person or entity has the right to request a hearing before an Administrative Law Judge pursuant to 5 U.S.C. 554–557, and that such request must be made within 30 days from the service of the Notice of Intent to Fine;

**(D)** That the Service will issue a final order in 45 days if a written request for a hearing is not timely received and that there will be no appeal of the final order.

**(d) Request for Hearing Before an Administrative Law Judge.** If a respondent contests the issuance of a Notice of Intent to Fine, the respondent must file with the INS, within thirty days of the service of the Notice of Intent to Fine, a written request for a hearing before an Administrative Law Judge. Any written request for a hearing in a foreign language must be accompanied by an English language translation. A request for a hearing is not deemed to be filed until received by the Service office designated in the Notice of Intent to Fine. In computing the thirty day period prescribed by this section, the day of service of the Notice of Intent to Fine shall not be included. If the Notice of Intent to Fine was served by mail, five days shall be added to the prescribed thirty day period. The respondent may, but is not required to, file with the INS an answer responding to each allegation listed in the Notice of Intent to Fine.

(e) **Failure to file a request for hearing.** If the respondent does not file a request for a hearing in writing within thirty days of the day of service of the Notice of Intent to Fine (thirty-five days if served by mail), the INS shall issue a final order from which there is no appeal.

[52 FR 16225, May 1, 1987, as amended at 53 FR 8613, March 16, 1988; 55 FR 25935, June 25, 1990]

# § 274a.10 Penalties.

(a) **Criminal penalties.** Any person or entity which engages in a pattern or practice of violations of subsection (a)(1)(A) or (a)(2) of the Act shall be fined not more than $3,000 for each unauthorized alien, imprisoned for not more than six months for the entire pattern or practice, or both, notwithstanding the provisions of any other Federal law relating to fine levels.

(b) **Civil penalties.** An employer or a recruiter or referrer for a fee may face civil penalties for a violation of section 274A of the Act. Civil penalties may be imposed by the Service or an Administrative Law Judge for violations under section 274A of the Act. In determining the level of the penalties that will be imposed, a finding of more than one violation in the course of a single proceeding or determination will be counted as a single offense. However, a single violation will include penalties for each unauthorized alien who is determined to have been knowingly hired or recruited or referred for a fee.

(1) A respondent found by the Service or an Administrative Law Judge to have knowingly hired, or to have knowingly recruited or referred for a fee, an unauthorized alien for employment in the United States or to have knowingly continued to employ an unauthorized alien, shall be subject to the following order:

(i) To cease and desist from such behavior;

(ii) To pay a civil fine according to the following schedule:

(A) First offense—not less than $250 and not more than $2,000 for each unauthorized alien, or

(B) Second offense—not less than $2,000 and not more than $5,000 for each unauthorized alien; or

(C) More than two offenses—not less than $3,000 and not more than $10,000 for each unauthorized alien; and

(iii) To comply with the requirements of section 274a.2(b) of this part, and to take such other remedial action as is appropriate.

(2) A respondent determined by the Service (if a respondent fails to request a hearing) or by an Administrative Law Judge to have failed to comply with the employment verification requirements as set forth in § 274a.2(b) of this part, shall be subject to a civil penalty in an amount of not less than $100 and not more than $1,000 for each individual with respect to whom such violation occurred. In determining the amount of the penalty, consideration shall be given to:

(i) The size of the business of the employer being charged;

(ii) The good faith of the employer;

(iii) The seriousness of the violation;

(iv) Whether or not the individual was an unauthorized alien; and

(v) The history of previous violations of the employer.

(3) Where an order is issued with respect to a respondent composed of distinct, physically separate subdivisions which does its own hiring, or its own recruiting or referring for a fee for employment (without reference to the practices of, and under the control of, or common control with another subdivision) the subdivision shall be considered a separate person or entity.

(c) **Enjoining pattern or practice violations.** If the Attorney General has reasonable cause to believe that a person or entity is engaged in a pattern or practice of employment, recruitment or referral in violation of section 274A(a)(1)(A) or (2) of the Act, the Attorney General may bring civil action in the appropriate United States District Court requesting relief, including a permanent or temporary injunction, restraining order, or other order against the person or entity, as the Attorney General deems necessary.

[52 FR 16225, May 1, 1987; 55 FR 25935, June 25, 1990]

## § 274a.11   [Reserved].

### SUBPART B—EMPLOYMENT AUTHORIZATION

## § 274a.12   Classes of aliens authorized to accept employment.

(a) **Aliens authorized employment incident to status.** Pursuant to the statutory or regulatory reference cited, the following classes of aliens are authorized to be employed in the United States without restrictions as to location or type of employment as a condition of their admission or subsequent change to one of the indicated classes and, except for paragraph (a)(12) of this section, specific employment authorization need not be requested:

410

(1) An alien who is a lawful permanent resident (with or without conditions pursuant to section 216 of the Act), as evidenced by Form I–151 or Form I–551 issued by the Service;

(2) An alien admitted to the United States as a lawful temporary resident pursuant to section 245A or 210 of the Act, as evidenced by an employment authorization document issued by the Service;

(3) An alien admitted to the United States as a refugee pursuant to section 207 of the Act for the period of time in that status, as evidenced by an employment authorization document issued by the Service;

(4) An alien paroled into the United States as a refugee for the period of time in that status, as evidenced by an employment authorization document issued by the Service;

(5) An alien granted asylum under section 208 of the Act for the period of time in that status, as evidenced by an employment authorization document issued by the Service;

(6) An alien admitted to the United States as a nonimmigrant fiance or fiancee pursuant to section 101(a)(15)(K) of the Act, or an alien admitted as the child of such alien, for the period of admission of the United States, as evidenced by an employment authorization document issued by the Service;

(7) An alien admitted as a parent (N–8) or dependent child (N–9) of an alien granted permanent residence under section 101(a)(27)(I) of the Act, as evidenced by an employment authorization document issued by the Service;

(8) An alien admitted to the United States as a citizen of the Federated States of Micronesia (CFA/FSM) or of the Marshall Islands (CFA/MIS) pursuant to agreements between the United States and the former trust territories, as evidenced by an employment authorization document issued by the Service;

(9) [Reserved].

(10) An alien granted withholding of deportation under section 243(h) of the Act for the period of time in that status, as evidenced by an employment authorization document issued by the Service; or

(11) An alien who has been granted extended voluntary departure by the Attorney General as a member of a nationality group pursuant to a request by the Secretary of State. Employment is authorized for the period of time in that status as evidenced by an employment authorization document issued by the Service;

(12) An alien granted Temporary Protected Status under section 244A of the Act for the period of time in that status, as evidenced by an employment authorization document issued by the Service.

**(b) Aliens authorized for employment with a specific employer incident to status.** The following classes of nonimmigrant aliens are authorized to be employed in the United States by the specific employer and subject to the restrictions described in the section(s) of this chapter indicated as a condition of their admission in, or subsequent change to, such classification. An alien in one of these classes is not issued an employment authorization document by the Service:

(1) A foreign government official (A–1 or A–2), pursuant to § 214.2(a) of this chapter. An alien in this status may be employed only by the foreign government entity;

(2) An employee of a foreign government official (A–3), pursuant to § 214.2(a) of this chapter. An alien in this status may be employed only by the foreign government official;

(3) A foreign government official in transit (C–2 or C–3), pursuant to § 214.2(c) of this chapter. An alien in this status may be employed only by the foreign government entity;

(4) [Reserved].

(5) A nonimmigrant treaty trader (E–1) or treaty investor (E–2), pursuant to § 214.2(e) of this chapter. An alien in this status may be employed only by the treaty-qualifying company through which the alien attained the status. Employment authorization does not extend to the dependents of the principal treaty trader or treaty investor (also designated "E–1" or "E–2"), other than those specified in paragraph (c)(2) of this section;

(6) A nonimmigrant student (F–1) who is in valid nonimmigrant student status and pursuant to 8 CFR 214.2(f) is seeking on-campus employment for not more than twenty hours per week while school is in session or full time when school is not in session if the student intends and is eligible to register for the next term or session. Part-time on-campus employment is authorized by the school and no specific endorsement by a school official or Service officer is necessary.

(7) A representative of an international organization (G–1, G–2, G–3, or G–4), pursuant to § 214.2(g) of this chapter. An alien in this status may be employed only by the foreign government entity or the international organization;

(8) A personal employee of an official or representative of an international organization (G–5), pursuant to § 214.2(g) of this chapter. An alien in this status may be employed only by the official or representative of the international organization;

(9) A temporary worker or trainee (H–1, H–2A, H–2B, or H–3), pursuant to § 214.2(h) of this chapter. An alien in this status may be employed only by the petitioner through whom the status was obtained;

(10) An information media representative (I), pursuant to § 214.2(i) of this chapter. An alien in this status may be employed only for the sponsoring foreign news agency or bureau. Employment authorization does not extend to the dependents of an information media representative (also designated "I");

(11) An exchange visitor (J–1), pursuant to § 214.2(j) of this chapter and 22 CFR 514.24. An alien in this status may be employed only by the exchange visitor program sponsor or appropriate designee and within the guidelines of the program approved by the United States Information Agency as set forth in the Certificate of Eligibility (Form IAP–66) issued by the program sponsor;

(12) An intra-company transferee (L–1), pursuant to § 214.2(1) of this chapter. An alien in this status may be employed only by the petitioner through whom the status was obtained;

(13) Officers and personnel of the armed services of nations of the North Atlantic Treaty Organization, and representatives, officials, and staff employees of NATO (NATO–1, NATO–2, NATO–3, NATO–4, NATO–5 and NATO–6), pursuant to § 214.2(o) of this chapter. An alien in this status may be employed only by NATO;

(14) An attendant, servant or personal employee (NATO–7) of an alien admitted as a NATO–1, NATO–2, NATO–3, NATO–4, NATO–5, or NATO–6, pursuant to § 214.2(o) of this chapter. An alien admitted under this classification may be employed only by the NATO alien through whom the status was obtained; or

(15) A nonimmigrant alien within the class of aliens described in paragraphs (b)(2), (b)(5), (b)(8), (b)(9), (b)(10), (b)(11), (b)(12), and (b)(16) of this section whose status has expired but who has filed a timely application for an extension of such status pursuant to § 214.2 of this chapter. These aliens are authorized to continue employment with the same employer for a period not to exceed 120 days beginning on the date of the expiration of the authorized period of stay. Such authorization shall be subject to any conditions and limitations noted on the initial authorization. However, if the district director or regional service center director adjudicates the application prior to the expiration of this 120 day period and denies the application for extension of status, the employment authorization under this paragraph shall automatically terminate upon notification of the denial decision.

(16) A nonimmigrant pursuant to section 214(e) of the Act. An alien in this status must be engaged in business activities at a professional level in accordance with the provisions of Chapter 15 of the United States-Canada Free-Trade Agreement (FTA).

(c) **Aliens who must apply for employment authorization.**

An alien within a class of aliens described in this section must apply for work authorization. If authorized, such an alien may accept employment subject to any restrictions indicated in the regulations or cited on the employment authorization document:

(1) An alien spouse or unmarried dependent child of a foreign government official (A–1 or A–2) pursuant to § 214.2(a)(2) of this chapter and who presents a fully executed Form I–566 bearing the endorsement of an authorized representative of the Department of State;

(2) An alien spouse or unmarried dependent son or daughter of an alien employee of the Coordination Council for North American Affairs (E–1) pursuant to § 214.2(e) of this chapter;

(3) A nonimmigrant (F–1) student who:

(i) Is seeking off-campus employment authorization due to economic necessity pursuant to § 214.2(f) of this chapter. A student authorized employment under this section may use a properly endorsed I–20 ID issued to the student to establish employment authorization pursuant to 8 CFR 274a.2(b)(1)(v)(C)-(7). To constitute a proper endorsement for this section, the Form I–20 ID must contain the date until which employment is authorized; a statement that the hours authorized per week while school is in session may not exceed 20 hours weekly; the identifying number of the Service officer; and the date and location of the endorsement.

(ii) Is seeking employment for purposes of practical training (including curricular practical training) pursuant to § 214.2(f) of this chapter, provided the alien will be employed only in an occupation which is directly related to his or her course of studies. A student authorized employment under this section may use a properly endorsed I–20 ID issued to the student, to establish employment authorization pursuant to 8 CFR 274a.2(b)(1)(v)(C)(7). A properly endorsed Form I–20 ID must contain the date until which employment is authorized; the occupation or field in which employment is authorized; the name, title and signature of the designated school official or the identifying number of the Service officer; and the date and location of the endorsement; or

(iii) Has been offered employment under the sponsorship of an international organization within the meaning of the International Organization Immunities Act (59 Stat. 669), if such international organization provides written certification to the district director having jurisdiction over the intended place of employment that the proposed employment is within the scope of the organization's sponsorship;

(4) An alien spouse or unmarried dependent child of an officer of, representative to, or employee of an international organization (G–1, G–3 or G–4) pursuant to § 214.2(g) of this chapter who

presents a fully executed Form I–566 bearing the endorsement of an authorized representative of the Department of State;

(5) An alien spouse or minor child of an exchange visitor (J–2) pursuant to § 214.2(j) of this chapter;

(6) A nonimmigrant (M–1) student seeking employment for practical training pursuant to § 214.2(m) of this chapter following completion of studies if such employment is directly related to the student's course of study;

(7) A dependent of an alien classified as NATO–1 through NATO–7 pursuant to § 214.2(n) of this chapter;

(8) An alien who has filed a non-frivolous application for asylum pursuant to part 208 of this chapter. Employment authorization shall be granted in increments not exceeding one year during the period the application is pending (including any period when an administrative appeal or judicial review is pending) and shall expire on a specified date;

(9) An alien who has filed an application for adjustment of status to lawful permanent resident pursuant to part 245 of this chapter. Employment authorization shall be granted in increments not exceeding one year during the period the application is pending (including any period when an administrative appeal or judicial review is pending) and shall expire on a specified date;

(10) An alien who has filed an application for suspension of deportation pursuant to part 244 of this chapter, if the alien establishes an economic need to work. Employment authorization shall be granted in increments not exceeding one year during the period the application is pending (including any period when an administrative appeal or judicial review is pending) and shall expire on a specified date;

(11) An alien paroled into the United States temporarily for emergent reasons or reasons deemed strictly in the public interest pursuant to § 212.5 of this chapter;

(12) A deportable alien granted voluntary departure, either prior to or after hearing, for reasons set forth in § 242.5(a)(2)(v), (a)(2)(vi), or (a)(2)(viii) of this chapter may be granted permission to be employed for that period of time prior to the date set for voluntary departure including any extension granted beyond such date. Factors which may be considered in adjudicating the application for [granting] employment authorization of such an alien granted voluntary departure include, but are not limited to, the following:

(i) The length of voluntary departure granted;

(ii) The existence of a dependent spouse and/or children in the United States who rely on the alien for support;

(iii) Whether there is a reasonable chance that legal status may ensue in the near future; and

(iv) Whether there is a reasonable basis for consideration of discretionary relief.

(13) Any non-detained alien against whom exclusion or deportation proceedings have been instituted and who does not have a final order of deportation or exclusion, may be granted temporary employment authorization if the district director determines that employment authorization is appropriate. Factors which may be considered by the district director in adjudicating the application for employment authorization include, but are not limited to, the following:

(i) The existence of economic necessity to be employed;

(ii) The existence of a dependent spouse and/or children in the United States who rely on the alien for support;

(iii) Whether there is a reasonable chance that legal status may ensue in the near future; and

(iv) Whether there is a reasonable basis for consideration of discretionary relief;

(14) An alien who has been granted deferred action, an act of administrative convenience to the government which gives some cases lower priority, if the alien establishes an economic necessity for employment;

(15) [Reserved].

(16) Any alien who has filed an application for creation of record of lawful admission for permanent residence pursuant to part 249 of this chapter. Employment authorization shall be granted in increments not exceeding one year during the period the application is pending (including any period when an administrative appeal or judicial review is pending) and shall expire on a specific date;

(17) A nonimmigrant visitor for business (B–1) who:

(i) Is a personal or domestic servant who is accompanying or following to join an employer who seeks admission into, or is already in, the United States as a nonimmigrant defined under sections 101(a)(15)(B), (E), (F), (H), (I), (J), (L) or section 214(e) of the Immigration and Nationality Act. The personal or domestic servant shall have a residence abroad which he or she has no intention of abandoning and shall demonstrate at least one year's experience as a personal or domestic servant. The nonimmigrant's employer shall demonstrate that the employer/employee relationship has existed for at least one year prior to the employer's admission to the United States; or, if the employer/employee relationship existed for less than one year, that the employer has regularly employed (either year-round or seasonally) personal or domestic servants over a period of several years preceding the employer's admission to the United States;

(ii) Is a domestic servant of a United States citizen accompanying or following to join his or her United States citizen employer who has a permanent home or is stationed in a foreign country, and who is visiting temporarily in the United States. The employer/employee relationship shall have existed prior to the commencement of the employer's visit to the United States; or

(iii) Is an employee of a foreign airline engaged in international transportation of passengers freight, whose position with the foreign airline would otherwise entitle the employee to classification under section 101(a)(15)(E)(i) of the Immigration and Nationality Act, and who is precluded from such classification solely because the employee is not a national of the country of the airline's nationality or because there is no treaty of commerce and navigation in effect between the United States and the country of the airline's nationality.

(18) [Reserved].

(19) An alien applying for Temporary Protected Status pursuant to section 244A of the Act shall apply for employment authorization only in accordance with the procedures set forth in part 240 of this chapter.

(d) **Basic criteria to establish economic necessity.** Title 45—Public Welfare, Poverty Guidelines, 45 CFR 1060.2 should be used as the basic criteria to establish eligibility for employment authorization when the alien's economic necessity is identified as a factor. The alien shall submit an application for employment authorization listing his or her assets, income, and expenses as evidence of his or her economic need to work. Permission to work granted on the basis of the alien's application for employment authorization may be revoked under § 274a.14 of this chapter upon a showing that the information contained in the statement was not true and correct.

[52 FR 16226, May 1, 1987, as amended at 53 FR 8614, March 16, 1988; 53 FR 46855, Nov. 21, 1988; 54 FR 16, Jan. 3, 1989; 55 FR 5576, Feb. 16, 1990; 55 FR 25935, June 25, 1990; 56 FR 624, Jan. 7, 1991]

## § 274a.13 Application for employment authorization.

(a) **General.** An application on Form I–765 for employment authorization by an alien under § 274a.12(a)(3) through (a)(8) and (a)(10) and (a)(11) and under § 274a.12(c) of this part shall be filed in accordance with the instructions on Form I–765 with the district director having jurisdiction over the applicant's residence or the district director having jurisdiction over the port of entry at which the alien applies. Where economic necessity has been identified as a factor, the alien must provide information regarding his or her assets, income, and expenses in accordance with instructions on the Form I–765.

**(b) Approval of application.**  If the application is granted, the alien shall be notified of the decision and issued an INS employment authorization document valid for a specific period and subject to any terms and conditions as noted.

**(c) Denial of application.**  If the application is denied, the applicant shall be notified in writing of the decision and the reasons for the denial.  There shall be no appeal from the denial of the application.

**(d) Interim employment authorization.**  The district director shall adjudicate the application within 60 days from the date of receipt of the application by the Service.  Failure to complete the adjudication within 60 days will result in the grant of an employment authorization document for a period not to exceed 120 days.  Such authorization shall be subject to any conditions noted on the employment authorization document.  However, if the district director adjudicates the application prior to the expiration date of the interim employment authorization and denies the individual's employment authorization application, the interim employment authorization granted under this section shall automatically terminate as of the date of the district director's adjudication and denial.

[52 FR 16228, May 1, 1987, as amended at 53 FR 8614, March 16, 1988; 55 FR 25931, June 25, 1990]

## § 274a.14  Termination of employment authorization.

### (a) Automatic termination of employment authorization.

(1) Employment authorization granted under § 274a.12(c) of this chapter shall automatically terminate upon the occurrence of one of the following events:

(i) The expiration date specified by the Service on the employment authorization document is reached;

(ii) Exclusion or deportation proceedings are instituted (however, this shall not preclude the authorization of employment pursuant to § 274a.12(c) of this part where appropriate); or

(iii) The alien is granted voluntary departure.

(2) Termination of employment authorization pursuant to this paragraph does not require the service of a notice of intent to revoke; employment authorization terminates upon the occurrence of any event enumerated in paragraph (a)(1) of this section.

However, automatic revocation under this section does not preclude reapplication for employment authorization under § 274.12(c) of this part.

**(b) Revocation of employment authorization—(1) Basis for revocation of employment authorization.**  Employment authorization granted under § 274a.12(c) of this chapter may be revoked by the district director:

(i) Prior to the expiration date, when it appears that any condition upon which it was granted has not been met or no longer exists, or for good cause shown; or

(ii) Upon a showing that the information contained in the application is not true and correct.

(2) **Notice of intent to revoke employment authorization.** When a district director determines that employment authorization should be revoked prior to the expiration date specified by the Service, he or she shall serve written notice of intent to revoke the employment authorization. The notice will cite the reasons indicating that revocation is warranted. The alien will be granted a period of fifteen days from the date of service of the notice within which to submit countervailing evidence. The decision by the district director shall be final and no appeal shall lie from the decision to revoke the authorization.

(c) **Automatic termination of temporary employment authorization granted prior to June 1, 1987.** (1) Temporary employment authorization granted prior to June 1, 1987, pursuant to 8 CFR 109.1(b), or its redesignation as § 274a.12(c) of this part, shall automatically terminate on the date specified by the Service on the document issued to the alien, or on June 1, 1988, whichever is earlier. Automatic termination of temporary employment authorization does not preclude a subsequent application for temporary employment authorization.

(2) A document issued by the Service prior to June 1, 1987, that authorizes temporary employment authorization for any period beyond June 1, 1988, is null and void pursuant to paragraph (c)(1) of this section, and must be surrendered to the Service on the date that the temporary employment authorization terminates or on June 1, 1988, whichever is earlier. The alien shall be issued a new employment authorization document at the time the document is surrendered to the Service if the alien is eligible for temporary employment authorization pursuant to § 274a.12(c) of this chapter.

(3) No notice of intent to revoke is necessary for the automatic termination of temporary employment authorization pursuant to this part.

[52 FR 16228, May 1, 1987, as amended at 53 FR 8614, March 16, 1988]

# INTERNATIONAL REFUGEE CONVENTIONS

## CONVENTION RELATING TO THE STATUS OF REFUGEES

**Done at Geneva, July 28, 1951**
**Entry into force, April 22, 1954**
**189 U.N.T.S. 137**

PREAMBLE

THE HIGH CONTRACTING PARTIES

*Considering* that the Charter of the United Nations and the Universal Declaration of Human Rights approved on 10 December 1948 by the General Assembly have affirmed the principle that human beings shall enjoy fundamental rights and freedoms without discrimination,

*Considering* that the United Nations has, on various occasions, manifested its profound concern for refugees and endeavoured to assure refugees the widest possible exercise of these fundamental rights and freedoms,

*Considering* that it is desirable to revise and consolidate previous international agreements relating to the status of refugees and to extend the scope of and the protection accorded by such instruments by means of a new agreement,

*Considering* that the grant of asylum may place unduly heavy burdens on certain countries, and that a satisfactory solution of a problem of which the United Nations has recognized the international scope and nature cannot therefore be achieved without international co-operation,

*Expressing* the wish that all States, recognizing the social and humanitarian nature of the problem of refugees, will do everything within their power to prevent this problem from becoming a cause of tension between States,

*Noting* that the United Nations High Commissioner for Refugees is charged with the task of supervising international conventions providing for the protection of Refugees, and recognizing that the effective co-ordination of measures taken to deal with this problem will depend upon the co-operation of States with the High Commissioner,

*Have agreed as follows.*

## Chapter I.  General Provisions

### Article 1.  Definition of the term "Refugee"

**A.**  For the purposes of the present Convention, the term "refugee" shall apply to any person who:

(1) Has been considered a refugee under the Arrangements of 12 May 1926 and 30 June 1928 or under the Conventions of 28 October 1933 and 10 February 1938, the Protocol of 14 September 1939 or the Constitution of the International Refugee Organization;

Decisions of non-eligibility taken by the International Refugee Organization during the period of its activities shall not prevent the status of refugee being accorded to persons who fulfil the conditions of paragraph 2 of this section;

(2) As a result of events occurring before 1 January 1951 and owing to well-founded fear of being persecuted for reasons of race, religion, nationality, membership of a particular social group or political opinion, is outside the country of his nationality and is unable or, owing to such fear, is unwilling to avail himself of the protection of that country; or who, not having a nationality and being outside the country of his former habitual residence as a result of such events, is unable or, owing to such fear, is unwilling to return to it.

In the case of a person who has more than one nationality, the term "the country of his nationality" shall mean each of the countries of which he is a national, and a person shall not be deemed to be lacking the protection of the country of his nationality if, without any valid reason based on well-founded fear, he has not availed himself of the protection of one of the countries of which he is a national.

**B.** (1) For the purposes of this Convention, the words "events occurring before 1 January 1951" in Article 1, Section A, shall be understood to mean either:

*(a)* "events occurring in Europe before 1 January 1951" or

*(b)* "events occurring in Europe or elsewhere before 1 January 1951" and each Contracting State shall make a declaration at the time of signature, ratification or accession, specifying which of these meanings it applies for the purpose of its obligations under this Convention.

(2) Any Contracting State which has adopted alternative *(a)* may at any time extend its obligations by adopting alternative *(b)* by means of a notification addressed to the Secretary–General of the United Nations.

**C.** This Convention shall cease to apply to any person falling under the terms of Section A if:

(1) He has voluntarily re-availed himself of the protection of the country of his nationality; or

(2) Having lost his nationality, he has voluntarily re-acquired it; or

(3) He has acquired a new nationality, and enjoys the protection of the country of his new nationality; or

(4) He has voluntarily re-established himself in the country which he left or outside which he remained owing to fear of persecution; or

(5) He can no longer, because the circumstances in connexion with which he has been recognized as a refugee have ceased to exist, continue to refuse to avail himself of the protection of the country of his nationality;

Provided that this paragraph shall not apply to a refugee falling under section A(1) of this Article who is able to invoke compelling reasons arising out of previous persecution for refusing to avail himself of the protection of the country of nationality;

(6) Being a person who has no nationality he is, because the circumstances in connexion with which he has been recognized as a refugee have ceased to exist, able to return to the country of his former habitual residence;

Provided that this paragraph shall not apply to a refugee falling under section A(1) of this Article who is able to invoke compelling reasons arising out of previous persecution for refusing to return to the country of his former habitual residence.

**D.** This Convention shall not apply to persons who are at present receiving from organs or agencies of the United Nations other than the United Nations High Commissioner for Refugees protection or assistance.

When such protection or assistance has ceased for any reason, without the position of such persons being definitively settled in accordance with the relevant resolutions adopted by the General Assembly of the United Nations, these persons shall *ipso facto* be entitled to the benefits of this Convention.

**E.** This Convention shall not apply to a person who is recognized by the competent authorities of the country in which he has taken residence as having the rights and obligations which are attached to the possession of the nationality of that country.

**F.** The provisions of this Convention shall not apply to any person with respect to whom there are serious reasons for considering that:

*(a)* he has committed a crime against peace, a war crime, or a crime against humanity, as defined in the international instruments drawn up to make provision in respect of such crimes;

*(b)* he has committed a serious non-political crime outside the country of refuge prior to his admission to that country as a refugee;

*(c)* he has been guilty of acts contrary to the purposes and principles of the United Nations.

### Article 2. General obligations

Every refugee has duties to the country in which he finds himself, which require in particular that he conform to its laws and regulations as well as to measures taken for the maintenance of public order.

### Article 3.   Non-discrimination

The Contracting States shall apply the provisions of this Convention to refugees without discrimination as to race, religion or country of origin.

### Article 4.   Religion

The Contracting States shall accord to refugees within their territories treatment at least as favourable as that accorded to their nationals with respect to freedom to practise their religion and freedom as regards the religious education of their children.

### Article 5.   Rights granted apart from this Convention

Nothing in this Convention shall be deemed to impair any rights and benefits granted by a Contracting State to refugees apart from this Convention.

### Article 6.   The term "in the same circumstances"

For the purpose of this Convention, the term "in the same circumstances" implies that any requirements (including requirements as to length and conditions of sojourn or residence) which the particular individual would have to fulfil for the enjoyment of the right in question, if he were not a refugee, must be fulfilled by him, with the exception of requirements which by their nature a refugee is incapable of fulfilling.

### Article 7.   Exemption from reciprocity

1.   Except where this Convention contains more favourable provisions, a Contracting State shall accord to refugees the same treatment as is accorded to aliens generally.

2.   After a period of three years' residence, all refugees shall enjoy exemption from legislative reciprocity in the territory of the Contracting States.

3.   Each Contracting State shall continue to accord to refugees the rights and benefits to which they were already entitled, in the absence of reciprocity, at the date of entry into force of this Convention for that State.

4.   The Contracting States shall consider favourably the possibility of according to refugees, in the absence of reciprocity, rights and benefits beyond those to which they are entitled according to paragraphs 2 and 3, and to extending exemption from reciprocity to refugees who do not fulfil the conditions provided for in paragraphs 2 and 3.

5.   The provisions of paragraphs 2 and 3 apply both to the rights and benefits referred to in articles 13, 18, 19, 21 and 22 of this Convention and to rights and benefits for which this Convention does not provide.

### Article 8.  Exemption from exceptional measures

With regard to exceptional measures which may be taken against the person, property or interests of nationals of a foreign State, the Contracting States shall not apply such measures to a refugee who is formally a national of the said State solely on account of such nationality.  Contracting States which, under their legislation, are prevented from applying the general principle expressed in this article, shall, in appropriate cases, grant exemptions in favour of such refugees.

### Article 9.  Provisional measures

Nothing in this Convention shall prevent a Contracting State, in time of war or other grave and exceptional circumstances, from taking provisionally measures which it considers to be essential to the national security in the case of a particular person, pending a determination by the Contracting State that that person is in fact a refugee and that the continuance of such measures is necessary in his case in the interests of national security.

### Article 10.  Continuity of residence

1.  Where a refugee has been forcibly displaced during the Second World War and removed to the territory of a Contracting State, and is resident there, the period of such enforced sojourn shall be considered to have been lawful residence within that territory.

2.  Where a refugee has been forcibly displaced during the Second World War from the territory of a Contracting State and has, prior to the date of entry into force of this Convention, returned there for the purpose of taking up residence, the period of residence before and after such enforced displacement shall be regarded as one uninterrupted period for any purposes for which uninterrupted residence is required.

### Article 11.  Refugee seamen

In the case of refugees regularly serving as crew members on board a ship flying the flag of a Contracting State, that State shall give sympathetic consideration to their establishment on its territory and the issue of travel documents to them on their temporary admission to its territory particularly with a view to facilitating their establishment in another country.

## Chapter II.  Juridical Status

### Article 12.  Personal status

1.  The personal status of a refugee shall be governed by the law of the country of his domicile or, if he has no domicile, by the law of the country of his residence.

2.  Rights previously acquired by a refugee and dependent on personal status, more particularly rights attaching to marriage, shall be respected by a Contracting State, subject to compliance, if this be

necessary, with the formalities required by the law of that State, provided that the right in question is one which would have been recognized by the law of that State had he not become a refugee.

### Article 13.  Movable and immovable property

The Contracting States shall accord to a refugee treatment as favourable as possible and, in any event, not less favourable than that accorded to aliens generally in the same circumstances as regards the acquisition of movable and immovable property and other rights pertaining thereto, and to leases and other contracts relating to movable and immovable property.

### Article 14.  Artistic rights and industrial property

In respect of the protection of industrial property, such as inventions, designs or models, trade marks, trade names, and of rights in literary, artistic and scientific works, a refugee shall be accorded in the country in which he has his habitual residence the same protection as is accorded to nationals of that country.  In the territory of any other Contracting State, he shall be accorded the same protection as is accorded in that territory to nationals of the country in which he has habitual residence.

### Article 15.  Right of association

As regards non-political and non-profit-making associations and trade unions the Contracting States shall accord to refugees lawfully staying in their territory the most favourable treatment accorded to nationals of a foreign country, in the same circumstances.

### Article 16.  Access to courts

1.  A refugee shall have free access to the courts of law on the territory of all Contracting States.

2.  A refugee shall enjoy in the Contracting State in which he has his habitual residence the same treatment as a national in matters pertaining to access to the Courts, including legal assistance and exemption from *cautio judicatum solvi.*

3.  A refugee shall be accorded in the matters referred to in paragraph 2 in countries other than that in which he has his habitual residence the treatment granted to a national of the country of his habitual residence.

## Chapter III.  Gainful Employment

### Article 17.  Wage-earning employment

1.  The Contracting State shall accord to refugees lawfully staying in their territory the most favourable treatment accorded to nationals of a foreign country in the same circumstances, as regards the right to engage in wage-earning employment.

2. In any case, restrictive measures imposed on aliens or the employment of aliens for the protection of the national labour market shall not be applied to a refugee who was already exempt from them at the date of entry into force of this Convention for the Contracting States concerned, or who fulfils one of the following conditions:

*(a)* He has completed three years' residence in the country;

*(b)* He has a spouse possessing the nationality of the country of residence. A refugee may not invoke the benefits of this provision if he has abandoned his spouse;

*(c)* He has one or more children possessing the nationality of the country of residence.

3. The Contracting States shall give sympathetic consideration to assimilating the rights of all refugees with regard to wage-earning employment to those of nationals, and in particular of those refugees who have entered their territory pursuant to programmes of labour recruitment or under immigration schemes.

### Article 18. Self-employment

The Contracting States shall accord to a refugee lawfully in their territory treatment as favourable as possible and, in any event, not less favourable than that accorded to aliens generally in the same circumstances, as regards the right to engage on his own account in agriculture, industry, handicrafts and commerce and to establish commercial and industrial companies.

### Article 19. Liberal professions

1. Each Contracting State shall accord to refugees lawfully staying in their territory who hold diplomas recognized by the competent authorities of that State, and who are desirous of practising a liberal profession, treatment as favourable as possible and, in any event, not less favourable than that accorded to aliens generally in the same circumstances.

2. The Contracting States shall use their best endeavours consistently with their laws and constitutions to secure the settlement of such refugees in the territories, other than the metropolitan territory, for whose international relations they are responsible.

## Chapter IV. Welfare

### Article 20. Rationing

Where a rationing system exists, which applies to the population at large and regulates the general distribution of products in short supply, refugees shall be accorded the same treatment as nationals.

### Article 21. Housing

As regards housing, the Contracting States, in so far as the matter is regulated by laws or regulations or is subject to the control of public authorities, shall accord to refugees lawfully staying in their territory treatment as favourable as possible and, in any event, not less favourable than that accorded to aliens generally in the same circumstances.

### Article 22. Public education

1. The Contracting States shall accord to refugees the same treatment as is accorded to nationals with respect to elementary education.

2. The Contracting States shall accord to refugees treatment as favourable as possible, and, in any event, not less favourable than that accorded to aliens generally in the same circumstances, with respect to education other than elementary education and, in particular, as regards access to studies, the recognition of foreign school certificates, diplomas and degrees, the remission of fees and charges and the award of scholarships.

### Article 23. Public relief

The Contracting States shall accord to refugees lawfully staying in their territory the same treatment with respect to public relief and assistance as is accorded to their nationals.

### Article 24. Labour legislation and social security

1. The Contracting States shall accord to refugees lawfully staying in their territory the same treatment as is accorded to nationals in respect of the following matters:

(a) In so far as such matters are governed by laws or regulations or are subject to the control of administrative authorities: remuneration, including family allowances where these form part of remuneration, hours of work, overtime arrangements, holidays with pay, restrictions on home work, minimum age of employment, apprenticeship and training, women's work and the work of young persons, and the enjoyment of the benefits of collective bargaining;

(b) Social security (legal provisions in respect of employment injury, occupational diseases, maternity, sickness, disability, old age, death, unemployment, family responsibilities and any other contingency which, according to national laws or regulations, is covered by a social security scheme), subject to the following limitations:

(i) There may be appropriate arrangements for the maintenance of acquired rights and rights in course of acquisition;

(ii) National laws or regulations of the country of residence may prescribe special arrangements concerning benefits or portions of benefits which are payable wholly out of public funds, and concerning allowances paid to persons who do not fulfil the contribution conditions prescribed for the award of a normal pension.

2. The right to compensation for the death of a refugee resulting from employment injury or from occupational disease shall not be

affected by the fact that the residence of the beneficiary is outside the territory of the Contracting State.

3. The Contracting States shall extend to refugees the benefits of agreements concluded between them, or which may be concluded between them in the future, concerning the maintenance of acquired rights and rights in the process of acquisition in regard to social security, subject only to the conditions which apply to nationals of the States signatory to the agreements in question.

4. The Contracting States will give sympathetic consideration to extending to refugees so far as possible the benefits of similar agreements which may at any time be in force between such Contracting States and non-contracting States.

# Chapter V.  Administrative Measures

### Article 25.  Administrative assistance

1. When the exercise of a right by a refugee would normally require the assistance of authorities of a foreign country to whom he cannot have recourse, the Contracting States in whose territory he is residing shall arrange that such assistance be afforded to him by their own authorities or by an international authority.

2. The authority or authorities mentioned in paragraph 1 shall deliver or cause to be delivered under their supervision to refugees such documents or certifications as would normally be delivered to aliens by or through their national authorities.

3. Documents or certifications so delivered shall stand in the stead of the official instruments delivered to aliens by or through their national authorities, and shall be given credence in the absence of proof to the contrary.

4. Subject to such exceptional treatment as may be granted to indigent persons, fees may be charged for the services mentioned herein, but such fees shall be moderate and commensurate with those charged to nationals for similar services.

5. The provisions of this article shall be without prejudice to articles 27 and 28.

### Article 26.  Freedom of movement

Each Contracting State shall accord to refugees lawfully in its territory the right to choose their place of residence and to move freely within its territory, subject to any regulations applicable to aliens generally in the same circumstances.

### Article 27.  Identity papers

The Contracting States shall issue identity papers to any refugee in their territory who does not possess a valid travel document.

### Article 28.   Travel documents

1.   The Contracting States shall issue to refugees lawfully staying in their territory travel documents for the purpose of travel outside their territory unless compelling reasons of national security or public order otherwise require, and the provisions of the Schedule to this Convention shall apply with respect to such documents.   The Contracting States may issue such a travel document to any other refugee in their territory;  they shall in particular give sympathetic consideration to the issue of such a travel document to refugees in their territory who are unable to obtain a travel document from the country of their lawful residence.

2.   Travel documents issued to refugees under previous international agreements by parties thereto shall be recognized and treated by the Contracting States in the same way as if they had been issued pursuant to this article.

### Article 29.   Fiscal charges

1.   The Contracting States shall not impose upon refugees duties, charges or taxes, of any description whatsoever, other or higher than those which are or may be levied on their nationals in similar situations.

2.   Nothing in the above paragraph shall prevent the application to refugees of the laws and regulations concerning charges in respect of the issue to aliens of administrative documents including identity papers.

### Article 30.   Transfer of assets

1.   A Contracting State shall, in conformity with its laws and regulations permit refugees to transfer assets which they have brought into its territory, to another country where they have been admitted for the purposes of resettlement.

2.   A Contracting State shall give sympathetic consideration to the application of refugees for permission to transfer assets wherever they may be and which are necessary for their resettlement in another country to which they have been admitted.

### Article 31.   Refugees unlawfully in the country of refuge

1.   The Contracting States shall not impose penalties, on account of their illegal entry or presence, on refugees who, coming directly from a territory where their life or freedom was threatened in the sense of Article 1, enter or are present in their territory without authorization, provided they present themselves without delay to the authorities and show good cause for their illegal entry or presence.

2.   The Contracting States shall not apply to the movements of such refugees restrictions other than those which are necessary and such restrictions shall only be applied until their status in the country is regularized or they obtain admission into another country.   The

Contracting States shall allow such refugees a reasonable period and all the necessary facilities to obtain admission into another country.

### Article 32. Expulsion

1. The Contracting States shall not expel a refugee lawfully in their territory save on grounds of national security or public order.

2. The expulsion of such a refugee shall be only in pursuance of a decision reached in accordance with due process of law. Except where compelling reasons of national security otherwise require, the refugee shall be allowed to submit evidence to clear himself, and to appeal to and be represented for the purpose before competent authority or a person or persons specially designated by the competent authority.

3. The Contracting States shall allow such a refugee a reasonable period within which to seek legal admission into another country. The Contracting States reserve the right to apply during that period such internal measures as they may deem necessary.

### Article 33. Prohibition of expulsion or return ("refoulement")

1. No Contracting State shall expel or return ("*refouler*") a refugee in any manner whatsoever to the frontiers of territories where his life or freedom would be threatened on account of his race, religion, nationality, membership of a particular social group or political opinion.

2. The benefit of the present provision may not, however, be claimed by a refugee whom there are reasonable grounds for regarding as a danger to the security of the country in which he is, or who, having been convicted by a final judgment of a particularly serious crime, constitutes a danger to the community of that country.

### Article 34. Naturalization

The Contracting States shall as far as possible facilitate the assimilation and naturalization of refugees. They shall in particular make every effort to expedite naturalization proceedings and to reduce as far as possible the charges and costs of such proceedings.

## Chapter VI. Executory and Transitory Provisions

### Article 35. Co-operation of the national authorities with the United Nations

1. The Contracting States undertake to co-operate with the Office of the United Nations High Commissioner for Refugees, or any other agency of the United Nations which may succeed it, in the exercise of its functions, and shall in particular facilitate its duty of supervising the application of the provisions of this Convention.

2. In order to enable the Office of the High Commissioner or any other agency of the United Nations which may succeed it, to make

reports to the competent organs of the United Nations, the Contracting States undertake to provide them in the appropriate form with information and and statistical data requested concerning:

(a) the condition of refugees,

(b) the implementation of this Convention, and

(c) laws, regulations and decrees which are, or may hereafter be, in force relating to refugees.

### Article 36.  Information on national legislation

The Contracting States shall communicate to the Secretary–General of the United Nations the laws and regulations which they may adopt to ensure the application of this Convention.

### Article 37.  Relation to previous conventions

Without prejudice to article 28, paragraph 2, of this Convention, this Convention replaces, as between parties to it, the Arrangements of 5 July 1922, 31 May 1924, 12 May 1926, 30 June 1928 and 30 July 1935, the Conventions of 28 October 1933 and 10 February 1938, the Protocol of 14 September 1939 and the Agreement of 15 October 1946.

## Chapter VII.  Final Clauses

### Article 38.  Settlement of disputes

Any dispute between parties to this Convention relating to its interpretation or application, which cannot be settled by other means, shall be referred to the International Court of Justice at the request of any one of the parties to the dispute.

### Article 39.  Signature, ratification and accession

1.  This Convention shall be opened for signature at Geneva on 28 July 1951 and shall thereafter be deposited with the Secretary–General of the United Nations.  It shall be open for signature at the European Office of the United Nations from 28 July to 31 August 1951 and shall be reopened for signature at the Headquarters of the United Nations from 17 September 1951 to 31 December 1952.

2.  This Convention shall be open for signature on behalf of all States Members of the United Nations, and also on behalf of any other State invited to attend the Conference of Plenipotentiaries on the Status of Refugees and Stateless Persons or to which an invitation to sign will have been addressed by the General Assembly.  It shall be ratified and the instruments of ratification shall be deposited with the Secretary–General of the United Nations.

3.  This Convention shall be open from 28 July 1951 for accession by the States referred to in paragraph 2 of this Article.  Accession shall be effected by the deposit of an instrument of accession with the Secretary–General of the United Nations.

## Article 40.  Territorial application clause

1.  Any State may, at the time of signature, ratification or accession, declare that this Convention shall extend to all or any of the territories for the international relations of which it is responsible. Such a declaration shall take effect when the Convention enters into force for the States concerned.

2.  At any time thereafter any such extension shall be made by notification addressed to the Secretary–General of the United Nations and shall take effect as from the ninetieth day after the day of receipt by the Secretary–General of the United Nations of this notification, or as from the date of entry into force of the Convention for the State concerned, whichever is the later.

3.  With respect to those territories to which this Convention is not extended at the time of signature, ratification or accession, each State concerned shall consider the possibility of taking the necessary steps in order to extend the application of this Convention to such territories, subject where necessary for constitutional reasons, to the consent of the governments of such territories.

## Article 41.  Federal clause

In the case of a Federal or non-unitary State, the following provisions shall apply:

*(a)* With respect to those articles of this Convention that come within the legislative jurisdiction of the federal legislative authority, the obligations of the Federal Government shall to this extent be the same as those of Parties which are not Federal States,

*(b)* With respect to those articles of this Convention that come within the legislative jurisdiction of constituent States, provinces or cantons which are not, under the constitutional system of the federation, bound to take legislative action, the Federal Government shall bring such articles with a favourable recommendation, to the notice of the appropriate authorities of States, provinces or cantons at the earliest possible moment.

*(c)* A Federal State Party to this Convention shall, at the request of any other Contracting State transmitted through the Secretary–General of the United Nations, supply a statement of the law and practice of the Federation and its constituent units in regard to any particular provision of the Convention showing the extent to which effect has been given to that provision by legislative or other action.

## Article 42.  Reservations

1.  At the time of signature, ratification or accession, any State may make reservations to articles of the Convention other than to articles 1, 3, 4, 16(1), 33, 36 to 46 inclusive.

2. Any State making a reservation in accordance with paragraph 1 of this article may at any time withdraw the reservation by a communication to that effect addressed to the Secretary-General of the United Nations.

### Article 43.  Entry into force

1. This Convention shall come into force on the ninetieth day following the day of deposit of the sixth instrument of ratification or accession.

2. For each State ratifying or acceding to the Convention after the deposit of the sixth instrument of ratification or accession, the Convention shall enter into force on the ninetieth day following the day of deposit by such State of its instrument of ratification or accession.

### Article 44.  Denunciation

1. Any Contracting State may denounce this Convention at any time by a notification addressed to the Secretary-General of the United Nations.

2. Such denunciation shall take effect for the Contracting State concerned one year from the date upon which it is received by the Secretary-General of the United Nations.

3. Any State which has made a declaration or notification under article 40 may, at any time thereafter, by a notification to the Secretary-General of the United Nations, declare that the Convention shall cease to extend to such territory one year after the date of receipt of the notification by the Secretary-General.

### Article 45.  Revision

1. Any Contracting State may request revision of this Convention at any time by a notification addressed to the Secretary-General of the United Nations.

2. The General Assembly of the United Nations shall recommend the steps, if any, to be taken in respect of such request.

### Article 46.  Notifications by the Secretary-General of the United Nations

The Secretary-General of the United Nations shall inform all Members of the United Nations and non-member States referred to in article 39:

(a) of declarations and notifications in accordance with Section B of Article 1;

(b) of signatures, ratifications and accessions in accordance with article 39;

(c) of declarations and notifications in accordance with article 40;

(d) of reservations and withdrawals in accordance with article 42;

*(e)* of the date on which this Convention will come into force in accordance with article 43;

*(f)* of denunciations and notifications in accordance with article 44;

*(g)* of requests for revision in accordance with article 45.

*In faith whereof* the undersigned, duly authorized, have signed this Convention on behalf of their respective Governments,

*Done* at Geneva, this twenty-eighth day of July, one thousand nine hundred and fifty-one, in a single copy, of which the English and French texts are equally authentic and which shall remain deposited in the archives of the United Nations, and certified true copies of which shall be delivered to all Members of the United Nations and to the non-member States referred to in article 39.

# PROTOCOL RELATING TO THE STATUS OF REFUGEES

**Done January 31, 1967**
**Entry into force, October 4, 1967**
**606 U.N.T.S. 267, 19 U.S.T. 6223, T.I.A.S. No. 6577**

*The States Parties* to the present Protocol,

*Considering* that the Convention relating to the Status of Refugees done at Geneva on 28 July 1951 (hereinafter referred to as the Convention) covers only those persons who have become refugees as a result of events occurring before 1 January 1951,

*Considering* that new refugee situations have arisen since the Convention was adopted and that the refugees concerned may therefore not fall within the scope of the Convention,

*Considering* that it is desirable that equal status should be enjoyed by all refugees covered by the definition in the Convention irrespective of the dateline 1 January 1951,

*Have agreed* as follows:

### Article I.  General provision

1.  The States Parties to the present Protocol undertake to apply articles 2 to 34 inclusive of the Convention to refugees as hereinafter defined.

2.  For the purpose of the present Protocol, the term "refugee" shall, except as regards the application of paragraph 3 of this article, mean any person within the definition of article 1 of the Convention as if the words "As a result of events occurring before 1 January 1951 and ..." and the words "... as a result of such events", in article 1A(2) were omitted.

3.  The present Protocol shall be applied by the States Parties hereto without any geographic limitation, save that existing declarations made by States already Parties to the Convention in accordance with article 1B(1)*(a)* of the Convention, shall, unless extended under article 1B(2) thereof, apply also under the present Protocol.

### Article II.  Co-operation of the national authorities with the United Nations

1.  The States Parties to the present Protocol undertake to co-operate with the Office of the United Nations High Commissioner for Refugees, or any other agency of the United Nations which may succeed it, in the exercise of its functions, and shall in particular facilitate its duty of supervising the application of the provisions of the present Protocol.

2. In order to enable the Office of the High Commissioner, or any other agency of the United Nations which may succeed it, to make reports to the competent organs of the United Nations, the States Parties to the present Protocol undertake to provide them with the information and statistical data requested, in the appropriate form, concerning:

*(a)* The condition of refugees;

*(b)* The implementation of the present Protocol;

*(c)* Laws, regulations and decrees which are, or may hereafter be, in force relating to refugees.

### Article III.  Information on national legislation

The States Parties to the present Protocol shall communicate to the Secretary–General of the United Nations the laws and regulations which they may adopt to ensure the application of the present Protocol.

### Article IV.  Settlement of disputes

Any dispute between States Parties to the present Protocol which relates to its interpretation or application and which cannot be settled by other means shall be referred to the International Court of Justice at the request of any one of the parties to the dispute.

### Article V.  Accession

The present Protocol shall be open for accession on behalf of all States Parties to the Convention and of any other State Member of the United Nations or member of any of the specialized agencies or to which an invitation to accede may have been addressed by the General Assembly of the United Nations.  Accession shall be effected by the deposit of an instrument of accession with the Secretary–General of the United Nations.

### Article VI.  Federal clause

In the case of a Federal or non-unitary State, the following provisions shall apply:

*(a)* With respect to those articles of the Convention to be applied in accordance with article I, paragraph 1, of the present Protocol that come within the legislative jurisdiction of the federal legislative authority, the obligations of the Federal Government shall to this extent be the same as those of States Parties which are not Federal States;

*(b)* With respect to those articles of the Convention to be applied in accordance with article I, paragraph 1, of the present Protocol that come within the legislative jurisdiction of constituent States, provinces or cantons which are not, under the constitutional system of the federation, bound to take legislative action, the Federal Government shall bring such articles with a favourable recommen-

dation to the notice of the appropriate authorities of States, provinces or cantons at the earliest possible moment;

*(c)* A Federal State Party to the present Protocol shall, at the request of any other State Party hereto transmitted through the Secretary–General of the United Nations, supply a statement of the law and practice of the Federation and its constituent units in regard to any particular provision of the Convention to be applied in accordance with article I, paragraph 1, of the present Protocol, showing the extent to which effect has been given to that provision by legislative or other action.

## Article VII.  Reservations and Declarations

1.  At the time of accession, any State may make reservations in respect of article IV of the present Protocol and in respect of the application in accordance with article I of the present Protocol of any provisions of the Convention other than those contained in articles 1, 3, 4, 16(1) and 33 thereof, provided that in the case of a State Party to the Convention reservations made under this article shall not extend to refugees in respect of whom the Convention applies.

2.  Reservations made by States Parties to the Convention in accordance with article 42 thereof shall, unless withdrawn, be applicable in relation to their obligations under the present Protocol.

3.  Any State making a reservation in accordance with paragraph 1 of this article may at any time withdraw such reservation by a communication to that effect addressed to the Secretary–General of the United Nations.

4.  Declarations made under article 40, paragraphs 1 and 2, of the Convention by a State Party thereto which accedes to the present Protocol shall be deemed to apply in respect of the present Protocol, unless upon accession a notification to the contrary is addressed by the State Party concerned to the Secretary–General of the United Nations. The provisions of article 40, paragraphs 2 and 3, and of article 44, paragraph 3, of the Convention shall be deemed to apply *mutatis mutandis* to the present Protocol.

## Article VIII.  Entry into force

1.  The present Protocol shall come into force on the day of deposit of the sixth instrument of accession.

2.  For each State acceding to the Protocol after the deposit of the sixth instrument of accession, the Protocol shall come into force on the date of deposit by such State of its instrument of accession.

## Article IX.  Denunciation

1.  Any State Party hereto may denounce this Protocol at any time by a notification addressed to the Secretary–General of the United Nations.

2. Such denunciation shall take effect for the State Party concerned one year from the date on which it is received by the Secretary-General of the United Nations.

### Article X. Notifications by the Secretary-General of the United Nations

The Secretary-General of the United Nations shall inform the States referred to in article V above of the date of entry into force, accessions, reservations and withdrawals of reservations to and denunciations of the present Protocol, and of declarations and notifications relating hereto.

### Article XI. Deposit in the Archives of the Secretariat of the United Nations

A copy of the present Protocol, of which the Chinese, English, French, Russian and Spanish texts are equally authentic, signed by the President of the General Assembly and by the Secretary-General of the United Nations, shall be deposited in the archives of the Secretariat of the United Nations. The Secretary-General will transmit certified copies thereof to all States Members of the United Nations and to the other States referred to in article V above.

# SELECTED IMMIGRATION FORMS

I-9       Employment eligibility verification.

I-94      Arrival—Departure Record.

I-130     Petition for alien relative.

ETA-750 Application for alien employment certification.

I-140     Petition for prospective immigrant employee.

I-485     Application for permanent residence.

I-551     Alien Registration Receipt Card.

———

# Form I-9  Employment eligibility verification

### EMPLOYMENT ELIGIBILITY VERIFICATION (Form I-9)

**1 EMPLOYEE INFORMATION AND VERIFICATION:** (To be completed and signed by employee.)

| Name: (Print or Type) Last | First | Middle | Birth Name |
|---|---|---|---|
| Address: Street Name and Number | City | State | ZIP Code |
| Date of Birth (Month/Day/Year) | | Social Security Number | |

I attest, under penalty of perjury, that I am (check a box):

☐ 1. A citizen or national of the United States.

☐ 2. An alien lawfully admitted for permanent residence (Alien Number A _____ ) .

☐ 3. An alien authorized by the Immigration and Naturalization Service to work in the United States (Alien Number A _____ ,
   or Admission Number _____ , expiration of employment authorization, if any _____ ) .

I attest, under penalty of perjury, the **documents that I have presented as evidence of identity and employment eligibility are genuine and relate to me. I am aware that** federal law provides for imprisonment and/or fine for any false statements or use of false documents in connection with this certificate.

| Signature | Date (Month/Day/Year) |
|---|---|

PREPARER/TRANSLATOR CERTIFICATION (To be completed if prepared by person other than the employee). I attest, under penalty of perjury, that the above was prepared by me at the request of the named individual and is based on all information of which I have any knowledge.

| Signature | Name (Print or Type) |
|---|---|
| Address (Street Name and Number) | City | State | Zip Code |

**2 EMPLOYER REVIEW AND VERIFICATION:** (To be completed and signed by employer.)

Instructions:

Examine one document from List A and check the appropriate box, **OR** examine one document from List B **and** one from List C and check the appropriate boxes. Provide the *Document Identification Number* and *Expiration Date* for the document checked.

| List A<br>Documents that Establish<br>Identity and Employment Eligibility | List B<br>Documents that Establish<br>Identity | and | List C<br>Documents that Establish<br>Employment Eligibility |
|---|---|---|---|
| ☐ 1. United States Passport | ☐ 1. A State-issued driver's license or a State-issued I.D. card with a photograph, or information, including name, sex, date of birth, height, weight, and color of eyes. (Specify State)_____ ) | | ☐ 1. Original Social Security Number Card (other than a card stating it is not valid for employment) |
| ☐ 2. Certificate of United States Citizenship | | | ☐ 2. A birth certificate issued by State, county, or municipal authority bearing a seal or other certification |
| ☐ 3. Certificate of Naturalization | ☐ 2. U.S. Military Card | | |
| ☐ 4. Unexpired foreign passport with attached Employment Authorization | ☐ 3. Other (Specify document and issuing authority) | | ☐ 3. Unexpired INS Employment Authorization Specify form # _____ |
| ☐ 5. Alien Registration Card with photograph | | | |
| *Document Identification* # _____ | *Document Identification* # _____ | | *Document Identification* # _____ |
| *Expiration Date (if any)* _____ | *Expiration Date (if any)* _____ | | *Expiration Date (if any)* _____ |

**CERTIFICATION: I attest, under penalty of perjury, that I have examined the documents presented by the above individual, that they appear to be genuine and to** relate to the individual named, and that the individual, to the best of my knowledge, is eligible to work in the United States.

| Signature | Name (Print or Type) | Title |
|---|---|---|
| Employer Name | Address | Date |

Form I-9 (05/07/87)
OMB No. 1115-0136

U.S. Department of Justice
Immigration and Naturalization Service

## Employment Eligibility Verification

> **NOTICE:** Authority for collecting the information on this form is in Title 8, United States Code, Section 1324A, which requires employers to verify employment eligibility of individuals on a form approved by the Attorney General. This form will be used to verify the individual's eligibility for employment in the United States. Failure to present this form for inspection to officers of the Immigration and Naturalization Service or Department of Labor within the time period specified by regulation, or improper completion or retention of this form, may be a violation of the above law and may result in a civil money penalty.

### Section 1. Instructions to Employee/Preparer for completing this form

*Instructions for the employee.*

All employees, upon being hired, must complete Section 1 of this form. Any person hired after November 6, 1986 must complete this form. (For the purpose of completion of this form the term "hired" applies to those employed, recruited or referred for a fee.)

All employees must print or type their complete name, address, date of birth, and Social Security Number. The block which correctly indicates the employee's immigration status must be checked. If the second block is checked, the employee's Alien Registration Number must be provided. If the third block is checked, the employee's Alien Registration Number *or* Admission Number must be provided, as well as the date of expiration of that status, if it expires.

All employees whose present names differ from birth names, because of marriage or other reasons, must print or type their birth names in the appropriate space of Section 1. Also, employees whose names change after employment verification should report these changes to their employer.

All employees must sign and date the form.

*Instructions for the preparer of the form, if not the employee.*

If a person assists the employee with completing this form, the preparer must certify the form by signing it and printing or typing his or her complete name and address.

### Section 2. Instructions to Employer for completing this form

(For the purpose of completion of this form, the term "employer" applies to employers and those who recruit or refer for a fee.)

Employers must complete this section by examining evidence of identity and employment eligibility, and:
- checking the appropriate box in List A *or* boxes in both Lists B and C;
- recording the document identification number and expiration date (if any);
- recording the type of form if not specifically identified in the list;
- signing the certification section.

***NOTE: Employers are responsible for reverifying employment eligibility of employees whose employment eligibility documents carry an expiration date.***

Copies of documentation presented by an individual for the purpose of establishing identity and employment eligibility may be copied and retained for the purpose of complying with the requirements of this form and no other purpose. Any copies of documentation made for this purpose should be maintained with this form.

Name changes of employees which occur after preparation of this form should be recorded on the form by lining through the old name, printing the new name and the reason (such as marriage), and dating and initialing the changes. Employers should not attempt to delete or erase the old name in any fashion.

### RETENTION OF RECORDS.

The completed form must be retained by the employer for:
- three years after the date of hiring; or
- one year after the date the employment is terminated, whichever is later.

> Employers may photocopy or reprint this form as necessary.

U.S. Department of Justice
Immigration and Naturalization Service

OMB #1115-0136
Form I-9 (05/07/87)
☆ U.S.G.P.O.: 1987- 183-918/69085

For sale by the Superintendent of Documents, U.S. Government Printing Office
Washington, D.C. 20402

# I-94  Arrival–Departure record

U.S. Department of Justice
Immigration and Naturalization Service

OMB 1115-0077
Expires 10-11-88

**Welcome to the United States**

Admission Number
123456789 00

I-94 Arrival/Departure Record - Instructions

This form must be completed by all persons except U.S. citizens, returning resident aliens, aliens with immigrant visas, and Canadian Citizens visiting or in transit.

Type or print legibly with pen in ALL CAPITAL LETTERS. Use English. Do not write on the back of this form.

This form is in two parts. Please complete both the Arrival Record (Items 1 through 13) and the Departure Record (Items 14 through 17).

When all items are completed, present this form to the U.S. Immigration and Naturalization Service Inspector.

Item 7 - If you are entering the United States by land, enter LAND in this space. If you are entering the United States by ship, enter SEA in this space.

Form I-94 (10-01-85)V

Admission Number
123456789 00

Immigration and
Naturalization Service
I-94
Arrival Record

1. Family Name

2. First (Given) Name                    3. Birth Date (Day Mo Yr)

4. Country of Citizenship              5. Sex (Male or Female)

6. Passport Number                     7. Airline and Flight Number

8. Country Where you Live            9. City Where You Boarded

10. City Where Visa Was Issued    11. Date Issued (Day Mo Yr)

12. Address While in the United States (Number and Street)

13. City and State

Departure Number
123456789 00

Immigration and
Naturalization Service
I-94
Departure Record

14 Family Name

15. First (Given) Name                  16. Birth Date (Day Mo Yr)

17. Country of Citizenship

See other Side                    **STAPLE HERE**

[FR Doc. 85-21553 Filed 9-9-85; 8:45 am]
BILLING CODE 4410-01-C

---

This Side For Government Use Only

Primary Inspection

Applicant's
Name _____

Date
Referred _____ Time _____ Insp. # _____

Reason Referred

☐ 212A  ☐ PP  ☐ Visa  ☐ Parole  ☐ SLB  ☐ TWOV

☐ Other _____

Secondary Inspection

End Secondary
Time _____ Insp. # _____

Disposition _____

| 18. Occupation | 19. Waivers |
| --- | --- |
| 20. INS File  A - | 21. INS FCO |
| 22. Petition Number | 23. Program Number |
| 24. ☐ Bond | 25. ☐ Prospective Student |

26. Itinerary Comments

27. TWOV Ticket Number

Warning - A nonimmigrant who accepts unauthorized employment is subject to deportation.

Important - Retain this permit in your possession; *you must surrender it when you leave the U.S.* Failure to do so may delay your entry into the U.S. in the future.

You are authorized to stay in the U.S. only until the date written on this form. To remain past this date, without permission from immigration authorities, is a violation of the law.

Surrender this permit when you leave the U.S.:
- By sea or air, to the transportation line;
- Across the Canadian border, to a Canadian Official;
- Across the Mexican border, to a U.S. Official.

Students planning to reenter the U.S. within 30 days to return to the same school, see "Arrival-Departure" on page 2 of Form I-20 prior to surrendering this permit.

Record of Changes

Port:                              **Departure Record**

Date:

Carrier:

Flight #/Ship Name:

# Form I–130  Petition for alien relative

U.S. Department of Justice
Immigration and Naturalization Service INS  **Petition for Alien Relative**

## Instructions

**Read the instructions carefully. If you do not follow the instructions, we may have to return your petition, which may delay final action. If more space is needed to complete an answer continue on separate sheet of paper.**

### 1. Who can file?

A citizen or lawful permanent resident of the United States can file this form to establish the relationship of certain alien relatives who may wish to immigrate to the United States. You must file a separate form for each eligible relative.

### 2. For whom can you file?

A. If you are a citizen, you may file this form for:
1) your husband, wife, or unmarried child under 21 years old
2) your unmarried child over 21, or married child of any age
3) your brother or sister if you are at least 21 years old
4) your parent if you are at least 21 years old.

B. If you are a lawful permanent resident you may file this form for:
1) your husband or wife
2) your unmarried child

NOTE: If your relative qualifies under instruction A(2) or A(3) above, separate petitions are not required for his or her husband or wife or unmarried children under 21 years old. If your relative qualifies under instruction B(2) above, separate petitions are not required for his or her unmarried children under 21 years old. These persons will be able to apply for the same type of immigrant visa as your relative.

### 3. For whom can you *not* file?.

You cannot file for people in the following categories:

A. An adoptive parent or adopted child, if the adoption took place after the child became 16 years old, or if the child has not been in the legal custody and living with the parent(s) for at least two years.

B. A natural parent if the United States citizen son or daughter gained permanent residence through adoption.

C. A stepparent or stepchild, if the marriage that created this relationship took place after the child became 18 years old.

D. A husband or wife, if you were not both physically present at the marriage ceremony, and the marriage was not consummated.

E. A husband or wife if you gained lawful permanent resident status by virtue of a prior marriage to a United States citizen or lawful permanent resident unless:
1) a period of five years has elapsed since you became a lawful permanent resident; OR
2) you can establish by clear and convincing evidence that the prior marriage (through which you gained your immigrant status) was not entered into for the purpose of evading any provision of the immigration laws; OR
3) your prior marriage (through which you gained your immigrant status) was terminated by the death of your former spouse.

F. A husband or wife if he or she was in exclusion, deportation, rescission, or judicial proceedings regarding his or her right to remain in the United States when the marriage took place, unless such spouse has resided outside the United States for a two-year period after the date of the marriage.

G. A husband or wife if the Attorney General has determined that such alien has attempted or conspired to enter into a marriage for the purpose of evading the immigration laws.

H. A grandparent, grandchild, nephew, niece, uncle, aunt, cousin, or in-law.

### 4. What documents do you need?

You must give INS certain documents with this form to show you are eligible to file. You must also give the INS certain documents to prove the family relationship between you and your relative.

A. For each document needed, give INS the original and one copy. However, because it is against the law to copy a Certificate of Naturalization, a Certificate of Citizenship or an Alien Registration Receipt Card (Form I-151 or I-551), give INS the original only. **Originals will be returned to you.**

B. If you do not wish to give INS the original document, you may give INS a copy. The copy must be certified by:
1) an INS or U.S. consular officer, or
2) an attorney admitted to practice law in the United States, or
3) an INS accredited representative (INS may still require originals).

C) Documents in a foreign language must be accompanied by a complete English translation. The translator must certify that the translation is accurate and that he or she is competent to translate.

### 5. What documents do you need to show you are a United States citizen?

A. If you were born in the United States, give INS your birth certificate.

B. If you were naturalized, give INS your original Certificate of Naturalization.

C. If you were born outside the United States, and you are a U.S. citizen through your parents, give INS:
1) your original Certificate of Citizenship, or
2) your Form FS-240 (Report of Birth Abroad of a United States Citizen).

D. In place of any of the above, you may give INS your valid unexpired U.S. passport that was initially issued for at least 5 years.

E. If you do not have any of the above and were born in the United States, see the instructions under 8, below. "What if a document is not available?"

### 6. What documents do you need to show you are a permanent resident?

You must give INS your alien registration receipt card (Form I-151 or Form I-551). Do not give INS a photocopy of the card.

### 7. What documents do you need to prove family relationship?

You have to prove that there is a family relationship between your relative and yourself.

In any case where a marriage certificate is required, if either the husband or wife was married before, you must give INS documents to show that all previous marriages were legally ended. In cases where the names shown on the supporting documents have changed, give INS legal documents to show how the name change occurred (for example a marriage certificate, adoption decree, court order, etc.)

Find the paragraph in the following list that applies to the relative you are filing for.

Form I-130 (Rev. 02-28-87)N

[F7498]

# Form I-130 SELECTED IMMIGRATION FORMS

If you are filing for your:

A. **husband or wife,** give INS:
  1) your marriage certificate
  2) a color photo of you and one of your husband or wife, taken within 30 days of the date of this petition. These photos must have a white background. They must be glossy, un-retouched, and not mounted. The dimension of the facial image should be about 1 inch from chin to top of hair in 3/4 frontal view, showing the right side of the face with the right ear visible. Using pencil or felt pen, lightly print name (and Alien Registration Number, if known) on the back of each photograph.
  3) a completed and signed Form G-325A (Biographic Information) for you and one for your husband or wife. Except for name and signature, you do not have to repeat on the G-325A the information given on your I-130 petition.

B. **child** and you are the **mother,** give the child's birth certificate showing your name and the name of your child.

C. **child** and you are the **father or stepparent,** give the child's birth certificate showing both parents' names and your marriage certificate. **Child** born out of wedlock and you are the **father,** give proof that a parent/child relationship exists or existed. For example, the child's birth certificate showing your name and evidence that you have financially supported the child. (A blood test may be necessary).

D. **brother or sister,** your birth certificate and the birth certificate of your brother or sister showing both parents' names. If you do not have the same mother, you must also give the marriage certificates of your father to both mothers.

E. **mother,** give your birth certificate showing your name and the name of your mother.

F. **father,** give your birth certificate showing the names of both parents and your parents' marriage certificate.

G. **stepparent,** give your birth certificate showing the names of both natural parents and the marriage certificate of your parent to your stepparent.

H. **adoptive parent or adopted child,** give a certified copy of the adoption decree, the legal custody decree if you obtained custody of the child before adoption, and a statement showing the dates and places you have lived together with the child.

## 8. What if a document is not available?.

If the documents needed above are not available, you can give INS the following instead. (INS may require a statement from the appropriate civil authority certifying that the needed document is not available.)

A. Church record: A certificate under the seal of the church where the baptism, dedication, or comparable rite occurred within two months after birth, showing the date and place of child's birth, date of the religious ceremony, and the names of the child's parents.

B. School record: A letter from the authorities of the school attended (preferably the first school), showing the date of admission to the school, child's date and place of birth, and the names and places of birth of parents, if shown in the school records.

C. Census record: State or federal census record showing the name, place of birth, and date of birth or the age of the person listed.

D. Affidavits: Written statements sworn to or affirmed by two persons who were living at the time and who have personal knowledge of the event you are trying to prove; for example, the date and place of birth, marriage, or death. The persons making the affidavits need not be citizens of the United States. Each affidavit should contain the following information regarding the person making the affidavit: his or her full name, address, date and place of birth, and his or her relationship to you, if any; full information concerning the event; and complete details concerning how the person acquired knowledge of the event.

## 9. How should you prepare this form?

A. Type or print legibly in ink.

B. If you need extra space to complete any item, attach a continuation sheet, indicate the item number, and date and sign each sheet.

C. Answer all questions fully and accurately. If any item does not apply, please write "N/A".

## 10. Where should you file this form?

A. If you live in the United States, send or take the form to the INS office that has jurisdiction over where you live.

B. If you live outside the United States, contact the nearest American Consulate to find out where to send or take the completed form.

## 11. What is the fee?

You must pay $35.00 to file this form. **The fee will not be refunded, whether the petition is approved or not.** DO NOT MAIL CASH. All checks or money orders, whether U.S. or foreign, must be payable in U.S. currency at a financial institution in the United States. When a check is drawn on the account of a person other than yourself, write your name on the face of the check. If the check is not honored, INS will charge you $5.00.

Pay by check or money order in the exact amount. Make the check or money order payable to "Immigration and Naturalization Service". However,

A. if you live in Guam: Make the check or money order payable to "Treasurer, Guam", or

B. if you live in the U.S. Virgin Islands: Make the check or money order payable to "Commissioner of Finance of the Virgin Islands".

## 12. When will a visa become available?

When a petition is approved for the husband, wife, parent, or unmarried minor child of a United States citizen, these relatives do not have to wait for a visa number, as they are not subject to the immigrant visa limit. However, for a child to qualify for this category, all processing must be completed and the child must enter the United States before his or her 21st birthday.

For all other alien relatives there are only a limited number of immigrant visas each year. The visas are given out in the order in which INS receives properly filed petitions. To be considered properly filed, a petition must be completed accurately and signed, the required documents must be attached, and the fee must be paid.

For a monthly update on dates for which immigrant visas are available, you may call (202) 663-1514.

## 13. What are the penalties for committing marriage fraud or submitting false information or both?

Title 8, United States Code, Section 1325 states that any individual who knowingly enters into a marriage contract for the purpose of evading any provision of the immigration laws shall be imprisoned for not more than five years, or fined not more than $250,000.00 or both.

Title 18, United States Code, Section 1001 states that whoever willfully and knowingly falsifies a material fact, makes a false statement, or makes use of a false document will be fined up to $10,000 or imprisoned up to five years, or both.

## 14. What is our authority for collecting this information?

We request the information on the form to carry out the immigration laws contained in Title 8, United States Code, Section 1154(a). We need this information to determine whether a person is eligible for immigration benefits. The information you provide may also be disclosed to other federal, state, local, and foreign law enforcement and regulatory agencies during the course of the investigation required by this Service. You do not have to give this information. However, if you refuse to give some or all of it, your petition may be denied.

**It is not possible to cover all the conditions for eligibility or to give instructions for every situation. If you have carefully read all the instructions and still have questions, please contact your nearest INS office.**

[F7499]

**U.S. Department of Justice (INS)**  **Petition for Alien Relative**  OMB No. 1115-0054

■ DO NOT WRITE IN THIS BLOCK — FOR EXAMINING OFFICE ONLY ■

| Case ID# | Action Stamp | Fee Stamp |
|---|---|---|
| A# | | |
| G-28 or Volag # | | |

Section of Law:
- ☐ 201 (b) spouse    ☐ 203 (a)(1)
- ☐ 201 (b) child     ☐ 203 (a)(2)
- ☐ 201 (b) parent    ☐ 203 (a)(4)
- ☐ 203 (a)(5)

AM CON:_____

REMARKS:

Petition was filed on _____ (priority date)
- ☐ Personal Interview        ☐ Previously Forwarded
- ☐ Pet .☐ Ben. "A" File Reviewed    ☐ Stateside Criteria
- ☐ Field Investigations      ☐ I-485 Simultaneously
- ☐ 204 (a)(2)(A) Resolved    ☐ 204 (h) Resolved

## A. Relationship

1. The alien relative is my:
☐ Husband/Wife  ☐ Parent  ☐ Brother/Sister  ☐ Child

2. Are you related by adoption?  ☐ Yes  ☐ No

3. Did you gain permanent residence through adoption?  ☐ Yes  ☐ No

## B. Information about you

1. Name (Family name in CAPS)    (First)    (Middle)

2. Address (Number and Street)    (Apartment Number)

(Town or City)    (State/Country)    (ZIP/Postal Code)

3. Place of Birth (Town or City)    (State/Country)

4. Date of Birth (Mo/Day/Year)

5. Sex
☐ Male
☐ Female

6. Marital Status
☐ Married  ☐ Single
☐ Widowed  ☐ Divorced

7. Other Names Used (including maiden name)

8. Date and Place of Present Marriage (if married)

9. Social Security number

10. Alien Registration Number (if any)

11. Names of Prior Husbands/Wives

12. Date(s) Marriage(s) Ended

13. If you are a U.S. citizen, complete the following:
My citizenship was acquired through (check one)
- ☐ Birth in the U.S.
- ☐ Naturalization
  Give number of certificate, date and place it was issued

- ☐ Parents
  Have you obtained a certificate of citizenship in your own name?
  ☐ Yes  ☐ No
  If "Yes," give number of certificate, date and place it was issued

14a. If you are a lawful permanent resident alien, complete the following:
Date and place of admission for, or adjustment to, lawful permanent residence, and class of admission:

14b. Did you gain permanent resident status through marriage to a United States citizen or lawful permanent resident?  ☐ Yes  ☐ No

## C. Information about your alien relative

1. Name (Family name in CAPS)    (First)    (Middle)

2. Address (Number and Street)    (Apartment Number)

(Town or City)    (State/Country)    (ZIP/Postal Code)

3. Place of Birth (Town or City)    (State/Country)

4. Date of Birth (Mo/Day/Year)

5. Sex
☐ Male
☐ Female

6. Marital Status
☐ Married  ☐ Single
☐ Widowed  ☐ Divorced

7. Other Names Used (including maiden name)

8. Date and Place of Present Marriage (if married)

9. Social Security number

10. Alien Registration Number (if any)

11. Names of Prior Husbands/Wives

12. Date(s) Marriage(s) Ended

13. Has your relative ever been in the U.S.?
☐ Yes  ☐ No

14. If your relative is currently in the U.S., complete the following:
He or she last arrived as a (visitor, student, stowaway, without inspection, etc.)

Arrival/Departure Record (I-94) Number    Date arrived (Month/Day/Year)

Date authorized stay expired, or will expire as shown on Form I-94 or I-95

15. Name and address of present employer (if any)

Date this employment began (Month/Day/Year)

16. Has your relative ever been under immigration proceedings?
☐ Yes  ☐ No  Where_____  When_____
☐ Exclusion  ☐ Deportation  ☐ Rescission  ☐ Judicial Proceedings

| INITIAL RECEIPT | RESUBMITTED | RELOCATED | | COMPLETED | | |
|---|---|---|---|---|---|---|
| | | Rec'd | Sent | Approved | Denied | Returned |
| | | | | | | |

Form I-130 (Rev. 02-28-87) N

[F7500]

# Form I-130  SELECTED IMMIGRATION FORMS

## C. (Continued) Information about your alien relative

16. List husband/wife and all children of your relative (if your relative is your husband/wife, list only his or her children).

| Name | Relationship | Date of Birth | Country of Birth |
|------|-------------|---------------|------------------|
|      |             |               |                  |
|      |             |               |                  |
|      |             |               |                  |

17. Address in the United States where your relative intends to reside

| (Number and Street) | (Town or City) | (State) |
|---------------------|----------------|---------|

18. Your relative's address abroad

| (Number and Street) | (Town or City) | (Province) | (Country) |
|---------------------|----------------|------------|-----------|

19. If your relative's native alphabet is other than Roman letters, write his/her name and address abroad in the native alphabet:

| (Name) | (Number and Street) | (Town or City) | (Province) | (Country) |
|--------|---------------------|----------------|------------|-----------|

20. If filing for your husband/wife, give last address at which you both lived together:  From  To

| (Name) | (Apt. No.) | (Town or City) | (State or Province) | (Country) | (Month) | (Year) | (Month) | (Year) |
|--------|-----------|----------------|---------------------|-----------|---------|--------|---------|--------|

21. Check the appropriate box below and give the information required for the box you checked:

☐ Your relative will apply for a visa abroad at the American Consulate in _____
(City)  (Country)

☐ Your relative is in the United States and will apply for adjustment of status to that of a lawful permanent resident in the office of the Immigration and Naturalization Service at _____ . If your relative is not eligible for adjustment of status, he or she will
(City)  (State)
apply for a visa abroad at the American Consulate in _____
(City)  (Country)

(Designation of a consulate outside the country of your relative's last residence does not guarantee acceptance for processing by that consulate. Acceptance is at the discretion of the designated consulate.)

## D. Other Information

1. If separate petitions are also being submitted for other relatives, give names of each and relationship.

2. Have you ever filed a petition for this or any other alien before?   ☐ Yes   ☐ No
If "Yes," give name, place and date of filing, and result.

**Warning:** The INS investigates claimed relationships and verifies the validity of documents. The INS seeks criminal prosecutions when family relationships are falsified to obtain visas.

**Penalties:** You may, by law be imprisoned for not more than five years, or fined $250,000, or both, for entering into a marriage contract for the purpose of evading any provision of the immigration laws and you may be fined up to $10,000 or imprisoned up to five years or both, for knowingly and willfully falsifying or concealing a material fact or using any false document in submitting this petition.

**Your Certification**

I certify, under penalty of perjury under the laws of the United States of America, that the foregoing is true and correct. Furthermore, I authorize the release of any information from my records which the Immigration and Naturalization Service needs to determine eligibility for the benefit that I am seeking.

Signature _____  Date _____  Phone Number _____

**Signature of Person Preparing Form if Other than Above**

I declare that I prepared this document at the request of the person above and that it is based on all information of which I have any knowledge.

| (Print Name) | (Address) | (Signature) | (Date) |
|--------------|-----------|-------------|--------|

Volag Number _____  ___  G-28 ID Number _____

[F7501]

446

**NOTICE TO PERSONS FILING FOR SPOUSES IF MARRIED LESS THAN TWO YEARS**

Pursuant to section 216 of the Immigration and Nationality Act, your alien spouse may be granted conditional permanent resident status in the United States as of the date he or she is admitted or adjusted to conditional status by an officer of the Immigration and Naturalization Service. Both you and your conditional permanent resident spouse are required to file a petition, Form I-751, Joint Petition to Remove Conditional Basis of Alien's Permanent Resident Status, during the ninety day period immediately before the second anniversary of the date your alien spouse was granted conditional permanent residence.

Otherwise, the rights, privileges, responsibilities and duties which apply to all other permanent residents apply equally to a conditional permanent resident. A conditional permanent resident is not limited to the right to apply for naturalization, to file petitions in behalf of qualifying relatives, or to reside permanently in the United States as an immigrant in accordance with the immigration laws.

> **Failure to file Form I-751, Joint Petition to Remove the Conditional Basis of Alien's Permanent Resident Status, will result in termination of permanent residence status and initiation of deportation proceedings.**

**NOTE: You must complete items 1 through 6 to assure that petition approval is recorded. Do not write in the section below item 6.**

1. Name of relative (Family name in CAPS)          (First)          (Middle)

2. Other names used by relative (Including maiden name)

3. Country of relative's birth          4. Date of relative's birth (Month/Day/Year)

5. Your name (Last name in CAPS)     (First)     (Middle)     6. Your phone number

Action Stamp

SECTION
- ☐ 201 (b)(spouse)
- ☐ 201 (b)(child)
- ☐ 201 (b)(parent)
- ☐ 203 (a)(1)
- ☐ 203 (a)(2)
- ☐ 203 (a)(4)
- ☐ 203 (a)(5)

DATE PETITION FILED

☐ STATESIDE
CRITERIA GRANTED

SENT TO CONSUL AT:

**CHECKLIST**

**Have you answered each question?**
**Have you signed the petition?**
**Have you enclosed:**

- ☐ The filing fee for each petition?
- ☐ Proof of your citizenship or lawful permanent residence?
- ☐ All required supporting documents for each petition?

**If you are filing for your husband or wife have you included:**

- ☐ Your picture?
- ☐ His or her picture?
- ☐ Your G-325A?
- ☐ His or her G-325A?

Relative Petition Card
Form I-130A (Rev. 02-25-87) N

[F7502]

# Form ETA 750 Application for alien employment certification

OMB Approval No. 44-R1301

U.S. DEPARTMENT OF LABOR
Employment and Training Administration

**APPLICATION
FOR
ALIEN EMPLOYMENT CERTIFICATION**

**IMPORTANT: READ CAREFULLY BEFORE COMPLETING THIS FORM**
*PRINT legibly in ink or use a typewriter. If you need more space to answer questions on this form, use a separate sheet. Identify each answer with the number of the corresponding question. SIGN AND DATE each sheet in original signature.*

*To knowingly furnish any false information in the preparation of this form and any supplement thereto or to aid, abet, or counsel another to do so is a felony punishable by $10,000 fine or 5 years in the penitentiary, or both (18 U.S.C. 1001).*

## PART A. OFFER OF EMPLOYMENT

1. Name of Alien (Family name in capital letter, First, Middle, Maiden)

2. Present Address of Alien (Number, Street, City and Town, State ZIP Code or Province, Country)

3. Type of Visa (If in U.S.)

The following information is submitted as evidence of an offer of employment.

4. Name of Employer (Full name of organization)

5. Telephone (Area Code and Number)

6. Address (Number, Street, City or Town, Country, State, ZIP Code)

7. Address Where Alien Will Work (if different from item 6)

| 8. Nature of Employer's Business Activity | 9. Name of Job Title | 10. Total Hours Per Week | | 11. Work Schedule (Hourly) | 12. Rate of Pay | |
|---|---|---|---|---|---|---|
| | | a. Basic | b. Overtime | | a. Basic | b. Overtime |
| | | | | a.m. p.m. | $ per ............ | $ per hour |

13. Describe Fully the Job to be Performed (Duties)

14. State in detail the MINIMUM education, training, and experience for a worker to perform satisfactorily the job duties described in item 13 above.

15. Other Special Requirements

| EDU-CATION (Enter number of years) | Grade School | High School | College | College Degree Required (specify) |
|---|---|---|---|---|
| | | | | Major Field of Study |

| TRAIN-ING | No. Yrs. | No. Mos. | Type of Training |
|---|---|---|---|

| EXPERI-ENCE | Job Offered | Related Occupation | Related Occupation (specify) |
|---|---|---|---|
| | Number Yrs. | Mos. | Yrs. | mos. |

16. Occupational Title of Person Who Will Be Alien's Immediate Supervisor ➤

17. Number of Employees Alien will Supervise ➤

**ENDORSEMENTS** (Make no entry in section - for government use only)

| Date Forms Received | |
|---|---|
| L.O. | S.O. |
| R.O. | N.O. |
| Ind. Code | Occ. Code |
| Occ. Title | |

*Replaces MA 7-50A, B and C (Apr. 1970 edition) which is obsolete.*

[F7477]

ETA 750 (Oct. 1976)

| 18. COMPLETE ITEMS ONLY IF JOB IS TEMPORARY | | 19. IF JOB IS UNIONIZED (Complete) | | |
|---|---|---|---|---|
| a. No. of Openings To Be Filled By Aliens Under Job Offer | b. Exact Dates You Expect To Employ Alien | a. Number of Local | b. Name of Local | |
| | From | To | | |
| | | | c. City and State | |

### 20. STATEMENT FOR LIVE-AT-WORK JOB OFFERS    (Complete for Private Household Job ONLY)

| a. Description of Residence | | b. No. Persons Residing at Place of Employment | | | | c. Will free board and private room not shared with anyone be provided? | ("X" one) |
|---|---|---|---|---|---|---|---|
| ("X" one) | Number of Rooms | Adults | | Children | Ages | | ☐ YES ☐ NO |
| ☐ House | | | BOYS | | | | |
| ☐ Apartment | | | GIRLS | | | | |

**21. DESCRIBE EFFORTS TO RECRUIT U.S. WORKERS AND THE RESULTS.** (Specify Sources of Recruitment by Name)



22.  Applications require various types of documentation. Please read PART II of the instructions to assure that appropriate supporting documentation is included with your application.

### 23. EMPLOYER CERTIFICATIONS

*By virtue of my signature below, I HEREBY CERTIFY the following conditions of employment.*

a.  I have enough funds available to pay the wage or salary offered the alien.

b.  The wage offered equals or exceeds the prevailing wage and I guarantee that, if a labor certification is granted, the wage paid to the alien when the alien begins work will equal or exceed the prevailing wage which is applicable at the time the alien begins work.

c.  The wage offered is not based on commissions, bonuses, or other incentives, unless I guarantee a wage paid on a weekly, bi-weekly or monthly basis.

d.  I will be able to place the alien on the payroll on or before the date of the alien's proposed entrance into the United States.

e.  The job opportunity does not involve unlawful discrimination by race, creed, color, national origin, age, sex, religion, handicap, or citizenship.

f.  The job opportunity is not:

(1)  Vacant because the former occupant is on strike or is being locked out in the course of a labor dispute involving a work stoppage.

(2)  At issue in a labor dispute involving a work stoppage.

g.  The job opportunity's terms, conditions and occupational environment are not contrary to Federal, State or local law.

h.  The job opportunity has been and is clearly open to any qualified U.S. worker.

### 24. DECLARATIONS

**DECLARATION OF EMPLOYER** ►    Pursuant to 28 U.S.C. 1746, I declare under penalty of perjury the foregoing is true and correct.

| SIGNATURE | DATE |
|---|---|
| | |

| NAME (Type or Print) | TITLE |
|---|---|
| | |

**AUTHORIZATION OF AGENT OF EMPLOYER** ►    I HEREBY DESIGNATE the agent below to represent me for the purposes of labor certification and I TAKE FULL RESPONSIBILITY for accuracy of any representations made by my agent.

| SIGNATURE OF EMPLOYER | DATE |
|---|---|
| | |

| NAME OF AGENT (Type or Print) | ADDRESS OF AGENT (Number, Street, City, State, ZIP Code) |
|---|---|
| | |

[F7478]

**15. WORK EXPERIENCE.** List all jobs held during past three (3) years. Also, list any other jobs related to the occupation for which the alien is seeking certification as indicated in item 9.

**a. NAME AND ADDRESS OF EMPLOYER**

| NAME OF JOB | DATE STARTED Month   Year | DATE LEFT Month   Year | KIND OF BUSINESS |
|---|---|---|---|

| DESCRIBE IN DETAILS THE DUTIES PERFORMED, INCLUDING THE USE OF TOOLS, MACHINES, OR EQUIPMENT | NO. OF HOURS PER WEEK |
|---|---|

**b. NAME AND ADDRESS OF EMPLOYER**

| NAME OF JOB | DATE STARTED Month   Year | DATE LEFT Month   Year | KIND OF BUSINESS |
|---|---|---|---|

| DESCRIBE IN DETAIL THE DUTIES PERFORMED, INCLUDING THE USE OF TOOLS, MACHINES, OR EQUIPMENT | NO. OF HOURS PER WEEK |
|---|---|

**c. NAME AND ADDRESS OF EMPLOYER**

| NAME OF JOB | DATE STARTED Month   Year | DATE LEFT Month   Year | KIND OF BUSINESS |
|---|---|---|---|

| DESCRIBE IN DETAIL THE DUTIES PERFORMED, INCLUDING THE USE OF TOOLS, MACHINES, OR EQUIPMENT | NO. OF HOURS PER WEEK |
|---|---|

## 16. DECLARATIONS

**DECLARATION OF ALIEN** ► ►  Pursuant to 28 U.S.C. 1746, I declare under penalty of perjury the foregoing is true and correct.

| SIGNATURE OF ALIEN | DATE |
|---|---|

**AUTHORIZATION OF AGENT OF ALIEN** ► ►  I hereby designate the agent below to represent me for the purposes of labor certification and I take full responsibility for accuracy of any representations made by my agent.

| SIGNATURE OF ALIEN | DATE |
|---|---|

| NAME OF AGENT (Type or print) | ADDRESS OF AGENT (No., Street, City, State, ZIP Code) |
|---|---|

[F7480]

# Form I-140   Petition for prospective immigrant employee

**U.S. Department of Justice**
Immigration and Naturalization Service (INS)

Petition for Prospective Immigrant Employee

---

## Instructions

**Read the instructions carefully. If you do not follow the instructions, we may have to return your petition which may delay final action.**

### Definitions

**Third Preference Immigrant** - A prospective employee who is a member of the professions, or who because of exceptional ability in the sciences or arts will substantially benefit the national economy, cultural interest, or welfare of the United States, and whose services are sought by an employer.

**Sixth Preference Immigrant** - A prospective employee who is capable of performing skilled or unskilled labor, not of a temporary or seasonal nature, for which there is a shortage of employable and willing persons in the United States.

**Schedule A** - A list of occupations for which it has already been determined that a shortage of U.S. workers exists. This list can be found in Title 20 CFR 656.10.

### 1. Who can file?

A. You may file this form under Third Preference if you are:

1) the prospective employer, or
2) the prospective employee, or
3) any other person applying on the prospective employee's behalf.

B. You may file this form under Sixth Preference only if you are the prospective employee's prospective employer.

If the petition is approved, the husband or wife and unmarried children under 21 years of age of the prospective employee will automatically be eligible to apply for a visa.

### 2. What documents do you need?

A. 1) In general, you must give INS certain documents with this form. For each document needed, give INS the original and one copy. **Originals will be returned to you.**

2) If you do not wish to give an original document, you may give INS a copy. The copy must be certified by:

a) an INS or U.S. consular officer, or

b) an attorney admitted to practice law in the United States, or

c) an INS accredited representative

(INS still may require originals).

3) Documents in a foreign language must be accompanied by a complete English translation. The translator must certify that the translation is accurate and that he or she is competent to translate.

B. You must give INS a completed Form ETA-750A&B "Application for Alien Employment Certification" bearing the Department of Labor's certification, unless the occupation is currently listed in Schedule A (see definitions).

C. You must document the prospective employee's qualifications:

1) If the prospective employee's qualifications are based on education, give INS:

a) diploma(s) and

b) a certified copy of school transcript(s).

2) If the prospective employee's qualifications are based on exceptional ability in the sciences or arts, give INS evidence of national or international recognition such as awards, prizes, specific products, publications, memberships in a national or international association that maintains standards of outstanding achievement in a specific field, etc.

3) If the prospective employee's qualifications are based on a profession requiring a license or other official permission to practice, give INS a copy of the license or other official permission.

4) If the prospective employee's qualifications are based on technical training or specialized experience, give INS affidavits or published material supporting this training or experience.

5) For physicians or surgeons, also give INS:

a) the results of Parts 1 and 2 of the National Board of Medical Examiners Examination, the Visa Qualifying Examination, or Foreign Medical Graduate Examination in Medical Sciences.

b) evidence of competency in oral and written English.

D. The prospective employer must give INS documentary evidence that establishes ability to pay the offered wage (e.g., latest annual report, last U.S. tax return, profit/loss statement, etc.)

E. Affidavits - These must come from independent sources, such as the prospective employee's former employers or recognized experts familiar with the prospective employee's work. The affidavits must:

a) identify the person making the affidavit, showing the capacity in which he or she is testifying

b) give the places and the dates during which the prospective employee gained his or her experience

c) describe in detail the duties the prospective employee performed, the tools he or she used, how he or she was supervised, and any supervisory tasks that he or she performed. A mere statement, for example, that the prospective employee was employed as a baker, is not adequate.

d) show the date on which the affidavit was signed.

### 3. How should you prepare this form?

A. Type or print legibly in ink.

[F7512]

Form I-140 (REV.3-2-87)Y

B. If you need extra space to complete any item, attach a continuation sheet, indicate the item number, and date and sign each sheet.

C. Answer all questions fully and accurately. If any item does not apply, please write "N/A".

### 4. Where should you file this form?

A. If you are in the United States, send or take the completed form and supporting documents to the INS office that has jurisdiction over the place of intended employment.

B. If you are outside the United States, contact the nearest American Consulate to find out where to send the completed form.

### 5. When will a visa become available?

The availability of an immigrant visa number depends on the number of aliens in the same visa classification who have an earlier priority date (date for which visas are available) on the visa waiting list.

Visa numbers are given out in the order in which Forms ETA-750A&B are filed with the Department of Labor or the order in which they are properly filed with INS in Schedule A cases. Since these numbers are limited each year, it is important to make sure the form is properly filed to put the prospective employee on the waiting list at the earliest possible date. To be properly filed, the form must be complete, the form must be signed, the necessary documents must be attached, and the fee must be paid. For a monthly update on dates for which immigrant visas are available, you may call (202) 663-1514

### 6. What is the fee?

You must pay $35.00 to file this form. **The fee will not be refunded, whether the petition is approved or not.** DO NOT MAIL CASH. All checks or money orders, whether U.S. or foreign, must be payable in U.S. currency at a financial institution in the United States. When a check is drawn on the account of a person other than yourself, write your name on the face of the check. If the check is not honored, INS will charge you $5.00.

Pay by check or money order in the exact amount. Make the check or money order payable to "Immigration and Naturalization Service". However,

A. if you live in Guam: Make the check or money order payable to "Treasurer, Guam", or

B. if you live in the U.S. Virgin Islands: Make the check or money order payable to "Commissioner of Finance of the Virgin Islands".

### 7. What are the penalties for submitting false information?

Title 18, United States Code, Section 1001 states that whoever willfully and knowingly falsifies a material fact, makes a false statement, or makes use of a false document will be fined up to $10,000 or imprisoned up to five years, or both.

### 8. What is our authority for collecting this information?

We request the information on this form to carry out the immigration laws contained in Title 8, United States Code, Section 1154(a). We need this information to determine whether a person is eligible for immigration benefits. The information you provide may also be disclosed to other federal, state, local, and foreign law enforcement and regulatory agencies during the course of the investigation required by this Service. You do not have to give this information. However, if you refuse to give some or all of it, your petition may be denied.

**It is not possible to cover all the conditions for eligibility or to give instructions for every situation. If you have carefully read all the instructions and still have questions, please contact your nearest INS office.**

[F7513]

**U.S. Department of Justice**
Immigration and Naturalization Service (INS)   **Petition for Prospective Immigrant Employee**   OMB # 1115-0061

| DO NOT WRITE IN THIS BLOCK | | |
|---|---|---|
| **Case ID#** | **Action Stamp** | **Fee Stamp** |
| **A#** | | |
| **G-28 or Volag#** | | |
| **Petition was filed on:** | | Petition is approved for status under section:<br>☐ 203(a)(3)   ☐ 203(a)(6)<br>Section 212(a)(14) certification<br>☐ Attached   ☐ Sched. A, Group _____ |
| _____ (Priority Date) | | |

## A. Information about this petition

This petition is being filed for a:   ☐ 3rd Preference Immigrant      (See instructions for definitions
☐ 6th Preference Immigrant      and check one block only)

## B. Information about employer

1. **Name** (Family name in CAPS) (First) (Middle)   or   (Company Name)

2. **Address** (Number and Street)

   (Town or City)      (State/Country)      (ZIP/Postal Code)

3. **Address where employee will work**   (If different)
   (Number and Street)

   (Town or City)      (State/Country)      (ZIP/Postal Code)

4. **Employer is:**   ☐ an organization   ☐ a permanent resident
   (check one)   ☐ a U.S. citizen   ☐ a nonimmigrant

5. **Social Security Number**   or   **IRS employer ID number**

6. **Alien Registration Number** (if any)

7. **Description of Business**   (Nature, number of employees, gross and net annual income, date established)   (If employer is an individual, state occupation and annual income).

8. **Have you ever filed a visa petition for an alien employee in this same capacity?**
   ☐ Yes   ☐ No   (If Yes, how many?)

9. **Are you and the prospective employee related by birth or marriage?**
   ☐ Yes   ☐ No

10. **Are separate petitions being filed at this time for other aliens?**
    ☐ Yes   ☐ No   (If Yes, list names)

11. **Title and salary of position offered**

12. **Is the position permanent?**   ☐ Yes   ☐ No
13. **Is the position full-time?**   ☐ Yes   ☐ No
14. **Is this a newly-created position?**   ☐ Yes   ☐ No
    (If No, how long has it existed?)

## C. Information about prospective employee

1. **Name** (Family name in CAPS) (First)      (Middle)

2. **Address** (Number and Street)      (Apartment Number)

   (Town or City)      (State/Country)      (ZIP/Postal Code)

3. **Place of Birth**   (Town or City)      (State/Country)

4. **Date of Birth**   5. **Sex**   6. **Marital Status**
   (Mo/Day/Yr)   ☐ Male   ☐ Married   ☐ Single
   ☐ Female   ☐ Widowed   ☐ Divorced

7. **Other names used** (including maiden name)

8. **Profession or occupation and years held**

9. **Social Security Number**   10. **Alien Registration Number**   (if any)

11. **Name and address of present employer** (Name)

   (Number and Street)

   (Town or City)      (State/Country)      (ZIP/Postal Code)

12. **Date employee began present employment**

13. **If employee is currently in the U.S., complete the following:**
    He or she last arrived as a (visitor, student, exchange alien, crewman, stowaway, temporary worker, without inspection, etc.)

**Arrival/Departure Record (I-94) Number**      Date arrived (Month/Day/Year)

| | | | | | | | | | | | | |
|---|---|---|---|---|---|---|---|---|---|---|---|---|

Date authorized stay expired, or will expire as shown on Form I-94 or I-95

14. **Has a visa petition ever been filed by or on behalf of this person?**
    ☐ Yes   ☐ No   (If Yes, explain)

| INITIAL RECEIPT | RESUBMITTED | RELOCATED | | COMPLETED | | |
|---|---|---|---|---|---|---|
| | | Rec'd | Sent | Approved | Denied | Returned |
| | | | | | | |

Form I-140 (REV.3-2-87)Y   [F7514]

# Form I-140   SELECTED IMMIGRATION FORMS

## C. (continued) Information about prospective employee

**15. List husband/wife and all children of prospective employee**

| Name | Relationship | Date of Birth | Country of Birth | Present Address |
|------|--------------|---------------|------------------|-----------------|
| | | | | |
| | | | | |
| | | | | |
| | | | | |
| | | | | |
| | | | | |

**16. Employee's address abroad**

(Number and Street)   (Town or City)   (Province)   (Country)

**17. If your employee's native alphabet is other than Roman letters, write his/her name and address abroad in the native alphabet:**

(Name)   (Number and Street)   (Town or City)   (Province)   (Country)

**18. Check the appropriate box below and give the information required for the box you checked:**

☐ The employee will apply for a visa abroad at the American Consulate in _____
(City)   (Country)

☐ The employee is in the United States and will apply for adjustment of status to that of a lawful resident in the office of the Immigration and Naturalization Service at _____   (City)   (State)   If the employee is not eligible for adjustment of status, he or she will apply for a visa abroad at the American Consulate in _____
(City)   (Country)

**Warning: The INS investigates employment experience. If the INS finds that employment experience is false, the application is denied and the person responsible for providing false information may be criminally prosecuted.**

**Penalties: You may, by law, be fined up to $10,000, imprisoned up to five years, or both, for knowingly and willfully falsifying or concealing a material fact or using any false document in submitting this petition.**

### Your Certification

This petition may only be filed by one of the following:

I am   ☐ the employer
☐ the prospective employee (only allowed for 3rd preference)
☐ a person filing on behalf of and authorized by the prospective employee (only allowed for 3rd preference)

I certify, under penalty of perjury under the laws of the United States of America, that the foregoing is true and correct. Furthermore, I authorize the release of any information from my records which the Immigration and Naturalization Service needs to determine eligibility for the benefit that I am seeking.

Print Name _____   Title _____

Signature _____   Date _____   Phone Number _____

### Signature of Person Preparing Form If Other than Above

I declare that I prepared this document at the request of the person above and that it is based on all information of which I have any knowledge.

(Print Name)   (Address)   (Signature)   (Date)

G-28 ID Number _____

Voleg Number _____

[F7515]

**NOTE: Fill in items 1–5 below so that your petition approval can be recorded by the Immigration Service.**

| 1. Name of Prospective Employee | A# |
|---|---|
| 2. Other Names Used | |
| 3. Country of Birth | 4. Date of Birth |
| 5. Name of Prospective Employer | |

| Action Stamp | Section | Priority Date |
|---|---|---|
| | ☐ 203(a)(3) | |
| | ☐ 203(a)(6) | Filing Date |
| | | Sent to Consul at: |

Petition for Prospective Immigrant Employee
Form I-140 (REV.3-2-87)Y

[F7516]

**CHECKLIST**

☐ Have you filled in all the information required on the form?

☐ Have you signed the form?

☐ Have you enclosed the Labor Department forms ETA 7-50 A & B?

☐ Have you enclosed all other required documents?

☐ Have you enclosed the fee?

# Form I-485   Application for permanent residence

**U.S. Department of Justice**

Immigration and Naturalization Service (INS)

## Application for Permanent Residence

### Instructions

**Read the instructions carefully. If you do not follow the instructions, we may have to return your application, which may delay final action.**

**You will be required to appear before an Immigration Officer to answer questions about this application. You must bring your temporary entry permit (Form I-94, Arrival Departure Record) and your passport to your interview.**

**If you plan to leave the U.S. to any country, including Canada or Mexico, before a decision is made on your application, contact the INS Office processing your Application for Permanent Residence before you depart, since a departure from the U.S. without written authorization will result in the termination of your application.**

**1.   Who can apply?**

You are eligible to apply for lawful permanent residence if you are in the U.S. and you:

A.   have an immigrant visa number immediately available to you (see below - "When will a visa become available?"), or

B.   entered with a fiance(e) visa and have married within ninety days, or

C.   have been granted asylum by the INS or an immigration judge one year or more ago, or

D.   are a member of a class of "special immigrants" which includes certain ministers of religion, certain former employees of the United States government abroad, certain retired officers or employees of international organizations, certain immediate relatives of officers or employees of international organizations, and certain physicians who were licensed to practice medicine in the United States prior to January 8, 1978, or

E.   have resided continuously in the United States since before January 1, 1972, or

F.   are filing a motion before an immigration judge, or

G.   are a former foreign government official, or a member of the immediate family of that official, or

H.   received the designation "Cuban/Haitian Entrant (Status Pending)", or are a national of Cuba or Haiti who arrived before January 1, 1982 who had an INS record established before that date, and who (unless you have filed for asylum prior to January 1, 1982) was not admitted to the U.S. as a nonimmigrant. You must apply prior to November 6, 1988.

**2.   Who may not apply?**

You are not eligible for lawful permanent residence if you entered the United States and you:

A.   were not inspected and admitted or paroled by a United States Immigration Officer, or

B.   continued in or accepted unauthorized employment, on or before January 1, 1977, unless you are the spouse, parent, or child of a United States citizen, or

C.   are not in legal immigration status on the date of filing your application, or have failed (other than through no fault of your own for technical reasons) to maintain continuously a legal status since entry into the United States, unless you are the spouse, parent, or child of a United States citizen, or

D.   are an exchange visitor subject to the two-year foreign residence requirement, or

FORM I-485 (REV. 2-27-87)N

E.   were in transit through the United States without a visa, or

F.   were admitted as a crewman of either a vessel or an aircraft.

NOTE: If you are included under 2 above but have lived here continuously since before January 1, 1972 or are applying under the Cuban/Haitian provisions, you may still apply.

**3.   When will a visa become available?**

If you are applying for a permanent residence as the relative of a U.S. citizen or lawful permanent resident, or as an immigrant employee, an immigrant visa petition (I-130 or I-140) must have been filed (or must be filed with your application). In addition, an immigrant visa number must be immediately available to you.

If you are the husband, wife, parent or minor unmarried child of a U.S. citizen, a visa is immediately available to you when your U.S. citizen relative's petition, Form I-130, for you is approved.

For all other applicants,, the availability of visa numbers is based on priority dates, which are determined by the filing of immigrant visa applications or labor certifications. When the priority date is reached for your approved petition, a visa number is immediately available to you. For a monthly update of the dates for which visa numbers are available, you may call (202)663-1514.

**4.   What documents do you need?**

A.   1) For each document needed, give INS the original and one copy. **Originals will be returned to you.**

2) If you do not wish to give INS an original document, you may give INS a copy. The copy must be certified by:

a) an INS or U.S. consular officer, or

b) an attorney admitted to practice law in the United States, or

c) an INS accredited representative

(INS still may require originals)

3) Documents in a foreign language must be accompanied by a complete English translation. The translator must certify that the translation is accurate and that he or she is competent to translate.

B.   You must also give INS the following documents:

1) Your birth certificate.

2) If you are between 14 and 79 years of age, Form G-325A (Biographic Information).

3) a) If you are employed, a letter from your present employer showing that you have employment of a permanent nature.

[F7524]

b) If you are not employed in a permanent job, a Form I-134 (Affadavit of Support) from a responsible person in the United States or other evidence to show that you are not likely to become a public charge.

4) If your husband or wife is filing an application for permanent residence with yours, he or she also must give INS your marraige certificate and proof for both of you that all prior marriages have been legally ended.

5) If your child is filing an application for permanent residence with yours, he or she also must give INS your marriage certificate and proof that all prior marriages for you and your husband or wife have been legally ended, unless those documents are being submitted with your husband or wife's application.

C. If you entered the U.S. as a fiance(e), give INS your marriage certificate. If you are the child of a fiance(e), give INS your birth certificate and the marriage certificate for your parent's present marriage.

D. If you have resided in the United States continuously since before January 1, 1972, give INS documentary evidence of that fact. Some examples of records that can be used to prove residence are bank, real estate, census, school, insurance, or business records, affidavits of credible witnesses, or any other document that relates to you and shows evidence of your presence in the United States during this period.

E. If you have resided in the United States continuously since before July 1, 1924, INS may be able to create a record of your lawful admission as of the date of your entry. Therefore, if you have resided continuously in the United States since a date before July 1, 1924, it is very important to give evidence establishing that fact.

F. If you are a foreign government official or a representative to an international organization, a member of the family, or a treaty trader or treaty investor or the spouse or child of that person, you must give INS Form I-508. Form I-508 waives all rights, privileges, exemptions, and immunities which you would otherwise have because of that status.

## 5. Photographs

Give INS two color photographs of yourself taken within 30 days of the date of this application. These photos must have a white background. They must be glossy, un-retouched, and not mounted. The dimension of the facial image must be about 1 inch from the chin to the top of the hair; your face should be in ¾ frontal view, showing the right side of the face with the right ear visible. Using pencil or felt pen, lightly print your name on the back of each photograph.

## 6. Fingerprints

Give INS a completed fingerprint card (Form FD-258) for each applicant between 14 and 79 years of age. Applicants may be fingerprinted by INS employees, other law enforcement officers, outreach centers, charitable and voluntary agencies, or other reputable persons or organizations. The fingerprint card (FD-258), the ink used, and the quality of the prints must meet standards prescribed by the Federal Bureau of Investigation. You must sign the card in the presence of the person taking your fingerprints. That person must then sign his or her name and enter the date in the spaces provided. It is important to give all the information called for on the card.

## 7. Medical Examination

Unless you are applying as a fiance(e) or dependent, or as an individual who has lived here continuously since before January 1, 1972, you will be required to have a medical examination in conjuction with this application. You may find out more from the INS office that will handle your application.

## 8. How should you prepare this form?

A. Type or print clearly in ink.

B. If you need extra space to complete any item, attach a continuation sheet, indicate the item number, and date and sign each sheet.

C. Answer all questions fully and accurately. If any item does not apply, please write "N/A".

## 9. Where must you file?

You must send or take this form and any other required documents to the INS office that has jurisdiction over the place where you live. You will be interviewed. You must bring your temporary entry permit (Form I-94, Arrival Departure Record), and your passport to your interview.

## 10. What is the fee?

You must pay $60.00 to file this form, unless you are filing under the Cuban/Haitian provisions. **The fee will not be refunded, whether your application is approved or not.** DO NOT MAIL CASH. All checks or money orders, whether U.S. or foreign, must be payable in U.S. currency at a financial institution in the United States. When a check is drawn on the account of a person other than yourself, write your name on the face of the check. If the check is not honored, INS will charge you $5.00.

Pay by check or money order in the exact amount. Make the check or money order payable to "Immigration and Naturalization Service". However,

A. if you live in Guam: Make the check or money order payable to "Treasurer, Guam", or

B. if you live in the U.S. Virgin Islands: Make the check or money order payable to "Commissioner of Finance of the Virgin Islands".

## 11. What are the penalties for submitting false information?

Title 18, United States Code, Section 1001 states that whoever willfully and knowingly falsifies a material fact, makes a false statement, or makes use of a false document will be fined up to $10,000 or imprisoned up to five years, or both.

## 12. What is our authority for collecting this information?

We request the information on this form to carry out the immigration laws contained in Title 8, United States Code, Section 1255. We need this information to determine whether a person is eligible for immigration benefits. The information you provide may also be disclosed to other federal, state, local, and foreign law enforcement and regulatory agencies during the course of the investigation required by this Service. You do not have to give this information. However, if you refuse to give some or all of it, your application may be denied.

**It is not possible to cover all the conditions for eligibility or to give instructions for every situation. If you have carefully read all the instructions and still have questions, please contact your nearest INS office.**

[F7525]

# Form I-485  SELECTED IMMIGRATION FORMS

**U.S. Department of Justice**
Immigration and Naturalization Service (INS)    **Application for Permanent Residence**    OMB # 1115-0053

## DO NOT WRITE IN THIS BLOCK

| Case ID# | Action Stamp | Fee Stamp |
|---|---|---|
| A# | | |
| G-28 or Volag# | | |

| Section of Law | | Eligibility Under Sec. 245 |
|---|---|---|
| ☐ Sec. 209(b), INA | | ☐ Approved Visa Petition |
| ☐ Sec. 214(d), INA | | ☐ Dependent of Principal Alien |
| ☐ Sec. 13, Act of 9/11/57 | | ☐ Special Immigrant |
| ☐ Sec. 245, INA | | ☐ Other _____ |
| ☐ Sec. 249, INA | Country Chargeable _____ | Preference _____ |

## A. Reason for this application

I am applying for lawful permanent residence for the following reason: (check the box that applies)

1. ☐ An immigrant visa number is immediately available to me because
   - ☐ A visa petition has already been approved for me (approval notice is attached)
   - ☐ A visa petition is being filed with this application
2. ☐ I entered as the fiance(e) of a U.S. citizen and married within 90 days (approval notice and marriage certificate are attached)
3. ☐ I am an asylee eligible for adjustment
4. ☐ Other: _____

## B. Information about you

1. **Name** (Family name in CAPS)    (First)    (Middle)

11. On what date did you last enter the U.S.?

2. **Address** (Number and Street)    (Apartment Number)

(Town or City)    (State/Country)    (ZIP/Postal Code)

12. Where did you last enter the U.S.? (City and State)

13. What means of travel did you use? (Plane, car, etc.)

3. **Place of Birth** (Town or City)    (State/Country)

14. Were you inspected by a U.S. immigration officer?
☐ Yes    ☐ No

4. Date of Birth (Mo/Day/Yr)    5. Sex    6. Marital Status
☐ Male    ☐ Married    ☐ Single
☐ Female    ☐ Widowed    ☐ Divorced

15. In what status did you last enter the U.S.?
(Visitor, student, exchange alien, crewman, temporary worker, without inspection, etc.)

7. Social Security Number    8. Alien Registration Number (if any)

16. Give your name EXACTLY as it appears on your Arrival/Departure Record (Form I-94).

9. Country of Citizenship

17. Arrival/Departure Record (I-94) Number    18. Visa Number

10. Have you ever applied for permanent resident status in the U.S.?
☐ Yes    ☐ No
(If Yes, give the date and place of filing and final disposition)

19. At what Consulate was your nonimmigrant visa issued?    Date (Mo/Day/Yr)

20. Have you ever been married before?    ☐ Yes    ☐ No
If Yes.    (Names of prior husbands/wives)

(Country of citizenship)    (Date marriage ended)

21. Has your husband/wife ever been married before?    ☐ Yes    ☐ No
If Yes.    (Names of prior husbands/wives)

(Country of citizenship)    (Date marriage ended)

| INITIAL RECEIPT | RESUBMITTED | RELOCATED | | COMPLETED | | |
|---|---|---|---|---|---|---|
| | | Rec'd | Sent | Approved | Denied | Returned |
| | | | | | | |

FORM I-485 (REV. 2-27-87)N

[F7526]

458

**22. List your present husband/wife, all of your sons and daughters, all of your brothers and sisters** (If you have none, write "N/A")

| Name | Relationship | Place of Birth | Date of Birth | Country of Residence | Applying With You? |
|---|---|---|---|---|---|
| | | | | | ☐ Yes ☐ No |
| | | | | | ☐ Yes ☐ No |
| | | | | | ☐ Yes ☐ No |
| | | | | | ☐ Yes ☐ No |
| | | | | | ☐ Yes ☐ No |
| | | | | | ☐ Yes ☐ No |
| | | | | | ☐ Yes ☐ No |
| | | | | | ☐ Yes ☐ No |
| | | | | | ☐ Yes ☐ No |
| | | | | | ☐ Yes ☐ No |

**23. List your present and past membership in or affiliation with every organization, association, fund, foundation, party, club, society or similar group in the United States or in any other country or place, and your foreign military service** (If this does not apply, write "N/A")

A _____ 19 ____ to 19 ____
B _____ 19 ____ to 19 ____
C _____ 19 ____ to 19 ____
D _____ 19 ____ to 19 ____
E _____ 19 ____ to 19 ____
F _____ 19 ____ to 19 ____
G _____ 19 ____ to 19 ____

**24. Have you ever, in or outside the United States:**

a) knowingly committed any crime for which you have not been arrested?   ☐ Yes ☐ No

b) been arrested, cited, charged, indicted, convicted, fined, or imprisoned for breaking or violating any law or ordinance, including traffic regulations?   ☐ Yes ☐ No

c) been the beneficiary of a pardon, amnesty, rehabilitation decree, other act of clemency or similar action?   ☐ Yes ☐ No

If you answered Yes to (a), (b), or (c) give the following information about each incident:

| Date | Place (City) | (State/Country) | Nature of offense | Outcome of case, if any |
|---|---|---|---|---|
| 1) | | | | |
| 2) | | | | |
| 3) | | | | |
| 4) | | | | |
| 5) | | | | |

**25. Have you ever received public assistance from any source, including the U.S. Government or any state, county, city or municipality?**

☐ Yes   ☐ No   (If Yes, explain, including the name(s) and Social Security number(s) you used.)

**26. Do any of the following relate to you?** (Answer Yes or No to each)

A  Have you been treated for a mental disorder, drug addiction, or alcoholism?   ☐ Yes ☐ No

B  Have you engaged in, or do you intend to engage in, any commercialized sexual activity?   ☐ Yes ☐ No

C  Are you or have you at any time been an anarchist, or a member of or affiliated with any Communist or other totalitarian party, including any subdivision or affiliate?   ☐ Yes ☐ No

D  Have you advocated or taught, by personal utterance, by written or printed matter, or through affiliation with an organization:
1) opposition to organized government   ☐ Yes ☐ No
2) the overthrow of government by force or violence   ☐ Yes ☐ No
3) the assaulting or killing of government officials because of their official character   ☐ Yes ☐ No
4) the unlawful destruction of property   ☐ Yes ☐ No
5) sabotage   ☐ Yes ☐ No
6) the doctrines of world communism, or the establishment of a totalitarian dictatorship in the United States?   ☐ Yes ☐ No

E  Have you engaged or do you intend to engage in prejudicial activities or unlawful activities of a subversive nature?   ☐ Yes ☐ No

F  During the period beginning March 23, 1933, and ending May 8, 1945, did you order, incite, assist, or otherwise participate in persecuting any person because of race, religion, national origin, or political opinion, under the direction of, or in association with any of the following:
1) the Nazi government in Germany   ☐ Yes ☐ No
2) any government in any area occupied by the military forces of the Nazi government in Germany   ☐ Yes ☐ No
3) any government established with the assistance or cooperation of the Nazi government of Germany   ☐ Yes ☐ No
4) any government that was an ally of the Nazi government of Germany   ☐ Yes ☐ No

G  Have you been convicted of a violation of any law or regulation relating to narcotic drugs or marijuana, or have you been an illicit trafficker in narcotic drugs or marijuana?   ☐ Yes ☐ No

[F7527]

# Form I–485   SELECTED IMMIGRATION FORMS

| | | |
|---|---|---|
| H Have you been involved in assisting any other aliens to enter the United States in violation of the law? | ☐ Yes | ☐ No |
| I Have you applied for exemption or discharge from training or service in the Armed Forces of the United States on the ground of alienage and have you been relieved or discharged from that training or service? | ☐ Yes | ☐ No |
| J Are you mentally retarded, insane, or have you suffered one or more attacks of insanity? | ☐ Yes | ☐ No |
| K Are you afflicted with psychopathic personality, sexual deviation, mental defect, narcotic drug addiction, chronic alcoholism, or any dangerous contagious disease? | ☐ Yes | ☐ No |
| L Do you have a physical defect, disease, or disability affecting your ability to earn a living? | ☐ Yes | ☐ No |
| M Are you a pauper, professional beggar, or vagrant? | ☐ Yes | ☐ No |
| N Are you likely to become a public charge? | ☐ Yes | ☐ No |
| O Are you a polygamist or do you advocate polygamy? | ☐ Yes | ☐ No |
| P Have you been excluded from the United States within the past year, or have you at any time been deported from the United States, or have you at any time been removed from the United States at government expense? | ☐ Yes | ☐ No |
| Q Have you procured or have you attempted to procure a visa by fraud or misrepresentation? | ☐ Yes | ☐ No |
| R Are you a former exchange visitor who is subject to, but has not complied with, the two-year foreign residence requirement? | ☐ Yes | ☐ No |
| S Are you a medical graduate coming principally to work as a member of the medical profession, without passing Parts I and II of the National Board of Medical Examiners Examination (or an equivalent examination)? | ☐ Yes | ☐ No |
| T Have you left the United States to avoid military service in time of war or national emergency? | ☐ Yes | ☐ No |
| U Have you committed or have you been convicted of a crime involving moral turpitude? | ☐ Yes | ☐ No |

**If you answered Yes to any question above, explain fully**  (Attach a continuation sheet if necessary):

_____
_____
_____
_____
_____

27. ☐ **Completed Form G-325A (Biographic Information) is signed, dated and attached as part of this application.** Print or type so that all copies are legible.   ☐ **Completed form G-325A (Biographic Information) is not attached because applicant is under 14 or over 79 years of age.**

**Penalties: You may, by law, be fined up to $10,000, imprisoned up to five years, or both, for knowingly and willfully falsifying or concealing a material fact or using any false document in submitting this application.**

## Your Certification

I certify, under penalty of perjury under the laws of the United States of America, that the above information is true and correct. Furthermore, I authorize the release of any information from my records which the Immigration and Naturalization Service needs to determine eligibility for the benefit that I am seeking.

Signature _____   Date _____   Phone Number _____

## Signature of Person Preparing Form if Other than Above

I declare that I prepared this document at the request of the person above and that it is based on all information of which I have any knowledge.

_____

(Print Name)         (Address)         (Signature)         (Date)

G-28 ID Number _____

## Stop Here

Volag Number _____

(Applicant is **not** to sign the application below until he or she appears before an officer of the Immigration and Naturalization Service for examination)

I, _____ swear (affirm) that I know the contents of this application that I am signing including the attached documents, that they are true to the best of my knowledge, and that corrections numbered (   ) to (   ) were made by me or at my request, and that I signed this application with my full, true name:

_____
(Complete and true signature of applicant)

Signed and sworn to before me by the above-named applicant at _____ on _____
                                                                    (Month)   (Day)   (Year)

_____
(Signature and title of officer)

※U.S. Government Printing Office: 1989-261-708/08044

[F7528]

# Form I-551   Alien registration receipt card

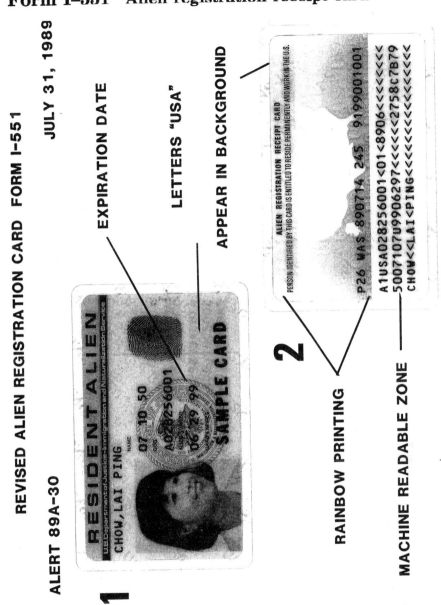

REVISED ALIEN REGISTRATION CARD  FORM I-551

ALERT 89A-30                                        JULY 31, 1989

EXPIRATION DATE

LETTERS "USA"

APPEAR IN BACKGROUND

RESIDENT ALIEN
U.S. Department of Justice-Immigration and Naturalization Service
CHOW, LAI PING
NAME
07 19 50
A028256001
06 29 99
SAMPLE CARD

1

2

ALIEN REGISTRATION RECEIPT CARD
PERSON IDENTIFIED BY THIS CARD IS ENTITLED TO RESIDE PERMANENTLY AND WORK IN THE U.S.

P26 WAS 890714 245  9199001001

A1USA028256001<01<8906<<<<<<<<
5007107U9906297<<<<<2758C7B79<
CHOW<<LAI<PING<<<<<<<<<<<<<<<<<

RAINBOW PRINTING

MACHINE READABLE ZONE

461

# TOPICAL INDEX

---

## CITATIONS

INA § ................................Section number of the Immigration and Nationality Act

8 USCA § ─ ..........................Title and section number of the U.S. Code

8 CFR § ─ ............................Title and section number of the Code of
Federal Regulations

Ap F ................................Appended forms

---

**ACTIONS AND PROCEEDINGS**
Deportation,
    Aliens, INA § 242
    Failure to appear, hearings, discretionary relief, INA § 242B
    Right to counsel, INA § 292
Unlawful employment, unfair immigration-related practices, aliens. Rules and Regula-
    tions, generally, this index

**ADJUSTMENT**
Status, generally, this index

**ADMINISTRATIVE LAW JUDGES**
Designation, authority, disqualification, etc., hearings, unnlawful employment and unfair
    immigration-related practices, 8 CFR § 68.24 et seq.
Hearings, document fraud, conduct of procedures, etc., INA § 242B

**ADMISSION**
Immigration,
    Aliens, this index

**AGGRAVATED FELONY**
Bar on reentry, aliens convicted of, INA § 212
Defined, expedited procedure, alien deportation, INA § 101
Deportation for, expedited proceedings, INA § 242A

**AGRICULTURAL WORKERS**
    See also, Labor and Employment, generally, this index
Immigration, Selection System,
    Determination, labor shortages and admission of additional special workers, INA
        § 210A
Special workers, INA § 210A
    Admission, determination, INA § 210A

**ALASKA**
Nationality, birth on or after certain date, INA § 304

**ALIENS**
Adjustment, status,
    Resident aliens to nonimmigrant status, exceptions, INA § 247
Admission,
    Essential aliens, limitation on number, 50 USCA § 403h
    Qualifications, H–2A temporary workers, INA § 218
Application, employment certification, Form ETA–750
Crewmen, this index
Deportation, this index

463

**ALIENS**—Continued
Penalties—Continued
    Unfair immigration-related practices, INA § 274B
    Unlawful bringing of aliens into U.S., INA § 273
    Unlawful employment, INA § 274A
Qualifications. Admission, ante, this subheading
Record, admission for permanent residence, entry into U.S. prior to certain date, INA
    § 249
Registered nurses, special classification, INA § 212
Registration, INA § 262
    Address, INA § 265
    Contents, INA § 261
    Entry, alien seeking, INA § 261
    Fingerprinting,
        Forms for, INA § 264
    Forms, INA § 264
    Penalties, violations, INA § 266
    Special groups, INA § 263
Removal, falling into distress, INA § 250
Travel control, INA § 215
Nationality, generally, this index
Nonimmigrant aliens, nurses, registered, "immigrant" as excluding, INA § 101

## AMERICAN INDIANS
Canada, birth in,
    Applicability of immigration provisions to, INA § 289

## APPEALS AND REVIEW
Aliens,
    Aggravated felony convictions, expedited proceedings, INA § 242A
    Deportation procedures, provisions, INA § 242B
Document fraud proceedings, decisions of Administrative Law Judge, INA § 274C
Orders of deportation and exclusion, judicial review, INA § 106

## APPLICATIONS
Forms, generally, this index

## ARMED FORCES
Foreign Countries, generally, this index
Immigration provisions, applicability to members of, INA § 284
Naturalization,
    Active duty service during World War I, World War II, hostilities, etc., INA § 329
    Deserters ineligible, INA § 314
    Nationality,
        Alien relieved of service due to alienage, denial of citizenship, etc., INA § 315
        Birth abroad before certain date, service parent, 8 USCA § 1401a
    Records, conclusiveness, citizenship denied alien relieved of service in Armed Forces,
        etc., INA § 315
    Service in, requirements, INA § 328

## ASYLUM
Immigration,
    Procedures, regulations, INA § 208; 8 CFR § 208.1 et seq.

## ATTORNEY GENERAL
Custody, aliens convicted of aggravated felonies, INA § 242
    Convicted of aggravated felonies, INA § 242
    Pending exclusion proceedings, convicted of aggravated felonies, INA § 236
Powers, duties, functions, etc.,
    Fraud prevention, control of illegal immigration, INA § 210
    Immigration and nationality, INA § 101 et seq.
    Nationality through naturalization, INA § 310
    Temporary protected status, INA § 244A
    Treatment of frivolous behavior, deportation proceedings, INA § 242B
Registration and fingerprinting, alien children, powers and duties, etc., INA § 262

# TOPICAL INDEX

# TOPICAL INDEX

467

# TOPICAL INDEX

# TOPICAL INDEX

# TOPICAL INDEX

# TOPICAL INDEX

**PARENT AND CHILD**—Continued

Naturalization,

    Birth outside U.S., INA § 322

        Alien parents, conditions, automatic citizenship, INA § 321

        One alien and one citizen parent, conditions, automatic citizenship, INA § 320

Registration and fingerprinting, alien children, waiver, INA § 262

Social Security, generally, this index

**PAROLE**

Power of Attorney General to grant, INA § 212

**PASSENGERS**

Immigration, entry and exclusion, lists of passengers arriving and departing, INA § 231

**PENALTIES**

See Fines, Penalties and Forfeitures, generally, this index

**PERMITS**

See Licenses and Permits, generally, this index

**PETITIONS AND PETITIONERS**

Forms, generally, this index

Immigration,

    Forms, generally, this index

Naturalization. Nationality, this index

**PHILIPPINES, REPUBLIC OF**

Naturalization, resident Philippine citizens exception from certain requirements, INA
    § 326

**PHOTOGRAPHS AND PHOTOGRAPHY**

Naturalization, number, INA § 333

**PILOT PROGRAM**

Visa waiver, certain visitors, INA § 217

**PRESUMPTIONS**

Deportability, aliens convicted of aggravated felonies, INA § 242A

**PRINTING**

Immigration, reentry permits and blank forms of manifest and crew lists, INA § 282

**PROCEEDINGS**

See Actions and Proceedings, generally, this index

**PUERTO RICO**

Nationality, birth on or after certain date, INA § 302

**REFUGEE ASSISTANCE**

Domestic resettlement and assistance to refugees, authorization for programs, INA § 412

Office of Refugee Resettlement, establishment, appointment of Director, functions, etc.,
    INA § 411 et seq.

Programs, domestic resettlement and assistance to refugees, authorization, INA § 412

Reports, Congressional committees, INA § 413

Secretary of State, powers, duties, etc., INA § 101 et seq., INA § 412 et seq.

United States Coordinator for Refugee Affairs, appointment, duties, functions, etc., 8
    USCA § 1525

**REFUGEES**

Assistance. Refugee Assistance, generally, this index

Immigration,

    Admission,

        Selection System, generally, post, this subheading

    Asylum, INA § 208; 8 C.F.R. § 208

    Selection System, admission, INA § 207

        Annual admission, INA § 207

        Emergency situation refugees, INA § 207

        Refugees and emergency situation refugees, INA § 207

        Status, adjustment, INA § 209

# TOPICAL INDEX

# TOPICAL INDEX

†